GW01143373

SMEs: INTERNATIONALIZATION, NETWO

SMEs: Internationalization, Networks and Strategy

Edited by

JOSÉ Mª VECIANA
Universitat Autònoma de Barcelona

Avebury

Aldershot · Brookfield USA · Hong Kong · Singapore · Sydney

© José Mª Veciana 1994

All rights reserved. No part of this publication may be reproduced, stored in a retrieval system, or transmitted in any form or by any means, electronic, mechanical, photocopying or otherwise without the prior permission of the publisher.

Published by
Avebury
Ashgate Publishing Limited
Gower House
Croft Road
Aldershot
Hants GU11 3HR
England

Ashgate Publishing Company
Old Post Road
Brookfield
Vermont 05036
USA

British Library Cataloguing in Publication Data

SMEs: Internationalization, Networks and Strategy
   I. Veciana, José M.
   338.04
 ISBN 1 85628 696 7

Library of Congress Cataloging-in-Publication Data

SMEs: internationalization, networks and strategy / José Mª Veciana
     p. cm.
  'Papers presented at the Sixth European Workshop on Recent Research on Entrepreneurship, ... November 1992'--Preface.
  ISBN 1-85628-696-7 : $68.95 (est.)
  1. Small businesses--Congresses. 2. International division of labor--Congresses. 3. Subcontracting--Congresses. 4. International business enterprises--Congresses. 5. Entrepreneurship--Congresses.
  I. Veciana, José Mª (José María), 1932-.
  HD2341.R352 1994
  658.4'21-dc20   94-14959
                                                                            CIP

Printed and Bound in Great Britain by
Athenaeum Press Ltd, Newcastle upon Tyne.

Contents

Preface ix

PART A: SMEs Internationalization

1) Methodological Problems in Assessing Awareness and Preparedness of SMEsTowards the Single European Market 3
   P. Rosa, M. Scott
2) Success Factors and Their Sensivity to Internationalization: Some Empirical Findings among Finnish SMEs 24
   L. Hurmerinta-Peltomäki
3) Modeling Key Success Factors in Manufacturing 38
   A. Haahti
4) Becoming International: Benefits and Pitfalls for Entrepreneurial SMEs: Experiences from Belgium 58
   R. Aerts
5) Internationalization of Finnish SMEs: Commitment, Internationalization Paths and Innovation 76
   L. Hyvärinen

PART B: Strategy / Organization

6) Flexible Companies in an Industrial District. 103
   The Case of the Gnosjö Region in Sweden
   J. Wiklund, C. Karlsson
7) Evaluating Growth Potential by Contingency Responsive Interaction 129
   T. Fuller
8) International Marketing Strategies of Dutch Small Firms 155
   R.M. Braaksma, H.G.J. Gankema, P.S. Zwart
9) Competitiveness, Autonomy and Business Relationships 174
   A.L. Duijnhouwer
10) The Small and Middle-Sized Enterprise in Cross-National Joint- 201
    Ventures: A Way of Inducing Renewal and Increasing Viability
    H. Gammelsaeter, B. Guvag
11) Japanese Retail Stores: Regulation, Demand and the Dual Labour 222
    Market
    J.C.A. Potjes, M.A. Carree, A.R. Thurik
12) Entrepreneurial Strategy-Making (A Norwegian Shipyard Facing 237
    the Soviet Market)
    J.A. Johannessen, A. Hauan, J. Olaisen
13) The Evolution of the Flexible Specialisation System: 252
    Some Italian Experiences
    A. Fumagalli, G. Mussati
14) The Oscillating Behavior of Small Innovative Firms: A Model 275
    M. Raffa, G. Zollo

PART C: Networks

15) A Relationships Typology in Firms Networks 305
    M. Raffa
16) Qualitative and Structural Changes of the Subcontracting Firms: 345
    A Micro-Analytical Approach to the Study of Inter-Firm Relationships
    E. Esposito, C.L. Storto

17) Internationalizing Subcontractors: Is Co-operation an Alternative?   359
N. Hovi

18) Community Brokers: Their Role in the Formation and Development of Business Ventures   380
S. Cromie, S. Birley, I. Callaghan

19) Barriers to Active Networks: Small Firms as Subcontractors in a Competitive Region   410
M. Monsted

20) Beyond Anarchy and Organization: Entrepreneur in Context   428
B. Johannisson, O. Alexanderson, K. Nowicki, K. Senneseth

PART D: Eastern Europe

21) Co-Operation Agreements Between Entrepreneurs from Developed and Developing Countries: Theoretical Considerations and Empirical Evidence from Belgium   473
J. Lambrecht

22) The Transfer of Organizational and Enterprise Patterns and The Creation of Market Economy in Eastern Europe   489
M. Aggestam

23) Women Entrepreneurs in Controlled Economies: A Hungarian Perspective   504
R. Hisrich, G. Fülop

24) Between Ikar's Flight and Heron's Boat: "The Choice of the Bulgarian Entrepreneur"   525
K. Todorov

25) Development of Small Business Sector in Poland as The Fisher-Pry Process   541
K. Wilczewska, W. Wilczewski

PART E: Entrepreneurs

26) Entrepreneurial Scripting 553
    D. Johnson
27) Psychological Profiling : Implications for the Training of Entrepreneurs 571
    R. Mulholland, E. McVeigh
28) Successful Women Entrepreneurs in Fiji: Their Profile, Vision and Motivation, an Exploratory Study 594
    K.K. Pang, G. Nair
29) Gender and Ownership in UK Small Firms 615
    P. Rosa, D. Hamilton, H. Burns

PART F: Venture Capital

30) Financial Structure and Profitability of SMEs vs Large Companies: An International Study 639
    E. Genescà, J.M. Veciana, T. Obis
31) Venture Capital Investment Process in a Decision Theory Framework 666
    H. Landström
32) The Impact of Venture Capital Funding on Small High Technology Manufacturing Firms in the United Kingdom 695
    H.I.M. Wilson

Preface

This publication contains the major papers presented at the Sixth European Workshop on **Recent Research on Entrepreneurship**, held at the Universitat Autònoma de Barcelona (UAB) in November 1992. The Workshop was organised by the European Institute for Advanced Studies in Management (EIASM) in collaboration with the European Council for Small Business (ECSB). The thirty two papers contained in this publication were presented and discussed in workshop sessions. In total over eighty leading researchers of entrepreneurship from across Europe attended the conference. Although covering a broad spectrum of research topics, the papers can be grouped into six distinct parts.

Part A deals with the topic of the **Internationalisation of SMEs** and opens with a discussion of the methodological problems in assessing awareness and preparedness of SMEs towards the single European Market (Rosa & Scott). Other papers in this section focus on success factors of internationalisation (Humerinta-Peltomäki and Haahti), and on the benefits and pitfalls of SMEs becoming international (Aerts).

Part B deals with the topic of **Strategy/Organization** and includes nine papers. Two papers centre on the question of flexibility; flexible companies (Karlsson & Wiklund); and the evolution of the flexible specialisation system in Italy (Fumagalli & Mussati). Others papers in this section refer to competitiveness, strategy-making, and organisation in small innovative firms.

The subject of **Networks,** which is attracting increasing attention of researchers, is covered in Part C. Raffa develops a relationships typology in firms networks; Johannisson, et. al. focus on the entrepreneur in context; and Monsted, Hovi and other researchers investigate subcontracting at a regional and/or international level.

Part D highlights the topical subject of **the Development of SMEs in Eastern Europe.** Lambrecht addresses the question of co-operation agreements between SMEs from developed and developing countries, Aggestam explores the transfer of organisational and enterprise patterns from West to East; and Todorov and Fülöp analyse the status of entrepreneurs and SMEs in Eastern Europe.

Entrepreneurs' personality and gender is the topic covered in Part E. Entrepreneurial scripting (Johnson) may contribute to the understanding of the entrepreneur, whereas psychological profiling (Mulholland & McVeigh) has implications for their training. Successful women entrepreneurs in Fiji, and Gender and ownership in UK small firms are the topics addressed by Pang and Rosa respectively.

Finally, in Part F, the topic of **Venture Capital** is discussed. Genescá, Veciana and Obis offer the results of an international study on the financial structure and profitability of SMEs versus large firms; Landström analyses the venture capital investment process in a decision theory framework. The last paper in this publication, by Wilson, analyses the impact of venture capital funding on small high technology manufacturing firms in the United Kingdom.

In conclusion, the proceedings of the RENT VI European Workshop provide 1) a plethora of research evidence in the field of entrepreneurship and SMEs; 2) stimulus for further research, and 3) an indication of the research interests of those active in the arena of research on entrepreneurship in SMEs across Europe.

José M. Veciana
Barcelona, November 1993.

Part A
SMEs' INTERNATIONALIZATION

1 Methodological problems in assessing awareness and preparedness of SMEs towards the Single European Market

Peter Rosa and Michael Scott

ABSTRACT:

As the Single European Market (SEM) nears completion, there is much policy concern within each country on whether the small business sector is responding positively to change. Acting on this concern, there have been many consultancy studies commissioned to predict or estimate the potential impact of the SEM on local firms, and on assessing their preparedness and internationalisation performance towards the SEM.

Most studies have adopted general, often ad hoc approaches to assessing preparedness and internationalisation performance. The paper illustrates from mainly Scottish research evidence that measuring these concepts is, in fact, a complex and difficult exercise. Estimates of "awareness" and "preparedness" can show marked variability according to which definition is employed, and according to the selection and composition of the sample base. This variability poses question marks on the reliability and usefulness of currents assessments of the preparedness of firms within the EEC as the SEM approaches.

Introduction

European policy makers have calculated that the completion of the Single Market by 1992 would lead to greater industrial efficiency as European industry, no longer protected by national legislation and subsidies, felt the full weight of competition (EC: White Paper 1985:4-9). Implicit in this reasoning is the idea that all efficient businesses, irrespective of size, can take advantage of the new freedoms and opportunities. In practice, the fear is that smaller business will tend to lose out by failing to identify and exploit new opportunities, and by succumbing to the more powerful competitive threats. As Sweeney points out, the main gainers in the SEM are likely to be large corporations, at the expense of the small business sector and at the cost of a decline in entrepreneurial vitality (Sweeney 1991:365).

The preparedness of smaller firms towards the advent of the SEM is thus a vital issue, particularly as they are the most numerous type of firm in all European economies, and are associated with a significant capacity for economic regeneration. Recognition of this has led to policy concern by regional and national policy makers that smaller firms may not be effectively meeting the challenge of "1992". Owner managers may be unaware of opportunities and threats, or while vaguely aware, may be complacent. A feeling also exists that the owner managers of many smaller firms lack understanding of how to exploit new opportunities, particularly in international markets within Europe. This concern led to the commissioning of many consultancy studies by Government and business organisations, which puported to measure accurately the state of awareness, preparedness or internationalisation of firms within Regions or particular industries. Thus for example, the national BBC breakfast news announced on the 13th October 1992 that a local survey by the Chamber of Commerce in Dulwich had reported that n 50 % of local firms were now prepared for the Single Market~. This kind of certainty is not confined to the local level. For example a survey of 2,000 SMEs in the UK, France and Denmark on how they are shaping up to the single market by Rant Thornton International reported very exact figures on the extent of preparations (43% of SMes in France; 37% in the UK; 60% in Denmark had taken action- source: The Times May 8th 1992). Even major government departments have shown confidence in the accuracy of these measures. From the findings of its commissioned studies, the Department of Trade and Industry was able to report in 1988 that, following a national campaign to raise the awareness of the Single Market amongst businesses, that 90 per cent of UK firms were aware of the importance of the Single Market

(Scottish Economic Bulletin December 1988). Such figures have percolated into academia. In a research paper from the Durham Business School, for example, Roe (1990:1) uncritically reiterates DTI figures in stating that "more than 95% of businesses in the UK are now aware of the Single Market".

Are concepts such as "awareness", "preparedness" amenable to simple measurement and interpretation for policy purposes? Is it possible to manipulate the definition to produce the desired result? This paper seeks to show that these concepts are in fact complex to measure. It uses evidence from the authors' own research on Scottish small firms to illustrate methodological problems in using such measures in relation to studying the reaction to the SEM by small firms, and in predicting trends.

Materials and methods

The focus of the study was on four industrial sectors in Central Region, Scotland, chosen on the basis of their major contribution to local employment (Scott, Rosa and McAlpine 1989:14ff). The sectors were mineral and chemical products, metal goods/ engineering, other manufacturing and transport/communications. The study achieved 146 face-to face interviews using a structured questionnaires of owner managers of firms in these four sectors. The response rate was 65 per cent. The sectoral distribution of firms amongst respondents was not significantly different than that amongst the total sample contacted (see Scott et al. 1989:18). The interview schedule comprised 73 questions on aspects of performance, export activity, awareness and preparedness of owner managers; the effects of the SEM on the firm; and perceived training needs.

This paper later also briefly refers to results from a secondary postal survey of 628 businesses from service sectors within Central Region, using a reduced version of the main interview questionnaire. The quality of this postal survey is well below that of the main interview survey in terms of response (only 20%) and representativeness. Basic information and results from the postal survey are described in Scott et al 1989.

Awareness of the single European Market

"Awareness" has been used vaguely in relation to the impact of the SEM on British firms. In a research paper from the Durham Business School, for example, Roe (1989:1) uncritically reiterates DTI figures in stating that "more than 95% of businesses in the UK are now aware of the Single Market". Awareness of the SEM, however, is not straightforward to measure. At its most general level, awareness may merely reflect that the owner or manager of a firm has heard of the phrases "l992" or "Single European Market". Awareness may often go no further than this. Beyond this level, awareness may become increasingly specific. Awareness may refer to the state of knowledge concerning new legislation, directives, quality standards and changes in customs regulations and other bureaucratic procedures specifically relevant to the firm.

Awareness may also refer to knowledge of the way the SEM may be affecting the business. Again the degree of specificity that could be encountered is variable - from hazy perceptions that "1992" presents some sort of threat or opportunity, down to detailed reasoning and informed knowledge of precisely how the SEM will affect or indeed HAS already affected the business.

Awareness of Measures:

The interview schedule contained questions designed to probe increasingly specific levels of awareness. Table 1 summarises the results. It illustrates that awareness falls appreciably as more specific measures of awareness are probed for. Over half the sample were generally aware of European legislation for the SEM, but this proportion drops to less than a fifth in terms of being able to specify a directive affecting the business. The distinction between vague and business specific knowledge of directives is the most marked. Of the 75 generally aware of directives a clear majority (68%) were able to give an example of a directive, whereas only 41% were aware of directives actually affecting their business.

TABLE 1 Awareness of new European legislation.

		N	% *
a)	General awareness of legislation	78	54
b)	Aware of directives	75	51
c)	Can give an example of a directive	51	35 (68% of b)
d)	Aware of directive(s) affecting business	31	21 (41% of b)
e)	Can specify a directive affecting business	26	18 (84% of d)

* Percentage of total sample (146).

The reporting of awareness levels of measures relating to the SEM thus depends crucially on the level of specificity used in designing the questions.

Effect on the Business

The Cecchini Report emphasised the heavy costs to European industry of the then existing physical and technical barriers to trade. The elimination of barriers would directly and indirectly (through promoting increased industrial competitiveness) lead eventually to considerable economic growth and net gains in aggregate GDP throughout the Community. Scott (1988: 15), however, points out that Cecchini is much vaguer on the negative consequences, which include major resource shifts that favour the centre at the expense of peripheral Regions, and painful social and economic readjustment. Neuberger (1988) also discusses the dangers of the growth of the power of large corporations, at the expense of smaller firms. Both Scott and Neuberger predict major threats to many sections of UK industry without an adequate response from the Government. It follows that all businesses should not only be alerted to the fact that the SEM will affect their business in some way, but should also be anticipating the nature of the opportunities or threats posed by the SEM

In assessing awareness of opportunities and threats, business owners can be categorised as falling into two groups - those aware that the single market is affecting their business and those who are not. These latter can be subdivided into business owners who are totally unaware or of the opportunities or threats of the SEM; and business owners who while aware, have calculated that the SEM has in practice little to offer and poses minimal dangers to their business. The extent to which the business is affected by the SEM, therefore, is not just a question of awareness, but also of **PERCEIVED RELEVANCE.**

On this issue, under half of the respondents (42%) believed they are or would be affected by the Single Market; fewer believed they would not (38%); and the remainder (20%) did not know. Two thirds of those indicating that the SEM would have an affect (28% of the total sample) thought they were **already** affected. Respondents who identified the Single Market as having an effect, expressed the effect in terms of offering greater opportunities to their business (39%), or in terms of increasing the competition (37%), or as a combination of the two. Overall, therefore, positive and negative perceptions were evenly balanced.

How realistic are the perceptions of opportunities and threats? Although this question was not systematically explored in the questionnaire, some clue can be gained by analysing answers relating to perceived threats from competitors products. Table 2 lists the distribution of specific threats for the WHOLE sample. It should be noted that we did not mention the SEM when the question on threats was asked. The answers can thus be treated as a guide on how business owners perceive threats from any quarter - mostly local competition and competition within the UK.

TABLE 2: Perceived threats from competitors' products.

	Of Total Reasons Offered			
	Product/Service A		Product/Service B	
	N	%	N	%
Lower Price	102	43	45	47
Better Quality	18	8	4	4
Better Delivery	25	11	6	6
Better Promotion/Advertising	14	6	6	6
Competitors Have A Stronger Hold On The Market	25	11	13	14
Competitors Are Better Resourced	27	11	13	14
Other	9	4	3	3
No Threats	15	6	5	5

Lower price is seen by far as the most dominant threat. These data were then crosstabulated according to whether the business owner thought that the SEM would be affecting the business. The distribution of lower price was not significant between the two groups, but two other threats were (see Table 3). Business owners perceiving an effect were much more likely to feel that their competitors were better resourced; and that they had a stronger hold on the market. These two threats are not easily quantifiable by busy owner managers, in contrast to lower price, which is. We can assume, therefore, that the two significant threats are possibly not too realistic. This implies that owner managers are "guessing" threats when relating to the SEM, rather than working them out systematically. Awareness of specific threats and opportunities, therefore, is likely to be much lower than is implied by a general perception of threats.

TABLE 3: Perceived relevance of Single Market against perceived threat from competitors' products.

Threat:		Relevant		Not Relevant	
		N	%	N	%
Lower Price					
	Yes	39	63	39	71
	No	23	37	16	29
	TOTAL	61	100	55	100
N.S.					
Better Resourced					
	Yes	18	29	4	7
	No	44	71	51	93
	TOTAL	62	100	55	100

Chi square: p=0.01

We now move to considering the issue of whether owner managers who believe that the SEM will not affect their business do so out of ignorance, complacency or reasonable judgement. Table 4 lists reasons for believing why the SEM would not affect the business. Many respondents seem to dismiss as irrelevant the possibility that European competition could seize their business. One small group found the SEM irrelevant as they were already successfully trading with Europe. The clear cut nature of the responses (hardly any availed themselves of the open ended "other" category) implies that basic non-awareness of possible opportunities and threats was less of a problem than possible complacency - the deliberate calculation that the SEM would be irrelevant.

TABLE 4 : Reasons for believing the SEM would not affect the respondent's business.

REASON:	N	%
No Plan To Market In Europe	23	42
Foreign Firms Could Not Compete Locally	21	38
Parent Company Would Deal With This	3	6
Already Market In Europe	4	7
Other	4	7
TOTAL	**55**	**100**

Charges of complacency against business owner managers are all too easily made, and tend to reinforce the stereotype of business owners held by many in the business support environment and some policy makers. For example in 1991 Doncaster Business Link reported that government initiatives to advise small and medium enterprises about 1992 had been largely ignored by smaller businesses in Doncaster. "Few recognised the need to adopt defensive as well as pro-active strategies. The initiative to act would not be taken if left solely to SMEs. The need was for a direct link between SMEs and the resources and help available. " (source: The Times July 12th 1991) . Again a survey by KPMG Peat Marwick's management consultancy arm comparing small companies with larger ones in their response to changing markets reported that small businesses are "none too enthusiastic about the advantages of the single European market. Three quarters of them said implementation of the market was not significant" (source the Times July 24th 1992).

At first sight Table 4 reinforces the stereotype. The results, however, like those of the surveys just quoted, do not show **HOW** relevance is calculated by owner managers. We may hypothesise that owner managers are reluctant to react to vague opportunities or threats no matter how theoretically beneficial or inevitable the "experts" think they are likely to be. Owner managers are only interested in concrete identifiable effects on their business. In their absence, failure to react may be quite a reasonable judgement. For example why should a local transport firm specialising in livestock transport from farm to local market fear competition from similar German, Greek or Danish firms? Theoretically a foreign firm could muscle in, but the chances of this happening are remote. Similarly how could the same business owner regularly meet the local needs of customers in, say, Sardinia without totally and unrealistically altering the scale of the business?

TABLE 5 : Experience of change in key areas of production/service.

	Major Change		Some Change		Affected By Single Market		
	N	%	N	%	%*	%t	*
Types of Product/ Service Sold	8	..6	51	35	25	(10)	
Types of Customer	9	6	42	29	31	(11)	
Skills of Workforce	9	6	47	32	28	(9)	
Skills of Management	12	8	73	50	26	(15)	
Size of Workforce	7	5	45	31	19	(7)	
Types of Production Equipment	11	8	48	33	17	(7)	
Administration/Office Procedures	8	6	60	41	22	(10)	
Stock Control Methods	9	6	30	21	10	(..3)	
Response to Competition	10	7	56	38	35	(16)	
Allocation of Senior Managers' Time	10	7	57	39	31	(15)	
Implementing BS5750	17	12	23	16	40	(11)	
Implementing QualityControl Not Registered With BS5750	9	6	27	19	30	(8)	
Implementing Just - In-Time	4	3	14	10	17	(2)	

* % = percentage of those indicating change
  %t = percentage of total sample (146).

The importance of concrete relevance is indicated by the fact that the survey shows that it is:
- large firms which operate in non local markets;
- firms that export;

- and firms which are subsidiaries of other firms outside Central Region; which are all much more likely to be aware of measures of the SEM, and to find the SEM has or will have an effect on their business. (For example around 60 per cent of exporting firms thought that the SEM would have an effect on their business, compared to 38 per cent trading UK wide only and 23 per cent trading locally only within Scotland).

An attempt was also made to assess the degree to which the SEM has affected firms in specific areas of management. Respondents were asked firstly to indicate whether they had experienced "major", "some" or "no" change in thirteen areas or management (see Table 5). Those experiencing change were then asked to indicate whether the change had anything to do with the SEM. Responses ranged between a quarter and a third who were experiencing change, were affected by the SEM in the area probed. In most cases this was around 10 to 15 per cent of the total sample. So the proportion able to pinpoint specific effects is much lower than the 28% who had previously stated in a more general question that the SEM was already affecting their business.

Preparedness

What does preparedness mean in relation to the Single Market? Lack of preparedness is at first sight straightforward to envisage. A firm which is not changing or planning to change any of its activities in response to the Single Market is not preparing itself. In practice few firms stay the same even over a period of a few weeks. Changes occur to varying extents. If these changes occur as a planned response to the Single Market, this is preparedness. Is it preparedness, however, if unplanned changes occur as a result of the pressure of the Single Market? Again is this measurable? Moreover can a firm ever be prepared enough? How can we measure high levels of preparedness? These questions illustrate that "preparedness" is a complex concept.

For the purposes of this study it was assumed that preparedness is a proactive process involving to varying degrees:

- Basic preparation if the firm reports:
    - a specific plan or strategy for preparing for the Single Market.

- seeking advice.
- More advanced preparation if the firm has:
    - allocated a budget for the strategy.
    - devised a timetable to implement the strategy - allocated responsibility for planning and implementation of a strategy.
    - acted upon advice received when thought useful.

These main indicators are augmented in the survey by preparedness in relation to quality standards, which are essential for many firms if they are to compete efficiently in Europe. Preparedness is indicated where the firm has registered or is intending to register with BS5750 and or with ISO9000. It should be stressed, however, that registration for these quality standards is not necessarily directly a consequence of the advent of the Single Market. They are thus less reliable measures of preparedness than the questions on plans and strategies.

TABLE 6: Preparedness of firms for the advent of the SEM.

	N	%
a) Have a specific plan or strategy to prepare	40	27
b) Have allocated responsibility to specific owners/managers.	29	20 (73% of a)
d) Have a timetable	21	14 (53% of a)
e) Have allocated a budget	16	11 (40% of a)
f) Have requested advice	18	12
g) Will act on advice	29	20

* Percentage of total sample (146).

The results for basic preparedness are summarised in Table 6. Nearly a third of respondents claimed to have some plan or strategy to prepare for the advent of the SEM. As more specific measures of preparedness are applied, the proportion prepared declines to a fifth in terms of allocating responsibility and acting on advice; and to less than 15% in terms of budgets, time tables and requesting advice. As in the case of awareness measurements, the proportion defined as prepared declines appreciably as specificity increases.

Awareness/ Preparedness: Variation by Sample Selection

The figures on awareness and preparedness that we have obtained so far will also vary according to the nature of the sampling base chosen and the representativeness of businesses that responded. The primary question, therefore, is whether this "sectoral" variation is likely to be large. The study provides useful insights on this issue, as we have information not just on interviewed firms from the four predominantly manufacturing sectors, but also on service sectors derived from a postal survey (see Methodology Section).

Table 7 illustrates some of the possible variation in terms of two basic measures of awareness and one of preparedness in the study common to both surveys. If data from both surveys (i.e the main survey and the postal survey of service sector firms) are combined, the general awareness of European legislation is 34 per cent. This masks a variation of 16% to 54% according to whether the sample base is predominantly drawn from the service sectors or from manufacturing sectors. If industrial sectors are compared singly, awareness is even more variable. Awareness of European legislation could have varied from 9% to 60% depending on which sector is chosen as a sample; and whether the SEM would affect the business from 14% to 44%.

TABLE 7. Variations of awarenees/preparedness by sample base.

Sectors	Manuf/g Sectors		Service Sectors		RANGE of All Sectors	
	N	%	N	%	Min %	Max %
General awareness of European legislation or the SEM	78	54	20	16	9	60
SEM will have/has effect on business	62	42	41	32	14	44
Business has a plan or strategy for preparing for SEM	40	28	10	8	0	30

This pattern is similar our basic measure of preparedness. There is a dramatic difference between the manufacturing and service sectors in the percentage of businesses claiming to have a plan or strategy to prepare for the SEM. The range of variation across individual sectors is from 0 to 30 per cent. The manufacturing sectors showed much less variation than the service sectors, varying from 24 to 30 per cent, compared from 0 to 12 per cent in the service sectors.

Variation by firm size:

Awareness and preparedness levels also vary considerably by **firm size**. Awareness of European legislation, for example, varies from extremely low in the smaller service firms (10% in businesses with less than 51 employees) to 100% for those employing more than 100. The variation for manufacturing firms is less, but still considerable (38% for firms with 5-10 employees, ranging to 100% for those with more than 500). Awareness and preparedness levels could thus vary appreciably according to whether a sample has excluded some firms on criteria of size- or whether there has been differential response between firms of different sizes. Given that sectoral mixes of businesses are never the same from one region to another, these results beg the question of what is a "random" sample of businesses? Comparing results across different samples is thus far from straightforward. (It should be noted that most studies of the exporting behaviour of small firms show low involvement, whereas this study produced relatively high levels of international behaviour. One possible explanation of this anomaly is that "random" samples across sectors under-represent the clustering of export experience which occurs in certain sectors - including the sectors we chose as our population. Vertical slices may give a truer picture of export behaviour than horizontal slices, no matter how random).

Predicting Preparedness

The main data set of manufacturing firms is based on interviews, has a high response rate, and contains based on questions that have systematically sought information on key measures. The overall questionnaire contained 73 questions. It would have been all too easy to have used these positive aspects as evidence that the data provide precise and meaningful variables for investigating predictive statistical models of preparedness.

Complexity of the dependent variable

Modelling of this kind, however, is fraught with difficulties. We have seen that the concepts of awareness and preparedness, our major dependent variables, are complex and not straightforward to measure meaningfully. In addition to these basic problems, there is the complexity of the relationship between key potential dependent variables. For example "awareness" and "perceived relevance" -(i.e the belief that the SEM is affecting the business) could both be viewed as different facets of general "preparedness". They would all qualify as dependent variables. Alternatively it is possible to argue that there is only one general measure of preparedness (actually doing something). "Awareness" and "perceived relevance" from this viewpoint are independent variables explaining preparedness.

Key independent variables: problems of causality

The major independent variables in the study were factors such as exporting activity (measured by a number of questions); sector, firm size; whether operating in an expanding or contracting market for its two main products; whether a business is a subsidiary of a larger group; the number of managerial functions delegated to the local plant. When simple non parametric statistics are applied to crosstabulations, such as Chi square; systematic and significant differences are clearly demonstrated between many of these independent factors and "awareness", "perceived relevance" and "preparedness" (see Scott, Rosa and McAlpine 1989). For example the percentage aware and prepared rises markedly with firms size; by exporting activity; and by having a parent company. Such variables, however, are significantly intercorrelated. Causality is difficult to identify without a much more focused study.

Results of analyses

These complexities mean that interpretation requires caution when applying multivariate statistics to test predictive models of awareness and of preparedness for the SEM. This point emerged clearly from initial analyses involved a series of multiple linear regressions (OLS) using measures of awareness, perceived relevance and preparedness as dependent variables, and exploring different combinations of independent variables. The general pattern of results showed:
- significant predictive results, but:
- that these results were questionable as the assumptions of normality were seriously broken. Even log and square transformations of the independent variables failed to significantly improve the fit of the models investigated, or to remedy the problems of normality.

It is thus inappropriate to expect a simple linear multivariate relationship between the dependent and the independent variables, where preparedness and awareness are viewed as measures increasing gradually and at the same rate all the way along the continuum. Rather the regression results (especially the analyses of residuals) imply significant polarisation, where the intensity of each measure of preparedness or awareness is especially strong at the extremes (i.e those not aware/prepared compared to those strongly aware/prepared).

Discriminant analysis:

Because of this, we felt that discriminant analysis was more appropriate. A dependent variable was produced where the sample was divided into three groups: (1) Not prepared at all; (2) some preparedness; (3) strongly prepared. There is no prior expectation as in regression that the three groups formed from the continuum of "preparedness" should be equally related in a linear fashion. Discriminant analysis rather emphasises the best linear fit of independent variables that separate each pair of groups in turn. Analyses were performed:
- treating "awareness" and "perceived relevance" as independent variables.
- regarding "awareness" and "perceived relevance" as co-dependent, and thus excluded from the list of independent variables in the analysis.

The results we achieved were much stronger than the multiple regressions (Table 8). Overall around 70% of cases were correctly classified in both analyses, and also when prior probabilities of group membership based on proportional group size were applied rather than probabilities distributed evenly across groups. These overall figures, however, masked notable differences:

- correct classification of the "not prepared" group rose to over 90% in both analyses when prior probabilities based on group size were used.
- The "strongly prepared" group, so important in terms of policy interest, fluctuated considerably, from a high correct classification of 82% When awareness measures were included and equal probabilities applied; to only 39% when awareness measures were excluded and size probabilities applied. Though still much greater than expected by chance, the results are too variable to place too much reliance on if used for practical policy or business support purposes.

In these analyses BOX M was used to gauge whether the underlying assumptions of equal variances were violated. The two analyses reported in Table 8 produced probabilities for BOX M of .02 and .07 showing that assumptions were violated to some extent. Moreover other discriminant analyses established that BOX M was especially sensitive to the inclusion and exclusion of specific independent variables. Although discriminant analysis is "robust" (Norusis 1985) it is clear that failing to meet assumptions is a further complication in obtaining clear predictions of preparedness.

Table 8: Classification results from discriminant analyses.

A: Awareness/perceived relevance included:

		PRIOR PROBABILITIES						
		EQUAL*				SIZE		
		1	2	3	P	1	2	3
NONE	83	**75%**	7%	18%	.6	**90%**	1%	8%
SOME	35	20%	**49%**	31%	.2	34%	**57%**	9%
STRONG	28	11%	7%	**82%**	.2	21%	25%	**54%**
TOTAL CORRECTLY CLASSIFIED		**70%**				**72%**		

* p=.33 per group.

B: Awareness/perceived relevance excluded:

		PRIOR PROBABILITIES						
		EQUAL*				SIZE		
		1	2	3	P	1	2	3
NONE	83	**76%**	11%	13%	.6	**95%**	1%	4%
SOME	35	23%	**57%**	20%	.2	37%	**46%**	17%
STRONG	28	21%	25%	**54%**	.2	36%	25%	**39%**
TOTAL CORRECTLY CLASSIFIED		**67%**				**73%**		

Conclusions

The late 1980s saw a burgeoning of commissioned consultancy research measuring awareness and preparedness of UK firms towards the advent of the SEM. It was not unusual for these studies to report precise figures for "general" awareness and preparedness in their sampled firms (eg. Roe 1990:1). Even the DTI, as mentioned earlier, was able to report 90 per cent nawareness" in 1988. It is probable that similar studies will recur in the future when government concern is again focused on UK competitiveness within the SEM.

This paper shows that any confidence in simple measures of awareness or preparedness is misplaced. Awareness and preparedness are complex concepts, and do not easily lend themselves to measurement in questionnaires - particularly in short "quick and dirty" consultancy surveys. The early sections of the paper have demonstrated that the degree of preparedness and awareness can vary substantially according to the specificity of the questions used. Given a range of measures, it is all too easy to select out the statistical figure that best suits one's argument. The variability reported also cast doubts on the meaningfulness of direct comparisons across surveys using even slightly different questions from each other.

The variation by question specificity is compounded by the variation by sector. This paper shows clearly that every single measure of awareness and preparedness considered in the study is especially variable across sectors and in terms of firm size. This raises three issues. Firstly if non respondents are not random in terms of sector, then reported awareness and preparedness levels could be seriously distorted. This has immense implications for local commissioned surveys, such as the CBI East Kilbride Survey (1988:3), which concluded:

"The number of replies received (nearly 25%) were well above the standard response for a postal survey of this type. So the picture presented of the reaction of East Kilbride business to 1992 can be taken as a fair and authoritative measure for all Scotland. Our worry must be for those that did not reply. If silence is the result of heads stuck firmly in the sand I fear for their future after the 1992 earthquake."

Secondly any attempt to exclude firms out of the sample on the basis of sector or size (for example omitting all firms over 500 employees or under 5 employees), cannot yield answers that are generally applicable to all firms in the spatial area studied. This would make comparison difficult or even impossible with results from other studies where different selection criteria were used. Thirdly no sample of firms has the same sectoral mix from one area to another. The significant variation by sector again makes inter-regional comparisons difficult.

It is also apparent from the analysis that the respondents were often guessing on what the perceived opportunities and threats may be, rather than systematically trying to work these out. It may be that much of the difficulty surrounding the concepts of "awareness" and "preparedness" stem from the basic uncertainty of many owner managers of what effect the SEM really will have on their business. Even informed economists commissioned by the EC are "guessing" on the likely effects of the SEM on the business environment. Given this it is scarcely surprising that uncertainty is also endemic amongst practising owner managers. The common view by many policy makers and business support agencies that small business owners are extremely complacent in the face of the SEM, must take account of this uncertainty in passing judgement. Reactions to threats by owner managers is likely to be much more calculated and positive where the threats are perceived to be immediate, concrete and easily identified.

The latter part of the paper demonstrates that misleadingly good predictions of preparedness towards the SEM can be achieved through multivariate analyses. Discriminant analysis producec much better results than those from OLS multiple regression, which were beset with problems of serious dePartures from linearity and normality. These results, however, are beset with underlying problems of measurement and optimisation. The interview questions that provided the measures for preparedness in this study could have been much more sophisticated and exhaustive. Even so, they provide the means to measure preparedness (as a dependent variable) in many different ways. How each measure relates to the use of different options in the discriminant procedure is again a complex issue. Different options produce considerable differences in predictive results. (For example we have seen in Table 8 how changing the prior probabilities causes significant variations). The use of such techniques to predict preparedness on the basis of independent characteristics for policy purposes is premature and inappropriate until we learn far more about the nature of preparedness and the interrelations of key predictors.

The above discussion on awareness/ preparedness for the SEM has implications too for other studies involving businesses' (and especially small businesses') responsiveness to government policies and cultural changes (for example environmental protection measures, changes in safety and employment law, taxation regimes, for example). We possess in the social sciences a capacity for statistical precision that is often far in advance of our ability to match it in the measurement of attitudinal data amongst business owners and managers.

References

BISPA (November 1988) *BISPA and the Single Internal Market.* p 1-31.

CBI Scotland, (April 1988) *1992 - completion of the Single Market. East Kilbride Survey.* p. 1-6

Cecchini, P. (1988) *The European Challenge - 1992: The Benefits of the Single Market.* English Edition- Aldershot: Wildwood House

Commission of the European Communities.(June 1985) *completing the Internal Market.* White Paper from the Commission to the European Council.

Marquand, D. (1988) The politics of 1992. What is likely to happen? *Manufacturers Preparing for 1992 Conference, November 1992.* p. 1-7.

Neuberger, H. (January 1989) *The Economics of 1992.* A Report Commissioned by the British Labour Group of Euro MPs.

Norusus, M.J. (1985) *SPSSX- Advanced Statistics Guide.* London: McGraw Hill.

Roe, D. (1990) Strategies for small firms in the Single Market. *DUBS Occasional Paper 9040. University of Durham.* p. 1-14.

Scott, A. and Reid, A.I. (August 1988). Scotland and the completed Internal Market. *STUC Conference: Delegates Discussion Paper.* p. 1-16.

Scott, A.; McKinnon, A. and Reid, A. (1988) Completing the Internal Market: Some implications for the Scottish Economy. *Working Paper, Department of Economics, Heriot-Watt Universiti.* p. 1-26.

Scott, M.; Rosa, P. and McAlpine, A. (July 1989). The preparedness of firms in Central Region for the Single European Market, and their information and training needs. *SEF Report Series No. 53/89, UniversitY of Stirling, Scotland.*

Sweeney, G.P (1991) Technical culture and local dimension of entrepreneurial vitality. *Entrepreneurship and Regional Development.* 3(4): p. 363-378

2 Success factors and their sensitivity to internationalization: Some empirical findings among Finnish SMEs

Leila Hurmerinta-Peltomäki

1. Introduction

Due to the present economic situation and less positive demand expectations in domestic markets, also small firms are increasingly directing their interest to foreign markets. It is also assumed that younger and smaller firms start exports because of European integration (Young 1990). The internationalization process is found to have become more rapid - today, the firms are not becoming passively internationalized but are actively internationalizing their business (Hurmerinta-Peltomäki 1991).

During the last years an increasing proportion of Finnish industrial exports has been attributable to SMEs (less than 500 employees), going up to 49 percent of total exports in 1990. Approximately 23 percent of SMEs' production goes abroad while the corresponding figure for large firms is 52 percent (Central Statistical Offlce of Finland, 20 March 1992). Thus SMEs appear to have a lot of export potential.

Internationalization is no longer regarded as an altemative but rather an essential prerequisite for growth, also for small businesses. Along with the growing interest and involvement of SMEs in exports the differences between domestic and export firms are suggested to be disappearing. Similarly with the globalization of markets furthered by European integration and increasing foreign investments, the division of markets into domestic and export markets can also become less relevant. This is supported by Gankema & Zwart (1992), who noticed in their research review, that the same export problems continually appeared during the past decade but the importance of these problems are diminishing over time.

For years, success and its determinants have been a topical theme in business studies. Export success, too, is a popular research area, which presumably builds on the idea of differences between export and domestic success factors. However, it is seldom explained why and how success factors make a difference between exporters and non-exporters (Gemunden 1991, 50) or how the success factors differ with the firm's export involvement. Export success studies have concentrated almost entirely on the fims' foreign activities without analysing the importance of home-based factors related to both foreign and domestic markets. At the time when domestic and foreign markets are approaching each other and internationalization has become a reality also for small businesses this question is of great practical and academic interest. The question is also closely related with the debate about the differences between international and domestic marketing, even if success factors include many more than marketing factors. There are four basic positions in this debate (Perry 1990):

(1) there are differences in nature, but a dominant and superior domestic model will prevail;
(2) there are fundamental and sustained differences in nature;
(3) there are no differences;
(4) the differences in local environments are being invalidated by the globalization of markets.

This debate can usefully be extended to the discussions about the differences between the market-related success factors.

This paper consists of three parts: Firstly, a short conceptual description of the concepts success factor and export involvement is presented. Secondly, the characteristics of internationalizing SMEs are described. Thirdly, the connections of the concepts success factor and export involvement are examined in the light of empirical survey data. The paper ends with conclusions and further research suggestions.

2. Conceptual framework

Success factor

All definitions of the success factor [also named as key variable, strategic factor, key success factor, key result area, pulse point (Leidecker et al. 1984), critical success factor (e.g. Boynton et al. 1984), critical mass (Attiyeh et al. 1979)] can be said to agree that a firm possesses only a few success factors and that they influence the firm's success. More detailed definitions of success factors depend on three issues: the purpose of the study, the definition of the concept success and the determinants of the model used.

The success factor research is based on Daniel's article of 1961, where the concept was first met. It was then used in developing management information systems helping the managers to cover their information needs (information-based approach). Afterwards the concept has been used in strategy planning (process-based approach), and more lately especially in finding a match between the firm and its environment (contextual approach). The success factor research has become more and more market-oriented (see Grunert & Ellegaard 1992). The purpose of this paper calls for a contextual approach, which is based on the idea that the environment a firm is operating in detemmines the success factors. Accordingly, Grunert & Ellegaard's (1992, 517) definition for the success factor is used:"...a skill or resource a business can invest in, which, on the market the business is operating on, explains a major part of the observable differences in perceived value and/or relative costs".

The market-based description of a success factor involves a question: does foreign environment demand different success factors than domestic environment? Or do the success factors differ related to the firm's export involvement? That is, when the emphasis of the firm's activities are foreign-oriented there should be differences compared to the domestic-oriented firms.

Export involvement

A classical statement for internationalization is that of Johanson & Vahlne (1977), who described internationalization as a gradual and successively increasing commitment to foreign markets. This commitment or internationalization process has been named as export involvement by many authors (see for a review, Makinen 1992). However, even if the stages theory is consistent, not all firms follow this pattern (Welch & Luostarinen 1988). There are also differences in how the stages model is operationalized by researchers. Export involvement has been measured here by four different patterns as follows:

	operationalization
(1) the export/non-export nature of the firm	(export/sales ratio 0 %) = non-exporter (export/sales ratio 1-100 %) = exporter
(2) the export ratio	export/sales ratio
(3) the export experience	the year of beginning to export
(4) the export stage	six stages (see chapter 3.2)

3. Success factors related to export involvement - some empirical findings

3.1 Methodology

The data used for empirical testing of differences between the success factors was collected by mail survey in spring 1989 as part of the regional business development project in South-Western Finland (VAKE-project). The aim of the research project was to give a general picture of the internationalization of the small and medium-sized industrial fims in South-Western Finland. The analysis is based on the response of 556 firms which met the size criterion of 499 or less employees. The sample consisted of 2613 SMEs; the response rate was 21 percent. The names and addresses of the firms were collected from a company register maintained by the Central Statistical Office of Finland. The questionnaires were mainly filled out by senior executives, who can be assumed to have an extensive view of the firms' goals and strategies.

As the data was not originally met for the purposes of this article, some restrictions have to be approved. The concept 'success factor' has been replaced by 'development area'. However, the content of the concept is quite the same: the firm is investing in those factors or functional areas which are perceived to be most important for the firm's perfommance (see chapter 2). The limitation is, that the data did not contain any performance indicators with which it would have been possible to verify the reliability of the managers' perceptions. Cross-sectional data also creates some limitations from the point of view a single firm's internationalization. The empirical results are mainly based on means and correlations.

3.2 Differences between high- and low-involvement SMEs

The export involvement was measured with four indicators which were related to the firm's development areas (= potential success factors) used in this paper. The association between the indicators and the development areas was measured with Pearson's multiple correlation coefficient.

Table 1. Correlations between export involvement and development areas

	Export involvement			
	Non-exp./ exporter	Export ratio	Export experience	Export stage
Development areas				
Production methods	-	-	-	x
Product development	xx	xx	-	xx
Marketing	-	-	-	xx
Export marketing	xx	xx	-	xx
Personnel management	xx	xx	x	xx
Data processing	xx	x	-	xx
Accounting	-	-	x	xx
Financing	-	-	-	xx

Notation: '-' denotes that there is no significant correlation between export involvement and development area, 'x' =significant at 99 percent confidence level and 'xx'=significant at 99.9 percent confidence level.

The table 1 shows that there are significant correlations between export involvement and how the firms emphasize different development areas. The export stage has the strongest relationship with the development areas. Therefore this article attempts to profile further only those differences related to the firms' export stage. The EXPORT STAGE model is divided into six stages that are:

		frequency	%
1	**DOMESTIC** stage	247	48
2	Pre-export stage with **INTEREST** in export	42	8
3	Pre-export stage with **PLAN** to export	53	11
4	**EXPERIMENTAL** involvement stage (export /sales ratio 1-9%)	56	11
5	**ACTIVE** involvement stage (export/sales ratio 10-39 %)	67	13
6	**COMMITTED** involvement stage (export /sales ratio 40 % or more)	45	9
	total	510 firms	100 %

Nearly half of the firms belonged to the domestic stage, while the other stages accounted for some 10 percent of the firms each. The following figures will use the numbering presented above for the stages of export involvement.

Characteristics of SMEs along export involvement

As seen in Figure 1, the number of employees in SMEs is growing almost linearly as export involvement increases. The greatest growth is linked with the stages from interest in export to experimental export and also from active export to committed export. This would confirm the general view that there exists a relationship between the growth behaviour and internationalization of small businesses. Also the firms' turnover increases in a similar fashion. There are clear differences in these growth indicators between the high- and low-involvement firms. The interesting point is, that after advancing to the experimental stage, the firms' turnover decreases close to that at the preexport stage, after which it increases again.

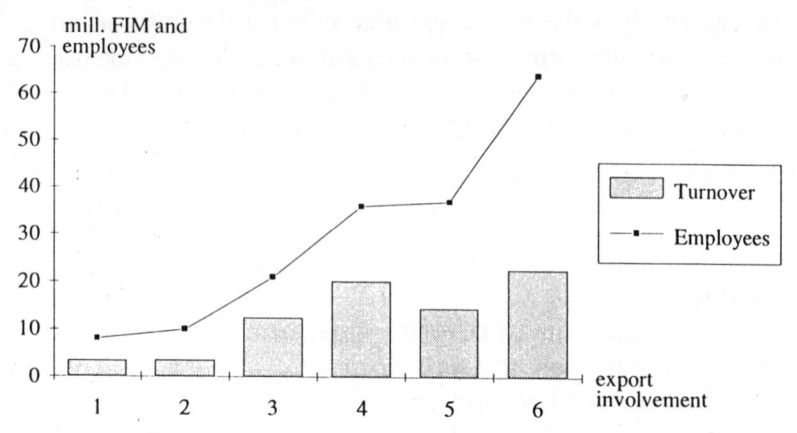

Figure 1. Turnover and number of employees along export involvement

A closer look at the ratio turnover/employees suggests that firms with higher export involvement are more efficient than firms with lower involvement as a whole (Figure 2). Although efficiency is continually increasing at preexport stages until the experimental stage, it goes down in the latter stages. Daniels & Bracker (1989) have tried to find an optimum point in the ratio of foreign to domestic activities. They succeeded to show that a significant difference in performance can be explained by the dependence on foreign operations.

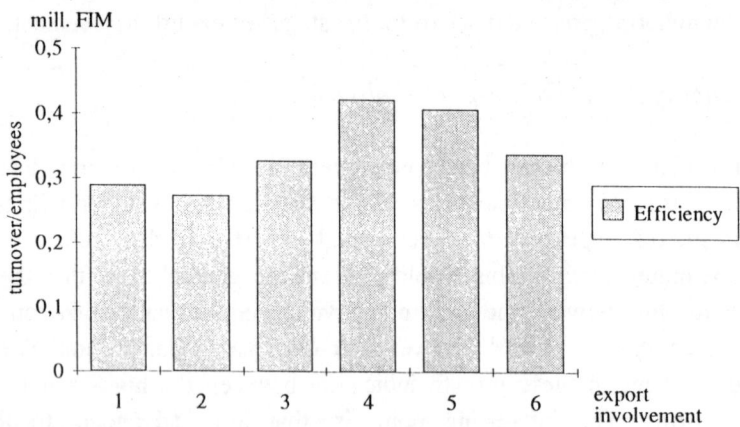

Figure 2. Efficiency along export involvement

Kinnunen (1991, 35) has recently noted that an internationalizing firm is more successful than its domestic counterpart as a whole. Foreign operations of an internationalizing firm are, however, less profitable than its domestic operations. This rises the question of foreign expansion as the result rather than the cause of good performance (see Daniels & Bracker 1989). There can also appear synergy between domestic and foreign operations: foreign operations improve the performance of domestic operations. This would support the idea of researching a firm's total performance and even in export studies emphasizing the role of the domestic base to export success.

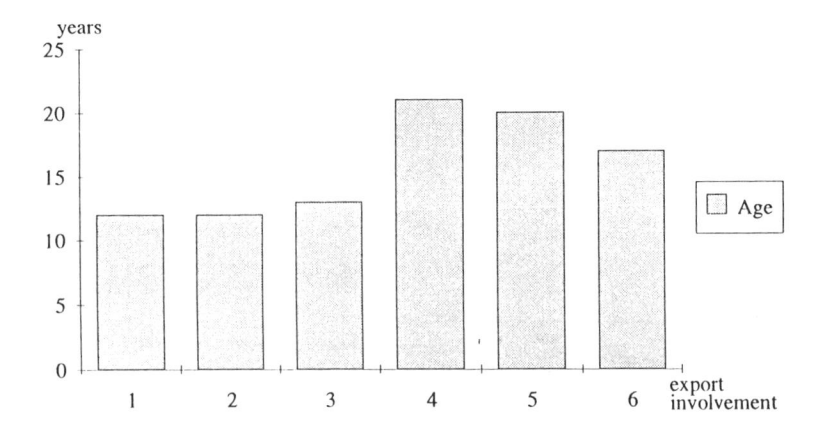

Figure 3. Age along export involvement

The firms' age is clearly higher at high-involvement stages than at lower stages (Figure 3). There are no noticeable differences in ages at preexport stages where ages varied from 12 to 13 years. At stages of higher involvement the trend was again declining from the age of 21 at the experimental stage to 17 at the committed stage. The stages approach questions the generally accepted conception of a single firm's internationalization process as a gradual and slow learning process. SMEs are nowadays more active and also aggressive in their internationalization. The stages are over jumped. This is shown by the fact that the firms' age structure at export levels of higher commitment is getting younger (see Hummerinta-Peltomaki 1991).

The firms are seen to expand their markets nationally before starting to export (Figure 4). Many factors thought to be related with export expansion appear also to be related with domestic expansion and vice versa (Yang et al. 1992). With expansion in domestic markets, a small firm develops its preconditions for successful export. At export stages the proportion between regional and national markets remained relatively stable (regional markets 40 percent and national markets 60 percent).

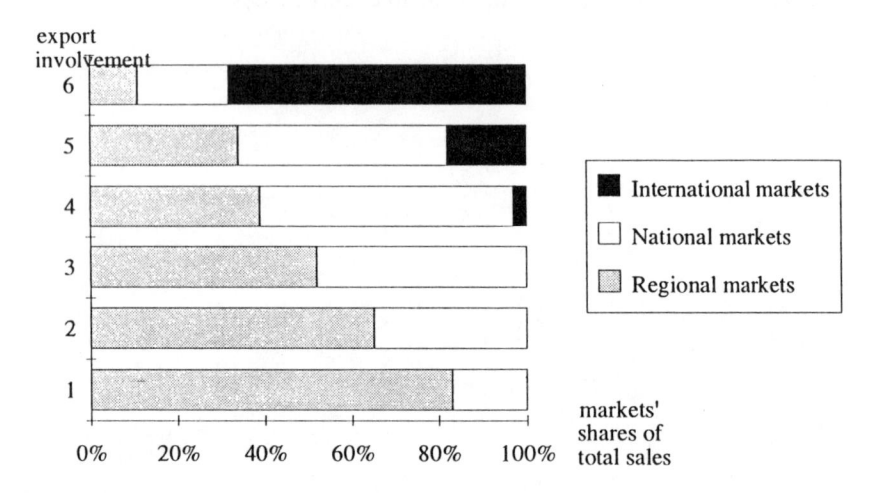

Figure 4. Shares of total sales between different markets along export involvement

Development areas of SMEs along export involvement

The development areas presented in this paper are internal to the firm and remain on a general level due to the data available. Generality is linked to information content: the more general the factor, the lower the information content. Alternatively the time span in which the factor is stable is longer (Grunert & Ellegaard 1992). At the extreme, a factor may be so general that it is true over a long time period almost by definition. One example may be market orientation, which has reached a critical position as a determinant of performance. Nevertheless, the data gives some indicative information about the functional areas in which the success factors should be found and how they relate with the firm's export involvement.

The first noteworthy fact is that the domestic firms with no interest to export emphasized all development areas less than any other group of the firms (Figure 5). They could be regarded as less development-oriented. Generally, the importance of development areas was positively correlated with the firm's stage of export involvement: the higher the stage of involvement, the more development-oriented the firms were. This applied to all the development areas of the firm.

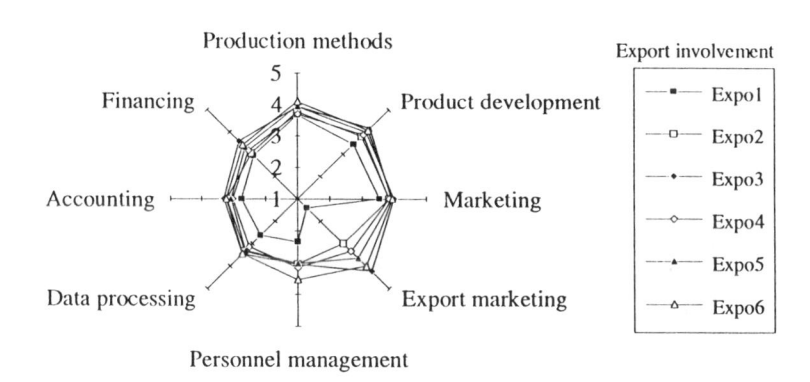

Figure 5. Development areas and their importance along export involvement

Scale: 1 = no importance...5 = very important.

The most obvious difference between the firms in emphasizing the development areas was undoubtedly concerned with export marketing and it was also in this area where the greatest variation occurred. The smallest variation was found in production methods and, if the domestic firms with no interest in exports are ignored, in marketing. But this showed only the absolute differences in evaluations of a single development area.

Even though there are differences in the degree of emphasis along export involvement, the differences are disappearing, when the comparison is based on relative importance between development areas obtained by a ranking list of the three most important areas. This "ranking"-system of managers' perceived success factors is the most common method in success factor research. The list of success factors becomes shorter, following the idea of the concept success factor - "... there are only a few success factors..."

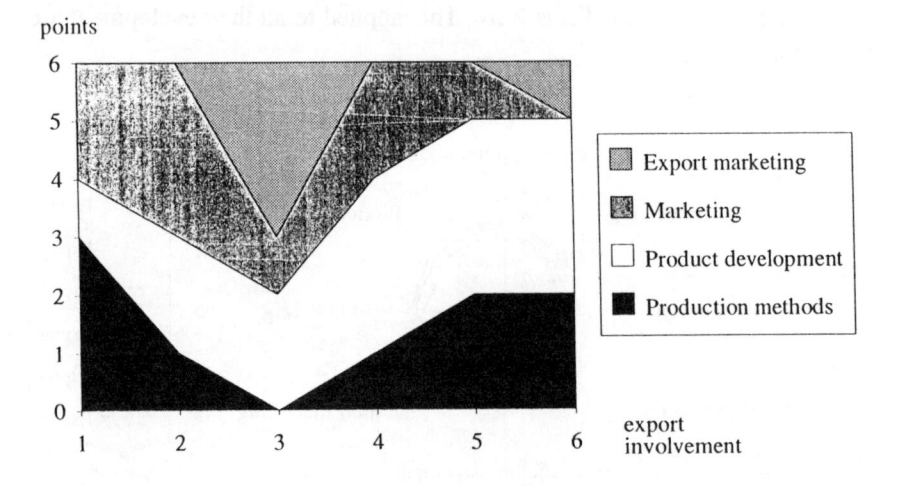

Figure 6. The three most important development areas along export involvement.

(scale: 3 points = the most important, 2 points = the second most important and 1 point = the third most important.)

The most important development areas were product development, production methods, marketing and export marketing, in this order (Figure 6). On the whole there seem to be only small differences between high- and low-involvement SMEs. Product development was an area which was regarded important regardless of the stage of export involvement. There were only two stages where notable variation existed: the pre-export stage of planning to export and the export stage of committed involvement. The firms at these stages ranked export marketing more important than marketing in general; yet the firms at the experimental and active stages of export considered general marketing more important.

This paper concentrated only on the export stages model. Measuring export involvement in the exporter/non-exporter categories would not have brought out differences in perceived success factors. Only in the preference order of these factors notable differences could have been detected. Both groups emphasized general marketing over export marketing.

4. Conclusions and suggestions for further research

This paper aimed at describing the possibilities to define market-related success factors and their relationship with the firm's export involvement measured by different indicators. The idea of the paper was based on the assumption that the differences between the firms' success factors related to domestic/export markets are diminishing with the increasing globalization of markets and the growing export involvement of SMEs. This assumption questions the reasons for studying export success factors in isolation of the firm's domestic success factors. This idea was tested by data collected in 1989 by mail survey. The analysis was based on the response of 556 industrial SMEs. As the data was not originally collected for this particular study, the analysis remained on a relatively general level. This is also why the concept 'success factor' was replaced by the 'development area'. The development areas and their evaluated importance were studied according to the firms' export involvement measured by four different indicators. The stages model of export involvement had the strongest relationship with the development areas and was thereby selected.

The differences between the high- and low-involvement firms were described. The firms with higher export involvement are bigger, more efficient, older and they function on a wider national scale than their domestic partners. The analysis showed, however, that the growth is not necessarily continuous. Firms at the pre-export stage with plans to export were much alike the firms at export stages.

The differences of success factors related to export involvement were small. The differences were more closely related with the preference order than the content of the success factors. Of the six stages only firms planning to export and firms with committed export diverged from the general trend. No differences were found between the exporters and non-exporters.

This paper showed that the success factors can be found from a few functional areas and the importance of these areas differed rather little along export involvement. This was partly due to the cursory survey of the subject. More detailed data is needed in future research to examine more deviating information. This would help managers to identify factors that are most critical for internationalization and therefore require flexibility. When the firm's export involvement increases, a bigger emphasis should be put on these sensitive factors to facilitate successful operation outside domestic markets.

References

Attiyeh, Robert S. and Wenner, David L. (1979), Critical Mass: Key to Export Profits, *Business Horizons*, December, Vol. 22, No. 6, pp. 28-38.

Boynton, Andrew C. and Zmud, Robert W. (1984), An Assessment of Critical Success Factors, *Sloan Management Review*, Vol. 25, No. 4, pp. 17-27.

Central Statistical Office of Finland, 20 March 1992.

Daniel, D. Ronald (1961), Management Information Crisis, *Harvard Business Review*, September-October, pp. 111-121.

Daniels, J. D: and Bracker, J. (1989), Profit Performance: Do Foreign Operations Make a Difference?, *Management International Review*, Vol. 29, No. 1, pp. 46-56.

Gankema, Harold G.J. and Zwart, Peter S. (1992), The relationship between film characteristics and export involvement of small firms. International Council for Small Business, 37th World Conference on Small Business and Entrepreneurship Development. Toronto, Canada June 18-21, Proceedings, pp. 2-16.

Gemünden, Hans Georg (1991), Success Factors of Export Marketing, A meta-analytic critique of the empirical studies, in Paliwoda, Stanley J. (ed.), *New Perspectives on International Marketing*, Routledge: London, pp. 33-62.

Grunert, Klaus G. and Ellegaard, Charlotte (1992), The Concept of Key Success Factors: Theory and Method, 21st Annual Conference of the European Marketing Academy: Marketing for Europe - Marketing for the Future, Aarhus May 26-29, Proceedings Competitive Papers, pp. 505-524.

Hurmerinta-Peltomäki, Leila (1991), PKT-*yritysten kansainvalistyminen Varsinais-Suomessa* (The Internationalization of the Small and Medium-sized Industrial Firms in South-Western Finland), Publications of the Turku School of Economics and Business Administration, Business Research Center, Series B 4, Turku.

Johanson, Jan and Vahlne, Jan-Erik (1977), The Internationalization Process of the Firm: A Model of Knowledge Development and Increasing Foreign Market Commitment, Journal of International Business Studies, Vol. 8, Spring/Summer, pp. 35-40.

Kinnunen, Helvi (1991), *Suomalaisten yritysten kansainvalistyminen: ulkomaantoiminnan kannattavuus ja vaikutus kotimaantalouteen*, Suomen Pankki A:80. Helsinki.

Leidecker, Joel K. and Bruno, Albert V. (1984), Identifying and Using Critical Success Factors, *Long Range Planning*, Vol. 17, No. 1, pp. 23-32.

Makinen, Helena (1992), Export Involvement of Small Exporting Firms: An Empirical Investigation, the 7th Nordic Conference on Small Business Research in Turku Finland, June 4-6, Proceedings, pp. 705-721.

Perry, Anne C. (1990), International versus Domestic Marketing: Four Conceptual Perspectives, *European Journal of Marketing*, Vol. 24, No. 6, pp. 41-54.

Welch, Lawrence S. and Luostarinen, Reijo (1988), Internationalization: Evolution of a Concept, *Journal of General Management*, Vol. 14, No. 2, Winter, pp. 34-55.

Yang, Yoo S., Leone, Robert P. and Alden, Dana L. (1992), A Market Expansion Ability Approach to Identify Potential Exporters, *Journal of Marketing*, Vol. 56, No. 1, January, pp. 84-96.

Young, Stephen (1990), Special issue on international marketing: Spotlight on Europe. Editorial. *Journal of Management*, Vol. 6, No. 3.

3 Modeling key success factors in manufacturing

Antti Haahti

Key Success Factors in Manufacturing

1.1 Purpose of the Study

The purpose of this paper is to explore success factors in manufacturing. As preliminary analyses within a longitudinal, comparative research program into pre-export, export and international operations of SME's in manufacturing industries (InterStratos, see appendix for short description), the broader intention is to develope hypotheses for further study. Given this purpose, the objectives of this paper are the following:
1. To describe differences and similarities of success factors, and
2. To investigate the structural characteristics of success factors, and
3. To test the effects of manager age and firm size on success factors and export sales.

The focus is on success factors as perceived by managers and entrepreneurs in SME's operative in textile and clothing industry, electronics industry, food industry, furniture-making and mechanical engineering industries in Austria, Belgium, Finland, Great Britain, Netherlands, Norway, Sweden and Switzerland during the year 1991.

1.2 Introduction

Identification and weighing the importance of success factors relative to the competitors is in the core of corporate strategy analysis. Success factors are those variables that managers can influence to gain advantageous competitive position in industry and these variables are derived from the interaction of economic and technological characteristics of the industry and the competitive weaponry used in that industry (Hofer and Schendel 1978).

In strategic planning literature, and specifically in the linear strategy models it is customary to model the planning process in stages starting with appraisal of the environment (see eg. Mintzberg, The design school model). The result of the external appraisal is a specification of the opportunities and threats in the (task) environment and the industry. The result of the internal appraisal is a determination of the strengths and weaknesses of the firm relative to the competing firms. This stage is better known as the SWOT-analysis, a starting point for strategic planning.

The former analysis, given it is an industry-wide study of competitive conditions in relevant product/market groups, will contribute in the determination of the key success factors of that specific competitive setting. The second analysis, given it is a through appraisal of the total organisation and the value chain within the firm (and the total value chain concerning the network of firms), will specify the distinctive competences of the firm.

The concept of distinctive competence was introduced by Selznik (1957) and was defined as a set of skills, capacity or ability to satisfy market needs comparatively better than the firm's competitors. By relating (fitting) the profile of distinctive competences of the firm with the industry profile of key success factors, the firm will be able to specify its competitive advantage(s) in product/market group and industry where it competes. In this transformation the two appraisals lead to the definition of competitive position of the firm. Corporate strategy is concerned with creating this edge against competitors, and with a continuous search for the sustainable strength relative to competitors.

In order to establish the competitive position of the firm, Hofer and Schendel (1978) recommend concentrating on only a few, most relevant key success factors. This is due to the fact that most often success factors differ in each industry or market where the firm operates and only few of these factors have a substantial impact on performance. The pragmatic problem is not identifying the factors, but weighting these to determine their relative effect on profitability or other measures of performance.

In the InterStratos study we are interested in the key success factors as a basis for export strategy. A starting point for economic choice is the scarceness of resources. Due to the market dynamism, the competitive advantages are typically discontinuous, much dependent on the technology, structure and stage of evolution of the industry and the product/markets. Therefore, as the market changes, the distinctive competences must be developed to precede (or follow) the requirements of the changing market. The allocation of the firm's resources should be based on a through understanding of the competitive conditions of the industry. Some factors are more relevant than others, and in each business and even in different product/market groups there is inherent logic of doing that business in order to succeed. Identification of these factors will facilitate the efficient allocation of resources to those product-market investments that contribute the highest economic rent. The fine tuning of the firm's distinctive competences to fit the relevant success factors is in the heart of creating a sustainable competitive advantage, and a necessary condition for successful performance.

The key success factors may differ between different product/markets or industries. The key factors of success may lie in different functions, areas and channels. The identification of success factors may need a through analysis of the total value chain or a comparison between winners and losers. Understanding the business logic is a result of a learning process. Mostly through experience within an industry a manager will learn the success factors in that industry and will learn to distinguish the key success factors among those influencing profitability. Whatever the nature of the factor, its identification is not enough to succeed since a thorough, effective and efficient implementation of the chosen strategy is needed.

Key success factors are of interest as such, but we are concerned with the links between selected exogenous variables and endogenous variables. Manager's experience, firm size, industry, competitive situation etc. may have effects on formulation of corporate and business strategy and export behavior.

Findings within organizational behavior literature support the causal relationship between size and functional specialization (Child 1973). It has also been shown that absolute size affects entry into foreign markets, and that export market expansion and export performance are distinguishable export activities that are not influenced by the same small-firm characteristics: export market expansion is strongly influenced by the presence of financial and human resources best represented by sales, assets, number of employees, whereas export performance was directly related to skill intensity of the small firm (Reid 1982, p.33). Therefore it is also of interest to study the relationship between the size of firm, skills and experience and the success factors, and their combined effects on export sales.

But key success factors seem not to have been of great interest to students of exporting and international operations. In Miesenbock's comprehensive review there are only indirect references to studies about (key) success factors in the context of export research (Miesenbock 1989). Neither do Turnbull & Palidowa touch on this issue in their review (1986). Since key success factors are important in the formulation of corporate strategy, it may be of interest to study key success factors also in the InterStratos design.

2.1 Key success factors by country

In the InterStratos we were satisfied with an attempt to describe the success factors identified as relatively important by the responding managers. There were altogether 19 items (see Table 1) collected from relevant literature (Stratos 1990, Ohmae 1982, Bamberger 1986).

The formulation of the question was as follows: On what factors do you put specific emphasis in order to achieve or maintain a competitive position in your main markets? 1 = no importance, 2 = low importance, 3 = medium importance, 4 = high importance, 5 = very high importance.

Table 1. Selected success factors (variable~ 201 to 219)

1.	Quality of management
2.	Reputation, local image
3.	Workers' skills
4.	Technology
5.	Technical problemsolving
6.	Product quality
7.	Aftersales service
8.	Creativity
9.	Distribution and selling
10.	Product design
11.	Pricing policy
12.	Low cost level
13.	Market share
14.	Financial strength
15.	Customer relations
16.	Flexibility
17.	Reliability of delivery
18.	Administration
19.	Product adaptation

The focus is here on the differences and similarities between firms from the eight countries participating in the study.

On the basis of mean values, rank orders were derived from the order of mean values for each country. Rank ordered means were given values in ascending order, where 1 = highest mean value (4.63) and 19 = lowest mean value (3.35). The results of this analysis are presented in Table 2.

Table 2. Rank order of importance of success factors in manufacturing by country. InterStratos 1991 sample, variables 201-219 (N=3243)

Success Factor	AUT	BEL	HOL	SWI	GBR	NOR	SWE	FIN	GRAND MEAN	RANK DIFF.
Quality of management	7	7	11	6	2	4	4	10	6	9
Reputation, local image	5	15	5	7	16	8	13	6	7	11
Workers' skills	3	6	6	5	6	5	5	4	4	3
Technology	13	12	12	14	12	16	14	12	15	4
Tech. problem solving	10	9	9	10	9	11	9	11	8	2
Product quality	1	1	1	1	-	1	1	1	1	0
Aftersales service	6	3	10	3	8	10	2	7	5	8
Creativity	9	14	14	8	14	12	6	16	13	10
Distribution & selling	12	13	16	9	7	13	7	9	11	11
Product design	16	18	18	15	10	18	10	17	16	8
Pricing policy	17	16	17	17	17	15	15	14	18	3
Low cost level	18	10	13	18	4	9	12	13	14	16
Market share	19	19	19	19	11	19	18	19	19	8
Financial strength	14	17	15	16	18	14	16	15	17	4
Customer relations	15	4	3	13	15	3	19	3	10	16
Flexibility	4	5	4	4	3	6	8	5	3	5
Reliability of delivery	2	2	2	2	1	2	3	2	2	2
Administration	8	8	8	11	5	17	17	18	12	13
Product adaptation	11	11	7	12	12	7	11	8	9	5

Rank order was derived from the order of mean values for each country. Rank ordered means were given values in ascending order, where 1 = highest mean value (4.63) 19 = lowest mean value (3.35) (Original scale: 1 = no importance...5 = very high importance). Rank difference = highest rank - smallest rank of a success factor.

Let's first focus on the ranks based on the grand means. The rank order of success factors in order of importance is then as follows.

1. Product quality
2. Reliability of delivery
3. Flexibility of the firm
4. Workers' skills
5. Aftersales service

and the five least important items:
15. Technology
16. Product design
17. Financial strength
18. Pricing policy
19. Market share

Product quality and reliability of delivery are perceived as the most important success factors for development of competitive advantage. The following most important success factors are the flexibility of the firm, workers' skills and the aftersales service.

The other end of the continuum presents peculiar results. For a marketer it should be disconcerting to note that the least important variables are some of the most relevant marketing weaponry. What else does there remain of marketing mix variables? Evidently, aspects of marketing strategy are estimated somewhat unimportant and we note this problem for further study.

2.2 Comparing individual ranks

Let us next focus on the individual ranks for each of the countries. It is clear that product quality is consistently regarded as the most important key success factor. There are slight, but insignificant variations in the second factor, the reliability of delivery. The third, success factor - flexibility - creates considerable variance. Actually its rank as the third factor is true only for British respondents. For all others it varies around fourth place, but for Swedes the derived rank was only eight. The difference between the highest rank (3 for British respondents) and lowest rank (8 for Swedes) is 5 rankings.

The fourth ranked item - workers' skills is quite consistently ranked as the fourth highest in importance. The rank difference is 3. The fifth factor of importance - aftersales service - shows high inconsistency and great differences between national samples. Swedes, Swiss and Belgian respondents rank it as a very important factor (second, third and third, respectively) and Dutch and Norwegian rank it both as the tenth in importance. The rank difference is 8.

The spread between opinions is even greater for the next factor - quality of management - with a grand mean of six. British respondents receive a derived second place, Norwegians and Swedes regard it as the fourth most important factor, Dutch and Finns rank it as the 11th and 10th in order of importance. The rank difference is 9.

The seventh most important success factor is reputation, and image factor. Dutch, Austrian and Finnish respondents rank it as the fifth (5,5,6) factor and British and Belgian rank it as a low 16 and 15. The rank difference is 11 implying high variation between different nationals.

Technical problemsolving ability is the rank 9 factor, which is consistently ranked between 9 and 11. Thus there are no or only slight national differences. The rank difference is 2. The next factor, customer relations, created much variation. Belgians, Dutch, Norwegian and Finns placed this factor as the third factor of importance (4,3,3,3). Swedes ranked it lowest as the 19th factor, and Swiss, Austrians and British respondents ranked it quite low (15,13,15). The rank difference is thus 16. The twelveth factor, administration, was ranked as fifth by British and 18th by Finns, a rank difference of 13.

Distribution and selling received a derived rank of 13 and (rank difference 10) the distribution of ranks shows somewhat high variation in responses between different nationalities. Low cost level - the 14th by grand mean - was ranked as number 4 by British respondents and 18th by Austrians and Swiss managers.

Technology (15th factor), product design (16th factor), financial strenght (17th factor), pricing policy (18th factor) and market share (19th factor) - were quite consistently regarded of about the same importance by all respondents. The greatest rank difference was 8.

To get some idea of the consistency of responses and variation in opinions, differences between the greatest rank and the smallest rank for each country by factor are presented in the last column of the Table 2. Clearly, success factors - low cost level (12.) and customer relations (15.) have the highest difference in responses. Considerable variation is also evident in administration (18.), distribution and selling (9.) and in reputation and local image (2.). The variation may be due to true differences between nationalities, due to some intervening variable or possibly due to unreliable results caused by some source of measurement error. The variation may be caused by differences between industries. To find out if this is the answer, an analysis of the means of success factors by industry was carried out. There were only insignificant differences in industry means.

3.1 Measurement Models of Rey Success Factors

In this part we focus on two questions: Is there structure to be found among the key success factors? If yes, what model best describes such structure?

Preliminary factor analysis with Finnish data suggests either a two factor model or a four factor model. In the latter description the factors were 1. product quality (6 + 7 + 8 +9 +10), 2. flexibility (15 + 16 + 17), 3. cost efficiency (11 + 12 + 13 + 14) and 4. technical competence (3 + 4 + 5). These numbers refer to those in Table 1. We start the development of measurement model and structural model by focusing on the correlation matrix (total 1991 InterStratos data, variables 201 to 219). In analysing the correlations, a possibility suggested by preliminary factor analysis with Finnish data was followed. Starting from the four factor hypothesis we explored the merits of the following measurement models presented in Table 3.

Table 3. Latent variables, Indicators and observed Items

Latent variable	Indicator	Item
Tecnical competence	worker's skills	var203
	technology	var204
	tecnical problem solving	var205
Customization	aftersales service	var207
	creativity	var208
	distribution & selling	var209
	product design	var210
Efficiency	pricing policy	var211
	low cost level	var212
	market share	var213
	financial strength	var214
Flexibility	flexibility	var216
	reliability of delivery	var217
	administration	var218
	product adaptation	var219

The presentation of the results follows the stages of the Lisrel7 analysis (Jöreskog and Sörbom 1988): 1. development of individual measurement models, 2. development of congeneric measurement model of key success factors, 3. development and tests of alternative structural models of key success factors.

We have above four latent variables with their indicators and items as their measures. Given the methodology of the holistic construal (Phillips and Bagozzi 1982) we start our preliminary analysis with the individual measurement models of the above named latent variables. A summary of the relevant results of the four congeneric measurement models is presented in Table 4.

Table 4. Indicators of fit for the measurement models

Latent variable	Chi sq.	(df)	p	GFI	AGFI	RMSR
Tecnical competence	0	(.00)	1.0	1.0	1.0	.000
Customization	106.8	(2)	.00	.99	.93	.034
Efficiency	121	(2)	.00	.98	.92	.04
Flexibility	23	(2)	.00	.99	.98	.02

(All standard errors < .054, all t-values > 19.2)

The only congeneric model that fits perfectly is the measurement model for technical competence. The standardized residuals for this latent variable are zeros and all standard errors are less than .05. Other measurement models are all also viable considering all the fit figures except chi squares-degrees of freedom and the standardized residuals. The unacceptably large ratio between chi square and degrees of freedom may be due to the large sample size (3243) but standardized residuals that exceed the critical value (about +, - 2.50) indicate unexplained variance. At this stage of the analysis these preliminary models are reasonably good for our purposes. Also, since we analyze the correlation matrix instead of covariances, this analysis is necessarily preliminary. Second, we are interested in the structure hypothesis among key success variables, in the context of building a larger explanatory model of export strategy. In that context these measurement models are reasonably good.

3.2 A first order congeneric model of key succes factors

What structure, if any, there is among the four latent variables: tecnical competence, customization, efficiency and flexibility? In analyzing the conceptual content of these variables we tested the following adhoc hypothesis above:

1. Flexibility, technical competence, customization and efficiency may be described as four latent variables.

Next we test whether:
2. The relations between the latent variables - technical competence, customization, efficiency and flexibility may be described as a causal structure.
3. Flexibility is a function of technical competence, customization and efficiency.

To test the second hypothesis, a first order congeneric model of key success factors was developed by correlating the four latent variables (see Figure 1). The theoretical correlations between the latent variables are quite low indicating high discriminating characteristics, but too low to imply any underlying (second order) theoretical variable.

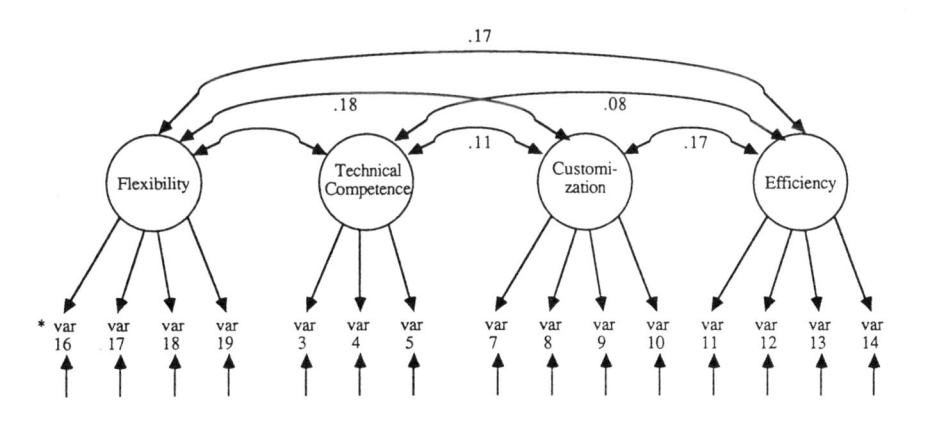

Figure 1. A Congeneric Measurement Model of Key Success Factors of SME's

(Source: Interestratos 1991 Data)

The indices of fit are the following: Chi square 1631, degrees of freedom = 84, p=.000, General index of fit: GFI = .93, Adjusted to sample size: AGFI = .90, Root mean square residuals:RMSR = .06, standardized residuals: max. +12.4, min. -10.1, standard errors, max. = .091, t-values min. = 11.1 . All the individual indicator loadings are fairly even and of about the same size as other indicator loadings for the same latent variables. All are around or above 1.0, and indicator loading for the technical competence are in the range of 1.7.

As with the individual measurement models the ratio between chi square and degrees of freedom is out of the ball park, the fit indices are low, but not discouraginly low, root mean square (rmsr) residuals are low, there are standardized residuals that exceed the critical values, standard errors are very low in this data and t-values are very high and, all the relations are highly significant.

In the light of these indices we do not reject the model. At the same time we accept that this model does not tap the available information to sufficient degree, ie. there are alternative, competing models given this data. Furthermore, since correlation matrix, not a covariance matrix was the source of information, identical analysis must be carried out with covariance structures before anything definitive is put forward.

3.3 Structural models of key success factors

Let us next turn to the third hypothesis that flexibility is a function of efficiency, technical competence and customization. Out of the score of alternative model specifications we chose the two most probable models presented in Figure 2 and 3.

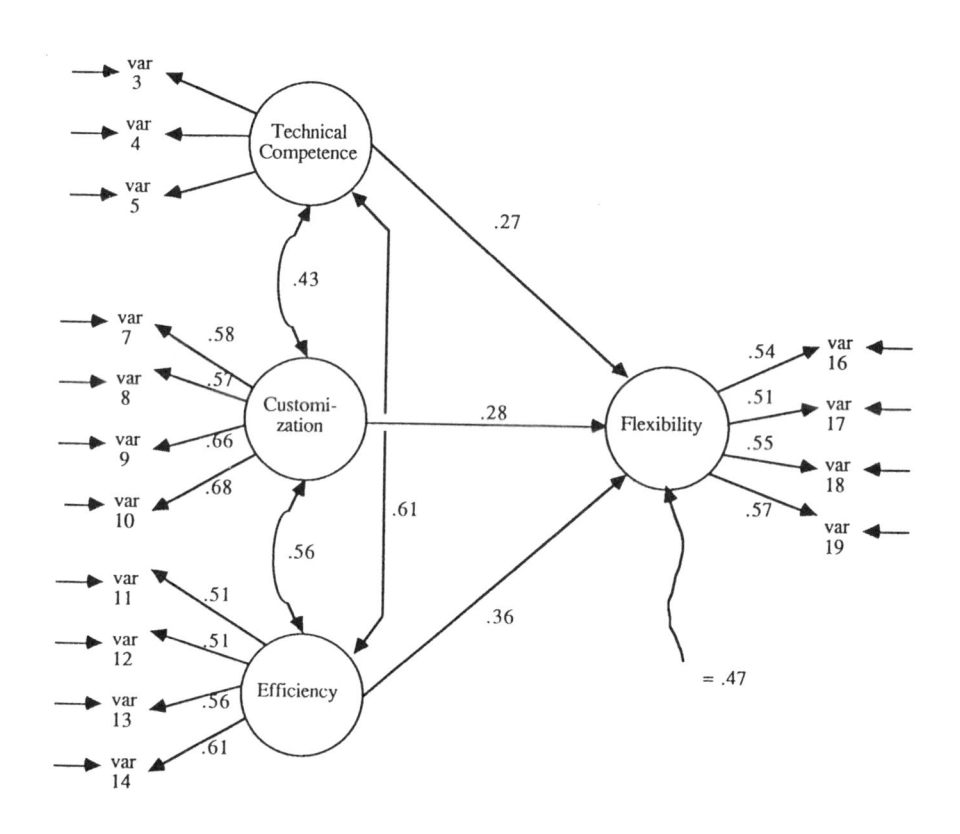

Figure 2. Model 2 Key Success Factors of SME's

(Source: Interestratos 1991 Data)

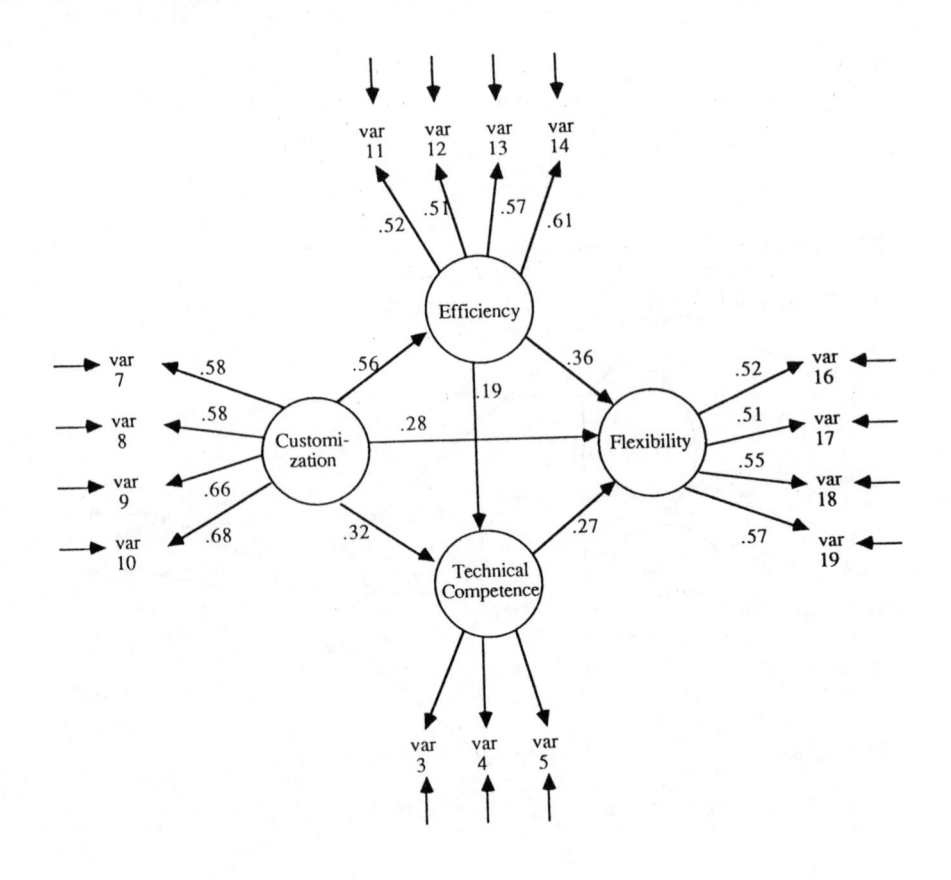

Chi square (df) = 1631.71 (84), p = .00
GFI = .93, AGFI = .90, RMSR = .06, n = 3243
all t-values > 5.5, all stand. errors > .091

Figure 3. Model 3 Key Success Factors of SME's

(Source: Interestratos 1991 Data)

Since there were no changes in any of the indicators or the latent variables and since we did not fix any of the measurement errors or theoretical errors, the indices of fit are identical with those of the first order congeneric measurement model with which we tested hypothesis 2.

There are interesting differences in structural characteristis however. In figure 2 Model 2, the theoretical correlations between the latent variables are much higher than the observed correlations, meaning that the observed correlations underestimate the true correlations. The effect of technical competence on flexibility is .27, the effect of customization is .28 and the effect of efficiency is strongest of the three and .36. In the third model (Model 3) the structural effects are more prevalent. The effect of customization on efficiency is .56 and the effect of efficiency on flexibility is .36. This is also the strongest route of influence. The total effects and indirect effects of customization on flexibility is strongest in comparing to all other effects.

All these preliminary submodels are of value at this stage of the InterStratos longitudinal research program. The models are competing hypotheses and eventhough they are only adequate we choose not to reject any of them. However, there is also strong reason to believe that more efficient models will be specified given further analysis of the data.

3.4 Firm and manager characteristics and success factor

Key success factors are of interest as such, but we are concerned with the links between selected exogenous variables and endogenous variables. Manager's experience, firm size, industry, competitive situation etc. may have effects on formulation of corporate and business strategy and export behavior. Therefore two tentative models are tested whereby the effects of size of firm (measured here simply with the number of full time employees) and manager's age on efficiency (one of the latent key success factors) on export sales (measured as a percentage of total sales) will give some hints for future modeling efforts.

The preliminary effects between size of the firm, efficiency and export sales (model 1) and the effects of manager age on efficiency and export sales (model 2) are shown below in Table 5.

Table 5. Effects of firm size, age of manager and efficiency on export sales: Two tentative models

	Efficiency	Export Sales
Size of Firm	.10	.89
Efficiency		.08
Age of Manager	.17	.14
Efficiency		.13
(Method of analysis GLS)		

Clearly the effects of age on efficiency and export sales are not strong. The effects of size of firm seems fairly small on efficiency and very strong on export sales reflecting the high bivariate correlations between these two variables. In both models success factors are not very much influenced by these two contextual variables. Also the effect of success factors on the export intensity is quite small (betas .08 and .13).

4. Summary

This paper is part of a longitudinal study into pre-export, export and international behavior in SME's in five industries and in eight European countries (InterStratos). This paper explores some preliminary questions for further study. The purpose of this paper was to explore the nature of success factors, describe the inherent structure among such factors in order to determine the key success factors and to explore the connections between contextual variables, success factors and export sales. In the first part we found that three most important success factors were product quality, reliability of delivery and flexibility. The least important, but important nevertheless, success factors were financial strength, pricing policy and market share, the ranking of which creates more questions than answers. Especially the marketing relatedness of success factors ranked as least important is a reminder of the dual thinking among sme's about marketing strategy - image and quality are regarded very important, but other parameters eg. pricing are regarded less so.

Competing models to describe the structure among the success factors were specified, and we found two which may be of value and adequate in the study of structural effects. Two tentative structural models were tested to clarify putative causal relations between size of firm, key success factors and export behavior. These preliminary models supported Reid's findings and suggested more exact specification of structural models.

There are several reservations to be made. The analysis of total aggregated data is necessarily not very meaningful except in the early stages of the research program. Meaningful partitions might have to be made eg. by country, industry, size class, stage of export behavior etc. before interesting relations may emerge. Methodologically it is misleading to use correlations, as we did here, instead of covariances as a basis of causal modeling. The results should be, therefore, regarded as only tentative.

References

Child,J.1973. "Predicting and Understanding Organizational Structure." *Administrative Science Quarterly* 18 (June), pp.168-196.

Bagozzi,R.P. and L.W.Phillips, 1982. "Representing and testing organizational theories: A holistic construal", *Administrative Science Quarterly,*27:3, pp.459-489.

Bamberger,I. 1986. *"The development of competitive advantages: theoretical bases and empirical results"*, Cahiers Strategie et Organisation, Rennes.

Hofer,C.W. and D.Schendel, 1978. *Strategy Formulation: Analytical Concepts.* St.Paul, Minn.: West Publishing Company.

InterStratos: H.Boter, R.Donckels, K.van Dijken, E.Fröhlich, I.Fröhlich, A.Haahti (Ed.), G.Hall, P.A.Havnes, R.van der Horst, C.Holmquist,

M.Habersaat, A.Lehtimaki, J-J.Obrecht, J.H.Pichler, H.J.Pleitner, A.Saether, P.Voithofer. (1993). Working Paper, European Institute of Advanced Studies in Management, Forthcoming.

Jöreskog,K. and D. Sörbom, 1988. LISREL 7. SPSS INC.Chicago.

Miesenbock,K.J. 1988. "Small Business and Exporting: A Literature Review", *International Small Business Journal,* 6:4, pp.42-57.

Mintzberg,H. 1990. Strategy Formation Schools of Thought. *Perspectives on Strategic Management.* (Ed.) J.W.Fredrickson, Harper-Row,112.

Ohmae,K. 1982. *The Mind of the Strategist.* Penguin Books: McGraw-Hill.

Reid,S.,1982, "The Impact of Size on Export Behavior in Small Firms", Chapter 2, in *Export Management: An International Context.* (Eds.) M. Czinkota and G.Tesar, New York.

Selznik,P. 1957. *Leadership in Administration.* Evanston, IL: Row,Peterson.

The Stratos Group, 1990. *The Strategic Orientations of Small European Businesses.* Gower Publishing.

Turnbull,P.W. and S.J.Paliwoda (Eds.), 1986. *Research in International Marketing.* Croom Hall, Dover.

Appendix

InterStratos Research Program

InterStratos - Internationalization of Strategic Orientations of Small to Medium-sized European enterprises - is a research project where researchers from eight European countries cooperate in studying international behavior of small to medium-sized firms.

The purpose of the longitudinal research program is to explore, describe and explain change in pre-export, export and international operations of sme's active in five industries - food industry, furniture industry, electronics industry, mechanical engineering industry and textile industry.

Data from Austria, Belgium, Finland, France, Great Britain, The Netherlands, Norway, Sweden and Switzerland are collected annually during a five-year period and these data will serve as a source of information when the researches collectively and individually publish results.

The work within the InterStratos group is organised according to a model where there is an interplay between collective and individual work. Today (1992) the group can be said to be in an initial stage and the collective efforts of presenting first year descriptive results are emphasised as well as further theoretical discussion, conceptualization and modeling to quide continuing analysis. The empirical data for the first year (1991) from the eight countries were compiled into one common data set during the spring 1992. First year country reports and descriptive working papers were discussed at the September 1992 conference in St.Gallen, Switzerland.

4 Becoming international: Benefits and pitfalls for entrepreneurial SMEs: Experiences from Belgium

Ria Aerts

1. Introduction

Research questions

The world we live in today is becoming increasingly international in outlook. The Free Trade Agreement between the United States, Canada and Mexico will increase the size of these countries' internal markets. The collapse of the Iron Curtain is creating new international opportunities for businesses in East and West alike, and the creation of the single European market is also a major new challenge.

Not so long ago, expanding into other countries was out of the question, except for some large companies. Only these latter would ever think of setting up any form of permanent representation abroad. Doing business in other countries was a costly and complex process: in short, it was not appropriate for SMEs.

This idea is no longer widely held as we become citizens of the global village. Everyone, SMEs included, will sooner or later become a part of the international network of goods, services, labour, capital and know-how.

The following are some of the most important questions that need to be addressed :

- How do entrepreneurs take their first steps into a foreign country?
- Where do entrepreneurs do business abroad?

- What are the benefits and pitfalls of these international adventures?
- What about 1993?

Data collection

In an attempt to reply to these questions, we carried out a detailed study of the literature and a large-scale empirical study.

The original empirical study consisted of four types of input: a written and a telephone questionnaire supplemented by case studies, and two round-table discussions. The first three were aimed at small business owners, and the fourth was a chance for people from business support services and government bodies to express their views. All the data were collected during 1991. The written questionnaire is part of an international research project being carried out in ten European countries (INTERSTRATOS, 1991).

Telephone survey

We used the standard European definition of an SME as one employing less than 500 people, thereby enabling comparisons to be made between countries. This definition was also used for the written survey.

The purpose of the telephone survey was to identify some of the characteristic features of SMEs doing business abroad, using large-scale fieldwork. The questionnaire covered three main topics: the extent to which the SME was involved in foreign business, details of the business itself and of its owner. The main purpose was to establish what kind of strategy the entrepreneur used in doing business abroad, how decisions were taken and what were the keys to international success. Other questions related to ways of gaining a foothold in foreign markets, personnel aspects, information, advisory and training services. The effects of 1993 were studied in the final section.

The businesses examined in the telephone survey were from the secondary and tertiary sectors. Table 1 is a summary by number of employees and sector.

Table 1. Breakdown of sample used in telephone survey by size and sector (number of businesses observed and percentage distribution)

Number of employees

Sector	00 - 09	10 - 19	20 - 49	50 - 99	100 - 500	Total
Secondary	239	179	215	142	160	935
	23%	18%	21%	14%	16%	92%
Tertiary	22	21	16	14	15	88
	2%	2%	2%	1%	1%	8%
Total	261	200	231	156	175	1023
	25%	20%	23%	15%	17%	100%

92% of the businesses sampled were in the secondary sector, and 8% in the tertiary sector. 71% were family businesses (businesses where more than 50% of the capital was family-owned).

Written survey

The purpose of this survey was to obtain a more detailed view of the companies' foreign involvement, and particularly to find out in which countries they did most of their business, their position in relation to their competitors, and any cooperation agreements with other SMEs at home and abroad.

The sample for the written survey was taken from the five largest sectors of industry : textiles, food, electrical engineering, furniture-making and mechanical engineering. As far as possible, observations were evenly distributed throughout the five sectors and six sizes of business. These are summarized in Table 2.

Table 2. Breakdown of sample used in written survey by size and sector (number of businesses observed and percentage distribution)

Number of employees

Sector	00 - 09	10 - 19	20 - 49	50 - 99	100 - 500	Total
Electrical engineer.	39 8%	7 1%	12 3%	7 1%	10 2%	75 15%
Furniture making	51 10%	6 1%	16 3%	11 2%	10 2%	94 18%
Mechanical engineer.	59 12%	10 2%	22 4%	12 2%	24 5%	127 25%
Textile	64 13%	2 1%	16 3%	18 4%	7 1%	107 22%
Food	46 9%	8 2%	11 2%	19 4%	15 3%	99 20%
Total	259 52%	33 7%	77 15%	67 13%	66 13%	502 100%

Table 2 clearly shows that small businesses formed the largest part of the sample, with 52% employing less than ten people. 77% of this sample were family-owned businesses.

Discussions with small business owners

More than ten owners of businesses took part in these discussions. They came from a variety of sectors of industry and so factors specific to their own sectors were reduced. All those taking part were involved in doing business abroad, and so were able to give a fairly clear picture of the situation. The owners did not take part in either the written or telephone surveys, and so were not influenced too much by the surveys. An open discussion was used to obtain detailed and critical information.

Round table discussions with support services

Two round-table discussions were held with specialists from the support sector and from government bodies. The support sector was represented by various institutions and organizations such as the Euro Info Centres, BC-Net, the Belgian Foreign Trade Service and a number of others. The role of training was also included, with a number of representatives from training centres specializing in the problems of SMEs and doing business abroad.

The legal, fiscal and financial aspects of the subject were also examined, using people with a theoretical and practical knowledge of doing business abroad.

Data processing

To process the data, we opted for a descriptive as well as an analytical approach. The descriptive element is based on frequency and cross-tables. The analytical processing consists of chi-squared tests, that compare the frequency distributions of random subsamples. The null hypothesis was that the distribution for the random subsamples was equal. As significance level, we used an alpha value of 0.05. In each table, we indicate the p-value as calculated by the SAS program.

2 Results

Type of foreign business

The telephone survey showed that 532, or nearly 52 % of the 1023 businesses examined, did business abroad. Of these, 89 % were involved in exports and 80 % in imports, with other forms of business being much less common. These figures are summarized in Table 3.

Table 3. Type of international business (N = 532) (more than one response possible)

Exports	89%
Imports	80%
Subsidiary	29%
Production or sale under license from foreign companies	18%
Production plant	17%
Issuing of licenses abroad	13%
Supply of services under license from foreign companies	12%

When analyzing these figures, it should be borne in mind that growth is often a gradual process. Companies start doing business in other countries because they find that there is a demand for Belgian products abroad. SMEs most often begin by testing the waters and exporting on an occasional basis. As their foreign clientele increases and they gain more experience, they adopt a more systematic approach to exporting, which involves deciding which markets they are going to deal with, and how. Often they will then start using importers and eventually agents.

Setting up a subsidiary in a foreign country is usually also a fairly gradual process. Companies start on a small scale by developing good local contacts in order to ensure that their products or services meet the needs of the local market. However some SMEs make a conscious decision not to set up subsidiaries abroad because of the huge expense involved. Another factor is that local people may be more familiar with the local market, but they may take a long time to develop the same work ethic and corporate culture as that of the parent company.

Those SMEs we interviewed who had set up a production facility abroad advised others to start by using less expensive methods, such as import companies. If the product proves a success, they can always invest in a production facility later on.

Licenses had not proved highly successful with SMEs, though this could change in 1993. The European Commission has issued a number of directives over recent years providing more effective and uniform protection for industrial and intellectual property at national and European level. This will considerably reduce the risk to smaller companies (The King Baudouin Foundation, 1991, pp. 53-56).

Geographical spread of foreign business

62% of those SMEs involved in doing business abroad exported to directly neighbouring countries. The next most common area was southern Europe, at only 14%. Similar figures apply to imports. These figures are summarized in Figure 1.

Imports

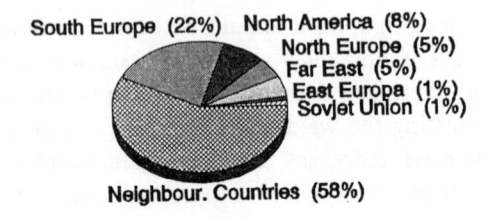

South Europe (22%) North America (8%)
North Europe (5%)
Far East (5%)
East Europa (1%)
Sovjet Union (1%)

Neighbour. Countries (58%)

Exports

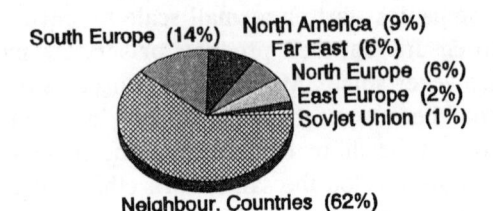

South Europe (14%) North America (9%)
Far East (6%)
North Europe (6%)
East Europe (2%)
Sovjet Union (1%)

Neighbour. Countries (62%)

Southern Europe: Italy, Greece, Turkey, Portugal, Spain, Yugoslavia
North America: Canada, USA
Far East: Japan, Indonesia, India, China, Taiwan
Northern Europe: Denmark, Norway, Sweden, Iceland, Finland
Eastern Europe: Bulgaria, Poland, Romania, Czechoslovakia, Hungary

Figure 1. Import and export countries: overall summary (N = 502)

Some SMEs do not confine themselves to neighbouring countries, or even to Europe. Limited demand for their products or services in nearby countries leads some companies to look further afield.

There are a number of reasons for dealing with countries directly adjoining one's own:

- SMEs prefer to adopt a step-by-step approach, beginning in the Belgian market and then spreading into nearby countries and venturing further away later on, when they have developed the experience and resources they need. Doing business abroad is often a case of working one's way up a learning curve for each new country.
- SMEs are often too small to rapidly increase production to meet demand from the rest of Europe or even outside.
- Some products are difficult to transport, and SMEs often decide to transport goods themselves to minimize costs.
- People in neighbouring countries are more likely to speak a language the entrepreneur understands and have a similar mentality to our own. This means that companies can often follow the same marketing strategy as the one they use in their own country.
- SMEs often do not receive large enough orders to justify expensive air fares and accommodation to give foreign clients the high level of service they need.
- Specific business trends may also play a part. For example, just-in-time production means that large customers are more likely to buy closer to home. As an exporter, there is little point in supplying to companies a long distance away in the knowledge that they operate a just-in-time system.
- Non-EC countries have different administrative procedures which often make it harder to do business there.
- Large exchange rate fluctuations can mean that SMEs have difficulty selling their products in a particular country because they are too expensive.
- In the United States, brand recognition is often more important than the actual product. Some SMEs find that advertising to achieve this level of recognition is too expensive and therefore tend to stay out of the American market.

Of the neighbouring countries, France is by far the biggest destination for exports, whilst the largest imports are from Germany (see Figure 2).

Imports

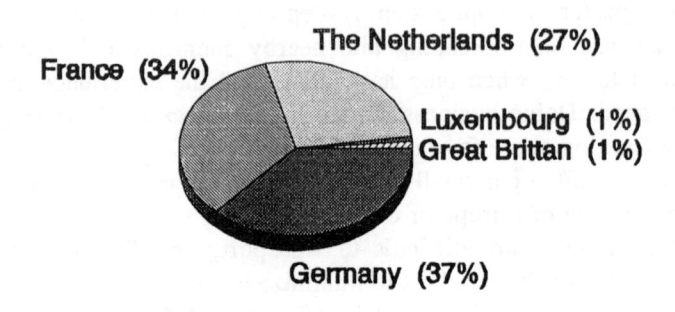

- France (34%)
- The Netherlands (27%)
- Luxembourg (1%)
- Great Brittan (1%)
- Germany (37%)

Exports

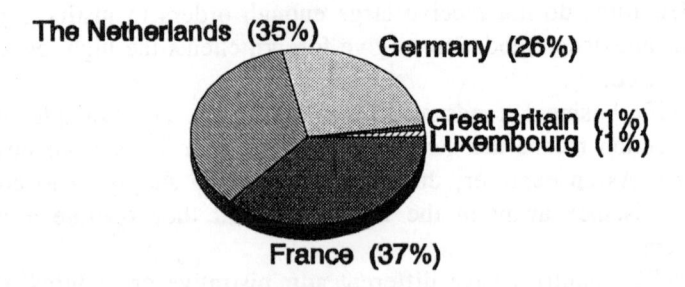

- The Netherlands (35%)
- Germany (26%)
- Great Britain (1%)
- Luxembourg (1%)
- France (37%)

Figure 2. Import and export countries: neighbouring countries (N= 502)

Few SMEs venture across the English Channel because they are wary of the fairly major differences in outlook. Those SMEs that do business in Britain often approach it in the same way as the Netherlands, France or Germany.

Benefits and pitfalls for SMEs doing business abroad

We will begin by discussing the benefits for SMEs of doing business abroad, and will then look at the factors affecting their success. Finally, we will discuss the pitfalls of exporting and importing.

Benefits

What makes SMEs start doing business abroad? 93% of Belgian SMEs said that demand for their products abroad was the key reason for venturing into other countries.

Table 4. Reasons for doing business abroad (N = 532) (more than one answer possible)

Demand from abroad	93%
To make growth possible	57%
Domestic market too limited	44%
Raw materials needed from abroad	43%
To make diversification of products and/or markets possible	30%
To strengthen competitive position abroad	19%
To keep abreast of developments abroad	14%

57% of SME owners said that they had moved into foreign markets to enable their business to grow. Both the literature on SMEs and our own empirical observations suggest that exporting is often the driving force behind expanding companies (3). The company outgrows the domestic market and therefore seeks markets for its products abroad.

Nearly 45% of SMEs obtain specific raw materials from abroad to make their production process as efficient as possible. It is therefore the production process itself which leads them to expand abroad.

30% of SMEs said that they operated outside Belgium in order to diversify in terms of products and/or markets.

Only a small number of companies said that they needed to keep pace with competition from abroad or use their business to keep up to date with events in the foreign markets.

Success factors

International success is very much dependent on the degree of specialization. Being the best in a specific part of the sector increases demand for the product at home and abroad. No fewer than 71% of SMEs said that specialization was the main factor in their success internationally (see Table 5).

Table 5. Factors determining international success (N = 532) (more than one answer possible)

Specialization	71%
Quality	67%
Inexpensive products	40%
Better approach than the competition	37%
Suitable personnel	32%
Good management	27%
Products and services geared to foreign customers	24%

Quality refers not just to quality of products and services, but also the service provided to customers. One company said this meant being able to get to the customer's premises quickly. Other SMEs said that the most important requirement was to provide products and services which met the customer's needs. For service companies, it was often important to inspire confidence by developing good relations between the two companies and between individual members of staff. This was one of the most important points which SMEs had in their favour, and many had made a conscious decision not to grow too large in order to maintain this personal service.

Good service also means making sure that it is no more difficult in terms of administration for a foreign customer to do business with a Belgian company than one in their own country. Another important factor is good after-sales service; the customer must be able to contact you at any time. Language skills are also an important factor in this respect.

One crucial determinant of success is finding a gap in the market. 37 % of SMEs said that being ahead of the competition in identifying opportunities, or doing better than their competitors, was a factor in their success.

The personality and experience of the owner and his or her employees are also important. If they are open to other cultures, they are more likely to succeed. Good language skills are also essential in many cases. In some areas of industry, such as the service sector, it is particularly important to develop good relations with clients by speaking their language, and if this is the case then geographical distance largely ceases to be a factor. 62% of the SME owners surveyed spoke three or four languages, and only 32% spoke one or two. People in companies doing business abroad spoke considerably more languages than those confining themselves to the home market, so it was very clear that language skills were an important factor (see Figure 3).

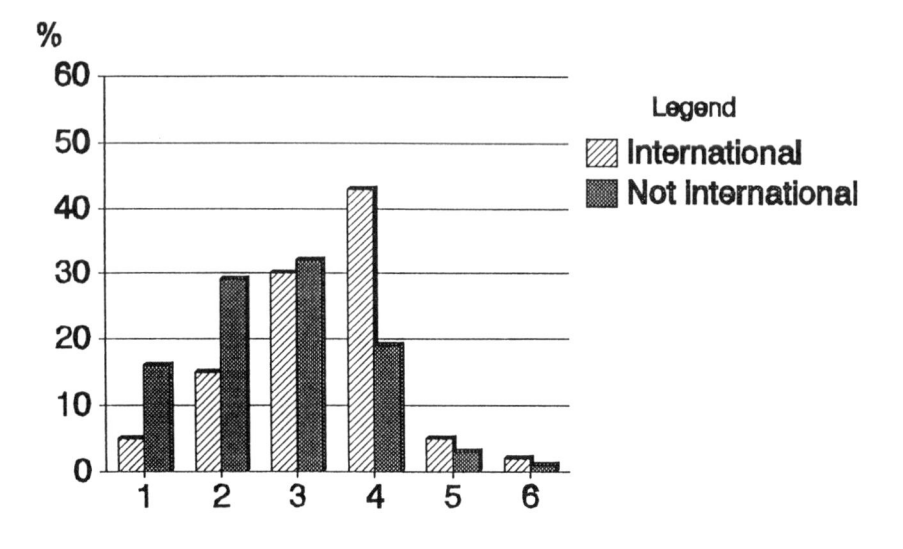

Figure 3. Languages spoken (N = 1011)
(Chi-squared test with prob = 0.000)

SME owners must also make a deliberate decision to do business abroad, which means not simply sitting and waiting for customers to appear, but going out to look for them. It also means persevering, even if it might appear at first sight that there is no market for one's products abroad or they are not immediately successful. It is very important to build up a network of contacts : many problems can be avoided by having someone in the country to point the company in the right direction. It is therefore very important to travel abroad oneself : the surveys showed clearly that SME owners who did business abroad travelled more than those who operated only in their own country. Travel is therefore a key factor, with major implications for the way business owners manage their time.

Another aspect which particularly affects family businesses is the fact that being family-owned can make it less easy to expand (Donckels and Hoebeke, 1992, pp. 155-164). Figure 4 shows that family companies are less likely to operate abroad. This very much reflects the findings of other research which has shown that family companies have a number of specific features, including their attitude to risk-taking and the limited resources they have available. These often lead to more conservative behaviour as a business (Donckels and Fröhlich, 1991, pp. 149-160). Launching a family business in the international markets also requires a suitable strategy (Gallo and Sveen, 1991, pp. 181-190).

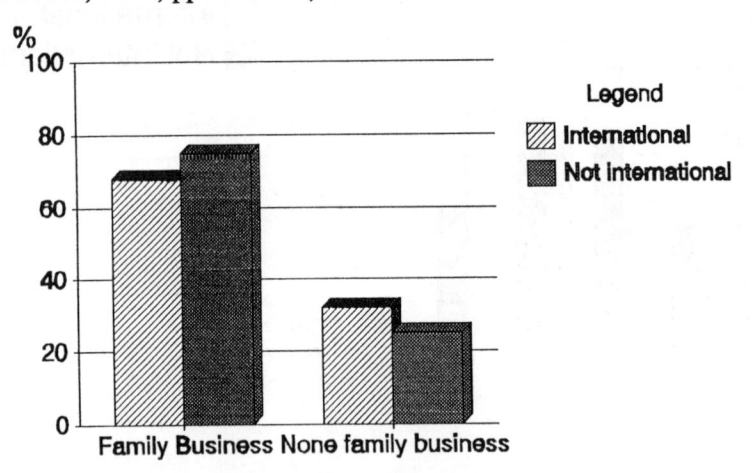

Figure 4 **Family-owned and non family-owned businesses (N = 1012) (Chi-squared test with prob = 0.011)**

Pitfalls

31% of SMEs engaged in exporting found that the biggest problems were obtaining payment and finance. The main currency for invoicing is the exporter's one, but smaller firms are often in a weak bargaining position with their customers and will therefore need to invoice in their customer's currency (Samuels, Greenfield and Mpuku, 1992, pp. 24-26). As a result, small companies run a greater currency risk than large ones.

Table 6. Top ten of the pitfalls (N = 1012)

Obtaining payment and finance	31%
Finding of the right contact person	30%
International laws and regulations	29%
Time for travelling	28%
Duration of the negotiations	27%
The way of doing business/mentality	26%
Filling in customs forms	26%
Correctness of the market information	25%
Setting the price for exports	20%
Languages	11%

Many entrepreneurs also find it very hard to find their way around the maze of international laws and regulations. They may be confused by company law, the tax system, ownership rights and uncertainty about their legal position.

All the staff are likely to be fully occupied in an SME, and it is not possible from a practical or financial point of view to send people abroad to assess the lie of the land and carry out on-the-spot negotiations or marketing. The owner of the company will often need to attend negotiations in person, especially in the final stages of a deal where customers like to be able to meet them face to face. However some company owners simply do not have the time for travel or lengthy negotiations. In many cases, success abroad simply requires a healthy dose of patience, and the situation may be complicated if there are major differences in outlook and ways of doing business.

Interestingly, 26% of SME owners believed that "filling in customs forms" was a barrier to foreign expansion. In the future, when these barriers are removed in 1993, life will be much easier for SMEs wishing to spread their wings abroad.

Setting an appropriate price for exports is also a problem for many SMEs, especially when these are affected by fluctuations in exchange rates. It is harder for small businesses to change their prices to reflect changes in rates, which can make their prices uncompetitive in foreign markets.

The majority of the SMEs covered by the survey did not have language problems. This is because Belgium is a multilingual country and therefore most owners of businesses have been taught foreign languages at school from a very young age.

Small businesses and 1993

Eighteen months before the beginning of 1993, more than half the SMEs surveyed had not taken any action in connection with the opening of the single European market, though 85% of them believed that 1993 would affect the way they did business in the future. Table 7 summarizes the changes which companies believed 1993 was likely to bring.

Table 7. Expected consequences of 1993 (N = 233) (more than one answer possible)

More joint ventures with companies abroad	81%
More opportunities for going international	80%
Possibility of merger	63%
More competition	60%
Possibility of being taken over	56%
More joint ventures with companies in Belgium	50%

Small business owners believe that 1993 will mean closer cooperation with other companies both in Belgium and abroad. Joining forces with others would make them much more competitive than going it alone. However some respondents believed that 1993 would not lead to any great internal changes in their company. The one fundamental change would be a reduction in red tape, which would make it easier for SMEs to do business in other countries.

63% of respondents said that in principle they might merge with another company, though this did not necessarily mean that they were interested in doing so. The bureaucracy and inertia inherent in some large groups of companies could affect their long-term competitiveness. Most SMEs therefore choose to remain independent, though they expected that SMEs would be most affected by takeovers. The surveys showed that more than half of people in small businesses saw this as a risk which they themselves faced.

60% believed that 1993 would lead to increased competition, though they believed that it was more likely that they would present a threat to their foreign competitors than vice versa. Their trump cards were the high quality of their products and personal service. Most entrepreneurs do not expect any radical changes to come out of 1993; markets have always been in a state of flux, and will continue to be, with or without 1993.

3 Concluding remarks

There are four main conclusions which can be drawn at this stage:

1. Companies must think carefully before venturing abroad.
   Exporting and importing are still by far the most common form of international business. However both are still the exception rather than the rule.
   It is a mistake to act on the spur of the moment. Expanding into foreign markets should be a gradual process, and it is vital to find out about the market and know one's own strengths. Careful monitoring of the market is vital. Companies also need to bear in mind the main potential drawbacks of doing business in other countries. Obtaining insurance and signing a contract may reduce the degree of risk involved.

2. Doing business abroad requires a different strategy.
   Companies should not forget the less business-oriented aspects such as culture, history, customs and laws, which are often very different abroad. This will often require changes in their products as well. The results of the surveys showed that a specialized, high-quality product is the most important determining factor in a company's success.

3. Doing business abroad should involve the whole company, not just the boss.
   Dealing with foreign companies will require a different degree of knowledge, commitment and use of time by managerial and other staff. However the boss should always remain the figurehead of the company.
   Everyone in the company will need to be persuaded of the importance of doing business abroad, and the changes will require them to be more flexible in their approach.

4. The company's foreign business will need to be critically evaluated on a periodic basis.
   This means assessing the financial implications and the effects on profitability of operating on an international basis. Employees must be involved in this exercise, and external help may also be useful. The most important thing to remember is keeping a close eye on the roots of the company. The home market may not be neglected.

Bibliography

Donckels, R., Fröhlich, E. (1991), 'Are family businesses really different? European Experiences from STRATOS', *Family Business Review*, Jossey-Bass Inc., San Francisco, volume 4, no. 2, pp. 149-160, Summer.

Donckels, R., Hoebeke, K. (1992), 'SME-led growth of the Belgian economy: fact or fiction ?' *Entrepreneurship and Regional Development*, Taylor & Francis, London and Washington DC, volume 4, no. 2, pp. 155-164, April-June.

Europe (1991), the King Baudouin Foundation, Brussels, pp. 53-56.

Gallo, M.A., Sveen, J. (1991), 'Internationalizing the family business : facilitating and restraining factors', *Family Business Review*, Jossey-Bass Inc., San Francisco, volume 4, no. 2, pp. 181-190, Summer.

INTERSTRATOS : project relating to international strategies of industrial SMEs in 10 countries : Austria, Belgium, Britain, Finland, France, Germany, Italy, The Netherlands, Sweden and Switzerland, 1991.

Samuels, J., Greenfield, S., Mpuku, H. (1992), 'Exporting and the smaller firm, *International small business journal*, Woodcock publications Ltd., volume 10, no. 2, pp. 24-26, January-March.

5 Internationalization of Finnish SMEs: Commitment, internationalization paths and innovation

Liisa Hyvärinen

Introduction

Internationalization was first considered as investment behaviour of enterprises. Later it has most often been defined as a time-related, gradual process of increasing involvement in international operations. Various objectives are sought through internationalization, for instance growth, improved profitability, or strengthening and sustaining the competitive position or removing a threat. Also motives of the decision-maker may be a reason to internationalize. (Ansoff, 1984, pp. 154-6, Dichtl et al., 1984, p. 50, Luostarinen, 1980, p.66, and Young et al., 1989, p. 268, among others)

Internationalization of Finnish small and medium-sized industrial enterprises, SMEs, is examined in this study. Unlike the generally adopted size limits, the enterprises dealt with in this study employ less than 200 persons. Those employing at least 5 but less than 30, are considered here as small enterprises. Thus it is possible to examine more homogeneous group of firms. SMEs cannot achieve economies of scale due to their small size and limited resources. Consequently, they have to compete with other means both in domestic and foreign markets. The most important person in SMEs is the manager/owner.

His often limited skills and knowledge, even personal attitudes, perceptions, and experience have a remarkable influence in the strategies and operations of the enterprise (Czinkota, 1982, Reid, 1981, and Samiee and Walters,1990).

Theoretical background

Gradual internationalization

The firm chooses its way to internationalize according to its strategies, general targets and competition situation. Luostarinen and Welch (1990, pp. 259-65) have summarized the earlier studies on gradual internationalization:

1) Internationalization is usually started from the neighbour countries or a country otherwise felt close to, e.g., an immigrant's native country.

2) The most common sequence of international operations presented in the literature is: The first stage is exports, which is followed by sales units abroad and later by manufacturing units abroad. The more a foreign operation requires investment and other involvement, the later that operation takes place in the internationalization process. Most studies on internationalization concentrate on one phase of internationalization. Usually the focus has been on export or production units abroad. However, for instance, Terpstra's definition (1981, pp. 9- 10) of an international firm leaves out the international marketing firm, i.e. the one that is exporting only. Import is usually the very first contact of an enterprise with foreign enterprises, suppliers and markets (Luostarinen and Welch, 1990, p. 249). However, it has seldom been notified in earlier studies on Internationalization.

3) The stages including foreign investments, like establishing an own unit abroad, generally take place in countries where the fimm previously has had less demanding foreign operations.

4) The offering to the international market also begins with the simplest form, goods. This is followed by services, and later by know-how and systems.

5) Evolution of internationalization pattem varies among firms. All enterprises do not apply all possibilities to internationalize.

In this study, Internationalization is viewed according to Luostarinen and Welch (1990, pp. 181-8 and pp. 192-3). They include indirect, direct and own exports, selling a license, know-how, franchising rights or projects, acting as a subcontractor or contractor, and being the foreign partner in joint/mixed venture in outward international operations. In inward international operations, they include indirect, direct and own import, buying a license, know-how, or franchising rights, importing projects, acting as a subcontractee or contractee, and being the local partner in joint/mixed venture. With co-operative international operations the partners work together in their own or in a third country, to achieve common agreed, shared goals. They also can exchange goods, services, know-how or systems with each other, with or without monetary flows.

In the literature, it has been stated that SMEs seldom have other international operations than importing raw materials etc., or indirect or direct export. SMEs' foreign operations are often regarded as irregular and unplanned. Moreover, only a small part of their total sales comes from export. (Kaynak et al., 1987, pp. 31-2, Lehtinen, 1983, and Aijo, 1977)

Commitment to internationalization

Few of the earlier studies consider commitment to Internationalization as a theoretical concept, often it is just mentioned. Christensen (1991, p. 51) lists resource commitment, management commitment and a general commitment of the organization to export. Luostarinen and Welch (1990, p. 269) mention commitment of resources and people to international operations. In this study, the commitment of small and medium-sized enterprises to Internationalization is divided into strategic and operational dimensions.

Strategic commitment Strategic decisions have
"enduring effects that are difficult to reverse, ... with the longest period worth considering" (Ackoff, 1970, pp. 4-5).

As components of a strategy, Ansoff (1971, pp. 97- 101) listed product-market scope, growth vector, competitive advantage, and synergy. The growth vector indicates the moves from present towards new products and missions. A strategy includes also measures for the present and future performance of the firm, and rules for developing the firm's relationship with its external environment, establishing the internal relationships and processes, and the rules by which the firm conducts its day-to-day business (Ansoff, 1984, p. 31). These can be found also in the internationalization strategies.

Mintzberg (1978, p.945) has distinguished intended strategies, part of which become realized and part remain unrealized due to various reasons, and emergent strategies, which get displaced along the way, and become realized.

This view is parallel to that of Johanson and Vahlne (1990, p. 22) who present the internationalization process being a mixture of strategic thinking, strategic action, emergent developments, chance and necessity.

A firm can be passively internationalized or it can actively internationalize itself (Lehtinen, 1983, and Piercy,1981). Most firms start with domestic operations, being disinterested in exports or manufacturing abroad. SMEs with irregular and unplanned export are passive or reactive in internationalization. Their internationalization process is pushed to motion by outside forces. (Kaynak et al., 1987, pp. 31-2, Lehtinen, 1983, and Aijo, 1977) Parallel to this view, Johanson and Vahlne (1990, pp.19-22) explain that if establishing relationships to foreign countries is found valuable, it becomes a continuous and active operation. Difficulties faced in other operations, or changing the manager(s) or organization otherwise may lead to higher readiness for foreign operations. Actively internationalizing enterprise has set targets, means and budgets also for international operations. Thus the impulse for internationalization comes from inside the enterprise. In SMEs, usually this is connected with high quality, special products for which the domestic market soon becomes saturated. Extending the life-cycle of a product (group) with market expansion abroad is the most typical product-market strategy for European small enterprises (Haahti, 1987).

Operational commitment. Operational or 'tactical' planning concerns with the shortest period worth considering, shorter than the strategic one, and with selecting means by which to pursue specified goals (Ackoff, 1970, pp.

4-5). Ansoff (1984) defines operational commitment to internationalization to include international day-to-day operating policy. This may be either an independent set of rules agreed for coincidental export or regular import, or an essential part of the strategy of a firm aiming at international markets. Or, as often in SMEs, it also may be a series of ad hoc operations taken when necessary. Often strategic planning does not exist in SMEs, neither do they have an internationalization strategy, at least not in the initial stage of internationalization. Most of the manager's time runs out in solving everyday problems of the enterprise, and planning has to be left to lesser attention. The object of operational decisions is "to maximize ... profitability of current operations. The major decision areas are resource allocation (budgeting) among functional areas and product lines, scheduling of operations, supervision of performance, and applying control actions. The key decisions involve pricing, establishing marketing strategy, setting production schedules and inventory levels, and relative expenditures in support of R & D (research and development), marketing, and operations." (Ansoff, 1971, p. 18)

Internationalization and innovations

Traditionally, an invention is understood as a solution to a problem, and an innovation a commercially successful use of an invention (e.g. OECD, 1982, and Bacon and Butler, 1981, p. 12). Innovations in the enterprises include creation of novelties, and adopting and using them, see e.g. Schumpeter (1949).

In this study, the innovation connected with internationalization is defined according to the views of Majaro (1982), Rogers (1983), and Drucker (1985). It is an idea, practice, or object that is perceived as new by an individual or other unit of adoption, and as a specific tool of entrepreneurs to exploit the change as an opportunity for different business or a different service. Innovation in Internationalization is seen here as a positive difference from the most frequent way of going international in the industry, group or market the enterprise is in.

An invention can be patented if its level of newness is high enough, and if it is a concrete thing, product, process or method that is 'not obvious to an average craftsman'. Nevertheless, patent does not automatically turn an invention into an innovation (Basberg,1987, p. 133, and Dror,1989, p. 243). On the other hand, the smallest enterprises do not protect their products or innovations although they would be remarkable technological improvements. Among reasons for this, are the expenses and time needed in the patenting process. Also 'protection' through marketing was considered too expensive. (Cannon, 1985, and OECD, 1982, p. 30)

Simmonds and Smith (1968) made the first exploratory study on outside originated stimulus to starting exports as an innovation adoption process in Great Britain. According to them,

> "Entry into the export market is just as much an innovation as the adoption of a new production process ... When the perspective is narrowed to the firm itself, the first export order can be considered an innovation within the closed environment of the firm" (p. 94).

After that, in USA, Lee and Brasch (1978) examined exports as innovation adoption process of a marketing strategy. Also in USA, Reid (1981) found the stages of export expansion process to correspond the ones of a new product development, innovation process. European research programmes on internationalization of small enterprises, STRATOS and its continuation INTERSTRATOS include no innovation aspect (Haahti,1987 and 1989, and Lehtimaki, 1992). Moreover, imports is notified only in INTERSTRATOS (Aerts, 1992 and 1993). None of the earlier studies is focusing on the innovations in SMEs' Internationalization.

Several types of innovations are separated in the literature. Basically, they are divided into radical and incremental ones. Even though an innovation usually is understood as a new product, or production process, the innovation can be also *non-technical,* i.e. economic, strategic, social and organizational, even financial (Drucker, 1985, Rickards, 1985, Ranta, 1987, and Heinonen, 1992, among others).

Often Internationalization is started when the domestic markets cannot fulfill the enterprise's growth targets anymore. Ansoff (1984) and Porter (1985) present that on the background of the firm's growth there must be a product or/and marketing innovation. According to OECD (1982), there is no real innovation without success in both product and marketing, whereas

Forsgren (1989, p. 11) presents, that internationalization can be based on a unique innovation. In the view of Harrison and Hart (1987, p.447), Internationalization means at least marketing innovation, although technological innovation also can be included. In this study, it is assumed that due to their limited resources, the internationalizing SMEs have the same products for both domestic and foreign markets. Still, some incremental product innovations may be necessary for adapting the products to the export markets.

In Schumpeter's (1949, p. 66) view, only the opening of a new market into which the particular sector of the country in question has not previously entered, or which has not existed before, is an innovation. Also creation of monopoly position or breaking it up, can be an innovation attached to Internationalization of those presented by Schumpeter (1949, p. 63). Nystrom (1990, p. 75) considers serving new customers with new products, processes and services as market innovations. Majaro (1982, pp. 254-6) presents innovation being possible in pricing, distribution, and communication in international marketing. In SMEs, all these marketing innovations in Internationalization are minor, incremental ones, though the change can be remarkable for the enterprise itself.

Innovating in international operations means implementing an operation different from the previous ones. That operation might not even be considered in the domestic markets. The change may be due to the demands from the new markets or, following an aggressive strategy, or responding to the acts of new competitors. Such innovations can be radical or incremental. For an SME, the requirement of adopting new operations may be restrictive, even lead to a negative decision concerning internationalization.

Financial, incremental innovations (Heinonen,1992) are rare in the SMEs' internationalization process. Kotabe (1990, p.624) states that set of management procedures in marketing the product and administering the business unit, can be considered as a component or source of the management innovation in internationalization process. These can be radical or incremental, and they are rare in small and medium-sized enterprises. Also the conquest of a new source of supply of raw materials or half-manufactured goods, irrespective of whether this source already exists or whether it first has to be created, is an innovation type presented by

Schumpeter (1949, p. 63), which can have a connection with internationalization. This innovation type is also rare in small enterprises.

In this study, innovations recognized by the SME managers, those verified by international patents, and differences from the competitors' internationalization as the managers saw it, are included in innovations in internationalization.

Internationalization of Finnish SMEs

Methodology and sample

Data for this study was gathered through a mail survey from Finnish small and medium-sized industrial enterprises in December 1992. The Finnish Association of Small Enterprises helped in mailing the inquiries to 856 Finnish SME managers picked from their member register. Altogether 245 answerswere received, of which 242 could be used in the analyses. Thus, the answering percentage is 28, which can be considered as satisfactory.

The research material is analyzed statistically and by clustering the enterprises. Both quantitative and qualitative aspects are notified, since the answers include both types of information. In some parts of the analysis, also case study is applied. When interpreting and generalizing the results of this study, we must remember that the material was based on the personal views of the SME managers on their own enterprises. To increase objectivity and reliability, results from different parts of the study are compared.

To homogenize the sample more, food, beverages and tobacco industries including bakeries, which is a common small enterprise type in Finland in this sector, are left outside. These enterprises mostly operate in local markets (Lehtimaki, 1992, p. 97). The so called high technology sectors, i.e. those manufacturing electrical machinery and appliances, and the ones manufacturing professional and scientific, measuring and controlling equipment also are excluded. They have been the most internationalized sectors in Finland, due to the specialized products (Lehtimaki, 1992, p. 97).

There are many earlier and on-going studies concentrating on this sector, presenting also results on their internationalization.

The enterprises manufacturing metal products make up 65 per cent of the sample but their share of the total industry in Finland is about 9 per cent only (PKT-tietoa, 1990, p. 3 and p. 5). Other sectors in the sample have the corresponding shares as in the whole industry. For more details, see Appendix 1. In 40 per cent of the SMEs, the main product group is manufactured products, and in 17 per cent, subcontracting.

Location of the enterprises in Finland is considered here as irrelevant because the Finnish home markets are so small, that specialized enterprises willing to expand will anyway go abroad despite their location. The sample covers the whole country, including both developing areas and industrialized cities. The shares of each province are about the same in the sample as they are in the whole Finnish industry.

Most of the enterprises in the sample are small, measured by both the number of employees and the turn over. 65 per cent of the enterprises employed 30 persons at most, and 84 per cent of them employed less than 50. In 43 per cent of the SMEs, the turn over in 1991 was less than 20 million FIM (about 3,1 million ECU). For more details, see Appendix 2.

International operations

193 SMEs, which is 80 per cent of the sample, have international operations, but only 42 of them (17 per cent of the sample) have also other foreign operations than imports and/or exports. Exports was the most common single international operation: 67 per cent of all the enterprises exported. Imports was almost as common, with 62 per cent of SMEs. All the other international operations were much less frequent. The most common form of international operations was combination of imports and exports, either regular or irregular. 151 SMEs, 78 per cent of the internationalized ones, had no other foreign operations than these two. That is the easiest way to internationalize, since at first they require no investment, special personnel or office. The bigger and older the enterprise was, the more often it had also other foreign operations than imports and exports in this sample. 10 per cent of internationalized SMEs had patents

abroad, 5 per cent foreign licensing contacts, 11 per cent a sales unit, and 2.5 per cent a manufacturing unit abroad.

In Finnish SMES, the 'basic model' to internationalize starts with either imports or exports. After both of them, follow foreign patenting and licensing contact(s), and later sales unit(s). Production unit(s) is the last phase of this process. However, there are many variations of this model, both in order and number of the phases as well as in the interval between them. Some examples of internationalization paths found in this sample, are presented in Figure 1. The variations originate to different strategies, markets, products, competition means and competition situations of the SMEs. Often the outside impulses have a great influence on internationalization process of SMEs.

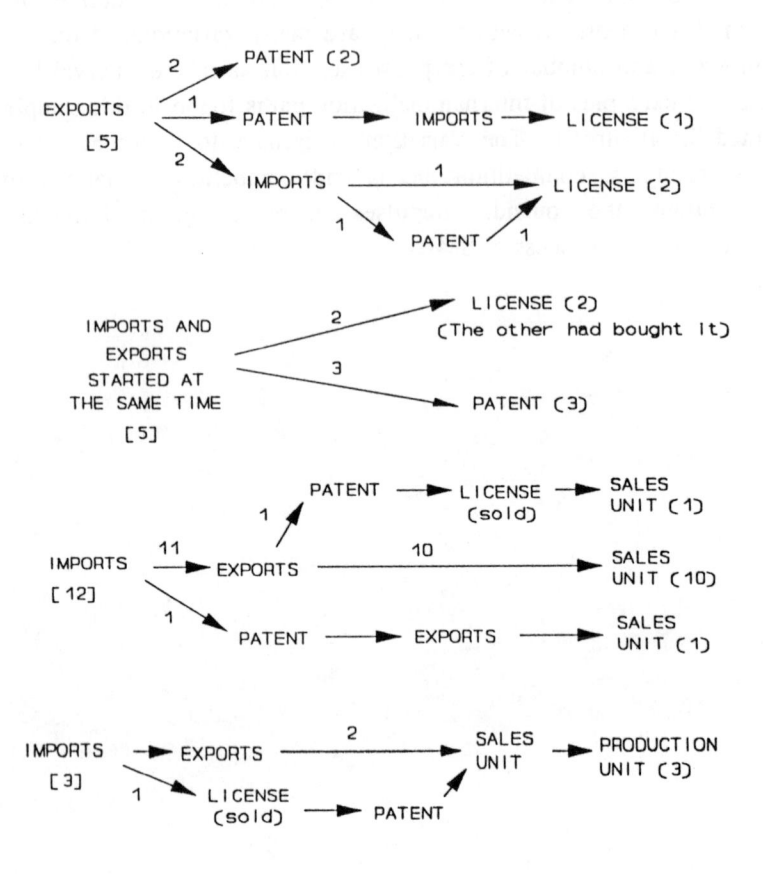

```
                    2    PATENT (2)
                   ↗
   EXPORTS   1
     [5]     →  PATENT  →  IMPORTS  →  LICENSE (1)
           ↘ 2
              IMPORTS ─────1─────→ LICENSE (2)
                      ↘ 1       ↗
                        PATENT  1
```

```
                              2      LICENSE (2)
   IMPORTS AND              ↗      (The other had bought it)
   EXPORTS
   STARTED AT                3
   THE SAME TIME              ↘   PATENT (3)
      [5]
```

```
                      PATENT  →  LICENSE  →  SALES
                    ↗ 1                (sold)   UNIT (1)
   IMPORTS   11                 10            SALES
    [12]     →  EXPORTS  ─────────────→      UNIT (10)
             ↘ 1
                PATENT  →  EXPORTS  →  SALES
                                       UNIT (1)
```

```
                            2     SALES  →  PRODUCTION
   IMPORTS  →  EXPORTS ───────→   UNIT       UNIT (3)
    [3]    ↘ 1                          ↗
              LICENSE  →  PATENT
              (sold)
```

Figure 1. Examples of internationalization paths of Finnish SMEs The numbers present the amount of enterprises in the sample having that path.

In this sample, majority, 100 of the 193 internationalized SMEs, 52 per cent, had started to internationalize with importing products, raw materials, services or/and sub-contracting. On the contrary, 51 enterprises, which is 26 per cent of the internationalized ones, exported first. 37 internationalized SMEs (19 per cent) had started importing and exporting in the same year. Independent of the first operation being imports or exports, starting internationalization was seen as positive by the managers: The first foreign operation encouraged to continue internationalization in about 53 per cent of the cases. There were some marginal differences between these two starts. Importing first lead the managers to changes in the forms of foreign operations practiced, in 12 per cent of the cases. Exporting first, made the managers more careful in the next foreign operations, according to 9 per cent of respondents. SME managers may consider imports more safe way first to try foreign operations than exports.

Commitment to internationalization

SMEs with domestic operations only make up 20 per cent of the sample, see Figure 2. The group of SMEs with not more than one quarter of total sales coming from exports is the biggest one in this sample, 45 per cent of all. Their export is mainly irregular and no personnel, separate units, or planning were involved. The remaining 35 per cent of Finnish SMEs of the sample, are committed to Internationalization. 20 per cent of the sample export for more than one quarter of their total annual turn over. However, they have no other international operations. Nor do they have any personnel or special units, budgeting or planning for their international operations. 6 per cent of SMEs get more than one quarter of their turn over from exports, and they have also employed someone to take care of these actions or started a special unit for them. 3 per cent of SMEs make budgets for their international operations, besides exporting more than a quarter and having employed personnel especially for these tasks.

The last thirteen Finnish SMEs in this sample, which is five per cent of the total sample, can be considered as strongly committed to Internationalization at the moment of inquiry, see Figure 2. Yet, the international operations of all of them are not very extensive. 5 SMEs export regularly, and 4 of them also import. 1 SME has patents abroad, 2 foreign licensing contacts, 3 sales unit, and 2 production unit abroad as the most extensive international operation. Besides getting more than one quarter of the total turn over from exports, these thirteen SMEs have personnel dedicated to international operations. Also budgets are made for foreign operations, and targets and ways to achieve them are planned in those enterprises.

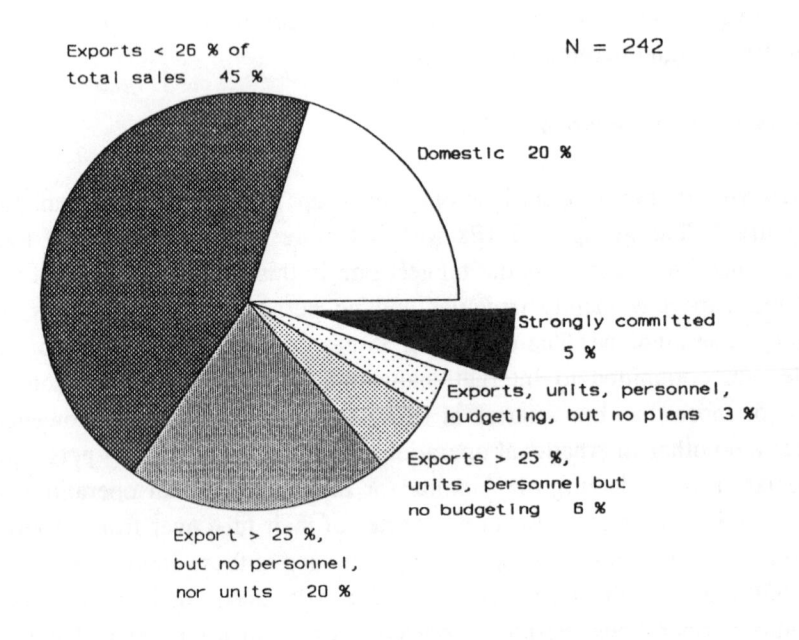

N = 242

- Exports < 26 % of total sales 45 %
- Domestic 20 %
- Strongly committed 5 %
- Exports, units, personnel, budgeting, but no plans 3 %
- Exports > 25 %, units, personnel but no budgeting 6 %
- Export > 25 %, but no personnel, nor units 20 %

Figure 2. Strategic and operational commitment of Finnish SMEs to international operations

Internationalization and innovations

Answering the question concerning innovations connected with internationalization seemed difficult to the Finnish SME managers. Only twenty four of them recognized innovations in Internationalization of their enterprises, see Figure 3. Innovation was defined in the covering letter of inquiry as presented earlier, to assure about similar understanding on it. One of these SMEs operated in home markets only but reported having international product innovations because it was sub-contractor to another firm that exports a lot. 2 SMEs had production unit(s) abroad, 3 foreign sales units, 2 licensing contacts, and 3 foreign patents as the most extensive international operation. 13 SMEs in this group imported and/or exported only. These SMEs are innovative also in the sense that usually their internationalization was started from an inside impulse, voluntarily.

Eleven of the recognized innovations were product innovations. Only in three further internationalized and established SMEs, the product innovations are verified with (several) foreign patents, see Figure 3. Concerning the rest eight, it is understandable, that the three new SMEs have not yet patented their products, but we can ask why not the five others, either. Those with patents are technology oriented in competition means while the others compete with know how, quality, and reliable deliveries, which are more typical for specialized SMEs.

Production innovations were connected with process innovations in five additional SMEs, and with marketing innovations in two. In two SMEs, (product) innovations could be verified by foreign patents. Other of them is in a sector, where there is no other Finnish firm, and the other was starting to internationalize. In one of these SMEs, a strategic innovation might be included, too. These SMEs compete with special production technology and high quality of products.

Other recognized innovation types were rare. Marketing innovations in Internationalization recognized by three SME managers were concerned with distribution and market expand. The first of these innovations was distribution directly to the retailers in target country nearby Finland. Increasing international demand has helped this enterprise to grow very fast to a large enterprise. The second SME exports through the same agent with five other enterprises, and the third innovation includes starting to market the present products to a larger group of customers, including foreign ones.

Process innovation connected with Internationalization was recognized by one SME manager, and innovation in strategy also by one. The process innovation of a small enterprise only importing and exporting, was to subcontract directly to the target of the foreign customer in a third country. Participating in projects is courageous and unusual way for an SME to operate abroad. The strategy innovation in internationalization was also uncommon. This small and extensively internationalized enterprise reported on an on-going research project conceming the SMEs' internationalizing problematics. The (product) innovations of this enterprise were also verified by foreign patents. One small enterprise manager did not define the type of innovation in Internationalization though he reported his enterprise to have one.

Fourteen other SME managers reported their enterprises to have foreign patents, mostly on products. Patenting was either their most extensive foreign operation or one operation among others, see Figure 3. Yet, these managers did not recognize them as innovations connected with Internationalization. However, we can ask, whether patenting abroad would have become necessaryif the SME was operating in home markets only. This group of enterprises was very heterogenous but their most common means of competition were various product characteristics, and price. Interestingly, one of these enterprises was a large one, whose manager did not report on any innovations connectedwith Internationalization although he mentioned the enterprise to *'have several kinds of innovations'* and to compete with *'innovation and high quality operations'*.

All the SMEs' innovations are not recognized by the managers, nor are they patented. The SME managers were also asked to compare the international operations of their fimms with those of the competitors when starting to internationalize, those at present, and the changes in international operations they plan for the future. Positive difference from the competitors may includean innovation. When starting the Internationalization, twenty three SMEs had differed from the competitors, according to the managers. In seven enterprises, the differences were concemed with the actual foreign operations: Co-operation with Finnish and foreign partners in international operations, having an agent if others had not and vice versa, connection to a market through the owner from that country, and being the first exporter in the sector. Market area of five SMEs was either broader or narrower than that of the competitors. Differences in internationalization strategies, i.e. forms of co-operation and contacts abroad, and trial of foreign operations were reported by four managers. Seven managers described their enterprise having differed from the competitors 'in many ways' when starting the internationalization. This includes the types presented above.

The present international operations differed from those of the competitors in twenty six SMEs. In eight of them, the present market area was different, usually broader than that of the competitors. Four SME managers considered the present international operations more 'efficient and economical' than those of others. In three SMEs, the present international strategies were considered different. 'Several differences', including the types presented above, was the most common type of present differences, identified by eleven managers.

Although the managers were often unable to define or see any differences from their competitors in the earlier international operations or those at present, changes to achieve such differences were set targets for the future in altogether eighty six SMEs. These changes may include making or adopting an innovation. 8 of these SMEs operated presently in the domestic markets, 52 imported and/or exported and the rest 26 had more extensive international operations. Thirty nine managers planned for a change in market area, and in 36 cases this meant expanding it. 5 of them operated presently in Finland only. Especially European markets were considered as interesting (17 cases), but also areas nearby Finland (8) (Scandinavia, Russia, the Baltic countries). The changes planned by nine SME managers on international operations would be concerned with everyday sales and marketing, starting a sales unit abroad, and promoting product development. Eleven managers planned for changes in the strategies of international operations. They include moving production and marketing abroad, concentrating on fewer products and searching buyers for them, searching for partners in certain markets, starting Internationalization (one of them operated now in the domestic markets), shifting from subcontracting to own products, improving planning and controlling, and marketing also products of Finnish partners abroad. The common motive for all these changes is "the necessity to internationalize" in the future, as one manager put it. Twenty seven managers planned for several changes, consisting of those described above, to be made in the future in their international operations. Most of these changes would mean considerable reorganizations in most of the firms' (international) operations.

N = 242

Domestic, no difference 17 %
Recognized Innovations domestic 0,4 %
Exports & Imports no difference 35 %
Recognized Innovations Internationalized 7 %
Recognized Innovations foreign patents 2 %
Foreign patents, no recognized Innovations 4 %
Patent & other operations no recognized Innovations 3 %
Difference(s) in International operations in the beginning 7 %
Difference(s) in International operations at present 3 %
Internationalized no difference 2 %
Change target in the future 21 %

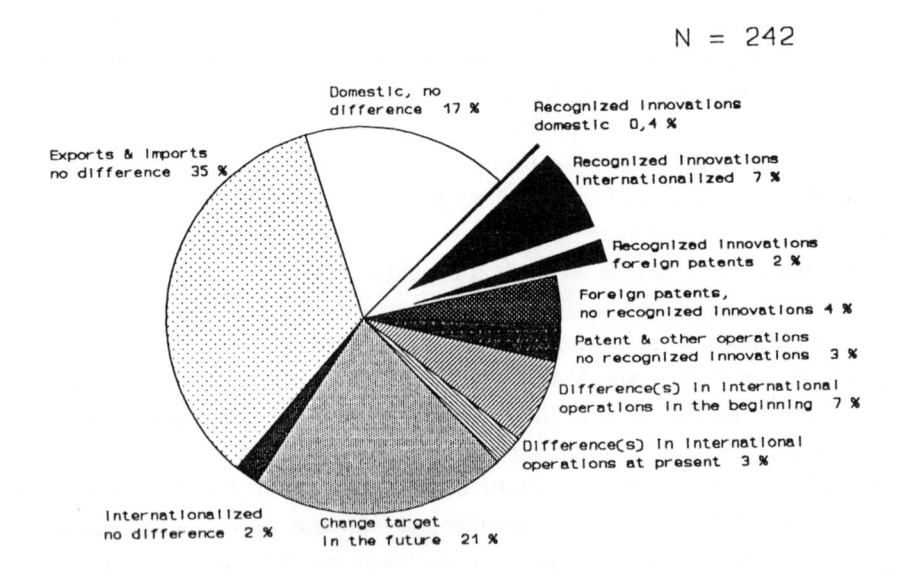

Figure 3. Innovations in internationalization of Finnish SMEs

Summary on innovations in Finnish SMEs' internationalization is presented in Figure 3. If we separate the groups of 24 enterprises having recognized innovations, 14 SMEs with foreign patents, 16 SMEs whose international operations were different from those of competitors when starting to internationalize, 8 SMEs with foreign operations different from competitors today, and 51 SMEs planning to change their foreign operations in the future, in this order, from 242 SMEs in the sample, there remains 129 enterprises. 40 of them are domestically operating ones, 85 importers and/or exporters and 4 further internationalized SMEs. The managers considered these entelprises as similar to the competitors. These SMEs have no patents or recognized innovations either. However, for instance opening a sales unit abroad points out that the SME has some competition potential in the foreign markets, too. Naturally, the results also present that part of Finnish SMEs are 'standard enterprises' even if they operate in international markets. In such cases, price and flexibility are their competition means, which unfortunately are not always the most economical and fortunate ones.

Discussion

The results achieved here present that gradual Internationalization takes place also in small firms and the internationalization models presented in the literature are valid also in this sample. However, the importance and frequency of imports in Finnish SMEs' internationalization process must be emphasized. Usually the earlier Internationalization models have not included imports. In this sample, majority of the 193 internationalized SMEs, 52 per cent, 100 enterprises, had started their Internationalization process with imports and only 51 enterprises, exported first. 37 internationalized SMEs had started importing and exporting in the same year.

The results on commitment to Internationalization achieved here are similar to those presented in the previous literature: Small and medium-sized enterprises seldom have other international operations than importing raw materials etc., or indirect or direct export. Seventy eight per cent of the internationalized SMEs in this sample only import and/or export. Furthermore, these operations are often irregular or/and unplanned, making up only a small part of their total sales. Only eight per cent of the SMEs examined here, plan their international operations. Five per cent are strongly committed to Internationalization in this sample.

Innovations in Finnish SMEs' Internationalization are rare. Only 24 managers recognized such innovations and most of these are product innovations. Also the number of reported foreign patents was small, 19 altogether. Usually they were also concerned with products. Identifying foreign patents and innovations connected with Internationalization do not always match among the SME managers. It seems that the SMEs' innovations are not always patented even if the SME operates in foreign markets. Moreover, it is difficult for the SME manager to compare his enterprise with its competitors. The SME managers seldom consider their enterprises different from the competitors, 23 did so concerning the start of the international operations, and 26 concerning those at present. But SMEs are looking forward a better future: Such differences were reported to be set targets for the future in 86 SMEs. This assumes arising of innovations or at least quick adoption of novelties in SMEs in the future. It would be interesting to study a few years later, how these SMEs have been able to reach the changes they reported having set targets for the future.

References

Aerts, Ria (1992), 'Becoming International: Benefits and Pitfalls for Entrepreneurial SMEs', Paper presented at RENT VI *Research in Entrepreneurship, 6th Workshop, Barcelona, Spain, November 26-27, 1992.*

Aerts, Ria (1993), 'Family Business and Internationalization' in Virtanen, Markku (ed.), *Proceedings of the Conference on The Development and the Strategies of SME's in 1990's, August 26-28, 1993, Mikkeli, Finland.* Volume 1. Helsinki School of Economics and Business Administration, The Small Business Center, Mikkeli. Pages 36-44.

Ackoff, Russell L. (1970), *A Concept of Corporate Planning*, Wiley-Interscience, New York.

Ansoff, Igor H. (1971), *Corporate Strategy. An Analytic Approach to Business Policy for Growth and Expansion,* Penguin Books, Bungay, Suffolk. Reprint.

Ansoff, Igor H. (1984), *Implanting Strategic Management*, Prentice-Hall Inc, Englewood Cliffs, New Jersey.

Bacon, Frank R. Jr. and Butler, Thomas W. Jr. (1981), *Planned Innovation*, The University of Michigan, Industrial Development Division, Institute of Science and Technology, Ann Arbor, MI, USA. Second edition.

Basberg, Bjorn L. (1987), 'Patents and the Measurement of Techno-logical Change: A Survey of the Literature', *Research Policy*, vol. 16, pp. 131-141.

Cannon, Tom (1985), 'Innovation, Creativity and Small Firm Organisation', *International Small Business Journal*, vol. 4, no. 1, pp. 33-41.

Christensen, Poul Rind (1991), 'The Small and Medium-Sized Exporters' Squeeze: Empirical Evidence and Model Reflections', *Entrepreneurship & Regional Development*, vol. 3, pp. 49-65.

Czinkota, Michael R. (1982), *Export Development Strategies*, U.S. Promotion Policy, Praeger Publishers, Westport, Connecticut.

Dichtl, E., Leibold, M., Koglmayr, H.-G. and Müller, S. (1984), 'The Export-decision of Small and Medium-sized Firms: A Review', *Management International Review*, vol. 24, no. 2, pp. 49-60.

Dror, Israel (1989), 'Technology Innovation Indicators', *R&D Management*, vol. 19, no. 3, pp. 243-9.

Drucker, Peter F. (1985), *Innovation and Entrepreneurship, Practice and Principles*, Heinemann, London.

Forsgren, Mats (1989), *Managing the Internationalization Process. The Swedish Case*, Routledge, London.

Haahti, Antti J. (1987), Product - *Market Strategies of Small and Medium-Sized European Firms*, Helsinki School of Economics, Working Paper, Series F, No. 169, Helsinki.

Haahti, Antti Juhani (1989), *Entrepreneurs' Strategic Orientation: Modeling Strategic Behavior In Small Industrial Owner-managed Firms*, Acta Academiae Oeconomicae Helsingiensis, Series A, No.64, Helsinki School of Economics and Business Administration, Helsinki.

Harrison, Richard T. and Hart, Mark (1987), *'Innovation and Marketing Development: The Experience of Small Firrns in a Peripheral Economy'*, *OMEGA International Journal of Management Science*, vol. 15, no. 6, pp. 445-54.

Heinonen, Tarja (1992), *Financial innovation,* Helsinki School of Economics, Series B, No. 122, Helsinki.

Johanson, Jan and Vahlne, Jan-Erik (1990), 'The Mechanism of Internationalization', *International Marketing Review,* vol. 7, no. 4, pp. 11-24.

Kaynak, Erdener, Ghauri, Pervez N. and Olofsson-Bredenlöw, Torbjöm (1987), 'Export Behaviour of Small Swedish Firms', *Journal of Small Business Management,* vol. 25, no. 2, April, pp. 26-32.

Kotabe, Masaaki (1990), 'The Relationship Between Offshore Sourcing and Innovativeness of U.S. Multinational Firms: An Empirical Investigation', *Journal of International Business Studies,* vol. 21, no. 4, Fourth quarter, pp. 623-638.

Lee, Woo-Young and Brasch, John J. (1978), 'The adoption of Export as an Innovative Strategy', *Journal of International Business Studies,* vol. 9, no. 2, pp. 85-93.

Lehtimäki, Allan (1992), *Product-Market Strategy Changes, Internationalization and Performance of European Small and Medium sized Enterprises,* Tampere University of Technology, Publication No. 105, Tampere.

Lehtinen, Uolevi (1983), *Yrityksen kansainvälistymisen peruspiirteet ja käsite* (The fundamental characteristics and the concept of internationalization of the firm), University of Tampere, School of Business Administration (Yrityksen taloustieteen ja yksityisoikeuden laitos), Series A 3, Working and Discussion Paper No. 1, Tampere. (In Finnish)

Luostarinen, Reijo (1980), *Internationalization of the Firm. An empirical study of tlle internationalization of firms with small and open domestic markets with special emphasis on lateral rigidity as a behavioral characteristic in strategic decision-making,* Acta Academiae Oeconomicae Helsingiensis, Series A No. 30, Helsinki. 2nd edition.

Luostarinen, Reijo and Welch, Lawrence (1990), *International Business Operations,* Kyriiri Oy, Helsinki.

Majaro, Simon (1982), *International Marketing: A Strategic Approach to World Markets,* George Allen & Unwin, London. Revised edition.

Mintzberg, Henry (1978), 'Patterns in Strategy Formation', *Management*

Science, vol. 24, no. 9, May, pp. 934-48.

Nyström, Harry (1990), *Technological and Market Innovation. Strategies for Product and Company Development,* John Wiley & Sons Ltd, Chichester.

OECD (1982), *Innovation in Small and Medium Firms. Background Reports,* OECD, Paris.

Piercy, Nigel (1981), 'Company Internationalization: Active and Reactive Exporting', *European Journal of Marketing,* vol. 15, no. 3, pp. 26-40.

PKT-*tietoa* (Data on SMEs) 1990, Central Organization of Finnish Industry (Teollisuuden Keskusliitto), Helsinki. (In Finnish)

Porter, Michael E. (1985), *Competitive Advantage. Creating and Sustaining Superior Performance,* The Free Press, New York, U.S.A.

Ranta, Jukka (1987), *Innovation, Invariances and Analogies. Comments on the Life-Cycle Theory and the Forecasting of Future Trends in the Flexible Production Automation,* SITRA (Finnish National Fund for Research and Development), Discussion paper No. 2, Helsinki.

Reid, Stan D. (1981), 'The Decision-Maker and Export Entry and Expansion', *Journal of International Business Studies,* Fall, pp. 101-12.

Rickards, Tudor (1985), *Stimulating Innovation. A Systems Approach,* Frances Pinter (Publishers), London.

Rogers, Everett M. (1983), *Diffusion of Innovations,* The Free Press, New York. 3rd edition.

Samiee, Saeed and Walters, Peter G. P. (1990), 'Influence of Firm Size on Export Planning and Performance', *Journal of Business Research,* vol. 20, no. 3, pp. 235-48.

Schumpeter, Joseph A. (1949), *The Theory of Economic Development. An Inquiry into Profits, Capital, Credit, Interest, and the Business Cycle,* Harvard University Press, Cambridge, Massachusetts. 3rd printing.

Simmonds, Kenneth and Smith, Helen (1968), 'The First Export Order: A Marketing Innovation', *British Journal of Marketing,* Summer, pp. 93-100.

Suomen yritykset (Corporate Enterprises and Personal Businesses in Finland) 1990, (Statistics) Central Statistical Office of Finland, Enterprises 1992:9, Helsinki. (In Finnish)

Terpstra, Vern (1981), *International Marketing*, The Dryden Press, Holt-Saunders Japan, Ltd, Tokyo. 2nd edition.

Young, S., Hamill, J., Wheeler, C. and Davies, J. R. (1989), *International Market Entry and Development. Strategies and Management*, Harvester Wheatsheaf, Prentice Hall, Exter.

Äijö, Toivo S. (1977), 'The Internationalization Process of Business Enterprise - A Theoretical Framework of Study', The Finnish *Journal of Business Economics* (Liiketaloudellinen Aikakauskirja), vol. 26, no. 4, pp. 379-88.

Appendix 1 Industrial sectors of SMEs in the sample and comparison to the sectors of total Finnish Industry

Industrial Sector	Sample (%)	Finnish SMEs [1]
Metal products	156 (65 %)	9 %
Metal, electronics	3 (1 %)	
Electronics	9 (4 %)	7 %
Wood products	16 (7 %)	12 % [2]
Wood prod. and metal	4 (2 %)	
Textile and clothing	9 (4 %)	10 %
Textile and metal	1 (0,4 %)	
Plastics and rubber	4 (2 %)	4 %
Stone and glass	14 (6 %)	5 %
Publishing, printing	7 (3 %)	11 %
Others	8 (3 %) [3]	
MISSING	11 (5 %)	
TOTAL	**242 (100 %)**	

1) Total Finnish SMEs in 1988. Personnel by sectors.
   Source: PKT-tietoa 1990, p.5.

2) Wood, Wood products and Furniture.

3) 2 in heating, air other utility service, and 4 in construction, in chemical industry, and 1 in maintenance service.

Some SMEs gave more than one sector but did not define the principal one.

Appendix 2   Size of SMEs in the sample by the number of employees and by turn over in 1991 and their shares compared to the total Finnish Industry

Information concerning amount of personnel and turn over is missing of 26 SMEs.

TURN OVER IN 1991 (million FIM)	PERSONNEL									TOTAL	Finnish Industrial enterprises1)
	5-10	11-20	21-30	31-50	51-75	75-100	101-150	Over 150		
Under 5 million	14	25	3						42 (19 %)	22.522 (84 %)
5-10 million	4	40	19	9	1				73 (34 %)	
11-20 million	1	6	22	22	4				55 (25 %)	
21-50 million		3	1	12	13	5	4	1 2)	39 (18 %)	1.498 (6 %)
51-100 million		1		1	1	1	2		6 (3 %)	
Over 100 million								1 3)	1 (0,5 %)	421 4) (2 %)
TOTAL	19 (9 %)	75 (35 %)	45 (21 %)	44 (20 %)	19 (9 %)	6 (3 %)	6 (3 %)	2 (1 %)	216	
Finnish industrial enterprises 5)	2,644 (10 %)	1,765 (7 %)	1,578 (6 %)		525 (2 %)		281 (1 %)			26,870

1) Source: *Suomen yritykset* 1990, p. 38.
2) The enterprise had 174 employees, turn over was 49 million FIM in 1991. (1 ECU = 6.5 FIM)
3) The enterprise had 300 employees, turn over was 156 million FIM in 1991.
4) Turn over class 10 million .... 49.999 million FIM.
5) Source: *Suomen yritykset* 1990, p. 34.

Part B
STRATEGY/ORGANIZATION

6 Flexible companies in an industrial district: The case of the Gnosjö region in Sweden

Johan Wiklund and Charlie Karlsson

Introduction

Economic change and the success of flexible industrial districts

During the 1970s and 1980s economic decline and the internationalisation of markets increased international competition. Fluctuations in the economy increased uncertainty. However, the incomes of large groups of consumers increased, their consumption turned more sophisticated and they demanded a greater variety of products to choose from. This led to a shortening of product life cycles and to increased product differentiation. To survive in the market place, firms needed to adjust to constant changes in market demand and develop the ability to supply the markets with customised products. Companies needed greater flexibility.

Many large mass producing firms had problems adjusting to the uncertainty. This resulted in economic problems such as stagnation and unemployment. However, a few localities, termed industrial districts, prospered in different countries in the Western World. These industrial districts rely on dense networks of small and medium sized enterprises (SMEs) with both competitive and co-operative relations. A combination of economic, social and institutional arrangements provide the necessary conditions for the formation of the networks. Industrial districts have been successful in many different industries, traditional labour intensive industries as well as modern, knowledge intensive industries. The Gnosjö Region in Sweden which in the literature has been compared to regions such as Rhône Alp, Silicon Valley, Route 128, Baden-Württemberg, Jutland and the Third Italy etc (Sabel, 1989) is one example of such a region.

In their book "The Second Industrial Divide" (1984), Piore and Sabel °highlight the importance of flexibility for the success of industrial districts, introducing the term flexible specialisation. They, as well as other researchers, suggest that the SMEs in industrial districts are flexible. The literature is concerned with flexibility at macro, meso and intra-firm level. However, few if any studies have been made at the firm level that explicitly investigate the flexibility of the firms in industrial districts.

Since the performance of the industrial district on the aggregated level is determined by the performance of the firms and their utilisation of the regional network, it is important to investigate more closely the flexibility of the firms at the firm level, especially since so much credit is given to the specialisation of production on the firm level and the economic autonomy of the firms (cf. Garofoli, 1990).

Aim of the paper

The aim of this paper is to develop a taxonomy that identifies the flexibility of the firms in industrial districts and to apply this taxonomy to empirical data from firms in an industrial district – the Gnosjö Region in Sweden. That is to say to investigate whether or not the firms in this industrial district are to be referred to as flexible, in what respect they are flexible and what sources they use to achieve this flexibility.

For this purpose a model is developed that identifies different elements of flexibility at the firm level and then structures these elements into four different components of flexibility; input flexibility, internal flexibility, output flexibility and network flexibility. The model describes how the four components interact to constitute the overall flexibility of the firm.

Different levels of analysis of flexibility in the literature on industrial districts

In the literature on industrial districts, flexibility is considered as one of the key factors for the success of these districts. The analyses of flexibility basically concern different aspects on the reconstruction of production following the crises of Fordism during the 1970s. Three distinct levels of analysis are covered in this literature, macro economic, meso economic and intra-firm analysis of flexibility.

The identification of three different levels of analysis does not mean that the literature consists of analyses on one level and leaves out the others. On the contrary, much effort is put into relating the different levels to each other, e.g. to explain how the development of CNC machinery facilitates the development of new industrial districts that are more fit to serve the rapidly changing demands of the consumers.

However, these analyses seem to leave out one important level of analysis - the level of the firm and in what respects it is flexible.

The macro level

The macro analysis of flexibility has its genesis in the French regulation school (cf. Aglietta, 1979) which explains the slow down in economic growth by the limitations of Fordist production processes. According to their view, mass production of standardised goods was considered the ideal economic system up until the oil crises in the 1970s when a period of uncertainty started. The uncertainty depends on many factors such as consumer demands for a greater variety of products to choose from, a shortening of product life cycles in combination with product differentiation and the development of CNC machines that facilitates the simultaneous production of different and alternative products on the same line. Mass production has come to an end, as well as the strict Tayloristic division of the mental and manual aspects of work. The Fordist model of economic development is no longer sustainable and has to be replaced by a dynamic post-Fordist growth model.

Post-Fordism has been criticised for giving insufficient evidence of the failure of mass production (Teague, 1990) as well as exaggerating the rigidity of mass production. Dunford and Benko (1991) identify a number of different possible developments from Fordism, including neo-Fordism as well as different forms of post-Fordism.

The point of departure for the post-Fordism model seems to be mainly theoretical. The modes of regulation vary across nations and it is questionable whether one universal post-Fordism model is applicable to such different economies as for example the Swedish and the British.

The meso level

On the meso level, the unit of analysis is the industrial district itself or networks of firms within the district. The firms in the industrial districts are said to be innovative and are therefore well suited to respond to the rapid changes in market demand. The firms in these districts cooperate and compete in such a fashion that the resources in the region are constantly combined in new ways. Piore and Sabel (1984) introduced the term flexible specialisation to describe these industrial districts. Due to their small size and their origin in craft production, the firms in industrial districts are flexible, using a skilled work force and flexible equipment in a non-Tayloristic, craftsmanlike production.

Criticisms of the meso analyses of flexibility are based on the lack of empirical evidence supporting the idea that flexible specialisation is a new production system, and the fact that the number of examples are too few (Teague, 1990). Martinelli and Schoenberger (1991) argue that the flexible specialised regions are unique and question the sectoral and geographical generalisability of the flexible specialisation model. They also question if the specialised network of small disintegrated firms really is more flexible than the large integrated firm.

The Third Italy is a very important source of empirical evidence supporting the flexible specialisation model. The literature describing the development in the Third Italy is now quite extensive. The theoretical framework of flexible specialisation is based on the history of industrial districts, starting in the 19th century and the development of the third Italy after WW II. The model has later been applied to other industrial districts with similar features.

The intra-firm level

The third level of analysis deals with the internal flexibility of the firm. The introduction of microprocessors and electronic interfaces enabled equipment to be more flexible. The use of flexible CNC machinery facilitated the production of small batches of differentiated products aimed at smaller, differentiated markets. Thus, the flexibility of the equipment was one important factor that facilitated the change of the Fordist production system.

Later, the success of the Japanese car manufacturing industry changed the focus to organisational means to achieve intra-firm flexibility. Just-in-time-production (Schoenberger, 1979) and later, lean production (Womak, 1990) are Japanese, non-Tayloristic organisation of work that has been introduced in larger parts of the world. The importance of the use of flexible work practices as well as polyvalent workers are important features in both forms.

In the literature on industrial districts, the non-Tayloristic organisation of work as well as the modern, flexible equipment is supposed to be well suited for the small firms in the districts. However, there is little support that the diffusion of information technology applications or non-Tayloristic organisations of work has been faster within industrial districts than in other geographical areas (cf. Martinelli and Schoenberger, 1991).

The need for a taxonomy for the flexibility of the industrial district

Much is said about flexiblity in the literature on industrial districts but there are no explicit definitions of flexibility. Flexibility is most commonly described in general terms such as the firm's ability to respond to the rapid changes in market demand (cf. Sabel, 1989). This is a very broad description that leaves out important information such as what the firm gains from the flexibility, in what respects the firm is flexible, what sources the firm uses to obtain the flexibility, the trade offs of flexibility, etc.

Benko and Dunford (1991) distinguish the different meanings of flexibility as follows. Flexibility in the production methods, the employment contracts, the wage determinants, the inter-firm relations, the structure of capital, the modes of consumption and the state interventions. However, none of these meanings of flexibility focuses on the firm.

In organisation theory, one important distinction is between proactive and reactive flexibility. There are two major aims of flexibility, to increase stability and to increase market shares, the former is a reactive and the latter an proactive strategy. Implicitly, these distinctions are used in the literature on industrial districts as well. Coriat (1991) uses the terminology "strategy of passive differentiation" and "strategy of offensive differentiation" for this distinction. Storper and Christopherson (1987) stress that firms in the motion picture industry market across industrial boundaries to reduce the uncertainty that is created by vertical disintegration, which is an example of reactive flexibility whereas Sabel (1989) emphasises the proactive elements of flexibility and stress that industrial districts:

"....constantly varied their products to satisfy changing tastes and extend their markets by defining new wants". (Sabel, 1989, p17).

This is an example of proactive flexibility.

Flexible specialisation regions are often described in the same manner, even though they are specialised in many different ways. Route 128 and Silicon Valley in the USA are specialised in high-tech, the motion picture industry is concentrated to Los Angeles, many of the industrial districts in the Third Italy are specialised in design etc.

Piore and Sabel (1984) have shown that there are a number of similarities between these districts, but there is also reason to believe that there are some vital differences between the flexibility of the firms in different industrial districts, due to their different specialities. The demands from the customers and the volatility of markets differ, as do the production processes. This implies a difference in the importance of flexibility between districts and that firms should be flexible in different ways.

To be able to focus on the flexibility of firms in industrial districts it is necessary to find a taxonomy of flexibility on the firm level. In the following section a model is developed that aims at defining the flexibility of the firm in an industrial district and to chategorise elements of flexibility found in existing literature on industrial districts.

The flexibility model of the firm

By illustrating the flexibility of the firm by a simple input/output model it is possible to capture the great variety of flexibility elements in the literature. However, first a general duscussion on the input/output model might be fruitful. To perform economic activities, the firm needs input from its environment. Processes witin the firm add value to the input and result in output on the market. Obviously, there is a close relationship between the input, the internal processes and the output. Changes in one affects the others as well as the overall performance of the firm.

It is also possible to use an input/output model for the *flexibility* of the firm. Input flexibility, internal flexibility and output flexibility are closely related and interact. However, since it is possible for the firm to obtain flexibility from the regional network of firms by other activities than purely economic, it is important to add a network dimension of flexibility (figure 1).

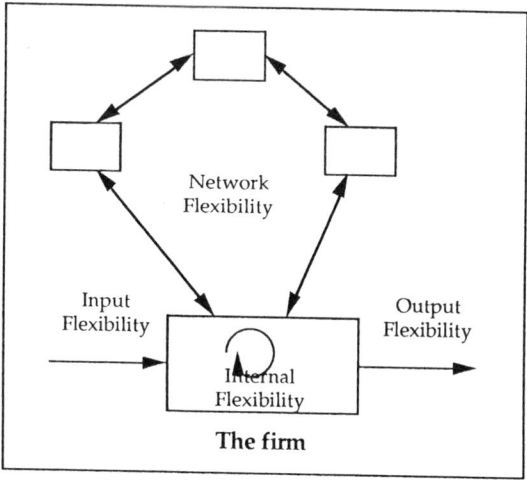

Figure 1   The flexibility model of the firm.

The model

The flexibility of the firm could be looked upon as *outcomes* and *sources* of flexibility. The outcomes of the flexibility refers to how the flexibility of the firm is appreciated in the market place, compared to its competitors. One way of describing this is in terms of the *output flexibility* of the firm.

To achieve this flexibility in relation to the market, the firm needs to utilise different sources of flexibility. There are *internal* and *external* sources of flexibility. Internal sources of flexibility refers to the ability to rapidly recombine the existing resources within the firm. Internal sources of flexibility are often covered in the intra-firm analyses of flexibility.

External sources of flexibility are sources that do not exist within the firm but can be obtained from the environment. Furthermore, it is necessary to make a distinction between two different kinds of external sources of flexibility, *input flexibility* and *network flexibility*. Input flexibility refers to flexible factor conditions. Network flexibility refers to flexibility in collaboration with other firms. Network flexibility is often covered in the meso analyses of flexibility.

Input flexibility

One way to obtain input flexibility is by rapid changes in the number of workers employed. Atkinson (1984) points to the following types of numerical flexibility: workers employed by subcontractors, self-employed workers, staff supplied by temporary employment agencies, the use of trainees, workers employed on short-term contracts, part timers and the use of job sharing.

Benko and Dunford (1991) point out the importance of flexible capital structures. To reduce the risks involved with investments in fixed assets, firms purchase goods from independent suppliers instead of producing them. It is also possible to reduce investments in fixed assets by leasing the equipment used. Another way to reduce the risk is to increase the share of external capital in the firm.

Internal flexibility

A common type of internal flexibility is the use of modern and multi-purpose flexible equipment that can perform a variety of different operations and/or quickly can be switched from one operation to another. Gerwin and Leung (1980) calls this technological flexibility and identify five dimensions of application of technological flexibility:

1. Design change flexibility refers to the possibility of modifying the process in accordance with the particular characteristics that can be introduced in the same basic products.

2. Mix flexibility has to do with the possibility of producing simultaneously, on the same line, different and alternative products that have certain basic elements in common.

3. Part flexibility concerns the fact that the processes as a whole can be made more simple or complex at low or no cost through the addition or subtraction of productive operations.

4. Volume flexibility denotes the possibility of altering the quantitative output of the line in accordance with variations in demand.

5. Routing flexibility refers to the capacity to route the product via segments of the process that are free or underemployed.

Coriat (1991) distinguishes economies of scope from economies of range, where economies of scope deals with a high degree of product differentiation, whereas economies of range is a scaled-down version of economies of scope, in which the differentiation that can be achieved is smaller.

The use of skilled, polyvalent workers that are able to conduct a number of different tasks and a work organisation that rapidly changes the tasks performed by the workers according to changes in demand are other internal sources of flexibility . Still another internal source of flexibility is the network organisation of large firms. Decentralised authority and independent operating units resembling autonomous small SMEs serving different markets facilitate flexibility through rapidly reorganised production to meet changes is demand.

Output flexibility

Output flexibility refers to the ability to respond to the changing needs of the customers. The output flexibility consists of two different parts, the ability to change customers and the ability to change products. The customer flexibility of the firm reduces the risk of remaining in declining market niches when market demands alter. Product flexibility means the ability to develop and produce new products for existing customers to keep moving to the left on the S-curve.

Customer and product flexibility of a firm could be combined in different ways. It is possible for a firm to have a high degree of flexibility in one of the dimensions and a low degree in the other, but still be a flexible firm. There are considerable differences between firms depending on their mix of customer and product flexibility.

In general, the product flexibility is related to flexibility of the production process, i. e. the ability to produce various products on the same line of production (cf Coriat, 1991), or else, the flexibility is related to the vertically disintegrated networks of specialised firms (cf Storper and Christopherson, 1987) that by different collaborative constallation vary their products. Unfortunately, very little is said in the literature about the firms' customer flexibility.

Network flexibility

The most important form of external flexibility is obtained by different kinds of cooperation with other firms, network flexibility. Piore and Sabel (1984) identify three different types of cooperation between firms that create flexibility. *Regional conglomerations* are networks of SMEs bound in a complex web of competition and cooperation. None of the firms in the network is permanently dominant and their roles in the network shift constantly. The networks are defined and held together by community ties, e.g. religion, rather then formal contracts.

The firms in *federated enterprises* are more tightly connected than the regional conglomerations both by interlocking personnel and financial agreements such as interlocking boards of directors as well as by family ties between the firms.

Solar firms are larger firms surrounded by orbiting subcontractors. Much of the value added is out sourced to subcontractors and they are treated as collaborators, not subordinates.

Storper and Christopherson (1987) stress that vertical disintegration under certain circumstances is better then integration. They identify three types of production subcontracting:

1. Specialised input that a integrated firm cannot produce as well as a specialised one.

2. Capacity subcontracting to respond to uncertainty or instability in output.

3. Supplier subcontracting may be advantageous when minimal optimal scales of output at different production stages are not equivalent and it is impossible to optimise capacity utilisation within the firm.

The Gnosjö firms

What is the relevance of the model developed in the previous section? To find out, the model is applied on data from a Swedish industrial district, the Gnosjö Region, where numerous studies have been brought out. Hewever, first of all it is important to find out in what respects the Gnosjö Region could be characterised as an industrial district.

The Gnosjö Region, a Swedish Industrial District

The Gnosjö Region (the municipality of Gnosjö with three surrounding municipalities) is located in the South Western part of the county of Jönköping, Sweden. The Gnosjö Region is well known in Sweden for its strong entrepreneurial spirit, known in Sweden as the Gnosjö spirit.

During the 1980s, the Gnosjö Region was the most successful industrial region in Sweden in terms of the relative increase in the number of employees in the manufacturing sector. While employment in the manufacturing sector in Sweden as a whole decreased by 12% during the period 1980-1988, it increased by over 10% in the Gnosjö Region (Statistics Sweden, 1990).

Compared to the total national employment in the manufacturing sector of more than 900,000 in 1990, the 20,452 employees in the Gnosjö Region might seem insignificant. However, the growth is endogenous and a result of expanding SMEs as well as the establishment of new firms. In the light of Sweden's small SME sector, the development of the manufacturing sector in the Gnosjö Region is remarkable.

From this point of view, the Gnosjö Region resembles an industrial district. The expansion of the manufacturing sector and the large share of small firms are two of the typical features that have made industrial districts famous.

To better judge whether or not the Gnosjö Region is an industrial district, it is possible to compare data from the Gnosjö Region to data from Italian industrial districts. In his definition of an industrial district, Brusco (1990) characterises the size as follows:

"Thus an industrial district is a small area in which (if we include both dependent and independent workers) there are perhaps 10.000 to 20.000 workers and around 1.000 to 3.000 firms with fewer than 20 employees". (Brusco, 1990, p14)

The Gnosjö Region meets this definition well with 20 452 employees and 1 326 firms with fewer than 20 employees within the manufacturing sector.

Sforzi (1990) identifies 61 Italian Marshallian industrial districts based on the characteristics that they are directed towards manufacturing and they are dominated by one particular industry. On average, the share of employees within manufacturing industry is 55% and the share of the dominant manufacturing industry in relation to the manufacturing industry is 50% in the 61 Italian Marshallian industrial districts. The corresponding figures for the Gnosjö Region are 45% employed within the manufacturing sector and 51% of these are employed within the metal goods industry. The share of employees within the manufacturing sector is somewhat below the Italian average, but still the highest figure in Sweden, whereas the concentration on the dominant industry is above the average of Italian Marshallian industrial districts.

A dense network of relations between the firms is another feature of an industrial district. Johannisson and Gustafsson (1984) have shown that the trust and number of contacts between managers within the Gnosjö Region is high. Further, Johannisson et al (1992) show that the Gnosjö firms have social and/or commercial linkages to a large number of other firms within the region.

To sum up, avaliable data from the Gnosjö Region strongly suggest that it should be considered as an industrial district.

The following sections cover an analysis of the empirical findings from this studies of the Gnosjö firms that shed light on aspects of flexibility. The empirical findings in this literature are related to the flexibility model that was formerly developed.

The regional production system

The results from an earlier multiple case study of eleven leading (100-200 employees) metal working firms in the Gnosjö Region (Wiklund, 1992a) shows that they mainly are directed towards the domestic market. New markets and products are developed slowly and carefully. The majority are subcontractors to the Swedish car manufacturing industry. However, all firms also serve other markets than the car manufacturing industry, either they subcontract to other large Swedish firms or they develop and market products directly to the final market.

The leading Gnosjö firms have developed profitable market niches. A purposeful development of relations with large, qualified and expanding customers has facilitated their expansion and development . Thanks to the broad product niches, they are able to operate in different industries simultaneously. This is a way of coping with the uncertainty that is transmitted down the subcontracting hierarchy by their large customers .

Swedish descriptions of such firms as the Gnosjö firms often resemble the "dependent subcontractor model" (Brusco, 1990). However, their autonomy in relation to their customers as well as their ability to change customers and/or products is often underestimated in these descriptions.

The car manufacturing industry is a very demanding and sophisticated customer and puts heavy pressure on the subcontractors to innovate and upgrade, whereas other customers are less demanding but more profitable. The mix of customers makes it possible to gain advantages from both types of customer relations.

The Gnosjö firms identify themselves by the specialised activities they perform (e.g. high quality lathing) or the product types (e.g. springs) they make rather than by the customers they serve. Specialisation is based on the production competence of the organisation, which has been turned into broad product niches based on a joint production technology. Most products are rather uncomplicated components, made from sheet metal or wire. Normally the products are developed by their customers.

The leading Gnosjö firms are production process oriented in the sense that the value that the firms add to the larger part consists of manufacturing rather then product development or marketing. Investments are mainly made in production systems. The leading Gnosjö firms are aiming to keep as much of the control and knowledge about the production process as possible within the firm. Raw material suppliers are large and localised to other parts of Sweden or the rest of Europe. However, local suppliers are used for service oriented inputs such as machine tools, computer service etc. Local, smaller firms deliver uncompicated component, often made from sheet metal, wire or plastic to the leading firms. They in turn, cooperate with other smaller firms and self employed workers. The principles of the regional production system could be illustrated by the figure below.

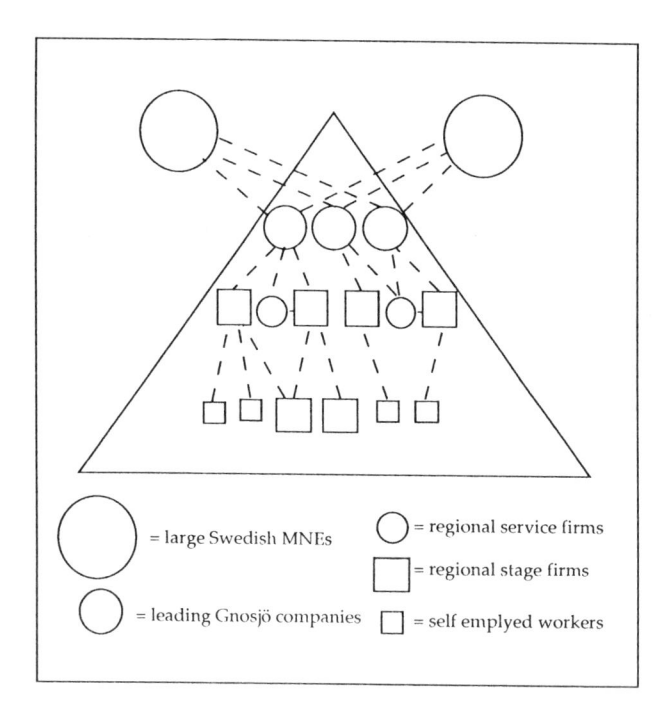

Figure 2 **Regional production system in the Gnosjö Region**

The firms in the regional production system interact by a complex web of linkages, both horisontal and vertical, both commercial and social (cf. Johannisson et al, 1992). Still there is a clear hierarchical structure, where the leading Gnosjö firms are the main interface to customers outside the Gnosjö Region and the smaller firms are "stage firms", involved in one or a few stages of down stream production.

Input flexibility

Swedish labour market legislation is very restrictive and severely limits the use of short term contracts or apprenticeship, which diminishes the possibility to rapidly adjust the number of employees, as compared to many other countries. Still, there are factors that indicate that the Gnosjö firms are eager to vary the number of workers and thus reach what Atkinson (1984) refers to as a high numerical flexibility.

The percentage of self-employed workers in the engineering industry in the Gnosjö Region is the highest in the country in 1989 (Statistics Sweden, 1991). The municipal executive board of Gnosjö has applied to the government to make an exception and allow for under-age children to work during their spare time, and a high percentage of the older student already work during their spare time, many of them without formal contracts of employment.

The worst recession since the 1930s occurred during 1991-92 within the manufacturing industry in Sweden and the unemployment rate increased rapidly. In this situation, many firms in the Gnosjö Region have chosen to work part time instead of laying people off. They do this partly because of social responsibility but also to ensure that the competence and capacity remains within the firms when market conditions alter.

To avoid the risk that markets for certain products disappear before the machinery´s cost is recovered and to regulate the capacity of production it is possible to out source production to independent suppliers (Benko and Dunford, 1991) or to lease machinery instead of buying it. As stated above, Gnosjö firms do not out source production and there are no indications that Gnosjö firms prefer to lease machinery to obtain flexibility. On the contrary, knowledge of what machinery to buy is considered as very important by the managers themselves in order to gain competitive advantages (Wiklund, 1992a). A high degree of external financing is another way of reducing risks (Benko and Dunford, 1991) that is not used by the Gnosjö firms that instead prefer a high degree of internal financing. This indicates that the capital structure of the Gnosjö firms is inflexible.

Input goods mainly consist of raw material that are purchased from suppliers outside the Gnosjö Region. The opportunities to switch suppliers are rare, mainly due to very few alternatives because of oligopolistic raw material markets. Since the suppliers are much larger then the Gnosjö firms and not dependent upon them, it is hard to get them to sign flexible delivery agreements, e.g. concerning volumes, delivery times or special qualities (Wiklund, 1992b). The Gnosjö firms only buy a few components. The components are uncomplicated and delivered from few different suppliers, mainly inside the region. This indicates that the Gnosjö firms have not disintegrated and that they have not transmitted the uncertainty backwards in the vertical market system.

Internal flexibility

The ambition of the leading firms to keep control of and knowledge about the production process within the firm implies a broad production system with the ability to perform a large number of different tasks. A number of different operations are conducted within the same factory and many different types of machines are used. Most firms employ specialists. Tool makers for example, are employed partly for maintenance and to produce less complicated tools, but the main reason for employing them is to keep the competence in-house. Since all the operations are in-house it is possible to rapidly combine them in different ways to obtain what Gerwin and Leung (1980) call design change flexibility . The wide range of different operations conducted by the firms also allows them to produce differentiated products.The product differentiation of the leading Gnosjö firms is not of a high degree and corresponds to "economies of range" as defined by Coriat (1991).

The Gnosjö firms give priority to employees with experience based competence rather then competence based on theoretical education. Most employees have worked in the firms for a long time and know the products and processes well, and are involved in major decisions such as what new production investments to make. Craftsmanship has a high status within the firms and craftsmen (e.g. tool makers) are among the highest paid employees.

The experience of the workers and their ability to conduct different operations in the production process also facilitates the design change flexibility.

The work shops are functionally organised with some job rotation within the different departments, which facilitates the capacity to route the same products in different ways through the work shop, to achieve what is called routing flexibility by Gerwin and Leung (1980).

Most literature describes CNC machinery, meaning multi-spindel cutting machinery with automatic tool changers, as the flexible alternative to inflexible product-specific machinery (cf. Piore and Sabel, 1984). Gnosjö firms engaged in milling use flexible CNC machinery. The majority of firms however, are specialised in sheet metal products and use general-purpose machinery. A variety of operations can be conducted using this machinery and a variety of different products can be produced. However, the set-up time is long which calls for large batches.

The major element of internal flexibility of the stage firms is their ability to rapidly variate their output levels, which is referred to as volume flexibility by Gerwin and Leung (1989). The variations in output is facilitated by the use of uncontracted students working part time and self employed workers (Wiklund, 1992a).

Output flexibility

Over a longer time span, the leading Gnosjö firms have been able to slide from customers in declining industries to more profitable customers. During the 1980s, the Swedish car industry had a major upswing. From 1985 to 1989, the number of employees within the car part industry in Sweden expanded by 7% whereas in the Gnosjö Region it expanded by 55%. The number of firms within the same sector expanded by 10% in Sweden and 46% in the Gnosjö Region (Statistics Sweden, 1991).

Leading Gnosjö firms already in the car part industry were able to increase their sales. Other customers were phased out and the relative share of sales to the car industry increased. In addition, leading Gnosjö firms not already in the industry were able to enter it during this decade.

Only minor changes appeared for stage firms that performed general purpose processes. They conducted the same, or at least similar, processes as before and sold them to the same customers. The major difference was that the end user of the product was the car industry. The leading Gnosjö firms deleted the linkages to stage firms that performed more specialised processes that did not fit in with the new products and established relations to new stage firms, both established firms, new firms and spin offs.

Network flexibility

The leading Gnosjö forms use the networks to put out operations that they do not perform in-house, which means that they are able to accept more complex orders. This should not be confused with the earlier statement about the small use of subcontractors. The putting out of processes does not refer to vertical disintegration and long term relations with close cooperation (which is the most common description of subcontracting) but to specialised input subcontracting (Storper and Christopherson, 1987) that involves more sporadic and short-term cooperation with specialised stage firms that conduct complementary operations. To give an example, springs are often integrated with plastic parts in electric components. A springmaker in the Gnosjö Region has started to collaborate with different neighbouring plastic moulders to deliver springs integrated with plastic parts. This is appreciated by the customers since it decreases the administrative purchasing costs. The spring maker adds more value which facilitates higher profits. But what is more important, the spring producer has been able to accept more complex orders that he had to turn down before, due to the small size of the firm in relation to its competitors.

The putting out implies that the Gnosjö firms are able to accept a greater variety of orders but it also means that they perform some of the coordination that usually is done by the customer, which also strengthens their market position. The coordination activities usually add some assembling operations that add more value to the products.

Gnosjö firms often spin off (Wendeberg, 1982 and Kolsgård et al, 1987). During booms, foremen of successful firms establish their own firms, first during their spare time, but later they give notice and work full time in their own firms. Their old employer is usually their main customer (at least in the beginning). This might seem strange, but the employer often encourages employees to start their own business since they, in their turn are able to accept more orders and to transfer less profitable operations (or whole orders) to the spin offs and in that way are able to increase their own profits. In this way, the firms are able to increase their capacity during booms and to concentrate on the more profitable orders and operations during this time, while during recessions they perform all operations in-house.

Another advantage of letting former employees establish spin offs is that the spin offs are closely tied to their old employer which makes cooperation easier, and that the spin offs, since they are new in the market place, are willing to accept less profitable orders from their old employer than other subcontractors would.

Stage firms transfer parts of the production volumes to other firms within the area to obtain volume flexibility. This is a form of horizontal capacity subcontracting (Storper and Christopherson, 1987). The operations of the firm are replicated in the subcontracting firm. In this way the firms are able to even out the uncertainty that occurs due to variations in the output levels.

Discussion

The traditional view of the industrial district as a network of firms with a complex web of cooperative and competitive linkages where no firm in the network is permanently dominant and their roles in the network constantly shift is somewhat idealised. There is a very complex web of cooperative and competitive linkages between the firms the Gnosjö Region, but there is also a clearly hierarchical structure, where the large, leading firms are the major interface to customers outside the district and smaller stage firms subcontract to the leading firms. As a result of this, there are distinct differences between the flexibility profile of the leading firms and the stage firms, table 5.1.

Table 1. Characteristic elements of leading and stage firms in relation to the four dimensions of flexibility.

Component of flexibility	leading firm	stage firm
input	minor significance	numerical flexibility
internal	design change flexibility	volume flexibility
output	product and customer variety and change	minor significance
network	complementary operations subcontracting; multiple, latent supplier relations	capacity subcontracting; multiple, latent customer relations

One striking element of flexibility of the leading Gnosjö firms is their output flexibility, i. e. their ability to change from customers in declining industries to more profitable ones. This is primarily a result of the production oriented specialisation of the Gnosjö firms (that facilitate broad product niches), the simultaneous operation of many market niches and the innumerous collaborative constellations that can be formed within the regional network of firms. Unfortunately, this ability of industrial districts to change market niches has not been highlighted in the literature. This is a major flaw since product differentiation and development of new profitable market niches is supposed to be one of the key factors underpinning the success of the industrial districts.

Let us now turn to the internal flexibility of the firm. Starting with Piore and Sabel (1984), much of the discussion of the flexibility of industrial districts has focused on the technological flexibility that derives from the exchange of inflexible technology for flexible. Their view is that the firms in the industrial districts were able to introduce this technology very rapidly thanks to a superior work organisation stemming from the pre-Fordist, craftlike organisation of work. One underlying logic in their argument is that the productivity gains from these investments are higher than the productivity gains from investments in traditional machinery. The productivity that the small firm in the industrial district gains, derive from the possibilities of differentiation. The differentiation allowed by the flexible machinery is amplified by the flexible relations to other firms in the district. However, Piore and Sabel overlook a vital point. A firm in an industrial district could be able to obtain a high degree of diffentiation by collaborating with other district firms, but still use traditional technology. In price competing, labour intensive industries, such as in the Gnosjö Region low production costs are essential. Therefore, they use traditional technology to cut costs, and flexibility is gained in other ways such as output and network flexibility.

The number of potential input and output linkages between the firms in the Gnosjö Region are enormous, but only a limited number is operated simultaneously. Johannisson et al, 1992, show that in Anderstorp, a part of the Gnosjö Region, the majority of firms have business ties to 10-30% of the other firms in Anderstorp, whereas they have acquaintance ties to 30-50% . Thus, the acquaintance networks are much larger and more intense than the commercial networks. The existing, commercial networks within the Gnosjö Region could be considered as primary networks, whereas the larger acquaintance network could be considered as a secondary network, among which commercial relations could be rapidly established.

Furthermore, due to the common social foundation, relations between firms within the region are standardised and informal. Investments and sunk costs involved with establishing and deleting input or output linkages to other firms within the region are low. Thus, firms can afford to operate many linkages and change linkages. The result is a rapid change of network constallations, which gives a high degree of flexibility in relation to the final customers. The leading firms are able to accept a wide range of complex orders from customers by diverse, rapid colloborative arrangements with stage firms. The regional network gives the specialised stage firms numerous potential customer relations to leading firms and also the opportunity to variate capacity by coooperations with other stage firms or self-emplyed workers. One indication of this flexibility is the expansion of the car part industry in the Gnosjö Region.

Conclusions and suggestions for further research

Traditionally, firms in industrial districts are described as having a high degree of internal flexibility (cf. Piore and Sabel, 1984). The research presented here suggests that flexibility is gained by various and changing interorganisational relations to firms within the regional network as well as to customers outside the district rather than by the flexibility of the firms themselves. This could be expressed as *external* economies of scope as opposed to *internal* economies of scope.

A present discussion concerns whether large firms are able to adapt flexible technology and flexible work organisation that will allow them to produce highly differentiated products in a similar fashion as the industrial districts. This paper indicates that neither the technology nor the work organisation gives flexibility to the industrial district. Thus the flexibility that large firms are able to achieve will differ from the flexibility on industrial districts.

Sabel (1989) stresses that large firms are turning their organisations from hierarchies to networks that resemble the organisation of industrial districts. Still, from a flexibility standpoint these intra-firm networks differ considerably from the inter firm networks in the industrial district. The flexibility of the network in the industrial district is primarily gained by the possibility of exchanging relations within the primary network to relations to firms presently in the secondary network rather than by flexible but stable relations within a permanent network structure.

This paper indicates that the overall flexibility of an industrial district could be achieved by various combinations of input, internal, output and network flexibility. It is likely that the optimal combination of these elements varies among districts dependent on their specialisation. So far, the discussion on the flexibility of industrial districts seems to have been mainly conceptual. Very little empirical evidence has been presented that sheds light on in what respects and to what extents the industrial districts are flexible. More research needs to be carried out that explicitly investigate the importance of flexibility for the success of industrial districts in general. The taxonomy developed in this paper could be a starting point for finding relevant operative measures of flexibility in industrial districts.

Turning to the Gnosjö Region, flexibility appears to be a characteristic feature of the Gnosjö firms. There are major differences between the flexibility profile of stage firms and leading firms, due to their different roles in the network. Research on aspects of flexibility and industrial districts has mainly focused on the flexibility within the districts and not on the flexibility in relation to customers outside the district. The ability of leading firms in the Gnosjö Region to change customers in accordance with the customers´stages in the life cycle is an essential characteristic of flexibility. This might not be a sustainable strategy if customers want to have close, long-term relations to their subcontractors.To find out the importance and sustainability of this output flexibility, it is possible to run time series of the composition of industries over long periods of time in the Gnosjö region as well as other districts.

References

Aglietta M. (1979) *A theory of capitalist regulation*, London: New Left Books

Andersson Å. E. et al (1990), *Regional vitalisering - en analys och vision för Jönköpings län*, Jönköping, Sweden: Länsstyrelsen i Jönköpings län.

Atkinson J. (1984) *Flexibility, uncertainty, and manpower management. Report of a study conducted under the co-operative research programme of the I.M.S.*, Falmer, Brighton: University of Sussex, Institute of Manpower Studes, Report no. 89.

Brusco S. (1990) The idea of the Industrial District: Its genisis, in Pyke F. et al (eds) (1990).

Cappellin R. and Nijkamp P. (eds) (1990) *The Spacial Context of Technological Development*, Aldershot, the Netherlands: Avebury

Coriat B (1991) Technical flexibility and mass production, in Dunford M. and Benko G. (eds) (1991).

Dunford M. and Benko G. (1991) Neo-Fordism or post-Fordism? Some conclusions and further remarks, in Dunford M. and Benko G. (eds) (1991).

Dunford M. and Benko G. (eds) (1991) *New Industrial Spaces.* London:

New Haven Press.
Garofoli G (1990) Local development: patterns and policy complications, in Cappellin R. and Nijkamp P. (eds) (1990).
Gerwin D. and Leung T. (1980) The organisational impacts of FMS: some initial findings, Trondheim, Norway: Institute of Social Reserarch in Industry, Discussion Paper.
Gidlund J and Törnqvist G. (eds) (1990) *European Networks (1990:2)*, CERUM, Umeå, Sweden: Umeå Universitet.
Hagedoorn J. (1990) *Partnering and Reorganisation of Research and Production*, in Gidlund and Törnqvist (eds) (1990).
Hirst P. and Zeitlin J (eds) (1989) *Reversing Industrial decline?: industrial structure and policy in Britain and her competitors*, Oxford: Berg.
Johannisson B and Gustafsson B-Å (1984) *Småföretagande på småort - Nätverksstrategier i informationssamhället*, Växjö, Sweden: Småskrifter nr 22, Växjö university.
Johannisson et al (1992) *Beyond Anarchy and Organization – Entrepreneurs in context*. Paper presented at RENT VI, Barcelona, Spain, November 26-27 1992.
Kolsgård et al (1987), *Gnosjöandan, verkligheten bakom myten....*, Linköping - Nässjö, Sweden: mimeo.
Martinelli F. and Schoenberger E. (1991) Oligopoly is alive and well, in Dunford M. and Benko G. (eds) (1991).
Piore M. and Sabel C. (1984) *The second industial divide*. New York: Basic books
Pyke F. et al (eds) (1990) *Industrial districts and inter-firm co-operation in Italy*, International Labour Organisation: Geneva.
Sabel C. (1989) Flexible specialisation and the re-emergence of regional economics, in Hirst P. and Zeitlin J (eds) (1989) pp 17-70.
Schonberger R. (1979) *Japanese Manufacturing Techniques: Nine hidden lessons in simplicity*, New York: Free Press.
Sforzi F. (1990) The quantitative importance of Marshallian industrial districts in the Italian economy, in Pyke F. et al (eds) (1990).
Storper M. and Christopherson S. (1987) Flexible Specialization and Regional Industrial Agglomerations: The Case of the U.S. Motion Picture Industry, *Annals of the Association of American Geographers*, 77(1):

104-117.

Teague P. (1990) The political Economy of the Regulation School and the Flexible Specialisation Scenario, *Journal of economic studies*, vol. 17 No.5.

Wendeberg B. (1982), *Gnosjöandan, myt eller verklighet*, Värnamo, Sweden: U B Wendeberg förlag.

Wiklund J. (1992a) *Företagsutveckling i Gnosjö under 1980-talet*, Stockholm: ERU, Arbetsmarknadsdepartementet.

Wiklund J. (1992b) *MA och flexibla underleverantörsnätverk i Jönköpings län (Business logistics and flexible subcontractor networks in the county of Jönköping)*, Jönköping, Sweden: Jönköping University, working paper, forthcoming.

Womak J. P. et al (1990) *The machine that changed the world*, Boston: MIT.

7 Evaluating growth potential by contingency responsive interaction

Ted Fuller

Abstract

This paper describes the key elements in the design of an expert system which enables "growth potential" of an individual firm to be evaluated. As such, it provides an overview of the "knowledge-base" on business growth from three perspectives: financial, market development, internal and external strategy.

The design of such a system requires considerable discipline in defining the parameters to be used and the way these are used, ie how the measurements taken are evaluated. The interaction between the user (typically the entrepreneur) and the system is an essential part of the process of evaluation and learning. The resulting evaluation is contingent on the characteristics of the firm, the entrepreneur, the environment and the growth plans or vision. These are reflected in the Users' responses stimulated by the interaction of the system.

The embodiment of business expertise in computer systems leads to the creation of a resource which can be used in many different ways. For example, in situations where professional advisors are unavailable, for instance in an environment where there is not a strong experience base of business management to draw on. The extent to which the design is internationally transferable is therefore discussed.

Introduction

There is quite a wide range of research related to theories of small business growth. These areas are noted in this paper, along with the more practical issues of stimulating growth and the pragmatics of intervention.

The desire to use new technology to assist in the process of stimulating growth led a number of economic development agencies to invest in a research project. The project, Enterprise Guidance Systems Initiative, is developing software tools for advising small businesses. These are for use by owner managers, with assistance from professional advisors where necessary. The objectives of this initiative are described, as are the two software tools being developed.

In designing one of these, a Business Review Tool, a framework of key growth criteria was established and a conceptual device, called "FUE Factors" was constructed to make this framework operational. The ideas behind this framework and the factors is described in some detail.

While the contents of an evaluation framework are important, the involvement of owner managers in the evaluation process is fundamental if changes in intention and behaviour are to result. The Review is grounded in well established business concepts, an interactive consultation metaphor and, of course, the data of the business itself. The overall process is intended to facilitate the development of the "vision" of the future business by using concrete factors in a feedback process. The feedback response is contingent on the actual situation. An example of how this design operates in practice is annexed to the paper.

The use of new technology to empower the owner manager, and the consultant, is becoming increasingly possible as improvements in IT continue. Generally speaking SME development organisations lag behind the technology in their ability to utilise it effectively. The paper ends by raising this issue.

How is growth potential evaluated or stimulated at a micro level?

How do you identify growth potential?

The evidence available on small business growth suggests that "success" is contingent on many factors. Currently there is no general theory of "growth", ie growth cannot, in general, be predicted. Numerous studies have also demonstrated that the decisions and actions of owners / managers are crucial to successful growth. Knowledge of the qualitative aspects of the small business stems from research in different areas of discipline, viz:

The entrepreneurial personality:
Personal goals, motivations, drives, preferences etc. of the owner(s) of the firms. (a personality-type assessment)

The organisation and development of the firm:
Critical mass, transaction costs, economies of scale, use of external / internal resources. (a resource use/cost efficiency assessment)

The management of the business:
Strategies for growth - product / market developments, managerial slack, planning (a process orientated assessment)

The market / sector influences
(external constraints and opportunities)

But these have not so far yielded the "answer" as to what constitutes growth.

"The analysis of the literature fails to provide convincing evidence of the determinants of small business growth as a base for informing policy makers (and) managers. The root of the problem is the absence of a comprehensive theory of small and medium sized enterprise development which brings together all the relevant parameters into a model and indicates how each part interacts with the other. The production of such a theory and explanation is the near future is unlikely." (Gibb AA, 1991)

Despite this lack of knowledge, practitioners make judgements about the viability of growth plans, of small businesses and of the capabilities of owner managers. In making these judgements, practitioners try to use the best tools they can. We know that through training and experience, certain methodologies are learnt and applied (eg ratio analysis). There exists numerous "check-lists" of the common areas to be addressed in small business evaluation. None of the published check-lists provide instructions on the calibration of the measures nor do they explain how inferences should be made from the evidence gathered. As far as can be seen, evaluation of "growth" firms is made subjectively and from the observers' own perspective.

Thus the situation is that theoretically the growth of an individual small business cannot be predicted, yet, each day, people make predictions about the growth of businesses and invest money on that prediction.

Can growth be stimulated?

Perhaps a more important question than whether growth can be predicted is whether growth can be stimulated; and if so how. Advocates of management development would argue that training and experience can lead to improved confidence of the entrepreneur, which in turn may lead to their willingness to run bigger businesses. Evaluations of management development programmes for small businesses tend to show increases in company performance as a result, though there has never been a satisfactory "clinical" evaluation of such programmes, nor, given the nature of the domain, is such evaluation possible.

The general approach to small business development is one of highly instrumental training. Focussing, for example, on the actual problems of the business and on the decisions which are to be implemented. Feedback on performance and the general approval of behaviour and values, generated by the promotion of role models and peer group learning, is a typical part of the process. Management programmes and individual counselling provide the time for reflection which is said to be important to the learning process (eg Honey and Mumford 1988, Kolb, 1973).

Improvements in business, leading to development and growth are also thought to be stimulated by consultancy intervention; providing the important managerial time unavailable within small firms. Development can also be stimulated by the provision of finance and other resources and through the creation of added value transactions (i.e. orders).

The provision of external resources to stimulate growth is frequently used as an economic development measure. For example, grant aid for capital investment or subsidies for consulting activities. A key question in the provider's mind is where to place the resources to be of best value. In practice, the identification of prime candidates may not be too difficult, but chosing investments of the more marginal cases is much more difficult. There is a belief among economic development organisations that they do not always reach the most appropriate firms with the most appropriate forms of stimulation.

Thus the position on stimulating growth seems to be that a number of forms of intervention are possible. Each of which is quite specific to the business. There is uncertainty about the effectiveness of each instrument and difficulty in identifying the most appropriate recipients, particularly in marginal cases.

The purpose of the Enterprise Guidance Systems Initiative is to automate some processes of identifying needs for intervention at a micro level and in stimulating growth in those small firms.

Enterprise guidance systems initiative

The Enterprise Guidance Systems Initiative is a project whose objective is to develop usable Enterprise Guidance Systems which help stimulate growth in SMEs. The concept of guidance for the managers of businesses is not new. The concept of enterprise guidance systems has been developed during the 1980's as a valuable and increasingly important application of the technologies of expert systems developed in the 1970's and early 1980's. The first developments in the UK of expert systems based counselling tools for small business is given in Fuller (1991). Two such systems were presented at an earlier RENT seminar (M□ller-B"ling and Kirchoff, 1991 and Senicourt, 1991).

The Initiative was formally started in July 1991. The main aim is to develop systems which enable small business and economic development agencies to achieve the following objectives:

- to reach existing businesses more effectively than is currently being done, ie increasing the efficiency of delivering information.
- to encourage small businesses to develop and grow, ie increasing the effectiveness of the communication with SMEs.
- to encourage the relationship between small businesses, the business assistance networks, and the economic development organisations, ie increasing the market efficiency of the support infrastructure.

Four tools have been outlined for development. The first two of which are actually being produced in the first phase. These are: (Fuller and Heslop 1992):

(i)   Business review/diagnostic tool
for use by the owner manager to carry out a 'Position Audit' of the SME, assisting in the identification of areas for change; it will assist in the definition of realistic goals and objectives; it will motivate the owner manager by illustrating possibilities in using a "Suppose I did ..." or "What if ..." facility; it will also assess the level of immediate growth potential.

(ii)   Immediate actions tool
targeted at companies assessed as needing a number of shorter term actions before having immediate growth potential; using information gathered by the Business Review, the tool will provide guidance on specific steps for enhancing the business, by defining and prioritising actions required to achieve shorter term goals; practical advice will be provided, with particular emphasis on the effective use of external consultants where appropriate; in particular, the tool will provide guidance on selection of consultants, development of expectations of consultancy assignments, and an outline on how to manage such an assignment.

The business review tool is described in more detail in this paper. In the design process key issues have been addressed, e.g. What aspects are important in relation to "growth potential", how these can be evaluated automatically, and how such a process can be put under the control of the owner manager. The way these issues have been tackled is described below.

Growth potential at the micro level - an operational framework

A framework of key criteria

From numerous sources of literature, some of which are referenced below, plus standard texts on business analysis, inputs from practitioner check-lists and focus groups, the following areas have been identified as those which need to be addressed in the evaluation of growth potential.

1. The business is able to finance growth:
e.g. issues such as meeting financial commitments, generation of internal finance, level of debt, accessibility to external funds.
The rules applied to small business in most cultures are that they have to service or reward the physical, financial and human resources used at market rates or near market rates. The variation in these rules is usually only a matter of timescale. Actual market rates vary from one country to another.

2. The business has a foundation for future profit generation:
e.g. previous trends in the growth of, and future trends in costs, prices and investment relative to competitors.
In practice, stakeholders put considerable importance on previous performance; perhaps the most common (and dangerous) practice of investors is to use previous growth as a predictor of future growth.
Small firms are not monopolistic, the importance of their ability to sustain advantages over their competitors is a well established axiom.

3. There is market potential:
e.g. attractive market (growth, changes, and the relative importance of entry barriers), the firm is aligned to the market (standards of quality, design etc, meeting needs), the firm is able to replicate business.

Growth is more likely to take place in a growing market, ie more customers or higher usage volumes. Entry barriers can play a role in defending or preventing the access to markets by the small firm. The degree to which the small firm is acceptable to their customers - ie meeting expectations or required contractual obligations - is a predicate to a transaction occurring. Most businesses depend on a formula for growth, e.g. a product or a repeatable service. Through this they are able to take advantage of the learning curve.

4. The business is customer orientated:
The bases of the relationship and the management of this, plus responses by and to the customers.
Relationships with the individual customer is generally accepted as an important thrust in marketing (See for example Hall, 1992). This stems from the growing sophistication of buyer-seller communications and the power of the buyer. The importance of relationships varies between market sectors, but the classical advantages of the small businesses - personal service, flexibility, problem solving, innovation - tend to imply strong individual relationships with customers. While the customer remains strong, and the relationship remains strong, then the small firm should develop.

5. The owner(s) is able to, and committed to, lead growth.
e.g key people's / owner(s)' willingness and ability to commit themselves to growth, personal commitment, delegation and strategic management.
Most small business literature recognises that the owner manager / entrepreneur is the key person, and that their time and commitment and strategic vision are fundamental to the development of the small business (eg Gibb and Scott, 1983, Filion, 1990).

6 The internal strategic approach is consistent with growth
e.g. quality of internal communications, management of and dependency on key resources, management experience of growth and change, approaches to development of people, ability to learn from mistakes, effectiveness of organisational design.
Filion (1990) identified that envisioning was insufficient without communication, both internally and externally. And, more mundanely, it is

important for workers in a small firm to have a sense of purpose and know what they are doing and why.

The extent of the dependencies of small firms is not an area which has been researched per se. Dependency on "networks", on stakeholders, on individuals (eg the owners), on a few customers etc. have been separately identified. All small business are dependent (a paradox for the "independent company"). The key issue is the way in which they manage their dependencies and reduce the risk associated with those dependencies.

Similarly, though "experience" has previously been identified as a key issue in Gibb and Scott (1983), no substantial research has examined the nature of what "experience" is important in the management of "growth". Logically, the lack of experience implies a longer or steeper learning curve, with its associated costs and risks.

In terms of organisational design, there are no valid models of how a growth firm should organise itself. An operational criterion is that its design should enable it to respond at the speed its customers require. Most literature on this subject addresses the problems caused by owners not able to change their style of self management or operational bias.

7. *The external strategic positioning is consistent with growth*
e.g. external communications, stakeholders' commitment to growth, management of dependent linkages,, degree of innovation or market leadership, validation of ideas, strategy relative to market leaders, differential advantage.

The points made above on communication, commitment, dependencies and experience apply equally to the external strategic positioning as to the internal design. A further point on strategy development is necessary however. Few firms "innovate" as market leaders might be thought of as doing, ie creating sea changes in market places. However, many consider that they innovate on a smaller scale (Hughes et al 1992). In particular, innovations in small firms have been found to fit a similar pattern within the same industries (eg clothing industry, see Smallbone, 1991).

The above seven main classifications have been developed and used as the framework for evaluating the growth potential of an individual small business. In the design, they are labelled Key Criteria.

Making the framework operational; the FUE factors

In the process of developing the above framework, numerous check-lists were analysed. They each had one common characteristic; they did not provide instructions on how to score the result on each dimension or concept used, nor on how to draw conclusions from the overall review.

A challenge for this project was therefore to make the above framework dynamic, so that the reasoning process could be automated. In some diagnostic tests, scoring systems are established to facilitate the calculation of results. This approach is only appropriate where a proven normalised scoring system exists, such as in some psychometric tests. Given the absence of adequate theory or norms in relation to business growth, 'scoring' is not a valid approach. Instead, one based on heuristic or rule of thumb methods employed by human experts was used.

The analysis of the growth potential of a small business typically uses a range of data about the business and its environment. Each data-point is relatively simple, but there are many relevant points of data which make up the whole picture. The information about an individual business is classified into a recognisable pattern by the human analyst or adviser. In simulating this process, the system design had to find a way of linking individual data-points to the broad classification framework in such a way as to provide a whole picture.

A construct was developed to achieve this. The construct is called a **FUE Factor.** FUE is the acronym developed by the design team as shorthand for:

- Favourable factors - those which are positive in the context of a firm's growth potential.
- Unfavourable factors - those which are negative in the context of a firm's growth potential
- Essential - those without which, growth is deemed difficult or even impossible.
- There is a fourth implied value, ie Missing Essential.

The FUEs are used as the building blocks for the system design. Overall conclusions about the ability of the business to grow are based on the presence or otherwise of evidence to support the FUEs.

FUES are pre-defined as an integral part of the Business Review Tool. Facts and opinions (the data) about the business are gathered through interaction with the owner manager. The dialogue is controlled by IF... THEN ... rules (Production Rules). In some cases the FUE is determined by a 1:1 mapping with an answer to a specific question. In other cases combinations of data may be used to determine the existence of a FUE. Some FUEs are selected by production rules and others by weighted evidence. The analysis of an individual case, eg one company, determines which FUEs are relevant to that particular case. The combination of the FUEs represent the system's evaluation of the growth potential of that business.

The combination of FUEs for each Key Criterion gives the profile for that criterion. The "score" for the Profile is given in terms of the proportion of "Favourable" factors identified and the proportion of "Unfavourable" factors identified. Where some "Essential" factors are missing, then the "Favourable" factors are relegated to being "Potentially Favourable". The defining characteristic of an Essential Factor is that without it, growth is difficult, if not impossible. This idea is demonstrated in the example provided in the annexe.

Stimulating the process of evaluation and learning

The Review process facilitated by the tool is intended to encourage learning. The consultation process is interactive. The interaction strategy employed by the business review tool is intended to influence the intentions of the owner of the small business. A theory that performance feedback can motivate changes in behaviour underpins the design. The style used draws on and further develops the established "provocateur" techniques of current Enterprise Guidance Systems (Fuller 1990).

The focus is on enabling the User: owner manager / entrepreneur / decision maker, to develop and clarify his or her "vision" of the future business (Filion 1990). There are two interlinked approaches to this. The first is through the use of an evaluation framework, and the second is by modelling. (see Figure 1 below).

The evaluation framework of FUEs is overlaid on previous and current performance and, to some extent on extrapolated future performance. Concrete factors from the current position are embedded into a model, with explicit assumptions of behaviour. This can be used to ask "what-if" questions. The end position of the modelling exercise is evaluated through use of the framework, so that there is consistency in analysis between what is, and what might be. The Business Review Tool provides feedback on the firm's actual performance based on the FUEs triggered by the data.

The system also provides guidance on interpretation of the feedback. However, the ultimate interpreter is the User.

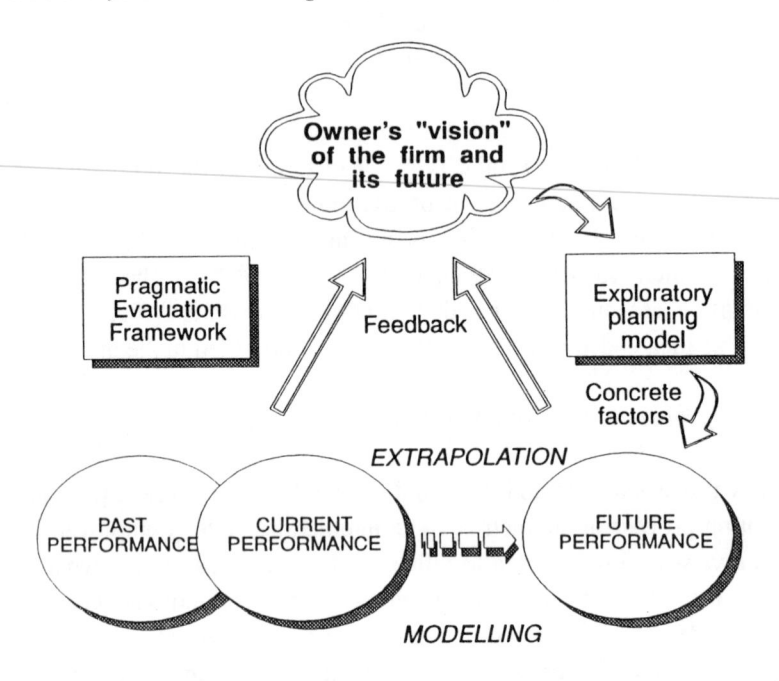

Figure 1. Encouraging the 'Emergent Vision'. An overview of the approach to stimulating growth taken by the EGSI Business Review Tool. Past and current performance is evaluated using well established criteria. This performance is extrapolated and re-evaluated. A modelling tool enables new assumptions to be made and evaluated.

The approach is therefore anchored in current activity of the firm and in established approaches to learning and development, though the process is innovative. In the context of SME development, this approach - of evaluating "what is" and of modelling "what if" - is not particularly new. To date, the use of such an approach relies almost entirely on human intervention and expertise; to make judgements on the current situation, to construct the model and to know the right "what-if" questions to ask. To automate the process is new. To make explicit the rules governing judgements and to interlink evaluation and modelling, is also new.

The business review tool from the user's perspective:

Consultation metaphor

A consultation metaphor is used as the basic interface design. The metaphor is developed in two ways. Firstly the counselling technique of involving the client in the process of data collection, analysis and decision-making is inherent in the design. Secondly the familiar concept of specialist consultants is used as a way of organising the overall consultation. The (relatively) familiar frameworks of The Accountant (or financial advisor), the Marketing Consultant and the Strategic Consultant are exercised.

Each metaphorical "Consultant" offers a variety of tools and frameworks to evaluate particular aspects of growth potential within the overall set of Key Criteria defined above. The outcomes of each consultation are a list of FUEs Factors for that particular business and a set of conclusions triggered by the specific combination of FUEs. In addition, specific information created through the modelling processes are also reported.

The accountant or financial consultant

The Accountant is concerned with the first two Key Criteria, "Is able to finance growth" and "Has a foundation for future profit generation". Past and current performance are evaluated. A substantial modelling tool which enables the picture of funds generation to be simulated for the next 12 months is included. The overall conclusions of the assessment are in terms of the rate of growth which can be financed under the assumptions given.

Accountant View

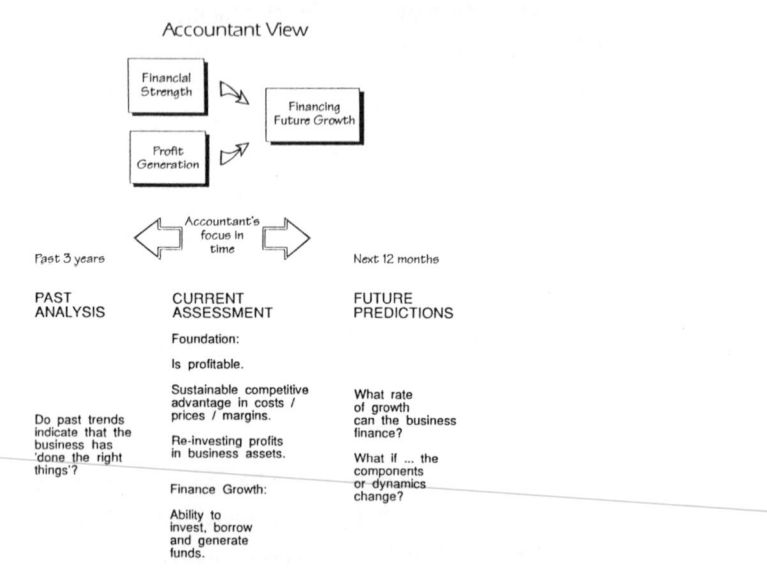

```
                    Financial
                    Strength
                                    Financing
                                    Future Growth
                    Profit
                    Generation

                    Accountant's
                    focus in
                    time
    Past 3 years                            Next 12 months

    PAST            CURRENT                 FUTURE
    ANALYSIS        ASSESSMENT              PREDICTIONS

                    Foundation:
                    Is profitable.

                    Sustainable competitive   What rate
                    advantage in costs /      of growth
    Do past trends  prices / margins.         can the business
    indicate that the                         finance?
    business has    Re-investing profits
    'done the right in business assets.       What if ... the
    things'?                                  components
                    Finance Growth:           or dynamics
                                              change?
                    Ability to
                    invest, borrow
                    and generate
                    funds.
```

Figure 2. Areas covered by the Accountant's Assessment in the Business Review Tool.

The marketing consultant

The Marketing consultant is concerned with the second two Key Criteria, ie "There is market potential" and "(the firm) has a customer orientation". The overall design of this View is reflected in Figure 3. The approach to evaluation is more subjective than with the financial data, however in-depth analysis of the current mix of customer / product / service / channel / geographic market is available to those with the ability and information to use it. The evaluation focuses on the nature and quality of relationships between the firm and its customers. It also addresses the attractiveness of the market in terms of future profitable sales (and hence incorporates such concepts as product portfolio and life cycle). From the analysis, conclusions are drawn as to the most attractive product/service/market development strategies for the firm.

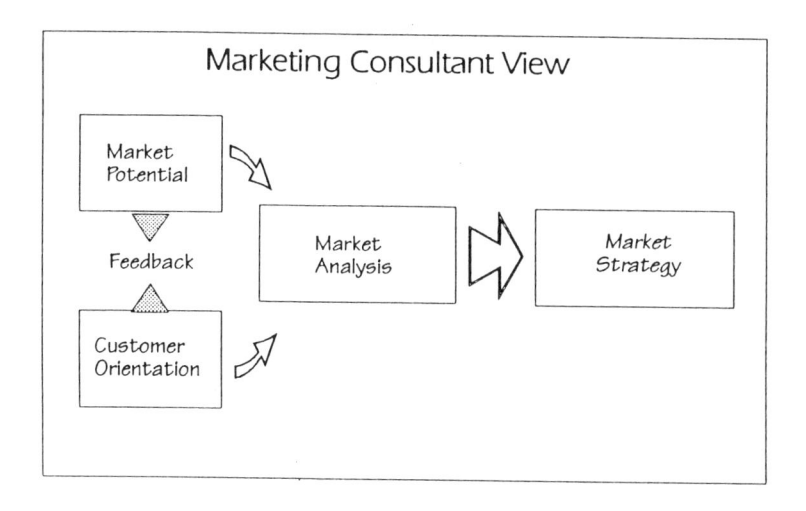

Figure 3. The Marketing Consultant

The strategic consultant

The overall design of this module is reflected in Figure 4. The evaluation is concerned with overall vision and commitment of the owners of the business and then how they manage the enactment of this. Issues such as communication, management of dependencies, depth of experience and positioning strategies are addressed in order to determine the strength of the firm in relation to the external environment and the inherent strength of the organisation. Conclusions are drawn on the coherence of the rationale and positioning for achieving growth.

The three Key Criteria used to classify the information gathered are "The Owner(s) is able to, and committed to, lead growth", "The internal strategic approach is consistent with growth" and "The external strategic positioning is consistent with growth".

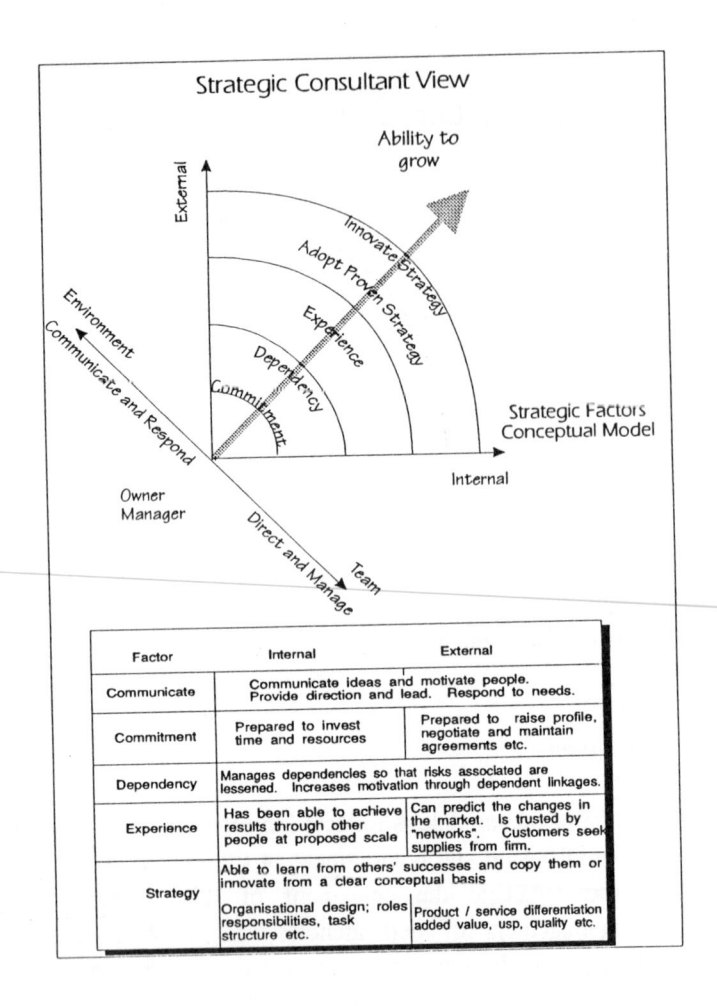

Figure 4. Details of the Strategic Consultant's View.

Overall profile of evaluation constructs

The three "Views" of the metaphorical consultants are put together as an overall profile. This profile summarises the "scores" of the main evaluation construct; the "FUE Factors". The "FUEs" are Favourable, Unfavourable and

Essential Factors related to growth potential. The Profile reflects the proportion of Favourable and Unfavourable Factors identified for each Key Criterion. Where "essential" factors are not identified (ie they are "Missing Essentials"), the firm's Favourable Factors are relegated to being only Potentially Favourable. They will only become Favourable when all the Essential Factors are present. Example FUEs are given in the Annexe.

Business review tool; design summary

Facts and opinions are gathered through a consultation process with the User. The User is typically the owner manager of the small business, possibly assisted by professional consultants and/or other members of the management team. The consultation process itself, and the feedback from it, stimulates learning.

The consultation takes place through a series of modules which are grouped in three main sections; the Accountant's View, the Marketing Consultant's View and the Strategic Consultant's View. Under each View, assessment is made from the information gathered. Key Favourable, Unfavourable and Essential Factors associated with growth are selected as relevant to the specific business. Some modules within a section enable more detailed analysis and modelling to be carried out under varying assumptions.

Combinations of the Key Factors and other indicators drawn from the data are used to select conclusions about the growth potential of the business. These, along with the Factors are fed back to the User on-screen and in printed reports.

An overall profile of each firm is given. This can be interrogated to identify its constituents. The User can present new information in a "what if" recapitulation of chosen modules. This may lead to a change in the firm's growth profile.

The role of enterprise guidance systems in promoting growth

How the systems are intended to be used

Retailers of Guidance Systems in the UK see a very bright prospect for them. For many business advisors in the UK, systems are becoming a vital part of the tool-kit. This tool-kit now includes the modern, powerful, portable personal computer, a spreadsheet package (used, for example, to assist owner managers in financial planning), a word processing package and a selection of Enterprise Guidance Systems. The business advisor is joining the ranks of professionals who use portable computer technology to ensure a high quality service, at reasonable cost. (Heslop 1992)

The current systems are intended to be part of an overall package of support for growth offered by the Initiative's sponsors (a group of ten economic development organisations). A typical overall package launched in 1993/4 by one of them might include:

Self administered automated overview of growth potential to stimulate interest and direction in respect of growth. This could be achieved by offering the EGSI systems, or more likely, parts of the systems, to owner managers. Interest could be stimulated by a "disk through the post" taster, which covered one portion of the overview.

Personal discussion with a business counsellor on what facilities and resources are available to growing businesses and the criteria for access to these. Discussion of feedback on growth potential from EGSI system could form the basis for further action.

Planning and diagnostic session by owner manager, management team and / or business advisor using the business modelling device in the Business Review Tool. The outcome of this would be a set of explicit assumptions about the future business. The business advisor could then construct a spreadsheet based model for operational planning.

Signposting, and possible financial support for actions required to bring the business to a point where it has a clear basis for "growth". The immediate actions are identified by the owners of the business with assistance from the EGSI system.

Grant aid for consultancy and training during the development and implementation of growth plans.

Links to loan and investment finance based on the needs identified through the exploratory planning process of EGSI.

The international potential

In the UK, the diffusion of this form of technology has been slow. Adoption has been mainly by new entrants to the business advisory market. Many existing intermediaries do not view the tools as additional resources, but as potential threats. However, as the tools become more powerful and designed to meet the needs of both the small firm and the intermediary, one expects the rate of diffusion to increase. Owner managers are, on the whole, fascinated by the use of these systems because they are highly relevant to their business. In early evaluation trials, the intentions of Users ware changed in over half the cases, and actual behaviour in over 25% of cases. (Fuller and LeRoi 1989)

The key aspect of these systems is that they contain useful and relatively rare expertise. The design of each system is to an extent culture and context specific, as well as exhibiting the biases of the designers. Despite this, such systems have a high degree of portability to other contexts. They rely on personal computers being available (IBM compatible, 640K and at least 3MB disk space).

Similar systems are becoming visible in European countries and the USA, though not widespread. It is suggested that one barrier to their more widespread utilisation is a lack experience in programming and designing these tools, which could be given more consideration by small business organisations in the next five years.

Summary

No theory is adequate to predict growth in an individual small firm, though people are well practiced in assessing growth potential; using a variety of heuristic methods to do so.

A number of types of intervention have been established as stimulating growth, or at least development, in small firms. Management development is among these. Economic development organisations have difficulty in reaching small firms and in assessing appropriate forms of intervention or assistance. The Enterprise Guidance Systems Initiative was established to produce computer tools to assist the process of influencing owners of small firms such that appropriate assistance can be provided.

The Business Review Tool is intended to stimulate growth orientation of owner managers of small businesses. It is an interactive system which responds according to the state of the business. It provides evaluation and planning frameworks within a consultation metaphor. Three consultants' views are given; The Accountant, The Marketing Consultant and the Strategic Consultant. The frameworks are derived from those in use in practice.

The creation of this tool has led to the conception of an evaluation construct, the "FUE". These Favourable, Unfavourable and Missing Essential Factors enable the automation of a reasoning process which maps data from the small business to an overall evaluation framework.

Feedback on the presence of favourable, unfavourable and essential growth factors is given during the consultation. Conclusions about future growth potential are determined from combinations of factors and needs for immediate actions are identified from the conclusions.

The systems developed under EGSI are intended to be used as part of an overall package of support to small businesses by the economic development organisations financing the project. The intention is to make the process of small business support more efficient and more effective.

Such effectiveness in small business development can be shared by any culture or context, given an appropriate design which reflects the needs of the end users and the intermediaries who are likely to deliver it. A barrier to such development is the ability of people to design and programme the systems. This is a need which should be addressed.

Details of the structure are described and exemplified by the following excerpt from a case study.

Bibliography

Davies L.G. and Gibb A.A., "Methodological Problems in the Development and Testing of a Growth Model of Business Enterprise Development", in Davies L.G. and Gibb A.A., *Recent Research in Entrepreneurship*, Avebury Press, Aldershot

Filion, L.J., (1991) Visions and Relations: elements for an entrepreneurial metamodel" *International Small Business Journal*

Fuller, E (1990) *Introduction to Enterprise Guidance Systems*, Durham University Business School.

Fuller, E (1992) *Encouraging the emergent vision*. Working paper, Durham University Business School, UK.

Fuller, E. and Heslop, J.M., (1992) "Encouraging growth orientation in SMEs by simulating advisers' viewpoints.", *proceeding of 15th UKEMRA Small Business Policy and Research Conference.*

Fuller, E. and LeRoi, C., (1989) "Computer Aided Guidance; a normal part of the professional adviser's toolkit", *Proceedings 12th UKEMRA National Small Firms Policy and Research Conference*

Gibb A.A., (1991) *Proceedings of Entrepreneurship and Growth, 21st EFMD Small Business Seminar*, ESADE, Barcelona. See also Davies and Gibb (1991)

Gibb, A.A., and Scott, M.G., (1985) Strategic Awareness, Personal Commitment and the Process of Planning in the Small Business, *Journal of Management Studies*, 22,6

Hall, D. (1992), *The Hallmarks for Successful Business*, Mercury Books, London.

Hughes, A. et al, (1992) *Working Papers, ESRC Small Business Research Initiative*, Dept of Applied Economics, Cambridge University, UK.

Heslop J.M., (1992) "Enterprise Guidance: an expert systems success story for the 1990s," *Forthcoming in Expert Systems '92*, Cambridge, UK.

Honey, P and Mumford A., (1986) "A Manual of Learning Styles", Published by Peter Honey, Maidenhead.

Müller-Böling, D. and Kirchoff, S., (1991) "Expert Systems for consulting in Business Start-up Phase", in Davies L.G. and Gibb A.A., *Recent Research in Entrepreneurship*, Avebury Press, Aldershot

Senicourt, P., (1991) "A methodology and Software for Financial Forecasting: PrefaceTM", in Davies L.G. and Gibb A.A., *Recent Research in Entrepreneurship*, Avebury Press, Aldershot

Smallbone, D.J., Leigh, R., and North, D. (1991) *Working Paper Series 1-4, ESRC Small Business Research Initiative*, Middlesex Polytechnic (as was), UK.

Annexe

Example

The following example is provided to indicate the structure of the analysis and conclusions. It does not show the questions asked, nor the complete framework for the module described. It should therefore not be viewed as a comprehensive coverage of the issues in "ability to finance growth"

Extract from accountant's assessment: "ability to finance growth"

The following example describes the response by the system in one of the key areas, "Ability to finance growth"

In this area a number of questions are posed (not shown) and financial information is collected. The questions posed relate to the following areas:

Ability to finance growth from the firms own resources
    Able to meet financial commitments
    Able to generate funds to finance growth
    Has funds to support growth

Ability to raise additional finance
    Immediate borrowing capacity
    Capitalising reserves
    Grants
    Increases in owners' capital
    External investment

FUE factors

The Accountant Assessment FUE Factors relevant to the questions in the above areas are as follows:

Essential factors (6)

1. Business can meet its financial commitments as they fall due.
2. Either
   Turnover sales above break-even (cf firm making a profit)
   OR
   Sales growth or profit (or lessening losses) growth last year and business can sustain losses until operating above break-even level
3. Trading generates funds for the business
4. Owners policy on further investment is known
5. Owners have fully investigated the possibility of grants for expansion
6. Owners have investigated external sources of long term capital.

Favourable Factors (7 or 12)

1. Break-even level below 50% of capacity
2. Has borrowing capacity of at least 20% of current funds (equity + borrowings)
3. Funds generated by trading at a faster rate than funds required by working capital
4. Owners would convert retained earnings to share capital
5. Owners willing and able to invest necessary additional capital
6. Owners willing and able to invest major proportion of additional capital
7. Owners would be prepared to borrow money if needed
8. AND if external finance is needed
8.1 Owners willing to consider external investor(s) for long term finance
8.2 Owner manager has experience in the use of external financial partners
8.3 Business can attract long term capital from external sources
8.4 Owner manager has made a detailed examination of sources of long term capital

8.5 Owners are actively seeking long term finance from external sources.

Unfavourable Factors (7 or 8)

1. Negative value of Net Current Assets
2. Break-even level at 80% or more of capacity
3. Currently the firm has no borrowing capacity (not able to borrow)
4. Funds required for working capital increase at a faster rate than funds generated by trading
5. No investments to cash into growth investment activities
6. Owners not willing to invest 50% of further equity
7. Owners unwilling to consider external long term finance
8. (If needed) Business is unable to attract external funding

Results of a consultation

Supposing that a consultation between the system and an owner manager resulted in the following FUEs being identified as relevant:

All Essential Factors were present, except that the owners had not looked at external finance because they felt they could invest sufficient themselves. They are quite reluctant to borrow money.

Favourable Factors identified were that the business has a low breakeven point and that the owners were prepared to invest in the business.

Unfavourable Factors identified were that the working capital requirements of the business were high compared to the cash generated (eg high stock levels or long payment terms by customers). Also the owners were unwilling to consider external finance.

Profile

The evaluation of the overall criterion "Ability to Finance Growth" would be as follows. The profile of these scores would also be shown graphically.

Favourable - Potentially the firm has 5 of 7 favourable factors. However they are not fully favourable until all the essential factors are present.

The Missing essential factor is that the owners are not prepared to borrow if needed. While they may decide not to use external finance, it is an important option for any growth firm.

Unfavourable Factors - the firm has 2 of 7 unfavourable factors. Working capital generation is not self funding and the owners are unwilling to consider external finance.

Conclusions

The conclusions on the ability to finance growth which would be drawn by the Accountant's Assessment from this analysis would be shown on-screen (and in a printed report) as follows:

Accountant's assessment:

Ability to Finance Growth
Essential Factors present:

> Business can meet financial commitments as they fall due
> Sales are above break even level.
> Owner's policy on further investment is known
> Owners have fully investigated grants for expansion

Favourable Growth Factors established:

> Break even sales are less than 50% of total capacity
> Owners are willing and able to invest necessary additional capital

Unfavourable Factors noted:

> Funds required by working capital increase at a faster rate than funds generated by trading
> Owners unwilling to consider external long term finance
> Factors which may need to be addressed before growth is possible:
> Owners to investigate external sources of long term capital

Conclusions:

- The business appears to be healthy in its ability to meet short term commitments.

- The firm is operating above break even level and, because it can break even at or below half its capacity, has considerable potential for making profits.

- You will have difficulty in financing growth from your operations because, on the current figures, you require more working capital than you generate by increased sales. Either you have to reduce your need for working capital or increase the profitability of your operations.

- The business has 50,000 internal funds to invest in growth. This is 10% of total assets and therefore implies the ability to finance growth by this level.

- From the answers provided to the questions, it would appear to be possible for the business to raise the following investment capital:

    Loans   [   ]
    Owners investment   [   ]
    Grants   [   ]
    External Finance   [   ]
    Other (specified)   [   ]

- It may also be possible to increase borrowings, linked to the new capital. This will depend on the availability of security for these borrowings."

8 International marketing strategies of Dutch small firms

R.M. Braaksma, Harold G.J. Gankema and Peter S. Zwart

Introduction

The environment of European small and medium-sized firms is changing rapidly. On the one hand global trends such as internationalization, concentration and globalization affect market developments in the long run, while on the other hand the establishment of the single market after December the 31st of this year, competition is expected to become stronger because of the abolishment of all trade barriers within the European Community. In order to survive, both international and local operating small firms will have to broaden their view and consider international market expansion.

A lot of research has been carried out concerning the problems small firms face while exporting or which internal and external factors contribute to the successfulness of the exporting activity. Little attention was paid to the influence of different strategies of internationalization chosen and whether certain strategies of internationalization are more successful than others. Our research objectives therefore are:

1) Which international marketing strategies are used by exporting small firms in the Netherlands?
2) Which relationship exits between the international marketing strategies chosen and the characteristics of the firm and conditions of the market?
3) Which international marketing strategies are more successful

considering the firm characteristics and market conditions?

Theoretical Background

A lot of research has been done about the motives of small firms to go international. Miesenbock (1988) distinguished between internal and external stimuli and found that the most important stimuli were external.

Unsolicited orders from abroad, saturated home market and more favorable market conditions are found to be important external stimuli (Rabino 1980, Kaynak and Stevenson 1982, Gankema and Zwart 1990). The most important internal stimuli are excessive capacity, a unique product, a differential advantage on technology or marketing and the attitude of the manager (Johnson and Czinkota 1982, Zwart and Gankema 1990). Our research therefore not examines the motives of small forms going international, but concentrates on the international marketing strategies. Theoretically we suggest a firm has to go through a <u>hierarchy of strategies with four levels</u>, each including various strategic options:

1. Market Expansion Strategies
2. Generic Competition Strategies
3. Geographic Segmentation Strategies
4. Market Entry Strategies.

These four levels are the starting-point for our analysis and as a consequence, will be discussed in some more detail hereafter.

Market Expansion Strategies

Decisions concerning entering new markets and choices concerning which products will be introduced at these markets have long term consequences for running the firm (Leeflang 1987). "Management should first review whether there are any furter opportunities for improving the performance of its existing business. Ansoff has proposed a product/market expansion grid for detecting new intensive growth opportunities" (Kotler 1988).

Choosing a **market penetration strategy** the firm tries to gain more market share with current products on current markets by encouragin current customer to use more, making competitors customers to switch brand or convincing non-users to buy the product. One can expect a great deal of small firms acting like this.

Selecting a **market development strategy** the firm is looking for new markets (other segments or abroad) whose needs are met by current products. Seifert and Ford (1989) and Gronhaug and Kvitastein (1992) found that small firms often use current products starting export activities.

A **product development strategy** is used when the former strategies offer insufficient opportunities and one has to consider product development possibilities.

A **diversification strategy** means introducing new products to new customers. This makes only sense when good opportunities can be found outside the present business (Kotler 1988).

Generic competition strategies

After a firm has decided in which way to expand, one has to decide what position among the existing competitors is desirable. Porter (1980) distinguished the following three generic strategies: overall cost leadership, differentiation and focus.

Overal cost leadership means that the firm can produce and distribute at lower costs than the competitors, e.g. because of economies of scale.

A strategy of **differentiation** means that the firm is exploiting a competitive differencial advantage in e.g. quality, design, service or brand. The product clearly distinguishes itself from other products.

Choosing a **focus** strategy a firm is concentrating on one or more narrow market segments and keeps looking for new niches to serve.

Geographic Segmentation Strategy

A number of factors like leadership style, managers' attitude towards foreign trade, history, culture, etc. account for the strategic predisposition of a firm on the international market. Heenan and Perlmutter (1979), described four distinct predispositions: ethnocentrism, polycentrism, regiocentrism and geocentrism.

Ethnocentrism is a predisposition where all strategic decisions are guided by the conditions of the domestic market.

Polycentrism is a predisposition where strategic decisions are tailored to meet the various market conditions in every country the firm completes.

Regiocentrism and **Geocentrism** are predispositions where strategic decisions are based on market conditions which several countries (a region) or global segments have in common. In this study these two are taken together as a **global orientation**.

Market Entry Strategies

Once a firm has decided to fulfil an occasional order from abroad or to introduce a product to a foreign market, it has to determine the best mode of distribution or market entry. Its broad choices are with increasing amount of commitment, risk and profitpotential: indirect exporting, direct exporting, licensing, joint ventures and direct investment (Kotler 1980).

An **indirect export** strategy means that the firm works through domestic based independent middleman. Goods are produced in the home country.

Choosing a **direct export** strategy, the firm handles its own export. Goods are still produced in the home country, but are sold by a domestic-based export department, export sales representatives, or foreign based agents or subsidiaries.

Licensing represents an agreement eith a foreign licensee, offering the right to use a manufacturing process, trade mark, patent, etc. for a fee or royalty. This study doesn't include this entry strategy.

In **joint ventures** the firm joins with foreign to create a local business in which they share a joint ownership and control.

A direct investment includes an investment in foreign-based assembly or manufacturing facilities.

Combining the various strategies we suggest the following hierarchy of international marketing strategies:

Market Expansion Strategies			
Market penetration	Product development	Market development	Diversification

Generic Competition Strategies		
Differentiation	Focus	Overall cost leadership

Geografic Segmentation Strategies		
Ethnocentric	Polycentric	Global

Market Entry Strategies			
Indirect Export	Direct Export	Joint Ventures	Direct Investment

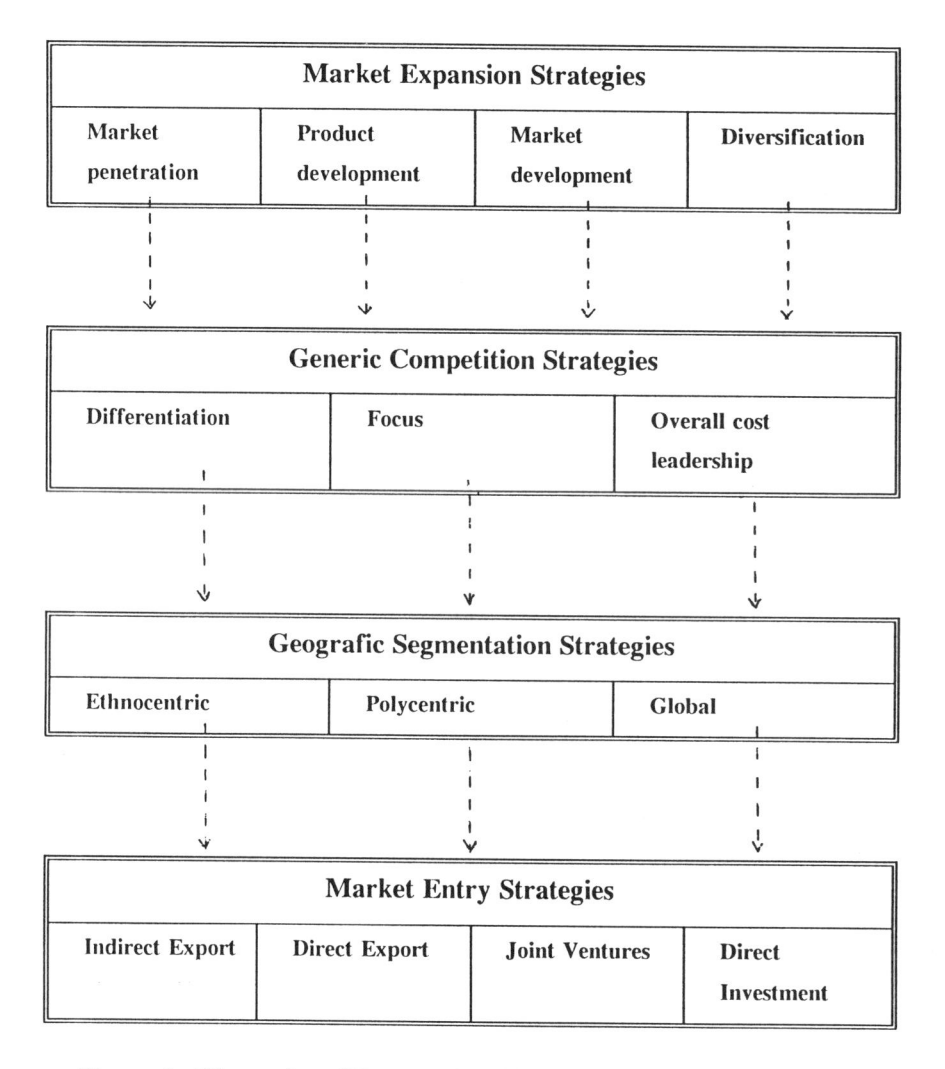

Figure 1. Hierarchy of International Marketing Strategies.

Small firms can be expected to choose other strategies and path's through the hierarchy of international marketing strategies than e,g, multinationals.

Research Methodology

The various international marketing strategies at the four levels will operationalized using the variables of the questionnaire of the Inter Stratos project. This project convers an annual survey research in several European countries for the time of five years, the first year being 1991. Characteristics of the firms measured by means of the Inter Stratos questionnaire are:

- number and type of products and markets
- export and internationalization
- last year changes in costumers', labour and financial markets
- management view toward internationalization.

The data used in this study are derived from 978 Dutch firms in 1991. The sample is stratified by firm size and branch. The five branches are:

1. Textile, footwear and clothing industry
2. Food, drink and tobacco industry
3. Electronical engineering
4. Timber and wooden furniture industry
5. Manufacture of metal articles and mechanical engineering.

The selection criteria to chose these branches were: high percentages of small and medium-sized enterprises, various degrees of internationalization, of types of market, technological developments, of roles of subcontracing, of sensitivities for the completion of the international market, of existence of economies of scale, of duration of the product live cycle and of the number of new entrants in the market.

A sample profile is shown in table 1,

Table 1. Sample profile

Sector	number of employees	1-9	10-19	20-49	50-99	100-500	total
Food, drink and tobacco industry		29	38	30	22	12	131
Textile, footwear and clothing industry		112	57	46	24	9	248
Timber and wooden furniture industries		40	46	35	21	12	154
Manufacture of metal articles and mechanical engineering		45	75	50	37	29	236
Electrical engineering		51	26	46	28	27	178
Total		277	242	207	132	89	947*

(*) Exclusive 30 cases which didn't respond to the number of employees and 1 case that didn't respond to the branche.

Method of analysis

Cluster analysis procedures were utilized todetermine which strategies firms choose at each level, according to the procedure recommended by Punj and Stewart (1983). This procedure is as follows:

1. Ward's hierarchical clustering method
2. Preliminary cluster solution
3. Select number of clusters

4. Iterative partitioning
5. Final solution

In step 1 the distance between two clusters is calculated as the sum of squares between the two clusters summed over all variables (Ward's method). According to Punj and Stewart (1983) this generally generates the best solution. As a result of this method a preliminary cluster solution is found in step 2. In step 3 the number of clusters is selected based on three criteria: a) the relative size of the clustering coefficients, b) the variance between the clusters and c) the number of respondents belonging to a cluster. Outliers are removed and the centroids of the clusters are obtained. In step 4 an interative partitioning procedure is performed, using the cluster centroids of the preliminary analysis as a starting point. In step 5 the final cluster solution is found.

Results

Market Expansion Strategies

In order to partition the sample into homogeneous groups of firms with the same Market Expansion Strategies, the following variables are used in the cluster analysis:

- the number of types of products
- the percentage of sales by the three most important products
- the number of types of customer
- the percentage of sales to the three most important customer
- the export / total sales ratio
- the local sales / total sales ratio.

The statistics didn't show an optimum within the number of clusters. Because of the small number of respondents in cluster seven and eight, a six clusters solution was subjectively selected.

Cluster 1 includes 104 firms. They carry a small number of types of products and have a small number of types of customers. therefore these firms have a very high percentage of sales both to the three most important customers and by the three most important products. They export quite a lot (68%) and do not sell very much local (8%). These forms seem to concentrate on the same type of customers, selling the same products internationally, which could be characterized as **market penetration** internationally. Of all clusters they have the highest sales abroad (16 million guilders on average), their number of employees is 72 people on average.

They meet the same degree of competiveness as the year before. This cluster includes few firms of the Furniture Industry.

Cluster 2 includes 266 firms which, as in cluster 1, have few products and customers, high percentages of sales of the three most important customers and the three most important products. However they export very little (8%) and sell not much locally. Therefore these forms seem to concentrate on the total Dutch market on few types of customers with few products. This could be characterized as a **market penetration strategy**. They have on average 35 employees and sell less than 1 million guilders abroad on average and indicate their competiveness didn't change. The Food Industry is underrepresented in this cluster.

Cluster 3 includes 104 firms. These forms sell quite a lot of products to uite a lot of customers. The most important three customers and products account both for about 60% of total sales. About 20% of sales is exported and about 32% is sold locally. Although not very clearly, these firms seem to follow a **diversification strategy**. The Food and Furniture Industries are underrepresented, while the Manufacture of metal products and Mechanical Engineering is overrepresented. On averege they have 61 employees and sell about 9 million guilders abroad.

Cluster 4 countains 206 firms shich have very few types of customers and products. They hardly sell abroad (2%)and concentrate sales on the local area (87%). These firms seem to follow a **market penetration strategy** on the local market. Electronical Engineering is underrepresented in this cluster, the firms are quite small (19 employees), and strongly belief competiveness in foreign remained unchanged.

Cluster 5 only contains 6 firms which claim to have an enormous number of types of products and a relative small number of types of customers. The three most important products only account for 18% of total sales, while the three most important customers account for 75% of total sales. They export quite a lot (29%) but sell most a locally (66%). In view of the number of products these frims seem to concentrate on a **product development strategy**. They can be characterized as the larger firms (131 employees on average).

Cluster 6 contains 8 firms which claim to have an enormous number of types of customers and a relative small number of products. Their export/sales ratio is small (11%) in local sales account for 29%. These firms seem to have concentrated on the dutch market following a strategy of (home) **market development**. They employ 64 people on average.

Generic Competition Strategies

In order to divide the sample in homogeneous groups that follow to the same generic competition strategies, a set of 19 variables is used. This set of variables concerned questions about the most important factors in achieving success and were measured on a 5-point scale from no importance to very high importance. To find out wether these 19 variables have some underlying dimensions in common, first a Factor analysis was carried out. This resulted in the following six factors used as input in the cluster analysis:

1. Marketing (after sales service, creativity, sales force, design)
2. Management (quality of management, reputation, PR)
3. Cost (lowest prices, lowest cost)
4. Technology (up-to-date technology, solve techn. problems)
5. Flexibility (respond quickly to changes, modify products)
6. Product Quality (product quality)

Because the statistics showed some contradiction, a six clutersolution was selected based on the relative small number of respondents in cluster seven.

Cluster 1 includes 136 firms which claim to stress the factors cost, flexibility and product quality in achieving success. They seem to follow a strategy a **cost leadership**, perhaps combined with a strategy of differentiation. The Textile, Footwear and Clothing Industry is clearly overrepresented in this group, while the Electronical Enginnering is clearly underrepresented. The sales volumes are quite high compared to the others clusters.

Cluster 2 differs from cluster 1 in that these 153 firms do not emphasize the factor costs at all. Because they stress the factors flexibility and product quality they seem to follow a strategy of **differentiation**. The export/sales ratio is among these six clusters the highest (26%).

Cluster 3 contains 131 firms which claim to stress all the six factors at one time. Because this does not seem to be very logical it seems that these firms are **not able to set any priorities**. Their sales volume is much lower than in cluster 1 and even cluster 2. The Food, Drink and Tobacco Industry are clearly underrepresented in this cluster.

Cluster 4 includes 111 firms which exclusively emphasize on the factor product quality. The factor technology however, is important. These firms are the smaller firms (21 employees) which do not export much (11%). They **don't** seem to **have a clear strategy** on this level. They strongly belief competitive conditions abroad remained unchanged. The Electronical Engineering clearly is underrepresented in this cluster.

Cluster 5 contains 157 firms that as contrasted with cluster 3, clain to stress none of the factors. These firms, as in cluster 3, **are not able to set any priorities**. Also in this cluster the Food, Drink and Tobacco Industry is clearly underrepresented. The Manufacture of metal articles and Mechanical Engineering is overrepresented. Their competitive strength became a bit wacker in the Netherlands.

Cluster 6 as in cluster 4, includes 91 firms that lay emphasis on product quality. Furthermore they stress the factor technology. Electronical Engineering and Manufacture of metal products and Mechanical Engineering are clearly overrepresented, while only three Food,Drink and Tobacco Industries are in this group. This cluster seems to **focus** on high quality, technologically advanced products.

Geografic Segmentation Strategies

The way a firm looks at a foreign market is expressed by its geografic segmentation strategy. Three variables are taken into the analysis to partition the sample into homogeneous groups:

- hunting for orders from abroad
- how often received orders from abroad
- ability to modify products.

The clustering coefficients showed an optimum at six clusters.

Cluster 1 includes 257 firms which hunted for orders from abroad. Only occasionally they receive orders from abroad, although they emphasis their ability to modify their products. these firms seem to have a **polycentric** predisposition. The Textile, Footwear and Clothing Industry is overrepresented in this group, while the Food and the Furniture Industries are slightly underrepresented. This cluster has the highest export/sales ratio of thes six clusters (42%). Their competitive position got worse a bit in the Netherlands as well as abroad. On average they employ 62 people.

Cluster 2 includes 106 firms who, as contrasted with cluster 1, do not hunt for orders from abroad. Despite of this these firms claim to regulary receive orders from abroad and to be able to modify their products. They are the smaller firms (28 employees) and do export only 6% of total sales. Their competitive strength decreased a bit in the Netherlands, but remained unchanged abroad. These firms seem to overemphasize their unsolicited orders from abroad and can to be expected to have a **ethnocentric** predisposition. The Food, Drink and Tobacco Industry clearly is very underrepresented in this cluster.

Cluster 3 Includes 191 firms which emphasize their ability to modify products. They donot hunt for or receive orders from abroad. These very small firms (17 employees) are found in all branches, do export only 3% of total sales and strongly think competitive situation abroad remained unchanged. These firms clearly have a **etnocentric** predisposition.

Cluster 5 includes 56 firms with on average 52 employees which, if necessary, modify their products. They don't hunt for an occasionally receive orders from abroad (25% of total sales). Their predisposition seems to be **ethnicentric**. The Food Industry is clearly underrepresented in this group, while the Electronical Engineering and Manufacturing of metal products and Mechanical Engineering are overrepresented.

Cluster 6 contains 86 firms which hunted for orders and occasionally received orders from abroad (35% of total sales). They do not emphasis their ability to modify their products and are therefore characterized as having a **global orientation**. Electronical Engineering is slightly underrepresented, while Mecahnical Engineering is slightly overepresented in this cluster.

Market Entry Strategies

To determine groups that are homogeneous the way they handle their export, the following variables are used in the clusering procedure:

- agents in the Netherlands
- dutch manufacturers who eventually export
- dutch distributors who export
- agents abroad
- license

- distribution subsidiaries abroad
- manufacturing subsidiaries abroad.

Because the statistics didn't show an optimum, a six cluster solution subjectively was selected, mainly based on the number of respondents in the clusters.

Cluster 1 contains 201 firms which all delivered direct to the customers abroad. Almost half of them also sold through agents abroad. None of them used other entry strategies, so this group clearly can be characterized as using a **direct export** strategy. The Textile, Footwear and Clothing and the Manufactures of metal products and Mechanical Engineering are clearly overrepresented, while the Food industry is clearly underrepresented in this cluster. They export about the average of all firms.

Cluster 2 contains 320 firms that sell through dutch agents, manufacturers and distributors, but also through agents abroad and direct to customers. These firms clearly combine **direct and indirect export** strategies. Food and Furniture Industries are underrepresented in this group of smaller firms (35 employees).

Cluster 3 includes 48 firms which, although they also sell through agents abroad and direct, nearly all have manufacturing subsidiaries abroad (**direct investment**). The Food and Furniture Industries are clearly underrepresented, while the Electronical Engineering is clearly overrepresented. These firms are the larger ones (90 employees) which sell about half of their sales abroad.

Cluster 4 includes 140 firms which **do not export** much (5%). They are the smaller firms (31 employees) in all branches.

Cluster 5 includes 82 firms which, except for the joint venture, use all the entry strategies. Most of them however, sell through a distribution subsidiary (**direct investment**). These firms employ on average 55 people and export 26% of total sales. Furniture Industry is clearly underrepresented in this cluster.

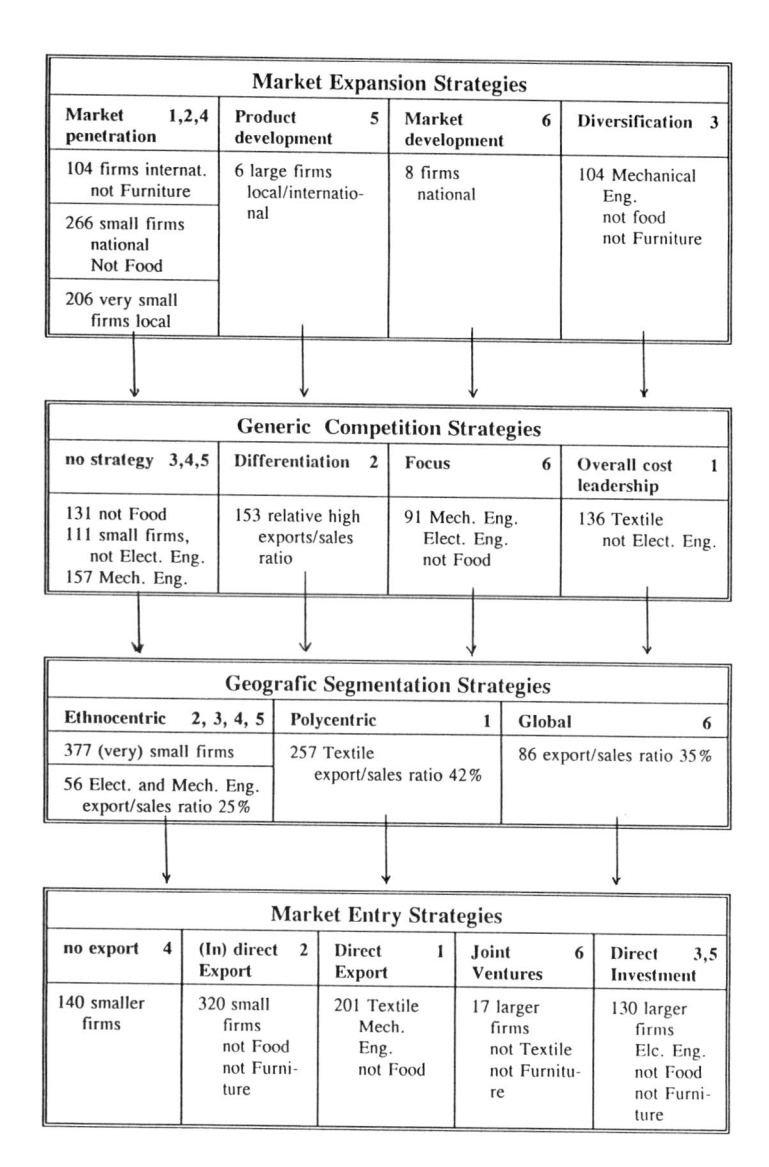

Market Expansion Strategies			
Market penetration 1,2,4	Product development 5	Market development 6	Diversification 3
104 firms internat. not Furniture	6 large firms local/international	8 firms national	104 Mechanical Eng. not food not Furniture
266 small firms national Not Food			
206 very small firms local			

Generic Competition Strategies			
no strategy 3,4,5	Differentiation 2	Focus 6	Overall cost leadership 1
131 not Food 111 small firms, not Elect. Eng. 157 Mech. Eng.	153 relative high exports/sales ratio	91 Mech. Eng. Elect. Eng. not Food	136 Textile not Elect. Eng.

Geografic Segmentation Strategies		
Ethnocentric 2, 3, 4, 5	Polycentric 1	Global 6
377 (very) small firms	257 Textile export/sales ratio 42%	86 export/sales ratio 35%
56 Elect. and Mech. Eng. export/sales ratio 25%		

Market Entry Strategies				
no export 4	(In) direct Export 2	Direct Export 1	Joint Ventures 6	Direct Investment 3,5
140 smaller firms	320 small firms not Food not Furniture	201 Textile Mech. Eng. not Food	17 larger firms not Textile not Furniture	130 larger firms Elc. Eng. not Food not Furniture

Figure 2. Overall results of the cluster analysis.

Cluster 6 includes the only 17 firms which set up a **joint venture**. Textile and Furniture industries are underrepresented, while the Mechanical Engineering is slightly overrepresented. These are the larger firms (94 employees) that sell 43% of total abroad.

The overall results of the cluster analysis are shown at figure 2.

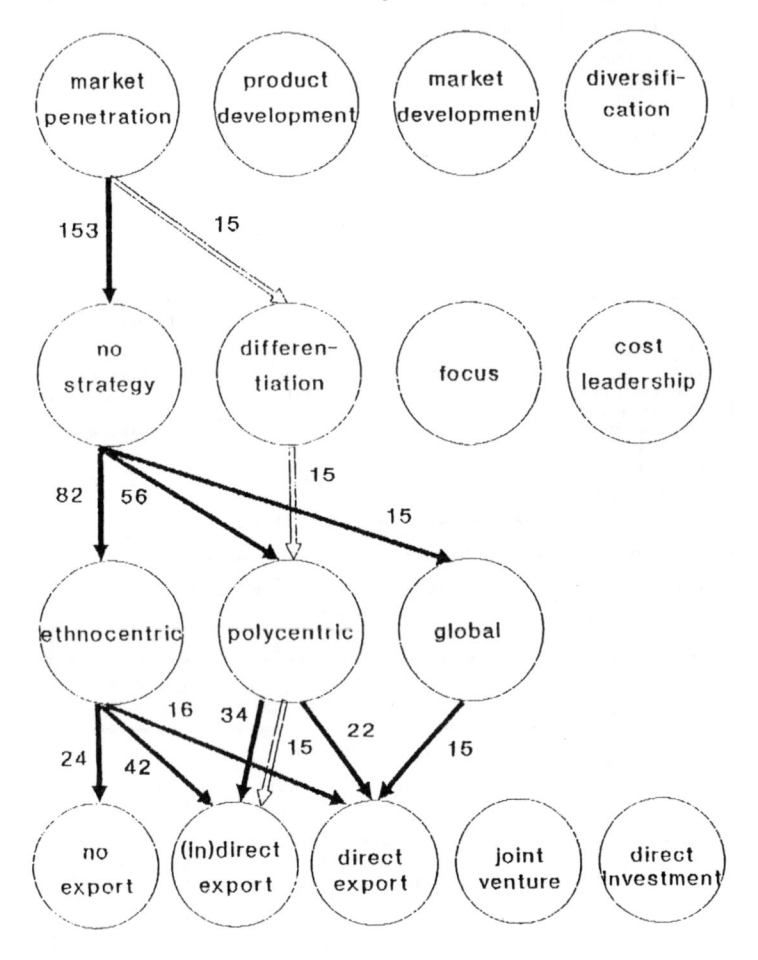

Figure 3. Paths througt the hierarchy of strategies with 15 or more firms.

Paths through the hierarchy of strategies

To get any insight in the relationship between the strategies chosen at each level, all the possible paths through the hierarchy of strategies were specified. This resulted in 4 x 4 x 3 x 5 = 240 paths to be investigated. Firms which could not be classified at one or more variables, can not be classified to one of the paths. Therefor only 470 out of the total sample of 978 firms appeared to be valid cases. Eightteen of these paths are followed by 9 or more firms.

Conclusion

From our results one can conclude that most of the investigated firms seem to follow a market penetration strategy. Only a relative small part of these firms penetrated on international markets.

Remarkably, a very substantial part of the firms don't follow a particular strategy on the level of generic competition, just a few seem to concentrate on a strategy of differentiation.

Most of the firms, which don't have a particular competition strategy, seem to have a global predisposition.

Of those with an ethnocentric orientation, some do export very rarely or not at all, most of them export direct and indirect.

Among those with a polycentric orientation, direct export is favourable, though indirect export is a used entry strategy too.

The few firms which seem to follow a differentiation strategy, all have a polycentric orientation and export both directly and indirectly.

All the firms however, which think more global, though lacking an obvious competition strategy, export only directly.

Although these results are preliminary, on general one can conclude that the small and medium-sized firms tend to go on the way they are used to, whithout concerning about their position among competitors.

They concentrate traditionally on the home country and, when selling abroad, mainly use export as an entry strategy.

Wellconsidered choices concerning alternative international marketing strategies are hardly made yet.

References

Ansoff, H.I. (1965): *"Corporate Strategy"*, McGraw-Hill, New York.

Gankema, H.G.J., ZWART P.S, (1992): *"The Relationship Between Firm Characteristics and Export Involvement of Small Firms"*, proceedings ICSB, Toronto, June 1992.

Gronhaug, K, Kvitastein, O.N., (1992): "Expansion Strategies in International Markets: An Exploratory, Study", *Scandianavian International Business Review*, Vol. 1, No.1. pp. 57-70.

Heenan, D.A., Perlmutter, H.V., (1979): *"Multinational Organized Developments A Social Araintecture Perspective"*, Reading Mass: Adisson Wessley, 1979.

Johnson, W.J., Czinkota, M.R., (1982): *"Managerial Motivations as Determinant of Industrial Export Behaviour, Export Management: An International Context"*, Praeger Publishers New York, pp. 3 t/m 17.

Kynak, E., Kothary, V., (1984): "Export Behaviour of Small and Medium Sized Manufactures", *Management International Review*, Vol. 24,2, pp. 61-9.

Kotler, P.H., (1980): *"Marketing Management, Analysis, Planning and Control"*, 4th edition, Prentice-Hall, Inc., Englewood Cliffs, N.J.

Kotler, P.H., (1988): *"Marketing Management, Analysis, Planning, Implementation and Control"*, 6th edition, Prentice-Hall, Inc., Englewood Cliffs, N.J.

Leeflang, P.S.H., (1987): *Probleemgebied Marketing een management benadring"*, 2e druk, H.E., Stenfert Kroese B.V., Leiden-Antwerpen.

Miesenbock, K.J, (1988): "Small Business and Exporting: A Literature Review", *International Small Business Journal*, Vol. 6.2., pp. 42-61.

Porter, M.E, (1980): *"Competitive Strategy: Techniques for Analysis Industries and Competitors"*, The Free Press, New York.

Punj G. Stewart (1983): "Cluster Analysis in Marketing Research: Review and Suggestions for Application", *Journal of Marketing Research*, May 1983, pp. 134-148.

Rabino, S., (1980): "An Examination of Barriers to Exporting Encountered by Small Manufacturing Companies", *Management International Review*, Vol. 20.1 pp. 67-73.

Seifert, B., Ford, J., (1989): "Are Exporting Firms Modifying Their Product, Pricing and Promotion Polices?", *International Marketing Review*, Vol. 6.6., pp. 53-67.

Zwart, P.S.., Gankema, H.G.J., (1990), *"Het Exportgedrag van het Midden - en Kleinbhedrijf in Noord-Nederland"*, Memorandum van het Instituut voor Economisch Onderzoek, Faculteit der Economische Wetenschappen Rijksuniversiteit Groningen, No. 393.

9 Competitiveness, autonomy and business relationships

A.L. Duijnhouwer

Introduction

Entrepreneurs are confronted with a number of (international) developments, such as the changing needs of consumers causing the product life cycles to decline, increasing competition forcing more efficient production and demanding a choice between production in-house or the necessity of subcontracting etc.

In response to these developments an increasing number of entrepreneurs is joining forces to achieve a positive synergic effect. Such business relationships can reinforce market strength and the competitive position of companies. By entering into business relationships some of the influence of various parties in the environment can be neutralized, a competitive edge can be gained and (improved) response to developments made possible. But at the same time, a business relationship will diminish the independence of an entrepreneur, as the entrepreneur becomes restricted in his ability to make decisions according to his own insight.

This paper is based on data for the Netherlands collected for an international comparative study in 8 European countries.[1]

> The purpose of the study is to determine in what way SME entrepreneurs perceive that different forms and areas of business relationships contribute (in a positive or negative sense) to their autonomy and to the competitive position of their company.

The company and its environment

The environment

In order to function, companies need resources such as raw materials, capital, manpower, political and social acceptance etc. Because the company itself does not have all these resources fully at its disposal, these will have to be acquired from third parties (suppliers of raw materials, banks, employees, the government etc.).

Therefore, companies have to enter into relationships with individuals, organizations or other companies. These groups are outside the immediate control of the company; rather, they are in the company's environment. Because the company is dependent on these groups in its environment for both resources and sales, it must take into account the wishes and needs of these groups (Pfeffer and Salancik, 1978). For example, the price and quality of the products supplied, the working conditions and remuneration of employees, environmentally sound production methods etc.

Each time the company requires resources or sales, it can enter into a relationship with parties in the environment to achieve the desired result (through market competition). Because the company cannot exercise full control over these parties, there is no guarantee that the required resources are available or that the sale can be realized. The company may be confronted with constantly changing conditions for supply or sales. This is even more the case if there is a shortage with regard to the availability of resources or sales potential.

An alternative strategy is to undertake a long-term or permanent relationship with one or more parties. By establishing such a relationship, it is possible to guarantee the availability of resources and ensure sales for a longer period of time. A long-term exchange relationship is entered into (Levine and White, 1961) .

Whether and to what degree a company enters into permanent relationships, rather than seeking contact with parties on an ad hoc basis, depends on a large number of factors. For example, the importance of the various resources to ensure the continued existence of the organization, the impossibility of obtaining these in another way or the availability of alternative choices, the ability to influence parties in the environment etc.

Developments in the environment

In recent years, companies have been increasingly confronted by a number of (internationally) interrelated developments and trends. These developments will have far-reaching consequences for company policy, also due to their influence on the availability of resources and on sales potential.

Although the developments and trends are strongly interrelated, three different areas can be distinguished (IMK, 1989). Firstly, changes in the market and in the needs and requirements of clients. Secondly, developments in the field of technology, generated on the one hand by changes in demand (demand-pull) and on the other hand by increased possibilities (technology-push). Thirdly, social developments that are associated with increased public awareness and the influence of the government on company policy. These developments are discussed here.

Present-day clients demand increasingly higher standards from products and services. This is true for consumers as well as for industrial clients. They not only demand an increasingly high quality from the product, which must also be supplied more rapidly and at lower prices, but they also demand an increasing number of product varieties available.

The consequences for company policy are most significant. In order to supply at lower prices, there is a growing tendency towards an increase in scale and further specialization. An increasing number of companies concentrate on core activities, by using external suppliers to supply parts and services on a subcontracting basis, to realize cost savings or to improve quality and flexibility. The contracting-out of all kinds of services by companies is a relatively new development that has led to an enormous growth in the number of specialized service companies. This is one of the reasons why the economy has seen a shift from goods production to the service industry.[2]

Another consequence of the fact that clients demand a new product at increasingly greater speeds is that the life cycle of products is diminishing. The period of time a product remains profitable is becoming shorter and shorter. Together with the creation of a world market, this has intensified international competition. The ongoing European unification has reinforced the process of internationalization in industry. A growing number of companies are involved in transactions across national boundaries, particularly within Europe. In addition, overseas companies are showing greater interest in European markets.

This intensified competition forces companies to incorporate the latest gimmicks and the newest technology into their product and to work with the newest machines. The life span of new techniques therefore decreases, while at the same time the cost and complexity of technology rise, particularly due to the use of micro-electronics. This makes it increasingly difficult to recoup investments in R&D, while the risk of these investments becomes greater.

Only those companies that have specialized know-how at their disposal are able to continue developing and introducing new techniques. In addition, a certain degree of specialization in production and sales is necessary to generate sufficient turnover to recoup the rising investment costs in product development or production technology.

The shorter time available for recovering the cost of technical devices and products has made it essential for manufacturers to come to an international agreement on standards. Only then will there be a sufficiently large international market to recover the costs. Familiar examples are the consumer electronics industry, e.g. in the field of video tapes and video recorders.

On a social plane, also, companies have to deal with a number of trends. The influence of politics on company policy is growing. The government is imposing more and more obligations on companies, e.g. in the field of employee participation, environmental protection, working conditions etc. The European integration has shifted the influence from a national to a European level to a certain extent. Presently, for example, there are European quality standards for products, a European regulation for product liability, all kinds of import and export restrictions etc.

Companies are also increasingly expected to act responsibly towards society. Both the government and other social groups ensure this. A company that tries to avoid its obligations can be confronted by a buyers' strike or by government intervention. The social responsibility of companies is a result of increased public awareness in general, and of employees in particular. In addition to requirements stipulated for products and production, requirements are also laid down for the quality of working conditions in and remuneration by the company. If these requirements are not met, companies may be confronted with considerable problems in attracting staff.

Possibilities and consequences for SME

The most important consequence of these developments is that the management of a company is becoming increasingly complex. The requirements imposed by the environment of the company on company policy are changing and increasing; the entrepreneur will have to take this into account. In addition, it is not enough to consider the immediate environment only, but (international) developments and trends must also be watched with greater vigilance.

The question is whether companies can respond to all of the above-mentioned changes in requirements and wishes.

Small and medium-sized enterprises (SME) can look more towards specialized markets. Due to the general trend towards increase in scale and greater specialization, special markets (market niches) can be created and become attractive for SME. Due to their small size, these 'niches' are not of interest to the very large companies. In contrast, this characteristic makes them interesting for smaller companies that wish to respond to this opportunity. Through closer contacts with clients and more direct transmission of signals, these companies can respond more efficiently to market demand than the very large companies.

Before it will be considered by the very large companies as a potential partner for the supply of products, semi-manufactured products or services, the company will also have to aim for (international) standards and quality requirements. In many cases, this will mean that investments will have to be made in (the development of) new production techniques. This is one of the reasons why many European governments have special programmes to improve the attention to quality in SME.

In addition, more attention will have to be paid to logistics. Shorter delivery times (Just In Time) are an important condition to be able to act as subcontractor. More attention for logistics is also essential to reduce the volume of resources held in stock and to control the greater variety of final products and semi-manufactured products.

As is true for large companies, SME must ask themselves whether they should still continue to perform all activities themselves. Contracting-out can offer advantages in the field of costs, quality and delivery time, factors that become more important as competition increases.

Problems may be anticipated with investments that are essential in order to meet the stringent requirements of clients. The development or acquisition of new products is becoming increasingly expensive, while recovery time is shorter. In addition, the level of know-how and training and the quality of management in many SME has not kept pace with the development in large companies. This is particularly important because the development and operation of machines and the development of products place an increasing demand on personnel.

To cope with the above-mentioned developments an entrepreneur has various options at his disposal. A long-standing policy is the 'go-it-alone' strategy, in which all activities are carried out 'in-house' or acquired by means of a market transaction. In other words, the target is reached through the hierarchy or the market as Williamson called it (Williamson, 1979). This concept of market versus hierarchy is being increasingly replaced by the idea that markets and hierarchies are two extremes on a continuum between which there are several forms of organizations presenting characteristics of both basic types. This applies to mergers, but also to business relationships.

Business relationships

Business relationships as an answer to these developments

During recent years, an increasing number of companies have been joining forces in the form of business relationships.

> A business relationship is understood to mean a consensus ad idem between two or several parties, entered into for a particular

period, where mutual rights and obligations are laid down and recognized by the parties involved. For the purpose of this study the term 'business relationships' denotes all dealings a company has with other companies which constitute more than a once-only agreement. Whether a certain agreement can be defined as a business relationship depends on whether mutual rights and bligations have been determined by the participating parties.

Relationships between companies which belong to the same concern are not considered as business relationships.

Business relationships can vary greatly in terms of their nature and the areas they relate to. The relationships may be either formally structured (e.g. by a joint-venture or contract) or verbally agreed upon. The partners may work together to develop activities, each partner may specialize in a particular activity, the partners may supply products or services to each other or contract-out production and services to each other. Examples of business relationships include cases where:
- the company recruits or trains new employees in cooperation with other companies;
- the company buys, sells, exports etc. jointly with other companies;
- the company develops new products or production techniques in cooperation with other companies;
- the company permanently contracts-out its bookkeeping activities to an external accounting or administration bureau;
- the company has a permanent relationship with a bank which finances all its activities;
- the company has an agreement with a leasing company for leasing of production resources etc.;
- the company has an agreement with a permanent supplier, client or service company that all purchases/sales/services be conducted through this company;
- the company has an agreement to produce goods or semi-manufactured products for a permanent client, or the company contracts-out such production to another company;
- etc.

Various forms of motivations can be given for entering into such business relationships. On the one hand, the above-mentioned developments in the environment have created interesting opportunities for companies. Modern developments are often so complex and demand so much effort from companies, that it becomes evident that the opportunities offered by these developments could be better exploited by working together with others to be able to respond to these developments adequately. By joining forces, a positive synergic effect can be realized and an optimum advantage achieved. This approach for entering into relationships can be characterized as active and offensive.

On the other hand, the above-mentioned developments could also represent a threat to the continued existence of the company. Companies will have to meet changing wishes and needs. Because the go-it-alone strategy is not possible for some companies, cooperation with others can provide the answer. Business relationships based on these considerations have a more passive and defensive character.

Advantages and disadvantages of business relationships

Possible advantages. The advantages of entering into business relationships are subdivided into a number of categories (See amongst others: Porter, 1986, Contractor and Lorange, 1988, and Commandeur and Den Hartog, 1991).

Scale effects and critical mass. Some activities are rewarding only when the company has reached a certain minimal size. If growth of the company is not considered possible or desirable, such activities can be realized sooner by making joint use of them. For example, joint export efforts or joint presentations at fairs.

By developing shared activities, an increase in scale can be realized leading to a cut in costs for each of the partners. This can be realized, for example, by joint purchasing enabling negotiation for discounts, or by mutual specialization in one or more activities that represents a strong point.

Gain access to (new) know-how, skills, markets, technologies etc. Due to the mutual relationship between the developments noted above, it is necessary to have disposal of know-how, skills, capital and sales potential etc. in a large number of fields to achieve a strong competitive position. Since for most companies this is not a feasible proposition on their own, it is also possible to choose to combine each other's strong points by means of a business relationship. Partners can then make use of each other's specific areas of strength and compensate each other in less well developed areas. By joining forces benefits from distribution channels, brand names, client circles or marketing concepts developed by other parties are obtained and the company's own core competencies strengthened.

Risk reduction. By developing joint activities, the risk for partners can be reduced.

Time-saving. In relation to the above-mentioned advantages, the time-saving factor of cooperation should be mentioned. The short life span of products and technology means that the recovery time is short, thereby increasing the risk. By entering into business relationships and combining know-how, skills, market access etc. a more rapid result can be obtained.

Reduce market competition. Uncertainties in the environment and therefore competition can be reduced by entering into agreements with other parties. These agreements can also make it more difficult for new competitors to enter the market.

Reduction in dependence/ensuring resource availability. As already stated, the company is dependent on 'parties' in the environment for the supply of all kinds of resources to enable it to function. In order to obtain these resources, the company must meet the wishes and demands of these parties. To avoid having to deal with constantly changing demands, agreements can be made with these groups. By making agreements with one group, a buffer can be formed against the demands of another group.

Acting together with other companies also strengthens the position of the company in respect of these parties. As a result, the company is less dependent on the demands of the parties.

Possible disadvantages. Of course, there are also disadvantages associated with a company entering into business relationships. These, logically, are strongly related to the advantages.

Firstly, the disadvantages may emerge from the possible abuse of, for example, know-how, skills etc. by the partner(s) because companies are then aware of each other's activities. This opportunistic behaviour of the partner can affect the competitive position in a negative sense.

Secondly, companies can become dependent on their business partner.

Thirdly, cooperation necessitates coordination, viz. contracting and controlling activities, which take time and money (Commandeur and Den Hartog, 1991).

Dimensions of business relationships

The advantages and disadvantages of a business relationship depend on the implementation of that relationship. Various dimensions of business relationships may be distinguished (Kaufman, 1990).

Offensive/defensive. If a company enters into a business relationship to take advantage of the possibilities, this is regarded as an offensive strategy. Such a relationship aims at gaining an edge over competitors. On the other hand, entering into a business relationship can ensue from a defensive strategy, where the company is not able to fend off the threat represented by a development on its own.

The difference between a defensive and an offensive business relationship is only a gradual one, however. If a large number of companies choose to enter into business relationships as an offensive strategy, and realize advantages (e.g. scale increase), a situation is created in the long run where companies that did not take part can no longer compete with these alliances. Those companies are also forced into increasing their scale or they will lose viability. So, developments which presently allow an offensive approach to be taken, may in the long run require a response in order to safeguard the existence of the company.

Horizontal/vertical/complementary. Business relationships between companies in the same branch of industry and operating in similar markets are known as horizontal forms of cooperation. Examples of this include the networks of accountancy companies that operate on a worldwide scale, or cooperations in retail trade aimed at joint purchasing.

Vertical business relationships are those where companies work together and act as each other's supplier or client. The companies carry out consecutive phases in the production process, e.g. cooperation between a wholesaler and retail shops.

With complementary relationships, the activities of companies in various (commercial) branches supplement each other, e.g. cooperation between banks and insurance companies.

Aim of the relationship. Is the primary aim intended to be an exchange of resources only, or is the main aim to pool resources to reach a mutual goal?

Intensity. There are very loose forms of relationships which aim only at gearing business functions, e.g. discount systems or standards. Partners continue to carry out these functions themselves. With more intensive forms there is mutual specialization in certain business functions. Ultimately, business functions may be transferred to a jointly established company, a joint venture or purchase organization.

Legal form. A distinction can also be made according to the legal form of business relationships, such as joint ventures, franchising, licences, agencies etc.

Degree of formalization. Are there verbal agreements only, are there contracts or a share exchange leading to changes in ownership relations? This dimension is partly related to the legal form of the company.

Business function. Business relationships are possible in all markets and in all areas of business where a company is developing activities.

Market and partner choice. One or more partners could be involved in the relation, either national or international, large or small. The relationship can be aimed at the national market or at the international market etc.

Business relationships and SME

Introduction

Previously in this paper, a number of factors that play a role in business relationships were presented, based on literature. A number of steps with, to some extent, a logical sequence may be identified.
- Companies interact with parties in the environment to obtain the means necessary to function.
- As a consequence of developments in the environment, a stimulus is created to enter into more permanent business relationships with those parties.
- It is also assumed that companies make a 'rational' choice based on economic motives only; only if it is not possible to utilize the opportunities or to respond to the developments independently, will a decision be made to join forces.

In this chapter some problems that arise when applying this (mechanical) approach to business relationships of SME in practice will be indicated. In particular a different way to classify business relationships than is normally used in the literature will be proposed.

SME entering into business relationships in practice

In literature the consideration of whether or not to enter into a business relationship is treated somewhat mechanically: rational behaviour and long-term strategy are assumed to play a significant role. However, in practice for SME the situation surrounding the commencement of business relationships can deviate markedly from theoretical assumptions. A number of reasons can be given for this.

Personal preferences of the entrepreneur. In general, theory does not consider the influence that individuals exert on decisions taken within the company. Companies are regarded as impersonal entities, within which the process of balancing up the pros and cons is based only on the interests and objectives of the company.

However, as we know from behavioural theory of the firm, the wishes and preferences of the individual most certainly play a role in the process of weighing up with regard to business relationships. This relates to both managers in large companies and to entrepreneurs in SME.

For many entrepreneurs, autonomy in running a company is an important factor of attraction of entrepreneurship. An entrepreneur will therefore weigh up the effect of entering into a business relationship against his autonomy. In addition, the contracting-out of activities (e.g. bookkeeping) can relieve the entrepreneur of tasks which he dislikes. This does not necessarily have to be a consideration based on clear economic advantages, but this can give the entrepreneur more time for other activities, or offer him more satisfaction in his work (Gales and Blackburn, 1990).

Thus, not only economic motives are taken into consideration when deciding to enter or not to enter into relationships.

Short-term goals instead of strategy. In literature, business relationships are entered into mainly to realize long-term aims that are part of company strategy. Many (small) companies, however, do not operate on the basis of a(n) (explicit or even implicit) business strategy, but act on the basis of 'operational' circumstances. In this way, the long-term aims may be unclear or remain implied only. This does not mean that entrepreneurs do not enter into business relationships. Business relationships can provide a worthwhile solution even for the purpose of attaining short-term goals.

Bounded rationality. Another reason for the difference between the literature and practice lies in the fact that companies are made up of persons that are unable to act in a totally rational way (Simon, 1976). It is impossible by definition to have all relevant information at hand, to know all the alternatives and to predict the consequences of all choices available. Therefore, the individual will have to make a choice from the available information. Whether a company is large or small is not so relevant. At most, this would play a greater role for SME than for the larger international companies. This is also true with regard to entering into business relationships. An entrepreneur is unable to collect information about all developments, all alternatives, all possible partners etc.

Lack of information. This is worsened by the lack of conscious information-seeking behaviour of many entrepreneurs. Information is a very important factor when weighing up the pros and cons of entering into a business relationship. For example, entrepreneurs must have access to information on pertinent developments in their environment. The possible advantages and disadvantages of the various strategies that may be adopted (such as entering into business relationships) must be known. In addition, the likely consequences of the choice of a particular field or type of business relationship or for a particular partner must be clear. If the alternatives are given due consideration and all information available is studied, the chances of making a sound decision are highest. However, partly due to lack of time, entrepreneurs concentrate mainly on the day-to-day running of the business. Lack of information could create a situation where business relationships are not considered as a serious option in company policy.

In addition, the familiarity with possible alternatives can be limited, so that the choice whether to enter into a (particular type of) relationship can be based on incorrect information.

The entrepreneur must also be aware that a choice, once made, is not permanent. The advantages and disadvantages of a business relationship will change in the course of time. It is necessary to assess regularly whether the business relationship is still pertinent. For a company that has recently commenced and must still capture a place in the market, commercial cooperation or a close relationship with a client can be very useful. However, once the company has built up a stronger market position, has grown in scope or wishes to expand, the obligations of a relationship may become restrictive. Requirements imposed on company policy may be such that they do not allow optimal exploitation of market potential.

Classification of business relationships

The classification of business relationships in many studies is based on the formal rights and obligations of the partners. Usually, the legal aspect is used to classify business relationships (joint ventures, licence agreements etc.). This is an understandable approach, because the number of legal forms is limited and leads to a clear number of alternatives. These forms are based on legal prescriptions so that the formal rights and obligations of the parties are known in advance. Without entering into details, the various legal forms of cooperation are even classified according to the degree of autonomy of the entrepreneur within such a relationship (IMK, 1989).

But, the autonomy of entrepreneurs within a business relationship is not merely determined by the (formally) established rights and obligations, but also by practice (Gales and Blackburn, 1990). For example, the relationship between subcontractor and client certainly has an effect on the autonomy of the entrepreneur, but the magnitude of these effects depends on how this relationship is actually implemented in practice. Knowledge of the legal form of the relationship is therefore not sufficient to determine the remaining autonomy of entrepreneurs.

In addition, a link is usually (implicitly) assumed between a certain form of cooperation and one or several business functions. Supply and contracting-out are included in the consideration, particularly in the field of manufacturing, but contracting-out bookkeeping is also an example of cooperation between firms. The fact that both forms of contracting-out exert a totally different influence on the autonomy of the entrepreneur will be apparent.

As long as it is the intention to describe the difference between the various relationships in a general sense, it suffices to give an overall indication on an 'autonomy scale'. Consequently, the legal classification will suffice and the study can be based on the assumed characteristics of the various relationships. This approach is less useful however in a study, in which it is the intention to enter more specifically and concretely into the relationship between dimensions of business relationships and autonomy and market strength.

Autonomy. Aside from the degree to which the entrepreneur can organize his own work (craftsmanship) and the degree to which he can shape the company on the basis of his own preferences (internal organization), the perception of autonomy is related to the degree to which the entrepreneur is obstructed by others in his freedom to make decisions according to his own insight (and undertake action) as regards the market (entrepreneurship) (Duijnhouwer, 1990). Autonomy implies that the entrepreneur is able to make decisions and can act without having to give an account to others. The property relationships within the organization are of great influence in this respect.

The areas in which an entrepreneur perceives autonomy depend on characteristics of the firm and the personal characteristics of entrepreneurs.

There are various business functions (purchase, sales, marketing, R&D, production, personnel policy etc.) within companies. Depending on the branch of industry, one or more of these functions can be regarded as an essential (core) activity. For example, production is one of the core activities for manufacturing, while sales and marketing have that function in trade. The degree to which an entrepreneur is able to carry out the core activity independently is of great influence on his perception of autonomy. For manufacturing entrepreneurs, autonomy as regards production will therefore be essential, while for entrepreneurs in trade it is marketing and sales.

In addition to the to some extent objectively determined degree of autonomy based on the various core activities of companies, the personal preferences of the entrepreneur are also of importance. For each entrepreneur there are certain business functions which he regards as important or likes to do himself.

Various studies conducted in The Netherlands have shown that for instance entrepreneurs in crafts and small retailing companies prefer the vocational aspects and find other business functions, such as administration, bookkeeping and personnel policy, tedious (Tillaart, et.al., 1981).

Another example is the 'traditional' entrepreneur in manufacturing who aims particularly at production, while an 'innovative' entrepreneur concentrates relatively more on R&D. The degree to which entrepreneurs perceive their autonomy will therefore be influenced to some degree by their self-directing capacity with regard to the business functions they prefer.

Market strength/competitiveness. Market strength is related to the degree to which a company creates a position of power in the market and is able to respond adequately to new developments or take advantage of market potential. Positions of power can therefore be built up in all 'markets', not only with regard to sales, but also in other market areas such as capital, labour, raw materials, know-how, technology etc. If the company has a position of strength in a particular market, it will be relatively independent (compared to companies that do not have this strong position) in terms of the influence exerted by the environment, to develop its own policy. A company without a position of strength will have to adapt its policy moreto the wishes and needs of the environment, and/or is not in a position to take full advantage of the market potential. The combination of positions of power in different markets will determine the viability and competitive position of the company as a whole.

Differences exist between companies as regards the degree to which the various markets influence the competitive position of the company as a whole. The importance of a position of power in a particular market is therefore dependent on the importance of that market for the competitive position and viability of the company as a whole.

The influence of business relationships on autonomy and market strength. The information given above indicates that autonomy and market strength are strongly related to business functions and markets. To start with the business function to classify business relationships seems the most obvious approach to studies into the connection between business relationships, autonomy and market strength.

Business relationships can reinforce market strength and the competitive position of companies. By entering into business relationships, some of the influences out of the environment can be neutralized and a possible competitive edge and better response to developments can be achieved.

Whether and to what degree a business relationship can reinforce the market strength of a company is primarily dependent on the business function (i.e. the market) to which the relationship applies. If this is one of the core activities (e.g. the production function in manufacturing), this may reinforce the competitive position of the company more than when this involves another function (e.g. canteen management).

The degree to which the entrepreneur experiences a change in his autonomy is also dependent on which business function is affected by the relationship. If this concerns one of the core functions (in the light of the branch of industry or preference of the entrepreneur), a greater influence will be exerted on autonomy than when it relates to a secondary function.

Some research findings

The field survey

The survey was carried out in eight European countries, i.e. The Netherlands, Austria, Switzerland, Denmark, Finland, Great Britain, Portugal and Ireland. Entrepreneurs in two sectors, road transport and metal products industries, were requested to fill in a postal questionnaire to provide information about the characteristics of the companies, their business relationships and the effect of these relationships on their autonomy and their competitive position.

The survey is based on the assumption that developments in the environment of the business could prove reason to enter into business relationships. As there are significant differences between sectors as to the degree to which businesses are confronted with certain developments, it was decided to limit the research to two sectors. This made it possible to compare businesses within one sector without having to take into account other circumstances or developments which could distort the picture too much (ceteris paribus condition). However, this also implies that the results of the survey cannot be applied to other sectors without restriction.

Two sectors are included in the field survey:
- firms manufacturing metal products;
- road transport (haulage) firms.

The manufacturing branch of industry is being confronted by increasing quality requirements imposed by clients and a greater complexity of production techniques. The road transport firms are facing requirements in the field of integrated services, the concentration of larger companies and an increase in scale, due to the impending European integration. These industries have sufficient reason to enter into business relationships and should provide interesting data for the study.

Linkage between the literature and research findings

Developments in the environment as a stimulus to enter into business relationships. The study started with the assumption that firms are being confronted with a number of developments in the environment which demand a strategic action of the SME entrepreneur. One of the major developments is the increasing influence on the company's decision-making exerted by various parties in the environment. Indeed, the entrepreneurs (90 per cent) in the survey indicate that they increasingly have to take account of the requirements of other parties, like the government, employees, suppliers, customers etc., in their decision-making. Partly as a consequence of these developments entrepreneurs (41 per cent) feel threatened in their independence.

Business relationships as a response to these developments. In the literature it is stated that business relationships are a possible means to cope with the increasing influence. From the survey it can be concluded that entering into a business relationship is indeed a possibility to reinforce the company's position in dealings with third parties (69 per cent). This is indicated very broadly: both firms with and without business relationships affirm this statement.

Characteristics of firms which have entered into business relationships. Many (70 per cent) small and medium-sized enterprises (SME) have entered into business relationships. There are little differences between the two sectors.

On average, companies maintaining business relationships are more market-orientated and show a more dynamic management profile as they put more emphasis on competitive factors and on information-gathering activities, including contacts in informal networks. This is coupled with more confidence on the part of the entrepreneurs in the future of the firm. They regard developments within their environment more as opportunities than as threats.

Motives to enter into business relationships. In the literature it is assumed that improving the competitive position of the company is a major important motive to enter into business relationships. As was indicated before, in practice SME entrepreneurs do not act completely according to these assumptions.

Though there are clearly parallels between the key factors for the competitive position of the firm (product quality, customer relations, service) and the motives to enter into business relationships (upgrading quality, acquisition of new customers) in the survey, there are some marked differences as well. Apparently there are other motives than improvement of the competitive position involved as well. Though these other factors are not explicitly incorporated in this study, one could think of contracting-out activities the entrepreneur does not like (e.g. administration, bookkeeping) or areas in which entrepreneurs are almost forced to enter into relationships (e.g. with a bank for financing).

Furthermore, entrepreneurs are indeed concerned with the influence on their independence as a consequence of entering into business relationships. This element is important in research concerning cooperation and SME.

Experiences with business relationships. The areas where firms currently maintain relationships are mostly related to essential business functions. So manufacturers cited most frequently purchasing, domestic sales and manufacturing activities, while hauliers stated transport, purchasing, sales and repair/maintenance activities. Nevertheless, many companies are engaged in relationships concerning administration/bookkeeping and financing/credit facilities.

The overall opinion about business relationships is very positive (85 per cent) for those entrepreneurs engaged in a relationship. This is not remarkable because most (75 per cent) of the firms report an improvement of the company's competitive position as a result of the business relationship.

From the literature it was assumed that entrepreneurs are reluctant to enter into relationships because of expected limitations of autonomy. However, although partners have some influence on the choice of strategy, autonomy remained the same in general. And even when autonomy decreased, this was not perceived to be a problem because of the improvement of the competitive position. In some cases autonomy in terms of decision-making even increased as a result of the business relationship.

Some 25 per cent of the entrepreneurs list areas in which they do not wish to enter into relationships, partly because they do not expect positive effects and partly because they do not tolerate any outside influence in this area. These areas particularly relate to staff management. However, almost 75 per cent of these entrepreneurs do have relationships in other areas.

The entrepreneur's overall opinion of the relationship is determined by two countervailing effects: the entrepreneur's valuation of the improvement in competitiveness of the firm is partly offset by the influence of the partner on decision-making and the assessment of the importance of changes in autonomy. In general it can be said that the influence on the choice of strategy and decision-making is accepted, provided that the business relationship leads to an improvement of the competitive position of the company.

The exception to this is formed by relationships in the area of administration/bookkeeping or finance/credit, where a great influence on the choice of strategy still results in a positive opinion on the whole even if no improvement in the competitive position was realized. Obviously, these relationships have to fulfil completely different requirements than relationships in other areas. In the case of administration/bookkeeping companies do not expect these relations to have an important impact on the company's competitive position. In the case of finance/credit the relationship is absolutely inevitable for the continuity of the firm so any influence on strategic decision-making is accepted out of necessity.

Differences between the two sectors. Transport companies seem to offer somewhat less resistance to business relationships than manufacturing companies. Transport companies have already entered into business relationships slightly more frequently and have somewhat fewer objections in principle to business relationships. However, few differences can be found between the characteristics of those transport companies that do join forces and those that do not. The reason for not entering into business relationships is not so much due to the characteristics of the entrepreneur (owner etc.) or of the company (size etc.), but is based on other factors. Although the competitive position of transport companies has not improved more often than those of manufacturing companies, and they are subject to a greater level of influence from, and greater dependence on their business partners, transport firms nevertheless express a positive opinion about their relationships with the same frequency as manufacturing companies.

Conclusions

Business relationships are entered into partly as a possibility to respond to developments in the environment. By entering into business relationships an entrepreneur wants to keep a grip on the influence of parties in the environment and to improve competitiveness.

1. Entering into business relationships indeed is a way for SME to cope with the developments in a firm's environment. The entrepreneur can stay in the driver's seat, even when the influence from parties in the environment is increasing. Although all firms seem to agree to this advantage, some firms have not entered into relationships yet.
2 Though it is only measured in a subjective way, the results of this study show an improvement of the competitive position of firms as a result of entering into business relationships.
3. Entrepreneurs who have entered into business relationships perform better both in employment and turnover development than their colleagues who have not. However, the causality of this relation is not clear, because these are also the entrepreneurs showing a more dynamic management profile, using more sources of information etc. Probably it is the market-orientation of the entrepreneur which has realized the better performance as well as the decision to enter into the business

relationship.

However, entering into business relationships can have negative implications for entrepreneurs as well. One of the most important negative consequences for SME entrepreneurs is the possibility that their autonomy in decision-making is reduced. Therefore, some entrepreneurs are reluctant to enter into relationships with other firms.

4. The reluctance of some firms to enter into business relationships can be the result of thoroughly weighing up the pros and cons. If that is the case it is of no use to persuade an entrepreneur to enter into a business relationship. In most cases however, a lack of good information about the consequences of business relationships appears to be the most important reason: firms without business relationships have more fear as regards the influence on autonomy and decision-making than firms with business relationships. So, firms which have entered into business relationships do not experience influence on autonomy at all, or when there is an influence on autonomy, firms do accept that because of the improvement of the competitive position; they have learned to manage the influence of others on strategic choices.
5 . Entrepreneurs do accept more influence on strategic decision-making by others and do accept a smaller improvement of the competitive position in some areas than is true for other areas. This is especially the case if the relationship is inevitable (e.g. with a bank) or if the relationship concerns an area of minor importance for the entrepreneur or for the enterprise.

Contrary to what normally is assumed in literature, more formalized relationships are not better for competitiveness or worse for autonomy than less formalized relationships.

6. The closeness and the legal status of a business relationship are less important than the functional area of the relationship in determining the impact of that relationship on the firm's competitive position and on the autonomy of the entrepreneur. Verbal agreements, for example, sometimes have much more influence on the competitive position than more formal contracts. The impact depends both on the enterprise and

on preferences of the entrepreneur himself. An entrepreneur should keep this in mind when choosing a particular form and area of relationship.
7. However, it appears that the magnitude of the influence on competitiveness is interrelated with the closeness of the relationships: the closer and formalized the relationships, the bigger the chance on great improvement or great decline of the competitive position. Probably the entrepreneur chooses a formalized form if he expects a major influence of the relationship on competitiveness.

Obtaining information about the possibilities and consequences of business relationships is very important, firstly because of removing the prejudices and secondly because of preventing the entrepreneur to make the wrong choice. Weighing up the pros and cons of entering into a business relationship, and including autonomy in this decision-making process, is possible only if alternative strategies are known and available. One of the possibilities for entrepreneurs to obtain information about business relationships is to use their normal sources of information.
8. The accountant/bookkeeper and the bank are major sources of information for all entrepreneurs. However, they are not reported to be involved when entering into business relationships.

To generate competitive enterprises or to increase the economic performance of firms it is not sufficient to stimulate cooperation between firms. Whether the entrepreneur considers cooperation as a strategy to improve competitiveness depends on his strategic orientation.
9. Entering into business relationships is considered to be a response to developments in the environment of the enterprise. It is therefore necessary that the entrepreneur observes these developments. Thus, stimulating information-seeking behaviour of entrepreneurs (so the entrepreneur observes developments) is a prerequisite for stimulating business relationships.
10. Activities to improve the strategic orientation of entrepreneurs should parallel activities to stimulate business relationships between firms.

Business relationships are not stable but develop over time. So do the

enterprise and the goals of the enterprise.
11. Therefore, the business relationship has to be reconsidered every now and then, to investigate whether goals of the enterprise and goals of the relationship still match. An adviser (e.g. accountant) can help the entrepreneur to remember this.

Methodological lessons for future research

12. Most research into cooperation and business relationships only considers the improvement of the competitive position to be relevant for the decision as to whether or not to enter into relationships. After weighing up the possible advantages and disadvantages a decision is supposed to be taken whether or not to enter into a relationship. This is partly due to the fact that these studies mainly consider big firms run by managers instead of entrepreneurs. In SME however, the personal opinion of the entrepreneur is of particular importance. This research has shown that except for motives concerning the competitive position of the company other motives are relevant for SME entrepreneurs as well.
13. As a consequence of the above the valuation of a business relationship by SME entrepreneurs will not be based only on the improvement of the competitive position. It appears from the survey that the influence on decision-making and autonomy is an important factor as regards the decision to enter into and the valuation of the relationship.
14. Because the functional area of the business relationship especially appears to influence the competitive position of the company as well as the perception of influence on autonomy of the entrepreneur, the business function as a focus of study is essential.

Notes

1. The international study has been performed by Ulrich Aschoff (Switzerland), Bill Clarke (Ireland), Arjen Frentz (The Netherlands), Leif Jakobsen (Denmark), Mariano dos Santos (Portugal), Adam Strange (England), Dietmar Roessl (Austria), Frits van Uxem (the Netherlands)

and Jukka Vesalainen (Finland). The author has coordinated the research.

The full report of the international study can be ordered at the EIM and costs ECU 25.

2. So partly this shift is real, but partly it is caused by registering the same economic activity (e.g. printing) in the service industry instead of in the manufacturing industry.

Bibliography

Commandeur, H.R. and G.J. den Hartog (1991), 'Voor- en nadelen van strategische samenwerking' (Advantages and disadvantages of strategic alliances), *Economisch Statistische Berichten*, vol. 76, nr. 3819, 31 July

Contractor, F.J. and P. Lorange (1988), *Cooperative strategies in international business*, Lexington Books, Massachusetts/Toronto

Duijnhouwer, A.L. (1990), *Management en groei* (Management and growth), EIM, Zoetermeer

Gales, L.M. and R.S. Blackburn (1990), 'An analysis of the impact of supplier strategies and relationships on small retailer actions, perceptions and performance', *Entrepreneurship theory and practice*, Fall

IMK (1989), Gids voor *internationale samenwerking* (Guide for International Cooperation), IMK, Diemen

Kaufman, F. (1990), *Europaische Kooperation, eine Strategie für den Mittelstand* (European cooperation; a strategy for SME), Mittelstand an der Schwelle zum EG-Binnenmarkt '92, Bonn

Levine, S. and P.E. White (1961), 'Exchange as a conceptual framework for the study of interorganizational relationships', *Administrative Science Quarterly*, No. 5

Pfeffer, J. and G.R. Salancik (1978), *The external control of organizations; a resource dependence perspective*, Harper and Row, New York

Porter, M.E. (ed.) (1986), *Competition in global industries*, Harvard Business School Press, Boston

Simon, H.A. (1976), *Administrative behaviour*, Free Press, New York

Tillaart, H.J.M. van den, H.C. van der Hoeven, F.W. van Uxem and J.M.

van Westerlaak (1981), *Zelfstandig Ondernemen* (Independent Enterprising), ITS, Nijmegendent

Williamson, O.E. (1979), 'Transaction cost economics, the governance of contractual relations', *The Journal of Law and Economics,* Vol. XXII (2), October

10 The small and middle-sized enterprise in cross-national joint-ventures: A way of inducing renewal and increasing viability

Hallgeir Gammelsaeter and Bjorn Guvag

Abstract

The paper discusses the necessity for renewal and change in the autonomous SME, and questions whether the problems of SMEs can be alleviated by establishing international joint ventures. The management and ownership conditions necessary for establishing viable international joint ventures in which learning can take place, are outlined. Finally, a review of the literature on the experiences with Japanese subsidiaries or Japanese partners in international joint ventures highlights some of the problems SMEs may confront in cooperating with an international partner.

Introduction

The establishing of international joint ventures is often recognized as a way independent companies exchange technology for market entry. For small and medium sized enterprises (SMEs), alliance with an international partner is seen as a way of bringing in expansion capital and getting access to international markets. The benefits on the part of the SMEs are the ability to expand the business and getting access to established sales and distribution networks.

The international joint-venture is not, however, a panacea to international success. Many SME owners or entrepreneurs see dangers and disanvantages in such alliances. They are not willing to risk their freedom as entrepreneurs and the unique technology of the enterprise by joining a partner that might have in mind a future take-over of the SME.

The focus of this paper is not whether the international joint-venture is a convenient vehicle for market entry or access to new technologies as such. Rather, the focus will be on the potential of the international joint-venture for inducing strategic as well as technological and managerial change in the autonomous manufacturing SME. Our point of departure is that international joint ventures can represent powerful arenas for cross-cultural learning. The question is *how* and *under what conditions* this can take place.

The paper starts out with briefly explicating the position taken on the question of the transferability of organizational practices across national cultures. Second, we discuss the necessity for change and learning in the SME in general. Third, we discuss what management and ownership conditions are necessary for establishing international joint ventures in which learning can flourish. Fourth, we review the meagre literature available on the experiences with Japanese partners in international joint ventures.

On cross-national transferability

Within the field of cross-national organizational research there are at least three different theoretical perspectives implying different answers to the question of the transferability of organizational or managerial systems and tecniques accross national cultures. Child & Tayeb (1983) hold that there are sharp differences between a radical political-economy perspective, a cultural perspective and a contingency perspective.

According to a radical political-economy perspective, differences between national cultures is secondary to influences on organizational practice deriving from characteristics of the political-economic system, i.e. feudalist, capitalist, socialist etc. Given that the nations in question are parts of the same system, organizational practices that are in accord with the political-economic system may be successfully transferred, although they may take different forms within different national cultures.

Within the cultural perspective, differences between organizational practices in different nations are explained as the consequence of specific national cultures. Emphasis is put on stable nation-specific value systems and social institutions as mechanisms of perpetuating these value systems. Transferability across nations is questioned on the ground that organizational practices are imbedded in national cultures. Instead of copying other nations, each nation should find its own distinct way to reach the same goal (the principle og equifinality).

The essence of the contingency perspective is that there exists a level of rational administration, depending on the organization's contingencies, that it is imperative to reach in order to ensure the survival of the organization. What accounts for rational administration is based on performance requirements, irrespective of national cultures or economic-political systems as such. Those organizations that best adapt their organizational practices to contingencies, have the best prospects for the future. Organizational practices is understood as universal in the way that they may be transferred between organizations within different nation-cultures. Successful copying, however, will depend on the receiving organization's ability to learn and implement practices invented within other national cultures.

The position taken in this paper is that organizational systems and techniques may be successfully transferred between nations, if not in its pure form, at least as adaptations. For some practices, differences in national cultures and social structures may cause severe difficulties and unsuccessful implementation. Other practices may be transferred and adapted to more easily (Kool & Lengnick-Hall, 1985). Thus, we do not believe that national cultures and social structures should be conceived of as monolithic configurations implying that there is always a close tie between those configurations and practices in organizations. We share Smith's (1988) view about Japanese industrial practices, namely that the "*composite ideal*" of Japanization "*is rarely, if ever, fully realized in any company practice -even in Japan*" (p.48). Different national cultures can have similar or common values that facilitate cross-national learning and adaptation of single organizational practices.

Enforcing renewal and change in the autonomous SME

The question of SMEs in joint ventures is readily turned into a question of the autonomy and survival of the SMEs. Is there any reason to maintain the autonomy of the SME once it has succeeded in inventing a new product and attracted the attention of larger companies capable of developing and selling the product worldwide? Should not the owners sell out and let the SME become a subsidiary of a larger enterprise?

Motives for autonomy

Our concern is not what might be the proper strategy of the owners of the SME, selling out or maintaining autonomy. After all, a lot of SMEs are subsidiaries already. We recognize, however, that there are a number of reasons for retaining the autonomy of the SME. The owners of SMEs, especially an entrepreneurial owner-manager, may not primarily have profit motives for running the business. Achievement, or the satisfaction that comes with creating, may often be the primary motive (Smith & Miner, 1983). Owners, not to speak of unions and governmental authorities, may also prefer that the enterprise is kept going within national or even local borders to retain employment and knowhow. Take-over by a larger multinational company may treathen these objectives. Thus, there is a fair number of legitimate objectives motivating stakeholders to work against external control of the SME.

The need for additonal managerial competence in the SME

At the same time as those involved in the SME try to guard the business from being sold out, the SME often faces problems that are difficult to handle satisfactorily without bringing in external partners. The classical problem is how to raise extra funds to expand activities, be it R&D or the marketing, selling and distribution of products or services. The problem we would like to emphasize, is the need for SMEs to bring in additional managerial competence. According to a life-cycle perspective on organizational growth (e.g. Greiner, 1972, Normann, 1975, Kimberly and Miles, 1980, Adizes, 1987, d'Amboise & Muldowney, 1988), small businesses go through various growth stages, each confronting the business with different requirements on management practices. To each stage are coupled different problems, threats and possibilities. Managerial competencies that are desireable and successful in managing the specific contingencies met in one stage, may be misplaced or even cause damage in another (Norman, 1975, Miller & Friesen, 1983, Adizes, 1987).

The managerial problem is even more important if the transition between stages is critical for the survival and further growth of the company (Normann, 1975, Kilmann & Covin, 1989). As some authors argue (e.g. Greiner, 1972, Mintzberg, 1984), the solution to the problems posed in one stage appears to contain forces that threaten to destroy the same solution once implemented, thus sowing the seed for another transitional crisis. SMEs, then, may now and then confront situations that demand deep transformations in strategy, structure and management. Such transformations may demand new ways of perceiving, thinking, and behaving (Kilmann & Covin, 1989).

In every organization there exists a set of values, beliefs, norms and attitudes which constitute the reality of organizational members. Normann (1975) refers to this as the system of ideas. He claims that the main reasons for organizational crises is the misfit between this system of ideas and the organization's actual situation.

Organizations' perceptions are never totally accurate, however. Organizations scan and interpret some aspects of their environments while ignoring others. Organizations may be seen as interpretation systems regulating what information is important to monitor and process (Daft & Weick, 1984). In small businesses, the values and beliefs of the entrepreneurial manager may constitute this system. In larger organizations the managerial team may represent a collective mindset. Organizational crises are often explained as occurring from perceptual distortions that cause managers to take inappropriate actions (Starbuck et al., 1978). Top managers may rationalize and defend their choices (Wildawsky, 1972), even in the face of negative feedback (Staw, 1981). Cognitive simplification processes, in some respects functional, may operate to reduce uncertainty, eliminate contradictions and paradoxes and thus attention to vital information (Schwenck, 1984).

Although the personality of the founder may be critical for the survival of the firm during its formative stages of its development, at later stages the founder's or entrepreneurial manager's psycological identification with the enterprise may cause heavy problems (Barry, 1980). Need for complementary expertise and a more formal organization structure may be ignored. Although growth may require delegation of decision-making, for instance, owner-managers are often reluctant to share power, even when they are obliged by law to do so (Geeraerts, 1984).

The problem of being "*blinded by its purposes*" (Quinn, 1990) is not confined to dominant and entrepreneurial owner-managers in small businesses. Teams of homogenous managers in SMEs may also be unable to sense and heed important changes taking place inside as well as outside the firm. In any case, growth in SMEs as well as in larger enterprises may require renewal through changes in management. Weinshall (1971), among others, contends that an exchange of the chief executive may be necessary to achieve this. A more ideal path, requiring an integrative top manager at the outset, is creating and recreating managerial teams consisting of heterogeneous individuals (Gammelsæter, 1991). It is nevertheless suspected that managerial renewal in SMEs often comes about as a result of mergers or acquisitions. The question is if not renewal through international joint ventures might sometimes have been a better alternative.

Although processes of organizational learning and change are difficult to create and nourish in general, SMEs suffer from some disanvantages compared to large companies. One disadvantage may be the lack of middle management. In many large companies middle management constitutes the channel through which changes in markets and technologies are monitored. In Japanese companies middle management is often looked upon as the company's acummulated compentencies (Prahalad & Pucik, 1989). Although inconsistent with our heroic theories of leadership, in Western companies middle managers may also act as the real change agents (Gammelsæter, 1994).

The lack of a tier of middle managers also makes it difficult to deliberately build countercultures into the organization. Surely, this may not frequently be accomplished, or even tried, in larger companies either. Still, Nonaka (1988) claims that Japanese companies nourish change by building *coexisting counter-cultures* into their organizations. Honda, for instance, is well known for a culture in which confrontation is encouraged among employees, regardless of function, level or rank. The belief is that contradictions, when stimulated and regarded positive, is necessary to produce new approaches.

Contrary to large firms whose actions and performance are scrutinized by many stakeholders, including the press, SMEs often suffer from the disadvantage of having boards of directors made up of members that are hardly interested in the operations of the enterprise. While the fate of large enterprises is a public matter, SMEs may go bankrupt with little more than a note in the local newspaper. Consequently, board members do not have to possess the requested ability or alertness to have a seat in the board. This often renders the general manager in situations where there is neither advice, nor airing of different perspectives or alternatives. Moreover, in family businesses, the boards may often be characterized by nepotism.

The international joint venture as a source of competence

Through joint ventures with international partners, SMEs may not only obtain expansion capital or access to new markets. Of equal importance may be the access to new perspectives and complementary or additive competence. This can of course be obtained with national partners also. In small countries with small home markets, like in the Scandinavian countries, potential national partners may not exist, however. And when potential national partners do exist, an alliance with an international partner may be preferable. Kuhn (1989), for instance, argue that American mid-size companies should seek strategic alliances with foreign, especially Japanese, partners. His argument is that medium size can mean competitive advantage in many consumer and industrial markets. As the mid-sized companies do not posess all the competencies necessary for continued success in hypercompetitive international markets, strategic alliancies, like joint ventures, should be established with foreign companies.

Ownership and managerial conditions for learning and change

Harrigan (1985) defined the joint-venture as a new entity established by to separate partners, like a child with two parents. Tyebjee (1988), however, argues that the claim for two parents is an unnecessary constraint which excludes situations where one partner buys an equity position in an existing enterprise, i.e. an operating division or subsidiary of another firm. We think Tyebjee's definition is the most applicable to SME joint ventures. Although SMEs may be born by two parents, a joint-venture may also be created when an external partner buys a substantial equity in an autonomous SME. In this case, the SME's original owner(s) may be regarded as the other partner.

As briefly mentioned in the introduction, the joint-venture may represent dangers as well as benefits for the SME. We propose that a viable joint-venture in which learning and change conditions prevail and the autonomy of the SME is preserved, will be contingent on characteristics of the ownership and management of the SME. Table 1 outlines what conditions are likely to occur when SMEs with different ownership and management characteristics establish joint ventures with larger companies. In reading table 1, we would like to remind the readers that the dimensions of management and ownership in real life are not dichotomic but continual. Thus, the four quadrants in table 1 outline very rough, if not extreme, conditions.

On the ownership dimension we roughly distinguish between concentrated and dispersed ownership. When ownership is *concentrated*, the SME is owned by one or a very small number of shareholders with clear intentions to keep the business independent and autonomous. This situation is most likely when the SME is owned by a larger company pursuing a hands-off strategy in dealing with its subsidiaries, an owner-manager, or by the Government. When ownership is *dispersed* there is a large number of shareholders, no one controlling the business entirely. This is a situation likely to occur i.e. in 3rd or 4th generation family-owned SMEs.

Table 1 Typology of conditions posed by characteristics of ownership and mangement in joint ventures between SMEs and larger partners

	Concentrated ownership	Dispersed own
Entrepreneurial management	*Joint-venture arena for exchange* I	*Rare and very unstable for organization* II
Professional management	*Joint-venture arena for learning and change* III	*Joint-venture arena for suspicion and infighting* IV

On the management dimension we distinguish entrepreneurial from professional management. *Entrepreneurial management* is management dominated by one manager acting as an entrepreneur. The entrepreneurial manager is characterized by a strong achievement motivation and likes to make his or her own decisions (McClelland & Winter, 1969). Mintzberg and Waters (1983) describe the entrepreneur as carrying "*a personal vision in a brain*", a vision that "*may sometimes get partly articulated, but for the most part remains locked inside the brain*" (p.64). Coupled to this preference for autonomy in decision-making may often be a craft orientation (Smith & Miner, 1983), a preferance for technical issues. Although the entrepreneur formally acts as a general manager being in charge of all the necessary functions in the enterprise, in practice he or she primarily focuses on the visionary and technical aspects of the business.

By *professional management* we understand a team of managers employed by the owners to run the business. Contrary to the entrepreneur, the professional top manager concentrates on the business as a whole. He or she is a general manager building a team of professionals around him or her to take care of different functional activities. Compared to the entrepreneur, the professional manager is more apt to lean on the advice of the subordinates and to adopt a planning mode of strategic decision-making (Mintzberg & Waters, 1983).

When crossing the dimensions of management and ownership characteristics, we get four quadrants proposing different conditions for establishing viable joint ventures between SMEs and larger companies (table 1). We propose joint ventures may be formed in the quadrant I, III and IV situations. In the quadrant II situation the joint-venture is unlikely to prevail for very long. SMEs with an entrepreneurial manager and at the same time dispersed ownership may be rare. The reason is that the entrepreneurial manager will vie for total control, thus putting the owners in the untolerable position to take risks on the entrepreneurial manager without having a say in strategic decisions.

In situations in which the SME has an entrepreneurial manager and centralized ownership (quadrant I), most likely in SMEs where the entrepreneur is also the dominant owner, we propose that joint ventures may be formed as arrangements where the SME exchanges market entry and investment capital for products and technology. The joint-venture may be formed by the external partner buying a minority of the SME. We will expect that the dominant owner, especially if an entrepreneurial owner-manager, will guard against the partner being too influential in the development and production processes in the enterprise. The joint-venture, then, will be an arena for exchange of complementary products and services, more than an arena for joint efforts in improving all parts of the value-added chain in the business. The main reason for keeping cooperation on arms-length, will be the entrepreneurial manager's need for freedom and autonomy to be truly entrepreneurial.

In situations in which the SME has a professional manager and centralized ownership (quadrant III), most likely in SMEs owned by another company or by the Government, we propose that the conditions will be good for learning and innovation through cooperation with a venturing partner. The combination of having one or a few dominant owners and a professional management, puts the SME at "equal" terms with the larger partner. Fear of being taken over by the larger partner is generally suppressed, provided the original owner's strategy is to retain the enterprise. This will be likely especially when the Government owns the SME. Unlike the entrepreneurial manager who depends on full autonomy to develop the business, the professional top manager is more likely to invite the venturing partner into the enterprise to improve and develop the business on the basis of the partner's know-how as regards experiences with other enterprises, the marketing of the products etc.

When the ownership of the SME is dispersed and the management is professional (quadrant IV), the conditions for establishing joint ventures as arenas for learning and renewal are lesser than when the owners are few. Employees may fear that the large venturing partner's intention is to aquire the enterprise in order to strip, move, or close it down. The fear will be accumulated if the large company is international and unknown to the local stakeholders. After all, the venturing partner will soon be the major owner of the SME. The insecure situation can easily cause suspicion and infigting within the company. The professional manager may choose to cooperate with the venturing partner, either to try to hinder aquisition, to diminish the harm made to the enterprise if the venturing partner bids for the majority of the shares, or to secure his or her own career in the partner company. The workers may be anxious about the arrangement, feeling unconvinced that the manager is dedicated to the task of securing their employment. If, on the other hand, the manager fights for the autonomy of the enterprise, he or she will be apt to resign as soon as the new partner exposes intentions of controlling the business. The conditions necessary for partners to commit themselves to cooperative efforts based on mutual trust, are not very likely to be present in any of these situations.

The reasoning above implies that SMEs in the quadrant III situation are most likely to gain from joint ventures with international partners. Nevertheless, we should not ignore the possibility that the formation of joint ventures in quadrants I, (II) and IV impose changing conditions on the SME. The most likely situation, given that the SME is not taken over by the partner, is that the venturing partner press on for creating quadrant III conditions, either by working for a further concentration of ownership, or by interferring with the owner-manager. Such transitions may take time, however.

The prospects of joint ventures with the Japanese

Joint ventures between Japanese and Western companies are focused in much of the literature on international joint ventures. One reason for this is of course the last centuries' success of the Japanese, including the growing Japanese investments in Western countries. Another reason is that the Japanese historically have been more willing than American and European multinationals to accept a minority position in a local firm. In contrast to Western companies which prefer to secure control and profits through ownership, the Japanese are more inclined to control through technology, informations and knowhow flows (Gregory, 1978).

Yet another reason for focusing on Japanese-Western joint ventures is the fact that many of the last years management fads, JIT (just-in-time management) and TQM (total quality management) to mention what is probably two of the most popular, have their origin in observations of the Japanese way of managing. As Smith (1988) points out, "*Japanization may usefully be understood to refer to programmes of industrial innovation inspired by a set of standards or ideals extrapolated from some aspects of Japanese practice, as observed by some observers*" (p.48). The question is whether Japanese-Western joint ventures are convenient vehicles for Westeners to adopt such practices.

The particular question that concerns us is whether SMEs in joint ventures with Japanese partners are able to adopt or adapt to Japanese, or "ideal", practices that improve their chances of growth and survival. Further, it is of interest to know what factors and processes inhabit or facilitate cross-national learning and change through the formation of international joint ventures. Unfortunately, the literature on SMEs' experiences with international joint ventures is meagre, especially studies that focus on the joint venture's impact on organizational or managerial practices in the SME. Experiences reported on joint ventures formed by large companies are more frequent, although not abundant. The same can be said about experiences reported on wholly owned subsidiaries of Japanese companies. Although these are not equivalent to joint ventures, similarities are present, for instance in the necessity of blending managerial styles, paying attention to industrial relations etc. In the following we review available literature on joint ventures with the Japanese in general, also including experiences with Japanese subsidiaries, in order to locate factors that may facilitate or hinder that SMEs learn from their international partner.

In a critical article concerning management practices of Japanese subsidiaries overseas, Negandi et al. (1985) identify five problem areas in which clashes between national backgrounds have surfaced. These are Japanese centralization of decision-making, low confidence in employees, low level of trust for local managers, ceiling on promotion for locally employed managers, and problems with unions and employment regulations. Before emerging on an extended review and a discussion of experiences in each of these areas, it is interesting to note the almost unison conclusion among observers that the "Japanization" of firms has improved firm effectiveness. Even Negandi et al. (1985), whose review cannot be said to romanticize the Japanese impact, state that there is no doubt that Japanese companies, abroad as well as at home, are relatively more effective than their Western counterparts. Also, in the business press both managers and employees of British-Japanese joint ventures are quoted on the improvements made in the wake of the Japanese entry. Japanese or Japanese-inspired techniques are adopted and quality and production standards are improved (Arbose, 1981, McEvedy, 1990). Likewise, White & Trevor (1983) report that a highly distinctive profile of working practices were implemented in the firms they studied. These practices, notably *"an organized and orderly approach, an emphasis on detail, an over-riding priority attached to quality, and a punctilious sense of dicipline"* (p.128) made up a structure or ensemble of interrelated parts on which the effects dwelled. That Japanese practices indeed are transferable, as these studies witness, does not mean that all Japanese practices that are known to us are implemented in overseas joint ventures or subsidiaries. Comparative studies show that there still are marked differences in systems used by the parent and the subsidiary respectively (Sin & Jain, 1987, Jain, 1990). What remains to be answered is what practices are transferable, at what costs and benefits are they transferable, and, not the least, under what conditions can the costs involved be reduced.

The autonomy of the SME in the international joint venture

The first problem area mentioned by Negandi et al. (1985) is the autonomy rendered the subsidiary (or joint-venture). Negandhi asserts that the Japanese style of decision-making in overseas subsidiaries is autocratic, thus implying centralization. Little evidence of the concensus-approach is reported. A study by Sullivan & Peterson (1982) supports the contention that trust-building in Japanese-American joint ventures is partly based on Japanese managers being in charge of operations as well as in a position to initiate and control important decision processes. Whether this is endemic for the Japanese or a general tendency of foreign partners, trust-building must be essential in any joint-venture. In Japanese-Western joint ventures, however, the manager in charge of the SME does not have to be Japanese, especially not when the Japanese partner holds the minority of the shares. The balancing of power and differences in motives between the venturing partners may turn out to influence the local manager's autonomy. For example, the general manager in a 50-50 joint-venture in Britain, reports that the autonomy left to him tends to be pretty high because the venturing partners' needs are not identical (Arbose, 1981).

The level of confidence in local employees' abilities

The second problem area mentioned by Negandhi et al. (1985) is that the Japanese tends to have a low level of confidence in the local employees' abilities, expresses in close supervision of workers. This conclusion was based on studies carried out in USA and in some Pacific countries. Gregory (1978) also reports examples of Japanese inability to integrate with local staff in joint ventures in countries like Spain and Australia. Other reports on Japanese joint ventures and subsidiaries, both in the business press (Arbose, 1981, McEvedy, 1990) and in empirical studies (White & Trevor, 1983), are more favorable. Incidentally or not, these reports are all based on Japanese investments in Britain. The general British impression is that the Japanese managers' dedication and commitment to their work, manifested in their working on the shop-floor, has bred a sense of equality among workers. In a series of comparative case-studies of Japanese subsidiaries in

Britain, carried out i the beginning of the 1980s by White & Trevor (1983), the authors even indicate that *"British managers may ... underestimate the extent to which workers are ready to reject the traditional shop-floor relationships of British industry"* (p.71). The workers expectations of what it is like to work under Japanese managers are reported to be high. This means that workers expect deep changes to take place. When changes are implemented slowly, workers show signs of impatience and disappointment. Moreover, due to the Japanese dedication to work and their work on the shop-floor, the reactions of British workers to management were more favourable the more the Japanese were present on the shop-floor. Critics were voiced of native managers who were either not living up to the standards set by the Japanese, or departing from the Japanese systems originally planned.

Trust in local managers

Negandhi et al. (1985) also argue that the Japanese have a low level of trust in local managers. What comes through in their commentary, however, is that it takes a long time to build trust because the Japanese does not trust people they do not know on a personal basis. Their confidence is not based on contractual agreements, like in the West, but on interpersonal relationships (see also Sullivan & Peterson, 1982). Local managers who are able to build a personal relationship with the Japanese managers will be treated as key local officials. Other local mangers will be kept on arms-length. The trusted local managers will, however, suffer from the problem of having to balance between two cultures and will easily find themselves in the middle of organizational conflict and miscommunication. The local manager's problem may be magnified by the problems mentioned by White and Trevor (1983), namely that local managers were not living up to the standards set by the Japanese, thereby losing the workers' respect relative to the Japanese managers. These problems were observed in wholly owned Japanese subsidiaries in Britain, but may well be present in international joint ventures also. In general, they point to the important integrating role of the general manager (Gregory, (1978). Surely, being a manager in an international firm will have to imply balancing between cultures, at least in the beginning of the partnership until "*a blend of styles*" (McEvedy, 1990, p.98) has taken place. For SMEs in particular, one of the biggest problems in joining an international partner will be the ability to find a manager who can play this integrating role.

Problems with unions and employment regulation

A fourth problem listed by Negandhi et al. (1985) is the Japanese partners' problems with unions and employment regulation, reported most frequently in developed countries. This problem, to be just, is not confined to Japanese companies (Tolchin & Tolchin, 1988). We assert that international joint ventures in which the autonomy of the SME is taken care of, violations of employment regulations is less of a problem than in subsidiaries owned by foreign companies. This is not to say that such problems will not emerge, i.e. as a consequence of changing organizational practices. The Japanese belief in and emphasis on flexible working, implying job-rotation, may for instance run counter to the systems of profession- or industry-based unions in many countries. Such constraints on the process of implementing practices that are customary in the international partner's home country, may more readily be recognized and appropriately acted upon in joint ventures. After all, in the kind of joint ventures we are taking about here, the position of local management is supposedly stronger than in subsidiaries of foreign companies.

Etnocentric staffing policies

Negandhi et al. (1985) also notice that Japanese companies are the most ethnocentric in their staffing policies, leading to a ceiling on promotion for locally employed managers. We do not regard this as a major problem in the kind of joint ventures discussed here, namely international joint ventures in which the SME keeps its autonomy. Given that SME autonomy also is the goal of local managers, it is unlikely that their vocational prospects will be closely connected to the foreign partner.

It is beyond doubt that true commited within-firm cooperation with a foreign partner is no easy task. This may not partain to cooperation with the

Japanese only. Still, it is of vital importance for organizations in general, and for SMEs especially, to secure that new and different perspectives flow into the decision-making body. Obviously, we would expect it easier to cooperate with partners located in nations with similar economic and social institutions. Apart from the fact that this is not always possible or attractive out of i.e. competance or competitive reasons, there always remains the necessity *"to be able to approach reality from each other's philosophical perspective - to understand and experience an epistemological framework different from one's own. Only then will the institutional context and the behaviour manifested within it truly be understood"* (Peterson & Shimada, 1978). Ability and will to understand the combination of values and intentions in the partner, and how it can be tied to local values and practices, is necessary to induce melting of ideas and adoption or innovation of new solutions.

Concluding remarks

In this paper the joint-venture mode of organization is introduced as a strategic option in securing renewal and innovation in SMEs. Specific problems of the SME have been highlighted, and the ownership and management conditions under which learning and change can take place, specified. A review of the literature has turned our attention to problem areas in the operation of international joint ventures. Successful cooperation with international partners may not come about without costs.

The apparent inconsistency in observations reported by different students of the Japanese impact on joint ventures or subsidiaries in different countries, is most easily explained by pointing to differencies in nation-culture and social and economic structure, and possible differences in firms' scale, ownership, managerial style, industry, market position, performance etc. There is also reason to question how representative the reports on Japanese operations in overseas companies in the 1960s-1980s are for present or future international cooperation. These experiences may be representative of an early learning-and-failing stage of Japanese globalization, rather than germane to the way the Japanese generally establish business and industrial relationships in other countries.

Unfortunately, the literature is not replete with studies on change processes of autonomous SMEs in international joint ventures. Surely, more research is needed to identify such problems. The authors hope to contribute to this reseach by investigating the change and conditions of change in a Norwegian-Japanese manufacturer of trucks.

Bibliography

Adizes, I. (1987): *Corporate Lifecycles. The Theory of How and Why Corporations Grow and Die and What to Do About it.* Ichak Adizes

Adizes I. (1979): Organizational Passages - Diagnosing and Treating Lifecycle Problems of Organizations. *Organizational Dynamics,* Summer; pp. 3-25

Arbose, J. R. (1981): Japanese Technology Saves a Welsh Factory. *International Management.* Vol 36. No.6; 41-44

Barry, B. (1980): Organizational Problems and Small Business Growth. *Management International Review.* Vol.1. No.20

Bateson, G. (1979): *Mind and Nature.* New York: Bantam Books,

Child, John and Monir Tayeb (1983): Theoretical Perspectives on Cross-National Organizational Research. *International Studies of Management and Organization,* Vol.7, No.3-4, pp. 23-70

d'Amboise, G. and M. Muldowney (1988): Management Theory for Small Business: Attempts and Requirements. *Academy of Management Review,* Vol.13, No.2: 226-240

Daft, R. L. and K. E. Weick (1984): Toward a Model of Organizations as Interpretation Systems. *Academy of Management Review,* Vol.9, No.2, pp. 284-295

Dill, William R. (1958): Environment as an Influence on Managerial Autonomy. *Administrative Science Quarterly,* Vol.2, pp. 409-443

Gammelsæter, H. (1991): *Organisasjonsendring gjennom generasjoner av ledere* (Organizational Change Through the Generations of Managers). Molde, Møreforsking Molde (doctoral dissertation)

Gammelsæter, H. (1994): Divisionalization: Structure or Process? Forthcoming in *The Scandinavion Journal of Management*

Geeraerts, G. (1984): The Effect of Ownership on the Organization Structure in Small Firms. *Administrative Science Quarterly*. Vol. 29

Gregory, G. (1978): Japanese Joint ventures Abroad. Sources of Tension. *Rivista Internazionale di Scienze Economiche e Commerciali*. Vol. 25, pp.753-774

Greiner, L. E. (1972): Evolution and revolution as organizations grow. *Harvard Business Review*, July-August, pp. 37-46.

Harrigan, K. (1985): *Strategies for Joint Ventures*. Lexington MA: D.C.Heath

Jain, S.K. (1980): Look to outsiders to strengthen small business boards. *Harvard Business Review*. Vol.58, No.4.

Jain, H. C. (1990): Human Resourse Management in Selected Japanese Firms, Their Foreign Subsidiaries and Locally Owned Counterparts. *International Labour Review*, Vol. 129, No.1, pp. 73-89

Kilmann, R.H. and T.J. Covin (1989): *Corporate Transformation*. Jossey-Bass

Kimberly, J. and R. Miles (1980): *The Organizational Life Cycle*. Jossey-Bass

Kool, K. O. and C. A. Lengnick-Hall (1985): Second Thoughts on the Transferability of the Japanese Management Style. *Organization Studies*. Vol 6. No.1; pp. 1-22

Kuhn, R. L. (1989): Japanese-American Strategic Alliances. *The Journal of Business Strategy*. March/April; pp.51-53

McClelland, D. C. (1961): *The Achieving Society*. Princeton, N.J.:Van Nostrand

McEvedy, I. (1990): Britain's Rising Sons. *Management Today*. May; pp. 98-100

Miller, D. and P. H. Friesen (1983): Successful and Unsuccessful Phases of the Corporate Life Cycle. *Organization Studies*. Vol. 4. No.4, pp. 339-356

Mintzberg, H. (1984): Power and Organization Life Cycles. *Academy of Management Review, Vol.9*, No.2, pp. 207-224

Mintzberg, H. and J. A. Waters (1983): The Mind of the Strategist(s). I S. Srivastva and Associates, *The Executive Mind.* Jossey-Bass

Negandhi, A. R., G. S. Eshghi and E. C. Yuen (1985): The Management Practices of Japanese Subsidiaries Overseas. *California Management Review*, Vol.27. No.4, pp. 93-1

Nonaka, I. (1988): Creating Organizational Order Out of Chaos: Self-Renewal in Japanese Firms. *California Management Review*, Spring; pp. 57-73

Normann, R. (1975): *Creative Management.* Stockholm: Aldus

Peterson, R. B. and J. Y. Shimada (1978): Sources of Management in Japanese-American Joint ventures. *Academy of Management Review*, Vol.3, pp. 796-805

Prahalad, C. K. and V. Pucik (1989): Can Entrepreneurs Find a Home in Big Business. *Business and Society Review.* Winter; pp. 9-12

Quinn, R. E. (1988): *Beyond Rational Management.* Jossey-Bass.

Schwenk, C. R. (1984): Cognitive Simplification Processes in Strategic Decision-Making. *Strategic Management Journal*, Vol.5, pp. 111-128

Sin, G. T. T and H. C. Jain (1987): Learning from the Japanese in Malaysia. *Euro-Asia Business Review*, No.1; pp. 41-45

Smith, D. (1988): The Japanese Example in South West Birmingham. *Industrial Relations Journal*, Vol.19, No.1, pp. 41-50

Smith, N. R. and J. B.Miner (1983): Type of Entrepreneur, Type of Firm, and Managerial Motivation: Implications for Organizational Life Cycle Theory. *Strategic Management Journal*, Vol.4: pp. 325-340

Starbuck, W. E., A. Greve and B. Hedberg (1978): Responding to Crises. *Journal of Business Administration*, Spring

Starbuck, W. H and B. Hedberg (1977): Saving an Organization from a Stagnating Environment. *In H. Torelli (eds.), Strategy + Structure = Performance.* Indiana University Press

Staw, B. M. (1981): The Escalation of Commitment to a Course of Action. *Academy of Management Review*, Vol.6, No.4, pp. 577-587

Sullivan, J. and R. B. Peterson (1982): Factors Associated With Trust in Japanese-American Joint ventures. *Management International Review.* Vol. 22. No.2; pp.30-40

Thompson, J.D. (1967): *Organizations in Action.* New York: McGraw Hill

Tolchin, M. and S. Tolchin (1988): U.S. Unions and Foreign Employers. A Clash of Cultures. *Management Review,* Vol.77, No.3, pp. 47-53

Tyebjee, T. (1988): A Typology of Joint Ventures: Japanese Strategies in the United States. *California Management Review.* Vol.31. No.1, pp. 75-86

Weinshall, T. D (1971): *Application of Two Conceptual Schemes of Organizational Behaviour in Case Study and General Organizational Research.* Berkhamsted, Hertfordshire, U.K. Ashridge Management College.

White, M. and M.Trevor (1983): *Under Japanese Management.* London: Heinemann

Wildavsky, A. (1972/73): The Self-Evaluating Organization. *Public Administration Review;* pp. 509-521

11 Japanese retail stores: Regulation, demand and the dual labour market

Jeroen C.A. Potjes, Martin A. Caree and A. Roy Thurik

In this empirical study, the regional development in number of stores in Japan is explained using legal, social, demographic and economic factors. Both demand and supply effects are found to have strong impact on change in number of stores. The efect of the Large Scale Retail Store Law seems only to be limited.

1. Introduction

The Japanese distribution system is generally considered to be inefficiently structured. The abundance of small stores is widely viewed as evidence to this. Additionally, the high number of small retail stores discourages US and EC companies to export to Japan because small Japanese stores are less inclined to sell products from unknown foreign producers [e.g. Batzer and Laumer (1989), Montgomery (1991), US International Trade Commission (1990)]. A decrease in number of stores would imply a trend towards larger stores and therefore also a promising route towards a more efficient Japanese distribution system and a more open Japanese market for European and American products. Insight is required in the determinants of the development in the number of stores. Clearly, this development is influenced by a complex of social-economic and demographic developments as well as government regulation. This study investigates the importance of a variety of determinants over the 1970-1985 period using a comprehensive data set, covering 58 shop-types and 53 regions.

Four main views on the abundance of small stores in Japan exist[1]. The most popular view, also advocated by the US Congress, concentrates on the effect of the Large Scale Retail Store Law (LSRS Law). This law favours small retailers by regulating the establishment of large stores. Caves and Uekusa (1976) and Patrick and Rohlen (1987) emphasize a supply side approach, arguing that many shopkeepers use self-employment as alternative to being unemployed. This contrasts with the demand side approach of Flath (1990) who shows that a large number of stores is economically feasible because of the small size of Japanese houses and the low degree of car ownership. Batzer and Laumer (1989) similarly stress that the Japanese customer is service- and quality-oriented, creating opportunities for nearby stores as a serviceenhancing characteristic of the distribution system. Furthermore, the traditional shopping behaviour prevails: housewives frequent neighbourhood stores on a daily basis, to buy fresh products and to get an update on the local news [Bestor (1989), Sletmo and Ibghy (1991)]. The importance of tight relations with wholesalers and clients is a fourth explanation. These tight relations create a protected environment for the retailer. Therefore, stores are able to maintain market positions and to generate a comfortable income for the shopkeeper and his family [Den Hertog, Potjes and Thurik (1992)][2].

The social-economic structure of Japan has been changing rapidly since World War II. Since 1970, houses have become larger, car-ownership has increased, consumer expenditure has increased, consumer behaviour has become more diversified, population has aged, more people have moved into densely populated areas and self-employment has decreased. These social-economic developments have had their impact on the Japanese retail structure. Among these are the introduction of supermarkets and large specialty store chains during the 1960s and 1970s. The small stores came

---

[1]See Potjes (1992) for a more detailed discussion of these views.
[2]Goldman (1991) argues that the tight relations in Japanese retailing are traditional features of the internal political economy in the distribution system. Sletmo and Ibghy (1991) claim that the close relations between retailer and client should be incorporated in efficiency models on Japanese retailing.

under pressure and in 1973 the LSRS Law came into force, putting an end to the rapid development of the superstores and specialty chain stores. In the 1980s the convenience store was introduced in Japan and it proved to be an enormous success. Flath (1990) estimated the effect of demand factors and the LSRS Law on number of stores in 47 regional areas in the year 1985. His conclusion (based on static analysis) is that free entry of large stores would not result in a serious diminution of small stores. In this paper, we extend the statistical analysis of Flath (1990). First, supply factors, such as the importance of self-employment, are included in addition to demand and legal factors also used by Flath (1990). Second, we estimate a dynamic model to investigate the effect of the rapidly changing social-economic and demographic setting of Japan. Third, our analysis uses a more extensive data set.

The outline of the paper is as follows. In the next section we expand on the different views on the Japanese retail sector and on current developments. We consecutively describe the demand for stores, the supply of stores by independent retailers and government intervention in retailing. In Section 3, we describe the determinants of the change in number of stores. We provide results of the regression analysis in Section 4 and discuss sign and significance of the determinants. Section 5 concludes the paper.

2. Japanese retail practice

The demand for stores

Flath (1990) argues that retail stores not only distribute consumer goods but also function as a warehouse for people living in the neighbourhood. Retailers perform this function, because Japanese houses are generally small. Little room is available for keeping stocks inside the house and people buy only small amounts of daily necessities. This makes it important for Japanese retailers to be located close to their clients, in order to make daily shopping possible. In recent years, however, in-house storage space has increased as houses have become larger. In 1970, the living space of a Japanese was 7 tatami mats (one tatami mat is approximately 1.5 square meter). It almost doubled to 13 tatami mats in 1985 [Japan Statistical Yearbook (1973,1988)]. Furthermore, car-ownership has increased rapidly, enabling more Japanese to shop by car instead of on foot. On the other hand, Japan has an ageing population, and elderly people are assumed to rely more on neighbourhood stores, because of their lower mobility and their preference for traditional ways of shopping.The Japanese population grew from 100 million people in 1970 to 120 million people in 1985. This growth was accompanied by a substantial growth in personal income and an increase in retail spending per person. The composition of expenditures became more varied per person, with more luxury goods and higher spending on clothing and household appliances. Furthermore, living habits became more and more differentiated [Fields (1988)], creating market niches for new types of retailing (i.e. supermarkets, convenience stores, boutiques, vending machines). The once homogeneous Japanese market [Reischauer (1977), Yoshino (1971)] became more and more fragmented [Dodwell Marketing Consultants (1988)].

The Japanese highly value services and quality products. They are keen on fresh products (in particular fish). Despite the demographic and social-economic developments the Japanese remain buying these fresh products on a daily basis. These persisting habits favour a high density of stores selling fresh products. Young people also eat fresh fish and other traditional Japanese dishes, in addition to bread, spaghetti, curry and other non-Japanese dishes. Their purchasing habit is different in that they would rather buy these products in supermarkets and convenience stores.

The supply of stores

In Patrick and Rohlen (1987), the large number of small stores is explained by peculiarities of the Japanese labour market. It is reasoned that by screening out certain groups, in particular women, and by retiring workers early, large firms create large pools of people having a high potential of starting their own firm. This duality of the labour market is described in Caves and Uekusa (1976). Compared to other available jobs, their entrepreneurial activity will give more job satisfaction and will create a higher income. Retailing is a sector in which these people have good chances because capital requirements are low, no special skills are required, and government .policies stimulate small scale retailing. Usually, these new retailers invest all their savings in the store and perceive the store as a long term investment aimed at providing a family income also after the retirement age.

The costs and profit structure of these small scale family enterprises differs substantially from that of large scale retailers. Their labour productivity, measured in total sales value per person engaged, is about half of that of the larger retail stores [Source: Census of Commerce]. The difference in productivity between small and large retail stores does not fail to affect the market share of small stores, which is in rapid decline. However, many small stores seem to survive, despite the competition of large stores [Carree, Potjes and Thurik (1992)].

Government regulations

The traditional retail institutions in Japan were the small scale family enterprises and the large, luxurious, department stores. During the 1960s, supermarkets were introduced in Japan. Many of these stores became large chain store corporations. Later, specialty chain store corporations emerged, establishing large stores selling only one product line. The large scale department stores, superstores, supermarkets and specialty stores constituted a major threat to the small-scale retailers [Dawson (1989), Dodwell Marketing Consultants (1988), Kurebayashi (1991), Maeda (1981), Tajima (1971), Yoshino (1971)].

The leading Liberal Democratic Party (LDP) in Japan has been strongly dependent upon the support of the numerous small and medium-sized entrepreneurs and their relatives. This is one of the reasons why government policies have been directed towards the protection of these small and medium-sized enterprises [Patrick and Rohlen (1987)]. Considerable political pressure from small retailers on the LDP has led to the Large-Scale Retail Store Law (LSRS Law)[3]. This law favours small stores in three ways.

---

[3]The LSRS law is discussed in Kirby (1983), Kurebayashi (1991) and Patrick and Rohlen (1987).

First, the small stores are allowed to have more flexible opening hours than the large stores. Second, the law only allows for the establishment of a large scale retail store with the prior consent of the small retailers in the area. Third, the procedures to obtain the consent of the retailers delays the establishment of the large scale stores considerably, sometimes by 10 years [US International Trade Commission.(1990)].

The position of small retailers is also strengthened by regulations that are only imposed upon large enterprises. For instance, small retailers are not obliged to administrate their transactions, pay less taxes, and do not have to collect the 3 percent consumer tax.

3. Determinants of number of stores

In this section, we shall present factors assumed to determine the change in number of stores, NUM. The determinants we consider are population growth, POP; growth in expenditures per head in the shop-type, EXP; growth in share of people living in densely populated areas, DEN; increase in car-ownership, MOB; growth in size of consumer's storage space, TAT; regulated increase in number of large retail stores, LRS; growth in share of people older than 65, OLD; and the growth in share of people that is self-employed or works in a family enterprise (all industries) on total population, SELF. For the definitions and sources of the variables we refer to the data appendix.

The variables POP and EXP constitute the changes in regional sales volume per shop-type. In periods of sales growth, entry will be higher in the retail market. We hypothesize that population growth has a higher impact on growth in number of stores than growth in expenditures does, because the capacity of a store is related to number of customers rather than to total sales value[4]. Handling of goods is usually less time consuming than contacts

---

[4]In Nooteboom (1982) and Thurik (1986), it is demonstrated that labour costs of a store are determined by the number of customers rather than by the volume of purchases per customer. In other words, labour productivity increases when average purchases per customer increase.

with the clients. This might be especially true in Japan, where retailers have close relations with their clients. Furthermore, higher expenditures are not only related to the purchase of larger quantities but also to the purchase of more expensive products of higher quality. Population growth also has a supply effect, because a growth in population implies an increase in labour supply and thus an increase in the number of potential retail entrepreneurs.

The daily shopping behaviour of the Japanese customers makes a high number of stores in the neighbourhoods economically feasible. In Flath (1990), the number of stores per household in 1985 was explained using the average size of the houses, TAT, the average number of automobiles per 1000 inhabitants, MOB, and the share of people living in densely populated areas, DEN. The rationale for the use of TAT is that in areas with small houses, people keep fewer stocks of non-durables, which means that more stores selling non-durables are needed. On the other hand, in these small houses a minimum amount of furniture is used implying fewer stores selling durables. In areas with a high number of cars per 1000 inhabitants, people can travel further to do their shopping at larger stores and usually purchase larger amounts at one time. Finally, the distance between customer and store is smaller in densely populated areas. The height of population density is inversely related to the number of stores sufficient for daily shopping practice.

We follow Flath (1990) in testing whether the growth in number of large scale stores, LRS, affects the number of stores. In Flath (1990), it is hypothesised that in areas with a large number of department stores, competition has been more severe and inefficient small stores were not able to survive, implying fewer stores. In our study, we use the change in number of stores larger than 500 square meters per main shop-type, LRS^{app}, LRS^{food}, LRS^{house} and LRS^{other}. We distinguish four main shop-types: apparel, food, housing and other shop-types. The number of department stores larger than 500 square meters is added to the number of large stores of all four main shop-types, because department stores sell products in all categories.

The ageing of the Japanese population, OLD, is hypothesized to have three effects on number of stores. First, elderly people are less mobile and do their shopping in the neighbourhood. Second, aged people are more traditional and do their shopping in the traditional small stores. Third, retired people have the opportunity to set up a store themselves from their lump sum pension [Patrick and Rohlen .(1987)]. We test whether the number of stores has grown in areas with an ageing population.

We include the regional change in share of self-employed and family workers in all industries on total population, SELF, to estimate the effect of the dual structure of the Japanese labour market on number of stores. In areas were there is a strong demand for labour in large businesses, many self-employed and family workers will change occupation and join a large enterprise. This reduces the supply of low-cost labour in retailing and diminishes incentives for small store establishment.

In summary, following the demand side approach we would expect growth of population, POP, per person expenditure, EXP, and ageing, OLD, to positively influence the change in number of stores and growth of population density, DEN, mobility, MOB, and house storage space, TAT, to negatively influence the change in number of stores, NUM. A supply side view would be supported in case population, POP, ageing, OLD, and increasing self-employment, SELF, have a positive effect on NUM, whereas the magnitude of the effect of the LSRS Law depends upon the extent to which changes in number of large stores, LRS, negatively effect NUM.

In contrast to Flath (1990), who used a stationary model to estimate the impact of these social-economic variables on the number of stores in 1985, we investigate the impact of the change in these social-economic variables in a dynamic approach to determine the impact on the level of change in number of stores from 1970 to 1985. This is of particular interest, because in this period living space per person has almost doubled, possession of automobiles has more than tripled, a growing number of people are living in densely populated areas, while the number of large scale stores almost remained stable and the percentage of people being self-employed or working in family business decreased.

4. Empirical results

We investigate the importance of the developments discussed in the preceding section, using a large data set of 58 shop-types for 53 regional entities[5] yielding a total of 3074 observations. All variables are taken in logarithms [cf. Flath (1990)]. We refer to the data appendix for a detailed description of the variables and the data sources. The .regression results are obtained by using weighted least squares with the total sales value of the respective shop-types in the respective regions as weights. Our data set has the characteristics of a panel data set, because the data have a shop-type and regional dimension. Regular estimation techniques for panel data include the technique of fixed effects [Judge et al (1985)]. Many of our exogenous variables however vary only in the regional dimension, viz. POP, DEN, MOB, TAT, LRS, OLD and SELF. Therefore we could only include fixed effects, α_{oi}, in the shop-type dimension. The following regression results are obtained (standard errors between brackets):

$$\dot{NUM}_{ip} = \hat{\alpha}_{0i} + \underset{(0.032)}{0.893^* \dot{POP}_p} + \underset{(0.011)}{0.370^* \dot{EXP}_{ip}} - \underset{(0.046)}{0.080\ \dot{DEN}_p} - \underset{(0.025)}{0.075^* \dot{MOB}_p}$$

$$+ \underset{(0.094)}{0.350^* d_i^{nd} \dot{TAT}_p} - \underset{(0.101)}{0.025\ d_i^{dur} \dot{TAT}_p}$$

$$- \underset{(0.035)}{0.138^* \dot{LRS}_{ip}^{app}} - \underset{(0.018)}{0.005\ \dot{LRS}_{ip}^{food}} + \underset{(0.034)}{0.104^* \dot{LRS}_{ip}^{house}} + \underset{(0.028)}{0.009\ \dot{LRS}_{ip}^{other}} \quad (1)$$

$$+ \underset{(0.047)}{0.122^* \dot{OLD}_p} + \underset{(0.045)}{0.132^* \dot{SELF}_p} \qquad n=3074,\ R^2=0.679$$

The population elasticity[6] is approximately 0.9. The number of retail facilities increases almost proportionally with population. This finding supports three views on Japanese retailing, the supply side explanation, the demand side explanation, and the closeness of retailer-client relations.

---

[5]The regional areas are 46 prefectures and 7 cities with more than one million inhabitants in 1970. The data cover entire Japan, except the islands of Okinawa, which have not been returned to Japan until 1974.

[6]With elasticity we mean the elasticity of the change in number of stores. i.e. the population elasticity is defined as: $\partial NUM/\partial POP$. One should bear in mind that all variables are expressed in logarithms.

Population growth implies an increase in the number of potential retail entrepreneurs and a higher demand for stores. Existing stores are not flexible enough to extend their customer capacity and keep market share, which may well be related to the close relations between Japanese retailers and their customers. The expenditure elasticity is 0.37. In shop-types and areas with growing demand new stores are needed but fewer than proportional to the growth in expenditures.

The hypothesis that growth of population density, DEN, is negatively related to growth in number of stores, NUM, is confirmed at the 10 percent significance level. The hypothesis that a higher degree of mobilization, MOB, leads to fewer stores is confirmed. The hypothesis that an increase in living space per person, TAT, leads to fewer stores selling non-durable goods is rejected[7]. In fact, a significant positive effect is found. A possible explanation for this remarkable fact is that the increase in living space is not used to increase consumer's storage capacity, leading to fewer stores, but is used by many to start a family business. This would imply that TAT becomes a supply factor.

The change in number of large scale stores per head of population, LRS, exerts a negative effect on the change in the number of stores dealing in apparel and a positive effect on stores dealing in household goods. It has no effect on the number of food and other stores. This implies that there would have been fewer apparel stores if the LSRS Law would not have been in effect. The effect of the LSRS Law on the number of food, household and other stores is not in accordance with Flath (1990). It is possible that the small retailers in these sectors have been successful in applying the LSRS Law to the extent that large scale stores only were permitted in areas where small retailers had nothing to fear of large store competition. The empirical model is not able to detect whether this is the case. However, there is no support for a strong effect of the LSRS Law, and we agree with Flath (1990) that the effect of the LSRS Law on the number of stores has only been limited and that the amendment of the law will not wipe out small stores.

---

[7]For shop-types selling non-durable goods, the dummy variable d_i^{nd} is one and it is zero for other shop-types. The dummy variable d_i^{dur} is one for shop-types selling durable goods and zero for other shop-t,vpes.

Our two social determinants, OLD and SELF both exert a strong positive effect on number of stores, confirming the hypothesis of supply side advocates that the dual structure of the Japanese labour market has a significant impact on the Japanese retail structure. The growing number of elderly enlarges the supply of potential entrepreneurial activity, while increases in job availability in large firms in manufacturing and service industries make self-employment as retailer less attractive.

5. Concluding remarks and implications

Several explanations on the abundance of retail stores in Japan have been tested in this empirical study. We conclude that the effect of the Large Scale Retail Store Law on number of stores is only limited. However, the dual character of the Japanese labour market and the demand for retail facilities have a significantly positive effect on the large number of stores in Japan. Furthermore, the results of the study allow for the argumentation that retailer-client relations are important in Japanese retailing. Extending these findings to future developments in Japanese retailing, we expect the number of stores per number of inhabitants to decline gradually. The shortages on the labour market are expected to become more and more intense, indicating the disappearance of the dual structure of the labour market. This means that fewer people are inclined to set up a store, because they can find employment in more prestigious sectors of the Japanese economy. Many small family stores will stop in the years to come, because the shopkeeper is too old and there is no successor [Suzuki (1991)]. Consumer behaviour seems to evolve slowly. Modern shop-types become more popular at the expense of small retail outlets. The amendments on the LSRS law will only limitedly facilitate the modernisation process of the Japanese retail sector.

Appendix Data

The following data have been obtained from the Census of Commerce (CoC) and the Japan Statistical Yearbook (JSY). The index i refers to shop-type, p to region and t to year.

variable	description	Source
NUM_{ipt}	number of stores	CoC 3.2
Q_{ipt}	total sales value	CoC 3.2
POP_{pt}	population	JSY
DEN_{pt}	share of persons living in densely populated area's	JSY
MOB_{pt}	number of cars per 1000 citizens	JSY
TAT_{pt}	living space per persons in tatami mats	JSY
DEP_{pt}	number of department stores larger than 500 square meters per inhabitant	CoC 3.5
LRS_{pt}^{app}	number of apparel stores larger than 500 square meters per inhabitant	CoC 3.5
LRS_{pt}^{food}	number of food stores larger than 500 square meters per inhabitant	CoC 3.5
LRS_{pt}^{house}	number of household stores larger than 500 square meters per inhabitant	CoC 3.5
LRS_{pt}^{other}	number of other stores larger than 500 square meters per inhabitant	CoC 3.5
OLD_{pt}	share of people of 65 and older on total population	JSY
$SELF_{pt}$	share of self-employed and family workers on total population	JSY

$\dot{NUM}_{ip}$ growth in number of stores from 1970 to 1985:

$$\dot{NUM}_{ip} = \ln(NUM_{ip1985}) - \ln(NUM_{ip1970})$$

$\dot{POP}_{ip}$ population growth:

$$\dot{POP}_{p} = \ln(POP_{p1985}) - \ln(POP_{p1970})$$

$\dot{EXP}_{ip}$ growth of expenditures per head in the shop-type:

$$\dot{EXP}_{ip} = \ln\left(\frac{Q_{ip1985}}{POP_{p1985}}\right) - \ln\left(\frac{Q_{ip1970}}{POP_{p1970}}\right)$$

$\dot{DEN}_p$ change in share of population living in densely populated areas:

$$\dot{DEN}_p = \ln(DEN_{p\,1985}) - \ln(DEN_{p\,1970})$$

$\dot{MOB}_p$ change in car-ownership:

$$\dot{MOB}_p = \ln(MOB_{p\,1985}) - \ln(MOB_{p\,1970})$$

$\dot{TAT}_p$ change in living space per capita:

$$\dot{TAT}_p = \ln(TAT_{p\,1985}) - \ln(TAT_{p\,1970})$$

$\dot{LRS}^k_{ip}$ change in number of large scale stores of main shop-type k;

$$\dot{LRS}^k_{ip} = \ln(LRS^k_{p\,1985} + DEP_{p\,1985}) - \ln(LRS^k_{p\,1970} + DEP_{p\,1970}) \quad \forall\ i \in k$$

$$= 0 \quad \forall\ i \notin k$$

$\dot{OLD}_p$ change in share of people older than 65:

$$\dot{OLD}_p = \ln(OLD_{p\,1985}) - \ln(OLD_{p\,1970})$$

$\dot{SELF}_p$ change in self and family employment;

$$\dot{SELF}_p = \ln(SELF_{p\,1985}) - \ln(SELF_{p\,1970})$$

References

Batzer, E. and H. Laumer (1989), *Marketing Strategies and Distribution Channels of Foreign Companies in Japan*, Boulder, CL: Westview Press.

Bestor, T.C. (1989), *Neighborhood Tokyo*, Stanford, CA: Stanford University Press.

Carree, M.A., J.C.A. Potjes and A.R. Thurik (1992), Small store presence in Japan, *Research Paper 9205*, Research Institute for Small and Medium-Sized Business in the Netherlands, Zoetermeer.

Caves, R.E. and M. Uekusa (1976), *Industrial Organisation in Japan*, Washington, DC: The Brookings Institute.

Census of Commerce (1970, 1985), Compiled by the Research and Statistics Department, Minister's Secretariat, Ministry of International Trade and

Industry, Tokyo.

Dawson, J.A. (1989), Japanese distribution; effectual yes, but is it efficient? *The Japanese Market: A Guide to Distribution*, London:, 10-23.

Den Hertog, R.G.J., J.C.A. Potjes and A.R. Thurik (1992), Retail profit margins in Japan and Germany, *International Journal of Research in Marketing*, (submitted) Dodwell Marketing Consultants (1988), Retail Distribution in Japan, Tokyo: Dodwell Marketing Consultants.

Fields, G. (1988), *The Japanese Market Culture*, Tolyo: Japan Times Ltd.

Flath, D. (1990), Why are there so many retail stores in Japan?, *Japan and the World Economy*, 2, 365-386.

Goldman, A. (1991), Japan's distribution system: Institutional structure, internal political economy, and modernization, *Journal of Retailing*, 67 (2), 154-183.

Japan Statistical Yearbook, (1973, 1988), Management Statistics Bureau and Coordination Agency (eds.), Tolyo: Japan Statistical Association.

Judge, G.G., W.E. Griffiths, R.C. Hill, H. Lütkepohl and T.C. Lee (1985), *The theory and Practice of Econometrics*, 2nd edition, New York: John Wiley and Sons.

Kirby, D.A. (1983), Government policies towards the small retail business in Japan, *International Small Business Journal*, 2, 44-58.

Kurebayashi, S. (1991), Present situation and future prospect of Japan's distribution system, *Japan and the World Economy*, 3, 39-60.

Maeda, K (1981), The evolution of retailing industries in Japan, in A. Okochi and K Shimokawa (eds.), *Development of Mass Marke-ting: The Automobile and Retailing Industries*, Proceedings of the Fuji Conference, Tokyo: University of Tokyo Press, 265-289.

Montgomery, D.B. (1991), Understanding the Japanese as customers, competitors and collaborators, *Japan and the World Economy*, 3, 61-91.

Nooteboom, B. (1982), A new theory of retailing costs, *European Economic Review*, 17, 163-186.

Patrick, H.T. and T.P. Rohlen (1987), Small-scale family enterprises, in K Yamamura and Y. Yasuba (eds.), *The Political Economy of Japan, Vol. 1: The Domestic Transformation*, Stanford, CA: Stanford University Press, 331-384.

Potjes, J.C.A. (1992), *Empirical Studies in Japanese Retailing*, Tinbergen

Institute Series, Thesis, Arnhem (forthcoming).

Reischauer E.O. (1977), *The Japanese Today: Change and Continuity*, Harvard University Press.

Sletmo, G.K and R. Ibghy (1991), Distribution and culture: The case of the Japanese retail store, *Cahier de Recherche no 91-002*, Ecole des Hautes Etudes Commerciales, Montreal.

Suzuki, Y. (1991), The Large Retail Store Law, presentation at the *Second Annual Global Marketing Conference: The Japanese Distribution System*, of the American Marketing Association, November 24-26, Honolulu, HI.

Tajima, Y. (1971), *How Goods and Distributed in Japan*, translated from Japanese by J. Seward, Tolyo: Walton-Ridgeway.

Thurik, A.R. (1986), Transaction per customer in supermarkets, *International Journal of Retailing*, 1, 33-42.

US International Trade Commission (1990), *Phase I: Japan's Distribution System and Options for Improving US Access*, USITC publication 2291, Washington DC.

Yoshino, M.Y. (1971), *Marketing in Japan: Adaptations and Innovations*, Cambridge, MA: The MIT Press.

12 Entrepreneurial strategy-making (A Norwegian shipyard facing the Soviet market)

J.A. Johannessen, A. Hauan and J. Olaisen

Abstract

In this article, the process of entrepreneurial strategy making of a norwegian shipyard gaining access to the Soviet market is described and appraised. The genesis of events prior to establishing the relationship is outlined, and so is the structure of the integrated network put in place to accomodate the exchanges of goods and services. Finally, the success of the strategy is interpreted in terms of actions on the part of the strategy- makers to develop means of monitoring their environments and implement organizational innovations that enable them to perform in a highly competitive market.

Introduction

This article is part of a larger project pertaining to an analysis of the company Sterkoder Ltd. in Kristiansund, Norway. Sterkoder is a medium-sized shipyard employing about 650 persons, that specializes in constructing advanced trawlers, special tank/chemical-carriers and offshore supply vessels. During the last couple of years, the company has been through major reorganizations as regards technological as well as organizational procedures. This paper represents an analysis of certain aspects of organizational functioning. The ambition of the project is to contribute to answering questions of the following nature: What factors, or pattern of factors, have led to an increase in productivity of work of 30% in two years? What are the basic structures, relational patterns and organizational processes producing such gains, and how do they effect the system as a whole as well as the people taking part in producing them?

Background

In 1989, the company signed a contract with a Soviet agency for a total of 15, later to become 20, trawlers to be completed by the end of 1992. This contract triggered a major technical reorganization of the shipyard as well as the launching of an ambitious productivity campaign aimed at a 50% overall increase in the productivity of work by the end of the campaign period.

Purpose

In this paper, the process of secondary strategy making is discussed. Furthermore, the efforts on the part of the company to implement a business strategy related to its task environment is analysed. Task environment is defined as the set of " competitors, suppliers, customers, and regulatory bodies with whom the organizations interacts and whose actions directly affect organizational goal attainment" (Bourgeis, 1980: 26). The discussion is focused on two aspects of strategy making at the secondary level (Bourgeis, 1980: 31): environmental scanning and objective setting.

Method

The investigation was conducted in close cooperation with people working in the company through a highly interactive, collaborative approach (Lincoln, 1985; Lincoln & Guba,1985; Lundin & Wirdenius,1990; Scott Morton,1990; Czarniawska-Joerges, 1991). Interpretations of the organizational reality is constructed through continuous and extensive dialogues with people at all levels of the company. Organizational life is characterized by multiple or counter realities that could become a source of tension, provoking innovation and creativity, or engendering disintegration anddisorganization (Putnam et. al,1983; Brown,1978; Burrell & Morgan,1982; Berger & Luckman,1967; Glaser & Strauss,1967).

The modes of dialogues were grounded on various kinds of "diversity inquiring models" ranging from multiple-question-designs to "auto-communicative inquiry" in which the persons involved totally "emptied" themselves of two years of accumulated experience of frustration, anger, despair, enthusiasm and joy associated with the major upheavals they had gone through. By alternating between overall strategic perspectives and scrutinizing certain well- defined problem-areas, we hope to obtain the kind of insight associated with the "hermeneutic circle" approach (Gadamer,1975). In our opinion, this approach is essential to the study of change processes in organizations being a kind of systems creating ample potential for "butterfly effects" while simultaneously being in need of a certain level of order and control.

About 50 interviews were conducted; the longest lasting for 10 hours with an average of 90 minutes per interview. All members of top-management were interviewed along with representatives of middle-management, engineering and operators from all areas of production. So were the present and former trade union leaders, all of which also held key positions in either production or special tasks related to worker-training programs and management of internal information. Special attention were given to the so-called "production coordinators", a local innovation aimed at bridging the gap between Engineering and Production. Additional, particularly significant information emerged from attending various formal and informal meetings, notably the weekly friday get-together of all "leading-skilled-workers", or LSWs, a company-induced innovation of a formal position somewhere between the traditional foreman and skilled workers.

The following written sources were examined: Annual reports, company newsletters for the last two years and newsletter files, official long-range-plans, group-meeting reports, project-manuals, a total of 654 so-called "change reports", or CRs, sections- and subsection drawings, procedures for the use of work-lists and material-flow-charts, written material on management principles including course-material used at management-training courses and, notably, statistics on productivity broken down by various production areas and operations.

The paper aims at reflecting some of the complexities of organizational realities by drawing on different "epistemologies" (information science, systems science, cybernetics and organizational sociology) and attempt to interpret them in terms of "holo-movement" (by analogy with Bohm,1983), thus adding a dynamic element to the static metaphor of the holography (Johannessen&Olaisen,1991).

Environmental Scanning

Environmental scanning involves here the process of contracting and financing and the maintenance of a Business Intelligence System (BIS) and is aimed at continuously developing and renewing policies and strategies.

Contracting/ Financing

In 1988, the company got an inquiry from their broker about the possibility of building a special trawler for an unspecified customer. There was no mention at that time of a "Russian connection", nor any allusions of the "Moscow Norodny Bank" being involved. By "coincidence", people from the company met the then Soviet Vice-minister of Fisheries, E.D.Shirajev, at a Technology Exhibition in Trondheim, Norway, about 150 miles from the company's home town of Kristiansund. They took contact and flew the minister in a private plane to have a look at the shipyard.

A Norwegian trawler that happened to be present for repairs was leased to take the Soviet VIP on a promotion tour (supported by ample supplies of Soviet-style refreshments). On going ashore, the Soviet official indicated that " I too would like a ship like this,.....only five meters longer".

Meanwhile, the company in Kristiansund was unaware of the fact that contact had been established between the broker, a Soviet Shipping company based in London, the Soviet Bank, also in London, and the Vice Minister of Fisheries. They eventually got a query from the broker as to whether they would be able to produce a series of five, ten, fifteen or maybe even twenty identical trawlers. Some time later, the broker leaked that the Soviets were behind the project. As it turned out, "Rider Shipping Company" which ordered fifteen trawlers and options for five more was financed by the Moscow Narodny Bank in London.

Rider Shipping is a joint-venture investment company. As far as we know, it is the first time in history that an investment company has chartered a fishing-vessel on a so -called B-boat charter. Rider has an agreement with the Ministry of Fisheries in Moscow on building ships in the West that are to be financed through "Soviet" banks like the one in London.

The Soviet have set up several shipping companies sailing under Western flags to earn Western currency. Such companies have been established in Tokio and London. From their London base, the Rider Shipping Company charters the ships to a Russian fishing company north of Japan in the city of Petropavlousk Kamtchatskij, on the Shakalin peninsula

To meet their financial commitments in Western currency, every second ship in the series is what is called a " currency-ship", e.g. they sell their catch to Japan, Korea or Singapore to get Western currency. This money is channeled to the shipping company in London who, in turn, pay the Moscow Narodny Bank in London. In this way, the impediments associated with the non-convertibility of the ruble, are circumvented.

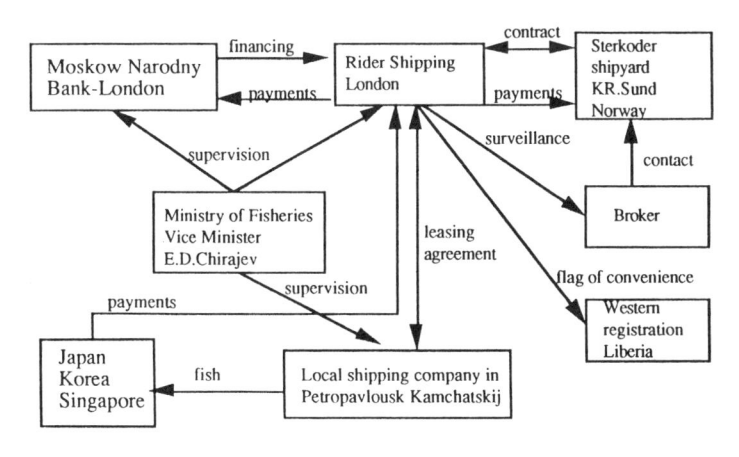

Fig.1. The "Fish for Pound" Network

The financing that the company achieved on the contract was extremely favorable. Normally, the contracting yard gets 5 % at the time of signing the contract, 10% at production startup, 5% when the ship is water- ready or launched and the rest on delivery. The Russians agreed to pay 25% down payment (500 mill. NOK) when signing the contract, and the rest upon delivery. The financial revenue thus derived amounted to 36 mill NOK in 1989.

The total Soviet fleet of trawlers consists approximately 2400 vessels. Sixty percent of these ought to be condemned within 3 years, forty percent of the rest within 3 to 5 years (Vice Minister E.D.Chirajev). The Shakalin company, for example, needs to replace 200 vessels in order to modernize its fleet which is badly worn out. Thus, the market potential is substantial. However, getting contracts in this market depends of the ability to obtain satisfactory financing backed by Government guarantees. For this particular contract, the contract with the Russians would not have emerged had it not been for the Government guaranteeing fulfillment of the contract. (Today ,1991, these guarantees are very difficult to obtain). Norway pursues a very restrictive policy with regard to Government financing of Norwegian-Soviet commercial contracts, whereas France, Spain and the Netherlands have developed an elaborate system of State-guarantees to accommodate their shipping industry.

The Shakalin company alone could conceivably keep an entire yard like Sterkoder busy for 28 years. In addition to the construction of trawlers, being able to offer management of the fleet to the Russians, is a major long term objective.

Through the depletion of the merchant marine in Norway as well as a large part of the fishing vessels, large numbers of people possessing considerable know-how in this field are today either out of work or working in other industries. The company already has a contract with the "Longva-group" on management of the fleet and training of personel. The product could conceivably be further "augmented" to include selling the catch in international markets. Competitive advantages in Norway is tied to the construction of ships that require complex technology and advanced organization, e.g. complex processes and equipment that make the price/kilo-ratio high, and managerial services connected with operations.

The most critical constraint is linked to the willingness on the part of the Government to back up contracts with State guarantees.

Business Intelligence System (BIS)

In 1990 the company worked out the specifications for the development of a Business Intelligence System expected to be completed in 1992. The system is intended to enable the company to scan internationally acclaimed statistical material from Lloyds and "Det Norske Veritas", it's Norwegian counterpart, on advanced vessels from 50-1SOtl60 meters that the company has focused on: advanced trawlers, special tank/chemical-carriers and offshore supply vessels. These are all "high-price per kilo"-ships with a high "technology to steel" ratio. When implemented, the system will be able to scan statistical material on shipping companies, types of ships, age distributions on types, competitors and their backlogs of orders etc... This way a "profile" may be derived for the "high price per kilo"-segment with respect to strategic features like:

a) shipping companies:
Who are the "high-tech" companies? Where are they localized? What is the age distribution of their fleet? When are ships to be replaced? Which brokers do they use?

b) Potential competitors:
Who are they? What is their economic situation? Are they Government supported through subsidies? Financing ? Do they have a backlog of orders?

Typically, the contract process follows this procedure:
1) Round of tender involving 12-15 yards.
2) Revisional round adjusting prices etc. 12-15 yards.
3) Technical round specifying technical requirements. 5-8 yards remain
4) Negotiating/contracting round,3 or 4 yards remain.
5) Contracting round, 1 yard remain.

The BIS system must be designed to be able to monitor all rounds on the basis of the questions specified in the system. The importance of a BIS system is inherent in this statement from the Marketing director: "If we know that we are competing with the worst-performance yards, we may add another 20 mill NOK to the contract and still get it !". The BIS provides a tool to systematically monitor the market for strategic information that, when combined with the informal information monitoring of experienced "old hands" in the industry, may create a substantial competitive edge.

Developing new strategies

What, then, would be the strategic options in Eastern European markets based on the company's experience with the Soviets ?
1. Eastern shipping companies commit themselves to the operation of "currency ships". The currency obtained may go directly to the Western bank financing the project through state guarantees.
2. A similar financial concept could be extended to the market for local maintenance and repairs. The demand for these services is going to increase with the proliferation of advanced trawlers.
3. The modernization of the fleet will lead to an increased demand for services that require management know-how.
4. A more radical strategy would be to move construction to Soviet or Eastern European sites. The lack of sophisticated technology could be overcome by transporting the more advanced tools and construction equipement, mobile cranes and section-carriers, as well as assembled parts of electronic equipement etc., to the less costly Eastern sites where the cruder construction of steel elements and outfitting could take place under supervision of Western management.

Objective Setting

Objective setting involves here: Competitors, Organizational Goal Attainment, Customers and Suppliers.

Shipyards may be divided into two main strategic categories depending on whether they pursue an **intensive** or **extensive** strategic concept. Intensive strategies require the ability to build highly specialized ships carrying sophisticated and expensive equipment that make the price-to-kilo ratio high, e.g. chemical tankers, offshore supply-vessels, freezers and fishing vessels etc. Extensive strategies involves focusing on the market for large tankers where the price of steel and labor costs are crucial competitive elements.

Throughout the last decades, the relatively higher wages in the Scandinavian countries have led to a restructuring of strategies in many shipyards, to a more intensive strategic concept.

Competitors

The Sterkoder company concentrates on the market segment of highly specialized ships of 50-150/160 meters. Their main competitors are to be found in the Netherlands, Germany, Finnland, Denmark and Spain. The far east, so far, seem to stick to a more extensive strategy. Most competitors, however, are able to take advantage of far more generous subsidies and other measures of financial support than the Norwegian shipyards.

To counter this, the Sterkoder company put an emphasis on productivity and the unique competences related to the cultural features of the nation as well as the social features of the local setting. By and large, industrial relations in Norway are favorable to accomplishing tasks that are complex and require fairly sophisticated social organization of work. The comparative advantage of such factors will conceivably increase as further integration and expansion of the EEC prohibits preferential treatment of national companies. The sharp focus on organizational procedures and management that is necessary in the competitive situation that prevails today, may prove to be an invaluable asset in a more "equal" homogenous competitive market of tomorrow.

The link between the compay's foci facing the competitors and internal goals of productivity is shown in fig.2

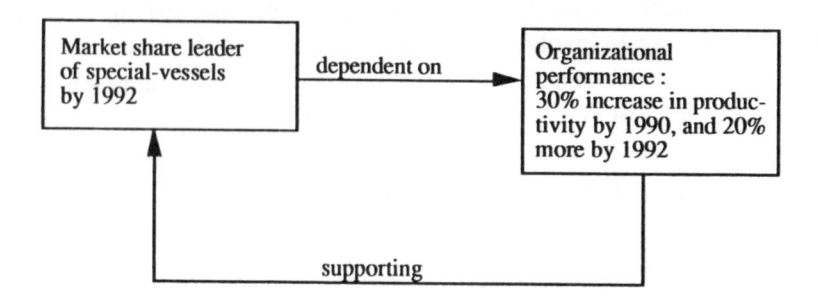

```
┌─────────────────────┐                    ┌──────────────────────┐
│ Market share leader │   dependent on     │ Organizational       │
│ of special-vessels  │ ─────────────────▶ │ performance :        │
│ by 1992             │                    │ 30% increase in produc-│
└─────────────────────┘                    │ tivity by 1990, and 20%│
           ▲                               │ more by 1992         │
           │                               └──────────────────────┘
           │                supporting                │
           └───────────────────────────────────────────┘
```

Fig.2. Productivity and strategy

Organizational goal attainment

As shown in fig.2, the company has already reached its productivity goal for the period 1988- 1990. This achievement is attributed to the combined effect of a major reorganization of the mode of production and a fundamental revision of the management philosophy. Technologically, production is now carried out in the fashion of the assembly line rather than the traditional docking. Essential features of the new mode of production are early-phase outfitting of subsections that are assembled into larger sections according to the building-block principle. To cope with the increase in governance and control requirements, CAD/CAM units are introduced that feature systemic integration through feedbackdesign and an elaborate logistics program. According to MacMillian, Hambrick and Day (1982) business performance is closely related to business strategy. The main strategy at Sterkoder for the period of 1988-1990 is related to productivity, full utilization of resources and product quality. The improvement in product quality is obtained through a routinization of organizational "bottom up" learning processes similar to quality circles, but also emphasizing individual change reporting, notably through the production coordinators.

Change in management philosophy is characterized by an attemt to overcome the shortcomings of the traditional hierarchical system of governance and control and become more heterarchical (Johannessen,J-A.,1991). The transition process has moved the company in the direction of becoming what has been named an "Information based Organization" (Drucker,1989)

Company strategy on "make or buy" decisions is permeatedy a overarching policy of internal specialization within a few select, vital areas: welding, plating and furnishing. Substantial investments are made to enable the company to perform with professional excellence in these fields.

Observing deadlines for delivery is of paramount concern to all shipbuilders. In fact, time considerations have a vital impact on the structuring of decision-making and action. There are several reasons for this preoccupation with deadlines:

a) Customers see it as a significant element of the total package of delivery. Overdue deliveries also normally have economic consequence that may seriously affect the overall profitability of a project.

b) Shortening construction time, thus increasing the turnover rate, generates net revenue. The more ships that can be buildt within a given time once the organization is aligned to a production series, the more money there will be to cover fixed costs and the more profits can be made. Saving time, therefore, is sometimes more important than saving money, at least in the short run.

Customers

The "Sterkoder-model" has itself become an important strategic asset in the market. In May 1991 the company got contract for the construction of a juice-carrier in the face of stiff competition from several other shipyards at home and abroad. The ship-owner explicitly stated that the innovations implemented at Sterkoder had a significant impact on his final decision. Furthermore, he emphasized the strong economic position of the shipyard as a result of its financial performance during the last years. Technological sophistication enables the customes representatives to closely monitor the development of the construction process. Turbulent times in the industry have made customers increasingly sensitive to any risk of orders not being completed due to economic problems. The fact that the Sterkoder company managed so well under extremely difficult circumstances within the industry further contributed to enhance their credibility and standing.

Suppliers

Altering standards of performance not only have consequences for customers. Increasingly productivity, quality and effectiveness requires the active cooperation of all levels in a chain of production that effect those measures. Subcontractors often account for a substantial amount of the cost (value) incurred. At Sterkoder, materials and equipment accounted for approximately 65% of total costs. Furthermore, keeping deadlines depends on subcontractors delivering on time. Economic efficiency, among other things, depend on minimizing inventories. The benefits associated with this, as reflected in e.g. just-in-time manufacturing, requires a vertical integration of subcontractors in the production process to an extent that is today unknown in the industry (Eisenhardt & Westcott, 1988). Rather than the typical sequential attention to goals (Cyert & March, 1963), just-in-time management requires a simultaneous attention to seemingly conflicting goals like quality and cost.

Increasing supplier-liability to end-users, combined with the considerable mutually interdependency in the subcontractor market that materialized as a result of landing the contracts, seem to have gradually altered the relationship between the Sterkoder company and its suppliers. Thus, changes in one organization may create reverberations in another due to networking effects. Furthermore, supplier responsibility is increasingly expanded to include tasks related to the "augmented product" (Porter, 1985) including services like supervising and trammg.

Conclusion

From a position of near bankruptcy, the Sterkoder company has been able to turn the tide in a slipping marked. By engaging in major innovations, a focusing of strategy, and luck (?), the company gained access to an hitherto unaccessible market in the Soviet Union. The increase in performance thus achieved further produced a competitive edge that helped improve the company's position in the market. This dual process is shown in fig.3

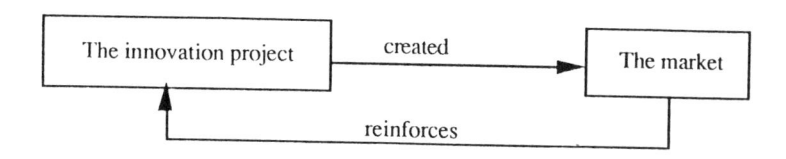

```
┌─────────────────────┐   created    ┌─────────────┐
│ The innovation project │ ───────────▶ │ The market  │
└─────────────────────┘              └─────────────┘
           ▲                                │
           └──────────── reinforces ────────┘
```

Fig.3 Innovation and market

Although the company did display pro-active behavior with respect to strategy and innovation, its market position was that of a "defender" in the typology of Miles & Snow (1978), concentrating on price, quality, delivery-time and service. In a dynamic world, however, few things are either/or. Sterkoder exhibit features of a "defender" experimenting with the possibility of becoming an "attacker". In the process, it went through a transition towards becoming one by setting new standards for delivery-time (every six weeks) and technical criteria.

References

Berger, P. & Luckman, T. *"The Social Construction of Reality"* 1967 Harmonthsworth Penguin Books, New York
Bohm, D. *"Wholeness and the Implicate Order"* 1983 ARK Paperbacks Routledge & Kegan Paul Ltd., London
Bourgeois, L.J.III "Strategy and Environment: A Conceptual Integration"

Academy of Management Review, 1980, 5, 9,: 25-39

Brown, R.H. "Bureaucracy as Praxis: Towards a Political Phenomenology of Formal Organizations" *Administrative Science Quarterly*, 23,1978 :83-105

Burrell, G & Morgan, G. *"Sociological Paradigms and Organizational Analysis"* 1982 Heineman, London

Cyert, R.M. & March, J.G. *"A Behavioral Theory of the Firm"* 1963 Englewood Cliffs,N.J.: Prentice Hall,N.Y.

Cziarnawska-Joerges, B. *"Exploring Complex Organizations. Towards an Antropological Perspective"* 1991 Beverly Hills CA: Sage, New York

Drucker, P. *"The New Realities"* 1989, Heinemann Professional Publishing, London.

Eisenhardt, K.M. & Westcott, B.J. "Paradoxical Demands and the Creation of Excellence: The Case of Just-in-time Manufacturing" In Quinn,R.E. & Cameron, K.S.:*"Paradox and Transformation"* 1988 Ballinger Publ. CompanyCambridge, Mass.

Gadamer *"Truth and Method"* 1975 Sheed and Ward, London1975

Glaser, B.G. & Straus, A.L. *"The Discovery of Grounded Theory"* 1967 Aldine, Chicago

Johannessen, J-A. "The Holographic Organization- A Design Model" *Cybernetics and Systems: An Intemational Journal,*22, 1991: 41-55

Johannessen, J-A. & Olaisen,J. "From Strategic Management to Creative Management". *International Journal of Information Resource Management*, Nov. 1991

Lincoln, Y.S. *"Organizational Theory and Inquiry: The Paradigm Revolution"* 1985 Sage, New York

Lincoln,Y.S. & Guba,E.G. *"Naturalistic Inquiry"* 1985 Sage: Beverly Hills, C.A.

Lundin, R.A. & Wirdenius,H. "Interactive Research" *Scandinavian Journal of Management*, Vol. 6,1990

MacMillian, I.C., Hambrick,D.C. and Day,D.L."The Product Portfolio and Profitability: A PIMS based Analysis of Industrial-Product Business" *Academy of Management Journal*, 25, 1982 :733-755.

Miles, R.E., and Snow,C.C. *"Organizational Strategy, Structure, and Process"* 1978, McGraw-Hill Book Company, New York

Porter,M. *"Competitive Advantage: Creating and Sustaining Superior Performance"* 1985,The Free Press, New York.

Putnam,L.L. et.al. *"Communication and Organizations: An Interpretive Approach"* 1983 Sage, Beverly Hills, C.A.

Scott Morton,M.S.(Ed.) *"The Corporation of the 1990's: Information Technology and Organizational Transformation"* 1991 Oxford University Press, Oxford

13 The evolution of the flexible specialisation system: Some Italian experiences

Andrea Fumagalli and Giuliano Mussati

1. Introduction

It is well recognized that the passage from the Seventies to the Eighties has represented a dramatic moment for the capitalistic economies. Different stylised facts confirm this opinion:

1. the productivity slowdown affected U.S. sconomy just during the mid-sixties and Europe at the beginning of the seventies;
2. the consensus on the keyenesian welfare policies begun- to decline in Europe at the end of the sixties through an arise of industrial conflictuality between unions and entrepreneurs associations;
3. the first oil-crisis of 1973 represent the last moment of a worsening situation, which was already ready to explode: the rise of inflation and the increasing unemployment was just the normal capitalistic way of a solution attempt. The "golden age" of the post-war period was definitely over.

We do not want to represent the economic story of that period. We'd only like to remind that the seventies represented the end of the fordistic way of production, that is the end of that productive and organizational cycle on

---

[1]Giuliano Mussati has written the paragraph 1 and 3. Andrea Fumagalli is responsible for the remaining paragraphes.

which the economic growth of post-war period was founded: the mixture of social intervention to keep demand up with an industrial organization based on mass consumption. Static scale economies together with incremental technical change was able to get high level of labour productivity and, therefore, constant increase in real wages. From an industrial point of view, the virtous circle of Kaldor-Verdoorn law was guaranteed.

The crisis of fordism is ctrictly related to the temporary decline of large companies as main economic object in determing employment, growth and technical change. The increasing role of small firms starts here, due to the contemporary decline of large companies and the diffusion of the new informatic technology.

The magic word became "flexibility", related both to technology and to labour organization. The dynamics of small firms has been analysed around this concept. Now, at the beginning of the ninties, the recessive conjuncture is highlighting a situation of crisis of the small firm world, which has to face new tupes of scale economy and technological and pro-ductive concentration.

This paper aims to analyse the dynamic of small firms in Italy in recent years, by discussing the characteristics of the new technological trajectory and the results of industrial restructuring process of the eighties, with special attention to the phenomenon of industrial district and to the evolution of the so-called flexible specialization model.

2. Flexibility, technology and labour organization

2.i.: Prologue

Peculiar emphasis has been - and still is - put upon "flexibility" as the way to get out from the productive stagnation of the Seventies. This decade represents the end of the "fordist way of production, based on a strict market hierarchy and production rigidity. That was the result of a "a rigorous standardisation of operating practises and a corresponding rigorous separation between the Organization and Methods Office and the shopfloor, between conception (design, engineering) on the one hand and manufacturing on the other hand" [1] . Taylorist revolution at the beginning of this century aimed to obtain gains in productivity in its strict meaning (physical efficiency of each operation) by the organised socialisation of collective "learning by doing". Further, an increase of the intensity of operatives' work was the second related aspect.

The immediate consequence of the fordist-taylorist pattern of industrialization deal with a rapid and prolongued rise in productivity (defined as the volume of goods produced per person) and a steady and general rise in volume of per capita fixed capital: in other words, what is commonly called "intensive accumulation" (counterbalanced by mass consumption).

The decrease of the rate of growth of productivity in the late Sixties and a growing capital/output ratio together with a worsening of the wage relations led to a fall in profitability. As Lipietz and Leborgne write [2], "the reaction of the management (through internationalization) and of State (through austerity policies) led to a crisis in employment, hence in Welfare State", with the double aims to minimize costs and weaken Unions. The less efficiency of mass production through large companies became evident to preserve profitability from decline. "Flexibility" then appeared as an adaptation to this aspect of the crisis, but the "profitability" aspect remains.

The concept of flexibility is normally used in many and diversifing meanings. Some clarifications are necessary. First of all, it is useful to divide among technological flexibility and labour flexibility.

2.ii.: Technological flexibility

The main future of technical change of the eighties is related to the introduction and spread of micro-electronics and informatic, not only within new products, but within the labour process itself. It is well known that product-innovation (home-computers, hi-fi, comunications in general) is likely to entail important cultural changes, even if from a macroeconomic

---

[1] - Leborgne-Lipietz (1987), pag. 5. See Boyer-Mistral (1978).

[2] - Leborgne-Lipietz (1987), pag. 9.

point of view we can say they do not provide a wide range of deep changes such as housing and automobile in fordism. Rather, it is the process innovations which appear to be more relevant, towards a full automatization of production organization.

We do not need to recall the effects of the introduction of automatic and/or semi-automatic production process, like CAD-CAM, robots, FMS and so on. Briefly, from an economic point of view, the new technologies have promoted the decreasing of static scale economies, the fall of barrier to entry and have encouraged the already existing process of productive decentralization, the externalization of different business functions: the result is a decrease of average size in manufacturing industries after three decades of increase.

On the other hand, new technologies have allowed a partial production automation even for small volume of output. From this point of view, small firms can result more efficient and obtain higher level of productivity at the same capital-output ratio than large companies in which transaction and indirect costs still represent a relevant share. At the same time, lower sizes allow more attention to the product quality and they are able to face the increasing level of demand differentiation better than standardized production.

Different degree of technological flexibility are possible, according to impact of new technologies, to the type of output and, in general, to the characteristics of the industry. One can highlight three main types:

1. full automatization of production: this may be the dream of a majority of bosses, faithful to the logic of taylorism. This implies the total expropriation of the direct operator from any initiative and the complete separation between intellect and monitoring functions from one side and some unskilled blue-collars serving some feeding and cleaning jobs from the other. In this case production flexibility is entirely due to and depends on the pure technology. Some attempts im this direction have been esperimented in USA and in Europe. The full robotisation with the pilot plant of Cassino and the introduction of L.A.M. system has been tried by

FIAT in Italy with not full succesfully results [3]. Some idyllic visions (mostly demagogic) like to see the future in this way and the same terrn "post-industrialism" comes from here.

2. a partial automatization of production, in which technical realisations depend on the involvement of the different components of work, both intellectual and manual. The new technologies are not able to "eliminate" the blue-collar functions but their sophistication does not allow a completely separation between execution and engeneering and design. The chance to direct production towards different outlets just due to technical innovations and flexibility lead to the building of a "know-how", whose essential properties should be systematically embedded into the hardware and software. The appropriability and cumulativeness of technical change, learning-by-doing and/or -by-using processes represent the conditions for the constant improvement of the way of production in terms of efficiency, productivity and so on. In this case, differing from the previous one, technological flexibility tries to reconnect what taylorism had disconnect: the manual and intellectual aspects of labour. This is what is called "total quality" [4].

3. the third type of flexibility is strictly connected to the output flexibility and to size. The possibility due to the new technologies to partially automathize the production even in presence of small volume of output without high cost of pay off encourage the process od decentralization and deverticalization. In this case, - as already noted - technological flexibility allows the decreasing of the size average, by giving the opportunity to small firms to become competitive from one hand and by minimizing management and indirect cost for large companies from the other.

---

[3] According to one of the Fiat major manager, "Having been created at a time when the social situation had become unmanageable, the L.A.M. is an interesting experiment which is not subject to generalization. It is an expensive sy- stem, it costs a lot, requires a lot of space and is more subject to default than less sophisticated ones" (Santilli, 1985, pag. 37).

[4] - Cfr. Aoki (1985).

Neverthless, it should be pointed out that technological flexibility is not itself the solution of the problems underlying the crisis of fordism. For inslance, contrary to an "overextimation" of the "new industrial divide" (Piore-Sabel, 1984), the flexibility entailed by electronics does not necessary imply the end of trend to technical and financial concentration of capital. Furthermore, technical flexibility to be success needs the implementation of a different labour organization, a sort of labour flexibility.

2.iii.: Labour flexibility.

It seems clear that labour flexibility is induced by technological flexibility, in the sense that technical conditions affect labour process and wage contract patterns, as it is normal in a capitalistic production.

The same characteristics of fordist system were based on the sort of counterbalancing between a rigid nexus wage-productivity due to the same production structure and a State able to redistribute income in indirect way (welfare, and so on).

The decline of fordism obviously opens the way to a rediscussion of wage collective bargaining. The monetarist shock succeded in changing the mechanism of wage formation, via delinking wage-price indexation, cuts in welfare, and so on.

The basic idea was to rebuild favourable conditions for profit, higher revenues, savings and investment. The possibility to get this result was through the renegotiation of wage contract mechanism. As big companies were too rigid and bureauchratic to face the new challenges of the crisis, so it was the wages formation.

Three alternatives are possible, according to the status of social relations:

1. the first one, which the japanese example made famous, consists in an **individual bargain** between the involvement of the worker and its sharing out of the improvements through bonus, career advantages, security of the work-place; this is the case in which labour flexibility reaches the highest degree;

2. the other alternative, examplified by sweedish attempt and some industrial agreement in Italy, France, is the **collective bargaining**. The union offers the involvement of its member in order to achieve the expected rate of growth in productivity and the quality standards, in exchange of the right to monitor working conditions and partnerships to the productivity gains; this situation implies the maintenance of high level of rigidity;
3. the third alternative is based on power relationship tolally favourable to the firms, in which Union power is minimized and the **exploitation** of labour force in term of productivity and low wages reaches its maximum: in this case, the flexibility is very high, but it represents a situation typical in many countries of the third and fourth world, in which unions organization are not allowed.

2.iv.: A taxonomy

After two decades of the emerging of the mith of flexibility, the differing experiences in the modern capitalistic economies says that flexibility is not an homogenous concept and that it empirical analysis shows different situations.

The same distinction between technological flexibility and labour flexibility (which can be specularly defined as rigidity in wage contracting) opens the way to a taxonomy, by combining them in different ways. This type of exercise has only sense if one takes account that technological conditions affect in a relevant way how wage bargain is contracted: in other words, that technological flexibility univocally affects labour flexibility:

Not all the combinations are possible in the western industrialized countries: the third case of labour flexibility (in which Trade Unions are illegal or somewhat similar) will not be considered. From this point of view, the following taxonomy can be advanced, by taking in account the most interesting cases:

a. the case of full authomatization process together with collective bargaining is the strict continuation of fordism and it was the main tendency in Europe and in USA in the late seventies. The inexistence of an adequate technology does not yet allow successful results to this type

of productive organization, since the increasing capital/output ratio is not accompanied by relevant increase in productivity. Neverthless, the end of the restructuring process of large companies, especially in Europe, and the tendency towards higher degree of concentration put this option as one of the most relevant hypothese in the future.
b. the second interesting case is a partial authomatization of production process together a more flexible wage contract through individual bargain. This situation implies an involment of workers in manufacturing and allows to optimize the microeconomical capacity of the firm to adapt volatility in demand and to obtain gains in productivity by constant capital/output ratio. From this point of view, this paradigm represents the main answer to the limit of the previous case. Contrary to the full authomatization process, the adequate technology does not necessary imply high degree of concentration and, therefore, a more rapid growth for large companies and the penalization of small firms. The japanese case represents an attempt in this direction, even it should be considered that the success of this type of productive organization lies on high rate of growth of demand and output.
c. the combination of decentralization strategies with collective and/or individual bargain in wage contract implies the existence of dualism in manufacturing. From one side, large companies adopt flexible production system by diversifying plants and establishments and from the other, small firms are mostly subcontractors or marginal, characterized by niche production.

These three types of paradigms are simultaneously present in capitalistic economies and not yet a paradigm has the supremacy on the others.

The first scenario seems for the moment not yet realistic, whilst the case b. appears much more possible. The third one is a sort of mixture of the two, with the difference that market hierachy are non put in discussion.

2.v. Flexibility and small firms

It is well known that flexibility and small firms has represented and still represents an unseparable link for many authors [5]. This idea lies upon the fact that smaller is the productive unit higher is the possibility to be flexible, greater is the chance to capture demand volability.

The implicit hypotheses is that flexibility (both technological and labour) and small firms are considered as something homogenous.

In the previous paragraphs, the concept of flexibility can have different meanings according to the considered scenario. Especially technological flexibility does not necessary imply favourable conditions for small size. Even the idea of small firm is not homogenous and, overall, completely independent from large corporations strategies. From this point of view, it is possible to suggest a taxonomy of SMEs [6]:

1. Schumpeterian **innovative SMEs**, recently founded and rapidly growing if the business idea is succesfully;
2. **SMEs in a district**, which can be defined as "smithians", based on the existence of a inter-firm network, cooperation structure, normally monoproduct;
3. **Sub-contracting SMEs,** subordinated to the investment strategies of a big corporation;
4. **Marginal SMEs**, autonomously operating in a market niche in industries with lower scale economies and barriers to entry;
5. **Specialized SMEs** in particular productions, about which they have the market leadership (es.: non generalized consumption or investment goods).

To each of this type of small firms is connected a different kind of flexibility, according to the fact that technological flexibility is more or less relevant than labour flexibility.

---

[5] - See most of literature on flexible specialization model. More in particular, Priore-Sabel (1981) and (1984), Brusco-Sabel (1981), Sabel-Zeitlin (1982), Brusco (1982) among others.

[6] - See Dosi (1988), Zanetti (1988), Fumagalli-Pompili (1990).

3. The flexible specialization model and the case of Italy

3.i.: Theoretical limits of the flexible specialization model [*]

The Italian experience represents a very good point of observations to discuss the dynamic of flexibility and small firms.

In the mid-seventies, especially after the first oil crisis, the role played in the italian industrial structure by small medium sized firms increased in a relevant way. A wide debate on the causes and origins on this phenomenon still characterizes non only the italian but also the international economic literature during the 80's [7]. The alternative explanations are mainly two:

1. according to the dualism and oligopoly literature, SME growth is considered as a transitory phenomenon, linked to a particular stage of the economic process (large corporations crisis, decrease in barriers to entry due to technical change, SME's higher flexibility, etc.); when this peculiar situation is over, the extent of the markets, the process of concentration of the new technologies due to the growth of dynamic scale economies, the loss of importance of flexibility as competitive factors only for SMEs lead to a better performance of large corporation, which are now able to gain market power, confining the small dimension in a subordinated role [8];
2. according to an alternative interpretation, growth on SMEs is the effect of a radical change in the production process and in the industrial organization and it becomes a permanent and structural character [9].

The last interpretation is particular significant with regards to the italian

---

[*] - This paragraph follows Fumagalli - Mussati (1992).

[7] - See, besides footnote (5), Landes (1987), Murray (1987), Sabel (1989), Zeitlin (1990), Pollert (1990), Amin-Robins i1991), Lazerson (1991), Fumagalli-Hussati (1992).

[8] - See Freeman-Clark-Soete (1982).

[9] - See Barca (1985).

case, where the presence of such organizative structures like "districts", "system-areas", etc. focussed the debate of the potential birth of the so-called "self-founded model" [10] . The autonomous role played by SMEs, recognized by different italian authors and especially by some foreigners, especially from United States (Priore, Sabel, Zeitlin), has led to the building of a theoretical model, that is .he "flexible-specialization model". In a productive system characterized by a sub-contracting process as it follows from the acceleration of technical change, small and medium firms are forced to specialize theirselves in some particular productions along the productive cycle. From this point of view, the "flexible-specialization model" includes all the organizational forms, like districts and so on, which are typical of italian industrial evolution during the Seventies and it is based on the existence of the following conditions [11] :

1. Changes in labour supply; the growth of "job dissatisfaction leads to the preference of self-employed jobs, even if the uncertainty is higher from one side, and the increase of the share of skilled workers on the total employment, from the other;
2. Increase in the degree of specialisation and diversification of demand, as result of the greater level of sophistication of mass consumption;
3. Increase of capital flexibility as result of technical change together with the diffusion of new techniques, which allow automatic working for small quantity of output.

It follows that:

a. in the "flexible-specialization model" the kind of technology plays a very important role, since is the technology itself which allows to diminuish the weight of scale economies and the constraints due to the existence of barriers to entry;
b. there is not a particular regional or local connotation at a general level; localism plays a role only in modelling some particular characteristics of

---

(10) - For a definition of these concepts, see Goodaman-BamfordSayer (989).

(11) - See Barca (1985) and Barca-Magnani (1989).

the productive structure or in highlightening some institutional (public, financial) constraints, which can lead to the birth of different organizational sub-forms;
c. the growth of a flexible specialized production structure needs the existence of a particular kind of small firms, in which the entrepreneurial character and dynamics is extremely high;

In conclusion, this kind of literature focusses the attention on the fact that SMEs are the best answer to the crisis of fordist model: a higher role of SMEs leads to the growth of flexible-specialized organization, which brings higher competitivity and efficiency and it is able to give a dynamic answer to the rigid and bureaucratic hierarchy induced by the dominance of the typical large fordist corporation in the last decade.

Peculiar attention has been paid and still it is to potential changes in the labour organization structure. According to an idyllic vision, the structural growth of the small firm can highlight new and different entrepreneurial models (especially in the Nec regions), which is able to lead to an overcome of the traditionally market hierarchies and competition towards form of inter-firms integration and cooperation (see, for example, the "district" experience).

Nevertheless, this theoretical literature does not deeply analyse the possibility of the whole small firms to be autonomous and independent from large companies strategies. As already seen, the disomogeneity of small firms lead to the necessity of considering different situations and the role played by flexibility in increasing the competitivness of small firms should be analysed according to the existing different contexts.

Now, the critical point of the "flexible specialization model" is that the empirical investigations refer to the first two types of SMEs (innovative and district firms), but the number of these firms is limited. Most of italian SMEs refer to the third and fourth category (subcontractors and marginals). From this point of view, the idea of an increase in the flexible and specialized production is valid, only in peculiar contexts.

Small firms which are really innovative have a small weight, moreless about 12% if only firm with less than 99 employees are considered. From Table 1, small firms which have at least adopted an innovation (whatever it is) are less than 75% of the total. If the type of innovation is considered, it is easy to see (cfr. Table 2) that only 17% has adopted an innovation through R&D function, for a total of 12%. This datum presumebly decreases if also small firms with less than 20 employess are considered. It follows that schumpeterian small firms are the minority in Italian experience.

Neverthless, at the beginning of the eighties, some researches show an increase in the number of schumpeterian small firms especially in some areas near big cities (i.e. north-east of Milano) as result of the increase of technological flexibility.

It is difficult to say if the number of this type of small firms has increased in the second half of the eighties. The growing of technological concentration and of fusions and acquisitions together with the obvious consideration that succesful innovative small firms tend to become bigger lead to hypothesize that the its share is presumibly remained constant.

For what concerns the so-called "district small firms", Sforzi (1989) estimated 57 districts areas, with an average presence of 7000-7500 firms for each districts. It follows that the estimated number of this type of small firms is about 420.000 maximum, moreless the 25% of the total number of small firms.

Therefore, small firms with higher degree of flexibility and independent from large companies strategies are less than 40% of the total. The "flexible specialization model" can be applied only to this kind of firms, which during the eighties represent the minority.

In fact, subcontractor small firms, if, from one side, are able to manage autonomously the production inputs, from the other, are subordinated in prevailing way to the large companies requirements for what concerns final prices and output. From this point of view, the increasing subordinated role played by small firms in general is highlighted by data analysis on subcontracting share. In 1983-88, given a value of 100 for medium size firms (200-499 employees), the ratio subcontracting works added value is 192,9 for small firms (20-49 employees) whilst for big firms (more than 1000 employees) it is 53.1 [12].

---

[12] - See in English, Rey (1989) and Amin (1990).

Marginal small firms represent the greatest share in italian industrial structure and they are characterized by niche production mostly in traditional industries. The degree of influence in active way on its own industry's structure is very low.

3.ii: Small firm performance in the Eighties.

Looking at the Smes performances (see Table 3 and 4), economic indicators draws upon some results of recent national surveys [13] , by presenting data from 1978 to 1988 on various performance measures for small and large firms. The data, in general, indicate that small enterprises (20-90 employees) do not compare well with their larger counterparts (more than 200 employees) in respect of productivity (output per capita), investment activity, especially after 1981. Even if the pay (real income) is lower for the small enterprises, the CLUP (Cost of labour per unit output) is higher (but decreasing). Gross profit indicators (see Table 4) shows that the early positive differentials for small firms is declining along the '80s and if ROE index is considered, there is a real overturn (from a positive differentials for small firms of points 13,6 in 1982 to a negative differential of points - 2.6 in 1988).

Some reflections can be useful:

1. technical change dynamics towards integrated systems of authomatization, increase of higher scale economies and barriers to entry due to a more relevant role played by "learning-by-doing" process in the late eighties than before, are all factors which represent source of a new kind of discrimination among Smes and bigger firms: innovative Smes, already on the technical frontier, will probably be able to grow and become larger (hence, they cannot be more considered as small), whilst the remaining small firms will probably see a reduction of their competitivness and efficiency.

2. Subcontractor Smes run the risk of increasing their dependency from

---

[13] - Source ISTAT, Yearly Bulletin on Industrial Structure.

large companies strategies, even if they are able to be technologically efficient. As already noted, the process of productive deverticalization in the Seventies, which led to an increase of the economic role of this type of Smes, no longer operates in the same directions. If tertiarization process seems now irreversible for some business functions, not the same can be said for what concerns productive stages. At the beginning of the Ninties, acuisition and fusions are the predominant strategies to monitor technology and production cycles, as externalization was in the Seventies.

3. The evidence on industrial districts is also less uncouraging for the future of small size. The italian experlence shows (10) that, with the concentration of information technology, horizontal competition is fierce, while vertical cooperation is weak. That means that inside most of the districts (see Prato), oligopolistic tendency is overcoming the previously cooperation system and, secondly, they are populated by small firms "producing the same finished or intermediate product for large subcontractors" (Amin, 1990). Moreover, and crucially, district's firms are engaged in the production of traditional consumer goods and not the high quality differentiated products. Innovative and schumpeterian SMEs are decreasing as the R&D and learning process are unilateraly dominated by size hierarchies.

In the district of Prato, according to a recent research by Nomisma, the division of work among subcontractors has decreased machinery intensity from 50% to 130% with a conseguent reduction of tarifs about 30% and the exit of the market of many small firms. At the same time, lenght of labour day has quite a lot increased, also as result of extension of transport time (from 3 to 5 hours, according to Nomisma). The transformation of a district in a hierarchical structure has led to a relevant loss of firms: in 1985, 16,839 were active in Prato, in 1991 they are 11,894 [14].

These transformations have more to do with restructuring process than with innovative activity. In fact, they are often accompanied by a higher

---

[14] - See Nomisma (1989). For some considerations on these phenomena, see Bologna (1992). See also Fumagalli-Vivarelli (1992)

degree of labour exploitation, without relevant improvement in labour and product quality. In the district of Carpi, the number of small subcontractors is about 85% of total (4.300 firms) in 1988. The average number of hours yearly worked by knitwear's craftsmen is 2,428 against 2,817 hours of weavers (that means, respectively, 9 and 10 and half hours per day, saturdays included) [15].

The recent crisis of district experience is linked to an increasing pressure on labour, as the only variable factor in cost structure. From this point of view, technical change is, unfortunately, a marginal aspect.

4. In the so-called "system areas", the changing direction of technical change in the Eighties can have a more direct effect as consequence of the "open" structure, more export oriented than district reality. The growth of international competitivness and the globalization process could lead to a brake in the dynamic of this industrial organizations.

The resulting picture is not very optimistic for the future of italian small firms structure. Once that flexibility no more represents a point of advantage respect to larger companies, the lower dimension has to face new challenges, too much similar to those of a typic and traditional dualistic model.

4. Conclusion

Which kind of conclusion can we draw from this picture at the beginning of a new decade? On our opinion, the flexible specialization model in no more valid after the second half of the '80s. The gains in productivity of large corporations, the increasing role of dynamic scale economies, the R&D expenditures as new forms of barriers to entry, the concentration of technology are all factors which previligizes the performance of large companies respect to that of small firms.

From this point of view, the economic result of the Eighties are more

---

[15] - See Lazerson (1991), pag. 127.

favorable to the neo-schumpeterian interpretation, even if some qualitative changes should be underlined, especially regarding the structure of the economic process. Manufacturing system play a lower quantitative role than before and the rise of new jobs in the tertiary sector is the confirmation of the definitive passage from a dicothomy structure, simply based on production and consumption, to a complex system of industrial and services interrelations, which needs more transactions to the consumption of the final goods. Immaterial inputs, like information, reliability, human capital, learning processes, are now crucial factors to be competitive in a market, which becomes wider and wider. Taking possession of these inputs is not costless and it origins new and differing forms of scale economies and barriers to entry. From this point of view, small firms return to face the same problems they had to face in the period of growth after the Second World War, when they played a marginal role in the accumulation process and when not, because they were operating in marginal or in particular sectors.

In the '70s "small firms flourished as the larger corporations, keen to shed high cost plants with strong unions, adopted a policy of decentralization (Murray, 1987, Amin 1990). Now there is evidence that the large firms regrouping and taking in the work previously put out to the smaller jobbing firms" [16] . Whether or not the small firms are able to survive this challenge remains to be seen, but it seems clear that it will come under mounting pressure from the conglomerates if the international competitivness increases. In this circumstances, the idea of a flexible system of production as form of a new labour organization and economic strategies (with all the implications of public policy) is strongly deteriorate and if the small firms are relatively profitable, this seems to reflect the prevalence of low wages and poor working conditions, not superior economic dynamism.

The recent facts about italian industrial relationships (stop to wage contracting till 1994 and abolition of any form of wage indexation) shows that labour flexibility has reached its maximum point, whilst technological flexibility is spread all over the industrial structure through adoption of partial automatized processes for what concerns firms on the technological

---

[16] - See O'Donnel-Nolan (1989), pag. 11.

frontiers from one side and through a wide range of organizational forms from the other.

From this point of view, the scenario is going to become predominant in Italy is characterized by the supremacy of individual bargain in wage-contracting, with a less relevant role played by Trade Unions, and a dualist productive structure, both flexible [17]:

a. an **offensive flexibility**, carried on by larger firms, according to technical change dynamics, in which competitivness and capitalistic efficiency lies on the fact to be able to capture demand volability, even in presence of standardized productive organization.

b. a **defensive flexibility**, as form of survival for most small firms, whose greater degree of dependency leads to an increment of pressure on labour force according to short term strategy.

Finally, the recent recession of 1991 has definitely pointed out the decline of small firms as principal subject of change and as "engine" of growth of output and productivity.

References

Amin A. (1990): "The flexible small firm in Italy: myths and reality", in Pollert A. (ed.) (1990).
Aoki M. (1985): "Learning by doing vs. the bounded-rational control: an approach to U.S. - Japan comparison of industrial organization", C.E.P.R. Publication n. 53, Stanford University, mimeo.
Barca F. (1985): "Tendenze nella struttura dimensionale dell'industria italiana: una verifica empirica del 'modello di specializzazione flessibile'", in *Politica Economica*, n. 1, pag. 71-110.
Barca F.- Magnani M. (1989): *L'industria tra capitale e lavoro*, Il Mulino, Bologna.

---

(17) - See Leborgne (1987).

Boyer R.- Mistral J. (1978): *Crise, accumulation et inflation*, PUF, Paris.

Bologna S. (1992): "Problematiche del lavoro autonomo in Italia (I)" in *Altre Ragioni*, n.1, pp. 197-231.

Brusco S. (1982): "The Emilian Model: productive decentralization and social integration", in *Cambridge Journal of Economics*, n. 6.

Brusco S.- Sabel C.F. (1981): "Artisan Production and Economic Growth" in Wilkinson F. (ed.) (1981).

Dosi G. (1988): "Innovazione e dinamica strutturale", in Zanetti G. (ed.) (1988).

Freeman C.- Clark J.- Soete L. (1982): *Unemployment and Technical Innovation*, F. Pinter, London.

Fumagalli A.- Pompili T. (1990): "Differenziazioni territoriali della strutturazione del processo produttivo nel settore manifatturiero italiano: 1971-81", in Mussati G. (ed.) (1990).

Fumagalli A.- Mussati G. (1992): "Italian Industrial Dynamics from the Seventies to the Eighties: some Reflections on the Entrepreneurial Activity" fortcoming in *Entrepreneurship and Regional Development*.

Fumagalli A.- Vivarelli M. (1992): "La crisi delle piccole imprese nell'attuale contesto competitivo e tecnologico", mimeo.

Goodman E.- Bamford J.- Saynor P. (1989) (eds.): *Small firms and industrial districts in Italy*, London, Routledge.

Landes D.S.(ed.) (1987): *A che servono i padroni?*, Torino, Boringhieri.

Lazarson M.H. (1991): "La subfornitura nell'industria della maglieria a Modena", in *Studi e Informazioni*, Quaderno n. 1, 1991, pp. 119-144.

Leborgne D.(1987): "Equipment flexibles et organisation productive", in *Aspects de la Crise*, CEPREMAP.

Leborgne D.- Lipietz A. (1987): "New Technologies, new modes of regulation: some spatial implications", CEPREMAP, Serie Orange, n.8726.

Murray R. (1987): "Flexible specialisation in the 'Third Italy'", in *Capital and Class*, Winter.

Nomisma (1989): *Ristrutturazione industriale e piccole imprese*, Bologna.

O'Donnel K.- Nolan P. (1989): "Flexible specialisation and the Cyprus industrial strategy", in *Cyprus Journal of Economics*, n. 2.

Piore M.J.- Sabel C.F. (1981): "Italian Small Business Development:

Lessons for U.S. Industrial Policy", MIT, Working Paper n. 288, August.
- (1984): *The Second Industrial Divide,* New York, Basic Books.

Pollert A. (1990) (ed.): *Farewell to flexibility. Ouestion of restructuring work and employment,* Oxford, Blackwell.

Rey G. (1989): "Small firms: profile and analysis, 1981-85", in Goodman E.- Bamford J.- Saynor P. (1989) (eds.).

Sabel C.F. (1982): *Works and Politics: the Division of Labour in Industry,* Cambridge, Cambridge University Press.
- (1989): "Flexible specialization and the re-emergence of regional economics", in Hirst P.- Zeitlin J. (eds.): *Reversing industrial decline? Industrial structure and policy in Britain and her competitors,* Oxford.

Sabel C.F. - Zeitlin J. (1982): "Alternative storiche alla produzione di massa", in *Stato e Mercato,* n. 5.

Sforzi F. (1989): "The geography of industrial district in Italy", in Goodman-Banford-Saynors (eds.) (1989).

Santilli G. (1985): "L'automatisation comme forme de controle sociale", *Travail,* n. 8, June.

Zanetti G. (ed.) (1988): *Alle radici della struttura produttiva italiana,* Roma, Sipi.

Zeitlin J. (1990): "The Third Italy: Inter-form cooperation and technological innovation", in Murray R. (ed.): *Technology strategies and local economic intervention,* Nottingham, Spokesmann Books, forthcoming.

Statistical Appendix

Tab. 1: Innovative activity in Italy by size: 1981-85.

Size	Firms introducing an innovation	Firms introducing no innovation
20-49	63.3%	36.7%
50-99	74.7%	25.3%
100-199	81.9%	18.1%
200-499	83.5%	16.5%
500	88.9%	11.1%
TOTAL	69.3%	30.7%

Source: Istat-CNR.

Tab. 2: Type of innovative activity in Italy by size: 1981-1985

Size	R&D	Engineering	Investment	Marketing
20-49	7.4%	15.1%	73.1%	4.4%
50-99	9.6%	17.5%	68.2%	4.7%
100-199	10.6%	18.3%	66.2%	4.9%
200-499	14.3%	16.1%	64.2%	5.4%
> 500	21.4%	29.5%	43.5%	5.6%
TOTAL	17.9%	25.2%	51.5%	5.4%

Source: CNR-Istat.

Table 3: Economic results of manufacturing firms: 1978-1988.								
	Small firms (20-99)				Large firms (>200)			
Variables	78-80	81-85	86-87	87-88	78-80	81-85	86-87	87-88
Variations % (yearly average)								
Investment (1)	6.6	2.3	5.2*	7.8*	-5.2	-1.0	10.5*	1.0*
Added Value (1)	6.1	5.8	...	...	2.0	0.7	5.2	...
Employment (2)	0.6	0.8	0.8*	2.3*	-1.2	-6.7	-1.9*	0.5*
Output p.c. (2)	5.5	5.0	3.4	...	3.3	8.0	7.2	...
Real income (3)	2.9	2.6	2.1	0.4	0.4	2.7	4.0	1.2
CLUP (4)	13.1	11.1	3.8	12.7	8.1	2.1	2.3	...
% Average share on added value								
Gross profit(5)	31.9	35.9	38.9	...	25.4	30.7	35.7	...
Investment	14.0	13.0	13.1	...	16.3	14.0	14.1	...

NOTES: (1) - At price 1980; (2) - Without C.I.G. (unemployment benefits); (3) - Deflated with consumption price index; (4) - Cost of labour per unit output; (5) - Added value - earned income; p.c. = per capita.

Sources: Istat;
* Banca d'Italia.

Table 4: Industrial Firms Profitability (%): 1982-88.							
Size	1982	1983	1984	1985	1986	1987	1988
ROI (1)							
20 - 49	15.1	13.6	14.2	13.8	13.8	13.8	12.4
50 - 99	14.7	13.4	14.3	13.8	13.9	13.0	12.3
100 - 199	14.0	12.2	11.7	12.5	12.1	12.2	11.7
200 - 499	12.7	11.7	13.1	12.8	12.6	11.3	11.3
500 - 999	12.3	11.0	11.2	10.3	11.3	10.9	11.9
> 1000	7.9	7.7	11.0	11.4	10.1	9.5	12.1
TOTAL	11.4	10.4	12.2	12.3	11.9	11.4	11.9
ROE (2)							
20 - 49	3.4	3.1	5.2	4.9	7.4	8.7	8.5
50 - 99	3.6	3.0	6.2	5.6	8.8	9.6	9.4
100 - 199	2.7	2.4	2.0	4.8	6.8	9.4	9.1
200 - 499	1.0	1.8	6.5	6.5	8.9	9.2	9.8
500 - 999	-1.0	-0.1	2.6	2.2	7.2	6.1	11.2
> 1000	-10.2	-11.4	0.4	4.0	5.0	6.3	11.1
TOTAL	-2.3	-2.9	3.2	4.6	6.9	8.4	10.0

NOTES: (1) (rectified net result + financial charges) / (internal funds + financial debts);
(2) (rectified net result) / (internal funds).

Source: "Centrali dei bilanci" databank

14 The oscillating behavior of small innovative firms: A model

Mario Raffa and Giuseppe Zollo

Summary

The paper illustrates the results of a research carried out on a sample of small Italian software firms and presents a *fuzzy firm* model for small innovative firms on the basis of the field data obtained. Their innovative behavior relies on the management of professionals, taking into account the opposite requirements of autonomy (to encourage innovation and motivation) and control (to gain reliability and productivity). During their life these small companies display an *oscillating behavior*: in the first phase their technical capabilities are mainly based on the internal expertise of the founder-entrepreneur. In the following phase the small firm opens to professionals by means of a wide range of employee-employer relationships. Finally, in the third phase the company tries to define internal routines to manage efficiently the maintenance and new releases of its products, and the relationships with a large number of customers. In so doing the small firm shifts from a maximum closing degree (the use of internal skills entrepreneur-embodied) to a maximum opening degree (where the support of external expertise prevails).

Foreword

This article presents a model of the innovative behavior of small firms, based on a decade's research carried out by the authors on a sample of small Italian software firms. The model relies on the distinction between two main features of the firm's abilities: a *certainty boundary*, defining what the firm can actually do, its memory, its rules, its routines; a *knowledge boundary*, defining the wider field of information, technologies, market opportunities scanned by the firm through its external networks.

Starting from the issues concerning the management of professionals, the authors state that small firms try to cope with the need to encourage innovation and productivity through time. Consequently, during their life, the *small innovative companies display an oscillating behavior*: in the first phase their technical capabilities are mainly based on the internal expertise of the founder-entrepreneur. In the following phase the small firm opens to professionals by means of a wide range of employee-employer relationships. Finally, in the third phase the company tries to define internal routines to manage efficiently the maintenance and new releases of its products, and the relationships with a large number of customers.

The management of professionals

We know that in a stable environment, with a long product life cycle and slow changing technology, firms may effectively exploit the strong linkages with their technological resources and select an internal development strategy. In cases where there is a very high potential for innovation, we would expect management to be oriented towards the establishment of loose linkages with their resources in order to limit the organizational effects derived from external changes. Usually, after the initial technological impulse by the inventor-founder-manager, the small innovative firms must open to external sources to sustain technological capabilities (Oakey, 1984; OECD, 1982; Rothwell, Zegveld, 1982). For this reason boundary-spanning activities are thought to be of the utmost importance to small innovative firms, especially if they are facing a turbulent environment and are engineering-oriented firms (Brown, Schwab, 1984; Galbraith, 1982; Rothwell, 1984).

As to small-sized software firms (SSFs), innovation management is strictly linked to technical personnel management (Raffa and Zollo, 1992). The behavior is barely formalized and work is carried out by groups of technicians organized into project teams. The firm has to solve some basic problems with regard to its personnel, because it cannot rely on experts' standardized skills to achieve coordination and innovation capabilities. Rather the firm must consider existing skills merely as the foundation on which new skills have to be built up, and integrate different competencies in multi-disciplinary work teams.

The differentiation of skills

At present there are a large number of categories of professional skills in software firms and in EDP departments of large companies. There are technical, organizational, and market reasons affecting this differentiation (Gallino, 1983; Kraft, 1979; OECD, 1986). The necessity to meet the varying needs of different users is the first reason for skills differentiation, because it is difficult to find the right balance between the user's need for the most friendly computer interfaces and instructions required by computer systems that necessarily have to be as close as possible to its internal structure. For this reason software firms create layers of different skills, some of them oriented towards technical hardware problems and others towards customer issues. This, together with the wide variety of programming languages available and the different application areas induces differentiated skills (Floyd, 1979; Kraft, 1979).

A second element leading to skill differentiation is the use of methodologies in software production. Methodologies, generally speaking, define the software development path and the distinction between activities, skills and responsibilities. With these tools, project managers can easily control the product implementation (Floyd, 1979; Kraft, 1979; Reifer, 1981).

A third factor contributing to differentiation is the complexity of programs (Daly, 1979; Reifer, 1981). This requires a product subdivision into increasingly simple parts (subprograms, modules, functions), for the production of which staff of graduated qualifications can be used.

In this approach crucial factors are, on the one hand, the breakdown process, which identifies small significant elements for the assignment of clear-cut tasks to every individual taking part in the development process, and establishes quality-control systems for each element of the project, and on the other, the management of work-groups, both in terms of staffing and work co-ordination (Reifer, 1981).

The integration of skills

The differentiation of professional skills and breakdown of specific stages may not be pushed beyond certain levels due to 3 basic reasons:

a) *labor breakdown* is limited by the size of the firm, by its market share, its portfolio of orders, and in general by its growth expectations. A work-group cannot be enlarged for a specific procedure and then risk being inactive for a certain period;
b) the ratio of coordination to operational activities grows as the work group expands;
c) *optimization requirements* become more problematic as breakdown increases. The optimization of a software package is not a linear function of the optimization of its single parts (OECD, 1982; Reifer, 1981).

Other aspects are also important, such as the relationship between programmer/analyst and co-workers, project leaders and users (Goldstein, 1982). Starting from these findings project managers should give each programmer/analyst complete control over a specific part of a system development project from system analysis to testing, in order to increase skill variety, task identity, autonomy, and through increased job satisfaction, high quality and productivity. Hauptman (1985) argued that software development is not only programming, but there are many additional activities such as design, maintenance, validation, documentation and many others. In other words, software development consists of "software engineering", with the typical features of an R&D activity (complex, unstructured and technologically volatile), and "software production", where the major concern is with manufacturing and productivity. From this latter perspective software projects require strong coordination and controlled interaction amongst individuals to gain the desired functionality, usability, reliability, maintainability, and flexibility of the developed system.

The management of labor relationships

The main features of SSFs can be summarized as follows: on the one hand the complexity of tasks, rapidly evolving technologies and unstructured methodologies push the management towards a policy based on loose-links and loose control over technical professionals, and on the other reliability and productivity commitments suggest the use of formal rules and regulations and a strict control over activities and technical professionals.

The resolution of innovation management issues in the engineering companies usually lies in effective management practices, good organizational structure and well-defined design methodologies (Daly, 1979). The concepts of organizational structure are meaningless to SSFs and the design methodologies are not explicit, but embodied in technical personnel, and in many cases there is no formal training of newly hired personnel. For these reasons the best solution, considering the need for control and the need to open to environmental resources, lies on the management practices of technical personnel. Past experience helps SSFs to establish the proper degree of control over activities and professionals to link the technical professional skills to the firm and to overcome difficulties arising from low motivation and high personnel turnover (Barocci, Wever, Lahey, 1983; Barocci, Wever, 1983; Gagnon, Krasner, 1990; Parden, 1981). Experience allows the exploration of the environment through technical professional people, and the acquisition of new ideas, new market opportunities and new technologies.

Autonomy and control

Quinn (1979, 1985), from the observation of many successful small technical/entrepreneurial ventures, sees a pattern in the factors leading to success. Some success factors are related to employee-employer relationships, or, to what Van de Ven (1986) calls part-whole relations. Van de Ven states that the most significant structural problem in innovation processes is the proliferation of ideas, people and transactions over time and difficulties of managing the consequent complexity. This is a major problem in large organizations, but it is also very important in small innovative firms where there is no formal organizational structure to reduce the number of transactions between management and staff. Van de Ven proposes that the management should relax its control over development unit in order to structure the proliferate parts of the innovation processes and to obtain better performances.

This point of view sheds light only on one aspect of the problem. An increasing number of authors suggest that the most effective organizations are also characterized by paradoxes, i.e. attributes that are simultaneously contradictory, even mutually exclusive (Cameron, 1986; Peters, Waterman, 1982; Quinn, Rohrbaugh, 1983). In an effective organization the opposites must exist simultaneously without one attribute prevailing on the other: they must exist in such a balance as to create the right level of tension that gives dynamism to the organization.

Feldman (1989) shows that, within an innovative organization, autonomy and control are interdependent. They are simultaneously managed in order to promote creativity and testing while integrating work and complying with the firm's constraints and goals (time, costs, specifications). From the analysis of a firm's case, Feldman draws some conclusions which are particularly interesting for this paper:

1) to produce innovation, autonomy must be exerted within a minimum framework managerial control;
2) management control is needed as a sort of switching station to regulate interaction and set and enforce priorities;

3) when control and autonomy are not in balance, a vicious circle can develop that undermines commitment to organizational goals;
4) innovation requires participants to have a highly developed sense of the legitimate possibilities of autonomy within the organization.

The management of paradoxes

The management of professionals is based on the paradox between autonomy and control. A paradox involves "contradictory, mutually exclusive elements that are present and operate equally at the same time" (Cameron and Quinn, 1988). Usually theorists, in search of rigor and coherence, try to eliminate contradictory assumptions, looking at the organizational reality as a multifaceted one, that can be adequately analyzed from several viewpoints (Morgan, 1986). Poole and Van de Ven (1989) suggest an alternative strategy, that is using tensions and oppositions to explain organizational arrangements. They suggest four different ways of working with paradoxes:

1) accept the paradoxes and learn to live with them (renouncing any further explanations);
2) assume that the horns of paradoxes operate at different levels (spatial separation);
3) assume that the horns of paradoxes operate at different times (temporal separation);
4) introduce new terms to resolve paradoxes (synthesis).

According to our experience, firms resort to all of these to deal with paradoxes. The organization is the *locus*, where provisional solutions to paradoxes are embedded.

To detect how the opposite requirements of autonomy and control are managed in order to encourage innovation, motivation, reliability and productivity we develop a model of a small innovative firm based on two assumptions:

a) the firm manages the requirements of autonomy and control by differentiating employer-employee relationships, ranging from full-time employee to external consultant. The variety of labor relationships allows the firm to balance the need to import technological information and explore new opportunities, with the opposite need of predictability of software development. Our hypothesis is that the most innovative firms display a larger variety of labor relationships than the less innovative ones. This solution corresponds to the spatial separation mode of working with paradoxes suggested by Poole and Van de Ven;

b) the second assumption is that firms do not have definitive solutions for their organizational features. Consequently they explore appropriate solutions through time, by varying the previous organizational equilibrium. In some periods the firm amplifies the dangers arising from loose control, and than tries to emphasize reliability and productivity. When these aspects outgrow themselves, the firm reverses its priority, and tries to encourage creativity and innovation. Looking at the firm's behavior over a long period of time we should find an oscillating path between the two opposite managerial practices of high control and high autonomy. Our hypothesis is that the most innovative companies display such an oscillating behavior, modifying their organization accordingly. This solution corresponds to the temporal separation mode suggested by Poole and Van de Ven.

The spatial solution: the fuzzy organization

The first assumption of the suggested model is that a wide range of labor relationships develop between the opposite requirements of autonomy and control.

For the implementation of autonomy, loose linkages and strong interactions between the firm and its environment are needed for scanning the environmental opportunities. The second requirement, control is linked with planning, predictability of production processes, and insulation from environmental turbulence, through the implementation of internal routines. Following Cameron's approach, for the firm to be effective the two requirements must not be mutually exclusive and therefore, as relationships between the firm and the external environment grow, the firm must develop internal routines. By this we mean that, as the *opening degree* increases, a higher *closing degree* is required in order to effectively process new information flows and new opportunities.

Figure 1 shows our model of SSF, where a distinction can be made between two main features:

a) a *certainty boundary*, defining what the firm can actually do, its memory, its rules, its routines;
b) a *knowledge boundary*, defining the wider field of information, technologies, market opportunities scanned by the firm.

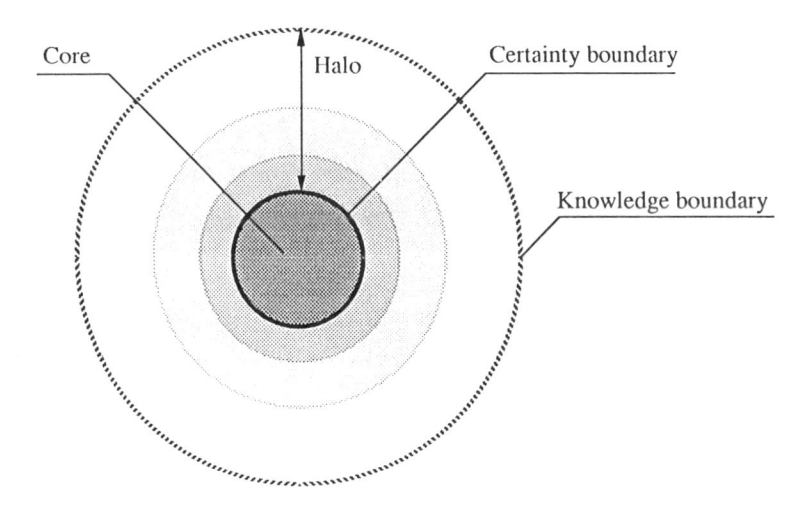

Figure 1 Fuzzy innovative firm model
Source: Raffa, Zollo, 1988

Within the certainty boundary the firm's *core* of operative procedures can be found, which enables it to achieve consistent performances. Around the core is the *halo* of fragmented knowledge, uncertain relations, and "experimental" relationships with the environment. The latter can be utilized by the firm to achieve future performances as alternatives and improvements in current procedures. This halo denotes the area of uncertainty managed by the firm through the wide range of labor relationships previously mentioned.

The extent of the knowledge boundary is an index of the firm's innovative capability. Thus the halo corresponds to the *technological potential*, defined as the set of alternatives explored by, or accessible to, a firm. This technological potential would be ineffective without the ability to convert it into explicit rules for the achievement of precise goals. For this reason technological innovative performances rely on the relationship between the extent of the knowledge boundaries and the certainty boundaries, that is between *halo* and *core*. We call this model a *"fuzzy firm model"*.

The application of the fuzzy firm model for analyzing SSF's performances requires the assessment of the relationships between firm and professionals, and the firm's capability of carrying out technological innovations

Relationships between firm and professionals: the variable OCD

The relationship between firm and professionals was evaluated by an index, denoting the *membership degree* of these professionals.

The membership degree was assessed on the basis of the "formal control" concept. The lower the degree of "formal control", the lower the membership degree. The formal control concept denotes the management's capability of influencing other's decisions and behavior. It represents the mix of two elements:

1) the Influence Power (IP), i.e. the management's decision scope as to the amount of working hours, the content of the individual's tasks, the relationship between subjects and environment, technologies and methods used by subjects in performing their activities;
2) the Work Ratio (WR), i.e. the ratio between professionals' man-days dedicated to the specific firm and their total yearly working days.

This approach is based on two issues:

a) overcoming the traditional subdivision between internal and external employees by using a more detailed analysis of professionals involved in small-sized software firms (Eccles, 1981);
b) allowing for the type of relationship between firm and professionals (see Appendix).

Technological innovation capabilities: the variable TID

To verify the relationship between organizations' closing degree (OCD) and firms' innovation capability an index of the firm's technological innovation capability must be defined. There are many methods available. Literature reports indirect and direct methods (Freeman, 1982; Meyer, Roberts, 1986; Rothwell, 1984). Usually, indirect methods are built either on the analysis of factors affecting innovation performances (number of employees involved in R&D and expenditures for R&D activities), or on the output indices of technical activities (such as number of patents or bibliographic measures). Direct methods use indices such as number of new products or successful new products, and revenues from new products. However, it is very difficult to establish how innovative a product is without considering its technical features, and users' viewpoint, and without comparing these aspects with previous and competitive products. Literature shows that each index presents some advantages but also some problems related to measurement and interpretation of results (Freeman, 1982).

The *Technological Innovation Degree* (TID) considers the number of new programs produced by the firm in one year. As the number of new programs also depends on the firm's size, in order to compare different-sized firms we broke them down into five classes, by yearly revenue. These classes were labeled from one to five; then the number of New software Program (NP) was divided by the Size class of the firm (S). The choice of using a size index instead of the exact revenue value came from the necessity to minimize the index sensitivity to small revenue variations and to take into account the approximation of respondents in filling in the questionnaire. Then the technological level of each software program was measured. For an easy management of this problem, the technological level was split into two components: technical complexity and size complexity.

The technical complexity was measured by asking respondents to focus on the new features of each new program and to rank them on a scale ranging from one to five. The size complexity of the software program was measured by allowing for the man-years needed for a program to be developed. Because some respondents were unable to provide a detailed answer for each new software program, the new software programs were grouped and an average for Technical Complexity (TC) and Size Complexity (SC) for each firm was considered (see Appendix).

Empirical evidence

In the years 1983-87 the authors investigated about 200 software firms located in different part of Italy. The results of this research are included in the book "Software, tecnologia e mercato" (Raffa and Zollo, 1988). In 1990 a new research was started in order to analyze software firms development trajectories and the organization and technology changes experienced by them during the '80s. At the same time, a new field survey was started aimed to investigating the firms already studied in the previous research and simultaneously at widening the sample. Fifty firms were investigated as *case studies* in order to collect not only the most accessible quantitative information but also to understand, by means of interviews with the business managers, the complex organization problems faced by a small firm introducing innovations.

The analysis of the organizational arrangements was realized on a sample of 79 firms (Table 1), for which data concerning the OCD variable and the TID variable were available. The average values show a high Organization's Closing Degree (OCD) whereas the Technological Innovative Degree (TID) is very low.

Table 1. Basic statistical data of the 79 investigated software firms

Variables	Minim.	Mean.	Maxim.	Variance	Std.Dev
Sales-revenue classes	1.000	3.228	5.000	1.537	1.240
Software sales revenue % Total sales revenue	5.000	43.608	100.000	727.831	26.978
Age	3.000	7.076	15.000	8.610	2.934
Total of employees	4.000	15.114	44.000	94.333	9.713
Software employees	1.000	9.291	30.000	41.824	6.467
Software —graduate —employees % Software —employees	0.000	20.047	100.000	499.581	22.351
TID	0.000	0.122	1.000	0.035	0.187
OCD(Total employees)	0.300	0.775	1.000	0.029	0.169
OCD(Software professionals only)	0.230	0.735	1.000	0.043	0.207

(*) Revenue classes: 1: < 100
(in millions of Lire)   2: 100-300
    3: 300-500
    4: 500-1000
    5: > 1000

Source: *ODISSEO-DIS, Faculty of Engineering, Naples*

Figs. 2 and 3 show the percentage of firms according to the OCD, respectively with reference to all employees, and to software employees only. It can be seen quite clearly that completely closed firms are a very small minority, both when the total number of employees and when the software employees are considered. Lorentz's index of concentration was used to analyze distribution of firms related to OCD. This index gives zero value if all firms are completely closed, and gradually increases as the closing degree decreases. The index values are 0.64 when considering the total number of employees, and 0.71 when only software employees are considered. This shows that, as to the software activities, there is as light shift towards a higher opening degree.

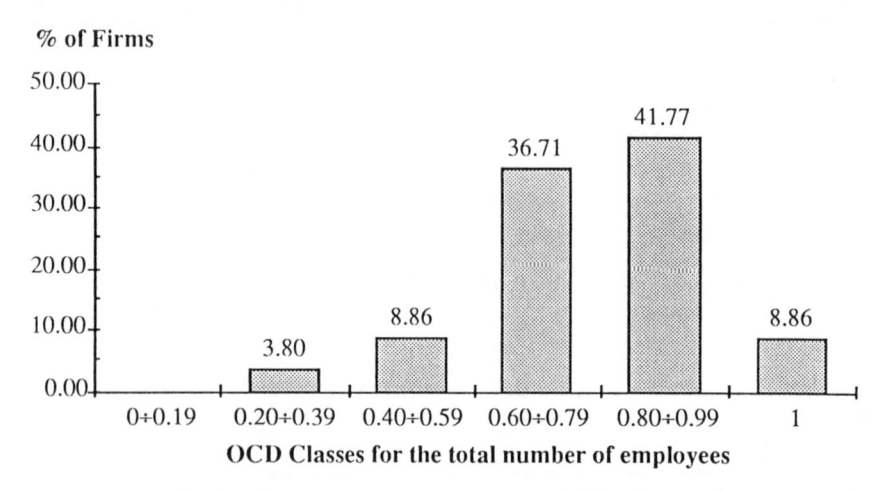

Figure 2. % distribution of firms according to OCD classes for the total of employees

Source: ODISSEO-DIS, Faculty of Engineering, Naples

Values (OCD Classes for the total number of employees):
- 0÷0.19: —
- 0.20÷0.39: 3.80
- 0.40÷0.59: 8.86
- 0.60÷0.79: 36.71
- 0.80÷0.99: 41.77
- 1: 8.86

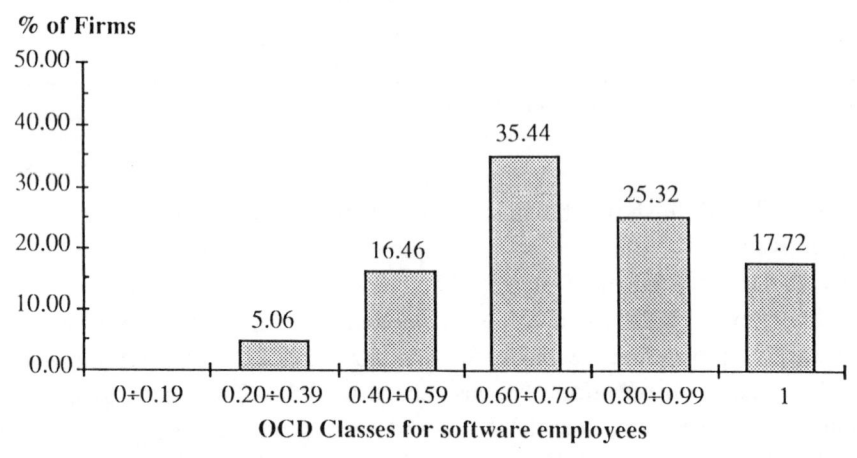

Figure 3. % distribution of firms according to OCD classes for software employees

Source: ODISSEO-DIS, Faculty of Engineering, Naples

Values (OCD Classes for software employees):
- 0÷0.19: —
- 0.20÷0.39: 5.06
- 0.40÷0.59: 16.46
- 0.60÷0.79: 35.44
- 0.80÷0.99: 25.32
- 1: 17.72

Figure 4 shows firms' distribution, with respect to TID: 29.11% of the firms studied show a TID of zero and most show an index less than 0.20. This is due both to a structural reason (because the sample includes a large number of not very innovative firms and only a small number of very innovative ones) and to a methodological reason (as the computing method squeezes the majority of firms towards a low TID value when the sample includes only one very innovative firm). Moreover, the TID index is very sensitive to the yearly variations in innovation capabilities. To reduce this sensitivity in ongoing research, the TID index is calculated on a three-year basis.

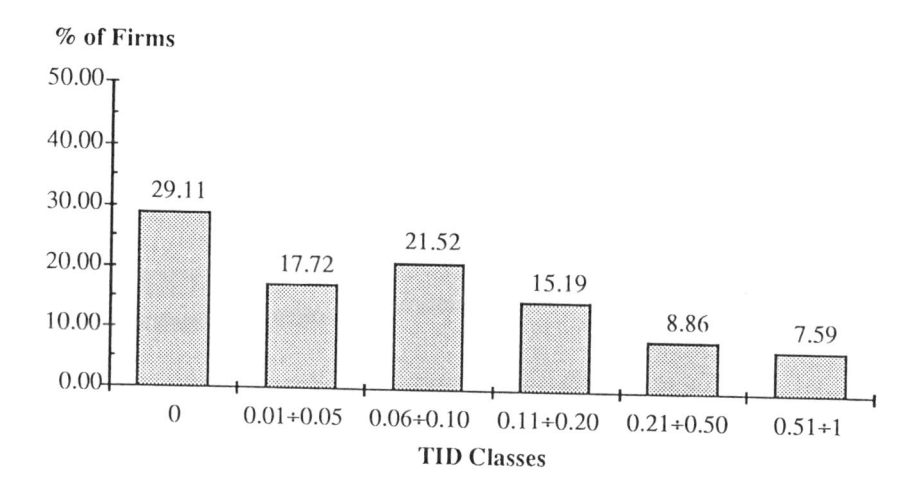

% of Firms

TID Class	% of Firms
0	29.11
0.01÷0.05	17.72
0.06÷0.10	21.52
0.11÷0.20	15.19
0.21÷0.50	8.86
0.51÷1	7.59

Figure 4. % distribution of firms according to TID classes
Source: *ODISSEO-DIS, Faculty of Engineering, Naples*

The OCD values, as to the total number of employees and software employees, are strictly correlated ($R=0.905$ with $p<0.05$); for this reason we can use both variables alternately. In the following analysis the OCD variable for the total number of employees was used. No linear correlation ($R=-0.033$) exists between the OCD and TID variables; this makes us assume that, in the case of one existing the relationship would be much more complex.

The statistical method used for investigating the existence of such a relation is the KMEANS non-hierarchic clustering method (program SYSTAT 5.0 for Macintosh). The chosen method requires a preliminary definition of the clusters' number. First four classes were defined, but one of them consisted of only one member. This anomalous case was ruled out and three clusters totaling 78 firms were defined.

Table 2 shows the statistical data related to the three clusters.

Table 2. Summary of the three clusters

Cluster #	Variable	Minimum	Mean	Maximum	Std.Dev.
#1 : 43 cases	TID	0.00	0.06	0.23	0.07
	OCD	0.75	0.89	1.00	0.08
#2 : 11 caes	TID	0.26	0.45	0.71	0.15
	OCD	0.39	0.75	0.96	0.16
#3 : 24 cases	TID	0.00	0.05	0.14	0.05
	OCD	0.30	0.59	0.72	0.11

	Variable	Between SS	DF	Within SS	DF	F-RATIO	Prob.
F-RATIO	TID	1.461	2	0.492	75	111.469	0.000
TEST	OCD	1.366	2	0.865	75	59.213	0.000

Cluster 1 is made up of 43 cases, with an OCD average of 0.89 and a TID average of 0.06. This cluster consists of by a set of firms with a high closing degree from the organizational standpoint, and a very low innovation capability degree. Cluster 2 is made up of 11 cases, with an OCD average value of 0.75 and a TID average of 0.45. These firms clearly show a medium-high organizational closing degree and an average innovation capability. Cluster 3 consists of 24 cases, with an OCD average value of 0.59 and a TID average of 0.05. The organizations' closing degree decreases and takes an intermediate value, whereas innovation capability is low.

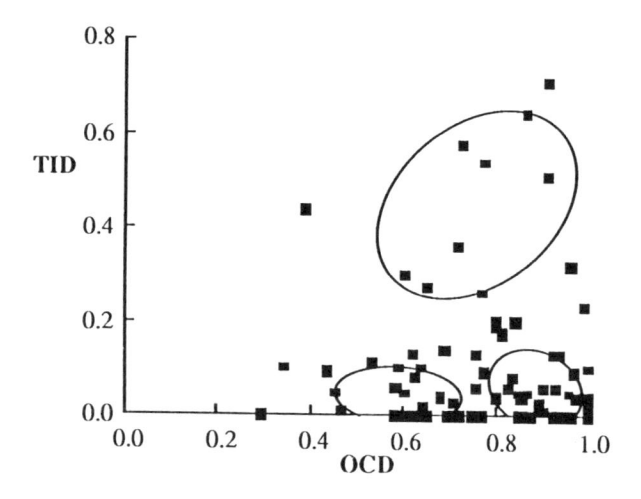

Figure 5. Representation of the three clusters by the ellipsoid method

In Figure 5 the three clusters are represented using the ellipsoid method where the three ellipses include at least 50% of the cases in the defined clusters. The F-Ratio test (Table 2) shows that the three clusters are representative of different phenomena. The assumption can then be made that we are dealing with three different classes of firms; the second cluster, characterized by a balance between the two opposite opening/closing requirements, shows a better performance as to innovation capabilities. These results seem to corroborate the assumption that the wide range of labor relationships between professionals and firms (being mixed), allows SSFs to obtain an inflow of technological information and to develop innovation capabilities.

The temporal solution: the oscillating path

To analyze the dynamics of small innovative firms and their organizational transformations 50 case studies of small software firms were made from 1990 to 1992. Furthermore, a comparison regarding 30 firms investigated both in 1984 and in 1990-91 was made to answer the central questions: how do small innovative firms evolve? How does the initial organizational pattern evolve? The analysis of the organization characteristics of the sample firms allows us to emphasize the non-linear path along which the small software firms can implement and define the boundaries of the internal expertise (core) and the extent of the external expertise (halo).

Most small software firms are established by technical entrepreneurs who are simultaneously responsible for management and development. Many firms maintain this organization arrangement for a very long time. In these firms the entrepreneurial group, or even the single entrepreneur, performs all the firm activities without any clear cut distinction amongst the various responsibilities and functions: entrepreneurs, in different forms, are directly involved also in project development. This organization is typical of the early stages of life of firms founded by technical entrepreneurs (Figure 6 stage I).

There are many two-headed firms where one of the entrepreneur-founders performs marketing and commercialization functions, while the other is concerned with technical issues and project development. This type of organization usually focuses on a single product and may have some difficulty in sustaining the innovation capability in the long term. In fact these firms, which at the beginning of their life experienced the highest technological introduction, professionally settle down to the lowest levels (new releases, programs up-dating) and end up managing only the current market. As a matter of fact the halo defined by the external expertise does not exist at all. All expertise is focused in the core. The critical event that leads to the overcoming of this organization is the distinction between management and development functions and the identification of the firm's new functions such as marketing and commercialization.

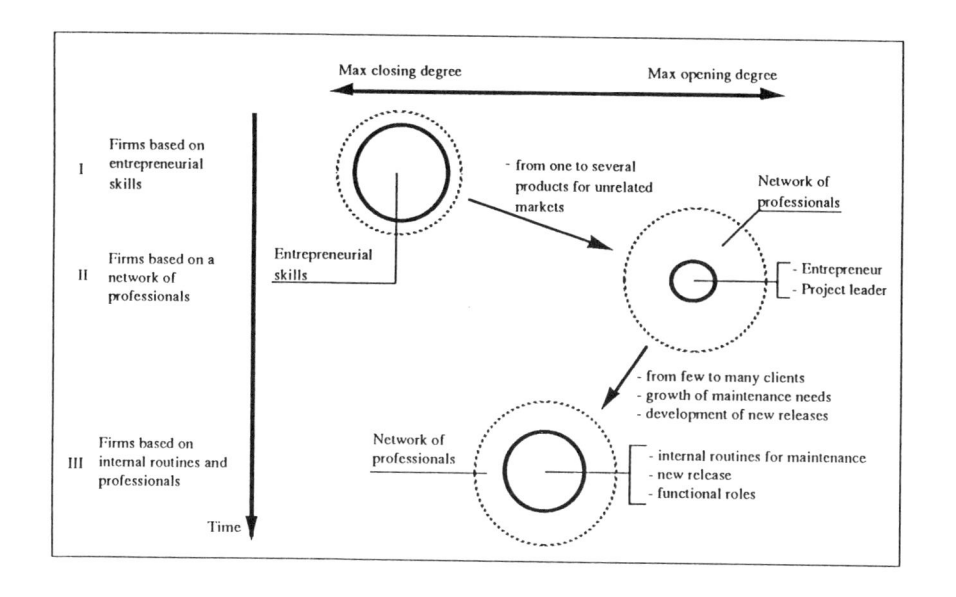

[Figure showing three stages (I, II, III) of firm evolution over time, with circles representing entrepreneurial skills, network of professionals, and internal routines, between "Max closing degree" and "Max opening degree" axes]

Figure 6. The oscillating behavior of small software firms
Source: Raffa, Zollo, 1994

Firms have two options:

a) to delegate the product development to technicians, with the entrepreneurial group holding the responsibility of business and other strategic functions;
b) to delegate both development responsibilities and the remaining business functions such as marketing. In this latter solution the entrepreneurial group holds only general responsibilities as to coordination and strategy definition.

The first factor affecting the delegation process is the customer typology. In firms producing almost exclusively for the public market (local bodies, hospitals, public administration, schools, etc), where the personal, formal and informal relation between customer and supplier is crucial, the entrepreneurial group has a direct relationship with the customer. Firms operating on the private market can hardly survive and develop in a specific market segment they supply specific products to. The small firm that overcame the early life stage must simultaneously explore various market segments with very different characteristics. This activity requires not only marketing but also entrepreneurial capabilities. In other words the opportunity of committing resources to explore a new kind of market must be assessed for each project.

A second factor, linked to the product and affecting in a remarkable way the firm's organization and professional skills, is the kind of software being manufactured. Larger firms work on orders rather than producing standardized packages for the market. The order acquisition is usually made by the entrepreneur.

A third factor, linked to the market, is the type of demand by the customer to the software house. The customer usually demands a set of services not confined solely to software manufacturing but also personnel training, hardware consultancy and, sometimes data entry. To meet this demand the software firm usually uses integrated professional skills rather than specialized ones: it is more useful to have a multi-function performing technician than an expert in an advanced technical field. When the entrepreneur is no longer concerned with the technical issue and takes care of the market and/or of management issues, the organization is deprived of the skills required to explore the supply of technologies appearing on the market.

The sample firms that are able to avoid the loss of technical expertise which might turn them out of the technological competition, are those whose entrepreneurial group is made up of two or more people who, when the critical event occurs, differentiate their responsibilities. Consequently some of them take care of marketing and management while the others are concerned with strategy issues and with technological issues as to the package development. In our sample these firms are 50% of the total.

The firms where the environmental factors (market, customer, etc.) are more favorable, decide more frequently to differentiate the entrepreneurial responsibilities, to delegate also marketing activities and to use specific professional skills. This technology and market specialization allows the firm to have various relations with the external environment (universities, research centers, laboratories, large firms, innovative customers, etc.) thus strengthening its competitive capabilities (Figure 6 stage II). The entrepreneurial group in some cases fully delegates technicians. In fact sometimes project development is fully delegated to external consultants. In most of the cases a member of the entrepreneurial group also performs the task of project leader, whereas analysts and programmers may be either full-time company employees or external consultants. The entrepreneurial group is mainly concerned with professional skills management and project team coordination. In all the firms of this cluster, that are the majority of the software firms, two problems arise: the need to have a constant rapport with the consultants as they are the carrying structure of the firm's technological capability and the need to update existing professional skills to gain access to new technologies. The extreme organization solutions show the following strengths and weaknesses: if professional skills are strongly linked to the firm (for instance technicians are full-time employees), the firm is able to control and stabilize its own know-how but meets serious problems as to its updating and replacement. On the other hand, if technicians are outside to the firm and are involved with a single project, the firm can have an easier access to updated knowledge but it does not have its own technical endowment to rely on. By means of this operational flexibility these firms can easily introduce high level innovations that, however, are not linked to an explicit innovation strategy but are targeted to catch the market opportunities consistent with the available professional resources.

Firms based on a network of specific professional skills have a point of weakness: their technological expertise are person-embodied. When an expert technician leaves the firm it irreversibly loses a parts of its own skills. This gives rise to many difficulties; first of all the maintenance and development of newly release programs carried out by the technician who left the firm. To solve this problem the firm can only develop its own technological endowment being partially independent of the employees' skills (Figure 6 stage III). The building up and management of this technological endowment brings about the second critical event; in fact the firm must transform both its organization pattern and its employees' professional skills. Two new functions become strategically crucial: the technology monitoring and the in-firm training. For these functions to be introduced a qualitative leap is required that very few firms were able to implement. As to the technological issues, the basic difference from the firms of the previous groups is that these firms acquired or developed internally a set of methodologies, techniques and development environments. From the operational standpoint, the project leader and the project team are not delegated the software development modes, but they must operate in conformance with standards and methods imposed by the firm. The relations between the entrepreneurial group, the project team and the set of the firm's methodologies are crucial to the success of innovation.

The entrepreneurial group not only chooses the required professional skills, but develops two new activities: a training plan for the research team in order to transfer the know-how needed to use the development methodologies, and technological monitoring to update or replace the held technologies. In this way a new activity of the entrepreneurial group is identified, the management of the technological endowment that allows these firms to implement innovations over the whole range of technologies. At any rate, just because of the need to exploit the scope economies due to their technological endowment these firms can hardly develop completely new innovations. It can be stated that this shift is the real challenge of the '90s for the whole Italian software industry.

Conclusion

This article outlines some aspects of professional management in small software firms. The results can be easily extended to small innovative companies, particularly small engineering-based companies. A conceptual framework was used asserting the presence of both autonomy and control in innovative firms. The model emerging from these considerations depicts a *firm with fuzzy boundaries*, with a core of consolidated routines surrounded by a halo of loosely planned activities aimed at exploring environmental opportunities. A dominant pattern will emerge over time, though in an unplanned way. We found a behavior wavering over time between two poles: a firm with an *oversized halo and a small core* -which depicts a very creative organization, and a firm with *a big core surrounded by a tiny halo* - which depicts a very productive organization.

Our analysis shows that a successful firm is a fuzzy firm oscillating between these poles without reaching them. Further development of this research will explore this assumption using quantitative methods on a larger sample.

The principal result is that the innovation abilities of small firms are fundamentally abilities in managing the path between opposite requirements, accordingly modifying organizational arrangements, goals and strategies. It is necessary to remove the static view of organization, which is a dynamic entity: if the management does nothing, the organization automatically pursues the previous direction, with the consequence of enhancing one side of the opposite requirements and eliminating the other. When this occurs, the firm faces serious difficulties in finding a new organizational arrangement, and, often, this is only reached after a general crisis.

There are no recipes for running the firm because the oscillations are determined by the specific conditions in which the firm operates. Then, the management should learn from experience how to use the various labor relationships within the larger horizontal network in order to run the business through time, to emphasize different needs for different phases.

In conclusion, we underline some observations, that can be starting points for further research: a) each organizational arrangement, such as the peer-group, is unable to sustain innovation over time; b) the differentiation of professional skills and the full delegation of decision-making to professionals limits the possibility for constant innovation; c) the management of people-embodied technology makes it difficult to routinize and update the firms' technological assets.

Acknowledgements

The research was funded by CNR n. 89.05320.CT13, CNR AI90.01585.13, CNR n.. 91.02505.PF74; CNR n. 91.04237.PF43 and MURST by 40% and 60%. A previous version of this article was presented to the *EIASM RENT VI Workshop in Barcellona,* November 26-27 1992, where it was awarded first prize as the best paper, and to the *First Venezuelan SME Management Seminar*, March 7-11, 1993. The authors thank the partecipants of the Conferences for their suggestions, particularly L. Fillion, B. Johannisson, A. Mettinen, M. Scott and C. Steyaert.

Appendix: The OCD and TID variables

The OCD variable

The membership degree has been assessed by interviewing managers of 79 software firms, who were called to define, for each professional role, their Influence Power (IP) on a scale ranging from one to five, and the Work Ratio (WR). For this purpose the following formula was utilized:

$$MD_{ij} = (IP_{ij}/5) \cdot (WR_{ij})$$

where:
- i = the i-th firm;
- j = the j-th employer-employee relationship (full-time consultant, part-time, etc.);
- MD_{ij} = membership degree relating to the i-th firm with an j-th employer-employee relationship;
- IP_{ij} = influence power relating to the i-th firm with an j-th employer-employee relationship;
- WR_{ij} = work ratio relating to the i-th firm with an j-th employer-employee relationship.

The membership degree enables the estimation of the "Work Potential" (WP), which provides us with more detailed measurements of the work controlled by a single firm and with a more precise index of the firm's size.

The formula used for this purpose is the following:

$$WP_i = \sum_j (N_{ij} \cdot MD_{ij})$$

where:

i = the i-th firm;
j = the j-th employer-employee relationship (full-time consultant, part-time, etc.);
WP_i = work potential of the i-th firm;
N_{ij} = number of employees of the i-th firm with an j-th employer-employee relationship;
MD_{ij} = membership degree relating to the i-th firm with an j-th employer-employee relationship.

The measurement of the *Organization's Closing Degree (OCD)* of the individual firm to the environment, is based on the following ratio:

$$OCD_i = WP_i / N_i$$

where:
i = the i-th firm;
OCD_i = organization's closing degree of the i-th firm;
WP_i = work potential of the i-th firm;
N_i = number of employees of the i-th firm.

According to our assumption the OCD index, (which increases when the firm is self-contained, i.e. with no external relationships, no consultants, experts, part-time programmers, etc.), should be somehow linked to firm's innovation capabilities.

The TID variable

The normalized values of Technological Innovation Degree (TID) is derived from the following formula:

$$TID^*_i = (NP_i / S_i) \cdot TC_i \cdot SC_i$$
$$TID_i = TID^*_i / \max(TID^*)$$

where:

i = the i-th firm;
TID^*_i = raw value of technological innovation degree of the i-th firm;
NP_i = number of new software programs delivered by the i-th firm in one year;
S_i = size index of the i-th firm;
TC_i = average technical complexity of new software programs;
SC_i = average size complexity of new software programs measured in man-years needed for them to be developed;
TID_i = normalized value of technological innovation degree of the i-th firm.

References

Barocci, T.A. and Wever, K.R. (1983), *Turn-over among Information Systems Professionals*, Working Paper WP 1480-83, Sloan School of Management, MIT, Cambridge (MA).

Barocci, T.A., Wever, K.R. and Lahey, R.A. (1983), *Human Resource Planning for Information Systems Personnel: Skills Mixes and Technological Trends*, Working Paper WP 1478-83, Sloan School of Management, MIT, Cambridge (MA).

Brown, W.B. and Schwab, R.C. (1984), 'Boundary-Spanning Activities in Electronics Firms', *IEEE Trans. Eng. Manag.*, Vol. 31, No. 3.

Cameron, K.S. (1986), 'Effectiveness as Paradox: Consensus and Conflict in Conceptions of Organizational Effectiveness', *Management Science*, Vol. 32, No. 5.

Cameron, K.S. and Quinn, R.E. (1988), 'Organizational Paradox and Trasformation', in Cameron, K.S. and Quinn, R.E. (eds.), *Paradox and Transformation: Toward a Theory of Change in Organization and Management*, Ballinger, Cambridge (MA).

Daly, E.B. (1979), 'Organizing for successful software development', *Datamation*, Dec.

Eccles, R.G. (1981), 'The Quasy-Firm in the Construction Industry', *Journal of Economic Behaviour and Organization*, Vol. 2, No. 2.

Feldman, S.M. (1989), 'The Broken Wheel: the Inseparability of the Autonomy and Control in Innovation within Organizations', *Journal of Management Studies*, Vol. 26, No. 2.

Floyd, R.W. (1979), *The Paradigms of Programming*, Communication of the ACM, Aug.

Freeman, C. (1982), *The Economics of Industrial Innovation*, Pinter, London.

Gagnon, R.J. and Krasner, J.D. (1990), 'The Optimal Mix of Internal/External Engineering Staff and Equipment with Different Levels of Capability and Performance', *IEEE Trans. Eng. Manag.*, Vol. 37, No. 1.

Galbraith, J.R. (1982), 'Designing the Innovating Organization', *Organizational Dynamics*, Winter.

Gallino, L. (1983), *Informatica e qualità del lavoro*, Einaudi, Torino.

Goldstein, D.K. (1982), *A Further Examination of the Determinants of the Job Satisfaction in Programmer/Analyst*, Working Paper WP 1370-82, Sloan School of Management, MIT, Cambridge (MA).

Hauptman, O. (1985), *Influence of Task Type on the Relation between Communication and Performance: the Case of Software Development*, Working Paper, WP 1712-85, Sloan School of Management, MIT, Cambridge (MA).

Kraft, P. (1979), 'The Industrialization of Computer Programming: From Programming to Software Production', in Zimbalist, A. (ed. by), *Case Studies on the Labor Process*, Monthly Review, New York.

Meyer, M.H. and Roberts E.B., (1986), 'New Product Strategy in Small Technology-Based Firms: a Pilot Study', *Management Science*, Vol. 32, No. 7.

Morgan, G. (1986), *Images of Organizations*, Sage, Beverly Hills.

Oakey, R. (1984), *High Technology Small Firms*, Pinter, London.

OECD, (1982), *Innovation in Small and Medium Firms*, Paris.

OECD, (1986), *Software: A New Industry*, Paris.

Parden, R.J. (1981), 'The Manager's Role and the High Mobility of Technical Specialists in the Santa Clara Valley', *IEEE Trans. Eng. Manag.*, Vol. 28, No. 1.

Peters, T.J. and Waterman, R.H. (1982), *In Search of Excellence: Lessons from America's Best Run Companies,* Harper & Row, New York.

Poole, M.S. and Van de Ven, A.H. (1989), 'Using Paradox to Build Management and Organization Theories, *Academy of Management Review*, Vol. 14, No. 4.

Quinn, J.B. (1979), 'Technological Innovation, Entrepreneurship and Strategy', *Sloan Management Review*, Vol. 20, No. 3.

Quinn, J.B. (1985), 'Managing Innovation: Controlled Chaos', *Harvard Business Review*, Vol. 63, No. 3.

Quinn, R.E. and Rohrbaugh, J. (1983), 'A Spatial Model of Effectiveness Criteria: Toward a Competing Approach to Organizational Effectiveness', *Management Science*, Vol. 29.

Raffa, M. and Zollo, G. (1988), *Software: tecnologia e mercato*, Il Mulino, Bologna.

Raffa, M. and Zollo, G. (1992), 'Il rapporto tra innovazione tecnologica e organizzazione nelle piccole imprese innovative', *Piccola Impresa / Small Business*, No. 2.

Raffa, M. and Zollo, G. (1994), 'Sources of innovations and professionals in small innovative firms', *International Journal of Technology Management*, Feb.-March.

Reifer, D.J. (1981), *Tutorial: Software Management*, IEEE Computer Society, Los Angeles.

Rothwell, R. and Zegveld, W. (1982), *Innovation and Small and Medium Sized Firm*, Pinter, London.

Rothwell, R. (1984), 'The Role of Small Firms in the Emergence of New Technologies', *Omega*, Vol. 12, No. 1.

Van de Ven, A.H. (1986), 'Central Problems in the Management of Innovation', *Management Science*, Vol. 32, No. 5.

Part C
NETWORKS

15 A relationships typology in firms networks

Mario Raffa

Summary

This paper highlights the special role played by sub-contracting relations in the very many changes occurring within the production system. These relations, as emerges from our *field survey*, are increasingly becoming a crucial element for the competitiveness of the firms and of the firms system as a whole. The analysis of the *collaboration relations* shows that the firms benefit more from the network system than from the traditional external relations. Namely they improve their *performance* and *competitiveness*. A new phenomenon is taking place: the stabilization of the firms' relations within a network brings about benefits other than the simple exchange relation. Collaboration is an alternative strategy to vertical integration. Alongside new forms of relations developed by firms, traditional relations can still be found. New *hybrid* types of management are emerging that have the advantage to preserve the flexibility and the positive elements of the market-balanced exchanges. In this hybrid management, co-ordination between firms results from both the mutual competition and the strategic benefits from the collaboration effort. The horizon of the long-term benefits usually guides the joint effort of the firms within the network. The *partnership* benefits are: cost reduction due to the relation-related economies of scale; lead time reduction; quality improvement and timely response to market needs.

Part I - Industrial changes and doctrines support

Firms in the different industrial systems are typified by various transformations. These relate to the conventional manufacturing and organization patterns, to the change in the relation with the external environment (in particular the demand and the service networks) and to the increasing importance of technology. The firm aims at managing the whole set of these elements so as to achieve a good dynamic efficiency (Bertelè and Mariotti, 1991). "The firm's trend is increasingly typified by differentiation processes: each large enterprise holds an innovation and self-creation capability that enables it to compete in global markets. These, in their turn, are differentiated as to demand requirements and roles played by economic-social institutions".

"However we must emphasize that the firm, operating in increasingly complex and dynamic contexts, is less able than before to plan the change and thus to forecast and assess all the effects of entrepreneurial choices. But, most interestingly, its decision making and operational processes are more flexible and rapid thus enabling it to face effectively an increasingly complex world". For this reason the firm - to achieve its targets - tries to involve "in its production efforts a set of knowledge and resources needed - even though insufficient - to cope with the growing complexity of the context it operates in". Consequently *final demand holders, skilled suppliers, suppliers of parts, products and intermediate services* are gaining more power. The firm is increasingly able to interact and co-operate "with a set of resources, skills, knowledge held by other autonomous decision centers (firms and other institutions) having their own specific targets" (Vaccà, 1991, p. 6). Competition takes different typology (Gros-Pietro and Zanetti, 1988); integration costs increase (Crozier, 1990); the role of the labor-force changes (Dertouzos, Lester and Solow, 1989); de-verticalization of the large firm's production cycles increases and takes different shapes.

The competitive strategy that must allow for internal and external resources (e.g. the sub-contractor's resources) develops. The effectiveness of the interfirm relations increases when a larger number of resources are available and the autonomy of each network firm is high. Alongside the *competitive actions*, described by Ansoff (1969) and Porter (1980, 1985) and defined by the strategic matrices built on the identification of the firm's relations with its competitors, the *co-operative interactions* - based on resource sharing and mutual interests - must also be allowed for.

Collaboration helps the firm develop its own competitive capability. This is particularly true in a historical stage in which competition is increasingly difficult and new rules for design and management of the innovative firm are being established (Filippini, Pagliarani and Petroni, 1992).

The theory of the firm and of the technological change must focus on the firm's internal structure, organizational rules, decision-making processes and relations with the external environment. For this reason it must resort to various doctrines concerned with the following; the correlation between *type of technology and organizational structure* (Woodward, 1983); the paradigm of the *strategic choices* (Child, 1972); the *effects of new technologies on labor* (Emery and Trist, 1960, 1965; Braverman, 1974); the relations between *technological innovation and firm's strategy* (Kay, 1984; Teece, 1986); the relation between *strategy and corporate structure* (Chandler, 1962); the *satisfactory rather than optimizing choices* (Simon, 1977); the *technological guidepost* (Sahal, 1981); the *technological paradigm* (Dosi, 1982); the notion developed by sociology and related to the *techno-economic networks* built by agents and intermediaries (Callon, 1987).

While the reference economic framework has been changing over the last fifty years, some basic thoughts on the role played by innovations can already be found in Schumpeter's works (Scherer and Perlman, 1992).

The different approaches focus either on the external or on the internal forces (Penrose, 1959; Williamson, 1976; Mintzberg, 1979; Porter, 1980; Teece, 1986; Shapiro, 1989). These approaches, even though typified by remarkable differences, provide useful elements to analyze the role of the *technical/economic networks* in which - in the different life stages - many agents operate. With reference to the firm these stages include design, manufacturing, distribution and diffusion of processes, products and services. All agents can play an active role to increase transactions. However the bonds between internal and external agents mainly relate to three poles: market, science and technology, with different linkages between them (Coombs, Saviotti and Walsh, 1992). Changes in the firms, in the inter-firm relations, in the firms/institutions relations, bring about *new hierarchies* and *new structures* where previous competitors, customers and sub-contractors are either replaced by new agents or change remarkably their nature and relation types[1]. For instance the sub-contractor's ability to gain profits and the customer's demand mutually interact thus becoming more important in the theory of the technology transmission (Metcalfe, 1988).

Part II. Networks of firms

Major contributions to the study of the firm networks and of the inter-firm relations are provided by many authors.

Birley (1985) highlighted how the network relations affect the firms' early life; Lorenzoni and Ornati (1988) analyzed their effect on the growth strategies; Zanoni (1984) studied the changes in the supply chain; Dioguardi (1992) analyzed the macro-firm operation and design; Larson (1991) underlined the small enterprise benefits from network relations. These authors, while investigating the issue from different stand-points, emphasize that the network development requires an accurate knowledge of its internal structure, in particular of the relations between the network agents. The knowledge of these relations allows both *the benefits for the network firms* to be assessed and *some managerial guidelines to be drawn*.

The interaction process between the firms is affected by technological, economic, logistical, and operational issues. These elements influence the individual firm's market strategy, the firm's internal mechanisms, and inter-firms relations, as summarized by Johanson's and Mattsson's model (Figure 1).

In the same paper the two above mentioned authors summarize some elements of the network approach which are very useful for the purposes of this paper and are therefore fully quoted.

The authors distinguish technical, planning, knowledge, socioeconomic, and legal bonds. They maintain: "These bonds can be exemplified by, respectively, product and process adjustments, logistical coordination, knowledge about the counterpart, personal confidence and liking, special credit agreements, and long-term contracts. The relationships imply that there are *specific inter-firm dependence* relations that are different in nature from the general dependence relationship to the market in the traditional market model."

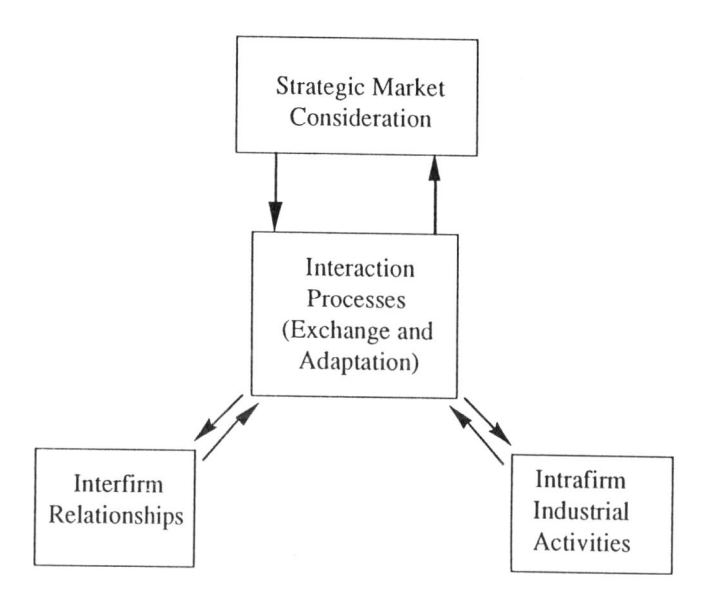

```
                    ┌─────────────────┐
                    │ Strategic Market│
                    │  Consideration  │
                    └─────────────────┘
                         ↕
                    ┌─────────────────┐
                    │   Interaction   │
                    │    Processes    │
                    │  (Exchange and  │
                    │   Adaptation)   │
                    └─────────────────┘
                       ↙         ↘
            ┌──────────────┐   ┌──────────────┐
            │  Interfirm   │   │  Intrafirm   │
            │Relationships │   │  Industrial  │
            │              │   │  Activities  │
            └──────────────┘   └──────────────┘
```

Figure 1 Basic causal relations of Johanson's and Mattsson's model
Source: Johanson and Mattsson, 1987, pp. 35-37

And then: "A basic assumption in the network model is that the individual firm is dependent on resources controlled by other firms. The firm gets access to these external resources through its network positions. In industrial networks, suppliers and customers establish, develop, and maintain lasting relationships with each other. Such relationships may be significant to the participants. They may reduce costs of exchange and production; they may give the parties some control over each other; they may be used as bridges to other firms; and they may be used when mobilizing partners against third parties" (Johanson and Mattsson, 1987, pp. 35-37).

The firm can be viewed as a core surrounded by uncertain boundaries and included in a wide external context where many forces operate: other firms, the network the firm is part of, the various institutions, the country's economic policy. Nowadays, *while there is an increase in the decentralization of the internal and external responsibilities and in the co-ordination role played by the parent company, standards and procedures become the language through which the audit of the supplying units* -and thus of all the firms linked to them *is performed*.

The linkage between the most formal and visible elements of the firm's structure and its strategies was already underlined (Chandler, 1962). Other informal internal elements and the modifications of the industrial pattern are also meaningful.

Some key words

Within a network there are many inter-firm relations. The type of bonds can significantly change; so they may be *technical, socioeconomic, commercial, legal* and *knowledge bonds*.

Hallen and Johanson (1989) maintain that technical bonds mainly depend on the technology and machine features. Social bonds depend on personal relations, that may be typified by mutual trust, confidence, etc. Knowledge bonds are based on the firm's knowledge of other firms' resources, strategies, and relations. Logistical bonds are based on common systems for planning and re-arrangement of stocks. Financial bonds are related to specific forms of credit, finance and payment. Legal bonds are the result of different contract forms (short-term, long-term contracts).

All these bonds can be caught if we are able to analyze the whole set of interactions between the various network agents. (Johanson and Vahlne, 1990).

These linkages are complex and transient. To catch these bonds, Hakansson (1987) exhibits a model based on the assessment of four variables: the *interaction process* and *its participants*, the *environment within which interactions take place*, the *strength and dependence degree as to the various interactions*. Participants are characterized by their technology, organizational features and staff. The set of these characteristics affects the linkages between the various participants and contributes to the implementation of an efficient system. Interactions are typified by the dynamics depending on the environment, on the strengths and characteristics of the various subjects, on the conflict or collaboration degree between them, on their closing degree and on the distance between them. Relations must be viewed as investments of the firms aiming at increasing their technical efficiency, productivity, information channels and their ability to control the system.

Strength of the linkages

Usually the network approach emphasizes mainly the network size and considers the relations with reference to some specific technologies or specific products. Similarly when reference is made to the geographical features we speak of local, national or multi-national networks. The *industrial network* is the result of a set of interacting firms. What is important is the *identification* and *boundary* of the investigated network. That is, if we make reference to the network firm, the *boundary* refers to all relations directly or indirectly linked to the investigated firm. The structure affecting an industrial network is crucial not only to the member firms but also to those interested in being part of it.

The characteristics and complexity of the inter-firm linkages are an indicator of their strength. For instance, if the relation between a customer and his sub-contractor involves the exchange of expensive technologies, agreed production scheduling, continuous and stable personal relations, then the linkage is strong. Only the measurement of a set of elements typifying the linkage enables us to assess its strength. An indirect way to measure the linkage strength is the evaluation of the factors preventing its breaking off. This allows the characteristics of the network in its different points to be clarified, possibly even quantified. For instance, the understanding and measurement of the linkage elements can help the firm forecast how to prevent the entry of new competitors.

The level of *structuring, concentration, density, variability* are the elements typifying the network (Rogers and Kincad, 1981)

These elements affect the capability of the network firm to develop technologically.

The features of the network result from its history and depend on its investment in relations, knowledge and routine etc. The influence of the various firms varies in relation to the degree of dependence.

Customer/sub-contractor linkages

In general the parties involved in a relationship are interested in getting information on their relevant resources, organizations and strategies. These bonds - aimed at collecting information - concern a wide range of areas, such as manufacturing, logistics, design and development, finance, services, quality control. The set of the inter-firm relations denotes the distribution channels set up between them. The duration of the relationship usually depends on the two parties' will to set up long-term relations. This holds mainly in a stage in which the change of the external scenario is highly dynamic.

The *type of relation* depends on the specific network agents (customer/sub-contractor, sub-contractor's sub-contractor, customer's customer, competitors). For this reason firms perform over time gradual adjustments leading to stable relations. In some cases, for instance, a sub-contractor uses significant resources to develop the design of a new product for an important customer. This behavior relates also to the development of specific orders and to short-medium term planning systems. Adjustment processes underlie a *mutual learning* of the involved parties and make the relation more stable.

Assessment model of the technology flow between two firms

Technology was defined as "the practical knowledge, know-how, skill and manufactured goods used to develop a new product or service and/or a new production/distribution system. Technology can be embodied into people, materials, physical and knowledge processes, plant, equipment and tools" (Burgelman, Kosnik and Van den Poel, 1987).

By defining technology as knowledge, skills and manufactured goods, it is clear that each organization makes use of a variety of technologies along the value chain - from the design stage to the manufacturing and distribution stage. Some structural mechanisms guiding the relations in the high-tech sectors are not basically different from those in the low-tech sectors. The user of high-tech technologies must focus on two uncertainties: *market* and *technology*. While the market uncertainty relates to the lack of knowledge with particular reference to its extension and customer needs, the technology uncertainty relates to the lack of information on the technology characteristics (Kosnic and Moriarty, 1989).

It is well known that today the process and product technology has become more complex as it must combine different technologies (mechanics, electronics, chemistry, etc.). To analyze all these areas, a firm should allocate a share of its resources to follow the different technological trajectories. Through the collaboration with a sub-supplier, the firm can increase its potential to specialize by focusing on some key areas. The development of relations can become a pre-condition to increase the in-house specialization in development processes. However these actions imply some limitations; some components have a strategic importance and must be internally developed so as to maintain a given balance between internal and external development.

Therefore there are some multi-lateral relations affected both by internal elements and by elements depending on the inter-firm relation.

The channels through which two firms interact can be investigated and analyzed by assessing the technology flow between them. *Channels can be viewed as linkage vectors between two firms carrying the different technology components*. The weight of the technology elements carried through the vectors can be assessed by means of the technology transmission model shown below (Figure 2).

In our model, by technology of a firm we mean the set of knowledge embodied into the hardware system, the software system and human resources (The Technology Atlas Team, 1987; Esposito and Raffa, 1991a; Raffa, 1992c). Technology is then constituted of a systemic application of various components: *machines, professional skills, documents, organizational rules*. *Machines* include all technologies embodied into objects, components, parts, devices and systems. *Professional skills* include human-embodied technologies, that is the whole set of human skills. *Documents* include technologies embodied -in the form of ideas and information- into manuals and other documents. *Organizational rules* include technologies in the form of procedures and organizational constraints. All these components are strictly inter-related; they can thus be viewed as cores of a system from which stimuli by the other members and the external environment flow in and flow out.

Whenever one of these cores undergoes a transformation process, information is immediately transmitted to coordinate the technological system. When one of the technology components changes, it affects the other components and, consequently, the previous system's technological equilibrium is modified as well.

The transformation process of one of the technology components can take place as a result of internal opportunities or because externally induced.

The suggested model includes two different levels.

At the first level we have the technological network that, as already mentioned, is viewed as a systematic application of the four components (materials, professional skills, documents and organizational rules).

At the second level we have the technology transmission channels. They are real vectors through which firms feed and modify their technology components.

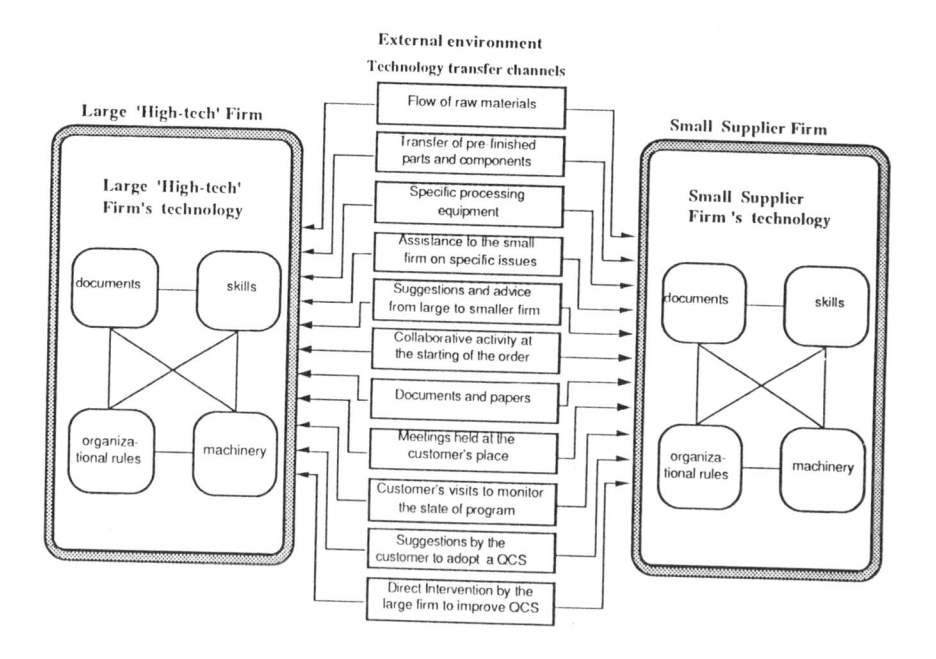

Figure 2 **The channels for technology transfer**
Source: Esposito, Raffa, 1991a

Methodologies for the network study

When a relation or a network is studied, the perspective can be either of the parties investigated or of the whole system. In the former case the focus is on one single unit, in the latter on the whole system. When the focus is on one single unit, its perspective prevails, to the detriment of the whole system perspective. In the former case we have a more partial vision, in the latter a more neutral one.

The external study of a network is quite difficult as the linkages between the various components are typified by composite relations. Moreover each relation is typified by a specific structure of the linkages; it is ambiguous with a variable strength (Hallen and Johanson, 1989). Therefore it is difficult to provide a framework including of all the elements typifying a relation without being part of it. Moreover, the different interconnections make the understanding even more difficult. *A given knowledge can be acquired by becoming part of the network and observing constantly its different points and relations.* By analyzing some networks is possible to identify the major explanatory variables of their relations and contents.

Part III - The dependence degree between the network firms

A characteristic of the network is the inter-dependence degree between firms. Given that product is the result of a set of relations, if we want to change it we must incur a certain cost (related, for instance, to the search for a new sub-contractor, the testing of his manufacturing and innovation skill, etc.), defined by Porter (1980) as *switching cost*, namely the switching to another sub-supplier involves a high cost. The higher these costs, the greater the difficulty to switch to other sub-contractors (Johanson and Vahlne, 1990). *The degree and type of dependence can be a hindrance or a contribution to change.* The most common types of dependence relate to technical, knowledge, administrative, logistical and social issues.

The inter-dependence between the various relations of the network implies that the change in the firm's position brings about a change also in the position of other firms (Hakansson, 1987). For instance, by tuning the strength of his relations with the sub-contractors, the customer can better exploit their resources. Therefore he is interested in making relations more stable and this is the condition that avoids the waste of an asset of information given and received (Rosenberg, 1982).

The manufacturing of a new product within a network system requires the manufacturers of complementary parts adjust themselves to the new situation by changing machines, procedures and relations. This in order to obtain a good efficiency of the network system that sometimes is a hindrance to a new product launching (Hakansson, 1987).

Within the system, inter-firm relations do not have only formal and explicit characteristics (as to the flow of components and parts between the firms). The analysis of the informal element enables us to explore the range of the collaboration/dependence relations between customers and sub-contractors. These relations are typified by formal and informal agreements between the network firms, and range from transient relations to symbiosis (Figure 3).

The assessment of the technology flow illustrated in the previous pages can be applied to the network by considering the firms as *couples*. This pattern (Figure 4) will help us identify the increasing collaboration between sub-contractors and customers in the investigated networks.

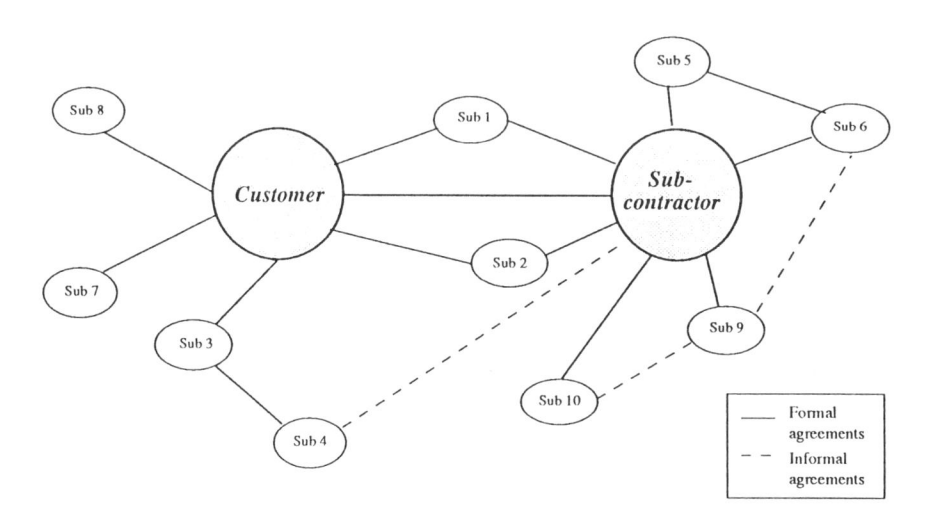

Figure 3. Formal and informal agreements amongst firms in the network

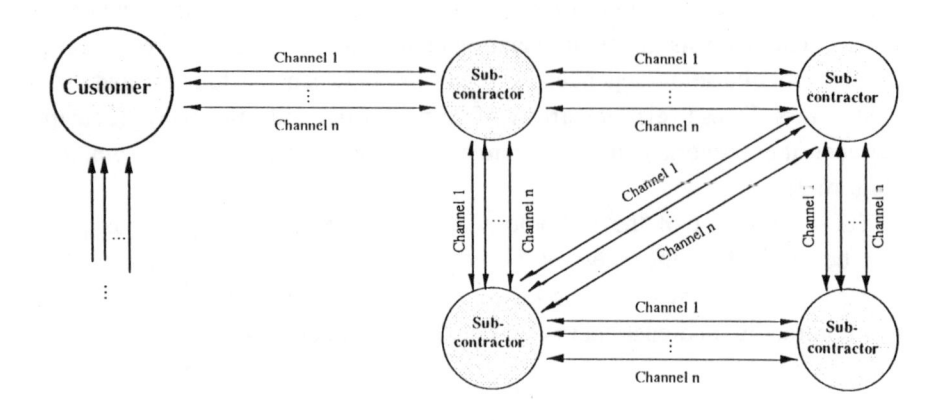

Figure 4 The channels for technology transfer between firms in the network

Matrix of firms' dependence

The two dependence indicators (Degree of the customer's dependence on his sub-contractor, Degree of the sub-contractor's dependence on his customer) illustrated in the appendix can be used to position the firms on the *sub-contractor/customer dependence matrix* (Figure 5).

This matrix, characterized by five areas (a, b, g, d, e) denoting the different values of the two indicators, allows the various possible typologies of the customer/sub-contractor relations to be analyzed.

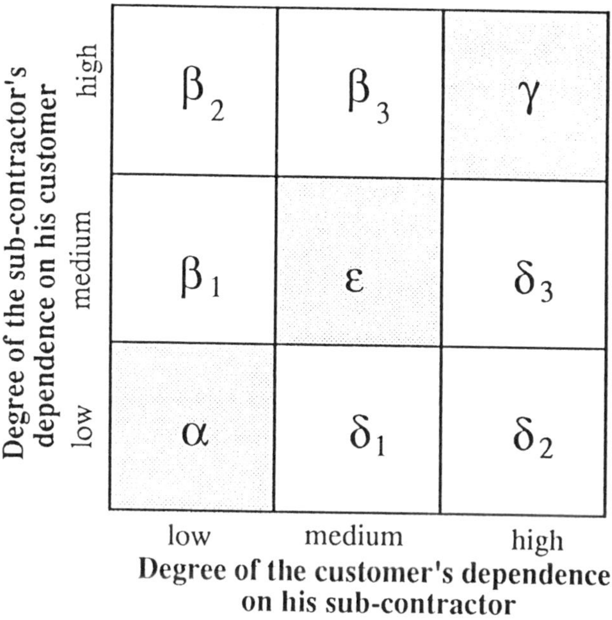

high	β_2	β_3	γ
medium	β_1	ε	δ_3
low	α	δ_1	δ_2
	low	medium	high

Degree of the sub-contractor's dependence on his customer (vertical axis)

Degree of the customer's dependence on his sub-contractor (horizontal axis)

Figure 5 Sub-contractor - customer dependence matrix

Area α. Occasional sub-contracting. This area includes sub-contracting relations typified by a low technology content; the collaboration degree is very low because technology transmission is quite limited. The order weight and importance is such as to imply a low dependence degree for both the sub-contractor and the customer. The customer can easily replace his sub-contractor and vice versa; the order weight has little impact on the small firm's sales revenue and strategy.

Area β (β1, β2, β3). Sub-contractor's weaknesses. The sub-contractor's dependence on his customer is always higher than the customer's dependence on his sub-contractor. In this case the collaboration is uneven as the customer's weight is higher compared to the sub-contractor's one. These relations usually imply a low technology exchange; however sub-contractor's dependence is high since most of his sales revenue is derived only from one customer. In particular in this area the customer holds a semi-monopsonistic position. In this case the sub-contractor does not implement a customer diversification policy. This area includes sub-contracting relations -typical of the skills externalization- and all those relations typified by the customer having a stronger bargaining power than his sub-contractor.

Area δ ($\delta 1$, $\delta 2$, $\delta 3$). Large firm's weaknesses. In this area the relationship is unbalanced, the customer's dependence degree is higher than the sub-contractor's one. This area includes those relations typified by the sub-contractor holding a know-how crucial to the customer's production cycle. In particular in the area d2 the sub-contractor holds *not only* the technologies necessary to the customer production cycle, but also an almost monopolistic position because his dependence degree is low whereas the customer's one is high. In this case the sub-contractor has a higher bargaining power as he plays a major role in his relation with the customer.

Area ε. Strategic sub-contract. Under many aspects this area can be viewed as the "area of the complex sub-supply", as the small firm is equipped to perform all operations, from design to industrialization and execution of the order. In the area e relations are balanced as the two involved parties are mutually and similarly dependent. The technological level is high and this demands strict collaboration. This area includes relations involving skills externalization: the large firm is one of the small firm's important partners and the small firm performs important stages of the large firm's production cycle.

Area γ Co-maker relations. In this area relations are typified by a high customer/sub-contractor mutual dependence. Between the two partners strict collaborative relations are established as the sub-contractor performs a significant share of the customer's production cycle. On the other hand the customer is the major sub-supplier's customer. The sub-contractor holds technologies which are able to interface with the customer's ones who is able to affect the sub-contractor technological development by imposing operational specifications and technological dynamics. In the area g the number of technology transmission channels being used is higher than in the area e. The shift from the occasional sub-contracting area a to the co-makership area g is accompanied by an increasing use of the technology transmission channels. *Even the co-makership relation is typified by a different degree of intensity.*

The empirical research

The research allowed the various inter-firm relations to be identified and the specificity of the relations underlying the co-operative partnership in which many sub-contracting firms and their customers are included to be assessed. We wondered how the nature of the relations, and in particular of the channels through which these relations are set up, affects the dependence relation and the competitiveness of the network firms.

The field survey concerned a sample of 61 firms representative of the most advanced Italian industrial sector. The survey was conducted from early 1991 to May 1992 through constant interviews and meetings with the firms' managers. The interviews were conducted through a semi-structured questionnaire aimed to catch both quantitative and qualitative elements. The exploratory survey to test the validity of the research approach was started in 1987; the firms investigated have been under examination and their data constantly up-dated.

The survey unit

The structure of the network can be described through the different patterns of relations between the agents. Two interacting firms constitute a *couple*.

The study of the couple is crucial to understand the nature and strength of the network structure the firms are part of. In a network, *exchanges* and *adjustments* take place thanks to the relation. For this reason in considering only two firms and their relations, we allow also for the set of relations between them, the other firms and the external world (Figure 6).

This statement, namely that the survey unit is representative of the set of interactions taking place within the network, can be easily understood by resorting to the *metaphor of the force field* (Melin, 1989). Everything concerning the firm A and the firm B (or core) denotes the force field gravitating round the firm A and the firm B. The extent of the relations between A and B denotes all forces in the network; thus the effect of the interactions between all network agents is measured through the assessment of the interactions within the couple A and B.

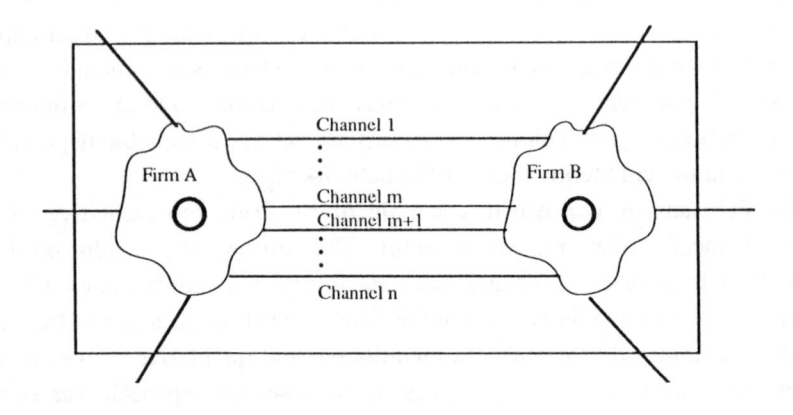

Figure 6 The research unit: the couple

The sample of the investigated firms

The investigated customers are: Augusta, Alenia, Alfa Avio, Ansaldo, FF.SS., Fiat, Iveco, Galileo, Indesit, Magnaghi, Merloni, Olivetti, Piaggio, Siemens, Sip, Zanussi. These firms selected belong to medium-high technological sectors. They are also representative of the major dynamics typifying our country. In particular sub-contracting involves the following sectors: aerospace (8 firms), automotive (20 firms), electromechanical (2 firms), machines for agrofood processing (6 firms), mechanics (17 firms), mechanical-textile (5 firms), telecommunications (6 firms) transportation (6 firms) other sectors (17 firms).

The investigated sub-contracting firms are broken down into the following size classes: 10 microfirms (less than 20 employees), 31 firms with 21 to 100 employees and 20 firms with more than 100 employees.

Some firms are leaders of a group of small and medium enterprises or are members of a group. From the geographical standpoint the firms are based in various Italian regions.

Manufacturing activities of the investigated sub-contractors

The manufacturing activities of the investigated firms represent some of the major transformations in the industrial firms of our country. They include high labor-intensive processing (such as painting and assembly) and highly automated processing (processing of rubber, iron powders, etc.). In some cases there is a man-machine integration.

The manufacturing activities of the sub-contracting firms range from the manufacturing of finished products to the assembly of complex components. Also when the activities have similar features, there is a high differentiation as to the mix of the four technology components: machines, information, human resources and organizational rules (Esposito and Raffa, 1991a).

Outcomes of the empirical survey

For each of the 61 sub-contractors of the sample, on the basis of the field research, two dependence indicators were derived related to their first, second and third customer. In this manner the respective dependence matrices were drawn. Figure 7 exhibits 157 relations between the 61 investigated firms and their first, second and third customer. A small number of heavy dependence relations can be easily observed ($\beta 2$, $\delta 2$). The number of firms along the diagonal is higher in the area α, it declines along the diagonal and becomes smaller in γ. This indicates that most of the firms are typified by a low inter-dependence.

Other more meaningful indications can be drawn by analyzing the relation of the sub-contractors with their first, second and third customer (Figures 8, 9 and 10).

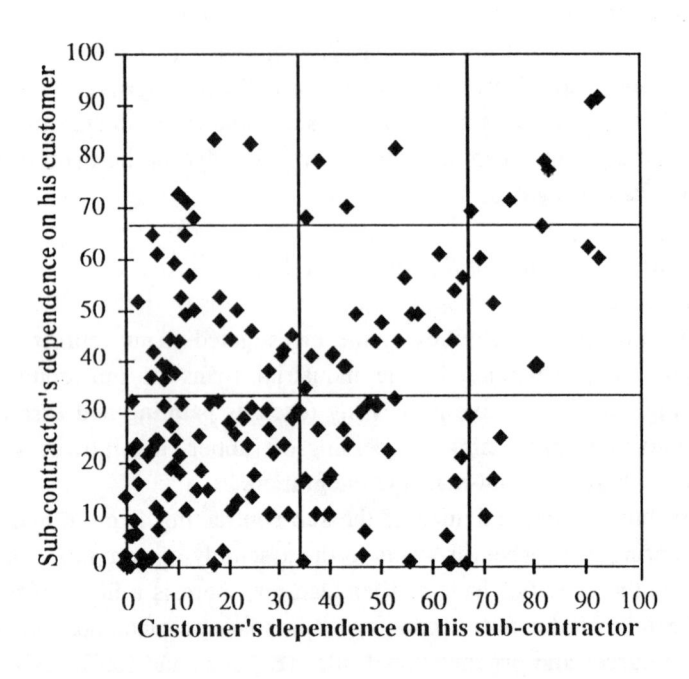

Figure 7. The dependence matrix related to 61 investigated sub-contractors and their first, second and third customer

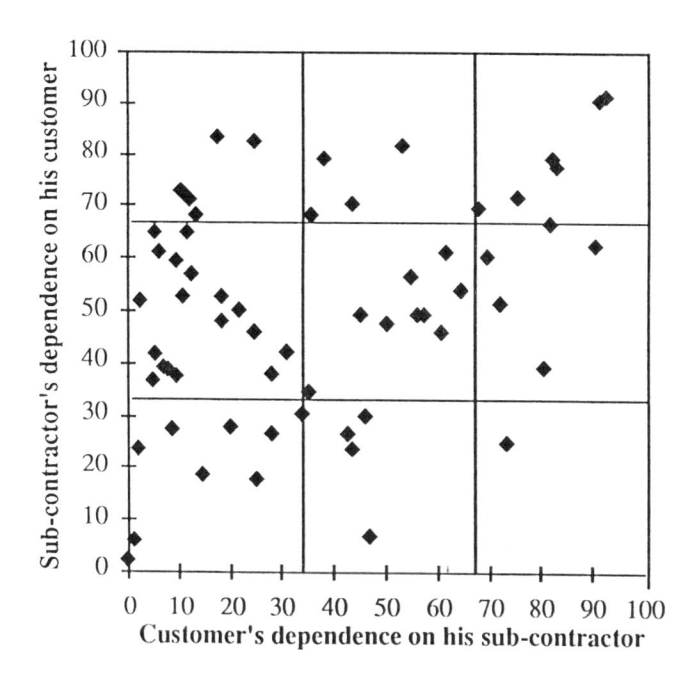

Figure 8. The dependence matrix related to 61 investigated sub-contractors and their first customer

It can be observed that from the first to the third customer, the customer's dependence on his sub-contractor increases. Namely only in the case of the relation with the first customer is the sub-contractor's dependence heavy (Figure 8). In general the firms distribution on the dependence matrix shows that we are in the presence of heterogeneous behaviors corresponding to different characteristics of the firms. Consequently there are different types of relations between customers and sub-contractors.

However we can observe that a meaningful number of the investigated firms are positioned below the main diagonal. This indicates that, as to systematic technology-based firms, the customer's dependence on his sub-contractor is heavy. Along the main diagonal the shift *from occasional to strategic sub-contracting and to early integration forms* is particularly significant.

The analysis of the Figure 9 is even more significant. It shows how the second customer's dependence on his sub-contractor is heavier than the first customer's. Namely the survey outcomes show that the sub-contractor tries to get orders also from firms positioned on a technological level lower than the first customer's. So doing the sub-contractor gains a bargaining power against the second and third customer but, above all, *he uses the know-how acquired and/or developed through the collaboration with the first customer. The sub-contracting firm thus becomes a vehicle for transmitting technological skills while achieving its institutional targets.*

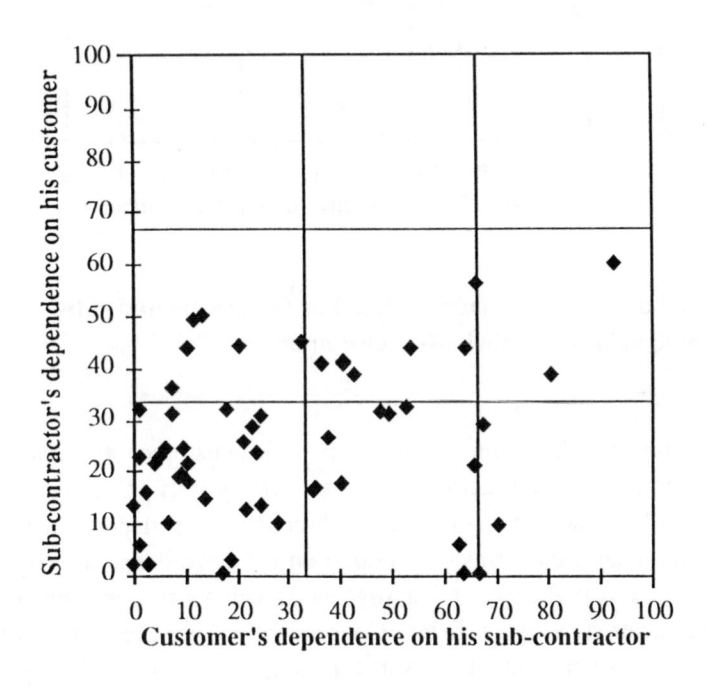

Figure 9 The dependence matrix related to 61 investigated sub-contractors and their second customer

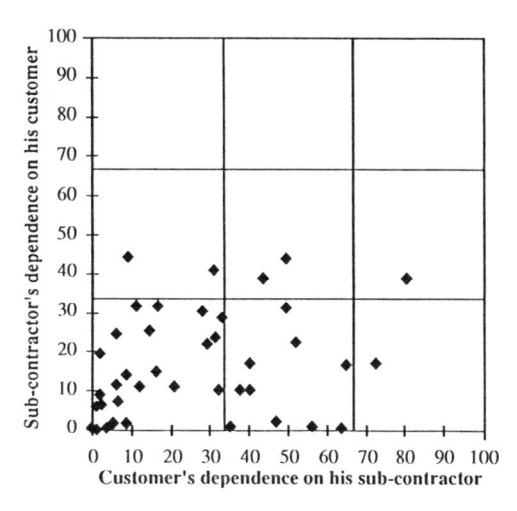

Figure 10. The dependence matrix related to 61 investigated sub-contractors and their third customer

Table 1. The importance of the technology transmission channels

Technology transmission channels	Customer		
	First	Second	Third
Raw material flow	6,6	6,2	4,9
Transfer of pre-finished parts and components	4,1	3,6	2,8
Equipment for specific manufacturing	5,0	4,4	5,4
Support through customer's training activities	4,1	4,7	4,2
Customer's visits and suggestions	5,7	5,5	5,9
Collaboration at the beginning of the order	6,2	5,8	6,1
Written documents (projects and other information flow)	7,0	7,0	7,4
Meetings at the customers'	5,7	5,4	5,6
Customer's visits to verify the state of the order	6,0	5,9	6,0
Customer's suggestions for the adoption of quality control	6,2	6,0	5,9
Customer's direct intervention to improve QC function	6,7	6,9	6,8

Source: ODISSEO-DIS, *Faculty of Engineering, Naples, Italy*

Table 2. The weight of the technology transmission channels

Technology transmission channels	Customer		
	First	Second	Third
Raw material flow	44,3%	34,4%	13,1%
Transfer of pre-finished parts and components	41,0%	24,6%	9,8%
Equipment for specific manufacturing	39,3%	27,9%	13,1%
Support through customer's training activities	37,7%	18,0%	8,2%
Customer's visits and suggestions	68,9%	44,3%	26,2%
Collaboration at the beginning of the order	85,2%	67,2%	41,0%
Written documents (projects and other information flow)	96,7%	80,3%	54,1%
Meetings at the customers'	65,6%	54,1%	29,5%
Customer's visits to verify the state of the order	86,9%	70,5%	39,3%
Customer's suggestions for the adoption of quality control	78,7%	55,7%	32,8%
Customer's direct intervention to improve QC function	62,3%	39,3%	21,3%

Source: ODISSEO-DIS, Faculty of Engineering, Naples, Italy

Tables 1 and 2 - exhibiting the weight and importance of the technology transmission channels to the various customers - confirm that just stated. It can be observed that the weight of the channels declines significantly when shifting from the first to the third customer. This is just because of *the sub-contractor/various customers asymmetrical relation*. On the other hand the importance of the channels does not vary significantly; this indicates the strong role of the technology channels in the different sub-contracting relations. The asymmetry between sub-contractors and customers varies in the different sectors as a function of the transformation process development in the inter-firm relations.

Figure 11, denoting the dependence matrix in the aerospace sector, highlights two broad firm clusters. The first cluster is typified by a heavy sub-contractors' dependence and involves conventional sub-contracting. The second cluster exhibits a heavy mutual dependence and indicates a *meaningful sub-contractor/customer integration process*. Allowing for the transformations experienced in the last few years by the aerospace industry, it can be stated that this process allowed the development of the strategic sub-contracting relations.

As regards the automotive industry (Figure 12) the survey outcomes show clearly that - alongside the conventional sub-contracting- a transformation process in the customer/sub-contractor relation was started involving early balanced relations. This process will continue in the next few years and will imply a further decline in the number sub-contractors. Indeed the customer will rather have only one sub-contractor being, in his turn, the leader of a sub-contractors chain.

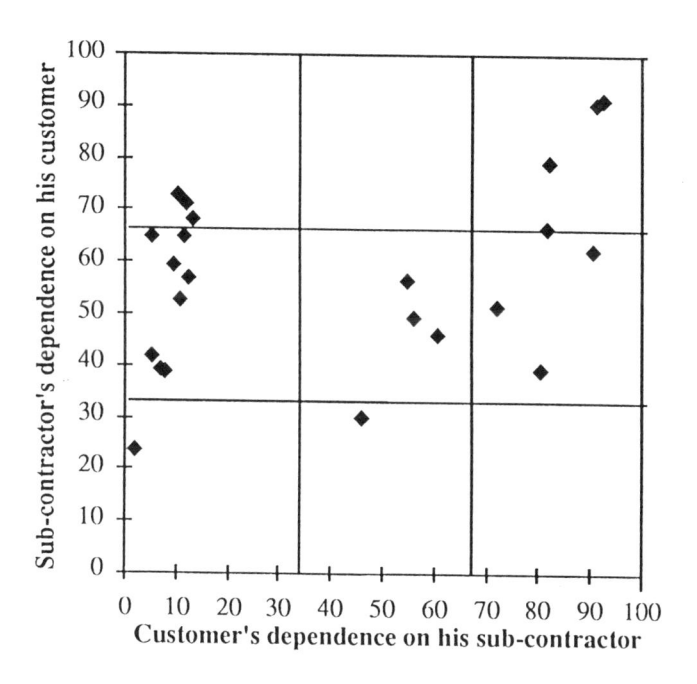

Figure 11. Dependence matrix related to the aerospace investigated firms and their customers

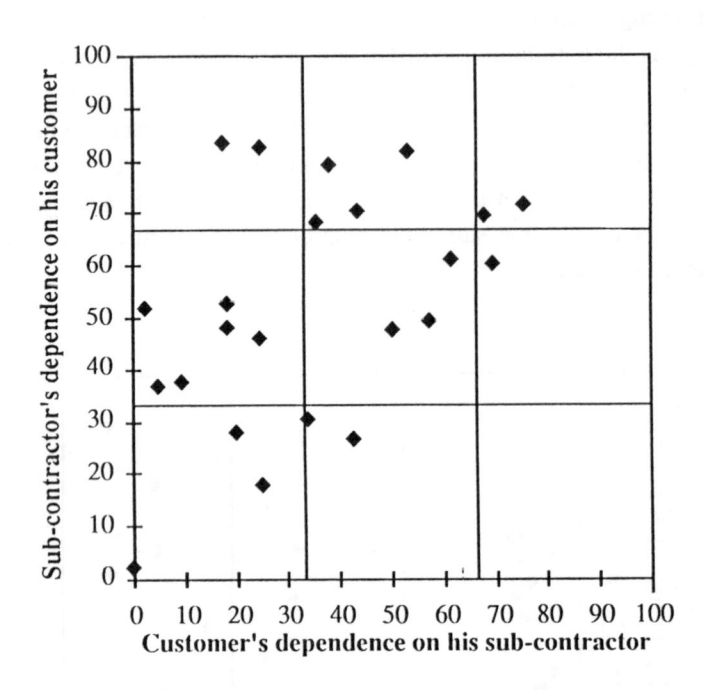

Figure 12. Dependence matrix related to the investigated automotive firms and their customers

The shift along the sub-contractor diagonal indicates his importance to the customer. The characteristics of this phenomenon are basically similar in the various countries (Hallen and Johanson, 1989).

Firms invest in the development of information, social and technical channels. Relations between them are then closer, and specific dependence relations develop. Under many aspects the parallel increase in transactions and production efficiency accounts for the sub-contractor's/customer's reluctance to change their partner, even to the detriment of *their autonomy* (Hallen, 1986). This trend emerges both in the *international sub-contracting relations* (customers and sub-contractors based in different countries), and in the *local and national sub-contracting relations*. Usually what varies is the strength of the relation that is usually stronger between sub-contractors and customers based in the same country.

Network knowledge and managerial behaviors

The empirical outcomes of the research help identify some managerial behavior. The knowledge of the network is crucial to design and plan the optimum resources mix. This knowledge can be acquired by actively joining all the network development stages. It is also important to understand the interaction between the various units and the processes of continuous mutual adjustments performed through capital investment (e.g. purchase of new machines) and daily rationalization operations (thousands of small adjustments increasing the efficiency of the processing activity and the product development).

For a network to operate effectively four conditions must exist (Hakansson, 1987):

1. Agents must speak a common language (i.e. have a common technology and a similar way of thinking about technical issues).
2. Agents must know each other very well (i.e. know their mutual skills and resources, how to organize them, how to behave with people.
3. Agents must trust each other (i.e. fair play as to the mutual exchange of information).
4. Agents must stimulate each other to improve their performance.

The literature mentions the sub-contractor benefit from the customer demand for appropriate performances to meet the product/service requirements.

The knowledge of some of the major features of the network agents enables the firm to have a timely and flexible decision making process as to the use of the various internal and external resources.

Some elements illustrated in this paper have some *regulatory* and *managerial* implications that may helps to position our own firm.

The dependence matrix, providing a quantitative assessment of the position of the various firms against the others, allows the assessment of the actions to be performed to occupy a given position. It may help identify the following: our own market segment and, consequently, the best customer or sub-contractor; the actions to improve our relations with the customer/customers; the way to compete with other sub-contractors. As to these issues, the technology uncertainty/market uncertainty matrix might be useful.

Conclusion and future research developments

This study illustrates in-depth the typologies of the inter-firm relations and allows new assumptions to be made and tested.

The notion of network used herein fits to describe and interpret the complex present reality of the manufacturing/service firms. However this notion has to be precisely limited and defined to assign it a precise theoretical meaning. This is in order to avoid using it as an ambiguous notion denoting all inter-organizational bonds between firms.

In this research the survey unit was a couple of firms being part of the environment. The focus on them allowed to major elements of the dynamics in the inter-firm relation to be understood. The identification of the technology transmission channels and their weight outlined an analytical framework of the inter-firm relations and in particular of their different degree of dependence, collaboration and/or competitiveness.

The research outcomes highlight that the co-makership success is related to the types of channels used to develop and preserve the relation. An effective management must then learn how to identify the network structure.

In the Italian case this process is slower than in other countries. It requires the simultaneous presence of various factors. Mention must be made of the importance of the sub-contractor's involvement starting from the design stage, and of the critical role played by human resources that on the one hand must act as sources facilitating relations amongst enterprises and on the other hand be components of the enterprise's inter-functionality (Mattana, 1991). According to the co-makership trend, enterprises strongly focusing on quality and reliability try to turn their conflictual relations with sub-contractors into collaborative relations (Hax and Majluf, 1990). Of course collaboration may range from an operational integration of some elements, to a deep integration leading to strategic convergences. From the operations standpoint double checks are eliminated after establishing the necessary reliance relation.

As a whole the firms may draw some benefits as to lead time reduction and timely response to market demand.

From a competitive perspective (Porter, 1985), allowing for the five competitive forces defining the competitiveness level, the most advantageous position to the customer is the area typified by a high sub-contractor's dependence. On the other hand the most advantageous position to the sub-contractor is the one where the customer's dependence is prevailing.

From the trade off between the different customer's and sub-contractor's interests a wide range of relations is generated and developed, whose characteristics depend on the weight and financial, economic and technological importance of the order, as well as on the two partners' strategies and the industry specificity.

The research exhibits - mainly in the medium-high technological sectors, whose competitiveness is quality- based - the early set up of balanced relations in which the equilibrium is guaranteed by mutual heavy dependence. Relations mainly involve the sectors typified by a complex organization of the production cycle. The achievement of high performance as to efficiency and effectiveness depends on the individual firm (then also on the sub-contractor), on the management of the network internal relations and on the inter-firm relation system.

Appendix - Definition of variables used in the model

Below we illustrate how the two dependence indicators, used in the model to draw the sub-contractor-customer dependence matrix related to the investigated firms, were defined. Table 3 summarizes the dependence indicators definition.

Table 3. Dependence indicator's definition

Indicator		Partial indicator		Value
Sub-contractor's dependence on his customer	DSC_{ij}			$100*\sqrt{\dfrac{A1^2+B2^2}{2}}$
		Customer's relative weight	A1	Sub-contractor's sales revenue share related to activities performed for the customer
		Collaboration degree in the customer/sub-contractor relation	B2	$\dfrac{1}{99}*\sum_{i=1}^{11}B1_i$
		Technological importance of each channel	$B1_i$	Value assessed by the researchers together with the managers of the investigated firms [1 to 9]
Customer's dependence on his sub-contractor	DCS_{ji}			$100*A2*\sqrt{\dfrac{C^2+B2^2}{2}}$
		Sub-contractor's relative weight	A2	percentage of activities performed by the sub-contractor for the specific order execution
		Importance to the customer of the component manufactured by the sub-contractor	C	Value assessed by the researchers together with the managers of the investigated firms [1 to 9]
		Collaboration degree in the customer/sub-contractor relation	B2	$\dfrac{1}{99}*\sum_{i=1}^{11}B1_i$
		Technological importance of each channel	$B1_i$	Value assessed by the researchers together with the managers of the investigated firms [1 to 9]

Source: ODISSEO-DIS, Faculty of Engineering, Naples, Italy

Firstly we identified and measured the following input variables related to:

A. firm (A1, A2);
B. relations (B1, B2);
C. product (C).

A. Variables related to firm

With reference to the firm the following variables were measured:

A1. Sub-contractor's sales revenue share related to activities performed for the customer, measured through the variable A1 denoting the *customer's relative weight*. Customer's relative weight refers to the share of the sub-contractor's sales revenue derived from activities performed for the customer. The assumption was made that this dependence follows a S-shaped curve. As the share of sales revenue increases, the sub-contractor's dependence initially grows slowly, then increases faster and finally slows down. A rule of the declining marginal dependence was assumed with reference to high values of the sales revenue percentage. Indeed the sub-contractor's adjustment process to the customer is very high when the latter is the most important sub-contractor's customer, even though he is not the only one. Therefore the sub-contractor's dependence on his customer is already very high as to the shares of sales revenue less than 100%. For this reason the choice was made to denote the sub-contractor's sales revenue related to activities performed for the customer through the sine

customer through the sine function. The formula is:

$$A1 = \frac{1}{2} * [1 + \sin(\frac{\%f}{100} * p - \frac{p}{2})]$$

where %f denotes the sales revenue percentage related to activities performed for the customer. All constants included in the formula are intended to make A1 vary between 0 and 1 respectively in correspondence to percentage values equal to 0 and 100.

A2. Activities performed by the sub-contractor for a specific order, measured through the variable A2, denoting the *collaboration intensity*. As for the variable A1 we have the following formula:

$$A2 = \frac{1}{2} * [1 + \sin(\frac{\%c}{100} * \pi - \frac{\pi}{2})]$$

where %c denotes the percentage of activities performed by the sub-contractor for the specific order execution.

B. *Variables related to relations*

With reference to the collaboration relations the following variables were measured:

B1. Technological importance of each channel (B1); the technological importance was assessed by the researchers together with the managers of the investigated firms through a value from 1 to 9.

B2. Collaboration degree in the customer/sub-contractor relation (B2). This is determined by the summation of the technological importance of all the technology transmission channels (B1) activated within the relationship. As the collaboration level calculated in this manner can have a maximum value equal to 99 (in a relationship where the eleven technology transmission channels are all activated and are of the most technological importance) it was divided by 99. So doing the results are always positive and less than 1, a value corresponding to a relationship with a technical skills exchange totally involving all technology transmission channels.

C. *Variables related to product*

With reference to the product an indicator was drawn denoting the technology importance to the customer of the component manufactured by the sub-contractor (C). The indicator was drawn by the researchers together with the managers of the investigated firm. The indicator takes a value from 1 to 9. The assigned value took into account if the firm was performing only product manufacturing, if it was involved in the product engineering and if it also performed the product design. The highest value is 9, corresponding to a high technology product. The value of 9 was divided so that C1 is always positive and less than 1 (high technology product designed by the sub-contractor).

Finally the two dependence indicators were determined: DSC_{ij} denotes the dependence of the sub-contractor "i" on the customer "j"; DCS_{ji} denotes the dependence of the customer "j" on the sub-contractor "i".

The following formulas were used:

$$DSC_{ij} = 100 * \sqrt{\frac{A1^2 + B2^2}{2}}$$

$$DCS_{ji} = 100 * A2 * \sqrt{\frac{C^2 + B2^2}{2}}$$

where the division by two and the multiplication by 100 are used to make the indices between 0 and 100 vary. 1 denotes a fully independent sub-contractor or customer and 100 a fully dependent sub-contractor or customer.

Acknowledgements

This research is part of the CNR (National Research Committee) Strategic Project "Trasferimento delle tecnologie dei progetti finalizzati". The research was also funded by CNR n. 92.03434.CT11 and CNR n. 91.02225.CT11. The outcomes herein presented are part of a study developed by the CNR Operational Unit of Naples.

Bibliography

Acs, Z.J. and Audretsch, D.B. (1990), *Innovation and Small Firm*, MIT Press, Cambridge (MA).

Aldrich, H.E. (1979), *Organizations and Environments*, Prentice-Hall, Englewood Cliffs.

Ansoff, I.H. (1969), *Business Strategy*, Penguin Books, Harmondsworth.

Ansoff, I.H. (1984), *Implanting Strategic Management*, Prentice-Hall, Englewood Cliffs.

Bertelé, U. and Mariotti, S. (eds.) (1991), *Impresa e competizione dinamica*, ETAS Libri, Milano.

Biggiero, L. (1991), 'Teoria dell'impresa: alcuni spunti di riflessione', *Economia e politica industriale*, n. 71.

Birley, W.S. (1985), 'The Role of Networks in the Entrepreneurial Process', *Journal of Business Venturing*, Vol. 1, No. 1, 107-117.

Braverman A. (1974), *Labor and Monopoly Capital*, Monthly Review, New York.

Burgelman, R. A., Kosnik, T.J. and Van den Poel, M. (1987), 'The Innovative Capabilities Audit Framework', in Burgelman, R.A. and Maidique, (eds), *Strategic Management of Technology and Innovation*, Irwin, Homewood.

Butera, F. (1991), 'Gestire la crescita di una impresa inconoscibile: la piccola e media impresa come 'pacchetto' di organizzazioni coesistenti e come nodo di reti organizzative', *L'Industria*, No. 2.

Callon, M. (1987), 'The Dynamics of Techno-economic Networks' in Combs, R., Saviotti, P. and Walsh, V., (eds), *Economics and Technological Change*, MacMillan, London.

Chandler, A. (1962), *Strategy and Structure*, MIT Press, Cambridge (MA).

Child, J. (1972), 'Organization Structure, Enviroment and Performance: the Role of Strategic Choice', *Sociology*, No. 6.

Child, P., Diederichs, R., Sanders, F.H. and Wisniowski (1991), 'SMR Forum: The Management of Complexity', *Sloan Management Review*, Fall.

Combs, R., Saviotti, P. and Walsh, V., (eds) (1987), *Economics and Technological Change*, MacMillan, London.

Commission of the European Communities. D.G. XXIII (1988), *Partnership Between Small and Large Firms*, Graham-Trotman, London.

Contractor, F.J. and Lorange P. (1990), *La cooperazione tra imprese*, Angeli, Milano.

Crozier, M. (1990), *L'impresa in ascolto*, Il Sole 24-Ore, Milano.

Cusumano, M.A and Takeishi, A. (1991), 'Supplier Relations and Management: A Survey of Japanese, Japanese-Transplant and U.S. Auto Plants', *Strategic Management Journal*, Vol. 12, pp. 563-585.

Dertouzos, M.L., Lester, R.K. and Solow, R.M. (1989), *Made in America*, MIT Press, Cambridge (MA).

Dioguardi, G. (1992), 'L'impresa flessibile', in. D'Antonio, M. (ed.), *Il Mezzogiorno. Sviluppo o stagnazione*, Il Mulino, Bologna.

Dioguardi, G (1983), 'Macrofirm: Construction Firms for the Computer Age', *Journal of Construction Engineering and Management*, ASCE, No. 1.

Dodgson, M. (1990), 'Technology Strategy in Small and Medium-Sized Firms', in Acs Z.J. and Audretsch, D.B., (eds.), *The Economics of Small Firms*, Kluwer Academic Publishers, Dordrecht.

Dosi, G. (1982), Paradigmi tecnologici e traiettorie tecnologiche, *Prometheus*, n.2, Franco Angeli, Milano.

Easton, G. and Araujo, L. (1989), 'The Network Approach: an Articulation', in Hallen, L. and Johanson, J., *Networks of Relationships in International Industrial Marketing*, JAI Press, Greenwich.

Emery, F.E. and Trist, E.L. (1960), 'Socio-technical Systems', in Churchman, C.W. and Verhulst, E.L., (eds), *Management Science, Models and Techniques*, Pergamon Press, London.

Emery, F.E. and Trist, E.L. (1965), 'The Causal Texture of Organizational Environments', *Human Relations*, No.18.

Esposito, E. and Raffa, M. (1991a), 'Supply in Hi-Tech Industry: the Role of the Small Businesses', *Proceedings of the 36th ICBS World Conference*, Wien, June 24-26.

Esposito, E. and Raffa, M. (1991b), 'Quality and supply in the Italian industry: outcomes from an empirical research', *Proceedings of the 8th Annual Conference ICSB 'Entrepreneurship, Small Business and Government Policies'*, Trois-Rivières (Québec), November 14-16.

Filippini, R., Pagliarani, G. and Petroni, G., (eds.), (1992), *Progettare e gestire l'impresa innovativa*, ETAS Libri, Milano.

Gros-Pietro, G.M. and Zanetti, G. (1988), 'Quale politica della concorrenza in Italia', in Bianchi, P. (eds.), *Antitrust e gruppi industriali*, Il Mulino, Bologna.

Hakansson, H., (ed.) (1987), *Industrial Technological Development: A Network Approach*, Routledge, London.

Hallen, L. (1986), 'A Comparison of Strategic Marketing Approaches', in Turnbull, P.W. and Valla, J.P., (eds), *Strategies for International Industrial Marketing*, Croom Helm, Beckenham.

Hallen, L. and Johanson, J. (1989), *Networks of Relationships in International Industrial Marketing*, JAI Press, Greenwich.

Hax, A. and Majluf, H. (1991), *The Strategy Concept and Progress: a pragmatic approach*, Prentice Hall, New York.

Ikeda, M. (1991), 'Development Networks in the Automotive Industry', *Proceedings of the International Symposium on 'The Production Strategies and Industrial Relations in the Process of Internalization'*, 14-18 October, Tohoku University, Sendai, Japan.

Imrie. R.F. and Morris, J. (1988), *Buyer-Supplier Relations in the British Economy: an Empirical Study*, University of Wales, College of Cardiff.

Imrie, R.F., Morris, J. (1992), *Transforming Buyer-Supplier Relations*, MacMillan, London.

Johannisson, B. (1988), 'Network Strategies: Management Technology for Entrepreneurship and Change', *International Small Business Journal*, Vol. 5, No.1.

Johannisson, B. (1990), 'Anarchists and Organizers: Entrepreneurs in a Network Prospective', *International Studies of Management & Organization*, Vol. 20, No. 4.

Johanson, J. and Mattsson, L.G. (1987), 'Interorganizational Relations in Industrial Systems: A Network Approach Compared with the Transaction-Cost Approach', *International Studies of Management & Organization*, Vol. 1.

Johanson, J. and Vahlne, J.E. (1990), 'The Mechanism of Internationalisation', *International Marketing Review*, Vol. 7, No. 4.

Kay, N.M. (1984), *The Emergent Firm*, MacMillan, London.

Kosnic, T.J. and Moriarty, R.T. (1989), 'High-Tech vs. Low-Tech Marketing: What's the difference?', in Hills, G.E., LaForge, R.W. and Parker, B.J., *Research at the Marketing/Entrepreneurship Interface*, Proceedings of the UIC Symposium, The University of Illinois at Chicago.

Lamming, R. (1986), *For Better or For Worse: Technical Change and Buyer - Supplier Relationships in the U. K. Automotive Component Industry*, Operations Management Association of Great Britain, Conference, University of Warwick, January 2-3.

Larson, A. (1991), 'Partner Networks: Leveraging External Ties to Improve Entrepreneurial Performance', *Journal of Business Venturing*, No. 6, pp. 173-188.

Lassini, A. and Mariti, P. (1991), 'Accordi di collaborazione costruttiva e crescita delle piccole e medie imprese innovative', *L'Industria*, No. 2.

Lazerson, M. (1990), *Subcontracting as an Alternative Organisational Form to Vertical-Integrated Production*, Department of Sociology, State University of New York.

Lorenzoni, G and Ornati, O.A. (1988), 'Costellations of Firms and New Ventures', *Journal of Business Venturing*, Vol. 3, No. 3, pp. 41-57.

Lorenzoni, G. (1990), *Architettura di sviluppo delle imprese minori*, Il Mulino, Bologna.

Lundvall, B. (1988), 'Innovation as an Interactive Process: from User-Producer Interaction to the National System of Innovation', in Dosi, G., Freeman, C., Nelson, R., Soete, L. and Silverberg, K., (eds), *Technical Change and Economic Theory*, Frances Pinter, London.

Mattana, G. (1991), 'La qualità nel rapporto fornitore-cliente', in *Come cambia il rapporto fornitore cliente*, Assoservizi, Milano.

Melin, L. (1989), 'The Field of Force Metaphor', in Hallen L., Johanson J., *Networks of Relationships in International Industrial Marketing*, JAI Press, Greenwich.

Metcalfe, J.S. (1988), 'The Diffusion of Innovation', in Dosi, G., Freeman, C., Nelson, R., Soete, L. and Silverberg, K., (eds), *Technical Change and Economic Theory*, Frances Pinter, London.

Mintzberg, H. (1979), *The Structuring of Organization*, Prentice-Hall, Englewood Cliffs.

Nelson, R.I. and Winter, S.O. (1982), *An Evolutionary Theory of Economic Change*, Belknap Harvard University, Cambridge (MA)

Oakey, R. (1984), *High Technology Small Firms*, Frances Pinter, London

Ouchi, W.G. (1980), 'Markets, Bureaucracies and Clans', *Administrative Science Quarterly*, Vol. 25, No. 1, pp. 129-141.

Penrose, E. (1959), *The Theory of the Growth of the Firm*, Basil Blackwell, Oxford.

Porter, M.E. (1980), *Competive Stragegy: Techniques for Analyzing Industries and Competitors*, Free Press, New York.

Porter, M.E. (1985), *Competitive Advantage*, Free Press, London.

Raffa, M. (1992a), 'Small and Large Firms Interdependence', *Proceedings of the 37th ICSB World Conference 'Enterprising in Partnership with the Environment'*, Toronto, June 18_21.

Raffa, M. (1992b), 'Interdependence Level between Small and Large Firms', *Proceedings of the 8th I.M.P. Conference*, Lione, September 3_5.

Raffa, M. (1992c), 'Strategie di cooperazione: l'evoluzione della subfornitura nei settori a tecnologia sistemica', in Filippini, R., Pagliarani, G. and Petroni, G., (eds.), *Progettare e gestire l'impresa innovativa*, ETAS Libri, Milano.

Rogers, E.M. and Kincaid, D.L. (1981), *Communication Networks. Towards a New Paradigm for Research*, Free Press, New York.

Rosenberg, N. (1982), *Inside the Black Box: Technology and Economics*, Cambridge University Press.

Rosenberg, N. (1987), *Le vie della tecnologia*, Rosenberg & Sellier, Torino.

Ruberti, A. (ed.) (1991), *Confronto, innovazione, tecnologia, società*, Laterza, Bari.

Sahal, D. (1981), *Patterns of Technological Innovation*, Addison-Wesley, Reading (MA).

Scherer, F.M. and Perlman, M., (eds.) (1992), *Entrepreneurship, Technological Innovation and Economic Growth-Studies in the Schumpeterian Tradition*, University of Michigan Press.

Scott, C. and Westbrook, R. (1991), 'New Strategic Tools for Supply Chain Management', *International Journal of Physical Distribution and Logistics Management*, Vol. 21, No. 1.

Shapiro, C. (1989), 'The Theory of Business Strategy', *Rand Journal of Economics*, Vol. 20, No. 5.

Simonn H.A. (1977), *The New Science of Management Decision*, Prentice-Hall, Englewood Cliffs.

Slowinski, E.J., Hull, F.M. and Seelig, G.L. (1990), *Managing High Tech Strategic Partnerships Between Large and Small Firms*, CIMS, Lehigh University, Pennsylvania.

Teece, D.J. (1986), 'Profiting from Technological Innovation', *Research Policy*, Vol. 15, pp. 285-305.

The Technology Atlas Team (1987), 'Components of Technology for Resources Transformation', *Technological Forecasting and Social Change*, Vol. 32, No. 1, pp. 19-35.

Thorelli, H.B. (1986), 'Networks: Between markets and hierarchies', *Strategic Management Journal*, Vol. 7, pp. 37-51.

Turnbull, P.W. and Valla J.P., (eds) (1986), *Strategies for* International *Industrial Marketing*, Croom Helm, Beckenham.

Turnbull, P.W., Oliver, N. and Wilkinson, D. (1992), 'Buyer-Supplier Relations in the U.K. Automotive Industry: Strategic Implication of JapaneseManufacturing Models', *Strategic Management Journal*, Vol. 13, pp. 159-168.

Utterback, J.M. and Abernathy, W.J. (1975), 'A Dynamic Model of Process and Product Innovation', *Omega*, Vol. 3, No. 6, pp. 639-56.

Vaccà, S. (1991), 'La grande impresa in transizione', *Economia e politica industriale*, No. 71.

Williamson, O.E. (1975), *Markets and Hierarchies: Analysis and Antitrust Implications*, Free Press, New York.

Woodward, J. (1983), *Comportamento e controllo nell'organizzazione industriale*, Rosenberg & Sellier, Torino.

Zanoni, A. (1992), 'Accordi tra imprese nell'area di produzione', in Lorenzoni, G. (ed.), *Accordi, reti e vantaggio competitivo*, ETASLIBRI, Milano.

Zanoni, A. (1984), *Gli approvigionamenti*, ETASLIBRI, Milano.

1. The inter-firm relations system creates synergy and increases productivity. The possibility to audit the phenomenon depends on the number of sub-contractors linked to the customer. Europe and the USA started many years ago imitating the Japanese practice to set up long-term relations only with a limited number of sub-contractors. Already at the beginning of 1987 official documents of the European Community claimed "European and USA manufacturers have attempted to imitate the Japanese model. In the last five years this has led to a dramatic reduction in sub-contracting. European manufacturers are trying to shift from a multiple sub-contracting system to a few sub-contractors based system. Crucial elements typifing the industry underlie this trend: the need to view price as only one of the competition factors, the increasing product differentiation, a more rapid entry of new products into the market".

16 Qualitative and structural changes of the subcontracting firms: A micro-analytical approach to the study of inter-firm relationships

Emilio Esposito and Corrado L. Storto

Summary

In medium-high technology industries, products must meet strict quality and reliability requirements achievable only through a deep and intense network of relationships between firms involved in product manufacturing. Far more frequently firms in different countries are involved in these alliance systems. Within the networks hierarchies of firms based on firms' technological and commercial competencies, and firms' size are determined. Production cycles are often organized on different levels. Generally, at the first level large global firms are positioned, at the intermediate level national firms, and at the last level small sized subcontracting firms. Among all these various relationships, the subcontracting relationships between large and small-sized firms are particularly relevant. Small-sized firms, due to their specific competencies, play different roles within the firms network. A micro-analytic study was conducted on a sample of firms subcontracting to large sized firms in medium-high technology industries (aerospace, automotive, telecommunications, transportation). This study allowed us to identify a typology of network subcontracting firms based on the analysis of the technology flows between firms: *closed firm, quasi-open firm, open firm, associative firm, leader firm, co-maker firm.*

Introduction

In medium-high technology sectors (such as the aerospace, automotive, components, machine tools, telecommunications transportation sectors) products are more and more frequently manufactured within alliance systems joined by firms from different countries. Within these networks some hierarchies are set, based on the firm's size and on its technological and commercial skills. Production cycles are often organized at different levels. In general, large firms operating on global markets are positioned at the first level, national firms at the intermediate level, and sub-contracting firms at the last level. Through the network the sub-contractor is included into international programs and develops a wide range of collaboration relationships.

In this manner the sub-contracting firm, traditionally closed, turns into an open firm and sets up deeper and more complex collaboration relationships with the customer and other sub-contractors. This meaningful trend can be found in different industries and countries.

Scope and methodology

This work aims at investigating some issues related to qualitative and structural changes that have been typifying the Italian industrial sub-contracting system in the last years. The analysis is made starting from the investigation of the various collaboration forms established by sub-contractors with their customers and other sub-contracting firms. From the analysis of their relationships with other firms, a *typology of sub-contracting firms* is identified.

The investigated firms supply companies operating in medium-high technology based sectors. In these sectors products must meet high reliability and quality standards, that can be achieved only through the commitment of all the firms involved into the production cycle. Customers then set up close collaborations with sub-contractors based on a high exchange of: *explicit and formal technology* (technical specifications, drawings, designs, manufacturing cycles, part programs for NC machines, handbooks);

informal and implicit technology (suggestions for quality management, meetings between the customer's technicians and technicians/entrepreneur of the sub-contracting firms to solve problems arising during the order execution, organizational procedures).

To understand and interpret the qualitative and structural changes in the different industrial sectors, an aggregate approach - comparing the trend of the phenomenon over the years or between different companies only from the *quantitative standpoint* - is inadequate. It is necessary to use a *microanalytical approach* that -from the analysis of the individual sub-contractors- investigates the *variety of inter-firms relationships* and the *qualitative changes* (Freeman, 1991). Based on these considerations we "*entered*" some networks and studied sub-contractors' response to the network stimuli and the re-arrangement of their relationships with the customer and other sub-contractors.

The field survey has been conducted in the last two years by a group of researchers of ODISSEO. The microanalytic study of the inter-firm relationship was conducted with the support of a semi-structured questionnaire and each of the firms of the sample was treated as a case study. All sub-contracting firms were studied through direct visits and interviews. In general each firm required more than one single visit.

The sample of the investigated firms

The sample is made above all of sub-contractors supplying medium-high technology sectors such as the aerospace, automotive and electronic industry. The sample of the investigated firms was stratified in order to obtain meaningful outcomes as to the Italian reality. The major customers of the 40 sub-contractors are plants of the following companies: Alenia, Fiat Auto, Magnaghi of Naples, Siemens, Ansaldo. The sample includes 12 sub-contractors with less than 20 employees (30%), 19 firms with 21 to 50 employees (47,5%), 5 firms with 50 to 100 employees, and 4 firms with more than 100 employees (10%).

Sub-contracting relationships: general problems

The research exhibits different sub-contracting characteristics as to quantity (volume of the sub-contractor's business with an individual customer or an industrial sector); quality and reliability (compliance with customer's procedures and standards); and type of activity (ranging from the manufacturing of mechanical parts to the assembly of sub-systems for aircraft or, in some cases, to the design and manufacturing of a complete set of equipment).

Sub-contractors reduce risks related to market turbulence by setting up a wide range of sub-contracting relationships with various customers often operating in different industries. As an average, *the firms of the sample set up stable relationships with three customers and their sub-contracting activity involves two different industrial sectors.*

For this reason firms have to assess the trade off between the need to adjust their technological asset to the asset of one single customer, and the need to have relationships with different customers. A technological asset adjusted to that of their customer's allows sub-contractors to achieve a higher level of efficiency and be more effective. Sometimes, as customers perform some stages of the production cycle by means of computer-based machines, sub-contractors are forced to equip themselves with NC machines tools, design and design/manufacturing interface systems so as to communicate with the customer technology.

On the other hand the portfolio diversification enables the sub-contractor to reduce risks related to the market demand trend.

Sub-contracting firms are able to solve this dilemma through:

a) *organizational flexibility*. The study shows that sub-contractors are undergoing remarkable restructuring and reorganization processes. These include: *mergers of firms* (operating in equal or similar sectors); *establishment of groups of companies* (aimed at exploiting the technological complementarity and decreasing costs and time); *creation of consortia* (to enter international markets and have joint specialized plants to exploit scale economies). In fact four sub-contracting firms plan to merge with other firms, while 15 firms have *established formal collaboration* relationships through associations and consortia with other sub-contractors. A large number of firms (53%) plan to expand their market geographical area. Many sub-contractors are themselves customers of other sub-contractors;

b) *acquisition of a technological asset allowing to operate with different customers*. In this field a major contribution was provided by the *new flexible automation technologies* (in particular the manufacturing/design technologies and the computer aided design/manufacturing interface technologies). These technologies affect in many ways the inter-firm collaboration: reduce the learning time; make the product quality constant from the very first sample; improve the customer/sub-contractor interface; decrease management costs and response times. Our survey shows that the use of NC and computer aided technologies has rapidly increased in the last years. Whereas in 1983 conventional machines stock amounted to 95% of the total, in 1988 the share of NC machines increased up to 23% and by 1993 firms' plans include the acquisition of a remarkable amount of NC technologies (38%). Presently 31 firms are endowed with NC technologies. Seventeen firms are equipped with design technologies and/or design/manufacturing interface technologies through which they can perform the drawing of a part or the NC machines work schedule.

Alongside these flexible technologies, more specific technologies can also be found such as plants for surface treatments (12 firms) and know how for manufacturing of parts made of compound materials (4 firms).

The investigated firms, alongside a sub-supply mainly based on manufacturing, are slowly replacing the customer in some stages of the production process. Namely, some of them design and manufacture equipment previously made by the customer, produce software for NC machines, production schedules and cycles. In some cases they also design parts and components for the end product and perform the final test of the in-house manufactured part.[1] All sub-contractors of our sample perform manufacturing, some of them engineering (17 out 40), design (6 out of 40) and final test (4 out of 40).

Sub-contracting firms are slowly playing a major role in the customer's overall manufacturing strategy. Sub-contractors, as well as customers, focus their efforts and resources on the most profitable activities of the value chain. Alongside this internal growth, new collaboration relationships (formal or informal, lasting or occasional) between the firms and the external environment are being set up. Within this network each firm plays a particular role according to its specific skills. Hereafter a *sub-contractor typology* is outlined, based on the analysis of the sub-contractor's relationships with the customer and other sub-contracting firms.

Sub-contractor typology

To identify a sub-contractor typology, each sample firm was investigated with reference to the characteristics of its exchange relationship with the customer and other sub-contractors (these, in their turn, may be directly or indirectly linked to the customer through their relationship with other firms). We allowed for the type, quality, frequency and intensity of the technology flows between customer and sub-contractors and between sub-contractors themselves.

When a sub-contractor interacts with another firm and sets up collaboration relationships, a complex exchange of materials, information, human resources and organizational rules takes place. These exchange flows vary in their intensity and direction depending on the various cases. In the customer/sub-contractor relationship, technology flows through many channels.2

Written documents are the most used channel viewed as crucial by thirty-nine sub-contractors of the sample.

A major role is also played by: *meetings joined by customer's and sub-contractor's representatives* (or even by the entrepreneur himself); *meetings and collaboration between the customer and the sub-contractor at the beginning of each order* (30 firms); *customer's or sub-contractor's suggestions* (30 firms); *customer direct intervention* (16 firms) for implementation of specific managerial procedures.

Table 1
Sub-contractors typology

	Closed sub-contracting firm (type A)	Quasi-open sub-contracting firm (type B)	Open sub-contracting firm (type C)
It interacts with	Customer	Customer sub-contractor	Customer sub-contractor (formal linkages); sub-contractor (informal linkages)
It has business exchanges with	High-tech and/or not high-tech end-customers	High-tech and/or not high-tech, sub-contractors of the end customers	Sub-contractors of high-tech end customers
Business exchanges with end customer relate to	Parts manufacturing (preforged and special alloys), equipment for nc machines, bonding	Manufactured parts (preforged and special alloys), equipment for nc machines	Manufactured parts (preforged and special alloys), parts sub-assembling, wiring, circuit board manufacturing
Exchanges frequency with end customer	High for bonding, low for the rest	High	High
Business exchanges with sub-contracting firms relate to		Not relevant stages of the production cycle	Relevant stages of the production cycle (complementary technologies)
Exchanges frequency with sub-contractors		Medium	High
Its position within the sub-contracting network	End ring of the production chain	End ring of the production chain or linkage point toward other sub-contractors	Linkage point toward other sub-contractors
Co-ordination mechanisms (customer/sub-contractor and sub-contractor/sub-contractor)	Meetings, check visits, customer engineers visits, technical drawings, written documents	Meetings, check visits, customer engineers visits, written documents, nc machines part-program, quality control handbook, customer suggestion, phone calls	Meetings, customer check visits, customer engineers visits, written documents, nc machines part-program, quality control handbook, customer suggestions, phone calls, production planning procedures
Input flow	Materials, technical specs, working schedules, training	Materials, equipment, assemblies, technical specs, working schedules, procedures, handbooks	Materials, equipment, technical specs, drawings, suggestions, knowledge transmitted through people
Output flow	Materials	Manufactured parts, written documents	Manufactured parts, equipment, written documents, suggestions to the customer

(continued)

	Associative sub-contracting firm (type D)	Leader sub-contracting firm (type E)	Co-maker sub-contracting firm (type F)
It interacts with	Customer sub-contractor (formal linkages); sub-contractor (formal linkages through associations, informal linkages through people meeting and collaborative agreements not formalized)	Customer sub-contractor	Customer sub-contractor (not determinant)
It has business exchanges with	High-tech end-customers sub-contractors	One or more high-tech end-customers several sub-contractors	Generally one high-tech customer some sub-contractors
Business exchanges with end customer relate to	Parts manufacturing (preforged and special alloys), parts sub-assembling, electronic boards test	All parts manufacturing for an aerospace component, assembling, specific equipment	Design and part manufacturing for a component, mechanical part treatment, assembling
Exchanges frequency with end customer	High	High	Very high
Business exchanges with sub-contracting firms relate to	Relevant and not relevant stages of the production cycle depending on the specific role of the firm as to the agreement	Relevant and not relevant stages of the production cycle. It depends on the specific role of the sub-contractor within the sub-contractor network	Relevant and not relevant stages of the production cycle.
Exchanges frequency with sub-contractors	High, especially in the case of the existence of formal agreements	High or low depending on the externalized activity	High or low depending on the kind of the externalized activity
Its position within the sub-contracting network	Part of a production chain	Vertex of a production pyramid	An extension of customer plant
Co-ordination mechanisms (customer/sub-contractor and sub-contractor/sub-contractor)	Meetings with the customer, check visits, customer engineers visits, meetings with other sub-contractors, nc part-program exchange with other sub-contractors, written documents, technical drawings, quality control handbook, phone calls, customer suggestions, technical reports, production planning procedures	Meetings with the customer and other sub-contractors, check visits, customer engineers visits, technicians transfer to other sub- contractors, written documents, quality control handbook, phone calls, customer suggestions, technical reports, technical specs and drawing equipment lent to other sub-contractors	Joint-design groups made of customer and sub-contractor's engineers and technicians, meetings with the customer, written documents, technical drawings, equipment, phone calls, technical reports, training, customer's engineers visits, production planning procedures
Input flow	Materials, equipment, technical specs, drawings, suggestions, knowledge transmitted through people, information software incorporated	Materials, equipment, technical specs, drawings, suggestions, knowledge transmitted through people	Materials, equipment, drawings, technical specs, knowledge transmitted through people
Output flow	Manufactured parts, equipment, sub-assemblies, written documents, suggestions to the customer	Manufactured parts, equipment, sub-assemblies, written documents, suggestions to the customer, technical reports	Manufactured parts, specific equipment, sub-assemblies, technical reports, written documents, suggestions to the customer

Source: ODISSEO-DIS, Faculty of Engineering, Naples, Italy

Also the interaction between two sub-contractors is quite complex. Formal relationships include: transfer of a remarkable share of an order production cycle (31 firms out of 40); externalization of operations unimportant to the contracting out firm's value chain (19 firms). The reasons underlying the contracting out of some production cycle stages are manifold and relate to: *technology, economic convenience, organizational simplification, plant capacity saturation*. Informal relationships between entrepreneurs or technicians of the various sub-contractors are also particular important. These relationships are usually aimed at exchanging technical information or software for NC machines (21 firms out of 40).

Sub-contractors' behavior is not univocal. The same firm has different behaviors and different sub-contracting relationships co-exist, according to the program they are involved into and to the type of order. Six behaviors were identified giving rise to the following typology (Table 1).3

Closed sub-contracting firms (type A)

These firms carry out internally the whole order (metal small parts, composite materials manufactured components) and do not feed any out-flows towards other sub-contractors. They keep relationships only with aerospace end-customers and other industries customers and their behavior is exclusive. These firms usually receive technology from the customer in the form of written documents (technical specifications, working schedule), rules (regulations and procedures for quality compliance), materials (pre-forged parts, special alloys, pre-impregnated fiber sheets, equipment for NC machines or assemblies) and, in some cases, professional skills (training of sub-contractor's employees at the customer premises). *Sub-contracting relationships with the customer may imply a long-term collaboration or occasional orders; closed sub-contracting firms are often the end ring of the sub-contracting chain.*

Quasi-open sub-contracting firms (type B)

These firms have few exchange relationships with other sub-contractors and contract out to other firms some not-relevant stages of the production cycle required by the order. This behavior is due to: cost-benefit trade off analysis; lack of specific know-how and equipment; temporary saturation of their production capacity. These firms receive technology from the customer (that may be the end-customer or another sub-contractor) in the form of: written documents (technical specifications, handbooks, part programs for NC machines, working schedules); materials (pre-forged parts, special alloy bars, equipment for NC machines and assemblies); professional skills (transfer of technicians to the sub-contracting firm, training and certification courses for Quality Controllers); rules (procedures for quality management). *The collaboration of this group of firms with the customer is usually lasting.*

Open sub-contracting firms (type C)

These firms, due to a strategic choice, contract out some important stages of the production cycle to firms *having a complementary technological asset*. In this manner they exploit their value chain by achieving higher effectiveness levels. Technical information exchange between technicians from different firms or between entrepreneurs is quite high. *Collaboration with customer feeds and, in its turn, is fed by frequent technology flows.* Some of these firms behave simultaneously as type B and type C firms according to the different orders.

Associative sub-contracting firms (type D)

These firms make formal or informal collaboration agreements with other sub-contractors for a joint benefit. In general formal agreements are targeted to a higher business strength (in particular on foreign markets) or to additional technological skills for reducing risks of failure. These collaborative relationships are also aimed to achieve a joint business volume such as to justify investment in specialized and expensive equipment and plants. As to our sample, sub-contractors in order to achieve these targets make *formal contracts* or establish *consortia*. Sometimes two or three open sub-contracting firms make an informal collaboration agreement.

This agreement can imply a role exchange for the management of different orders: the firm getting the order commits itself to contract out a share of the activities to other sub-contractors involved in the informal agreements. Through this associative relationship sub-contractors strengthen their bargaining power and establish joint strategies. In general associative firms show different opening degrees, according to their flows towards other sub-contractors or to the joint manufacturing plants created as a result of collaborative agreements.4

Leader sub-contracting firms (type E)

These firms become themselves customers of other sub-contractors performing in different sub-sectors (10-15 firms of our sample). The leader firm gets the order from the aerospace customer for manufacturing a complex component or a sub-assembly -the production of which implies different manufacturing stages. Depending on technological requirements and available resources, this sub-contractor/customer allocates production work to various firms. It becomes the top of a pyramid-shaped production system it is responsible for. Sometimes these firms are members of an industrial group. The arising of leader firms falls within the restructuring process of the manufacturing system managed by the customer. This phenomenon is comparable to what can already be found in the Japanese automotive industry and partly in other European countries. *The leader behavior of some sub-contracting firms supports activities coordination, improves information flows and increases quality and reliability standards.*

Co-maker sub-contracting firms (type F)

Relationships established by these firms with their customers are quite similar to the co-maker relationships. In this case sub-contractor/customer collaboration is very close (both ways frequent and high technology flows). This collaboration implies often a transfer of technicians from the customer to the sub-contractor and vice-versa.

Co-maker sub-contractor are responsible for the manufacturing of a product part or sub-assembly, or of specific equipment. Their responsibility starts from the design specifications choice.

Conclusion

The study of the collaboration relationships set up by sub-contractors with their customers and other sub-contracting firms, allowed to *identify a sub-contractor typology*. This relates to *six different firm's behaviors*: *closed, quasi-open, open, associative, leader, co-maker*.

With the exception of the closed firm, a behavior is not exclusive. For instance co-makers are typified by a leader, associative and open behavior. Likewise, some open firms contract out unimportant stages of the production cycle (quasi-open behavior). The sub-contractor's trajectory develops through subsequent stages: from closed firm to open firm, up to the last stage of co-makership.

The difficulties sub-contractors have to cope with (both internally as to the product/process, and externally as to the environment and market turbulence) drive them to establishing a system of new relationships. In this system, small and large enterprises contribute, according to different hierarchic roles, to the product realization. This conclusion paves the way to the assumption that the sub-contracting firm, traditionally closed, can develop by turning into an open firm and setting up stronger and complex relationships with the customer, the other sub-contractors and the environment.

That highlights the increasing and complementary role being played by the small and medium enterprise in the present industrial development stage.

Acknowledgements

This research is part of the CNR Strategic Project "Trasferimento delle tecnologie dei progetti finalizzati". The research was also funded by the CNR 92.03434.CT11 "Technology transfer between small and large firms". The authors thank Olav Spilling for their precious suggestions.

Bibliography

Allen, T.J. (1988), *Managing the Flow of Technology*, MIT Press, Cambridge (MA).

Bertelè, U. and Mariotti, S., (eds.), (1991), *Impresa e competizione dinamica. Complessità economica, efficienza d'impresa e cambiamento industriale*, ETAS LIBRI, Milano.

Birley, S. (1985), 'The Role of Networks in the Entrepreneurial Process', *Journal of Business Venturing*, No. 1.

EEC, (1990), *The competitive challenge facing the EC automotive components industry*, EEC, London.

Del Monte, A. (1991), 'Alcuni modelli di interpretazione nei rapporti fra grandi e piccole imprese', *Proceedings of the Conference 'Rapporti di collaborazione tra grandi e piccole imprese'*, Napoli, May 12.

Dioguardi, G. (1991), 'L'impresa flessibile: una risposta alla competizione globale', in Bertelè, U. and Mariotti S. (eds.), *Impresa e competizione dinamica. Complessità economica, efficienza d'impresa e cambiamento industriale*, ETAS LIBRI, Milano.

Esposito, E. and lo Storto, C. (1992), 'Il sistema della subfornitura', *Sviluppo & Organizzazione*, No. 130.

Esposito, E. and Raffa, M. (1991a), 'Supply in Hi-Tech Industry: the Role of the Small Businesses', *Proceedings of the 36th ICSB World Conference*, Wien, June 24-26.

Esposito, E., and Raffa, M., (1991b), 'Quality and supply in the Italian industry: Outcomes from an empirical research', *Proceedings of the 8th Annual ICSB Conference*, Trois-Rivières (Québec), November 14-16.

Filippini, R., Pagliarani, G. and Petroni, G. (eds.), (1992), *Progettare e gestire l'impresa innovativa*, ETAS LIBRI, Milano.

Freeman C., (1991), 'Networks of innovators: A synthesis of research issues', *Research Policy*, Vol. 20, No. 5.

Gros-Pietro, G.M. (1990), 'Ruolo della subfornitura in un sistema industriale avanzato', *Proceedings of the Conference 'Tendenze e prospettive della Subfornitura'*, Milano, November 27.

Jarillo, C.J. (1988), 'On Strategic Networks', *Strategic Management Journal*, Vol. 9, No. 1.

Jarillo, J.C. (1989), 'Entrepreneurship and Growth: The Strategic Use of External Resources', *Journal of Business Venturing*, Vol. 4.

Johannisson, B. (1988), 'Network Strategies: Management Technology for Entrepreneurship and Change', *International Small Business Journal*, Vol. 5, No. 1.

Johannisson, B. (1990), 'Anarchists and Organizers: Entrepreneurs in a Network Prospective', *International Studies of Management & Organization*, Vol. 20, No. 4.

Raffa, M. (1991), "Un modello di valutazione del grado di dipendenza tra le grandi e le piccole imprese", *Proceedings of the Conference 'I processi innovativi nella piccola impresa'*, Università degli Studi di Urbino, October 17-18.

Saget, F. (1988), 'Partnership Between Small and Large Firms: What Does It Entail? How Is It Developing?', in AA.VV., *Partnership Between Small and Large Firms*, Graham & Trotman, London.

Sako, M. (1988), 'Partnership Between Small and Large Firms: The Case of Japan', in AA.VV., *Partnership Between Small and Large Firms*, Graham & Trotman, London.

Slowinsky, E.J., Hull, F.M. and Seelig, G.L. (1988), 'Managing High-Tech Strategic Partnerships Between Large and Small Firms', *Interim Report*, CIMS, Lehigh University, Benthlehem (Pennsylvania).

---

1. Del Monte (1991) and Slowinsky, Hull and Seelig (1988) highlighted the sub-contractors' crucial role in product definition within their relation with large firms. In some cases they also perform R&D and design for the large firms.
2. A detailed description of the technology transmission channel between customer and sub-contractor can be found in Esposito and Raffa (1991) while some outcomes can be found in the paper "A Relationships Typology in Firms Networks" by Mario Raffa.
3. Empirical evidences herein included confirm Dioguardi's model of the multi-pole firm positioned within the system defined by him as macro-firm (Dioguardi, 1991, pp. 180-186).
4. For instance the consortium between some sub-contracting firms for the establishment of a surface treatment center.

17 Internationalizing subcontractors: Is co-operation an alternative?

Niina Hovi

Besides describing an important business phenomenon, this paper aims at raising more questions than answering them. However, the paper can be considered as a preliminary report of a pilot study which is to be followed later by others. The emphasis of this paper has been on description of the current situation of subcontracting in Finland, and especially on the subcontractors' internationalization. We can conclude that the subcontractors' have only very limited knowledge and experience of the international markets, and also their willingness to enter these markets is relatively low. However, as the structural change rearranges the market of subcontractors at least in some cases subcontractors are compelled to seek foreign customers. Alternatives how to lower subcontractors' barriers to export are discussed. Interfirm co-operation appears to result in advantages which could be a solution. Nevertheless, in order to determine the precise effects of co-operation as well as find out how and when co-operation lowers these barriers, further research should be conducted of the subject.

1. Introduction

The importance of subcontractors has been rapidly increasing during the last decade. In Finland for example, the proportion of subcontracting in the metal and engineering industry exceeds 20 % of the industry's annual turnover. The increasing interest in subcontracting has also affected academic research on the matter. Numerous articles have been recently published in academic journals and conference proceedings, but only a few academic studies with empirical material are available. However, also empirical studies will probably be reported in the near future as the interest in the subject appears still to be growing.

Nevertheless, the future research will presumably seek different perspectives than those used in previous studies, since subcontractors are encountering the negative effects of the turbulent environment and economic decline. The subcontracting system in general and consequently also the requirements on subcontractors have changed. Subcontractors have to adapt themselves to increasing specialization, more integrated production systems, growing internationalization, higher quality standards in production, and co-operation of customers (see e.g. Andersson 1992, Andersson & Hovi 1992).

This adaptation should begin with a thorough evaluation of skills and resources and also of strengths and weaknesses. One weakness of subcontractors - which probably has been crucial in this situation - is the subcontractors' dependence on few, often large customers. At the moment when large companies suffer liquidity problems and are strongly reducing their costs, the amount of subcontracting is also decreasing. Subcontractors are compelled to look for new customers, also from abroad, but with their customer-specific, often "tailor-made" production it is not easy.

This paper consists of two parts: firstly a review of the situation of subcontractors and their internationalization, and secondly a discussion of one alternative way of acting, viz. co-operation. The review is based on an empirical survey, which was conducted among the small business in South-Western Finland. The purpose of the discussion is to compare the topical situation of subcontractors and the opportunities which could be offered by co-operation. We attempt to find answers to questions like: Could co-operation help subcontractors to find new customers ? Does co-operation offer means to facilitate subcontractors' internationalization ? In this paper barriers to internationalization and outcomes of co-operation are compared and some conclusions are drawn from the comparison. Based on these conclusions, topics for further research will be suggested at the end of the paper.

2. Subcontractors and previous research of internationalization

We - as many other researchers (cf. Miesenbock 1988) - assume that small and medium-sized businesses differ from larger ones in their internationalization. We consider e.g. their decision-making, international activities, internationalization process and stimuli for exporting to be different. However, despite the growing interest also in academic circles, no conclusive theory of small business internationalization has been developed yet (Miesenbock 1988).

Subcontractors are a subgroup of small firms which are often characterized as firms that operate mostly at domestic markets with relatively few customers. Therefore, from their perspective the most interesting issue in the previous research is probably the research on the reasons for non-exporting. As very few subcontractors are involved in international operations, it would be very rewarding to find out the factors that prevent subcontractors from exporting. Is it possible to find a way that would facilitate subcontractor's entry to international markets ?

The existing research of barriers to exporting is somewhat problematic. Firstly, it is strongly biased to countries like the United States, which have a very large domestic market, on which small firms can easily operate. There is no such need to internationalize as in smaller countries. In these studies small firms' internationalization is naturally seen from different perspective than in e.g. European studies, in which international markets are considered as the only source of potential growth for SMEs.

In addition to the bias to some countries, or possibly because of it, the generalizability of results is in some cases questionable. For example Sullivan and Bauerschmidt (1989) state that too many researchers have assumed their findings of one single nation to be generalizable to situations in other countries, which could be of different character. The economic structure differs country by country: e.g. a small firm in the US is not identical with a small firm in Scandinavian countries. Consequently, differences in findings of barriers to exporting may be due to definition or more fundamental factors as e.g. SMEs' different position in economy or available resources. Because of lacking comparative research it is impossible to state the explaining factors.

The problems become even more evident if we list barriers of export used in some previous research (see Table 1, collected from Bilkey 1978, Bauerschmidt, Sullivan and Gillespie 1986, Sharkey et al. 1989 and Sullivan & Bauerschmidt 1989). From our point of view these barriers do not seem very relevant, instead we agree more with Johanson and Vahlne (1977) who stated in a very general way in their study of small Swedish firms that the most important barriers are lack of managerial knowledge and resources.

Most of the barriers in Table 1 do not seem relevant for Finnish subcontractors. In our opinion, when studying barriers to exporting (or SMEs in general) the tools for the study should be "tailor-made" in order to achieve the best results. Therefore in this study we apply a list of barriers to exporting (see chapter 4) which is a combination of the lists applied earlier in studies of Finnish small firms and their internationalization (e.g. Hurmerinta-Peltomaki 1991, Toivonen 1991, Tuulenmaki 1990, Tuulenmaki-Virtanen 1990 and 1989). In our opinion these lists describe more accurately the true barriers that prevent subcontractors from exporting.

Table 1. Barriers to exporting in some previous studies

```
INTERNAL
        - insufficient finances
        - insufficient knowledge
        - lack of foreign market connections
        - lack of export commitment
        - lack of capital to finance expansion into foreign markets
        - lack of productive capacity to dedicate to foreign markets
        - lack of foreign channels of distribution
        - management emphasis on developing domestic markets
EXTERNAL
        Governmental
        - foreign government restrictions
        - national export policy
        - lack of governmental assistance in overcoming export barriers
        - lack of tax incentives for companies that export
        - high value of our currency relative to those in export markets
        - high foreign tariffs on imported products
        - confusing foreign import regulations and procedures
        - complexity of trade documentation
        - enforcement of national legal codes regulating exports
        Other
        - comparative market distance
        - exogenous economic constraints
        - competition from other firms in foreign markets
        - differences in product usage in foreign markets
        - differences in product specifications in foreign markets
        - language and cultural differences
        - complexity of shipping services to overseas buyers
        - high transportation costs to ship products to foreign markets
        - risks involved in selling abroad
```

3. Empirical data of subcontractors - the KANSA study

In autumn 1990, a survey was conducted in the Satakunta Region in SouthWestern Finland. The survey was called "Kansainvälistyvä Satakunta - KANSA" (Internationalizing Satakunta Region). The questionnaire was sent to 1695 small and medium-sized businesses. The sample consisted of industrial firms which employ less than 500 employees. 582 firms, or 34 % of the sample, returned the questionnaire.[1]

---

[1] Other results of the same survey have been previously reported in three other publications: Toivonen

Of the 582 respondents in the survey, 140 firms obtained 50 per cent or more of their annual turnover from subcontracting. This review focuses on these firms. 50 per cent of the firm's turnover is considered as a suitable limit between subcontractors and non-subcontractors because it helps us to focus on firms which are strongly dependent on subcontracting.

No generally accepted definition of subcontracting or a subcontracting firm exists in the literature. Only a few researchers[2] have tried to develop and define the ambiguous concept. In this paper, subcontracting is defined as in everyday language: "manufacturing products which are used as components in the customer's manufacturing process". A more accurate definition of subcontracting can not be used here as the concept was not defined in the questionnaire.

3.1 Elementary information of the respondents

Although subcontracting is a common way of doing business in Finland, the data of the subcontracting firms is surprisingly lacking. For example, the Central Statistical Bureau of Finland does not collect any information on subcontracting and neither do the interest groups of different industries. One reason for the lack of information might be the complexity of the concept subcontracting itself. However, without any statistical data, knowledge of subcontracting, its structure and position in the Finnish economy is mainly based on "gut reaction", not empirical data.

Some generally accepted beliefs about subcontracting do exist. One objective of this paper was to see if these beliefs and the results of the KANSA study actually fit together. For example, it is generally assumed that subcontracting firms are very small. At least the results of this study verify this assumption. Although the annual turnover of the firms varied from less than 1 million FIM (approx. 200 000 ECU) to over 100 million FIM (approx. 20 million ECU), the majority of companies were very small: 50 % of the firms had an annual turnover below 1 million FIM. The distribution of the firms by their turnover (%) is illustrated in Figure 1.

1991, Uotila 1991 and Veromaa 1991.
[2] One example is Andersson (1990).

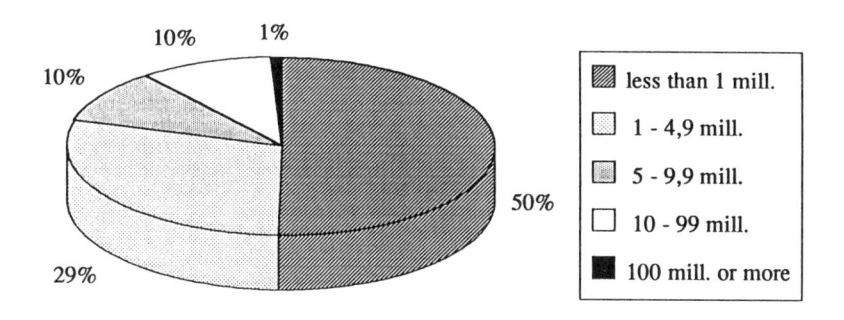

Figure 1. The estimated turnover of subcontractors in 1990

The number of personnel also indicates that we are studying very small firms. The majority of the firms employed less than ten employees, almost two thirds less than five employees. Distribution of the firms by the number of personnel is presented in Figure 2.

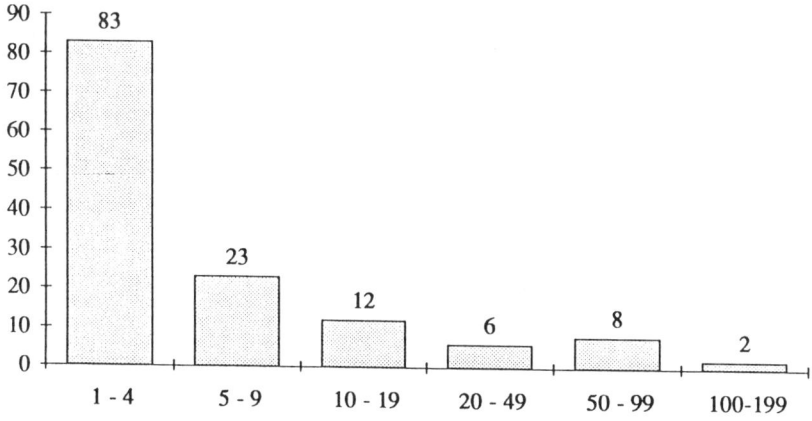

Figure 2. Number of personnel in subcontracting firms

However, according to the results the subcontractors do not substantially differ from the total sample of 582 firms. On the contrary, their size distribution was almost equal to that of small businesses in general. Nevertheless, the subcontractors appeared to be slightly smaller than the rest of the respondents. We must also keep in mind that the smallest firms (1-4 employees) are slightly underrepresented among the respondents (see Toivonen 1991), and it is therefore possible - even probable - that in reality the difference between subcontractors and other small firms is more clear than the results indicate.

Subcontracting is believed to be strongly concentrated to certain industries in Finland. The results of the KANSA study show this assumption to be principally true. Almost 60 per cent of the subcontractors were firms in the metal and engineering industry. Other industries were relatively evenly represented in the sample. When we compare the subcontractors with all the respondents of the survey, we notice that the bias toward metal and engineering is significant: The firms in the metal and engineering industry account for only 34 per cent of the total sample (Toivonen 1991). The division of subcontractors in different industries (in percentages) is illustrated in Figure 3. The category "other industries" includes printing and publishing (7 firms), textile (4), furniture (3), electrotechnical products (3)

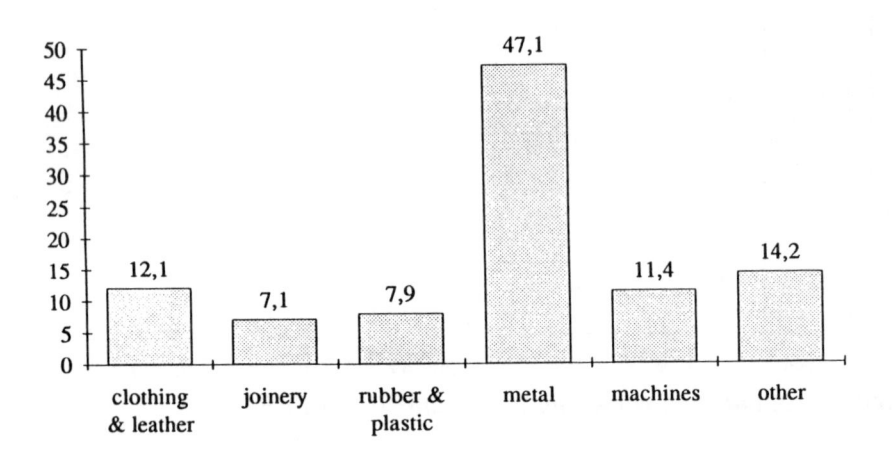

Figure 3. Subcontractors in the Satakunta Region by industry

It is also often suggested that *the boom in Finnish economy in the late 1980s increased substantially the number of firms and especially the number of subcontractors.* At that time, due to the lack of production capacity in larger firms, some tasks were given to smaller firms as subcontracts. Many subcontracting firms were also established as spinn-offs from larger companies. Our results show that although all small businesses are young (Toivonen 1991), we can assume subcontractors to be in an even younger category: 75 per cent of the subcontractors were established less than ten years ago (the percentage in the total sample was 64 %). However, in our opinion the results are only suggestive and do not allow us to draw firm conclusions of the age difference between subcontractors and small businesses in general.

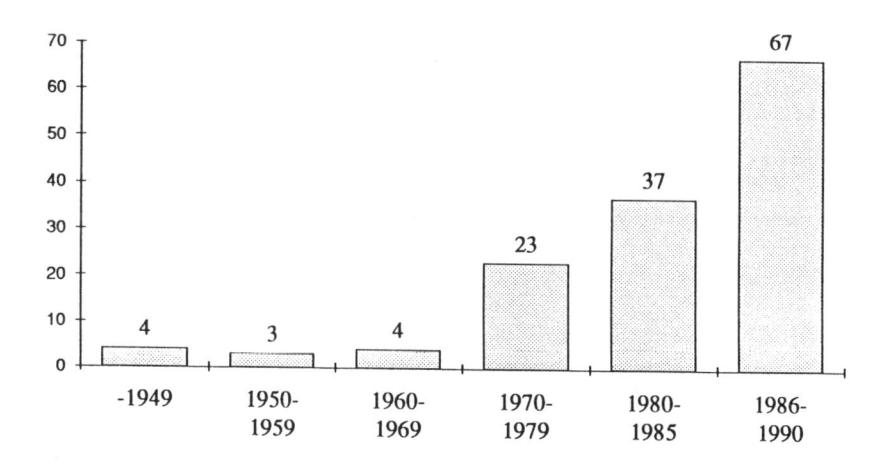

Figure 4. The year of establishment of the subcontracting firms

So, at least according to the KANSA survey, subcontractors seem to have the general characteristics they are supposed to have: i.e. they are small, young and mainly concentrated to the metal and engineering industry. However, in order to analyze subcontractors' internationalization, we have to get further information of their production and clientele.

3.2 Production and clientele

Subcontracting firms are supposed to have a very specialized production. Most of the firms have a long relationship with one or a few main contractors. For example, 70 per cent of the subcontractors in the KANSA study sold the majority of their production - 90 per cent or more - as subcontracted, "tailormade" special products. Without a product of their own, the subcontractors are very dependent on their customers and therefore especially vulnerable to fluctuations in the economy.

The customer structure does not help the position of the subcontractors either. Usually *they have just one or a couple of important customers who buy the majority of their production.* In this study 44 of the 140 firms stated that the share of the biggest customer accounted for more than 90 per cent of their annual sales. In more than 100 firms the main customer's share of annual sales rose to 50 per cent or more. The customers are located close by, and are mostly domestic. The average customer structure (based on mean values), 50 per cent local, 23 per cent regional, 22 per cent other Finnish and 5 per cent foreign customers, is illustrated in Figure 5.

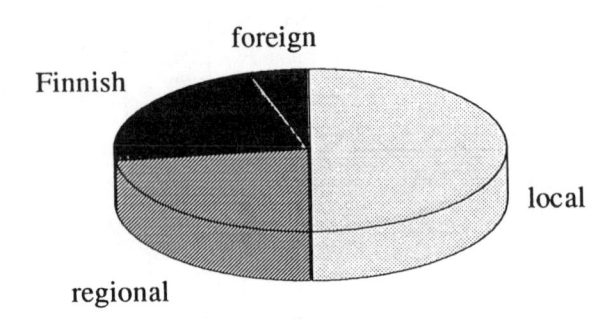

Figure 5. Subcontractor's customer structure

The concentration to a domestic customer-base is noticeable; for example, in a comparative Swedish study subcontractors had considerably more foreign contacts (Braunerhjelm 1991). However, some of this difference may be due to different definition: Braunerhjelm defines a film to be subcontractor if the proportion of subcontracted products exceeds 20 per cent of turnover. In addition, he excluded the smallest firms (personnel 1-20) from his study, whereas they formed a considerable part of the sample in the KANSA study.

In conclusion, both the subcontractors' production and markets are strongly concentrated. In the present economic recession and turbulent environment both of these characteristics can be seen undesirable as they make subcontractors dependent on their customer's performance. In order to survive search for new alternatives will be inevitable.

4. Subcontractors and internationalization

From the traditional, "Ansoffian" point of view[3] subcontractors have four alternative ways to act in the future: to continue business as before, to seek either for new products or new markets, or diversify both products and markets (see also Andersson 1992 and Andersson & Hovi 1992). When describing the future of subcontractors we use the term "alternative" in order to avoid the term "strategy" which has been used in some studies (e.g. Andersson 1992). Terms "strategy" and "strategic" are complex and ambiguous enough to warrant studies of their own.

Continuing with existing business does not seem to bring any solution to the subcontractors' problems in the long run, and diversifying both products and markets simultaneously probably exceeds the resources of most subcontractors. Of the two remaining relevant alternatives this paper focuses on the latter, finding new markets.

As the results of the KANSA survey indicated, most of the subcontractors' present customers were located close by. This is natural, as the firms are usually established to fulfill the needs of one larger customer. As subcontractors have relatively few experiences of international markets (Braunerhjelm 1991, see also the results of KANSA below), we can assume that they probably first try to broaden their customer structure in Finland.

---

[3] For Ansoff's growth strategies, see Ansoff 1965.

However, the Finnish economy is small and especially during the present recession they may find the number of potential customers very limited. Consequently, also foreign customers are considered.

As stated earlier, however, very few subcontractors have experiences of international markets. In the KANSA survey the degree of internationalization among the subcontractors was measured as the amount of export, because exporting is the most common form of internationalization of SMEs. Most of the respondent firms had never tried exports, and only 10 firms of the 140 subcontractors had regular export activities. The division of firms according to their involvement in export activities is presented in Figure 6.

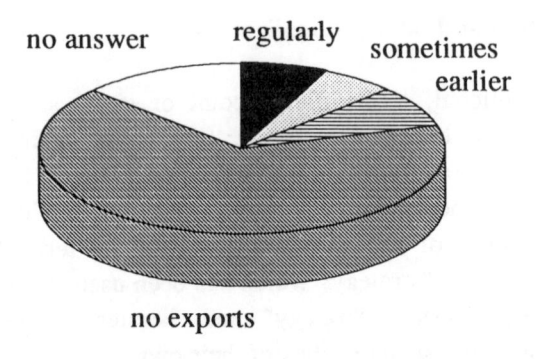

Figure 6. Export activities of subcontractors

Besides actually exporting, also the willingness to export was meagre. Only 19 per cent of the subcontractors expressed a willingness to export. However, the number of non-respondents in this question was considerable, 26 per cent. Why then, this lack of interest in exporting ? An export decision is based on internal and external factors of the firm and a very important internal factor is the decision-maker's perception of the firm's resources and ability to enter new markets. According to the respondents of the KANSA survey, subcontractors appear not to believe in their capabilities in entering foreign markets.

In the survey respondents were asked to state the most significant barriers to exporting. The suggested alternatives were:
- lack of suitable product (PRODUCT)
- insufficient production capacity (CAPACITY) -non-competitive price (PRICE)
- lack of skilled labour (LABOUR) -difficulties finding customers (CUSTOMERS)
- lack of experience in export marketing (EXPERIENCE) -problems in finance (FINANCE)
- lack of experienced export personnel (PERSONNEL) -insufficient knowledge of export markets (MARKETS)
- severe competition in export markets (COMPETITION) -barriers to trade (BARRIERS)
- lack of knowledge in foreign business and culture (CULTURE) - lack of language skills (LANGUAGE)
- sufficient domestic markets (DOMESTIC)

According to the results of KANSA, issues related to information, experience and skills seemed to be the most significant barriers to enter foreign markets (see Figure 7). This was not surprising, as other Finnish studies have also shown that factors connected with knowledge and competence especially restrict small businesses (Tuulenmaki & Virtanen 1989, Tuulenmaki & Virtanen 1990). Also compared with all the respondents of the KANSA survey subcontractors seemed not to differ significantly in this respect (see Toivonen 1991).

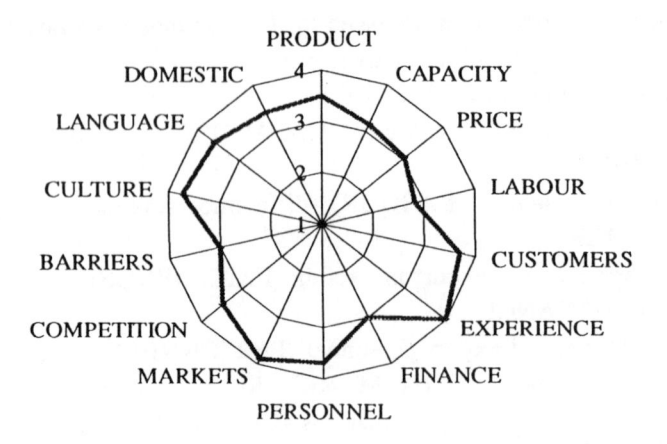

```
                    PRODUCT
        DOMESTIC      4      CAPACITY
   LANGUAGE                      PRICE
                      3
      CULTURE          2         LABOUR
                       1
     BARRIERS                    CUSTOMERS

    COMPETITION                  EXPERIENCE
             MARKETS      FINANCE
                  PERSONNEL
```

Figure 7. Subcontractors' barriers to exporting

(Likert scale from 1 to 5 was used in the questionnaire, i.e. 1= not significant, 2= not very significant, 3= some significance, 4=quite significant)

However, both among all the respondents of the KANSA study and also among the domestic firms of another study made among SMEs in South-Westem Finland (Hurmerinta-Peltomaki 1991) the lack of production capacity was a very important barrier to exporting. Because of the economic upturn in 1990, we did expect that this would have ranked higher among the subcontractors than it eventually did. This is probably due to subcontractors' awareness of their weaknesses concerning internationalization. On the other hand, the fact that 'lack of suitable product' and 'non-competitive price' did not seem to be very significant barriers to exports may also be due to subcontractors' limited knowledge and experience of international markets.

In general we can conclude that all barriers that were mentioned in the questionnaire ranked relatively high. Because of these barriers subcontractors' are neither willing nor able to start internationalizing their operations. What could be done to lower or remove these barriers ?

5. Co-operation as an alternative

As the empirical results in the previous chapter show, the willingness to internationalize lies very low among subcontractors. This was not due to sufficient markets in the home country as could have been expected at the time when the survey was conducted. Rather, the respondents felt their material and immaterial resources limited. With little or no experience of international markets they are not encouraged to engage in activities in foreign markets.

One alternative solution which is often suggested for small businesses is co-operation. It is said that small businesses should join their forces in order to obtain competitive advantage, which they would not have when working alone. Co-operation is supposed to give the partners better possibilities to enter new markets as well.

However, despite all the encouragement, co-operation among small businesses is not very popular. For example, among the respondents of the KANSA study only very few had experiences of co-operation. Approximately one third of the respondents had no previous experiences of co-operation. Especially co-operation in exporting occurred very seldom. The most common form of co-operation seemed to be co-operation in production: 36 per cent of firms had some experiences and 12 per cent co-operated very much in production.

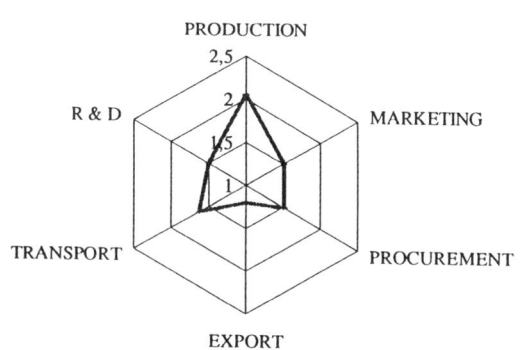

Figure 8. Subcontractors' co-operation among the respondents of the KANSA survey
(1= not at all, 2= a little, 3= very much)

Why subcontractors do not co-operate ? There are probably numerous reasons why small businesses do not co-operate, but one of them might be the fact that the results of co-operation seem to vary. Additionally, knowledge of the precise outcomes of existing cooperative ventures is not generally available. The media has obviously not been interested in publishing this kind of information; and the few research results seem more or less contradictory. As a result perceptions of co-operation and its outcomes are mostly based on "hearsay". Unfortunately also existing academic studies offer mainly theory-based lists of the advantages and disadvantages of co-operation. For example, the following advantages and disadvantages are suggested to be results of co-operation:[4]

Table 2. Advantages and disadvantages of interfirm co-operation

ADVANTAGES
- increased efficiency, e.g.
- economies of scale
- rationalization
- critical mass
- improved resources, e.g.
- utilization of partner's skills
- complementary resources
- financial support
- ability to concentrate on firm's distinctive competency
- learning from partner
- decreasing risk
- easier access to market, e.g.
- overcoming governmental trade or investment barriers
- facilitation of initial international expansion
- improved competitive position
- reduced competition
- fulfillment of strategic needs
- reinforcement in competitive strength
DISADVANTAGES
- risk of partner's opportunism
- uncertainty of the outcome
- loss of flexibility
- mutual dependence
- division of authority and decision-making power
- loss of top management time and energy
- utilization of own skills by partner

---

[4] Sources: Gullander 1975, Andersson 1979, Contractor & Lorange 1988, James 1989, Parkhe 1989 and Jarillo & Stevenson 1991.

This list on previous page is a combination of several, very different studies, which are not directly comparable with each other. Moreover, the researchers have been more interested in larger firms and their "alliances" than in the future alternatives of small businesses, i.e. we are confronted with the same bias as previously with research on internationalization. This bias probably affects the findings, and we have to be aware of the possibility that the list in Table 2 may be partially defective from our perspective.

Nevertheless, despite its defects we can conclude from the list above that co-operation offers some advantages which can also lower the barriers to exporting. With the help of partners it might be possible for instance to decrease the costs and risks connected with exports. In other words, co-operation seems to be a way to avoid the basic problems of initiating exports: creating a competitive product and decreasing the financial costs and risks involved.

However, according to the results of the KANSA survey most of the respondents did not perceive product and finance related issues critical to exporting. On the contrary, important barriers for the subcontractors were issues related to knowledge and competence, such as lack of experience and skilled personnel as well as insufficient information of the markets. According to the list presented in Table 2, only co-operation with an experienced partner would seem to bring solution to these problems. Co-operation with other small businesses appears to be less beneficial, or at least would require more partners with complementary skills and resources.

In addition to the benefits also potential disadvantages may be an explanation for the non-cooperativeness. Uncertainty of outcome, which was suggested as disadvantage of co-operation in Table 2, might be relatively more significant to smaller than larger firms. Also loss of authority and dependence of other partners matter: entrepreneurs in small businesses are generally considered to be independent and relatively dominating decision-makers. The change from authoritative decision-maker to collective consensus is a slow process.

However, in spite of the mentioned obstacles some cooperative ventures between small subcontractors do exist, and a few of them have expressed entering international markets one of their objectives. Considering the fact that some of these ventures have been established years ago and partners have stayed together, we can assume that co-operation has had more positive than negative outcomes. Their existence suggests that our list of advantages has some serious flaws: maybe the perceived advantages and disadvantages of SMEs' co-operation are different ? Nevertheless, in order to draw further conclusions, a deeper analysis is needed.

4. Discussion

The main objective of this paper was not to answer many questions, but rather to raise them. As a basis for these questions, also few answers were given. In the beginning of this paper the current situation of subcontracting was described with the help of empirical research results. Common assumptions of the characteristics as well as production and clientele of subcontractors were verified by the empirical data. As expected, subcontractors rely strongly on domestic markets and are not very interested in expanding their operations to international markets. However, as their business environment has changed remarkably since the survey data was collected, we assume that several subcontracting firms have at least an attempt of exports behind them at present.

It is yet unclear how subcontractors did succeed in these attempts to export. Did they overcome the barriers that were measured in the survey ? How did they acquire the lacking knowledge of export markets and customers ? Where did they find the experienced and skilled personnel ? And perhaps the most interesting question, what was the significance of co-operation in this learning process ?

We are not yet able to answer these questions. However, we strongly emphasize the need of this kind of research in the future. Information of the positive outcomes as well as existing successful cooperative arrangements should be delivered to entrepreneurs in order to facilitate their way to international markets. In addition to this managerial contribution, outcomes of interfirm co-operation offer also a theoretically challenging research subject. No deep theoretical analysis of the outcomes exist and researchers are tempted by an unexplored path.

References

Andersson, Göran (1979) *Samverkan mellan småföretag* (Co-operation Between Small Firms), Doctoral dissertation, University of Lund, Studentlitteratur: Lund, Sweden

Andersson, Göran (1990) Underleverantörsroller (The Roles of Subcontractors), Paper presented at the 6th Nordic *Conference on Small Business*, June 13-17 1990, Copenhagen

Andersson, Göran (1992) Strategier för underleverantörer (Strategies for Subcontractors), Paper presented at the 7th Nordic *Conference on Small Business*, June 4-6 1992, Turku, Finland

Andersson, Jens - Hovi, Niina (1992) Subcontractor Networks. Future from Two Alternative Points of View, Paper presented at the 7th *Nordic Conference on Small Business*, June pp. 4-6 1992, Turku, Finland

Ansoff, H. Igor (1965) *Corporate Strategy*, McGraw-Hill: New York

Bauerschmidt, Alan - Sullivan, Daniel - Gillespie, K. (1986) Common Factors Underlying Barriers to Export: Studies in the U.S. Paper Industries, *Journal of International Business Studies*, Vol.16 Fall 1986, pp.111- 123

Bilkey, W. (1978) An Attempted Integration of the Literature on the Export Behavior of Firms, *Journal of International Business Studies*, Vol.9 Spring-Summer 1978, pp. 33-46

Braunerhjelm, Pontus (1991) Svenska underleverantorer och småföretag i det nya Europa (Swedish Subcontractors and Small Firms in the New Europe), *Industriens utredningsinstitut*, Forskningsrapport Nr.38:1991, Stockholm 1991

Contractor, Farok J. - Lorange, Peter (1988) Why Should Firms Cooperate? The Strategy and Economics Basis for Cooperative Ventures, IN: *Cooperative Strategies in International Business* (eds. Contractor, F. Lorange, P.), Lexington Books: Lexington, Mass., pp. 3-28

Gullander, Staffan (1975) *An Exploratory Study of Inter-Firm Co-operation of Swedish Firms*, Unpublished doctoral dissertation, Columbia University, New York

Hurmerinta-Peltomäki, Leila (1991) *Pkt-yritysten kansainvälistyminen Varsinais-Suomessa* (Internationalization of SMEs in South-Western

Finland), Publications of Turku School of Economics and Business Administration, Business Research Center, Series B 4, Turku

James, Barne G. (1989) Alliance: The New Strategic Focus, *The Best of Long Range Planning* No.2: Entrepreneurship: Creating and Managing New Ventures, pp. 111 - 116

Jarillo, J. Carlos - Stevenson, Howard H. (1991) Cooperative Strategies - The Payoffs and the Pitfalls, *Long Range Planning*, Vol.24 No.1 1991, pp. 64-

Johanson, Jan .- Vahlne, Jan-Erik (1977) The Internationalization Process of the Firm - A Model of Knowledge Development and Increasing Foreign Market Commitments, *Journal of International Business Studies*, Vol.8, pp. 23.-32

Miesenbock, Kurt J. (1988) Small Business and Exporting: A Literature Review, *International Small Business Journal*, Vol.6 No.2 1988, 42-61

Parkhe, Arvind (1989) *Interfirm Strategic Alliances: Empirical Test of a Game-Theoretic Model*, Doctoral dissertation, Temple University, UMI: Ann Arbor

Sharkey, Thomas W. - Lim, Jeen-Su - Kim, Ken I. (1989) Export Development and Perceived Export Barriers: An Empirical Analysis of Small Firms, *Management International Review*, Vol.29 No.2 1989, pp. 33-40

Sullivan, Daniel - Bauerschmidt, Alan (1989) Common Factors Underlying Barriers to Export: A Comparative Study in the European and U.S. Paper Industry, *Management International Review*, Vol.29 No.2 1989, pp. 17-32

Toivonen, Jouko (1991) *Kansainvälistyminen ja Satakunnan pieni ja keskisuuri teollisuus* (Internationalization and SMEs in Satakunta Region), Publications of Turku School of Economics and Business Administration, Pori Research Center Nr.3, Pori 1991

Tuulenmäki, Heli (1990) *Pienten ja keskisuurten yritysten sopeutuminen Euroopan yhdentymiseen* (SMEs' Adaptation to European Integration), Publications of Helsinki School of Economics and Business Administration, Small Business Center, Series M-.46, Mikkeli

Tuulenmäki, Heli - Virtanen, Markku (1989) *Yritysten vientikynnykset* (Barriers to Exporting in Firms), Publications of Helsinki School of

Economics, Small Business Center, Series M-36, Mikkeli

Tuulenmäki, Heli - Virtanen, Markku (1990) *Export Thresholds Encountered by Finnish SMEs in Global Market,* Publications of Helsinki School of Economics, Small Business Center, Series S-2 Discussion and Working Papers, Mikkeli

Uotila, Tuomo (1991) *Satakuntalaisten yritysten kilpailutavat* (Competitive Strategies of SMEs in Satakunta Region), Publications of Turku School of Economics and Business Administration, Pori Research Center No.5, Pori 1991

Veromaa, Veli-Matti (1991) *Porilaisten pkt-yritysten vientitoiminta ja kansainvälistyminen* (SMEs and Internationalization in the Town of Pori), Publications in Turku School of Economics and Business Administration, Pori Research Center No.4, Pori 1991

18 Community brokers: Their role in the formation and development of business ventures[+]

Stanley Cromie, Sue Birley and Ian Callaghan

1. Introduction

In common with many regions in the United Kingdom, Northern Ireland experienced serious structural unemployment in the 1980's; indeed, by 1986 22% of all adults were without a permanent job. Inward investment, a recurrent feature of the 1960's and early 1970's, dwindled and but for the dominance of employment in the public sector things would have been very much worse (Harvey 1989).

During the 1980's small firms, together with support for an enterprise culture, received a boost and statistics reveal that in 1986 there were 1,679 small firms in the manufacturing sector in the Province with an additional 1,200 in the very small firms' category (Enderwick et al. 1990). While, in aggregate, small firms have increased their employment between 1973 and 1986 by around 50%, strenuous efforts are needed to expand further the size of the small firms sector if significant economic development is to occur in Northern Ireland.

To increase the supply of new firms it is essential that an adequate supply of individuals with viable business ideas, skills and resources emerge and

---

[+] This paper was originally published in Entrepreneurship and Regional Development, Volume 5 (1993) pp.247-264. It is reproduced with the permission of the publisher, Taylor and Francis Ltd.

that these persons are highly motivated to succeed (Gibb and Ritchie 1982). To generate business ideas Drucker (1985) argues that entrepreneurs must analyse the changes that are taking place in society and recognise how they can allow businessmen to provide customers with what they want. Business founders who are seeking new markets for existing products or entirely new markets must be fully in touch with what is happening in a community. They must develop intelligence gathering mechanisms to inform themselves of demographic, social, structural, market and technical changes and the likely opportunities that these changes present. If they want to develop their businesses beyond the immediate community they must extend their data collection into national and international arenas by extending their network of informants (Dubini and Aldrich 1991).

Individual action may be sufficient to produce business ideas and innovations in some situations but it will not sufflce in others. Biemans (1992) notes that in stable consumer goods markets individual manufacturers may well be able to identify and meet customer needs. However, in industrial markets ideas for product innovations often originate from customers (von Hippel 1976, 1977). They may recognise a need, develop a solution, build a prototype and then approach a manufacturer to see if the new product is commercially viable. 'Customer active paradigms' (CAP) are often successful in industrial markets because the 'number of potential customers is relatively small, user requirements are changing quickly, and new products need to be developed quickly in response to urgent problems' (Biemans 1992, pp.67-68).

The basic CAP model envisages the customer as launching a new product idea but Biemans reports that subsequent work on customer inaugurated innovations by the International Marketing and Purchasing Project Group (Hakansson, 1982, Ford, 1984, Voss 1985 and Foxall 1989) indicates that the innovative process is characterised by multiple interconnections not only between manufacturers and customers but also between these principals and third parties such as university staff, competitors, government agents etc. These groups share information, debate issues, undertake speciflc parts of the innovative process and generally, collaborate rather than compete. It is important for the would be innovator to identify cadres of 'technological gatekeepers' (Allen and Cohen 1969), to pinpoint their knowledge base, and to develop a working-relationship with these contacts. Relationships develop with time and Biemans suggests that effective innovators need to be skilled at building and maintaining networks of useful contacts and setting up relationships 'based on co-operation, trust and loyalty' (p.79).

In essence, the innovative process is best undertaken through collective rather than individual action. Similar sentiments are expressed by Johannisson and Nowicki (1992) when they argue that the inexperienced entrepreneur may well need some assistance to complete the task of business formation. They argue further that the emergence of new firms through the instinctive identification of market opportunities may need to be supplemented by 'locally initiated economic development' programmes.

Spotting an opportunity is one thing but the creation or development of a venture involves the mobilisation and organisation of resources and the harnessing of skill. Most entrepreneurs will have determined where they can acquire key resources but organisations normally require a myriad of supplies and the owner manager will be hard pushed to identify a range of suppliers and arrange for a flow of assets into his firm. In large bureaucratic organisations Perrow (1971) notes that a host of staff specialists; purchasing officers, personnel managers, treasury managers and the like will scan the environment for sources of supply and create administrative rules and procedures to ensure a steady flow of crucial resources into the organisation. In contrast, the entrepreneurial world is volatile, (Mintzberg 1979), and planning is difficult. Informed guesswork and trial and error are the order of the day and it is important for the entrepreneur to be flexible and to know who to turn to for assistance in acquiring resources or solving problems. Therefore, the business proprietor will have an interest in building a good working relationship with a collection of business contacts to secure a steady supply of resources.

Dubini and Aldrich (1991) argue that good working relationships are vital for reciprocal influence between persons and they note that influence is greatest when strong ties exist between associates and that trust, predictability and a willingness to negotiate over difficulties are the hallmarks of strong ties. If strong ties exist these authors argue that 'the other party will do something to assist you when things do not go according to plan' (p.307). They note, also, that when parties know that they will be dealing with one another over time trust is often reciprocated and individuals can get on with their own tasks in the knowledge that they don't have to keep a constant eye on others and that they will be alerted to an opportunity or problems by those personal contacts with whom they have strong ties.

In essence, the formation of a network of strong ties is indispensable to the business founder when gathering pertinent information on demographic, cultural, technological, legal, political and economic factors which are relevant to his business and in ensuring that appropriate resources flow into his organisation. Entrepreneurs can 'increase their span of actions through their personal networks and gain access at a limited cost to resources otherwise unavailable' (Dubini and Aldrich 1991, p.308).

2. Assistance with networking

Networking and other skills are essential for successful entrepreneurship but we must recognise that 'the only occupations for which there is no formal institutional selection are those involving new enterprise formation', (Vroom 1964, p.56), and consequently many entrepreneurs are poorly prepared for the tasks they face. The reasonably well prepared entrepreneur is not immune from difficulties either. Johannisson and Nowicki (1992) note that the new entrepreneur needs to increase his self confidence and that this may be an unlikely outcome in a harsh economic environment. In addition they observe that the newness of the entrepreneurial role for many persons and the problems associated with smallness suggest that many business proprietors 'must get support to acquire legitimacy'. In these situations expert assistant in launching, developing and expanding a business could be invaluable and Johannisson and Nillson (1989) argue that community entrepreneurs, people who help others to create and develop their ventures, are particularly useful. They note that 'the community entrepreneur make [s] the individual would-be entrepreneur aware of how his or her capabilities as a member of the local community can be turned into a business venture' (p. 4).

The community entrepreneur is likely to adopt an informal, 'catalytic' consulting stance and help the entrepreneur 'to widen his or her view of the situation by gaining additional information or by verifying existing data' (Blake and Mouton 1976, p.86). They often function as coordinators, aim to limit the dependence of the entrepreneur on themselves and coach the latter until he can be left to his own devices (Johannisson and Nillson 1989).

This informal approach can be effective but a formal, prescriptne approach is often required too. Specific information on taxation, instruction on how to operate new technology or clear guidance on developing new markets is often indispensable. In addition, to counteract the resource deficiencies of small ventures several policy makers support the creation of 'industrial districts'. A constellation of small firms in a locale may be able to develop their inter-organisational relationships to such a degree that they function like a large concern and reap some of the benefits of large scale organisations.

In summary, the individual entrepreneur is likely to make his way more effectively in a complex world if a range of supporting mechanisms exist. Community brokers can adopt a non directive or a prescriptive approach to helping their clients but in both instances they will need to develop a large cluster of personal contacts if they are to assist numerous businessmen and meet their manifold needs. An effective community entrepreneur/broker will help to create linkages between the personal contact networks of individual entrepreneurs and therefore create extended networks which will expand the capacity of business founders to gather information and acquire resources. (Johannisson 1990, p. 79) notes that 'the community entrepreneur promotes the community and individual ventures by either linking his own personal network to the collective network or by expanding it through the creation of new arenas'.

There are many individuals in Northern Ireland who resemble Johannisson's community entrepreneurs although their approach is normally more formal and prescriptive. Most prominent are the area managers of the Local Enterprise Development Unit and the managers of around forty Local Enterprise Agencies (LEAs). These persons are charged with assisting business development by acting as role models for aspiring entrepreneurs, by providing certain necessary resources and above all by developing a web of contacts in an extended network within a locality. Networking is clearly a key competence for both business founders and community entrepreneurs and in this study we propose to compare the networking activities of these groups of actors.

We feel it is important to do so because a study by (Birley et al. 1991) on the networking activities of autonomous entrepreneurs in Northern Ireland reveals that the latter have smaller direct and indirect personal contact networks than international comparison groups. If entrepreneurial supporters in Northern Ireland are to surmount this apparent weakness of Irish entrepreneurs it is incumbent on them to excel at personal networking. Gibb and Manu (1990) suggest that the best small business support agencies closely resemble entrepreneurial firms but it seems plausible to suggest that LEA managers should be more active at networking than business proprietors if they are to help improve the competitiveness of the local small firms sector. We will develop some hypotheses about networking by our two comparator groups shortly but let us discuss, first of all, some features of networks.

3. Features of Networks

We have argued that in many instances innovators and entrepreneurs develop permanent as opposed to transient relationships with their contacts and that these relationships allow them to identify opportunities and resources rapidly. However, networks are not easily observed and consequently they are rather difficult to analyse. They have been studied from the perspective of the focal individual, from the perspective of both individuals in a dyad or from the frame of reference of all the persons in network triads. In this study we focus on the images of networks by individual entrepreneurs and community brokers. Following Aldrich and Zimmer (1986) these issues are addressed: network size, density and diversity together with the strength of ties and the presence of brokers. Networking is action oriented and entails making contact and building a relationship with other individuals. The network is then utilised to gain access to the knowledge and information that contacts possess. Some individuals devote lots of energy to these activities and will have several direct associates together with indirect contacts who are employed vicariously. The greater the number of direct and indirect contacts available to an entrepreneur the greater, other things being equal, are the chances of him acquiring the information and resource he needs at minimum cost. A large number of contacts are not courted without effort and it is important to note the amount of time focal individuals spend in developing their networks. While a large number of contacts are important the strength of the ties together with the frequency with which contacts interact are important too. Casual acquaintances are unlikely to act as intelligence gathering bodies for the entrepreneur's business; indeed knowing that the relationship is ephemeral a casual contact might behave badly (Axlerod 1984).

On the other hand a committed contact may frequently act on the entrepreneur's behalf and this can help increase the flow of relevant information and reduce uncertainty. In addition networks must be employed to be useful; indeed they need to be tested at regular intervals to discover if a particular source is still useful.

A large number of strong ties should guarantee a steady supply of relevant information to the focal individual but the density of a network is important too. A dense network is one in which everybody knows everyone else and in compiling their measure of network density (Aldrich et al. 1986) note the proportion of ties which actually exist in a network and compare this with the above. In a dense network information will flow rapidly along its channels to the focal entrepreneur but as Dubini and Aldrich (1991) note if individuals in a dense network have similar status or views then contact with one member puts the focal entrepreneur in touch with all opinions. To gain access to different sections of the environment strong ties with a range of persons is required.

The diversity of network contacts is the final issue addressed by Aldrich and his associates. Individuals occupying different roles and statuses and those holding different opinions will improve the quality of information available to the entrepreneur. He will hear counter-arguments, may develop different perspectives on issues and have a breadth of knowledge which should prove invaluable in recognising the societal, market and technical changes which can be exploited commercially.

4. This Study

To date we have argued that network formation is an essential aspect of industrial innovation and business development and that it is a key activity for entrepreneurs. We have also suggested that community entrepreneurs can assist in the developmental process. In view of the fact that the enterprise supporters in N Ireland are less embedded in the community and adopt a more prescriptive approach than Johannisson's community entrepreneurs in Sweden, henceforth we will refer to the Irish helpers as community brokers. Given that the community broker is developing contacts for the benefit of other people and given that they will normally have large numbers of clients it seems reasonable to suggest that community brokers will engage in networking to a greater extent than their entrepreneurial clients. Accordingly we suggest that:

(a) community brokers will have larger direct and indirect contacts networks than autonomous entrepreneurs;
(b) they will devote more time to networking;
(c) they will be more proactive in seeking contacts and more liberal in sharing their contacts than autonomous entrepreneurs;
(d) community brokers will have more dense networks than autonomous entrepreneurs; and
(e) they will have more diverse contacts than business founders and will include less family and friends in their personal contact networks.

4.1 The Sample

To test the validity of these proposals we interviewed 65 chief executives of organisations in Northern Ireland which actively support the development of small firms. These organisations range from the Local Enterprise Agencies which were explicitly set up to boost entrepreneurship in localities, to management consultants and university departments with a strong interest in small business development, to employment agencies for whom the encouragement of entrepreneurship is within their remit but not a mainstream activity.

The mean number of employees in these organisations is 50 but this is heavily skewed. The median number is six and is more representative. The senior executives have a mean age of 41.8 years and they had worked for between four and five other organisation before taking up their current posts. They are well educated; indeed two-thirds have degrees or postgraduate qualifications. A quarter of the sample had previously owned their own firm and 23% are females. Just over 50% were employed in the private sector immediately prior to taking their current job, around 40% worked for the government and merely 3% were selfemployed.

The comparison group of 274 owner managers were the subjects of a previous study by Birley et al. (1991). This sample is fully described in Birley et al. but a few points should be noted. Around one third of the sample had been trading for less than two years, 25% for between two and five years and approximately 40% had traded for more than five years. The mean number of employees was 10.1 which indicates that the sample were mainly small firms. Almost none of the owners emerged from the ranks of the unemployed. In Table 1 some comparative background data are presented on the samples of autonomous entrepreneurs and community brokers in Northern Ireland together with information on the same issues from two Swedish samples.

Table 1. Some background data on autonomous entrepreneurs, community brokers and community entrepreneurs in Northern Ireland and Sweden

	N Ireland		Sweden	
	A Ent	C Brk	A Ent	C Ent
Age	38	42	40	47
Sample size	274	65	183	33
% women	23	25	20	33
% with University ed	N/A	64	35	55

Source for Swedish Data: Johannisson and Nillson (1989)

4.2 The Questions

To investigate their networking activity community brokers were asked to answer a series of questions, based on a questionnaire developed by Aldrich et al. (1986), during personal interviews. The same questions had been answered by the 274 autonomous entrepreneurs in Birley et al.'s study. In assessing network activity the samples were questioned on the number of direct contacts they had in their personal network, on the amount of time spent during a typical week in developing and maintaining contacts and on the number of hours per month they spent on 'networking journeys'. Furthermore, respondents were asked to mention five individuals with whom they had regular business contacts. Information was collected on the frequency of interaction with these people and on how long the focal individual had known them. We mentioned earlier that direct contacts can lead to indirect contacts and we assessed the size of these secondary networks by asking if the five people in the direct personal contact network had large or small networks of their own.

On the process of making contact we asked whether the focal individual, his contact or a third party (intermediary) initiated the original contact and we asked the sample how they went about seeking out useful contacts.

Making a contact is one thing; making use of one is another. We asked the sample therefore to what extent they encouraged their own staff and their clients to make use of their own personal contacts.

The sample were questioned on how well the five people in the personal contact network knew one another. They were asked if each pair of individuals: (a) did not know each other at all; (b) knew each other slightly; (c) knew each other well; or (d) if they did not know whether they were known to one another. Aldrich measures network density by noting the proportion of strangers, i.e., density = $[A+D]/[A+B+C+D]$.

Network diversity was our last area of interest. We have argued that different perspectives are important in formulating sound decisions and we questioned the sample on the type of people they made contact with. We enquired if they were male or female, if they were professional people, entrepreneurs, friends or relations. In the questionnaire we did not present respondents with forced choice questions on the latter issues; rather we enquired about the type of the relationship they had with personal contacts and the connection in which they first met.

5. Results

5.1 Networking Activity

In this section of the paper we report on the networking activity of autonomous entrepreneurs and community brokers in Northern Ireland and because a sample of entrepreneurs and community activists in Sweden completed a very similar questionnaire we have an opportunity to compare results of networking activity in Ireland with those in Sweden.

In the first instance we discover that community brokers have very many more direct contacts in their networks than autonomous entrepreneurs. As Table 2 reveals, 75.4% of community brokers have more than ten persons in their networks whereas the equivalent figures for the comparison group is 19%. When we compute a 2 x 2 chi-squared test for this data we find that the differences are very significant ($X^2 = 78.4$, df= 1, $p = 0.0$). Johannisson and Nillson report that the corresponding percentages from Sweden are 74.1% and 29.7% which confirms that community brokers, who network for themselves and others, are much more active than business proprietors.

Table 2 The number of community brokers and autonomous entrepreneurs in Northern Ireland with <10 and >10 direct contacts in their personal networks

	Com Brok	Aut Ents
Less than 10	16	221
More than 10	49	53
Total	65	274

Direct contacts are important for networkers but indirect contacts may be reached via direct associates. Accordingly we enquired about the size of the networks of each of the five persons in the personal contact network of each community broker and, as Table 3 shows, their indirect networks in Northern Ireland are much larger than those of the comparison group of business founders.

These differences are confirmed statistically in Table 3 when we compute z-tests for differences in sample proportions between community brokers and autonomous entrepreneurs. The relevant z scores for contacts 1, 2, 4 and 5 are significant at the 0.01 level. For contact 3 the difference is not statistically significant ($p = 0.237$, $q = 0.763$, $z = 1.8$). The large indirect networks of our community brokers offers them an opportunity to extend their networks and create a web of interlinked associates across the Province.

Table 3. The percentage of secondary networks that are perceived as being very big by community brokers and autonomous entrepreneurs in Northern Ireland

	Personal Contact Network				
	1	2	3	4	5
NI Comm Brokers	55	51	32	57	31
NI Aut Entrepreneurs	31	21	21	15	15
z-score (diff of proportions)	3.6	4.8	1.9	6.7	2.7

When we enquire about the number of hours per week devoted to networking we discover that 84% of our community brokers spend less than ten hours a week in seeking out new contacts: indeed 47% spend less than five hours a week on this activity. The latter is very close to the 48% reported by Johannisson and Nillson in Sweden. We have no strictly comparable data for autonomous entrepreneurs because their questions differentiated between contacts with customers and non-customers. If we ignore contact with customers we find that almost 94% of our sample of business founders spend less than 10 hours per week on developing new contacts which would suggest that community entrepreneurs devote some more time to networking than their business counterparts. However, we did note in our introduction that contact with customers can be a very important source for innovative ideas. We must therefore treat this indicator of superior networking activity by our community brokers with some caution.

Turning to the maintenance of contact we find, again, that community brokers are most active. Around a quarter devote more than ten hours a week to this activity whereas 13% of autonomous entrepreneurs spend this amount of time in maintaining contact with non-customers. When we make a comparison with Sweden on this issue the contrast is quite striking: in Northern Ireland 60% of community brokers devote five hours or more to maintaining contacts while the comparable figure for community entrepreneurs in Sweden is 48%. The lower figure in Sweden could arise of course because community entrepreneurs have long established informal contacts in their locality which do not require a great deal of maintenance.

The three topics discussed so far reveal that community brokers are much more active networkers than autonomous entrepreneurs: they include more people in their networks and they spend more time in developing and maintaining contacts. They also spend more hours per month on journeys in relation to the development of contacts with associates. As can be seen in Table 4, 78% of community brokers in Northern Ireland as opposed to 70% of autonomous entrepreneurs spend in excess of 5 hours per month travelling to make contacts. Comparative data in Table 4 reveals that community brokers and autonomous entrepreneurs in Ireland spend more time on networking journeys than their Swedish counterparts. Given the limited geographical size of Northern Ireland this suggests that the local community brokers and autonomous entrepreneurs regularly get out of the office and seek contacts. It is also possible that the community entrepreneurs in Sweden, having developed extensive informal contacts in their localities, do not need to spend a great deal of time 'on the road'.

Table 4. Percentage of persons spending 5 hours or more per month making networking journeys

	Northern Ireland %		Sweden %	
	Comm Bks	Aut Ent	Comm Ent	Aut Ent
Spend 5 hours or more	78%	70%	63%	45%

Turning to the smaller proportion of autonomous entrepreneurs in Sweden who devote more than five hours per month to travelling in support of networking it is possible that this occurs because Swedish autonomous entrepreneurs have well developed inter-organisational networks. In our introduction we showed that interactions between customers, suppliers, universities, competitors, etc. can highlight business opportunities and facilitate low cost, highly productive business development. In Sweden, industrial structures in which firms simultaneously collaborate and complete are more highly developed than in Ireland. Autonomous entrepreneurs in Sweden, having developed and institutionalised their inter firm associations, may have less need to make networking journeys.

The expenditure of time and energy indicates that networking is important to our sample but contacts can come about through proactive endeavour on the part of the focal entrepreneur or because the other party approaches the central individual.

In Table 5 we present results of a question which asked the sample about the proportion of new contacts which came about through others coming to them and we discover that there is some evidence to suggest that others make contact with community brokers more often than they do with autonomous entrepreneurs. In Table 5 more autonomous entrepreneurs (55%) than community brokers (30%) report that less than 25% of contacts emerge from others approaching them. In view of the more active networking of the latter as reported above this result is somewhat surprising. However, when we reflect on the position of the community brokers in a locality this may be less surprising. His or her organisation exists to act as an example to business proprietors, to assist in acquiring appropriate resources and to develop a community wide network of contacts. As more and more people learn about the role of the community broker it is likely that many people will want to make contact with him. While there is some suggestion of more proactive action by autonomous business founders when we create a 2 x 2 contingency table from Table 5 (those in the less than 50% category in one cell, those in the 51%+ groupings in another) and compute a chi-squared statistic we find that there are no significant differences between the two groups $x^2 = 0.76$, df= 1, p > 0.25.

Table 5. Percentage of new contacts resulting from other people making contact with focal entrepreneurs

	Comm Bks %	Aut Ent %
<25%	30	55
26 - 50%	39	19
51 - 75%	25	11
76 - 99%	5	9
All of them	1	6

5.2 The Utilization of Networks

The size of a network and the time devoted to developing it is important but networks must be used to be effective. An extensive web of associates who are rarely called upon to provide information are an under-utilised resource. To get some indication of the utilisation of networks we asked our sample how often they had business related discussions per month with associates and results, presented in Table 6 show that, in general community brokers discuss business more frequently than business founders. Community brokers are more likely than business owners to meet contacts on eleven or more occasions per month. If we divide the 'times discussed business' categories presented in Table 6 into 10 hours or less and 11 hours and more and compute a series of 2 x 2 chi-squared tests for contacts 1 through 5 the associated x^2 values are 4.2, 5.9, 5.4, 3.6 and 3.81. Since the critical value for x^2 with one degree of freedom at the 5% level is 3.84 we can see that there are significant differences in the frequency with which associates 1, 2 and 3 are spoken to by community brokers and autonomous entrepreneurs. For contacts 4 and 5 the x^2 value is close to the critical value.

Table 6. Percentage of community brokers and autonomous entrepreneurs who discuss business with contacts with given frequencies per month

Times Discussed Business	Contact 1		2		3		4		5	
	CB	AE	CB	AE	CB	AE	CB	AE	CB	AE
5 or less	26	43	39	46	33	50	40	53	37	52
5 - 10	24	21	18	27	28	26	29	24	23	23
11 - 20	12	14	20	14	20	11	16	12	29	12
21 - 50	13	10	15	9	13	6	13	8	7	8
51+	15	12	8	5	6	7	2	4	4	5

The community broker is charged with increasing the flow of relevant information within the small business community and he will be a key actor in the process. However, the staff in his/her organisation may be equally important in disseminating information. In our previous study of business founders we discovered that owners were reluctant to share network contacts with their employees; networking was their sole preserve. In contrast we find that community brokers are much happier to share their own contacts with their employees (see Table 7).

Table 7. The percentage of the community broker's and autonomous entrepreneur's contacts who also have contact with other employees

Percentage	Northern Ireland %	
	Comm Brk	Aut Ent
<25%	24%	69%
>25%	76%	31%

When we compute a chi-squared statistic for the data in Table 7 we find that the difference between community brokers and autonomous entrepreneurs is highly significant $x^2 = 43.6$, df = 1, $p > .005$). The community broker and his staff occupy a central role in the dissemination of information to the business populace and it makes little sense for the managers of Local Enterprise Associations and similar organisations to insist that networking is their exclusive preserve.

Community brokers are required to act as go-betweens. It is part of their job to make it easier for those with relevant information to get in touch with individuals who need it. We surmised that the personal contacts of community brokers could, on occasions, be useful to their clients and we asked to what extent they make their own contacts available to business founders in the locality. Thirty-five percent reported that they were available to 'little' or 'some extent' and 65% said that they were available to 'much' or a 'great extent'. Clearly our respondents are happy to share their contacts with local businessmen if they consider that relevant information will be disbursed throughout the business locality.

Drucker (1985) argues that the skills of entrepreneurship can be taught and we wanted to know to what extent our sample gave their clients advice and training on the key entrepreneurial skill of networking. Only 40% of respondents did this to 'much' or a 'great' extent but most of the remainder did give some advice on this issue. If networking is so vital and if the skills can be developed, then community brokers could be charged with the relevant training. However, let us leave our discussion on this issue to the concluding section of this paper.

5.3 Networking Process

In our presentation to date we find that our sample of community brokers are more active than a comparison group of business founders on almost every networking variable of interest and that in some instances they have been more active than a sample of community entrepreneurs from Sweden. Before we conclude this section on networking activity, however, we want to say something about the process of networking. We are keen to know something about how contacts are sought and where they are approached. It turns out that a majority of our community brokers deliberately attend functions or events where they are likely to come into contact with useful associates. Mention was made of attending 'appropriate events', 'ceremonies', 'competitions', 'launches', 'network clubs' and the like with the aim of approaching people with information, ideas and resources.

Another approach is to keep in close association with an agency which has lots of contacts. Rather than seeking indirect affiliates through one of their personal allies the community entrepreneur is recognising the groundwork that has been done by others and he tries to tap into an appropriate source of information. Respondents mentioned the 'local EC office', 'district councils', the 'training agency', and 'the bank' as relevant orgamsatlons.

Another method of making contact is through direct calls on individuals or organisations. The sample make cold calls, send letters, use mail shots, tour relevant organisations and the like to develop new contacts or revive old ones. Respondents also keep their ear to the ground, scan relevant publications, advertise their services, and try, though the use of various publications, to discover what is happening in a locality which might be of interest to their clients or themselves. Finally, some respondents said that while they had no conscious plan for networking when fortuitous events happened they took full advantage of the situation.

On the issue of where contacts are made the most common venue is at formal gatherings of business people. Social venues are used also but not to any great extent. Purposive calls to the premises of other organisations are also made and once again chance meetings with likely affiliates are gratefully accepted. Clearly, our respondents are aware of the importance of linking with useful others and use a variety of approaches to gain access to information. Formalised instruction on developing network contacts could be as relevant to community entrepreneurs as it is to business founders and a sharing of approaches might stimulate the development of a more effective system of networking across the Province.

5.4 Network Density

A dense network is one where the direct interconnections between members is extensive and information travels along its channels at speed. This will facilitate the processing of information and ensure that opportunities which are drawn to the attention of any member of the network are passed on to relevant persons. If all associations with the focal entrepreneur are on a bilateral basis the network structure will resemble a wheel (Leavitt 1951) and the speed at which information flows will depend on the capacity of the focal person to gather and disseminate information. If associations are multilateral the structure will resemble the circle (Leavitt 1951) and information will move to key individuals without delay.

In a previous study of the networks of business founders we found that the average proportion of strangers was approximately 49%. In this study we find that it is approximately 22% which suggests that the networks of community brokers are much more dense that those of autonomous entrepreneurs. In Table 8 we present the proportion of strangers for each of the ten pairings of individuals in the personal contact networks of autonomous entrepreneurs and community brokers and we compute z scores for the differences in sample proportions for each pairing.

Table 8. The proportion of strangers for each pair of associates in the personal contact networks of community brokers and autonomous entrepreneurs

Contact Persons	1-2	1-3	1-4	1-5	2-3	2-4	2-5	3-4	3-5	4-5
Comm Brks (% Sgrs)	10.8	13.8	20.6	24.1	15.4	23.8	27.6	31.7	32.8	19.0
Aut Ents (% Sgrs)	40.8	42.1	53.6	52.1	48.2	55.7	51.2	47.1	55.9	51.5
z-score (diff of proport)	4.5	4.2	4.5	3.7	4.8	4.6	3.1	2.1	3.0	4.3

All of the z-scores exceed the critical value of z at the 5% level of significance (1.96 for a two tail test) and all but one exceed the critical value at the 1% level (2.58, two tail test). The density of the networks for each pairing of contacts in the community broker's personal contact network are therefore significantly higher than those of business founders. Since the cornmunity broker aims to create a socio-economic network and extend it to the farthest reaches of a locality the denseness of his networks will assist in this process. Since a great many persons in the personal network are interconnected the size and scope of the indirect networks will increase significantly. If persons A, B and C are in direct contact with the focal entrepreneur and each has his/her own personal contact X, Y and Z respectively in a dense network A will gain speedy access to Y, B to Z etc. A dense network will help create an extended network and significantly increase the flow of information throughout all network channels. However, if the persons in a dense network are homogeneous the increased volume of information will not greatly enhance its quality. Diversity is crucial and we now propose to examine some aspects of network diversity.

5.5 Diversity

The first issue for consideration in this part of the paper is the gender of contacts. Approximately 77% of our sample of comrnunity brokers are men and as Table 9 shows both they and a significant number of female respondents invariably turn to a man for their primary contact. A similar situation occurs with contact two but thereafter women are more likely to be included in personal contact networks. Further analysis of the gender pattern of the personal contact network was conducted by calculating the percentage of people in the networks who are of the opposite gender - the 'cross ties'. These results are also compared with those for the sample of owner-managers. [Table 10].

Table 9. The gender and age of the personal contact networks of community brokers and autonomous entrepreneurs

Contact	Percentage of Males		Mean Age	
	Comm Brks	Aut Ents	Comm Brks	Aut Ents
1	91	85	46	43
2	88	81	46	42
3	74	81	42	42
4	76	83	44	42
5	78	83	40	41

In both cases men are most likely to talk to males, although this is especially so in the case of the principal contact of community brokers. Women also regularly consult men but women do form part of the personal contact network of both community brokers and owner-managers.

When we consider that contacts are approached with a view to expanding the entrepreneur's capacity to generate relevant information it is not surprising that men are preferred. Men occupy the dominant positions of power in most communities and as a consequence they have privileged access to information. As Tables 9 and 10 reveal, this line of reasoning seems to prevail in the case of autonomous entrepreneurs.

Table 10. Percentage cross ties

Contact	Community Brokers		Owner Managers	
	Male	Female	Male	Female
1	4	71	14	94
2	12	93	13	65
3	22	60	13	68
4	21	72	14	64
5	23	79	13	71

Turning to the average age of contacts we can see from Table 9 that they are primarily in their forties. A more detailed look at the relevant frequency distributions reveals that two thirds of all personal contacts are over forty and virtually none are under thirty. In general, people acquire more knowledge as they get older and they normally take more responsible roles. This could well explain the absence of young persons among personal contacts. In addition, people tend to associate with those from their own age group. Our sample have a mean age of 42 which may explain why they tend to associate with people in their forties.

It was suggested above that strong ties which are characterised by mutual obligations, stability and a willingness to compromise are highly desirable in network contacts. In our present study we did not ask direct questions on the strength of ties but we presupposed that the length of time that associates knew one another could act as a surrogate for the strength of ties. In Table 11 we report on the average length of time that contacts knew one another and we find that the time scale is quite short. By comparison the autonomous entrepreneurs in our previous study knew their contacts for considerably longer. These differences are confirmed statistically when we compute z-scores for the differences of sample means in Table 11. In all cases the difference is significant at the 5% level (2 tail test) and in four out of five cases the significant level is 1% (2 tail test). The relatively short association with contacts on the part of community brokers might arise because a number of these agencies are of recent origin. Unlike the community entrepreneurs in Sweden, who have often developed elaborate informal networks for use by autonomous entrepreneurs, community brokers in Northern Ireland are still in the process of developing a network structure.

Table 11. The average amount of time community brokers and autonomous entrepreneurs have known their personal contacts

	Contacts									
	1		2		3		4		5	
Mean Years	CB	AE	CB	AE	CB	AE	CB	AE	CB	AE
Known	4.9	9.6	4.7	7.4	5.1	8.2	5.6	7.7	4.8	7.1
z-score	5.3		3.3		3.5		2.1		2.6	

5.6. Type of Relationship

When we investigate the type of relationship our sample have with affiliates (see Table 12), we find that friends (27%) predominate. Business relations which develop into friendships can strengthen the network but unless a friend has information which is relevant to the core duties of the entrepreneur he may be a less valuable resource than other contacts. When we add family contacts to friends, we discover that family and friends together comprise 29% of all personal contacts.

External business contacts, consultants, professionals, peers, suppliers, competitors and customers comprise 42% of contacts. In some instances these individuals are merely described as 'a businessman' or 'a Director', while in others, mention is made of individuals occupying specific business functions.

In the previous studies of networking by autonomous entrepreneurs family, friends and business contacts were the only type of relationship alluded to. However, an important new group is mentioned by community brokers: their peers. Twelve percent of contacts are peers and this indicates that several of our sample see significant benefit in collaborating with people in similar jobs to themselves. This is important in terms of sharing experiences and solving common problems but it is important also in extending the scope of personal networks. If two community brokers from different localities make contact on a regular basis and develop strong ties this will significantly increase the ability of the community brokers' clients to gain access to valuable resources. This finding is in marked contrast to our previous findings for autonomous entrepreneurs. Very few owner managers were members of the personal contact networks of autonomous entrepreneurs.

Table 12. Type of relationship between community brokers in N Ireland and their main contacts (number of responses)

Contacts	1	2	3	4	5	N	%
Board Member	13	7	6	8	4	38	8.5
Boss	14	8	3	4	4	33	7.4
Subordinate	11	15	18	8	7	59	13.2
Bus/Prof Cont	13	13	14	8	7	55	12.4
Consult/Adv	8	10	10	15	10	53	11.9
Peer	6	6	12	12	16	52	11.7
Com/Cus/Sup	4	4	6	9	3	26	5.8
Family	1	3	1	2	2	9	2.0
Friend	26	29	20	21	23	119	26.8

Another contrast with the previous study just mentioned is the inclusion of staff from the community broker's own organisation (29%) within their personal contact networks. Subordinates (13%) are numerically most important and the others are evenly divided among board members and chairmen. Employees and board members were noticeably absent from the networks of autonomous entrepreneurs.

In most cases the sample mention one type of relationship only with an afflliate but where more than one is mentioned they tend to combine a business and a friendly relationship. Indeed 18% of the sample reveal that the sole reason for including an individual in a personal contact network is friendship. Looking at the single responses and comparing them with those of owner-managers, we find that the owner-managers are even more likely to call upon the support of their friendship network, whilst the community brokers are more likely to call upon the support of their business network.

The final area of interest in this paper relates to the connection in which our sample first meet their contacts. By analysing this topic we are able to add to our information on the process of networking and to understand more fully where contacts come from.

In Table 13 we present a summary of information on first meetings and it can be seen that the great majority of meetings first occur in a business context. On well over 40% of occasions the pairings met on a business occasion. For example, one contact acted as a legal adviser before developing a regular association, another was a customer of a former employer of one of our respondents, others met when being interviewed by our respondents for jobs. On other occasions the first meeting took place at a business meeting, seminar or exhibition or at the premises of one of the major small business support agencies. In all, around 79% of first discussions occurred in a business context and this is in line with the reported first meetings of autonomous entrepreneurs.

Table 13. Connection in which community brokers first met contact (Percentages)

Connection	Contact					Total
	1	2	3	4	5	
Business Association	46	44	45	47	46	45
Business Event	27	30	33	31	20	29
Business Meeting	9	6	3	2	5	5
Relation	0	2	0	3	4	2
Social	16	10	12	7	9	11
Consultant	0	3	2	3	4	2
Employee	2	2	0	2	2	2
School	0	3	5	5	10	4

Smaller numbers of respondents made their connections in social and family settings (13%) and around 4% of associations date back to schooldays. The remainder of link-ups occurred as a results of a consulting assignment or from a previous employment relationship.

While the personal contacts of community brokers are rather more diverse than those of business founders the principal type of relationships and meeting venues are business, social and family contexts. However, the inclusion of peers and employees is indicative of the extent to which community brokers adopt a more collaborative stance to networking than the typical business founder.

6. Conclusions

Many writers have argued recently that networking represents the essence of entrepreneurship (Birley 1985, Johannisson 1988, Johannisson and Nilson 1989, Dubini and Aldrich 1991). The individual entrepreneur, operating as he does in a volatile context where planning is difficult, develops relationship with persons in the community for the purpose of developing and evaluating business proposals, solving problems and acquiring requisite resources. Johannisson (1988) argues that the success of the entrepreneurial venture will depend, to no small extent, on the size and diversity of the relevant network which the entrepreneur develops. His or her forays into the community in search of personal contacts links the business proprietor strongly with the local community.

However, Johannisson and others recognise that networks do not emerge overnight and that it can be quite a daunting task to make the necessary contacts with creative individuals, suppliers, customers etc. For this reason Johannisson (1988, p.5) suggests that the new business founder 'does not have access to a qualified network and will need support while launching her or his venture'. For many entrepreneurs the 'organising context' for their venture is the local community and we argued above that community brokers, people who facilitate the formation of contacts between business founders and who gather and disseminate information for the use of others, are an indispensable community resource. Community brokers are the linchpins in the process of business creation and development and their success will be based on their own social networks and upon their willingness and ability to use them to forge associations between individuals and organisations.

In essence the effective performance of the role of community broker requires the latter to be an even better networker than a business proprietor and in this study we hypothesised that the former would have larger direct and indirect networks, expend more energy on networking activity, be more proactive, be more willing to share contacts with others, have more dense and more diverse networks than autonomous entrepreneurs. Apart from our suggestion that community brokers would be more proactive networkers than autonomous entrepreneurs, our hypotheses were confirmed in all cases and it seems clear that the community brokers in this study have the potential to make a significant contribution to the development of diverse personal contact networks by business founders in the Northern Ireland community.

Individual organisations which support enterprise will facilitate the development of embryo and developing firms but an integrated and holistic approach by support organisations across Northern Ireland could be even more beneficial. As Saxenian (1988, p.74) notes, the expansion of an economically active region requires more than the financing of singular organisations. Efforts must be directed towards 'building institutions and relationships ... that support the development of innovative enterprises'. In the field of inter-organisational relationships Scott (1992, p.129) drawing on the work of (Warren 1967) notes that a variety of relationships can exist. At one extreme 'all decisions are made at the level of the individual units', at another 'each organisational unit has its own decision making apparatus ... but collaborates informally and on an ad hoc bases' while in some cases organisations 'have individual goals but also participate in a structure in order to set more inclusive goals.' A recent report by (Cromie et al. 1992) reveals that enterprise support agencies in the Province do have resource dependencies, are aware of the goals and services offered by sister organisations, communicate regularly with their counterparts, share a limited consensus on the needs of their clients, have a degree of domain similarity, refer clients to one another and exchange technical information.

These are key variables in the field of inter-organisational relations (Van de Ven and Ferry 1980) and it appears therefore, that while our enterprise supporters do not agree on 'inclusive goals' they do at least work together on an informal basis.

The fact that the local community brokers do interact augers well for the possibility of creating extended entrepreneurial networks within Northern Ireland. The community entrepreneurs are in a strategic position to create a network of enterprise support agencies. If they succeed then the 'organising context' for local autonomous entrepreneurs could expand beyond the local area, into the wider community, and ultimately into the whole of the region and beyond.

Acknowledgement

The authors wish to thank the Department of Economic Development (Northern Ireland) and the Local Enterprise Development Unit for funding this study.

References

Aldrich, H. and Zimmer, C. (1986), Enterprise through social networks. In D. L. Sexton and R. W. Smilor, (eds) *The Art and Science of Entrepreneurship* (Cambridge, Massachusetts: Ballinger).

Aldrich, H., Rosen, B. and Woodward, W. (1986), *A Social Role Perspective of Entrepreneurship: Preliminary Findings from an Empirical Study*, Chapel Hill, University of North Carolina, unpublished paper.

Allen, T.J. and Cohen, S.J. (1969), Information flow in two R & D Laboratories, *Administrative Science Quarterly*, 14, pp. 234-242.

Axelrod, R. (1984), *The Evolution of Co-operation* (New York: Basic Books).

Biemans, W.G. (1992), *Managing Innovation Within Networks* (London: Routledge).

Birley, S. (1985), The role of networks in the entrepreneurial process,

Journal of Business Venturing, 1, pp. 107-117.

Birley, S., Cromie, S. and Myers, A. (1991), Entrepreneurial Networks: Their Emergence in Ireland and Overseas, *International Small Business Journal*, 9, pp. 56-74.

Cromie, S. Birley, S. and Callaghan, I. (1992), *Networking by Business Support Agencies in Northern Ireland*, Belfast, Department of Economic Development, unpublished report.

Drucker, P.F. (1985), *Innovation and Entrepreneurship: Practice and Principles* (New York: Harper & Row).

Dubini, P. and Aldrich, H. (1991), Personal and Extended Networks are Central to the Entrepreneurial Process, *Journal of Business Venturing*, 6, pp. 305-313.

Enderwick, P., Gudgin, G. and Hitchens, D. (1990), The Role of the Firm in Manufacturing. In Harris, R., Jefferson, C. and Spenser, J., *The Northern Ireland Economy* (London: Longman).

Ford, D. (1984), Buyer-Seller Relationships in International Industrial Markets, *Industrial Marketing Management*, 13, pp. 101-112.

Foxall, G.R. (1989), User Initiated Product Innovations, *Industrial Marketing Management*, 18, pp. 95-104.

Gibb, A.A. and Manu, G. (1990), Design of Extension and Support Services for Small Scale Enterprise Development, *International Small Business Journal*, 8, pp. 10-26.

Gibb, A. A. and Ritchie, J. (1982), Understanding the process of starting a small business, *International Small Business Journal*, 1, pp. 26-46.

Hakansson, H. (ed.) (1982), *International Marketing and Purchasing of Industrial Goods: An Interaction Approach* (Chichester: Wiley).

Harvey, S. (1989), The Local Enterprise Programme: a Strategy, *Journal of Irish Business and Administrative Research*, 10, pp.45-58.

Johannisson, B. (1988), Regional Variations in Emerging Entrepreneurial Networks paper, presented to the 28th Congress of the European Regional Science Association, Stockholm, August.

Johannisson, B. (1990), Community entrepreneurship - cases and conceptualisation, *Entrepreneurship and Regional Development*, 2, pp. 71-88.

Johannisson, B. and Nilsson, A. (1989), Community entrepreneurs:

networking for Local Development, *Entrepreneurship and Regional Development*, 1, pp. 3-19.

Johannisson, B. and Nowicki, K. (1992), Using Networks to Organise Support for Entrepreneurs, paper presented to the Babson College Entrepreneurship Research Conference, INSEAD, Fontainbleau, France.

Leavitt, H.J. (1951), Some effects of certain communication patterns on group performance, *Journal of Abnormal and Social Psychology*, 46, pp. 38-50.

Mintzberg, H. (1979), *The Structuring of Organisations* (Englewood Cliffs, NJ: Prentice-Hall).

Perrow, C. (1971), *Organisational Analysis* (London: Tavistock).

Saxenian, A. (1988), The Cheshire Cat's Grin: Innovation and Regional Development in England, *Technological Review*, February/March, pp. 67-75.

Scott, W. R. (1982), *Organisations: Rational, Natural and Open Systems* (Englewood Cliffs, NJ: Prentice-Hall)

Van de Ven, A.H. and Ferry, D.L. (1980) *Measuring and Assessing Organisations* (New York: Wiley).

von Hippel, E. (1976), The Dominant Role of Users in the Scientific Instlument Innovation Process, *Research Policy*, 5, pp. 212-239.

von Hippel, E. (1977), The Dominant Role of the User in Semiconductor and Electronic Subassembly Process Innovation, *IEEE Transactions on Engineering Management*, EM-4, pp. 60-71.

Voss, C.A. (1985), The Role of Users inthe Development of Applications Software, *Journal of Product Innovation Management*, 2, pp. 113-121.

Vroom, V. (1964), *Work and Motivation* (New York: Wiley).

Warren, R.L. (1967), The Interorganisational Field as a Focus for Investigation, *Administrative Science Quarterly*, 12, pp. 396-419.

19 Barriers to active networks: Small firms as subcontractors in a competitive region

Mette Monsted

1. Introduction

A study of small and medium sized firms in a local area – a municipality, was tied up to a regional development programme LOKE, which focused the search for innovative potentials for new production.[1] (Tetzschner, Herlau, Nyberg, 1992). The potential should be tied to the local industry, and the study of small firms was mainly related to their role in the community, their supplier and sales network, and use of consultants.

The profile of the region is heavily dominated by small firms, but slightly less than most other regions in Denmark, as there are a few large manufacturing firms within food-production. They are daughter firms of large companies. The region is 100 km. away from Copenhagen. There are some commuters to Copenhagen, but the distance and transport limit the number of commuters.

The area is close to the one end of the construction of the tunnel and bridge of Storebælt, between two of the larger islands in Denmark. This is a real big construction, and was seen very much as an opportunity for the local firms, when the first part of the construction works started 3 years ago.

The town of Slagelse is an old trading centre for the west of Zealand. Apart from retail trade, and centre for personal services for the Western Region, there is a good industrial service. Educational institutions cover both technical schools for apprentices, and for some further technical educations. There is a section of a Business School, and a commercial school, apart from a teachers college.

Within 30 km. there are several other towns, most are not as big, and do not have the variety of services. But especially one of them has had a better development in industry.

2. Regional industrial structure

The large enterprises of more than 100 employees, are mostly in food production: dairy, sweets-production, and related to packaging, or some combined production and trading in food and beverages. There are however also a few large enterprises within the machine industry.

Western Zealand county is very close to the average in the country with respect to distribution of enterprises, and to the size of the enterprises, though with a slightly more favourable distribution of medium sized firms from 20-100 and over 1000.

Table 1. Persons in employment by industry. pct.

Industry	Slagelse		Westzealand		Denmark	
	1970	1984	1970	1985	1970	1985
Agriculture	7%	4%	15%	9%	11%	7%
Manufacturing	30%	20%	28%	19%	29%	20%
Construction	10%	6%	12%	9%	8%	7%
Commerce[1]	17%	18%	13%	15%	16%	16%
Transport	6%	5%	7%	7%	7%	7%
Financing	2%	6%	2%	6%	3%	8%
Administration, liberal professions	21%	36%	18%	30%	21%	30%
Other services	3%	5%	3%	5%	4%	5%
Industry not stated	(566)		(3.190)	(1.604)	(31.200)	(28.379)
N =	14.969	18.685	117.955	143.325	2.380.200	2.674.535

1) Inclusive restaurants and exclusive financing

Also in terms of the growth this has been steady, and stable, though not very high. Most of the growth in employment in the 1980'es has been generated by the expansion of the hospital to a regional hospital. The growth in industry has been more modest.

The size structure shows the distribution, which is characteristic foremost of Denmark, with the very many small firms. Even within manufacturing industry, this pattern is persistent. The few large firms gives a small bias in Slagelse, as to a few more in the larger size groups.

Table 2. Places of work by size within manufacturing. pct.

Size classification by number of employees	Slagelse municipality 1988	West-Zealand county 1984	Denmark 1984
1-5	44%	49%	45%
6-19	25%	33%	33%
20-99	21%	17%	19%
100 and more	8%	4%	4%
Total numbers of work places N =	113	1.046	20.946

One of the main purposes with the development project was to work with the collaboration between the local industry and between industry and the public sector. To study and use the innovation potentials, and also exploit the potentials developed in relation to the very large scale new bridge construction work 20 km. away.

There is a local political support to develop the innovation potential. The kind of collaboration and power relations between the firms are then important for evaluation of the innovation potential of the region, as also Sweeney (1987) stressed in his analysis of different regions in Europe.

Metalworking firms, such as mechanical engineering, machine fabrication, mechanical workshops and blacksmiths, are quite well represented in the region, and as these had shown to be a growth sector around the time of starting up the project (1988), these were specially selected for interviewing.

In all 18 manufacturing firms were interviewed, mostly within machinery and mechanical industry. On top of these 12 firms represent industrial service, as well as a few construction firms.

The profile of the industry could be a very promising one, for the self-sustained growth development. If comparing with the demands Sweeney sets up, the profile appear to both be strong in engineering and have firms in the small to medium sized range. There is no large plant or one branch totally dominating the area.

The political leaders have been very active to try to develop projects, and the big bridge-construction, has generated the kind of mega-event, with high expectations, and a chance for firms to work together to bid on subsupplies. The exploitation of the plans though, has not been so successful by the firms.

In terms of technological level, it is very different in the machinery producing enterprises. Some are very advanced machine tools making firms, some are working with very advanced machinery, and a group could be seen as more classic blacksmith/metalworking workshops.

There has been an economic depression during the period, and many of the smaller metalworking firms, have been changing types of work, expanding their work-numbers to adjust and be flexible. Most of them do not refuse any new orders, as they did earlier.

3. Vertical collaboration - subcontracting

Many of the firms are subcontracting, but some consider themselves more as suppliers to the industrial market. The role as subcontractor is not necessarily a problem. Only in cases where the firm is a subcontractor for one firm, or have a very high dependency on one or just a few firms, it is considered dangerous.

The concept of the subcontractor is not a clearly defined concept (Andersson, 1990, Braunerhjelm, 1991). In some studies, large firms with limited amount of subcontracting are also considered subcontractors. Among subcontractors with more than 20 employees, with a minimum sale of 20% to one customer, and open to international competition, as the customer firm buys international, they are much more vulnerable to the crisis, than other firms (Braunershjelm, 1991).

In a survey of starters from 1977-80, subcontracting is not specifically defined, but asked whether they are subcontracting to other firms, 42% of manufacturing firms confirmed this. The level is higher, i.e. 58%, for metal-machine production (Wickmann, 1983).

A recent survey on starters in manufacturing (1985), showed that half of them are by the survey in early 1992 subcontractors, and 1/4 have more then 50% of the turnover as subcontractor (Andersen a.o., 1992). A few of these will be supplying the industrial market, but 16% sell 40-70% of the turnover to one customer (ibid., and are thus very dependent. Also the fastest growing firms started as spin-offs from their earlier employer, and many of these started up mainly as subsuppliers.

The problems in these subcontracting relations, are tied to the power relations. On the one hand most of the small firms are happy to have a large contract with a large and stable firm. This provides some kind of feeling of security of having one large "reliable" customer.

The role of subcontractor is not always a weak role. In a study in Sweden, some of the subcontractors had special qualities, either special skills or special equipment, which made them strong subsuppliers in an industrial market. The weak subsuppliers are those who provide a standardised capacity production, that may be easily replaced (Färnström & Kedström,1975).

In the statistics, even the manufacturing firms above 6 employees, the county of Western Zealand has an overrepresentation of subcontractors (Maskell, 1992). The interviews with the firms confirmed this pattern. There are many subcontractors within the metal industry, and there is a very tough competition between them. Several interview-persons defined the market as stagnating, and that "there were too many on general metalwork".

A few have been feeling very confident, being servicing the printing machinery of the local newspaper. When the paper closed down, and was merged with a neighbouring paper, the firm had specialized, and had only very few contacts to other customers. Even with a large modern equipment and skills to solve many problems for other local firms, the contacts were not established, and this created severe problems.

A small electronic firm, is more and more subcontractor for firms in the Copenhagen area. They have been working long for a few large firms, but have very few contacts in their own region.

Another small electronic firm suddenly lost 30% of the turnover, as the customer wanted to buy the customized wire in the new British daughter-company.

Some of the firms, are themselves daughter companies to firms in the Copenhagen area. They do not themselves have any capacity to establish new contacts, and develop new markets for their products.

There are many firms who feel very dependent in the role of subsupplier, and regionally the large firms appear to think of the area as one of production, rather than one of development of new products. The perception of a stable subsupplier market is relatively clear.

Most of the large firms in the area have the main sales and development headquarter in the capital, and only production in Slagelse. This increase the perception of the area as a satellite or periphery to the greater Copenhagen.

One of the dominating large firms producing machinery for the graphic industry, is very concerned of quality control, and use this as an argument *not* to use subsuppliers. They feel they have to produce practically everything within the firms own strict quality control systems, and do not leave out jobs and orders for other local industries. The interviews were carried out in the region before the ISO 9000 discussion of quality control really began among SMEs. The pressure on subsuppliers is as recent as in 1991-1992, and thus only gradually beginning to play any role.

Regionally there may be many good arguments for supplying the capital rather than other Western Zealand firms. The transport net has been very easy to the capital. Both by road and by rail.

The structure of the region as a subcontracting region is felt in many ways. The competition is very hard between the firms, with many firms subsupplying within the same products. Visiting the majority of the firms within metalwork, the firms criticise each other very hard for imitation of products, for underbidding tenders, and for bias in the competition by a "protected workshop" - a public workshop for training persons under special programmes, mostly for handicapped persons.

The many complaints provides a characteristic of a highly competitive region, but not the kind of competition Porter is discussing in his Competitive advantage of nations (1990). It is not a very fruitful competition used to improve the firms own products, but rather a negative competition, which is not providing neither better products, nor any regional strength in competition toward other regions.

4. Vertical collaboration - Infrastructure and industrial service

In a growth perspective, the lack of main headquarters is a barrier to a certain self-centred growth. One of the other variables is the access to relevant infrastructure and industrial service. The access to industrial service is one of the coupling mechanisms that may generate spin-off growth in the area. If the large firms have most of the services in house, this is not so important for these firms, but is important for the SMEs.

The access to industrial and business service was especially in the growth centre/ development centre seen as the necessary infrastructure to support local industrial development (Kuklinsky, 1972, Mønsted, 1974). If the access to necessary industrial service is not available , as is the case for many smaller towns than Slagelse, then this is a local barrier towards growth (Pedersen, 1986)

The access to more standardized types of business service in the financial and accountancy area, is not standardized and widespread all over the country. Slagelse is an old trading centre, and is very well supplied, better than neighbouring towns, with all these services.

In relation to other types of services for the metalwork and metal/machineproduction , the area is generally a very well equipped. Most of the machineindustries characterize the area, of being very well in terms of access to: cylinder-service, painting and other surface treatment, supplies and services of tools and machinery, administrative information technology, though not for CAD-CAM, which is very centralised in the country.

The tradition for being a trading and service centre is maintained in terms of these services offered. Recently, many services tied to industry is also, and in some cases more developed in a neighbouring town of Næstved, 30 km. away.

The firms providing industrial service, service not only the local area, but have been specializing, and to some extend have a larger regional market. The provision of an elaborated sales and service of machines and tools has been expanded recently, and provide specialized services for machine, metal and construction work in a large part Western Zealand. One of these suppliers of machines and tools for the "black industry" is not in a crisis, even if the general level of activity in the metal-sector is very low.

The general infrastructural service for these SMEs in the metal working sector is good, but there is a very limited provision of qualified services within sectors demanding highly educated personnel, such as engineering, specialized technicians for computing etc. This may be related to the relative dependent development of the firms, but also provides a barrier to change this structure.

Business service for sales and export is hard to find. The channels for trading is very different for the different firms, and most use old network contacts. The dependency structure implies, that they as most SMEs are good to maintain old contacts, but have many difficulties in establishing new contacts. With the general stagnation and depression in the construction and industry, the old customer network is not enough for the subcontracting firms.

It is necessary for many metalworking and electronical equipment firms to search for new customers, and new types and groups of customers. The search for new customers among many subcontractors without too much specialization, implies a higher competition for the same customers. There are very few options in the local area, and the contacts are not well established to potential customers in other areas.

A few of those who have access to salesfirms, complain that they are very dependent on one saleschannel, who are not active enough to sell more.

The tough competition and difficulties in finding customers, implies that many firms are trying to spread their activities. They take in new products, and some find problems of adjusting to new or other quality demands, than they were used to in their core-production (Christensen, 1988). Having a core-skill in metalwork and welding as a black-smith, the expansion to areas of welding, where the quality control is more strict such as new tests at the public welding centre, implies large changes. These are both in terms of work, qualifications among staff, and routines, but also problems of dealing with new customers and other customer relations.

A few very specialized firms have the sales situation, that most dream of. They do not do very much to find customers, as they have a very good reputation to solve problems of making specialized machinery. Even if the owner-manager emphasize that they do not do anything, he goes to exhibitions, and he makes and brings videos of the machinery he already made for very large international companies. His firms is recommended from others, but he is very active in the sales, though not having to overcome the first barrier of making himself known.

The export is not very important, as so many are subcontractors for Danish firms. Even if many are producing for the export market, most do not themselves have the contacts.

Because of the problems at the home market, several firms have been thinking of reviving some earlier foreign contacts to expand on the export market. An electromechanical firm is now expanding in the Nordic countries, using a large sales firm in Copenhagen to establish contacts. They realize they have no chance of overcoming the first export barriers themselves. One of the firms repairing and selling farm machinery has been in exports to Thailand, Turkey and Eastern Europe. Poland and also other parts of Eastern Europe has been considered very tough for small firms to handle.

During the interview period, many small firms started using computers for administrative purposes. A special survey was made of computing services and the introduction of information technology, revealing that the area was not very well supplied in this field. Most firms had tried some contacts in Copenhagen, and others found assistance in a neighbouring town (Næstved) (Mønsted, 1989).

In all of the survey, small firms were very dependent on informal networks in the introduction of information technology. In the Slagelse region, there were quite a few barriers due to a relative weak supply of services in the early phase. The firms who had many informal contacts, especially certain trades: electricians and plumbers, were better to get access to information, and to manage the adaptation to the technology, as they had a network of trouble-shooters with some experience.

In relation to the information exchange and access to technological information, the infrastructure should be relatively good in Slagelse, having both technical and commercial school, and a department of the Business school. Especially the technical schools, not only train apprentices, but also have further educations for technicians, should provide access to new information, not available in most other regions outside the biggest cities. One of the larger firms collaborate with the technical school on the computing. The contact between the technical school and the firms is quite good, as many regular courses are also provided for the staff.

5. Horizontal collaboration - networks

The concept of network is used for many different purposes. Some of the roles as vertical relations, and industrial service is already covered. In this section, there is an emphasis on the both formal and informal collaborations between firms. In relation to the development project, this is based on the economic strong regions building on a network and collaborations between firms (Sabel, 1989, Courlet et al., 1988, Johannisson & Spilling, 1986). The strong development areas exploit the network both for services, information, and to work together on large orders.

In Denmark the Network programme in the Industrial policy is geared to make small firms work together to gain certain large-scale-benefits (Gjelsing & Knop, 1991). The more formal collaboration is however only a small part of the process of collaboration. The many informal contacts are important indicators both of:

- access to information
- the efficiency in the exchange of information
- the support for recommending services (Mønsted 1985 and 1991)

Sweeneys analysis is especially characterizing the differences in the access and exchange of information, that is the information intensity as one of the major indicators of development in a region (Sweeney, 1987). The access to information through the formal channels should be relatively good in Slagelse, though not on the very high technology, and research based technology, e.g. an example mentioned by a firm was that of optics. There are not very many university educated in the area, and it is difficult to persuade them to move to the area.

In most areas the informal network is expected to play an important role to diffuse and structure information. But in an area as Slagelse, this seems to be highly affected by the domination of the competition. Even if one of the benefits of the network is to open access to information and other firms, the reservations and many negative statements about other firms, seems to put a barrier for many of the informal networks.

Informal networks are found, especially among a few of the very strong firms in machine building. But the competition is so strong, that several attempt from firms and public institutions to make arrangement to bid for joint large tenders, and make some purchasing arrangements, have come out without any result. Several firms said they would rather refuse an order, than to go together with others about it.

There has however been a few cases of collaborations between electricians. Generally the electricians and the plumbers are better than any others to form and exploit networks. Their contacts to other "colleagues" are better than in most other trades, as they often have to join courses in the trade association (Mønsted, 1989).

One of the firms have been contacted from a firms outside the area, to go together on export of construction projects and parts to Eastern parts of Germany. The project only reached the early planning stage.

The expectations of using the "mega-event" of the bridge and tunnel construction for collaboration projects, and bids for joint orders was discussed at a few meetings arranged by the public and parastatal institutions. But this never materialised. Generally the impact on the orders in the region has been very meagre, and the expectations to the large constructions has not come through. Only a few have very little supplementary supplies for the construction, but it plays a very limited role in the industry of the region. The main construction firm has kept orders inside their own system of suppliers, only supplementing little locally.

Generally the network contacts are meagre, and most contacts seem to go to other areas. The local synergy is not impressing, and makes it difficult for the firms to get access to new contacts when the local depression is hard. The contacts to the customers in Copenhagen, and the lack of other local contacts, make it more difficult to get access to new jobs, and new kinds of orders. If firms are known, such as regional firms may have many formal and informal and personal contacts may give access also to other kinds of not standardised jobs. This is much more difficult, if many firms are tied to large customers outside the region, and many new potential contacts are not available.

6. Regional network perspectives for self sustained growth or for internationalization

In the discussion of regional structure and the firms, the level of analysis becomes important. Even in strong regions, not all firms are powerful and progressive, and in some of the weaker regions, there may be a few very strong and progressive firms.

It is a problem to generalize from regional level to firm level. The survey in this case has been working on both levels, as there are many interviews in the same area, and therefore information of quite a large share of the manufacturing firms. This gives information on the regional level also.

Comparing with some of the criteria, that Sweeney develops (1987), partly on the basis of Malecki (1981), there are traits in the area could be characterized basically as a "Technically progressive and Entrepreneurial Region" (Sweeney, 1987 p. 207-8). The model is not easily adaptable on any region, but there are certainly some of the most important traits as a relatively prosperous area, but there are also some missing links and barriers: both in terms of innovation, and in terms of information intensity and -networks.

Some of the problem in relation to the information intensity is the lack of highly educated research staff in the area. The limited network is a hindrance further for easy access to information. The barriers imply that, the quick access to information within the psychological half-hour contacts is difficult in the area.

Two of the large firms in machine fabrication and metal works however did not -by principle - want to have any interviews or firm visits. They are both very closed to the region, and also the local newspaper is not providing any positive news about the firms, whereas a few other large firms, clearly use the local news as a part of their image in the region (Ipsen & Mønsted, 1992).

Two of the large firms could be classified as some kind of innovators, and have very many contacts also outside the region. The local network and collaboration however is limited. Only the collaboration with the technical school, is the exception. The firms do not see the area as an innovative area. There are many qualified skilled labourers, but there is no real high-tech research and development. This development is in the Copenhagen area.

Looking at the region in a entrepreneurial perspective, it is not high. The turnover of firms is limited, and not high in terms of closed firms either (Maskell, 1992). The definition of new establishment and closed firms are however biased, as it is based on industrial statistics, which only include firms with more than 6 employees. New firms thus increase beyond the 6 employees, and closed, are decreasing under 6 employees. In terms of "new" establishments, the rate is actually quite good in both high-tech and medium technological fields.

Table 3. Establishing ratios[1] for high, middle and low technological industry in 1985-89, by counties

	Cph. Frb.	Cph.	Fr. borg	Rosk	West-seal.	Stor-strøm	Fyn	South jutl.	Ribe	Vejle	Ringk øb.	År hus	Vi-borg	No. jutl.
High technology	1,1	2,5	1,8	1,1	1,2	0,9	1,0	0,1	0,7	0,5	0,2	0,8	0,6	0,9
Middle technology	0,5	0,7	1,2	0,8	1,2	0,7	1,1	1,1	1,7	1,3	1,0	0,9	1,3	1,1
Low technology	0,8	0,7	0,8	0,8	1,1	1,1	0,9	1,1	1,1	1,1	1,6	1,0	1,2	1,0

[1] The establishing ratio state the relationship between every regions part of the total number of new firms in the whole country in a single industry, and the corresponding part for manufacturing. Average calculation for 1985-1989.

A number of firms are spin-offs from larger establishments, and run by earlier middle-managers. These appear to be very good firms, and have very many contacts from their earlier jobs. In a new survey of entrepreneurs these types of entrepreneurs/firms are characterised as the fast growing firms (Andersen et al., 1992). Also in the survey in Slagelse, the spin-off entrepreneurs were much better established, with more experience and much better network to solve problems. They do not suffer from the problem of isolation, and seem to have more contacts both within and outside the region.

The lack of network contacts, put a barrier both on the joint institutions "industrial councils", but also makes it difficult to make any kind of a joint regional strategy for growth.

The networks do not seem to be active. There are a few, but they are very passive, and the energy to expand and secure collaboration projects to come through, is not available. Most of the firms complain about the lack of new contacts, are used to be in the dependent part of the network. They are the dependent and neither the active nor the powerful part of the network.

This implies, that they are not tied to any active or balanced part of networks. Some would even not call this network, as it does not allow for temporary imbalances, and access through the other network contacts to new persons/firms.

The power relations of the network relations are not very well covered in research. The lack of power and lack of active access in the subcontracting firms are threatening. They can see the perspective of the networks, but are not forwarded as prosperous by other network contacts. They are therefore isolated, when old contacts are broken, and they do not have local informal contacts to other firms to exploit as new network contacts. Communication to development institutions and consultants show the desperate need to get new contacts and new customers.

The limited capacity to develop new contacts, and the dependency on old customers is an old clear pattern in the research on SMEs. The study of networks in existing small enterprise-areas are many, but the study of successfully building up, and expanding networks for non-prosperous regions, is more limited.

The larger and successful firms expand, but make expansion outside the region, either at the export market or in the Copenhagen region. Even if the success of the firm is perceived as very important in the region, also from newspaper articles, the expansion has very little to do with regional network contacts.

7. Conclusions

In a local development project, small firms within metalworking was interviewed. This group would normally constitute a group of firms, where networks both formal and informal play an important role. Earlier studies have emphasized the role of networks to both get information, to structure and solve problems, and to find new products and customers (Johannisson, 1986, Mønsted, 1989 & 1991). Looking at the single firms, there are a few network contacts, but the surprise in the regional study is the dominance of the competitive milieu setting barriers to the construction of local networks. The firms in this way are going much more into the role as subsuppliers, and role as dependent on the development in the firms in the Copenhagen area, and has little adjustment and alternatives, when their few contacts are not providing enough orders to them.

The apparent close collaboration between the public sector and the firms, and the initiatives by the municipality revealed, that the contacts were very few, and actually the networks did not trespass the border between public sector and the private sector. The actual contacts by the public sector were very few, and network contacts between the top officials in large firms and the political and municipal authority, were not active and possible to implement. The more informal contacts at the middle level of the organisations - private and public - did not exist, and thus made a barrier between the different networks.

Methodologically it is a problem to have contacts to many different parts of the public administration, political management and educational institutions, as well as to the smaller firms. The municipal institutions on the one hand say they have contacts, but can never apply them, and the small firms ask for contacts. The barriers build up and are difficult to overcome.

References

Andersen, Ib, Barnholdt-Jensen, T., Pedersen, K, Stuhr, S. (1992), *Succes-kriterier for iværksættere. En Undersøgelse af, hvordan virksomheder, etableret i fremstillingssektoren i 1985, har klaret sig*, Industry og Handelsstyrelsen, Copenhagen

Andersson, Göran (1990), *Underleverantörsroller*, paper presented at 6. Nordiske forskerseminar om små virksomheder 13.-17.juni 1990 Copenhagen

Braunerhjelm, Pontus (1991), *Svenske underleverantörer och småföretag i det nya Europa. Struktur, kompetens och internationalisering*, Industriens utredningsinstitut, Stockholm

Christensen, Poul Rind (1988), "Enterprise Flexibility and Regional Networks", *Industrial Flexibility and Work. French and Danish Perspectives, Cahiers IREP Development*, 12

Courlet, Claude, Pecqueur, B. & Roussier, N. (1988), "Etude sur les Politiques industrielles locales dans le cadre de la promotion des petites et moyennes entreprises", *IREP-D*. Université Grenoble

Danmarks Statistik (1988), *Erhvervsgrupperingskode af 1. april 1977*", 4. udgave

Danmarks Statistik, *Statistiske Efterretninger*, 1988:12, 1989:16, 1990:1, Copenhagen

Danmarks Statistik (1987), *Vejviser i Statistikken*, Copenhagen

Danmarks Statistik og Teknologirådet (1990), *Nye virksomheder. Statistisk belysning af virksomheder etableret i 1985 og 1986*, Copenhagen

Färnström, Bent O. & Kedström, Christer (1975) *Makt och beroende i samarbetsrelationer. En studie av mindre och medelstora underleverantörsföretag*, Lund

Gjelsing, Lars & Knop (1991) *Status i netværksprogrammet*, Industry- og Handelsstyrelsen, Copenhagen

Ipsen, Jytte og Mønsted, Mette (1992), *Analyse af forandringer i lokalt erhvervsliv gennem indholdsanalyse af lokalavisen*, Project LOKE, Center for Innovation & Entrepreneurship, Copenhagen

Johannisson, Bengt: Network Strategies (1986), "Management Technology for entrepreneurship and change", *International Small Business Journal* 5:1

Johannisson, Bengt & Spilling, Olav (1986), *Entreprenørskap og nettverksstrategier i noen norske og svenske kommuner*, Universitetsforlaget, Oslo

Kuklinsky, A. (ed.) (1972), *Growth Poles and Growth Centers in Regional Planning*, The Hague

Malecki, E.J. (1981), "Science, technology and regional economic development review and prospects", *Research Policy, 10*

Maskell, Peter (1992), *Nyetableringer i industrien - industristrukturens udvikling*, Handelshøjskolens forlag, Copenhagen

Mønsted, Mette (1974), "Francois Perroux' theory of "growth Pole" and "development Pole" - A Critique", *Antipode: A radical Journal of Geography*. vol. 6, no. 2

Mønsted, Mette (1991), *Regional Network Processes: Networks for Service or Development of Entrepreneurs?*, paper presented at the

International Workshop: "The Formation, Mangement and Organization of Small and Medium Sized Enterprises", Jönköping 25th-27th September

Mønsted, Mette (1989), "Small Enterprises Coping with the Challenges of Information Technology", Borum, F. & Kristensen P.Hull (eds.): *Technological Innovation and Organizational Change. - Danish Patterns of Knowledge, Network and Culture*, Copenhagen

Mønsted, Mette (1985), *Små virksomheder i rådgivningssystemet*, Nyt fra Samfundsvidenskaberne, Copenhagen

Nielsen, Peter Bøegh (1990), *Nye Virksomheder. Statistisk belysning af virksomheder etablerert i 1985 og 1986*, Danmarks Statistik og Teknologirådet

Pedersen, Poul O. (1986), "The Role of Business Services in Regional Development - A new growth centre strategy", *Scandinavian Housing and Planning Research 3:1986*

Porter, Michael (1990), *The Competitive Advantage of Nations*, London

Sabel, Charles F. (1989), *The Reemergence of Regional Economies*, Forschungsschwerpunkt Arbeitsmarkt und Beschäftigung (IIMV). Berlin

Sweeney, G. P. (1987), *Innovation, entrepreneurs and regional development*, N.Y.

Tetzschner, Helge, Herlau, Henrik & Nyberg, John (1992), *Uddannelsesbaseret erhvervsudvikling - forløbsrapport fra projekt LOKE*, Center for Innovation & Entrepreneurship, Copenhagen Business School, Copenhagen

Wickmann, Jane (1983), *Ungskoven i dansk erhvervsliv. Iværksættere 1977-80*, Report 1. Håndværksrådet, Copenhagen

Notes

[1] Project LOKE, Local Development had many different modules. The project was launched together with the municipality, who wanted to have both a more active industrial development, and be successful in a special "green project". The project had many different elements; teaching courses, introduction of projects, collaboration with local firms etc.

20 Beyond anarchy and organization: Entrepreneur in context

Bengt Johannisson, Ola Alexanderson, Krzysztof Nowicki and Knut Senneseth

Abstract

Three phenomena have dominated the interface joining research, management practice and public industrial policy during the 1980s: the revival of industrial districts, the creation of science parks and the promotion of corporate entrepreneurship. As a contribution to the understanding of the potential of entrepreneurship in such close settings, in its "contexts", we present a conceptual framework which focusses on the need for contextual rationales which can deal with the paradoxes ruling each empirical context. The network metaphor is introduced as a generic analytical tool in this endeavour.

Three contexts are studied, namely, the industrial district Västbo, the science park Ideon and the corporation Telub Service. In each context between 40 and 70 entrepreneurs/intrapreneurs are surveyed. Single-stranded network linkages including both business ties and social ties are identified and these are in turn combined to form multiplex ties. The network analyses concern both the firm and the context level.

The findings reveal the outstanding socioeconomic texture of an industrial district, one far more elaborate than in both the science park and the corporate setting. The industrial district is unique with respect to frequent complex social ties parallel with the business exchange relationships. In addition, the members of the industrial district exhibit much more homogeneity with respect to contextual networking, although this is supplemented to a considerable extent with networks in the business and societal environment at large. The findings suggest further that contextual networking is a necessary but not sufficient road to venture success.

1. The Need for a Contextual Approach to Entrepreneurship

The entrepreneurial function is recognized in many shapes other than that of the self-made founder-manager who independently carries out the venturing process. Corporate entrepreneurs and academic entrepreneurs represent special breeds in the market and social and political entrepreneurs create new societal settings for new ventures. The existence of these "alternative" entrepreneurs means that the notion of the entrepreneur as an anarchist has to be reconciled with the image of the entrepreneur as a tamed administrative man. Elsewhere we have suggested that this paradox can be dealt with by introducing the notion of the "organizing context" as an intermediate structure between the individual entrepreneur/venture and the global environment (Johannisson 1988, Johannisson & Senneseth 1990).

We see at least five reasons for introducing the notion of context. First, during the 1980s there was a debate concerning national strategies for the creation of competitiveness other than those of huge multinationals who lead the development, exploiting smaller firms as subcontractors. The Marshallian concept of "industrial districts", promoted by e.g. Piore & Sabel 1984 and Pyke et al. 1990, highlights the way agglomerations of small firms may unintentionally create a local texture which compensates for individual firms' lack of resources and regions' isolation.

Second, today a considerable part of the discussion concerning, on the one hand small-firm entrepreneurship and on the other hand renewal of large corporations, focusses on differences between spontaneous and induced entrepreneurship. The science park institution and locally initiated economic development are phenomena which to a very great extent belong to the 80s. These strategies for development are both based on the idea that creating a critical mass of emerging ventures will make sustainable economic development possible.

Third, the need for young firms to overcome the liabilities of newness and uniqueness has increased in the 80s. The dominance of large multinationals in the corporatist societies in Western Europe has created a political and institutional system that is biased towards large-scale operations. Given such a situation new firms without a track record obviously must get support to acquire legitimacy.

Fourth, adoption of the Kirzner (1973) definition of the entrepreneur suggests that (s)he is capable of alertly and serendipitously identifying and materializing opportunities in the market. Considering that entrepreneurship is perpetual learning by action an unexperienced entrepreneur will have difficulties in recognizing opportunities in distant markets. The natural frame of reference should be markets that are not too well known - because that makes one take things for granted - and not too alien - because then it will not be possible to acquire a holistic overview. A rich context thus provides the proper milieu for the emerging enterprise.

Fifth, since genuine entrepreneurship means management of ambiguity, the entrepreneur will need a "habitat" where personal self-confidence can be accumulated to balance the equivocality of the commercial operations. This place of rest is provided by e.g. a local or corporate context where the entrepreneur feels at home.

The "organizing context" represents the socioeconomic texture in which the entrepreneur and the venturing process are embedded. Drawing upon the cognitive approach to organizing provided by Weick (1979), the context then is defined as a provider of

> "...ends and means for the enactment, selection and retention subprocesses. It may operate as a springboard (supporting ecological change/enactment), a gear-box (supporting selection), and as a shock absorber or defence wall (supporting retention) between the entrepreneur and the environments beyond the context."
> (Johannisson, 1988, p 88)

We thus propose that the context carries the generic function to balance the entrepreneur's need for stability and change, for guidelines and independence. The role of the context can be further separated into different subfunctions which are summarized in Table 1. The table also indicates which partial functions we hypothesize to dominate in different kinds of empirical contexts. We are going to discuss these assumptions throughout this article. The table suggests what three subfunctions are given highest priority in each context throughout the venturing process. Cf. Alexanderson et al. 1992.

In the industrial district, where being an owner-manager is a life-style, the need for adaption due to external changes can be postponed by first taking on a subcontracting role in one's entrepreneurial career. When expansion opportunities emerge the venture can trade upon colleagues' experiences gained by trial and error and use contextual network control to enchance own recources. Vitality is upheld by using the context as an amplifier in the sense that even vague signals concerning the need for change will reach the firm in the district through a variety of channels.

Table 1. Generic Functions of the Entrepreneurial Context - Illustrations

Function of the context	*The industrial district*	*The science park*	*The corporation*
SUPPORT			
* Incubator		X	X
* Shock absorber	X		
VENTURING			
* Spring board		X	X
* Experience bank	X		
RENEWAL			
* Selector		X	
* Amplifier	X		X

The science park operates as an incubator for academic entrepreneurs who, due to the double membership of the scientific and the business communities, need special care. Once a market niche has been focused, the context can be used as an intermediate structure to reach sources of further competence within the university. The science park also provides a selection mechanism by which the existing stock of scientific knowledge can be scrutinized with respect to potential for commercialization.

The <u>corporation</u> as well has to provide an incubator function for intrapreneurs who will need active support in their venturing process while unlearning corporate practices. Once a venture is launched the intrapreneur can trade upon e.g. the marketing resources of the corporations, thereby easily multifolding his/her own capabilities and resources. The emerging venture can use the corporate context to amplify vague market signals when the venture has matured and needs elaboration.

Thus far, we have argued that entrepreneurs operate their ventures differently depending upon the context and its characteristics. In Section 2 we therefore conceptualize the different logics of the contexts introduced above: the industrial district, the science park and the corporation. We argue further that the personal network of the entrepreneur is an appropiate tool for mapping the context and its logic. In Section 3, an empirical study, its methodology and data are presented. The final section summarizes the findings and provides some suggestions for further research as well as implications for practitioners.

2. Conceptualizing Contextual Logic and Networking

The "logic" of a collective, whether a corporation, a trade association or a community, is formed by the values, attitudes and action rationales which are taken for granted as vehicles to success. In Table 2 below, the logic of each of the three contexts is illustrated with reference to the generic paradox the context copes with and the contextual action rationale adopted by the entrepreneur. We have elsewhere argued that there is much justification for analyzing entrepreneurship with the help of paradox (e.g. Johannisson & Senneseth 1990).

Table 2. Alternative Contextual Logics for Entrepreneurship

CONTEXT	GENERIC PARADOX	ACTION RATIONALE
Industrial district	Cooperation and competition	Economies of overview
Science park	Separation and integration	Shopping mall for problems solutions
Innovative corporation	Order or chaos	Skunk works and social resource management

In the industrial district <u>cooperation and competition</u> characterize business exchange, cf. e.g. Pyke et al. 1990, Zeitlin 1989. On the one hand, local firms for example may compete for an order, on the other, they may share the same order once it has been assigned to one party. Preconditions for both competition and cooperation are the focus on one industry, flexible specialization and co-existing social and business lives in the community.

The dual principles characterizing the science park are <u>separation and integration</u>. University scientists considering an entrepreneurial career must get away from the academic setting where basic research is focused and business is seen with suspicion. The corporate venturing unit which had moved into the park also needs separation. The highly specialized knowledge being commercialized for new niche markets is easily choked by routine formal structures. The university academics who populate the science park will become part of the world of business while the corporate scientists will reconstruct their linkages to the university. Cf. Stankiewicz 1986.

In the corporation <u>law and chaos</u> must coexist, cf. e.g. Quinn 1979. On the one hand the hierarchical structure must be respected, on the other disobedient behaviour in terms of e.g. using social resources for unsolicited initiatives must be accepted, or at least not banned, cf. Starr & McMillan 1990. A counterculture is needed in order to provoke tensions and change.

The action rationale in the industrial district is <u>economies of overview</u>, i.e. simultaneously adopting a helicopter and a grassroot perspective. Overview facilitates the identification of opportunities, whether they represent new-ventures ideas or solutions to problems that the entrepreneur has run into. The action rationale of the science park is to operate as a <u>market for problems and solutions</u> where serendipity combines with goal-directed behaviour, i.e. where ideas are both generated and tested. In the innovative corporation, finally, entrepreneurial action is guided by surprise and exploitation of the corporate masochistic admiration of innovation and deviant behaviour, cf. e.g. Peters & Waterman 1982, Kuratko et al. 1990. Hypocracy is institutionalized through the explicit promotion of holistic corporate strategies by CEOs who at the same time shut their eyes to the use of social resources for individual venturing, cf. Starr & McMillan 1990.

The existence of different logics places differing demands upon networks as organizing vehicles from the point of view of entrepreneurs as well as when considered from the perspective of contexts. The basic differences between the three contexts can be stated by differentiating the social and business sides of networks.

The needed simultaneous consideration of cooperation and competition for exploiting economies of overview in the industrial district calls for dense networks where ties are multiplex and social and business concerns overlap. Only then can asymmetries in individual ties be balanced; only then can the delicate matter of defining what is a "cost" or an "investment" in exchange between contextual parties be settled.

In the science park the logic calls for single-stranded relationships and separated networks; unwanted ties will otherwise be created, which means commitment beyond the role of the network as a vehicle for information exchange an opportunity/problem management. Overly integrated contextual networks would compete with the science-park entrepreneurs' need for ties to their academic domicile.

In the innovative corporation the networks should make it possible to maintain the double standard of a holistic corporate strategy and a continuous struggle between traditionalists and those pushing for change. This means that even if the social and business networks are contextually separated, individual ties very well may combine the two sides of entrepreneurial networking.

The network metaphor has become increasingly utilized within the social sciences in general (Easton & Araujo 1991), and in entrepreneurship research in particular since the mid-80s (Birley 1985, Aldrich & Zimmer 1986). Beyond the metaphorical and illustrative use (cf. e.g. Segal Quince Wickstead 1988), previous network studies restrict themselves to computations of dyads, possibly of dyads with bundles of further ties and triads (Aldrich et al. 1987, Johannisson 1990). Even the rich conceptual and empirical material on the Italian industrial districts lacks a thorough network analysis.

Elsewhere we have argued that the personal networks of entrepreneurs and their (small) firms/ventures combine social and business dimensions (Johannisson 1990). Since the entrepreneur personifies the new small venture, a critical methodological problem in network studies can be avoided. In the large firm an employee representing the organization may, between decisions switch over from a business to a social orientation, refering to either himself as a person or the company as a corporation. The entrepreneur on the other hand wants to and has to cope with both choice dimensions simultaneously. (S)he is existentially motivated and builds the organization around the own personality.

Studying contextual networks, it is, to our mind, too simplistic to distiguish solely between social and business ties in order to separate different contextual logics. First, in most entrepreneurial contexts in general and in the corporate in particular there are static structures which have become formalized by design or by organic sedimentation. Second, the social networks include ties that vary with respect to e. g. affective loading and exchange activity. "Acquaintances" represent a potential for both solicited and unsolicited exchange, while "talk" networks include both an instrumental communication dimension and socializing based on affection. Third, business networks include straightforward commercial exchange on a cash or barter basis as well as professional exchange of problem- or opportunity-oriented information. In Table 3 on the next page these specifications concerning the personal networks of entrepreneurs are further elaborated with respect to the three different contexts for entrepreneurship introduced above.

The formal structure is generic to the corporation, carrying the basic management control functions. However, it has to be kept in mind that the formal, chain-of-command, hierarchy is quite a simplistic structure when compared with the general potential of mutual linkages. Given a span of control of eight, an enterprise with two management echolons may encompass 73 people, interconnected with only 72 ties. The total network potential, considering unidimensional linkages, though, is 73x72/2, i.e. 2,628 ties!

Formal structures in terms of organizations especially created to deal with collective concerns also exist in industrial districts and science parks. In the industrial district these often operate as either gatekeepers, e.g. keeping unions and other pressure groups out, or as collective training and development agencies. Within science parks administrative units are created either to manage the property and auxiliary activities or to produce/intermediate professional services to the tenants. However, these formal structures within the industrial district and the science park do not include all context members in an ascribed structure, as is the case in the corporation.

Table 3 Towards Contextual Definitions of Social and Business Networks

		Relational Structure			
	FORMAL	SOCIAL		BUSINESS	
CONTEXT		Talk	Acquaintance	Commercial	Professional
Industrial district	(Operate as a gatekeeper, provide joint R&D)	Acquire information	Enforce norms/ resource bank	Provide a local market	Realize change
Science park	(Supply management resources)	Complete production function	Legitimate role as entrepreneur	Select niches	Create/test problems/ solutions
Corporation	Enforce norms	Generate ideas/reflect formal structure	Provide social support	Implement projects	Test venture ideas

The "social network" is here separated into a "talk network" and an "acquaintance network". Within the industrial district the function of the talk network is to communicate information concerning business as well as social life. In Sweden young entreprenerus build networks which include both social and commercial ties and their social arenas, e.g. the local organizational life, are used for discussing business matters (Johannisson 1990). Social and business activity spheres are organically integrated in the industrial district. In the science park, with its knowledge-based firms, "talk" is the major interogranizational production media, where some of the exchange is problem-oriented (see below) and some is spontaneous. In the corporative context talk furnishes on the one hand the formal structure with information and on the other generates new ideas.

The <u>acquaintance network</u> in the industrial district reflects the grid of social control that embeds all local activities. Personal ties also create social resources which may be activated when needed. In the science park the peers known bring a feeling of being legitimate to the academic entrepreneurs who are challenging (without abandoning) their origin at the university, cf. Stankiewicz 1986. Analogically the acquaintance network in the corporate context supports the intraprenerus in their venturing activities when confronted with formal policy.

The "<u>business network</u>" is here divided into a "commercial network" and a "professional" network. In the industrial district the <u>commercial network</u> reflects the local market, which, due to the logic of the context, is crucial not only to young firms but to business in general. While such production networks supposedly are dense in industrial districts, they are expected to be quite selective in the science park. Since the firms focus on unique competence and associated market niches, the potential for contextual commercial exchange is limited by definition. In the corporate context, finally, the exchange of goods and services reported in a network study basically reflects corporate strategy. The exchange in the emerging intrapreneurial counterculture will be confined to quantitatively relatively insignificant social resources.

The <u>professional network</u>, which here reflects problem-oriented information retrieval, in the industrial district reflects the incremental change process whereby product concepts are elaborated and new markets developed. In the science park this exchange provides both unexpected problems which will need further elaboration, and solutions to these, as well as problems generated in other ways. The professional network in the corporate context may be used by intrapreneurs to test their emerging business concepts.

Obviously the single-stranded networks introduced in Table 3 all contribute to the making of a context for entrepreneurship. However, while we hypothesize that the industrial district builds elaborate networks generally, the other two contexts nurture networks more selectively. In the science park the talk and problem-solving networks are most elaborate while in the corporation the talk network, due to proximity, is quite elaborate. However, we also expect the innovative corporation to provide an internal market with intense commercial networking.

3. Methodology and Basic Data

3.1. Data Collection. Basic Definitions.

In 1990 background and network data were collected in three entrepreneurial contexts - a community, a science park and a corporation - all located in the southern part of Sweden. The community Anderstorp with its approx. 5,000 inhabitants is (part of) an internationally recoganized industrial district in a small-business region, cf. e.g. Johannisson 1987, Zeitlin 1989. The science park Ideon, on the Lund University campus in Scania, was established in 1983 and is now the third largest in Europe. Telub Service is a company specializing in maintaining and developing computer hardware. The company dominates its market nationally and is located in Växjö.

The data were collected in a postal survey approaching all firms/entrepreneurs in the three contexts, i.e. 138 in Anderstorp and 100 in Ideon. In the corporate context (Telub Service) the 119 potential intrapreneurs were selected with the help of the management (the company has altogether 192 employees in its domestic operations). In Anderstorp the local business

Table 4 Three Contexts - a Presentation

CHARACTERISTIC	VENTURE CONTEXT		
	Anderstorp	Ideon	Telub Service (1)
Firm structure			
Number of firms	138	100	59
(respondents, generally)	(100)	(68)	(59)
(respondents, network data)	(67)	(42)	(57)
Firm size (employees) (2)	10(28.8)	3(12.5)	5(7.8)
Venture management (3)			
Founder manager (%)	39.2	58.5	50.9
Owner manager (%)	84.5	65.2	100.0
General venture network			
Portion of entrepreneurs who have discussed business venturing with more than 5 people over the last six months (%)	61.5	60.0	56.4
Most important business relationship within the context (%) (5)	18.8	12.7	81.8
Primary network within context (%) (5)	43.6	25.8	73.7
Market location (%) (2)			
Selling, contextual	5 (16,5)	0 (4,8)	-
international	5 (10,0)	5 (29,8)	-
Purchasing, contextual	10 (14,8)	5 (11,9)	-
international	5 (18,0)	0 (10,0)	-

(1) In this context, a "task force" or a "project" is defined as the (venture/firm) unit of analysis and "owned" by those recognizing responsability.
(2) Medians (means within parentheses). Refer to gross responses.
(3) In Telub Service, formation and ownership are operationalized as initiative to, and (partial) responsability for, a task force/project.
(4) Importance was defined with respect to how long time it would take to replace the contact (person/firm).
(5) The respondents were asked to identify the five persons they favour when discussing their business/work in general and to locate these persons.

association was contacted and in the science park, Ideon, the study was approved by the board of the property association. The response rate concerning background information, including late respondents contacted by phone, was satisfactory. The response rate concerning network data was, though, considerably lower in Anderstorp and Ideon as indicated in Table 4. Analysis of this secondary non-response with the help of available background information however reports little bias.

In Anderstorp we can report complete network data concerning 67 firms, implying a gross response rate of 48.5% and 67.0% net, i.e. as a percentage of those responses providing background information. Network data concerning 42 firms at Ideon show a response rate of gross 42.0%, net 61.8%.

Telub Service provides network data on all but two of the 59 "intrapreneurs", i.e. employees who were identified as potential project champions by management and who, returning the questionnaire, acknowledged (partial) personal responsability in a project.

With respect to data content, general background information and network data were collected. Some basic facts concerning the contexts are summarized in Table 4. The table, among other things, states that the science park includes a higher proportion of founder-managers than the industrial district but also that ventures to a lesser extent are owned by science-park entrepreneurs. A general finding is that ventures in each context are generally small. This is typical for the mature industrial district, to be expected in a rather young science park and natural in the corporate context where projects by definition are restricted in size and temporary constructs.

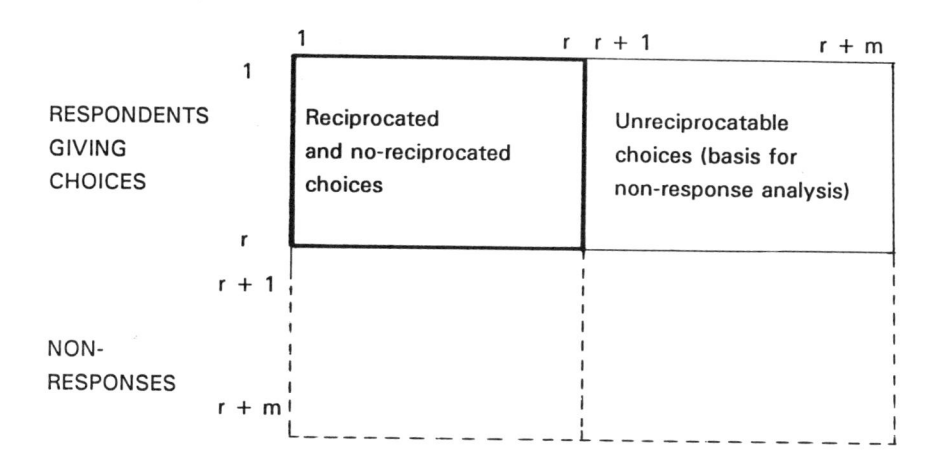

```
                        1              r  r + 1           r + m
                    1  ┌─────────────────┬──────────────────┐
RESPONDENTS            │ Reciprocated    │ Unreciprocatable │
GIVING                 │ and no-reciprocated │ choices (basis for │
CHOICES                │ choices         │ non-response analysis) │
                    r  │                 │                  │
                  r + 1│                 │                  │
NON-                   │                 │                  │
RESPONSES              │                 │                  │
                  r + m└─────────────────┴──────────────────┘
```

Legend: r = responses
         m = total number of contextual ventures

Figure 1 The Network Data Matrix

In the network data collection in Anderstorp and Ideon each entrepreneur was provided with a list of all 138/100 firms and their CEOs. In Telub Service a corresponding list of 119 (potential) intrapreneurs was distributed. The respondents then only had to mark (with an "x") if they and/or their firm were linked in each of the four possible ways with the other contextual units. In Telub Service the organization chart provided in addition a fifth, formal, chain-of-command network. Thus the repondents generated a matrix where it is possible to identify mutual choices or one-sided choices, which means that the network analyses are based on directed graphs. Cf. Figure 1.

The size of the network data matrices and the scope of the associated analyses depend on the response rates, cf. above. In Anderstorp we deal with a 67 x 67 matrix with regard to incoming as well as outgoing ties. With respect to outgoing ties alone, in the Anderstorp case we can operate a 67 x 138 matrix. In Ideon the symmetric is 42 x 42 and the overall matrix 42 x 100. In Telub Service the mutual matrix is 57 x 57 and the larger matrix 57 x 119.

The five single-stranded networks are defined as follows, cf. Johannisson & Nowicki 1992:

SOCIAL

Talk whether there was a face-to face or telephone meeting with the senior management of the firm (Anderstorp)/fellow employee (Telub Service) over the las 30 days. The conversation should have lasted for at least five minutes and concerned things other than weather;

Acquaintance whether the CEO or anyone else in senior management and on the board is personally known (Anderstorp)/whether the fellow employee is personally known;

BUSINESS

Commercial whether there was a business (including lending/borrowing and barter) transaction with the firm over the last nine months (Anderstorp)/whether there was any special deal with the fellow employee (Telub Service);

Professional whether the staff of the firm (Anderstorp)/fellow employee (Telub Service) would be approached if an ingenious or challeging problem turned up;

FORMAL whether there is an ascribed link according to the formal organization chart. (Telub Service)

Since our database provides basic information on directed ties, it is possible for us to study both symmetric, i.e. reciprocated, and asymmetric ties. All single-stranded networks besides the professional one assume reciprocity and we therefore for reliability reasons only include symmetric talk, acquaintance and commercial ties in the analysis. This implies that these three networks are treated as undirected in the presentation below. The professional network is here turned into an undirected graph by symmetrizing the tie between each pair of nodes. A professional tie is assumed to exist if either or both entrepreneurs use the other for solving problems. This means that the professional network reaches disproportionate frequencies and densities when compared with the other networks. The formal network by definition is symmetric.

We also define and elaborate upon the double-stranded, symmetric "friendship network". In the friendship network each tie consists of a reciprocated talk tie as well as a reciprocated acquaintance tie. Friendship here thus means an acquaintanceship which is regularly activated, and must be considered as a strong tie, cf. Granovetter 1973, 1982 and also Burt 1983.

In single-stranded, double-stranded or multi-stranded networks, three different kinds of network analyses will be presented (cf. also Alexanderson et al. 1992, Johannisson & Nowicki 1992):

Node level, e.g., characteristics based on ties from/to a firm or an entrepreneur;

Local level, e.g., dyads or triads, i.e. interaction between two or three firms/entrepreneurs;

Global level, i.e., structural properties relating to the whole graph, e.g. components and blocks.

In accordance with our research focus and conceptual framework, we focus here on network data. We will demonstrate the different levels of analysis on our contextual data. For a more general discussion concerning optional network concepts in socio-economic settings, see Tichy et al. 1979, Aldrich & Whetten 1981. Galtung 1967 and Burt 1982 present optional ways of classifying properties of network models.

The data analysis was carried out with the help of the UCINET IV computer package (Borgatti et al. 1992).

3.2. Findings

Node Level

The findings suggest that all single-stranded networks discriminate betweem the three contexts, cf. Table 5. Independent firms in the industrial district have slightly more frequent commercial exchanges than employees in the corporate context. The intrapreneurs'slightly higher degree of oral communication probably reflects routine information exchange based on physical proximity. In both the industrial district and the corporate context, commercial exchange however is considerably higher than in the science park where every second entrepreneur has no commercial exchange whatever with contextual peers. Even in the mos elaborate science-park networks, the talk an acquaintance textures, one third of the respondents has no exchange at all within the context.

Table 5 Distribution of Ties in Single-Stranded Networks

Accumulated distributions of firms (%)

Percent of potential number of dyadic ties	ANDERSTORP			IDEON			TELUB SERVICE		
	Business	Talk	Acquaintance	Business	Talk	Acquaintance	Business	Talk	Acquaintance
0	3.0	7.5	4.5	50.0	35.6	33.3	15.8	0.0	66.7
5	17.9	38.8	11.9	88.1	81.0	85.7	33.3	1.8	89.5
10	32.8	53.7	23.9	95.2	92.9	95.2	50.8	14.0	100.0
15	56.7	64.2	28.4	100.0	95.2	97.6	68.4	26.3	
20	79.1	88.1	32.8		97.6	100.0	78.9	36.8	
30	93.9	100.0	41.8		100.0		98.2	57.8	
50	98.5		82.1				100.0	100.0	
100	100.0		100.0						

There are some radical differences between Anderstorp and Ideon as contexts for independent entrepreneurship on the one hand, Telub Service on the other. In the former two and particularily in Anderstorp, there is a much denser web of voluntary and spontaneour acquaintanceships, which is also reflected in high frequencies of friendship ties, that is, social linkages with regular exchange. Two our of three of the industrial-district entrepreneurs know more than 20% of their local colleagues personally and almos half of them nurture friendship ties with between 10 and 30% of their peer entrepreneurs. In the corporation, in contrast, about two thirds of the intrapreneurs have not developed any qualified social relationships whatsoever. Little emotional energy for true entrepreneurship seems to be mobilized in that context.

In Table 2 above we suggest that different action rationales characterize each context. We furthermore assume that these rationales ares reflected in the structuring of contextual activity in networks. Consequently, different networks will have different antecedents and outcomes due to context concerned. E.g. it may be proposed that in the industrial district founders build more extensive social networks than non-founders because they once used the social network to launch their ventures, cf. Johannisson 1990. The commercial and professional, i.e. business, networks, in contrast, are not expected to differ because successors and immigrant leaders are attracted by the commercial dynamism created by flexible specialization. Owner-managers running small firms and marketing their products nationally are assumingly more dependent both socially and commercially on the local context than larger firms or those penetrating international markets. In addition it is reasonable to assume that success, as perceived by the entrepreneurs, relates to elaborate business networks but not to the structuring of social exchange in the context.

In the science park, due to its less dominant role in the existential being of entrepreneurs and, in this case, short existence, the networks are still emerging and thus less determined. We propose then that the contextual networks generally vary little according to entrepreneur and firm characteristics.

In the innovative corporation we suggest that project founders operate contextual social networks more actively than non-founders because of greater dependence upon social resources (Starr & McMillan 1990). Furthermore we expect smaller venture teams to pursue business exchange on the internal market to a greater extent than larger, more self-sufficient project groups. Success in corporate venturing is proposed to be associated with intensive networking.

Table 6. Antecedents and Implications of Contextual Networks (1)

Accumulated distributions of firms (%)

Percent of potential number of dyadic ties(2)	ANDERSTORP			IDEON			TELUB SERVICE		
	Commer-cial	Talk	Profes-sional	Commer-cial	Talk	Profes-sional	Commer-cial	Talk	Profes-sional
VENTURE ORIGIN									
Founders									
0	3.7	7.4	0.0	50.0	45.8	12.5	0.0	0.0	0.0
5	29.6	33.3	18.5	91.7	87.5	70.8	10.7	3.6	0.0
10	44.4	48.1	18.5	95.8	95.8	91.7	28.6	3.6	0.0
20	77.8	85.2	59.3	100.0	95.8	95.8	64.3	17.9	10.7
Non-founders									
0	2.5	7.5	2.5	50.0	22.2	16.7	31.0	0.0	0.0
5	10.0	42.5	12.5	83.3	72.2	44.4	55.2	0.0	0.0
10	25.0	57.5	22.5	94.4	88.9	100.0	72.4	24.1	3.4
20	80.0	90.0	55.0	100.0	100.0		83.1	55.2	27.6
VENTURE SIZE									
Small									
0	2.9	8.8	0.0	52.2	22.2	4.3	22.7	0.0	0.0
5	20.6	38.2	17.6	91.3	87.0	71.4	45.5	4.5	0.0
10	35.3	61.8	26.5	91.3	91.3	91.3	63.6	27.3	9.1
20	85.3	94.1	67.6	100.0	95.6	95.6	95.5	54.5	36.4
Large									
0	3.0	6.1	3.0	47.4	47.4	26.3	11.4	0.0	0.0
5	15.1	39.4	12.1	84.2	73.7	52.6	25.7	0.0	0.0
10	30.3	45.5	15.2	100.0	94.7	78.9	42.9	5.7	0.0
20	72.7	81.8	45.5		100.0	100.0	68.6	25.7	8.6

Table 6. Antecedents and Implications of Contextual Networks (1) (Cont.)

Accumulated distributions of firms (%)

	ANDERSTORP			IDEON			TELUB SERVICE		
Percent of potential number of dyadic ties(2)	Commercial	Talk	Professional	Commercial	Talk	Professional	Commercial	Talk	Professional
MARKET SCOPE									
Domestic									
0	0.0	5.8	2.2	55.0	35.0	15.0			
5	15.2	38.2	20.6	85.0	85.0	55.0			
10	39.4	58.8	20.6	95.0	95.0	90.0			
20	87.9	88.2	58.8	100.0	100.0	100.0			
International									
0	5.9	9.1	0.0	45.5	36.4	16.6			
5	20.6	39.4	9.1	90.4	77.3	63.6			
10	26.5	48.5	21.2	95.5	90.9	81.8			
20	70.6	82.9	54.5	100.0	95.5	95.5			
PERFORMANCE									
Success									
0	3.5	13.8	3.4	55.6	38.9	11.1	26.9	0.0	0.0
5	20.7	34.5	13.8	88.9	88.9	61.1	42.3	3.8	0.0
10	37.9	41.4	20.7	100.0	100.0	94.4	61.5	15.4	7.7
20	75.9	82.8	58.6			100.0	80.0	42.3	19.2
No success									
0	2.6	2.6	0.0	45.8	33.2	16.7	6.5	0.0	0.0
5	15.8	42.1	15.8	87.5	75.0	58.3	25.8	0.0	0.0
10	28.9	63.2	21.1	91.7	87.5	79.2	41.9	12.9	0.0
20	81.6	92.1	55.3	100.0	95.8	95.8	64.5	32.2	19.4

1. The variables and their dichotomizatins are presented in the text.
2. The percentages thus refer to the potential number of ties to all members of the context as defined by the network data base.

In Table 6 we provide data on subnetworks which are clustered according to determinants such as venture origin, size and international orientation. First the respondents in each context are classified according to whether or not the firm/project is run by the founder/initiator or not. Second, we have dichotomized the firms according to size (employees). In Anderstorp and Ideon we, in addition, distinguish between whether they have international operations (exports 5% or more) or not.

Table 6 also reports dichotomized data on firm/project performance as perceived by the entrepreneurs/intrapreneurs. In the corporate context the respondents were asked to judge whether they considered their projects to be more, equally or less successful than others in the corporation. In Anderstorp the entrepreneurs were asked to rate their business success with respect to industry averages with regards to in part growth, in part profitability. In the table the respondents are dichotomized according to a combined measure. (With few exceptions perceptions of relative profitability and relative growth are the same.)

The findings with regard to the community Anderstorp confirm that commercial exchange within the context is evenly distributed over the stated background variables. Large firms, though, build larger professional networks than small firms, possibly because more employees can be involved in problem-solving activities. Looking at the social dimension then, founders are not more dependent upon social networks than successors, probably because of the favourable local business climate legitimizing any business initiative. Data concerning the talk network also indicate that large and/or successful firms are bimodally distributed: a significant portion has little social exchange locally and an equally significant portion reports the opposite.

With respect to the commercial network, the science park Ideon reports the same, uniform, findings as what regards the industrial district. Neither does the professional network vary with international orientation or business success. However, small firms pursue professional exchange to a considerably higher degree than large firms. These findings confirm that the science park is used as a context for high-tech venturing for different purposes: by (small) founders as an incubator and by large immigrant firms as a gateway to the university. The report on the talk network indicates that founders hardly exploit the science-parl context for mere conversation; more that other park members they ration plain social exchange.

The findings concerning the corporate context Telub Service are the most diverse and surprising ones. First, the intrapreneurs who have founded their ventures to a greater extent than others exploit both their commercial and their professional networks. In addition, contrasting our assumptions, those in charge of large ventures are more keen on making use of collective corporate resources. Obviously, though, this does not mean that the ventures are more successful, suggesting that external resources must be brought in as well. Neither does social exchange in the talk network relate to venture success. Beside the fact that founder-managed ventures have more extensive social networks than others the findings thus differ considerably from what is assumed in the literature on corporate entrepreneurship. A reasonable explanation is that most ventures in Telub Service represent designed projects of an adhocracy, not anarchistic attempts to realize personal dreams with the help of corporate resources.

Local Level

In Table 7 we report network data concerning "density". The findings confirm, albeit from a different angle, the findings in Table 4, i.e., that the industrial district and the corporate context are about equally organized with respect to business exchange and communication while the industrial district is considerably more elaborate as a socioeconomic structure, including acquaintances, and, thus, friendship ties. Although the social networks in the science park are more elaborate than in the corporate context they are still underdeveloped compared with those of the industrial district. This suggests that it is difficulst, if not impossible, to create contextual networks with affective commitment through planning. In Anderstorp they have emerged over several hundred years. The high frequencies/density of the talk network in the corporate venture context, Telub Service, is astonishing and cannot be explained by the formal structure ascribing communication.The data include only 54 ascribed dyads in the corporate context. Telub Service also stands out because of its low density in the acquaintance network. The high density in the professional corporate network suggests a lateral structuring which is far beyond vertical and horizontal specialization.

Table 7. Network Density in Three Contexts - Symmetric and Asymmetric Ties (1)

	Relational Structure (2)							
	SOCIAL					BUSINESS		
	Talk		Acquanintance		Frienship	Commercial		Professional
CONTEXT	Symetric	All	Symetric	All	Symetric	Symetric	All	All
Anderstorp	.101	.183	.313	.460	.086	.144	.211	.138
Ideon	.039	.063	.035	.075	.016	.026	.041	.039
Telub Service	.264	.342	.012	.044	.011	.113	.192	.215

1) Line density is defined as the realized symmetric or symmetric as well as asymmetric ("All") linkages as a proportion of the potential number, i.e. r(r-1)/2 (Symmetric) and r(r-1) (All), where r is the number of respondents.
2) The problem-solving, professional, network was not designed as reciprocal, and the friendship network, not as asymmetrical, cf. above.

In Table 8 a more detailed analysis of single- and multi-stranded ties in the realized networks in the three contexts is reported. "Professional alone" defines a relationship where the firms/entrepreneurs are interrelated by way of problem-solving, mutual or not, and no other strand. Again the overrating of the professional network with respect to frequency and density measures has to be kept in mind, cf. above. "Commercial" and "Friendship" mean that the commercial and friendship strands as defined above are realized, single or in any combination. A "Complex" is a tie which includes all possible strands: commercial, friendship and professional.

A majority of the potential contextual linkages as defined are not realized in the first place. In Anderstorp 29.4% (649 out of 2211 (67x66/2)), in

Ideon 6.9% (59 out of 861 (42x41/2))and in Telub Service 35.8% (571 out of 1596 (57x56/2)) of the network potential is exploited. Table 8 shows what portion of the realized ties can be ascribed to the stated characteristics. In all three contexts the networks obviously include commercial exchange and "crude" professional support to a considerable extent.

Table 8 Conditioned Frequencies of Single- and Multi-Stranded Ties (1)

Portion of realized network (%)

THE CHARACTERISTIC	ANDERSTORP	IDEON	TELUB SERVICE
Commercial	49.0	37.3	31.5
Friendship	29.3	23.7	3.0
Professional only	38.8	52.7	66.9
Complex	13.7	13.6	1.4

Note: The frequencies reported in the table represent percentages of all realized ties (commercial and/or friendship and/or professional). Since multi-stranded ties are included, tie categories overlap and the percentages do not add to 100.

The contexts for autonomous entrepreneurship, the industrial district and the science park are considerably different from the intrapreneurial context with respect to how they mobilize the social dimension of entrepreneurial networks for business venturing. In Anderstorp and Ideon every fourth tie includes a qualified social strand; in the corporate context the social impact on networking in this respect is negligible. Complex ties, including all strands identified in the study, are quite frequent in the industrial district and the science park as well; in the corporate context they are obviously minimal.

Global Level

The dyadic analysis on the local level as reported in Table 7 has provided some information concerning the different logics of the industrial district, the science park and the corporate context. However, the analysis suffers from lack of methods to grasp network characteristics beyond dyads. Turning to global graph properties we are able to provide more comprehensive images of the differences in contextual complexity and logic. In Table 8 we introduce three global concepts, namely

Components, blocks and one/two-cliques.

In a connected network there is a path between every pair of nodes; the graph consists of one component. When a network is disconnected there are two or more components. The size of the component gives the number of firms/entrepreneurs interconnected by any path through the network. Obviously it may take many steps for e.g. information to extend through the network component but ultimately all component members will be reached.

The findings show that in all four networks there are very few isolates in Anderstorp; on the contrary, almost all firms/entrepreneurs make one large component. Not only does the science-park network have a considerably smaller maximum component but the robust block structure identified does not exceed 10 and in the commercial network the maximum block is not very much larger than a third of the component size. In Telub Service the talk and business networks, not surprisingly, provide large components. In contrast the genuinely social networks - acquaintance and friendship - reveal themselves to be quite fragmented in the corporate setting. These findings confirm the existence of the general organizing function of the context but also emphasize the generic differences between the three contexts with respect to prevailing logic for organizing business venturing.

Table 9. Contextual Substructures - Components, Blocks and Cliques (1)

	Relational Structure			
		SOCIAL		BUSINESS
CONTEXT	Talk	Acquaintance	Frienship	Commercial
ANDERSTORP				
- Components	1/62, 5/1	1/64, 3/1	1/59, 8/1	1/65, 2/1
- Maximum block	50	63	47	63
- Two-cliques	88/24	1/52	4/22	2/35
- One-cliques	1/6	6/14	1/6	1/6
IDEON				
- Components	1/23, 1/4, 15/1	1/22, 1/4, 1/2, 14/1	1/9, 1/3, 3/2, 28/1	1/22, 21/1
- Maximum block	7	10	3	8
- Two-cliques	1/10	1/8	2/5	1/7
- One-cliques	8/3	3/3	1/3	-
TELUB SERVICE				
- Components	1/57	1/6, 1/5, 1/4, 1/3, 39/1	1/6, 1/5, 1/4, 2/2, 38/1	1/48, 9/1
- Maximum block	56	4	4	45
- Two-cliques	26/35	1/6	1/6	3/21
- One-cliques	4/10	1/4	3/3	6/7

1) Symmetric ties only which means that the professional network is excluded. Only the largest cliques are reported.

Analyzing "blocks", we can also consider the fragility or robustness of established networks as e.g. defined by each component. A <u>block</u> is a network structure where there is no "cutpoint", i.e., a single node on which the completeness of the network depends. Consider e.g. the commercial network in Anderstorp, where 63 out of 67 firms are interlinked in such a way that even if one firm closes down, the remaining 62 in the network would still be interconnected by business transactions! Obviously networks provide a very strong mechanism for e.g. innovation diffusion in the industrial district. Not only does the science-park network have a considerably smaller maximum component but the robust block structure identified does not exceed 10. In the commercial network the maximum block is not very much larger than a third of the component size. The existence of quite large blocks in the talk and business networks in Telub Service suggests that possible gatekeepers in the formal hierarchical system are by-passed by lateral linkages.

The "clique" concept makes it possible to increase the level of organizing even beyond the block. An <u>n-clique</u> defines how many firms/entrepreneurs are mutually interconnected by an n-path- This means that in a one-clique all members are directly connected, while in a two-clique all firms/entrepreneurs are related, either directly ("primary network") or through another firm/entrepreneur ("secondary network"). It is recognized both in studies of industrial networks (Håkansson 1982) and entrepreneurial networks (Aldrich et al 1987, Johannisson 1990) that is difficult to take in cliques of a higher degree.

In the industrial district Anderstorp one two-clique in the acquaintance network includes 52 entrepreneurs and the commercial network encompasses two two-cliques of size 35, which obviously overlap. This means that 52 entrepreneurs are interconnected, directly or through friencds, and that threre are two commercial networks of equal strength which each encompass more than half the firms. The largest two-clique in Ideon is in the talk network, which to some extent supports the notion of the science parl as an arena for exchange of ideas. However, even in this respect, the artifically created science parl is by far surpassed by the organically evolving industrial district. Large two-cliques in Telub Service mainly appear in the talk and business networks, which suggests that there are optional network patterns.

The existence of one-cliques means that there are some network members who are directly related to each other, thus representing what Aldrich and Whetten (1981) call an "action set". Others more implicitly refer to the one-clique as a "strategic alliance", cf. e.g. Lorenzano & Ornati 1988. Focussing on the commercial network, we find a maximum "strategic alliance" of six firms in Anderstorp. In Ideon no strategic alliance can be identified, which again underlines the highly specialized, almost individualism-promoting character of the science park. The corporate context, in contrast, contains six alliances, each with 7 participants. Considering that the orientation of intrapreneurs is more contextual than that of autonomous entrepreneurs, cf. Table 4, this finding is not surprising.

3.3. Exploring Hidden Structures

Our analyses have so far concerned interrelated individual network nodes (entrepreneurs and their firms), providing network characteristics on different levels. By introducing background or "contingency" variables, conceptual assumptions based on entrepreneurial characteristics were put on the agenda for analysis, cf. Table 6. Innovation and entrepreneurship mean however dealing with chaos and paradox (Quinn 1979, Johannisson & Senneseth 1990). Any a priori conceptual structuring of data thus runs the risk of misconceiving important idiosyncratic features of entrepreneurial contexts. Consequently an unconditioned approach to the empirical investigation of networks is needed.

The analytical technique, "structural equivalence", provides an approach to teh exploration of disguised structures in networks (cf. e.g. Burt 1976, 1982). Network nodes are then clustered in shared "social positions", implying that all members of the cluster have approximately the same profile with respect to (asymmetric dyadic) linkages to other network members. One technique, which is adopted here (using UCINET IV) is to cluster the nodes with respect to the correlation between node vectors as defined by each node's in- and outgoing dyadic linkages. The structural-equivalence analysis presents data by way of a "r x r" asymmetric matrix (cf. Figure 1), where the network nodes are ordered with respect to their social positioning. Clusters of entrepreneurs/ventures may be demarcated by using analytical or ad-hoc criteria.

It is reasonable to assume that a shared socioeconomic position facilitates and reinforces cooperation - group members have the same frame of reference, which builds confidence in individual and collective action. Our notion of action rationale, cf. Table 2, suggests that the way entrepreneurs organize individual and joint action in the context depends upon kind of context. The identification of contextual substructures is therefore preferably based on both the interconnections between the members of the substructure and the members' linkages to the context at large. By applying a "structural-equivalence" analysis technique to our contextual network data in each context heuristically, i.e. through visual inspection we identified three (Ideon) orfour (Anderstorp/Telub Service) clusters of interrelated entrepreneurs/firms. these groups thus represent cooperative structures of nodes which enjoy the same exchange within the context.

The analyses encompass all network strands other than the acquaintance network in Anderstorp which, with its extremely high density, cf. Table 5, may hide more selective structures. Supplementing the preliminary identification of groups with the graphical analysis adopted by Burt (1976, Tables x -y), the robustness of each group was estimated. - Not surprisingly, the groups generated in Telub Service are the most robust ones - the formal structure conditions informal networking. In Anderstorp all groups are near equally robust. Two out of three (I1 and I2) groups in Ideon are very robust considering the voluntary and diverse setting.

Whether or not groups will promote innovation - i.e. represent "innovative nucleuses" in the context - is conditioned by factors indicated in the conceptual presentation in Section 2. The general conclusion is that entrepreneurship is far beyond management and notions of orchestrated change. Elaborating further we suggest that such prerequisites for innovative potential include group <u>diversity,</u> <u>loose/tight coupling</u> and <u>external orientation</u>.

<u>Intra-group diversity</u> with respect to member characteristics is needed to mobilize tensions with respect to world-views and experiences, a foundation for creativity, cf. e.g. Koestler 1964. The general advantages, besides that of promoting (local) innovation, of organizations which are not too tight but rather loosely coupled are elaborated by Weick (1976). The need for external orientation in personal networking of innovative corporations was stated already by Burns & Stalker (1961) and elaborated with regard to small firms and contexts by Johannisson (1988).

Intra-group diversity in the industrial district refers to the ratio between number of industries (two-digit level) represented and number of group members. In the corporate setting the corresponding ratio is calculated by substituing industry with functional department according to the organization chart. In the science park a direct application of the standard industrial classification system appeared too blunt and therefore the directory of the member firms was used to catergorize the firms into different "competence areas". Often this area consists of a dominating competence, e.g. biochemical analyses, and auxiliary competences. The ratio between number of such areas represented and group members defines intra-group diversity in the science park. The value of this indicator varies between $1/n$, where n is the number of members of the group, and 1, indicating maximum innovativeness.

Group cohesiveness is defined by the ratio between all realized single-stranded, asymmetric dyadic ties and the total number of potential linkages between group members. This measure is then equivalent with the one used to identify groups in the first place, cf. above. This measures varies theroretically between 0 and 1 and, considering the need fro coupling, albeit loosely, innovativeness means avoiding the extremes.

The entrepreneurs were asked to identify the five persons with whom they prefer to discuss their business or project (Telub Service). these members of the "primary" network were identified with repect to e.g. location, kind of relationship (professional/social and peer) and frequency (Johannisson 1990). The variable external orientation then reports what share of these network members is to be found outside the context. Since there were some internal non-responses, the portion for each member was calculated and used for estimating group average. This indicator of condition for innovativeness varies between 0 and 1, the higher value supposed to represent a maximum. - In Table 10 contextual groups are identified by size (number of members and member size), general networking and the criteria of innovativeness introduced.

Table 10 Groups of Structurally Equivalent Firms in Three Contexts

Variables	Anderstorp				Ideon			Telub Service			
	A1	A2	A3	A4	I1	I2	I3	T1	T2	T3	T4
Group size (firms)	5	7	7	4	3	4	5	7	5	6	12
Firm size (median)	9	11	20	29	3	15	3	6	4	9	8
General network (1)	1.6	2.3	2.4	3.0	1.6	3.3	2.0	1.8	1.4	1.8	2.4
Group diversity	.80	.85	.60	75	.33	.25	1.0	.28	.40	.17	.23
Group cohesiveness	.53	.48	.58	.64	.67	.71	.39	.43	.88	.78	.55
External orientation of group	.67	.67	.64	.57	.40	.65	.56	.33	.31	.17	.27

1) Cf. definition in association with Table 4

The findings according to Figure 2 report that the groups identified in the industrial district Anderstorp all meet the two requirements for innovative organizing depicted in the diagram: <u>group diversity and loose/tight mutual coupling</u>.

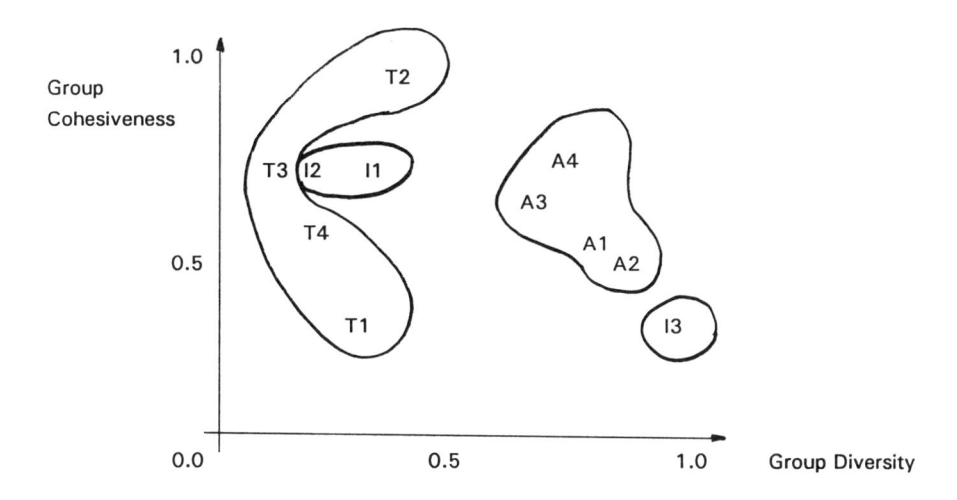

Legend: A1-4, I1-3 and T1-4 represent the groups in Anderstorp (A), Ideon (I) and Telub (T). The dimensions of the diagram are defined in the text.

Figure 2. Socieconomic Positioning - Cohesiveness and Variability

The Ideon groups seem to represent two different subsamples of firms. the first one includes firms which are located in the science park in order to enforce a unique competence and focussed strategy (groups I1 and I2). Group I3, in contrast, seems to represent those firms which locate in a science park in order to enhance more generally the creative input for the operations. In the corporate context the groups, as indicated, are composed of members who are close to the formal structure (e.g. Group T4 is made up of the two highest echelons in the corporation), which probably means that routine exchange is given priority. With respect to loose/tight coupling, though, three out of four corporate groups seem nevertheless more or less to meet the requirements. Altogether, the corporate structural analysis reports ambiguous findings and further criteria to identify innovativeness are needed.

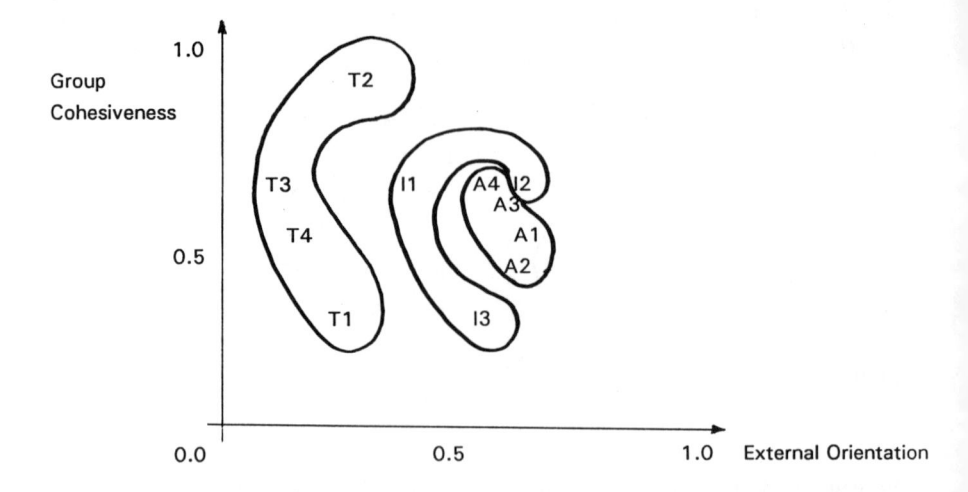

Legend: A1-4, I1-3 and T1-4 represent the groups in Anderstorp (A), Ideon (I) and Telub (T). The dimensions of the diagram are defined in the text.

Figure 3. Socieconomic Positioning - Cohesiveness and External Orientation

Replacing group diversity in the diagram with the dimension <u>external orientation</u> of group members does not change the picture very much (Figure 3). Groups within Anderstorp appear similar; to a great extent they all supplement contextual networking with global exchange. the autonomous entrepreneurs in the science park are equal with respect to external orientation, both between themselves and when compared with the industrial-district entrepreneurs. The corporate group members, in contrast, seem to ration networking beyond organizational boundaries. Obviously both the industrial district and the science park can provide the appropiate mixture of contextual and global networking that supports entrepreneurship.

4. Conclusions and some Implication for Researches and Practitioners

The industrial district is outstanding in all respects as an organically integrated texture encompassing all network strands. Anderstorp appears to be a self-organizing arena for entrepreneurship- Although the corporate context is the most elaborate with respect to communication and problem-solving networks, the corporate entrepreneurs may not be able to mobilize social resources. Complex ties are rare and this suggests that the social-resorce system is quite fragile. In the science park networks are generally quite loosely coupled, but, as expected, relatively elaborate with regard to communication and problem-solving. Altogether the conceptual and empirical research reported above suggests that the promotion of venturing in different contexts calls for different organizing principles.

One important finding is that the functions of the context have to be expanded to include the role of legitimizing an entrepreneurial career. the networks in the science park (Ideon) are too loose to build a particular (entrepreneurial) culture, including e.g. shared language. One explanation we have put forward is competing ideologies. Although the science-park networks never cluster into e.g. commercial one-cliques (strategic alliances), our structural-equivalance analysis revealed "islands of shared competences" in the rather thin science-park network atmosphere. Further inquiries into the consequences to this contextual logic will reveal whether this means that business development through contextual interaction is substituted for exchange with partners outside the context. This is an outcome which may be favourable to both the science-park entrepreneurs and to the economy at large. A basic challenge for further research is to more precisely position the science park as a construct between the fragmented market and the integrated organization.

Further studies are also needed to discriminate the influence of the character of the context and of e.g. the age of the context/firm upon the way the context carries out its supportive functions. Ideon has an almost negligible history in comparison with that of Anderstorp. This however is an empirical phenomenon that belongs to the postwar period - Ideon is merely ten years old. The corporate context is interesting with respect to history since strategic and cultural change in a large, well-established company may, over not too many years, restate the conditions for intrapreneuship.

Although tentatively adopted, the structural-equivalence analysis suggests that there are many more aspects of graph analysis to tap in order to - conceptually and empirically - state the organizational conditions for innovation and entrepreneurship. However, we argued that the findings prove the necessity of including both instrumental and social aspects in such inquiries. Social networks, which provide "economies of trust", are especially nurtured in industrial districts where business and social lives intermingle in an entrepreneurial culture. We thus propose that the pressure for functional organization according to the transactio-cost approach in stable environments is parallelled by a pressure for spatial organizing in dynamic environments. Along with Porter (1990) we argue that the recognition of site-specific investments in turbulent times calls for formal separation an spatial integration of venturing processes. Socioeconomic network approaches and the associated graph analyses appear to be indispensible as instruments with which to investigate how this complexity is related to innovation and entrepreneurship.

Induced entrepreneurship, here illustrated by corporate entrepreneurship/intrapreneurship but also appearing e.g. in science parks, has become increasingly relevant. The contradiction between top management's need for control and the individual's need for discretion in the venturing process has to be dealt with. We argue that further studies into the interaction between the formal, hierarchical network and the networking characteristics of the intrapreneurs will facilitate the exploration into corporate strategies to promote an entrepreneurial culture.

Applying the organization -or rather organizing - metaphor to entrepreneurs in context, alternative generic structures come to the fore. Cf. also Johannisson et al. 1992. Beside the traditional hierarchy and organic network, two options are close at hand: the federation and the heterarchy. - The federation then suggests that legally independent organizations voluntarily establish a joint unit to cope with shared problems and opportunities. The cooperative movement generally adopts this structure but also operative adhocracies formally structured as joint stock companies appear as federations. Some would even advocate that the decentralized corporation and franchising system ideally represent federations. However, for many reasons both conceptually and empirically stated, federative structures are fragile if not "impossible", cf. Bonus 1986, Strujan 1988. Our findings concerning Telub Service suggests that the hierarchical structure dominates federative features originating in the image of that corporation as an operative adhocracy (Mintzberg 1988).

There is a basic problem applying the federative metaphor to the industrial district or the science park. The crux is not that the commercial structures are embedded in an ideology - in Anderstorp a strong local culture and in Ideon academic professionalism. The critical issue is rather that these ideological textures are ascribed, not voluntarily adopted by the entrepreneurs concerned. In Anderstorp these are encultured by birth and ideologically the science park basically reflects university values. Science-park academic entrepreneurs are neither detached from their origin, nor attached to their new domicile - they remain intermediaries. Thus, for quite different reasons the federation is not appropiate as an ideal structure to any of the three empirical forms of entrepreneurial contexts introduced here.

The notion of "heterarchy" is elaborated by Herbst (1976) and suggests that in an interrelated population of individuals/groups the leading system varies according to the challenges which the total system experiences. No central unit is thus needed but rather a dense (communication) network to offer the overview the dynamic heterarchical organizing calls for. In Telub Service the heterarchy however is dominated by corporate management and in Ideon the networks appear to be too thin to support such an organization. In Anderstorp, though, where the features of the ideal industrial districts seem to be realized, the heterarchical ideal seems to be reachable. This e.g. suggests that initiative and leadership are taken by the entrepreneur/firm which possesses the distinctive compentences for a project; the other contextual members follow as resource providers. Dynamic specialization characterizing the industrial district suggests that the leading role varies depending on the challenges met.

We have throughout this paper focussed (socioeconomic) exchange networks for several reasons. First, they encompass, conceptually, information (diffusion) networks and normative networks of influence. Second. since e.g. transfer of technology is a social process in contexts such as the industrial district, reciprocal exchange ties appear to be indispensable. Third, our conceptual stand, the entrepreneur's need for an "organizing context", conditions exchange networks.

The conceptual perspective on entrepreneurship which we have developed and illustrated above has also implications for public policy and the support of new and small firms. In a recent study of business venturing we have applied four different firm-formatin models to Swedish data from the second half of the 1980s. We found that all models can satisfactorily explain regional variations in start-up frequencies, with a small advantage to the market model (Johannisson 1992). In Table 11 we suggest appropiate support measures related to each model. the incentives can all be looked upon as ways of enhancing the competitiveness of emerging firms.

The support thus may focus the individual entrepreneur/firm, the context at large or the contextual networks. Direct support for individual ventures, which dominates public policy today, is only one approach, and not necessarily the most efficient one. Contextual support in contrast works indirectly by increasing the legitimacy of entrepreneurial initiatives by providing a shopping mall for potential support, but in all else leaves the entrepreneur alone. Finally, existing and would-be networks may themselves be the focus of support. This paper has tried to provide some generic arguments for such measures whereby the firm is integrated with both the contextual and the external market.

Table 11 Firm Formation Models and Alternative Support Strategies

<u>Optional Support Measures with Different Focusses</u>

Formation Model	FIRM	NETWORK	CONTEXT
MARKET	Encourage local market surveys	Sponsor subcontrating and extrapreneurship	Organize local trade shows and promote privatization
RESOURCE	Subsidize rented premises	Organize private investors' network	Establish collective R&D centre
MILIEU	Encourage immigrant internships	Stimulate local organizational activities	Invest in leisure and cultural infrastructure
CAREER	Establish a "marriage" agency for partnerships	Create a pool of role models and mentors	Promote an enterprising prising community in the schools

Source: Johannisson 1992

Acknowledgements

The research reported here has been financially supported by the Ruben Rausing Foundation (Bengt Johannisson, Ola Alexanderson and Knut Senneseth). The research for this article was perfomed while Krzysztof Nowicki visited the Department of Statistics at the University of California, Berkeley. The visit was supported by the Swedish Council for Research in the Humanities and Social Sciences.

References

Aldrich, H & Zimmer, C 1986 "Entrepreneurship through Social Networks." In Sexton, D & Smilor, R (Eds.) *The Art and Science of Entrepreneuship*. New York, N.Y.: Ballinger. Pp 3-23.

Aldrich, H & Rosen, B & Woodward, W 1987 "The Impact of Social Networks on Business Foundation and Profit: a Longitudinal Study." Paper presented at the *1987 babson Entrepreneurship Conference*. Pepperdine University, Malibu, Ca., April 29 - May 2.

Aldrich, H & Whetten, D 1981 "*Organization-Sets, Action-Sets and Networks.*" In Nystrom, P & Starbuck, W (Eds.) Handbook of Organization Design, vol 1. Pp 385-408. Oxford: Oxford University Press.

Alexanderson, O & Johannisson, B & Senneseth, K 1992 "Organizing Entrepreneurs - Coping with Paradox through Contextual Networks." Paper presented at the *7th Nordic Conference on Small Business Research*. June 4-6, 1992, Turku, Finland

Birley, H 1985 "The role of Networks in the Entrepreneurial Process." *Journal of Business Venturing*, Vol 1, No 1, pp 107-117.

Bonus, H 1986 "The Cooperative Association of a Business Enterprise - A Study in the Economics of Transactions." *Journal of Institutional and Theoretical Economics*, Vol 14, No 2, pp 310-339.

Borgatti, Everett & Freeman 1992 *UCINET IV Version 1.0 Reference Manual*. Columbia: Analytical Technologies.

Burns, T & Stalker, G 1961 *The Management of Innovation*. London: Tavistock.

Burt, R S 1976 "Positions in Networks." *Social Forces*, Vol 55, pp 93-122.

Burt, R S 1982 *Toward a Structural Theory of Action: Network Models of Social Structure, Perception, and Action*. New York, N.Y.: Academic Press.

Burt, R S 1983 "Distinguishing Relational Contents." In Burt, R S & Minor, M J (Eds.) *Applied Network Analysis*. Beverly Hills, Cal.: Sage. Pp 35-74.

Easton, G & Araujo, L 1991 "Language, Metaphors and Networks." Paper presented at the *7th I.M.P. conference on International Business Networks,* Uppsala, Sweden. September 1991.

Galtung, J 1969 *Theory and Methods of Social Research.* Oslo: Universitetsforlaget.

Granovetter, M S 1973 "The Strength of Weak Ties." *American Journal of Sociology,* Vol 78, No 6, pp. 1360-1380.

Granovetter, M S 1982 "The Strength of Weak Ties: A Network Theory Revisited". In Marsden, P V & Lin, N (Eds.) *Social Structure and Netwok Analysis.* Beverly Hills, Ca.: Sage. Pp 105-130.

Herbst, Ph G 1976 *Alternatives to Hierarchies.* Leiden: Martinus Nijhoff.

Håkansson, B 1982 *International Marketing and Purchasing of Industrial Goods. An Interaction Approach.* Chichester: Wiley.

Johannisson, B 1987 "Toward a Theory of Local Entrepreneurship. In Wyckman, R G & Meredith, L N & Bushe, G R (Eds.) *The Spirit of Entrepreneurship.* Vancouver, B.C.: Simon Fraser University. Pp 1-14.

Johannisson, B 1988 "Business Formation - A Network Approach." *Scandinavian Journal of Management.* Vol 4, No 3/4, pp 83-99.

Johannisson, B 1990 "Building an Entrepreneurial Career in a Mixed Economy: Need for Social and Business Ties in Personal Networks. Paper presented at the *Academy of Management Annual Meeting,* San Francisco, USA. August 12-15, 1990.

Johannisson, B 1992 "Designing Supportive Contexts for Emerging Enterprises". *To be published* at Routledge in a volume edited by Johannisson, B & Karlsson, C & Storey, D.

Johannisson, B & Nowicki, K 1992 "Using Networks to Organize Support for Entrepreneuship - a Graph Analysis of Swedish Contexts." Paper presented at the *1992 Babson College Entrepreneurship Research Conference,* INSEAD, Fontainebleau, June 28 - July 1, 1992.

Johannisson, B & Senneseth, K 1990 "Paradoxes of Entrepreneurship." Paper presented at the *4th Workshop on Recent Research in Entrepreneurship.* Cologne, Germany, November 29-30 1990.

Kirzner, I M 1973 *Competition and Entrepreneurship.* Chicago, Ill.: The University of Chicago Press.

Koestler, A 1964 *The Act of Creation.* London: Hutchinson.

Kuratko, D F & Montagno, R V & Hornsby, J S 1990 "Developing an Intraprenerial Assessment Instrument for an Effective Corporate Entrepreneurial Environment." *Strategic Management Journal*, Vol 11, pp 49-58.

Laumann, E O & Galaskiewicz, J & Marsden, P V 1978 "Community Structure as Interorganizational Linkages". *Annual Review of Sociology*, No 4, pp 455-88.

Lawrence, P R & Lorsch, J W 1967 *Organization and Environment*. Boston, Ma.: Harvard University Press.

Lorenzoni, G & Ornati, O A 1988 "Constellations of Firms and New Ventures." *Journal of Business Venturing*, Vol 3, No 1, pp 41-57.

Mintzberg, H 1988 "The Adhocracy." I Quinn, J B et al. (Eds.) *The Strategy Process*. Englewood Cliffs, N.J.: Prentice Hall. Pp 607-627.

Peters, T J & Waterman, R H 1982 *In Search of Excellence*. New York, N.Y: Warner.

Piore, M J & Sabel, C F 1984 *The Second Industrial Divide*. New York, N.Y.: Basic Books.

Porter, M 1990 "The Competitive Advantage of Nations." *Harvard Business Review,* March-April, pp. 73-93.

Pyke, F & Becattini, G & Sengenberger, W (Eds.) 1990 *Industrial Districts and Inter-Firm Co-operation in Italy*. Geneva: ILO.

Quinn, J B 1979 "Techonological Innovation, Entrepreneurship, and Strategy." *Sloan Management Review,* Vol 20, Spring 1979, pp 19-30.

Sabel, C F et al. 1989 "Regional Prosperities Compared: Massachusetts and Baden-Würtenberg in the 1980s." *Economy and Society*, Vol 18, No 4, pp 374-404.

Segal Quince Wickstead 1988 *Universities, Enterprise and Local Economic Development*. London: HMSO.

Stankewicz, R 1986 *Academics and Entrepreneurs. Developing University-Industry Relations*. New York, N.Y.: St. Martin.

Starr, J A & MacMillan, I C 1990 "Resource Cooptation Via Social Contracting: Resource Acquisition Strategies for New Ventures." *Strategic Management Journal,* Vol 11, Special Issue on Corporate Entrepreneurship. Pp 79-92.

Stryjan, Y 1989 *Impossible Organizations. Self-Management and Organizational Reproduction*. Westport, Con.. Geenwood.

Tichy, N M & Tushman, M L & Fombrun, C 1979 "Social Network Analysis for Organizations." *Academy of Management Review*, Vol 4, No 4, pp 507-519.

Weick, K E 1976 "Educational Organizations as Loosely Coupled Systems." *Administrative Science Quarterly*, Vol 21, pp 1-19.

Weick, K E 1979 *The Social Psychology of Organizing*. Reading, Ma.: Addison-Wesley.

Zeitlin, J (Ed.) 1989 *Local Industrial Strategies*. Special issue of *Economy and Society*, Vol 18, No 4.

Part D
EASTERN EUROPE

21 Co-operation agreements between entrepreneurs from developed and developing countries: Theoretical considerations and empirical evidence from Belgium

Johan Lambrecht

Abstract

Several developing countries recognize the importance of entrepreneurship for their development. Therefore, they have improved the macro-economic environment and have taken care of the entrepreneurs. This healthier entrepreneurial climate is also crucial to attract the SMEs from developed countries. Their "raison d'être" explains why they can stem the tide of the deterioration in the Third World.

This article discusses the relationship of the entrepreneurs from industrialized countries with developing countries in general, and with the local entrepreneurs in particular. It has the following specific objectives :
1. to portray the interviewed Belgian entrepreneurs and their SMEs who have an economic tie with developing countries.
2. to present a theoretical framework on co-operation agreements between entrepreneurs from developed and developing countries.

Introduction

The recent peripeteias in the world economy do not leave the microeconomic entities unaffected. Companies must now already take up a favorable position in order to face the increasing competition. To this end they may opt for the offensive policy option. In that case, international activities are started up or further developed. We see more and more businesses, small ones too, entering into alliances in order to implement their offensive strategy.

The literature devotes ample attention to such associations, though chiefly from the point of view of large companies. We are breaking entirely new ground here by examining the possibilities for co-operation between small businesses from developed and developing countries in Africa, Asia and Latin America. The present article will focus on this issue in full detail.

1. Conceptual model

In Figure 1 we see the entrepreneur operating in an influencing and influencable environment. Moreover, the tentacles of cooperating entrepreneurs become interwoven. This is represented by the shaded concentric sections. In this article we will concentrate on the interrelation of entrepreneurs and their small businesses.

DEVELOPED COUNTRY   DEVELOPING COUNTRY

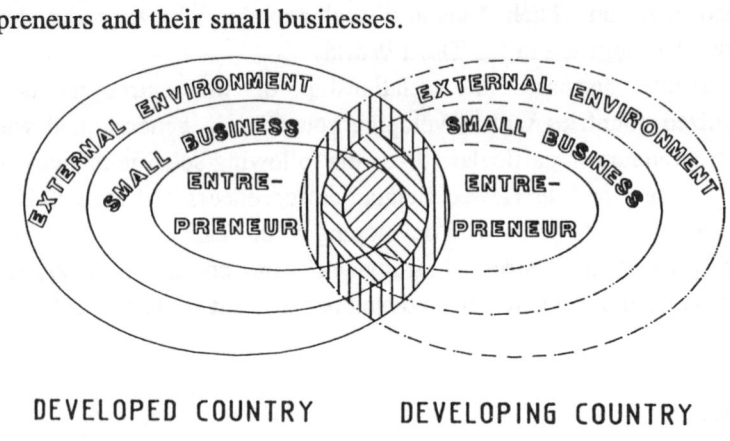

Figure 1   The factors of co-operation

2. Methodology

Research questions

Our aim is to answer the following questions :
- What is the profile of the interviewed entrepreneurs and their firms who are doing business with developing countries ?
- Why should entrepreneurs from developed and developing countries collaborate ?
- Which association matches the motives for collaboration most closely ?
- How should the ideal form of co-operation best be achieved ?

Compilation of data

The investigation began in 1992 with an in-depth study of the literature and with interviews of 65 selected witnesses from the supporting infrastructure in Belgium. We discussed the following topics with them : inhibitions to co-operation, ingredients of a successful recipe for co-operation, additional policy measures, the significance of entrepreneurship for the developing countries and the role of the Belgian entrepreneurs. The respondents and the literature provided sufficient source material to compile the survey.

We opted for a telephone survey among 1,000 entrepreneurs : 500 who are currently doing business with a developing country (active respondents) and 500 who are not (non-active respondents). This subdivision was chosen in order to sound out the interest in developing countries of non-active respondents, and on the other hand to find out about problems and possible solutions from the active respondents. The questionnaire was different for the two groups, although some questions were the same. The active respondents were selected at random from catalogues and from the data bank of the Belgian Foreign Trade Office. A marketing agency made a random selection of non-active respondents. The staff criterion for both samples was up to 100 employees. We considered the low-income and lower middle-income economies in Africa, Asia and Latin America as developing countries. Their GNP was less than US$ 2,450/capita in 1989 (criterion used by the World Bank). Before the telephone survey the entrepreneurs received an introductory letter and a list of developing countries. In the end there were 980 valid telephone surveys : 480 active respondents and 500 non-active respondents.

Statistical processing

The theoretical considerations for the developed countries are empirically tested on the basis of our data from Belgium. This is done descriptively by giving relative frequencies as well as analytically. The latter approach compares frequency tables of subsamples (dealing and not dealing with developing countries) in order to identify statistically significant differences. The first research question is dealt with by employing regression analysis with maximum likelihood estimates. We used this technique because the dependent variable is binary (for more technical details, see WONNACOT, WONNACOT, 1979).

3. Profile of the entrepreneur and SME dealing with developing countries

In order to draw a picture of the interviewed entrepreneurs and small businesses who are dealing with developing countries, we need to include entrepreneur- and company-related variables in the regression equation. The first category includes the level of training (TRA), the number of years of professional experience in the branch (EXP) and the number of languages which the entrepreneur knows (LANG). The second category comprises the family nature of the business, which is determined by the ownership structure (FAM = 1 = family business ; FAM = 2 = non-family business) and the size of the company (SZ). The dependent variable is the fact of whether or not dealing with a developing country (ACT = 1 = active, ACT = 0 = not active). The logit analysis gives the following results (in brackets the standard error and the significant coefficients on a significance level of 5% or less is marked with *):

ACT = - 1.1774 + 0.3685* TRA + 0.0460 EXP + 0.7025* LANG + 0.3256* FAM - 0.5878* SZ.
     (0.4656) (0.1445)   (0.1386)   (0.2049)   (0.1454)   (0.1517)

We see how entrepreneurs deal more with a developing country as their level of training and language knowledge increase. Worth noting is the negative correlation between being active and the size of the business. A possible explanation might be that smaller businesses want to expand and try to achieve this by opening up the markets in those countries. Our figures show that doing business with developing countries constitutes a significant growth lever for those firms. Nearly 37% of the businesses with fewer than 50 staff derive more than half of their total turnover from exports to developing countries, such in sharp contrast with the larger businesses where that percentage is only 23%. It is hardly surprising that significantly more non-family businesses turn to developing countries. Family businesses are significantly less internationally oriented (see DONCKELS, FRÖHLICH, 1991 and DONCKELS, AERTS, 1992). Finally, the EXP coefficient is not significant, yet does have the expected symbol.

4. Why co-operate ?

The regression equation revealed that the small businesses surveyed also develop activities with developing countries in order to grow. For this and other purposes the entrepreneurs are advised to look for a partner on the spot, who will also have specific reasons to co-operate. Both parties' motives for co-operation will be examined in this section.

Entrepreneur of the developed country and his business

Equation (1), which we will explain below, gives the co-operation objectives of the entrepreneurs from the industrialized countries :

$$S = f(E_{1r}, M_2, K_1, G_{1r}, SP_{2r}(PB_2)) \qquad (1)$$

in which :

S   = co-operation
E   = moral principles
1   = entrepreneur from the developed country
r   = type of association
M   = market knowledge of the partner
2   = partner from the developing country
K   = capital of the entrepreneur from the developed country
G   = growth of the small business from the industrialized country
SP = stable political factor
PB = political involvement.

Moral principles

In spite of the fact that business considerations come first, the entrepreneurs from the industrialized countries may also be guided by E. It may be part of their social responsibility to reach out to an entrepreneur from a developing country. We put this proposition to the Belgian entrepreneurs and we see in Table I that significantly more entrepreneurs dealing with developing countries agree. The implementation of E naturally also depends on r.

Table 1. Working together with an entrepreneur from a developing country is part of the social responsibility of a growing business (row percentages)

Relationship with developing countries	Agreed	Don't know	Not agreed	Chi-quare test
Active (N = 451)	40.4	20.4	39.2	$p > 0.05$
Not active (N = 475)	32.6	27.6	39.8	

Market knowledge

It is very difficult to penetrate into the markets of developing countries. Not only a geographical, but also a psychological distance needs to be bridged, for we cannot escape the fact that on the other side there is a totally different culture. It is essential to assimilate this culture if good results are to be achieved there. Of the active entrepreneurs, 76% regard knowledge of the developing country and 70% a thorough market survey as essential determinants of success.

In order to acquaint themselves with the local customs and practices, the entrepreneurs are advised to contact a local partner. The amount of M they receive will depend on the local entrepreneur and on r. If α_{2r} represents the amount of M furnished by the local entrepreneur, we may arrive at the following condition : $0 \leq \alpha_{2r} \leq 1$, in which $\alpha_{2r} \to 0$ if the partner fails.

Limited capital

The figure below shows the relation between S and K (S is represented as binary: 1 = co-operation). To formalize the interdependence between S and K, we equate S with aK. This gives the following four equations :

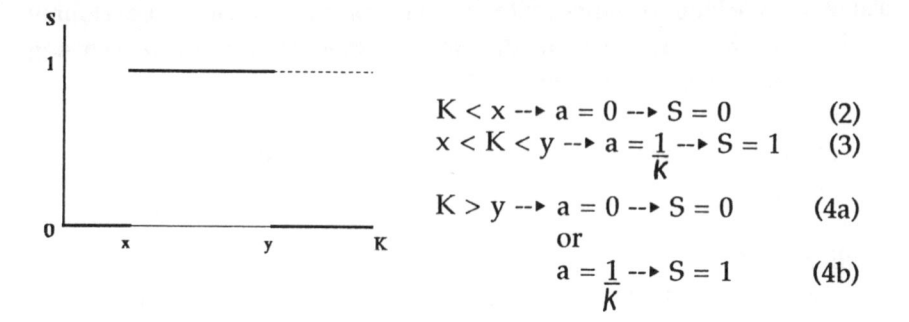

$$K < x \longrightarrow a = 0 \longrightarrow S = 0 \quad (2)$$
$$x < K < y \longrightarrow a = \frac{1}{K} \longrightarrow S = 1 \quad (3)$$
$$K > y \longrightarrow a = 0 \longrightarrow S = 0 \quad (4a)$$
$$\text{or}$$
$$a = \frac{1}{K} \longrightarrow S = 1 \quad (4b)$$

Figure 2. The relation between S and K

Relation (2) shows how setting up operations with developing countries requires considerable financial resources at least equal to x. More than 60% of the active businesses faced payment and financing problems when entering into business relations with developing countries. This stumbling block has led nearly 60% of the entrepreneurs who were active in the past to stop doing business with developing countries. In equation (3) a local entrepreneur breaks out of the financial straitjacket which can restrict entrepreneurs from the industrialized countries. However, if financial resources are amply available (more than y), the entrepreneur can approach the developing country independently (4a). He may also decide to look for a partner all the same (4b and represented by the dotted line in Figure 2).

Growth lever

In paragraph 3 we inferred from the greater involvement of smaller businesses that business relations with developing countries are naturally regarded as an interesting growth lever. This is confirmed in Table II, where significantly more active entrepreneurs agree with the growth theory. We also found that of the active entrepreneurs mainly the smaller ones agree with the proposition (75% compared to 25% of the small businesses with at least 50 staff). This confirms the finding that in our sample the small-scale businesses do significantly more business with developing countries because of the growth prospects. The table also teaches us that many non-active entrepreneurs, too, regard doing business with developing countries as a useful instrument for achieving growth. Of those who want to become active, 73 % quote the growth of their business as the prime motive.

Table 2. Doing business with developing countries is an interesting growth lever (row percentages)

Relation-ship with developing countries	Agreed	Don't know	Not agreed	Chi-quare test
Active (N = 451)	73.6	10.0	16.4	$p > 0.01$
Not active (N = 482)	48.8	31.3	19.9	

Because of the limitations of time, manpower and funds, it is advisable for the entrepreneur to develop his growth activities with a local entrepreneur (SCHILLACI, 1987). If the entrepreneur takes the internal route, where only his own company is involved, he will risk overreaching himself. By taking the external route, though, which stands for mergers and takeovers, he is also likely to hurt himself badly.

Stable political factor

Entrepreneurs who want to start doing business with developing countries must take into account that they could find themselves in troubled political waters. 61% of the interviewed entrepreneurs who were active in the past quoted the political and economic instability as their main reason for (provisionally) suspending their business dealings with developing countries. The entrepreneurs who are currently still dealing with developing countries also experience the instability there as the principal obstacle (74%). In turbulent political conditions, a local entrepreneur may act as a lifebuoy (SP) (CONTRACTOR, LORANGE, 1988). The degree in which this is possible will depend on r and PB. SP and PB are positively correlated if the political regime is stable. As we have pointed out above, the latter is usually not the case. Prudence is called for when dealing with a partner who is too closely involved in the current political circles (DAGEVOS, DE GROOT, 1990).

Entrepreneur of the developing country and his business

The objectives of co-operation of the entrepreneur from the developing country are formulated in equation (5). The variables are explained in detail in the next paragraph :

$$S = f(T_1, MA_1, K_2, G_{2r}(T_1, MA_1)) \quad (5)$$

in which :
S = co-operation
T = technical know-how and technology of the entrepreneur from the developed country
1 = partner from the industrialized country
MA = management know-how of the entrepreneur from the industrialized country
K = capital of the entrepreneur from the developing country
2 = entrepreneur from the developing country
G = exogenous growth of the local firm.
r = type of association

Technology, technical and management know-how and exogenous growth

The local entrepreneur will work together with an entrepreneur from an industrialized country who has T and MA. The technical know-how and technology ($ß_{1r}$) and the management know-how (Γ_{1r}) to which he has access is dependent on the partner and on r. Strategic alliances are the best training for him if $ß_{1r}$ and Γ_{1r} tend towards 1 ($0 \leq ß_{1r}, \Gamma_{1r} \leq 1$). In addition, he must be willing and able to learn and he and his partner must be frank with each other (HAMEL, 1991).

A sound technical and management infrastructure will not only strengthen the local firm on the local market, it will make it more resilient on the international scene too (DATTA, 1988). Moreover, it will overcome the growing pains more easily because they are of an exogenous nature. The firm has a welcome partner standing by in its precarious financial situation (K_2).

5. Why a joint venture?

The objectives that we discussed are represented below in Figure 3. The entrepreneurs are clearly the driving force. They need to develop an organization in which their objectives are geared to each other. In addition, it needs to push α_{2r}, β_{1r} and Γ_{1r} towards 1. In this section we will try to demonstrate why a joint venture is the most suitable form of co-operation. A joint venture is defined as a subsidiary of a small business from the developed country, in which the equity is shared with a local entrepreneur. It is clear from the definition that multicultural entrepreneurship culminates in this close association. After all, a joint venture in a developing country is a melting pot of a traditional and non-traditional entrepreneurial culture. It will take highly motivated entrepreneurs who are not averse to taking risks to make a success of this synergy.

```
                Small business                         Small business
     Limited                        Exogenous
     capital                         growth
  Moral
  principles    Entre-                    Technological,  Entre-
              preneur  COOPERATION        technical and  preneur
  Market                                   management
  knowledge                                know-how

     Growth lever                         Limited capital
```

DEVELOPED COUNTRY   DEVELOPING COUNTRY

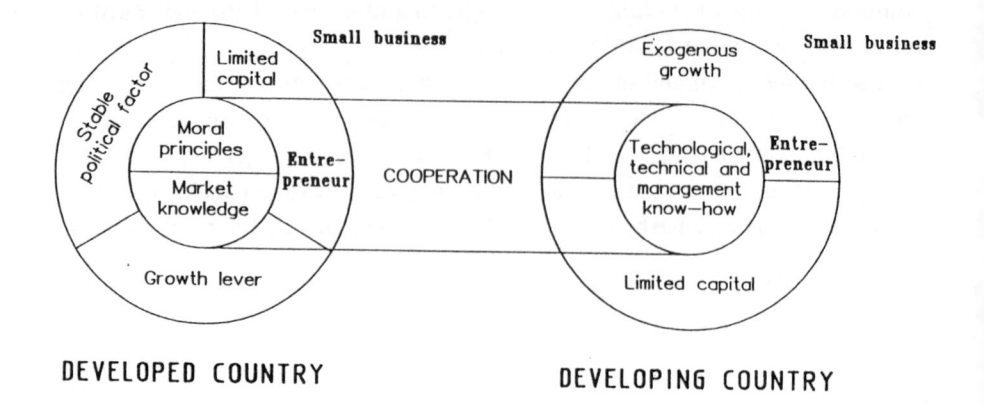

Figure 3. Objectives of co-operation

The entrepreneur and small business from the developed country

Moral principles

An entrepreneur will be able to indulge all his moral preoccupations in a joint venture. This is so because the partners rarely join forces and resources so much as in such an association (HARRIGAN, 1988). According to KOGUT (1988), joint ventures are the ideal vehicle for exchanging information and technology and for achieving good results. He attributes this to the "mutual hostageship" arising from the joint commitment of assets and sharing of the costs and profits. Joint ventures are therefore the best guarantee that α_{2r}, β_{1r} and Γ_{1r} go to 1.

Market knowledge

The interviewed entrepreneurs who will be entering into a joint venture later are doing so first of all in order to penetrate the local and other markets more effectively. A partner affords a better view of the competition, consumer behavior, the sector and the distribution system in that particular country (SCHILLACI, 1987). Naturally markets can also be penetrated through other avenues of co-operation. Licenses allow a rapid market representation at a relatively small investment (LEI, SLOCUM, 1991). However, there is specific knowledge, such as that of the characteristics of the country (M), which can almost only be transferred in a joint venture. This is particularly the case if there are considerable cultural differences between the countries of the partners. KOGUT and SINGH (see KOGUT, 1988) found that joint ventures occur relatively more frequently when the cultural gap is widest.

Growth

A good market penetration in developing countries through a joint venture is important for small businesses that embrace G as a principle. Such an association makes it possible to canvass a market from the inside. Capacity increase, vertical integration or diversification also make the joint venture a source of growth (SCHILLACI, 1987).

Stable political factor and limited capital

Joint ventures afford protection against political risks (SP). The financial contribution of the local partner is an antidote for appropriation by political authorities. By sharing the capital, the entrepreneurs provide each other with the necessary life support. Nevertheless, for a joint venture they must have a considerable financial capacity. The high cost and the considerable risk involved dissuade many respondents from entering into a joint venture in a developing country.

The entrepreneur and small business from the developing country

Technology, technical and management know-how

T and MA cannot be entirely contained in designs or manuals, encapsulated as they are in the individual (HENNART, 1988). Exchange of

T and MA will therefore need to be based on close human contact, which is the case in joint ventures. They are used for transferring intrinsic know-how. In the survey by BEAMISH (1987) the local entrepreneurs confirm that T and MA constitute the partner's most important contribution.

Exogenous growth

Thanks to $ß_{1r}T_1$ and $\Gamma_{1r}MA_1$, the small business and the other firm of the local entrepreneur are entirely developed in a more professional manner (G_{2r}). This enables the local firms to manifest themselves more strongly at the national and international level. The survey by BEAMISH (1987) suggests that the local entrepreneurs will be expecting a great deal from their partners in the area of export.

6. Why other forms of co-operation first?

Joint ventures are regarded as the most favourable, but also as difficult and fragile agreements (NEWMAN, 1992). That is why it is advisable for the partners first to become engaged through other forms of co-operation. This will allow the entrepreneurs to get to understand each other's culture, improve communication and build up confidence (CASCIO, SERAPIO, 1991). Another advantage of first entering into another type of association is that the local entrepreneur can work his way gradually through the learning process. Joint ventures will always remain a thing of the future if the abilities of the entrepreneurs differ too strongly (HAMEL, 1991). The local entrepreneur must primarily know how his partner has grown and developed. If the learning process has progressed satisfactorily and the entrepreneurs truly believe in each other, then they might be ready to undertake a closer commitment. Our survey and that of UNIDO in France (see **PASQUET**, 1988) show that most entrepreneurs do in fact first start off by setting up a looser association.

7. Conclusions

The interviewed entrepreneurs who are engaged in business operations with developing countries are characterized by a high level of training and a wide knowledge of languages. Their firms tend to be non-family businesses and on a small scale. It is the growth prospects, among other things, which in all probability stimulate the smaller entrepreneurs to do business with developing countries. In so doing, they are advised to enlist the assistance of a local partner who knows the ins and outs of his country and who can extend a helping hand in times of political turmoil. Co-operation will enable this local entrepreneur to improve his technical and management know-how in order to make his business more resilient on the market. In view of of the limited financial resources the entrepreneurs are also advised to join hands. Both will benefit most by a joint venture. However, it is advisable to start off in a looser association as the first step in the development process of a joint venture, since the chances of success of that final breakthrough will to a great extent be determined by the way in which the entrepreneurial attitude and spirit of the partners converge.

Bibliography

BEAMISH, P.W. (1987), 'Joint ventures in LDCs : partner selection and performance', *Management International Review*, 1, pp. 23-37.

CASCIO, W.F., SERAPIO, M.G. (1991), 'Human resources systems in an international alliance : the undoing of a done deal ?', *Organizational Dynamics*, pp. 63-74, Winter.

CONTRACTOR, F.J., LORANGE, P. (1988), 'Competition vs. co-operation : a benefit/cost framework for choosing between fully-owned investments and cooperative relationships', *Management International Review*, Special issue, pp. 5-18.

DAGEVOS, J., DE GROOT, G. (1990), 'Brabants bedrijfsleven en ontwikkelingslanden' *(Enterprises in Brabant and developing countries) (Tilburg : Development Research Institute)*, Monografie no. 42.

DATTA, D.K. (1988), 'International joint ventures : a framework for

analysis', *Journal of General Management*, 2, pp. 78-91.
DONCKELS, R., FRÖHLICH, E. (1991), 'Are family businesses really different? European experiences from STRATOS', *Family Business Review*, 2, pp. 149-160.
DONCKELS, R., AERTS, R.(1992), *KMO's en internationalisering* (SMEs and internationalization), Brussels, King Baudouin Foundation, CERA, Small Business Research Institute.
HAMEL, G. (1991), 'Competition for competence and interpartner learning within international strategic alliances', *Strategic Management Journal*, Special issue Summer, pp. 83-103.
HARRIGAN, K.R. (1988), 'Joint ventures and competitive strategy', *Strategic Management Journal*, 2, pp. 141-158.
HENNART, J.F. (1988), 'A transaction costs theory of equity joint ventures', *Strategic Management Journal*, 4, pp. 361-374.
KOGUT, B. (1988), 'Joint ventures : theoretical and empirical perspectives', *Strategic Management Journal*, 4, pp. 319-332.
LEI, D., SLOCUM, J.W. (1991), 'Global strategic alliances : payoffs and pitfalls', *Organizational Dynamics*, pp. 44-62, Winter.
NEWMAN, W.H. (1992), "Focused joint ventures" in transforming economies', *The Executive*, 1, pp. 67-75.
PASQUET, P. (1988), 'Co-operation industrielle - la "joint venture"' *(Industrial co-operation - the joint venture)*, *Le MOCI*, pp. 15-38.
SCHILLACI, C.E. (1987), 'Designing successful joint ventures', *Journal of Business Strategy*, 2, pp. 59-63.
WONNACOT, T.H., WONNACOT, R.J. (1979), *Econometrics*, New York, Wiley.

22 The transfer of organizational and enterprise patterns and the creation of market economy in Eastern Europe

Maria Aggestam

The transfer of an organizational pattern from one society to another, whether it be accomplished through conscious or unconscious innovation, inevitably results in deviations from the original pattern. The transferred pattern can never be completely replicated in the new setting.

The purpose of this paper is:

1 to describe the process of transfers and imitations of managerial models that take place between Western and former East European countries.

2 to discuss and to analyse the ability of the firms to adopt new managerial patterns in the transformation process from planned economy towards market economy.

Although it is one given model that is transferred from a Western to an Eastern country, it is highly unlikely that it remains unchanged in the process. The managerial model is exposed to various cultural modification which lead to very different results. It is thus possible to analyse the transfer/imitation process as a two directional phenomenon:

- the *detrimental direction*, which leads to 'mismanagement' and
- the *creative direction*, which leads to 'innovative management'.

The discussion focuses first on the conceptual distinction between the two faces of the process as related to the notions of transferability and imitability of Western models into the former East European economies. Then I give a characterisation of that influenceable absorbent faculty that firms have, and of the process of unlearning old habits and of learning new patterns.

The discussion is based on the relevant characteristics of the context in which the firms operate.

Introduction

The transfer of organizational patterns from one society to another, via innovation, invention as well as imitation, inevitably accomplishes results in deviations from the original pattern. But the transferred pattern can never be completely replicated in the new setting.

Through identifying the range of factors behind these deviations, we can understand how the national, socio-cultural environment and the recently introduced organizational patterns interact. An understanding of this phenomenon is crucial to the grasping of the process of cross-societal emulation which lies behind the creation of a market economy in Eastern Europe.

Although the imitation phenomenon is a well observed process, it is difficult to specify and to understand. It is clear that firms imitate other firms, but the process by which it is done is not well defined or understood.

This paper is based upon the premise that imitation is not replication and that the way in which the process is purved is a very important factor determining the development of a market economy in Eastern Europe. Thus, it might *lead to very different results.*

First, the character of the outcome might be *detrimental,* the organization has been led to a state of 'mismanagement' and second, it can be *creative* which means that the firm is being managed in an innovative fashion.

General problems concerning the transfer of organizational patterns major concepts

A study of the literature on determining factors reveals that the major emphasis is put on the management core and its impact on the strategic behaviour and on the performance of the organization. On one widely held perspective on the management core is that in which it is seen as exerting influence on the members of the organization through their shared perceptions and associated judgement of environmental events and organizational capabilities in different fields. It means, that managers listen to their employees and let them influence their strategy. To put it differently, the individual-level cognition by the management core contributes to organizational form-level strategies. This strategy, if misused, can lead towards what I call *detrimental management* if, however, the innovatively omnipotent factors of the socio-cultural environment are taken into proper account, it can lead towards *innovative management*.

Prahalad and Bettis (1986), related these shared values to the general knowledge structure that can store a shared dominant general management perspective. The transfer of organizational patterns by direct transfer or imitation i.e. of technology, expresses as I see it the firm's learning capacity and its ability to converge it into practice.

Many studies reconfirm the view, that the transfer of patterns and models of technology between different settings is strongly conditioned by both the technological and by the educational levels in the countries involved. The particular firm in question is then depending on these contextual conditions and levels. Volti (1980); Hall and Johnson (1970); Imai, Nonaka, Takeuchi (1985).

The unique features of previous experience and technological capability often determine the process of transfer and imitation of patterns done in order to be innovative in firm management. This was stressed by Fagerberg (1988); Cohen and Levinthal (1980). They pointed out the importance of pre-training of managers in order to better understand the meaning of imitation.

The organization and its context are constantly being fed with information. As the task of the firm stabilises and become less ambiguous, the firm develops information channels and filters that allow it to identify what is ost crucial in the information flow. Daft and Weick (1984).

Another view was presented by Cyert and March (1963) and Nelson and Winter (1982). They argued, that firms usually build their capability and knowledge around the recurrent tasks that they perform. Thus, to my mind it is difficult to understand the development of the firm's creative capacity without understanding the way in which it was shaped. It is difficult to perceive without first understanding how the organization structure was once build up. Their past and present performance and their context have to be chartered. What is important in this case is its own context and the possible influence exercised by transferred patterns.

As we experience it, reality is socially constructed and exists irrespectively of the perception of managers. It is through transfer and imitation of organizational patterns from the 'Western' society that knowledge about the attitudes and the roles of the management core is created. Because this individual perception is the basis for human praxis and since it is reconstructed in organizational actions, it is important to recognise the imitated options applied to organization in order to view their strategic options for the future. This means, what elements are there due to imitation in order to foresee their strategic possibilities for the future. These strategies will operate in the *detrimental direction*, if the new model is applied without *'nesting within'* the home context. If it is not used creatively it will not lead to innovative management actions. Where there is a constantly changing context, the contextual events have to be retained and included in the knowledge structure, thus causing a new association to be developed (ayer, 1982). This new knowledge structure is in the former Eastern countries built upon the basis established by past experience and by the different transfers and imitations of patterns fro the 'west'.

The choice of organizational patterns is a result of a complex process of imitation and innovation. This process is, in turn determined both by the local resources and by access to resources of foreign origin.

The degree to which the new technology is accessible to the organization depends on the role this particular type of technology is intended to play in the new setting and also on the firs network relations with the possessors of the desired patterns. Allen and Cohen (1969), called it 'the role of the gatekeepers who link their organization to the scientific community through their own dual allegiance'.[1]

A successful transformation of the economy under the conditions of cross-societal organizational emulation lessens the distinction between copying imitation and innovation. An effective imitation of foreign organizational patterns requires *local creativity*, which in turn can lead to innovative management actions.

The concept of diffussion of innovation has been defined in diverse ways with substantial variation between different approaches. The first attempt at a definition of technology transfer be found in study by Rogers[2] (1985, p. 5): "the process by which an innovation is comunicated through certain channels over time among the members of social system". Roger's and other diffusion researchers [3], concept of technology transfer emphasised four main factors as crucial to the transfer of patterns (communication channels, time, human beings and society with its social system). In order to accoplish particular actions they had to be connected to a wider context of time, communication, individuals and their social context.

There are two main ways of transferring and imitating new patterns - direct by patent or licensing, joint venture or other alliances or indirect, by observation. The term 'transfer' is used here to include both the intended and the unintended spread of ideas and models from Western societies to the former planned economies. 'Transfer', it is assumed, refers to a greater mechanism behind the diffusion, while it, in its more limited meaning, often refers to the imitation process itself. However, both the transfer itself and imitation as a form of transferring patterns, are very important to the process of creation of market economies in fomer Eastern Europe.

Alchain (1950) identified the interplay between imitation and innovation in the process of development of organizational forms. He said the following:

> ... while there certainly are those who consciously innovate, there are those who, in their imperfect attempts to imitate others, unconsciously innovate by unwittingly acquiring some unexpected or unsought unique attributes which under the prevailing circumstances prove partly responsible for the success. Others, in turn, will attepmt to copy the

uniqueness, and the innovation-imitation process continues.

Formally speaking, the performance of actors within the process of imitation is both *complex* and *diverse*. Complex when it comes to dealing with actors and their attitudes, beliefs and interactions within their own context in order to derive a particular behaviour. Diverse when referring to the uniqueness of the actor or society. These factors of contextual complexity, if left unconsidered during the process of imitation, might lead towards *detrimental* management.

Imitation permits a combination of structural and motivational aspects of the firm, thereby creating a hope for improvement and change as well as that of overcoming the traditional gap between 'past' experience and the new approach. If this is put within the frame of what is feasible, it might lead towards a *creative* way of managing the firm.

Nelson and Winter (1974, p. 123) related imitation to the process by which firm tries to reach beyond its limits by duplicating an incompletely observed successful performance. They said as follows:

> This implies that the copy is at best, likely to constitute a substantial mutation of the original. Embodying different responses to a large number of the specific challenges posed by the overall production problem. However, the imitator is not directly concerned with creating a likeness, but with achieving an economic success preferably, an economic success at least equal to that of the original.

The most desirable determinant of firm survival is the introduction of innovations in the production or service process by the transfer of technology[4]. This determinant has to be creative to produce an innovative outcome of the process.

To summarise briefly, to imitate successfully and creatively a combined innovative and traditional organizational experience taken from within as well as from without the area in question is required.

Specific problems concerning the transfer of soft technology

To return to the objects of my study, we can see that the transfer of technology has increased considerably unlike that of managerial practices.

Compare the situation of Great Britain at present, ... Every improvement, which we have since made, has arisen from our imitation of foreigners; and we ought so far esteem it happy, that they had previously made advances in art and ingenuity...
>from David Hume " Of the Jealousy of Trade" published in 1758 (quoted in Lyons, 1987).

That kind of 'borrowing' of patterns or models of managerial innovations, which originated in other countries, contributed to the development of the Western know-how and was further disseminated throughout the world.

Baranson (1970), however pointed out the differences between transferring internally within the national borders and doing so internationally. This latter form of transfer is often given a separate evaluation by transmitters. This is mainly due to problems brought about by differences in legal systems, conflicts between different political and economical interests, and the uncertainties of exchange rates. Teece (1976) approached the problems associated with the acceptance of new 'imported' technological patterns and their adaptation to local conditions, through contrasting different countries' infrastructure, internal distances and communication costs.

Furthermore, my overall impression from the bulk of literature is, that the time determinants are closely connected to hard technology. 'Hard' technology refers to the technical development that often occurs very rapidly, while 'soft' technology refers to management technology and takes time to develop. Soft technology is more timeconsuming and is chosen more carefully. Hard technology is often transitted all around the world shortly after its introduction. However there are certain types of technology transfer including such dealing with hard technology which take a very long time to develop and which proceed by degree. Other fors involving mature, codified technologies are often transformed more rapidly. The time factor is very important then, and the success of the transfer depends on how fast it is carried through. Because soft technology is implemented slower and after a long period of observation of the particular pattern, there is both time and space for the firm to use all its innovative and creative power in order to adjust the model to the organization.

The definitions above reflect a few important conceptual distinctions that require further elaboration towards exposing the phenomenon of imitation.

According to Bassalla's (1988) approach, the selecting individuals are active, productive individuals capable of making the choices needed in order to change and to shape the material world as they see fit. The selectors do not represent all segments of society, as Bassalla pointed out, and are not always concerned with the public good. But they have the power to make certain choices and decide which of the committing novelties should be replicated and incorporated into the socio-economic life. They have the opportunity to select and to make changes in the existing pattern of society. Using the economical perspective and having organizations in mind, we can see that the managers are in this position. They can either work in a detrimental or creative fashion. What is important to remeber is that the former East European countries did not require that any such model be transmitted, it was taken for granted that they needed one. In that way a pattern, often not relating to their macro-structures was imposed upon them.

Imitation, as a basic phenomenon, is a theoretical construct introduced a priori and as such it can not be in lack of empirical justification. Therefore, the point of departure is necessarily a theoretical one. Its empirical justification can be found in contexts such as leadership, effectiveness, goals of firms, networking within the firm and with the surrounding context (communication).

The capacity of the East European countries to transfer and to imitate foreign patterns

An important illustration of the imitation phenomenon is an example of a long-range imitation of different economic systems by a society.

When Japan (around 1870) acquired progressive modern western organizational forms through large-scale transfer and imitation, many issues were raised.

What was the motivation for selecting these particular systems? Why did the Japanese adopt the 'Western' type of organising into their own organizations? The Japanese navy was modelled on the British, and the army on the French and German systems, and the communication system on the British one, the police and legal system on the French and banking on the American system. The imitation of the 'Western' patterns influenced almost all parts of life there from newspapers, political parties, to enterprises etc. According to Westney (1987, p. 5), the reasons for that phenomenon to happen in Japanese society was "lack of originality and even the intellectual piracy... copying is less estimable than inventing, imitation is less honourable than innovation". At this point, it seems that it was easier for the Japanese to pick up the most progressive and recent system and apply it to their own socio-economic context. In the light of this, it has to be mentioned that another selective factor for Japan's choosing those organizational models was their international prestige. Prestige was therefore an important factor for choosing what to imitate. However, pursuing the imitation process through copying organizational systems also implies a selective invocation of elements of the past within the scope of present needs. This was very important in Meiji Japan and is even very urgent today. The British postal system model adopted by Japan and India in the XIX century was recreated following the pattern of the then prevailing socio-cultural values. Consequently, having women in top positions in India was explicitly rejected.

Indeed, should imitation of a certain model be a part of the process of building organizational system, that model must be implemented in such a way that individuals, on entering the organization meet with an implicit model of roles and structures based on their past experience and values. This is one of the most important conditions of creative management in the process of transformation from planned economy towards market economy. This also means, that the study of former East European management practices *must be firly anchored in time and space, providing a proper historical context analysis*. This is one of the most important requirements for procuring the *creative* way of firm management.

Berger and Luckmann (1967) suggested, that when an individual becomes committed to an organization, there must be an immersion in and commitment to the new reality. This immersion in and commitment to the new reality is simply lacking in the former Eastern countries. It is the acquisition of experience and knowledge that creates a mutual identification among managers and because of the time shortage, this is not developed to the same extent as are 'Western' thoughts.

The actual methods of transfer and imitation of different patterns and the ability of recipients to assimilate the transferred models are rarely discussed in literature. The study made by March and Olsen (1983) pointed out the difficulty the firms are having within the process of identifying what pattern is to be transferred or imitated. In the case of the former East European countries, the firm's ability to identify the best model is even more difficult to grasp, simply because they lack experience from the past. In the planned economy, one indigenous model was applied, which was never questioned or evaluated by outside knowledge. The choice between patterns suitable to transfer is often accoplished by an identification at the meso-level with the firm displaying the best performance results and by an evaluation of those contextual factors which determinate its performance. Since in the former East European countries firs are lacking in previous experience and since no coparative experimentation within the related area has been performed, the shift might cause *value-sensitive reactions and lead to detrimental action on the part of managers.*

But if some criticism could be put forward, I would like to quote Czaiawska-Joerges (1992) p. 158 who says as follows: "As a result of historical irony, Western researchers are now paying back by selling to the 'East' a second-hand knowledge that is no longer considered valuable in the countries of origin".

This means that the picture which has been created of Eastern Europe under communist rule is due not only to the native managers and their way of organising but the Western countries have also had a *detrimental* impact upon it.

The strength in the transfer of patterns and in the imitation of such lies in the firm's experience, and as I see it, is an indicator of the educational level of the firm context. Experience gives rise to a common understanding, using which the firm learns how to transfer or imitate more successfully over time. A lack of experience can lead towards *detrimental* magement routines and mismanagement.

In the case of Eastern Europe, the long term experience is lacking. This means, that firms consume more time to establish suitable routines and to build a common understanding of problems related to the new patterns and technology. When the stock of experience and knowledge is limited, the firms have to exploit all possible internal and external knowledge within their social context.

It is also difficult for East European organization to get access to the new soft technology. If it is introduced, it is with some limitation.

The transferability and imitability of the new socio-economic patterns i.e. organizational or technological, into the new setting is determined by the social context of the past, the level of educational experience and on whether this context is understood within and among the firms. Consequently, these factors can be seen as tools, which rationally designed can lead to a *creative* way of firm management or when neglected, to a *detrimental* one.

The firms in East European countries do not pay attention to learning about alteative possibilities, but they keep trying to learn more about the dominant and enforced model. Since the new model appears to create stability in the Western context, the East European firms rely mainly on these adopted routines and procedures. This tendency means that firms become caught in these procedures and in an early stage of development. They tend to further these procedures by different communication channels without them having been advised or completed. There is no time for refinement of the patterns, especially of those of proved contextual dependency.

Firms with 'planned economy' as their heritage are overwhelmed not only by the new information but they also use past experience it being a vital part of their context. The habits of the past were very much alive within the national context in the last half of the century, and are still crucial to the building of the new information system. The fact that the old system left traces within the firm causes both tensions and critical interactions within the firm and between these. These truly terrifying facts about individuals found at the meso-level are very powerful factors leading management towards in a detrimental direction.

Once the firm has decided on the suitable pattern for current development, the process of the unlearning old patterns should be introduced.

The new strategies for the East European countries, which have emerged using different information systems and communication channels, must take into consideration the important process of unlearning in order for those countries to cope with the complexity of the new systems. Once the firm has recognised how different the new pattern is to handle, it ought to invest time and resources in learning about the new model or pattern. Louis and Sutton (1989) argued, that firms are often handicapped in their attepts to develop, both by the difficulty all firms experience in switching from one model of operation to another, and by the fact that they must build a new understanding in a context in which some part of their past might still be relevant.

The firms, in order to develop, must change their orientation from the position in which they are now to one of quick search for new methods of solving the problems of an unstable and constantly changing context. But the process of systemic transformation and change does not automatically mean progress. To be prospective, firms have to pay more attention to the characteristics of the creative way of management operation and be more sensitive towards the detrimental domain. New establishments, most often not so strongly committed to certain established ways of acting when working within their own operational context, often find it easier to build up an organizational flexibility and to abandon the 'negative' part of the former ways of acting, all this being required by progress. Once the firm has reoriented itself, the creation of a new condition within a constantly changing context still, however, takes time and resources. Because of the strong mental barriers, which can be seen as *detrimental* to the labour force, it is even more difficult to identify the problems, then to solve them and yet again to enforce the new mode. To my mind, it is difficult and time-consuming to enforce the new fashion of acting, which is a creative one, when the firms persist using old organizational tools in the creation of a new contextual order.

Conclusion

Imitation has become a phenomenon of increasing presence within and outside all the traditional fields of human society. The phenomena of transfer and imitation of patterns are *unique* and *diverse* in terms of its character. Unique, because the transferred pattern can never be completely replicated in the new setting. And diverse, because its main strength has to do with the creation of novel fors of organising.

The challenge of this paper has been the presentation of the complexity both of the present situation in the former planned economies and of the categories of disjointed organizational competence in management. This competence was found to be twofold; *detrimental,* on the one hand, which in turn leads to unwanted mismanagement and *creative* on the other, leading towards innovative management and the creation of novel forms of organising. Creative management adds substantial value to the development despite the obstacles. And as Anderson (1983) emphasised, the strategic responses to the new situation, in which East European economies find themselves, may be the result of generalising from the existing structure of knowledge. It is a knowledge structure whose characteristics are socially constructed, and which is fundamental to our understanding of the ongoing process.

Bibliography

Alchian, A.A. (1950) 'Uncertainty, Evolution and Economic Theory', *Journal of Political Economy*, 58.

Allen, T. & Cohen, S. (1969) 'Information Flow in Research and Development Laboratories'. *Administrative Science Quarterly*,14, pp. 1 2-20.

Baranson, J. (1970) 'Technology Transfer Through the International Firm'. *American Economic Review*, May, pp.435-40.

Basalla, G.(1990) *The Evolution of Technology*, Cambridge History of Science Series.

Berger, P.L. & Luckmann, T. (1971) *The Social Construction of Reality,*

Penguin, Harondsworth, UK.

Cohen, W. & Levinthal, D. (1990) 'Absorptive Capacity: A New Perspective on Learning and Innovation', *Administrative Science Quarterly*, 35, pp. 128-52.

Cyert, R.& March, J.G. (1963) *A Behavioural Theory of the Firm*, Prentice-Hall, Englewood Cliffs, NJ.

Czarniawska Joerges, B. (1992) *Exploring Complex Organizations*, Sage Publications.

Daft, R. & Weick, K. (1984) 'Towards a Model of Organizations as Interpretation systems', *Academy of Management Review*, 9 (2), pp. 284-95.

Fagerberg, J. (1988) 'International Competitiveness', *Economic Journal*, 98, pp. 355-74.

Hall, G. & Johnson, R. (1970) 'Transfers of United States Aerospace Technology to Japan', in Vernon, R. (ed.), *The Technology Factor in International Trade*, National Bureau of Economic Research, Columbia University Press, New York, NY.

Imai, K. Nonaka & Takeuchi, H. (1985) 'Managing the new Product development Process: How Japanese Companies Learn and Unlearn', in Clark, K, Hayes, R & Lorenz, C. *The Uneasy Alliance,. Managing the Productivity-Technology Dilea*, Harvard Business School Press, Boston.

Mansfield, E. et al (1982) *Technology Transfer, Productivity and Economic Policy*, W.W. Norton, London.

Mansfield, E. (1968) *Industrial Research and Technological Innovation - An Econometric Analysis*, Norton, New York, NY.

March, J & Olsen, J. (1976) *Ambiguity and Choice in Organization.*, Universitetsforlaget, Bergen.

Nelson, R.R. & Winter, S.G. (1974) 'Neoclassical vs. Evolutionary Theories of Economic Growth: Critique and Prospectus', *Economic Journal*, Deceber.

Teece, D.J. (1976) *The Multinational Corporation and the Resource Cost of International Technology Transfer*, Ballinger, Cabridge. Rogers, E.. (1983) *Diffusion of Innovation*, Free Press, New York, NY.

Westney, D.E. (1987) *Imitation and Innovation: The Transfer of Western Organizational Patterns to Meji Japan*, Harvard University Press,

Cambridge, A.
Wilkins, . (1974) *The Maturing of Multinational Enterprise: American Business Abroad from 1914 to 1970*, Harvard University Press, Cambridge, A.
Volti, R. (1980) 'The Absorption and assimilation of Acquired Technology', in Baum, R. (ed), *China's Four Modernisation*, Westview Press, Boulder, Colorado.

Notes

1. In 'The Transfer and Imitation of the New Technologies' by Kogut and Zander (1990), Wharton School, University of Pennsylvania, first draft, p. 6.
2. See Tarde, G., 1903, "The Laws of Imitation", New York.
3. Note, that the definition of 'diffusion' is different from what is here called imitation. Wilkins (1974) suggests, that technology transfer across national boarders by an MNC is only diffused to other firms if it 'spills over' to suppliers or customers in the host country, or if it is imitated by other, indigenous firms. Mansfield (1968) and Mansfield et al (1982) labelled both technology transfer and imitation 'diffusion', arguing that both inter and intra-firm rates of diffusion vary a lot. Mansfield argued, that the rate of inter-firm diffusion depends on the success of the new technology, the differentiation among firms, the number and the size of the firms, and the amount they spend on R&D. The intrafirm diffusion indicates the importance of the firm's size and liquidity and its competitive position on the market.
4. The term 'transfer of technology' is used here to describe the transfer of specific know-how, which patented or not, can be transferred from one firm to another.

23 Women entrepreneurs in controlled economies: A Hungarian perspective

Robert D. Hisrich and Gyula Fülöp

Abstract

While the role of women entrepreneurs has received some attention in more developed Western economies the topic has received little attention in the once controlled economies of former Eastern and Central Europe. This paper explores this area by interviewing women entrepreneurs in Hungary. The results indicate that women entrepreneurs are forming a wide variety of businesses in Hungary, are similar in many ways to their Western counterparts in terms of personal characteristics and new ventures formed; and need some changes in education, business, and government infrastructures to better form new ventures in the future.

Introduction

The topic of women entrepreneurs is of increasing interest to educators, business people, government officials, and the general populace. The number of businesses created by women is growing in both developed and developing countries, particularly in Europe and the United States. The growth in the number of women-owned businesses should continue in many of these countries (OECD, 1986 "Local . . . "; Silvestri and Lucasiewiecz, 1987) and in most at a rate faster than for men. Significant growth in women entrepreneurs has occurred in the United States, where the annual increase in female self-employment in non-farm sole proprietorships (a proxy to the number of entrepreneurs) grew by 56 percent (versus 26 percent for men) between 1975 and 19B5 (OECD, 1986 - "Local . . . "). It is estimated that by the year 2000, 50% of the selfemployed in the United States will be women.

The growth in women-owned businesses on an international basis has followed the same pattern that has been occurring in the United States. In the United Kingdom, the number of women-owned businesses is growing at a rate of about 10 per cent per year with the total number increasing by 50 per cent between 1981 and 1986 (OECD, 1987 - United Kingdom). During a similar time period 1980-1985, in West Germany, self-employment by women increased 4 per cent with women currently accounting for nearly 30 per cent of all those self-employed while founding every third new firm (OECD, 1987 - Germany). In Norway, similar results occurred as the proportion of new ventures started by women increased from 14 per cent in 1982 to 19 per cent in 1985 (OECD, 1987 - Norway).

Background research

Interest and research on women as business owners is not only increasing but is now focusing on a wide range of issues in the United States. While earlier studies focused on the background (Hisrich and Obrien, 1981; Hisrich and O'Brien, 1982; Hisrich and Brush, 1983; Egge, 1987), motivations (Schwartz, 1979; Kaplan, 1988), characteristics and business ventures of women entrepreneurs, this research broadened to include investigations of such areas as management practices (Cuba, Decenzo, and Anish, 1983; Chaganti, 1986; Hisrich and Brush, 1987), skills (Hisrich and Brush, 1987), and problem areas (Pellegrino and Reece, 1982; Sexton and Bowman-Upton, 1988; Longstreth, Stafford, and Mauldin, 1987).

Understanding the international research on women entrepreneurs has even more problems than the US research, due to the different classification of businesses in the countries. Some of the terms used to categorize women's businesses include: employers, female-owned sole proprietorships, incorporated self-employed, independent self-employed, new entrepreneurships, and unincorporated self-employed. The term "entrepreneur" may include small businesses (Canada), new firms (West Germany), or selfemployed (Finland).

Where did these women tend to form ventures? Women internationally followed the same pattern as their American counterparts in forming ventures in traditional areas of female employment such as the retail trade and service sectors (OECD, 1987). Of the five million women selfemployed in several European countries, 46 per cent are in retail trade, 12 per cent in beauty and health care, 10 per cent in liberal professions, 9 per cent in handicrafts, and only 1 per cent in industry (Center for Research, 1987). The types of businesses vary within countries. Women in rural areas of countries tend to form craft, textile, and agriculturally based companies, while their urban counterparts tend to form clerical, hotel-restaurant, retail sales and service companies (Halpern, 1987). And, of course, the educational background (or lack thereof) as well as work experience affects the type of business created, with women entrepreneurs feeling discouraged and in some cases restricted from creating or acquiring high technology, financial services, or manufacturing businesses (van der Wees and Romijn, 1987). The growth of women-owned businesses in the service sector reflects: the knowledge and skill of the women relevant to the opportunity (Center for Research, 1987); the difficulty in raising start-up capital in quantities sufficient to start a business in more capital-intensive industries (OECD, 1986 - "Local . . ."); and the shift in industrial distribution throughout OECD countries (as well as The United States) from manufacturing to service.

Although information on the status and size of women-owned businesses, all businesses for that matter, is consistent across countries, the majority of women-owned ventures in Europe are registered as single-person businesses; 86 per cent are classified as sole proprietorships and 14 per cent as companies (Center for Research, 1987). Co-operatives, particularly in consumer, credit, and agricultural business areas, are becoming more popular as a legal form of business ownership for women in Greece, Italy, Portugal, Spain, and Turkey. The co-operative Organizational form is a great one for women starting a new venture as it provides flexible work schedules, participative decision making, and networking.

Regardless of the organizational form and the significant growth in the number, the size of women-owned businesses in terms of sales and number of employees is small. A European Commission study of 17,000 women indicated that more than half had no employees, one-fifth employed family members, and a quarter employed salaried workers other than family members (Center for Research, 1987). While in Great Britain more than 40 per cent had no employees (Geoffee and Scase, 1985), in Finland, 67 per cent had employees with only 5 per cent having more than five employees (OECD, 1987 - Finland). Similarly, most women-owned businesses in Ireland and Germany have between one and ten employees (O'Connor, 1987).

The sizes and types of business formed internationally reflect the background of the women entrepreneurs as they tend to have worked predominantly in the service areas with previous employment in secretarial, nursing, and teaching. Few have worked in high-level management or technical positions (United Nations, 1987). The career path of a woman entrepreneur is often interrupted by marriage, childbirth, and family responsibilities (ELISE, 1988). These interruptions can limit a woman's career path to having a high-level management experience and the informal networks and routines. In spite of these interruptions, women start businesses at an increasing rate for a wide variety of reasons. These include: a cultural center for women in Denmark; an independent veterinary clinic in Spain; an environmental protection service in Italy; a health food business in Germany; a publishing business in Wales (O'Connor and Humphreys, 1988).

These and other women business owners provide the few role models so needed by women desiring to start and operate new ventures. The image of a successful entrepreneur in nearly all countries is male and most international business literature and publicity is aimed in this direction. This can actually reinforce a woman's lack of confidence in her ability to start a venture (OECD, 1986). In Ireland, family role models had the most influence on women in their decision to pursue self-employment (O'Connor and Humphreys, 1988).

While many countries have implemented policies to promote the creation of new ventures by women. the scope and focus of these vary widely. In

Sweden, there are special arrangements and support to encourage enterprise development by women. Besides national trade fairs and seminars informing women about self-employment opportunities, the Swedish Regional Development Fund offers courses as well as special start-up grants just for women (OECD, 1987 - Sweden). Similar activities have occurred in two other Nordic countries, - Norway and Finland. While Norway has developed a Small Business Development Project that provides loans and training for women, Finland has start-up allowances to encourage women to start new ventures.

Small-scale industry for women, particularly in such areas as textiles and clothing, is promoted in Turkey. In Spain, the National Institute for Women encourages women to start a business and provides the appropriate training through ten offices across that country (OECD, 1986 - "Local . . ."). Encouraging women to start their own ventures is also a key element in the economic programmes of the Netherlands and France. In addition to the general promotion encouraging entrepreneurial activity, a special experimental scheme of financial assistance is offered to women in the Netherlands (OECD, 1987 - Netherlands). The Ministry of Women's Rights in France offers overall encouragement to women and assisted in launching 65 firms between 1981 and 1984 by direct financial support and providing training (OECD, 1986 - "Local . . ."). In Scotland, the Scottish Enterprise Foundation conducts research to determine the problems and needs of women business owner and provides gender-specific training (Rosa, 1988).

The environment of Hungary

To understand the development of a market oriented economy in Hungary from a previously planned economy it is necessary to look at events occurring before 1982 and events from 1982 when Hungary started its democratic transformation to 1992.

Pre-1982 Period

Both the Marxist philosophy and Stalinism and its Eastern European manifestation rejected the concepts of private ownership and entrepreneurship. In 1947-48, often referred to by historians as the "decisive year," the communist takeover of Hungary resulted in the elimination of private ownership in large enterprises. By 1950, the private ownership of small-scale ventures with ten employees or less was eliminated. A total nationalization of all forms of private property was achieved during this same period of time resulting in socialization of the assets based on the ideology of the regime.

Although every citizen in the country experienced an economic system that was suffering from operational disturbances of a structural origin and lived in a planned economy where even the most basic goods were sometimes difficult to obtain, the true nature of the problem was recognized by only a limited group of intellectuals. Due to the.structure of the Hungarian Communist Party, such information was available only to those who adopted the Stalinist ideology. This resulted in the early reform concepts coming from politicians and economists within the ranks of the prevailing Stalinist philosophy. These first reform concepts were therefore aimed at changing (rather than eliminating) the existing governmental framework. Three reform movements emulated form this ideological group each of which had significant impact: (1) the reform endeavors of 1953 championed by Imre Nagy, who is often called the reformist; (2) the reform committee of 1957-58; and (3) the gradual unfolding of the reform process of 1968, known as the "New Economic Mechanism."

Each of these reform movements developed by the small group of "Stalinists intellectuals" to improve the operation of the existing system failed. Groups of "elite party intellectuals" with the support of the established communist party government ridiculed the reformist group thereby helping to ensure that the reform concepts were not the dominant ideology of the era.

By the end of the 1970's, the fact that there would be no evidence of any strong economic performance became widely recognized. As a result, a fourth reform movement, stronger than previous ones, started. Naturally, even this reform movement had some limitations.

1982-1992 Period

In order to reduce the economic tension in a pragmatic way in 1980, the political leadership, adopted the slogan of "What cannot be prohibited should be permitted."

During this period, many semi-private or fully private entities (the so-called second or black economy) outperformed the official, statistically recorded state sector. The evolving civil society became strong in two areas. First, due to a loophole in Civil Code, new economic formations developed rapidly under the name of civil law association beginning in 1980. The first trial organization was established by a group of intellectuals in order to develop and produce software. The civil law association established by the software producers was a group of independent entrepreneurs developing software products for its clients.

One form of civil law associations - the "economic working community" - was codified and subject to a corporate taxation, which was then only three percent and covered by social insurance. The number of employees had to be a minimum of two and a maximum of thirty and could be employed on either a full or part time basis. If the economic working community was established by the employees of a specific company, the activities beyond the regular working hours were subject to a license and facility availability granted by the company. These organizations were called contract working communities.

Another new form of association within the co-operative sector was the institute of small co-operatives. A minimum of fifteen and a maximum of a hundred people could form a small co-operative. Compared to the former co-operatives set up on the basis or initiatives from the government where the members behaved much more like employees than owners, the new small co-operatives were grassroots and voluntary with members having an ownership approach and strong loyalty to the co-operative. Also, within the co-operative sector, specialized industrial and service groups with a minimum membership of five persons and no upper limit on membership were allowed to be established.

A second new economic formation indicating the start of more radical changes was the operation of catering facilities by private individuals on a contract basis. This new formation, due primarily to the efforts of Tibor Liska, developed into a special form of leasing by self-employed persons peculiar to Hungary.

For the state-owned company sector, two new alternative organizational forms were created by the package of decrees: (1) the ability to establish a subsidiary whereby individual operations could be transformed into independent legal entities; and (2) the ability to form small ventures with less than a hundred employees. These small ventures were subject to a preferential wage, taxation and record keeping treatment in comparison to the larger organization. Even with these advantages, these two forms of association did not spread throughout the Hungarian economy as was anticipated with less than one hundred being formed.

During the period from 1982 to 1985, the number of private ventures doubled almost every year, as did the number employed by such ventures. These increases allowed the Hungarian economy to exist during this period without any severe economic or political shock. Contract working communities operated within the framework of some companies had the most growth and represented two thirds of the associations by 1985.

Between 1982 and 1987, enterprise-work partnerships rose from 2,775 units employing 29,300 people to 19,169 units employing 252,100. Similarly, business-work partnerships increased from 2,341 in 1982 to 11,164 employing 74,500 people in 1987. In 1982 there were 121,400 artisans and 11,300 shopkeepers. These numbers rose in 1987 to 1,154,600 artisans and 31,800 shopkeepers (Bod, 1990).

Due to fiscal irresponsibility, greediness, and ideological aspects, the government in 1986 started to impose heavier and heavier tax burdens and restrictions on the new forms of associations. As a result, the initial legal principle was reversed to a new one - "everything is free that is permitted." Every sector of the economy began creating lists of the activities allowed and not allowed by each association. The rate of corporate tax increased from three to six percent; the tax rate then increased to ten percent and eventually to twenty percent. The amounts centralized by virtue of social insurance and personal income tax also increased. Although the number of new ventures decreased from 1986 to 1988, the entrepreneurial spirit in Hungary was not totally eliminated.

By 1988, significant economic, political and social changes had taken place in Hungary. The former reform thinking was reflected in Act VI of 1988 which allowed non Economic Associations. While previously there was no legal form of association available for private individuals to jointly undertake a new venture, Act IV on Economic Associations created several alternative forms for this purpose. The Act made it possible for small-scale producers to develop medium-scale enterprises. By raising the earlier quota of thirty people to five hundred the possibility for the development of medium-scale private enterprises was established. In April, 199o, the quota of five hundred people was abolished. The Act on Economic Associations also reintroduced and codified the institutions of the limited liability company and the joint stock company making it possible for private individuals to participate in such organizations as foundation members or partners.

Also, a section of small ventures in the Chamber of Economics became more and more efficient in organizing the enterprise and their interests. When the legal obstacles were removed by Act IV, the small venture section separated from the Chamber of Economics and established an independent organization under the name of National Association of Entrepreneurs (VOSZ), the first independent economic interest federation.

Hungary also opened a stock exchange on January 1, 1989 (Shapero and Sokol, 1982), that provided a mechanism to facilitate domestic and foreign private ownership. The political and economic reform beginning in 1988 and sustained by the Soviet withdrawal in 1989 stimulated the development of the banking and commercial infrastructure. Institutions began to offer services critical to capital formation and market conduct.

In April, 1990, a new act based on the concept - "In the Hungarian Republic, enterprising is a civic right" - was passed hat regulated private ventures by individuals. In the first six months, 150 companies transformed themselves into stock companies (Shapero and Sokol, 1982). Between January 1, 1989 and January 1, 1991, an estimated 2,500 joint ventures, worth more than $20 million in equity capital were established in Hungary. About 10% of these involved U.S. firms (Stepanek, 1991). It is estimated that small and medium firms may account for as much as 25% of Hungary's GDP. Estimates that include the "gray" or "informal" private sector suggest that the impact may be as high as 50% (Arvay, 1992). These legal enterprises have to overcome such difficulties as operating with a minimum of employees, heavy tax burdens, and little capital, and various economic, political, and infrastructure barriers.

Research design

In order to determine the role of women entrepreneurs in the Hungarian economy, fifty (50) women entrepreneurs were surveyed using a modified version of a questionnaire that was previously used in studies of women entrepreneurs in the United States, Republic of Ireland, Northern Ireland, Puerto Rico, People's Republic of China, and the new Russia. The questionnaire used dichotomous, rating scale, and open ended questions to delineate the characteristics of the entrepreneurs and their ventures created; the managerial skills and abilities of the women entrepreneurs; the problems encountered in creating a new venture; and their recommendations for improvement in infrastructure to better facilitate the new venture creation process. Several of these women entrepreneurs were also personally interviewed. While there are comparisons available since there is limited data in this once controlled economy and this is the first survey of women entrepreneurs in Hungary, it appears that the women entrepreneurs are representative on all the usual characteristics.

Findings

The findings will be discussed in terms of the: profile of the woman entrepreneur; starting the venture; profile of the new venture created; managerial skills and problems; and recommendations for improvement for future entrepreneurs.

Profile of Woman Entrepreneur

The woman entrepreneurs ranged in age from 22 to 68 with an average

age of 38.5 years. These entrepreneurs grew up primarily in middle (42%) or lower middle (26%) social class families where the occupation the father's occupation was mostly professional/technical (30%) followed by blue collar (28%), then self-employed (10%) and the mother's occupation was housewife (38%), professional technical (24%), or blue collar (22%). Many had older brothers or sisters and a few had a younger brother or sister.

Most were married (78%) with children. The occupation of their spouse was professional/technical (34%), followed by self-employed (22%), managerial (16%), and blue collar (8%). The woman entrepreneurs were highly educated as were their spouses. Eighty percent (80%) of the women entrepreneurs and 78% of their spouses had at least some college. While 34% of the women entrepreneurs and 33% of the spouses had graduate degrees, 24% of the women entrepreneurs and 31% of their spouses had an undergraduate college degree. The remainder (22% of women entrepreneurs and 14% of their spouses) had at least some college. The degree of the woman entrepreneurs varied greatly and included: trading, accounting, library science, foreign trade, engineering, finance, nursing, catering, economics, management, law, economics, and teaching. Their majors led to a variety of occupations just before starting their businesses: accountant, librarian, dressmaker, bookstore manager, project manager, economist, architect, training manager, sales executive, teacher, secretary, head of department, and engineer.

The self assessment of their personality characteristics is indicated in Figure 1. The woman entrepreneurs in Hungary felt they were extremely energetic and social and high in terms of independence, selfconfidence, perfectionist, anxious, flexible, and goal oriented. The three traits receiving a lower rating were: competitive/ noncompetitive, idealistic/ realistic, and generalist/ specialist.

The current income levels of the woman entrepreneur as well as her spouse were surprisingly lower than expected. The majority of women entrepreneurs (67%) had incomes below $9,999, with most of the others (31%) had incomes between 10,000 and $19,999. Only one woman entrepreneur had a current income between $20,000 and $29,999. Their spouses primary income was below $9,999 (65%) followed by $10,000 -

$19,999 (21%), and $20,000 - $29,999 (10%). One spouse had income in the $30,000 - $39,999 category.

Starting the Venture

For the majority of the women entrepreneurs (80%) this was their first venture creation effort. Of the remaining ten, four indicated it was their second venture and two their third. Four of the ten did not indicate which venture it was. Their departures were similar to that of most women entrepreneurs in Western economies: 60% (30) were interested in the area of business; 20% (10) were experiencing job frustration; 12% (6) were terminated from their jobs; 8% (4) moved; and 2% (1) was widowed. While most of the women entrepreneurs (88%) were sole founders, the remainder did co-found the new venture with a friend. What motivated them to start this new venture? The number of times mentioned for each rank order of motivation from 1 to 9 with 1 being the first priority is indicated in Table 1. When evaluating the motives receiving a 1 or 2 ranking, the women entrepreneur were somewhat similar to women entrepreneurs in Western cultures. Independence (25) received the highest number of first and second place rankings, followed by opportunity (23), money (16), economic necessity (15), and lack of job satisfaction (11).

Profile of New Venture Created

The new ventures created were in a wide variety of business areas and had many different legal forms. The nature of the businesses included: optician, trading, manufacturing, bookkeeping, private nursery, dressmaking, service, travel agency, retailing, training, tax advising, consulting, foreign trading, bakery, restaurant, and other service companies. 56% of the women entrepreneurs formed their new venture in a field in which they had previous work experience, education, or both. As is the case in Western cultures, most (74%) of the new ventures formed were in the service area.

Many different legal forms also occurred. The legal forms included: proprietorship, partnership, limited partnership, deposit company, small scale industry, cooperative, limited liability company, and deposit company. Following the trend of women entrepreneurs in Western cultures, the new venture was financed from savings personal assets, or retirement funds. No woman entrepreneur in Hungary had any external sources of financing.

Many of the ventures were 1 - 2 years (16) or 3 - 4 years (12) old. While a few had been established for 7 or more years (5), some were less than 6 months old (8), or 7 months to one year old (8). As would be expected, the size of the business was relative small. 26 ventures employed 5 - 9 full time employees and 16 employed 1 - 4 full time employees (see Table 2). Correspondingly, revenues were also low, with 25 firms having revenues less than $29,999 in 1991 and 23 had revenues at this level in 1992. Four firms had revenues in the $1,000,000 - $4,999,999 range in 1991 and six had revenues in this category in 1992. One firm in 1992 had revenues above $5,000,000.

Management Skills and Problems

The women entrepreneurs in Hungary generally rated themselves low on all management skills - finance, management, marketing, innovation, operations, and planning (see Figure 2). The areas receiving the lowest self assessment were finance and marketing while overall management received the highest rating. The major problems at start up were obtaining credit (28), weak collateral position (17), and demands of company on personal relations (17). These start up problems were followed in decreasing order by: lack of guidance and counsel (15), lack of management experience (15), lack of respect for women in business (15), lack of experience in hiring outside services (13), lack of experience in financial planning (13), lack of involvement with business colleagues (12), lack of busine-ss training (10), legal problems (9), and personal problems (7). Other start up problems mentioned were: lack of well-organized market economy, shortage of venture capital, narrow market, and a short period of ownership.

While the number of problems mentioned decreased in current operations, financial problems were still the most frequently mentioned; obtaining credit (16) and weak collateral position (11). Other problems in current operations were: lack of experience in hiring outside services (13), legal problems (8), lack of respect for business women (6), lack of involvement with business colleagues (6), demands of company on personal relations (6), personal problems (6), lack of experience in financial planning (6), lack of guidance and counselling (5), lack of business training (4), lack of management experience (4). Two other current operation problems mentioned were: a narrow market and the European Community. The most frequently mentioned risks at start up were: financial (39) and psychological (12), and the most frequently mentioned risks during current operations were financial (23), family (11), and psychological (8).

While only twenty two (44%) of the women entrepreneurs had a mentor, they indicated a wide variety of supporters: husband/fiance (29), friend (8), child (7), business associate (6), relative (4), boyfriend (3), and business partner (2). Two women entrepreneurs indicated that they did not have any supporters. The majority of the women entrepreneurs also networked. The networks included: close friends/family (30), trade associations (14), community organizations (5), women's professional groups (4), college alumni (4), political groups (2), foreign relations (1), trainers (1), and chamber of commerce (1).

Recommendations for Entrepreneurship Development

Finally, the women entrepreneurs were asked to indicate any recommendations they would make in terms of the educational system, business support system, and the government to make it easier for people to be successful entrepreneurs. In general, the women entrepreneurs recommended a Western style business education system. Specific courses mentioned included: international (5), business management (4), entrepreneurship (3), marketing (2), finance, investment, public relations, accounting, tax, legal, strategic planning, computer language, and basic business. Other recommendations for improvements in education included: continuous management training (5), professional training (3), training more skilled workers (2), training courses for city council (2), and entrepreneurship courses for middle and high school students.

In addition to the general comments, the suggestions for improvement in the business support system can be classified into three areas: consulting, credit, and infrastructure. In terms of consulting, women entrepreneurs felt there should be advising organizations established for new entrepreneurs as well as a free advice and counselling network in addition to professional advising. In the overall area of credit, they felt there should be better credit conditions, better credit possibilities, better loan conditions, a credit guarantee system, easier credit, favorable tax and credit systems, and more financial support. In terms of business infrastructure, women entrepreneurs recommended: a banking system, better bank relations, a better data system, guidance and counseling network, general business network, and an incubator system. General suggestions for improvements in the business support system included: city council help, regional concentration, qualified business partners, tax discounts, and tax relief.

The most numerous recommendations were in the area of government improvements. In addition to general comments, these recommendations clustered in terms of tax, credit, and consulting. In the tax area, eight women entrepreneurs recommended better tax conditions, seven specifically recommended tax discounts, one tax reduction, and one tax relief. Other tax recommendations included: tax advice, modification of taxation, and introduction of family taxation. The credit area also had a concentration of responses. Twelve women entrepreneurs recommended better credit conditions, three a favorable credit system, two an interest discount, and one each a credit discount, a credit guarantee, long term credit, more flexible credit, and more credit possibilities. The advising area had less recommendations. Those mentioned were: advising (6) enterprise advising (1), financial advising (1), and taxation advising (1).

While there were a wide variety of general government recommendations, the three mentioned more than once were: banking system (6), enterprise friendly policy (3), and a reduction in social insurance (2). Other suggestions being mentioned once included: better working conditions, bureaucratic authorities, business training, changing exchange control regulations, better conditions for suitable income retention, control liquidity of national economy, develop financing discipline, an economic information system, financial conditions, financial help, financial support, flexibility, flexible banking system, improve the economic position of Hungary, increase living standard of Hungarian people, provide information about privatization of former state large companies, legal advice, social security reform, stable economic position for Hungary, stable legal regulations in the long term which would provide some relief for entrepreneurs, support national culture, and support the starting of a business.

Conclusions and recommendations

For Hungary to continue to move toward a market economy, it is important that the small business/entrepreneurial sector be established. Women as well as men need to be encouraged to form new ventures in a number of different industries. Women entrepreneurs have created many successful businesses to date with their profile and the profile of their ventures being similar to those of their counterparts in Western countries.

In order for women and men entrepreneurs to be a vibrant part of the Hungarian economy, of particular importance are more Western business courses, a more favorable tax system, better credit conditions, free advising support, and a better banking system. With these and other improvements women entrepreneurs will be able to form more successful new ventures enabling the Hungarian economy to become more and more market oriented.

References

Arvay, J. (1992) "The impact of the "informal" private sector on the Hungary economy." Presentation at the Hungarian Blue Ribbon Commission Meeting, Budapest, Hungary.

Bod, P. A. (1990) "Privatization by proxy: New forms of entrepreneurship in Hungary." *Proceedings*, Conference on Political and Social Environment in Entrepreneurship, George Washington University, 1-8.

Center for Research on European Women (1987) "Women's businesses: legal, administrative and financial environment - some examples."

Chaganti, R. (1986) "Management in women-owned enterprises," *Journal of Small Business Management*, 24, 4, 18-29.

Cuba, R., Decenzo, D., and Anish, A. (1983) "Management practices of successful female business owners," *American Journal of Small Business*, VIII, 2, 40-5.

Egge, K. (1987) "Expectations vs. reality among founders of recent start-ups," *Proceedings*, 1987 Conference on Entrepreneurship, 322-36.

ELISE (1988) "Women in business: a career as an entrepreneur, 20 project profiles," Local Employment Initiatives in Europe, Information Network, 1-20.

Geoffee, R. and Scase, R. (1985) "Women in change: the experiences of female entrepreneurs," George Allen and Unwin, London.

Halpern, M. (1987) "Business creation by women: motivation, situation, and perspectives - final report of a study for the EEC."

Hisrich, R.D., and Brush, C.G. (1983) "The woman entrepreneur: implications of family, educational and occupational experience," *Proceedings*, 1983 Conference on Entrepreneurship, 255-70.

Hisrich, R.D., and Brush, C.G. (1986) "The woman entrepreneur: starting, managing, and financing a successful new business," Lexington Books, Lexington, MA.

Hisrich, R.D., and Brush, C.G. (1987) "Women entrepreneurs: a longitudinal study," *Proceedings*, 1987 Conference on Entrepreneurship, 187-99.

Hisrich, R.D. and O'Brien, M. (1982) "The woman entrepreneur as a reflection of the type of business," *Proceedings*, 1982 Conference on Entrepreneurship, 632-65.

Hisrich, R.D., and O'Brien, M. (1981) "The woman entrepreneur from a business and sociological perspective," *Proceedings*, 1981 Conference on Entrepreneurship, 21-39.

Kaplan, E. (1988) "Women entrepreneurs: constructing a framework to examine venture success and failure," *Proceedings*, 1988 Conference on Entrepreneurship, 643-65

Longstreth, M., Stafford, K., and Mauldin, T., (1987) "Self-employed women and their families: time use and socio-economic characteristics," *Journal of Small Business Management*, 25, 3, 30-37.

Mescon, T.S., Stevens, G.H., and Vozikis, G.S. (1983,1984) "Women as entrepreneurs: an empirical evaluation," Wisconsin *Small Business*

Forum, 2, 2, 7-17.

Neider, L. (1987) "A preliminary investigation of female entrepreneurs in Florida," *Journal of Small Business Management*, 25, 3, 22-9.

O'Connor, J. (1987) "Women in enterprise," Industrial Development Authority and Office of Minister of State for Women's Affairs, Dublin.

O'Connor, J. and Humphreys, E. (1988) "Entrepreneurial women," Social Research Centre, Limerick, Industrial Development Authority and Office of the minister of State for Women's Affairs.

OECD (1987) "Country report for Finland," OECD, Oslo.

OECD (1987) "Country report for the Netherlands," OECD, Oslo.

OECD (1987) "Country report'for Norway," OECD, Oslo.

OECD (1987) Country report for Republic of Germany," OECD, oslo.

OECD (1987) "Country report for Sweden," OECD, Oslo.

OECD (1987) "Country report for the United Kingdom," OECD, oslo.

OECD (1986) "Local initiatives for employment creation," 6, OECD, Paris.

OECD (1987) "Women - local initiatives - job creation, issues paper," W/2594V-D/0277V, OECD, Paris.

Pellegrino, E.T., and Reece, B. L. (1982) "Perceived formation and operational problems encountered by female entrepreneurs in retail and service firms," *Journal of Small Business Management*, 15-24.

Rosa, P. (1988) "Research in the Scottish enterprise foundation," Scottish Enterprise Foundation.

Schares, G. (1989) "Hungary: much done, much to do." *Business Week*, 73-76.

Shapero, A. and Sokol, L. (1982) "The social dimensions of entrepreneurship," C. Kent, D. Sexton, K. Vesper (Eds.), *Encyclopedia of Entrepreneurship*, Englewood Cliffs, NJ: Prentice-Hall.

Schwartz, E.B. (1979) "Entrepreneurship: A new female frontier," *Journal of Contemporary Business*, 47-76.

Scott, C.E. (1986) "Why more women are becoming entrepreneurs," *Journal of Small Business Management*, 24, 4, 37-44.

Sexton, D. and Bowman-Upton, N. (1988) "Sexual stereotyping of female entrepreneurs: a comparative psychological trait analysis of female and male entrepreneurs," *Proceedings*. 1988 Conference on entrepreneurship, 654-5.

Silvestri, G. and Lucasiewiecz, J. (1987) "A look at occupational employment trends to the year 200," *Monthly Labor Review*, U.S. Department of Labor, 46-63.

Stepanek, M. (1991) "Bright ideas." *World Trade*, 4, 1, 66-69.

United Nations (1987) "The economic role of women in the ECE region," United Nations, New York.

Van der Wees, C. and Romijn, H. (1987) "Entrepreneurship and small enterprise development for women in developing countries: an agenda of unanswered questions," International Labor Office, Geneva.

Appendix

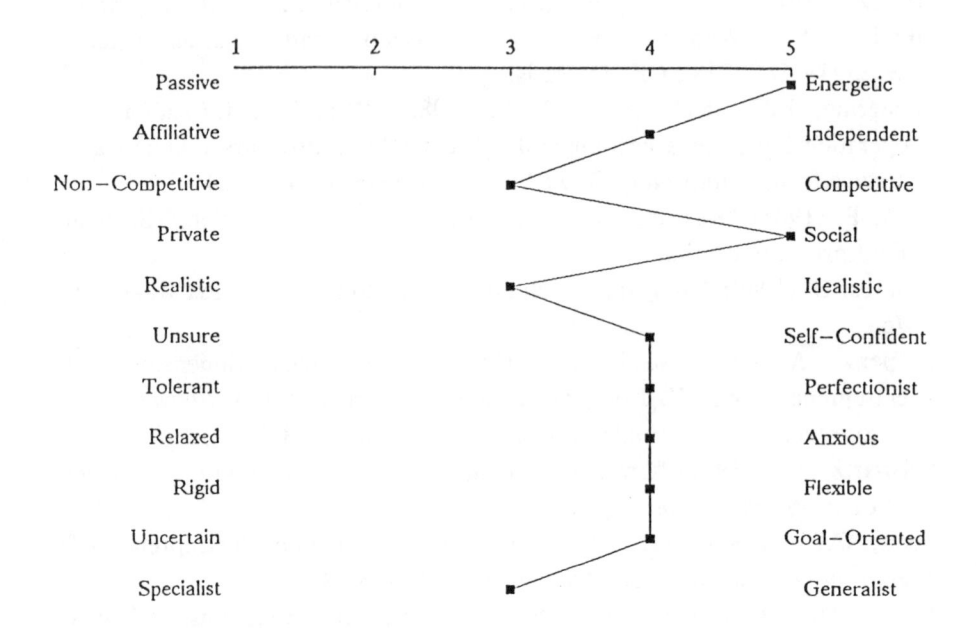

	1	2	3	4	5	
Passive					■	Energetic
Affiliative				■		Independent
Non–Competitive			■			Competitive
Private					■	Social
Realistic			■			Idealistic
Unsure				■		Self–Confident
Tolerant				■		Perfectionist
Relaxed				■		Anxious
Rigid				■		Flexible
Uncertain				■		Goal–Oriented
Specialist			■			Generalist

Figure 1. Self Assessment of Personality Traits

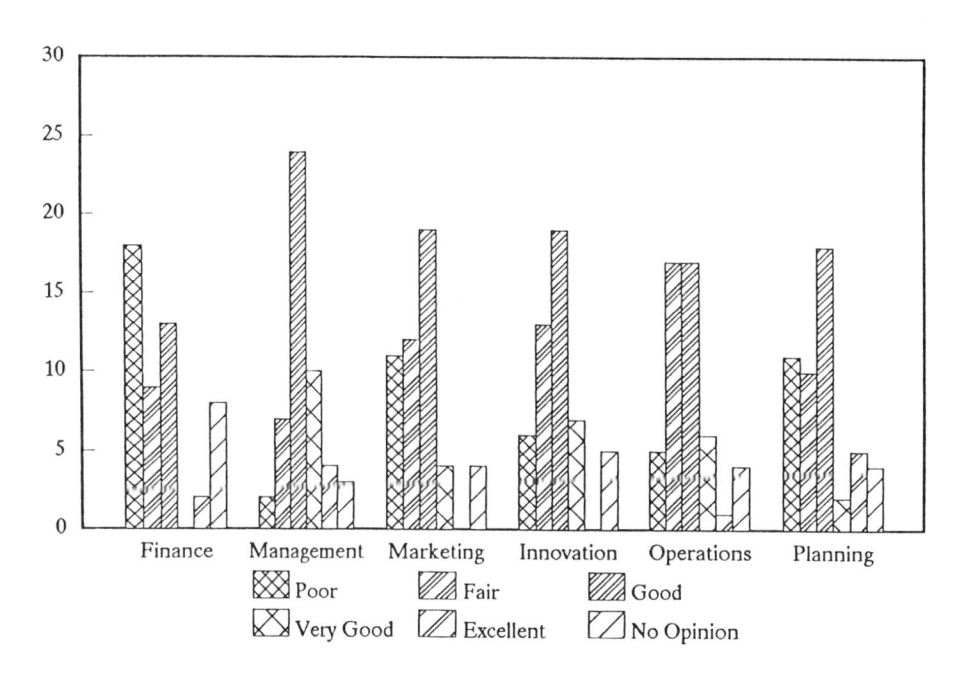

Figure 2. Self-Assessment of Skills

Table 1. Number of Times Motives for Starting their Business Mentioned

Ranking Indicated	Achievement	Job Satisfaction	Opportunity	Status/Prestige	Independence	Power	Money	Economic necessity	Career/Security
1	1	8	8	2	14	1	8	8	0
2	5	3	15	1	11	4	8	7	3
3	6	6	10	3	8	3	4	5	3
4	10	6	5	3	5	4	5	2	3
5	9	7	4	9	3	4	4	5	2
6	4	3	4	8	3	3	4	4	8
7	3	5	0	7	2	6	8	4	5
8	5	6	0	4	2	10	3	7	3
9	2	3	1	4	1	6	0	4	14

Table 2. Size of Venture

	Number of Employees				Revenues	
	Full time	Part Time	Family		1991	1992
1-4	16	31	29	<$29,000	25	23
5-9	26	15	18	$30,000-$49,999	0	0
10-19	1	1	0	$50,000-$99,000	6	8
20-49	3	0	0	$100,000-$499,999	7	5
50-99	1	0	0	$500,000-$999,999	0	2
100 or more	0	0	0	$1,000,000-$4,999,999	4	6
				>$5,000,000	0	1

24 Between Ikar's flight and Heron's boat: 'The choice of the Bulgarian entrepreneur'

Kiril Todorov

Introduction

Along with the other results, the present ongoing changes in Eastern Europe lead to the development of the private sector and entrepreneurial activity. Bulgaria does not make an exception in this aspect. The appearance and development of this new phenomenon in the economic system accompanies overcoming great difficulties that are common to some extent, but are also specific for each country.

We can observe interesting and often difficult to explain facts in Bulgaria. The economic environment is still far from market economy requirements though the monetary phase of the economic reform is nearly over. What we have in mind here is the construction of separate market elements and the chaotic and turbulent environment. We can also add that LSE's monopoly is not over to a large extent (the state still supports them directly or indirectly in contrast to private enterprises). The private sector is developing rather dynamically on this unclear economic background (though irregular in branches). The number of private firms by the end of August 1992 in Bulgaria is over 250,000 with a population less than 9 million.

Therefore a question arises here: What is hiding behind that growth, what are the problems and tendencies of its development? And further on: Who is the Bulgarian entrepreneur - with his motives, skills and problems? It is not a secret that many of the Bulgarian entrepreneurs attract "special attention" from some institutions and people but on the other hand they are an object for imitation and admiration. It would not sound unreal to say they are the heroes (in and without inverted commas) of the present situation which is not that conductive for entrepreneurial activity.

In other words the defining and analysis of the existing challenges to the economy, private sector and entrepreneurial activity are of some interest in terms of their further development. Future tendencies for development and ways for solving problems have to be outlined. That is why it is important to understand (on the background of the ongoing unique but specific in each country transition to market economy) to what extent the existing theory and practice in industrial countries can be used in describing foreseeing the development of the private entrepreneurial sector and entrepreneurs particularly.

Economic background for private entrepreneurial sector development

Let us start with some specific characteristics of the Bulgarian economy and industry (as its main component):

- Total dominance of state property and state owned enterprises in the country's economic and industrial structure (compared even to Poland and Hungary where private property has a larger share and stronger traditions). The private properties share now is about 94 per cent of the total property volume but its share in GNP and NI is less - 89,3 per cent and 84,1 per cent respectively (Annual Statistic Journal, 1992).
- Irrational economic and industrial structure. On the background of the country's size (as territory and population) the disposable resources and national traditions the former orientation toward mining industry, metallurgy, heavy chemistry and industrial electronics is at least inadequate. Moreover the structure was built at the expense of agriculture and that is why we have the present situation - non efficient industry and declining agriculture.
- One-sided orientation toward markets of goods and raw materials. Up to 1989 more than half of the Bulgarian export was for the former

COMECOM members and mainly for the former USSR. Nearly 65 per cent of the used raw materials were imported mainly from these countries.
- Large concentration of production capacities and a big average enterprise size (in comparison with other East- European countries). As a result large enterprises with monopolistic behaviour dominate the Bulgarian economy.
- Complicated and clumsy hierarchy management structure. The monopoly of LSEs went along with bureaucratic and ineffective management. Strategic planning did not exist in return to "perspective plans" - the tendency was to plan on the basis of the present situation and on the account of former tendencies' extrapolation.

Despite these specific negative characteristics and due to some circumstances as: large export to the former USSR and in return cheap raw materials and petrol, part of which was re exported for hard currencies; strong military-industrial complex with large profits and well-developed cargo transport (TIR), plus the favourable situation till 1985, the Bulgarian economy and life standard had a relatively good level.

The big problems came after 1985. The Bulgarian economy fell into a more difficult situation in comparison with the rest of the East-European countries since Gorbachov was in power and USSR as a market and basic supplier was on decline. Foreign obligations increased threefold and became $ 10.5 milliard for only five years - till 1990.

Therefore the November 1989 changes found a collapsing economy with irrational priorities, serious disproportions and a large foreign debt. Having in mind the specific characteristics and the economic situation the coalition government began the monetary phase of the economic reform in the end of January 1990 with the help of the so-called "shock therapy". Many important changes have been carried out thanks to the IMF and WB support, mainly aiming at financial stabilization and formulation of the basic elements of the newly created market environment. Combined with the policy of "small privatization" and the appearance of small private firms - mainly commercial and service - these facts lead to a balance of demand and supply in the summer of 1991 and to higher foreign currency reserves - they were $

100 million in the summer of 1990 and became $ 1,300 million at the end of August 1992.

The structural phase or "the large privatization" was delayed considerably because of political reasons (elections on the Parliament and President in October 1991 and January 1992). That is why and to some extent because of restrictive monetary policy, production decreased drastically. Another reason is the break-up of the USSR and COMECOM. The reduction according to official information is about 20 per cent but unofficially it accounts to 30 per cent. A new phenomenon appeared - unemployment (it was unfamiliar to the socialist society). The number of unemployed is 500,000 and that is 12 per cent of the total number of employed persons.

One of the most important results of the ongoing deep economic reform is the creation of private entrepreneurial sector. Despite unclear state policy, lack of preferences, limiting fiscal policy, lack of investments and unentrepreneurial behaviour of banks, the private sector development is quite considerable, especially in commercial and service spheres where about 50 per cent of the turnover belongs to it. As we will see later, though the structural phase and privatization have not started yet, a dynamically developing private sector is on hand and its importance in the national economy is increasing.

The private entrepreneurial sector development in the national economy

Till 1944 (the year when the communist regime came to power) small and middle-sized enterprises (SME) dominated the Bulgarian economy. Cooperative movement was well developed too. During the communist regime the situation was changed beyond recognition - starting with nationalization in 1948 and ending with monopolization of LSEs of economic space in late 1980s.

Two main periods in the present new history of small business can be outlined: 1982-1989 and from 1989 up to now.

1982-1989

A different economic policy faintly began to make its way in the early 1980s as a reaction to the first more serious symptoms of economic failure in the 1970s. It confirmed and acknowledged the role of SMEs in the economic structure and aimed at forming such enterprises though based on state property. The foundations were laid by two government acts - No. 12/1982 and No. 33/1984 and new SMEs appeared while the Bulgarian Industrial Association (BIA) had considerable role as the main co-ordinator of the
process. Some partial results were achieved as a consequence of this policy: diversity of national market utilization of local raw materials; higher technological level of some economic sectors; solution of local social tasks. That policy as a whole was only a cosmetic attempt to improve the socialist economic system without real changes. State property, the incentive on creating these enterprises and the lack of adequate economic (competitive and market) environment a priori predetermined the results of these intentions. It is also necessary to point out that a large part of SMEs did not answer criteria because they were either dependent structures within LSEs or production units but were never independent separate units. Thus LSEs took their profits and SMEs often could not reproduce and in the end went bankrupt.

From 1989 up to now

The fundamental changes in society and economic system unlocked enormous social forces especially in the sphere of private entrepreneurship and they were supported by the new liberal legislation. A dynamically growing private sector resulted from (and despite!) the first phase of the economic reform[1]. In 1989 the number of registered firms was 13,625. It went up quickly for the next two years (see Table 1).

---

[1] We have in mind the lack of preferences for the private sector and restrictive monetary policy that includes: high raw materials' prices; lack of initial capital; high credits interest; restrictive fiscal policy.

Table 1. Total number of newly registered enterprises on September 1st, 1991 and on February 24th, 1992 in activity sector

BRANCHES	1 SEPTEMBER 1991		24 FEBRUARY 1992	
	Absolute	in %	Absolute	in %
Industry	9,120	7.0	14,532	7.8
Building	5,061	3.9	6,768	3.6
Agriculture	7,664	5.9	13,609	7.3
Forestry enterprise	71	0.0	88	0.0
Transport	20,879	16.1	26,633	14.3
Communication	25	0.0	38	0.0
Trade	32,311	24.8	47,451	25.4
Other branches of material production	28,984	22.3	41,691	22.3
Public utilities	8,541	6.6	13,452	7.2
Science and services	1,235	1.0	1,427	0.8
Education	404	0.3	536	0.3
Culture and art	1,546	1.2	1,893	1.0
Healthcare, tourism, sport	977	0.8	1,437	0.8
Finances, credits	141	0.1	181	0.1
Management	89	0.1	123	0.1
Other branches of non material production	13,054	10.0	16,902	9.0
Total	130,102	100.0	186,788	100.0

Source: An Investigation of Small Business Sector in Bulgaria (by Programme PHARE); Ministry of Industry, Sofia 1992

The table does not include the registered firms in 1989 (13,625) because the statistic observations began later on. So, if we add that number to the total sum in Table 1, the number of private firms on 24 February 1992 will be 200,000. Unofficially they are over 250,000 by the end of August, 1992.

Therefore though the economic reform and its monetary phase brought about difficulties for the private entrepreneurial sector they had significant role in "letting the spirit out of the bottle" (the role of forced entrepreneurship due to unemployment was considerable). In a country like Bulgaria, where LSEs dominate the development of that sector is of vital importance for improvement of economy's competitiveness and increase in the economic efficiency. The solution of serious social problems is not less important unemployment in the first place. For example (as we said before), the unemployed are about 500,000 while the employed in the private sector are 450,000 . Conclusions are evident.

Who is the Bulgarian entrepreneur and what is he like?

Unfortunately, up to now we lack representative comprehensive studies that can give us a full picture of entrepreneurial activities and entrepreneurs. The problem is both in the short period of time since the beginning of that activity and in the lack of adequate information on certain dimensions in that sphere. In order to get a close answer of the question asked we will use our own study of 25 industrial firms with the help of BIA questionnaire that we renewed (Research project Entrepreneur Activity, UNWE,, 1991 -1992). Firstly as a result of our study we determined: The number of factors that determine entrepreneurial inclination.

That group of factors, on its part, can be divided into two subgroups: Factors concerning characteristics of people's psychology. Generally, they influence positively the inclination to entrepreneurship. We can point out here the rich and interesting history, the geographical situation, the mixture of different cultures through centuries. This leads to forming such basic features as: patience to the different value systems, tenacity in critical situations, inclination to look for the new (that is the Bulgarian hunger for knowledge). There are some characteristics that influence entrepreneurial activity negatively: conservative thinking and suspicion to "the entirely new", envy towards someone's success.

The second subgroup includes *The influence of the present social and political situation on the entrepreneurial activity*. Firstly, that is the intensity of the ongoing changes. We can see "the effect of the liberated spirit of the bottle" that freed internal man's power and the desire to prove oneself and to get high results. The influence of the still unsatisfied market and of empty niches as a consequence of breaking up the LSEs monopoly is not to be underestimated. The increasing unemployment rate is also of some importance because it leads to "forced entrepreneurship". We must not underestimate the influence of newly adopted liberal normative legislation.

So, who is the Bulgarian entrepreneur and what is he like?

To answer this question we shall shortly comment the results of our study. It shows that people's psychology, background and education determine the inclination to entrepreneurship. The data shows strong family environment influence. Most entrepreneurs have parents who are well-educated or have good professional training (44 per cent and 28 per cent of the respondent respectively). entrepreneurs have high education (that makes a difference to the popular opposite opinion in literature - see Monsted in Todorov and Nikolov, 1992). An entrepreneur is usually 35-49 years old and has about 10 years professional practice. Most entrepreneurs have technical education, good initial knowledge and skills to start own business. The highest number of entrepreneurs is in Plovdiv and its region where the unemployment rate is also the highest. Here is another interesting fact: a great location of entrepreneurs is noticed in smaller towns with rich craftsman traditions.

Table 2. Motives for entrepreneurial behaviour

Motives (in order of frequency they are pointed as main)	Frequency Number*	per cent %	Ranking of the motives
1. Desire for practical realization of an own idea	15	29	3
2. Need to be independent	11	21	2
3. Possibility to get high income	10	19	1
4. Desire to complete things	7	14	5
5. Challenge to do something the others can't	4	8	4
6. Others	3	8	4
7. Freedom to explore new spheres	1	1	7
8. Desire to manage people	0	0	8
Total	51	100	

* The answers are more than the respondents because some have pointed 2 and more motives.

This confirms some former studies of these traditions and their strong influence on entrepreneurship (see Pier Kristensen in Todorov, Nikolov, 1992).The motives for the entrepreneurial behaviour shown in Table 2 are of greatest interest.

It is obvious the leading motives are "possibility to get high income" and "need to be independent". We can explain the high ranking of the second motive (need to be independent) with the fact that the majority of entrepreneurs came from LSEs with monopolistic behaviour and they "get rid of inferiority complexes kept-down incentive" trough their own business. Of course it is not possible here to make a full interpretation of the results we got but we can summarize them concluding that the motivation of the Bulgarian entrepreneur (having in mind "who is he") is an expression of internal motives and stimuli. As we shall see later, the unclear and undefined environment that still does not have "rules of the game" ensures so little grounds for external motivation.

The challenges for the Bulgarian entrepreneur: taking Ikar's role or Heron' boat

The defined results and problems that appeared after the monetary phase was over do not create the best possible environment for entrepreneurship on the background of lost traditional markets and suppliers. In this sense the entrepreneurial activity naturally is laid on commercial and service spheres mainly because of the less needed initial capital, its quick turnover and the high profit. The former studies on small business in the country (An Investigation of Small Business Sector in Bulgaria by PHARE programme, 1992) show the large dominance of private firms in these two sectors. At the same time, unofficially, only 7-8 per cent of registered private firms operate in the industrial sphere (see Table 1).

Though not so big, the experience we have in entrepreneurship for the last three years shows some tendencies are at hand:

Forming and functioning of commercial firms with various objects of activity. These entrepreneurs take advantage of the market deficit of some goods and they get high profits. Therefore we can call them speculators instead of entrepreneurs. But the market gradually becomes sufflcient and competition more serious so a question arises in front of these businessmen - how to keep and develop accumulated capital and they do not posses the necessary knowledge to answer that question. Therefore the quick advancement and "flight" become more and more difficult and at the same time the danger their fragile wax wings to melt in the rapidly changing temperature i.e. environment. These firms and entrepreneurs rely on making a fortune quickly i.e. on so called "blows" without studying the environment and making a good base for their business. After quick success these firms and entrepreneurs generally are doomed to failure and practice shows they exist no longer than 2 years.

Firms and entrepreneurs who rely on commerce and partly on services in the very beginning and after accumulating initial capital they reorientate their activity to a more serious business - in material production or banking activity and services[2]. Entrepreneurs-owners of these firms have good knowledge, skills and sometimes solid informal relationships. While dealing with trade they are preparing their future activity, they think everything over at the same time and instinctively time has come for a more serious business. Therefore these firms and entrepreneurs are "waiting for their time to come" and balance various objects of activity.

Firms and entrepreneurs who rely only on production activity. Their object of activity can be figuratively called "risk" in the present market situation and the macroeconomic situation - raw materials' prices, high interest rates and high taxes. These entrepreneurs usually have own invention or technical idea and they want to make it a reality despite all difficulties. But at the background of production stagnation and restrictive economic policy they always take the risk to go on bankruptcy and to be passengers in Heron's boat. Some of them pass through entrepreneurial phase successfully having well prepared projects and luck and they show considerable growth.

Let us discuss two cases in brief. They represent us empirical information as a proof of these tendencies and as a topic of discussion.

Vek 22 Publishing House

The firm was found in the summer of 1990 and its main object of activity is publishing business literature. The change of the economic system will naturally lead to a boom in the demand of new economic and management literature - that is the presumption of the two partners who found the company. One of them is an ex-chief of a state publishing house and the other was the economic editor-in-chief in the same publishing house. The firm started with a very small sum (that was before price liberalization). The first edition was the memoirs of one of the greatest Bulgarian politicians of

---

[2]As we shall see later there are opposite cases as well.

the 1930s and 1940s whose memoirs were read illegally during the communist regime. The right estimation of the market situation and the potential demand allows the entrepreneurs (they are the beginners in this branch) to publish more books of the same kind. Thus they get on their feet and as they say they can move further on to something more difficult - to publish business literature. They consult their actions with lecturers from the Economic University and publish successfully some translated books or Bulgarian ones. Therefore they take a position on that specific market. Vek 22 began publishing *Manager* - a prestige magazine addressed to state and private enterprise managers that can help their image.

In the spring of 1992 the market slowly became satisfied as a consequence of new competitors (including foreign publishers) and the powerful firm (financially powerful) felt limited in its activity. The firm decided to diverse its activity having in mind the present situation (high prices of polygraphic services) and to enter new spheres, for example commerce and cargo transport. It goes on publishing at the same time, prepares its best-sellers and is waiting for the right time to come.

Tribo

It was founded in the autumn of 1990 by a family of engineers. The husband has an invention for using cheap materials for production of composite elements for brake's lining. The invention was tested and the results were very good while the inventor was working in the State Scientific Institute of Transport. He had to leave because of bureaucratic attitude of institute leaders and the endless promises of help. At last he decided to start his own business. The wife (they have two children aged 5 and 3) graduated a business-school and attended several courses in small business management. They started up after enormous difficulties (in preparing the instrument equipment) and after receiving a loan from a commercial bank (surprisingly quickly for Bulgarian conditions). They hired three workers in the beginning who had to maintain the equipment in a small production building. The models had very good qualities and the first orders came up. The husband dealt with technological-product part and the wife was the manager. The production went well and there were orders for an year in advance. The firm exported to Greece, Egypt and the Near East. The workers are fifteen now. The firm will be growing up in future.

These two cases show some important facts. The opportunity to be among beginners (as is the first case) gives you advantages in any case. But that lasts shortly, especially when the activity is performed in specific sector as publishing is. The firm has accumulated financial assets and has hired high qualified people by that time. The situation does not allow diversity of activity on the basis of main object of activity because the costs increase disproportionally to the results. It is obvious that the entrepreneurs want to grow - the question here is how and where. And is the growing favourable in strategic aspect?

In the case with Tribo the firm entered a perspective niche thanks to its own invention. The product approbation made during the former work in scientific institute is also of some help. Thus they save time and money for testing equipment. The firm quickly enters the market and the question of its growing is on having in mind the personnel number and the constant demand. While there are difficulties in further choice for Vek 22, the growth is easier for Tribo.

Therefore, the same question are facing both firms: where to go? To develop or not? I.e. where is the margin of reaching the critical point for beginning (and for stopping) the growth?

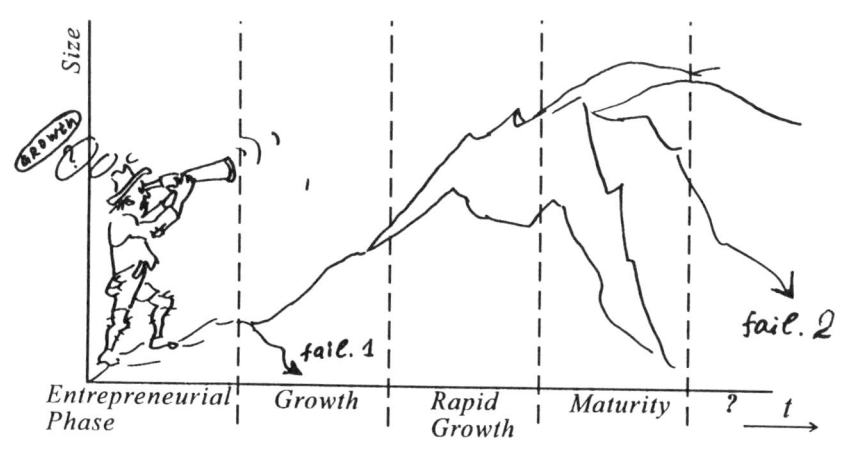

Figure 1. To grow or not to grow?

Entrepreneurial theory and practice (see for example Johannisson in references) represents us interesting approaches and discussions in this aspect. Firstly, that is the question about the kind of growth - internal or external. The external growth is far behind because of the level of market economy and its specific characteristics in Bulgaria (partly developed market and firm relations, people's psychology - the problem to balance one's ego and cooperation with an enemy). As to Vek 22, our opinion is they need external growth - partnership with a similar firm. Thus they will have a larger market share and will achieve the "scale effect". In practice they can not have internal growth because of the position they are in (because of already pointed reasons).

The situation with Tribo is different. They can show growth alone at least by now. The market is on hand, the invention has some potential, the wife has management qualification and the experience, the bank is benevolent. Therefore, as they realize internal growth (qualitative and quantitive - see Johannisson) they face the problem of growth ceiling and the price of that growth. What we mean here is not only the dynamics of the proportion results - costs but also the consequences for the entrepreneurs - stress, exhaustion, level of competence. The owners have to consider carefully the situation and to react in adequate way (see Figure 1).

Summary

In this analysis of the entrepreneurial activity and the private sector development allows us (though conditionally to some extent) to make some conclusions:

1. We can observe a dynamic development of the private entrepreneurial sector in a situation of a unique specific transaction to market economy on the background of still unclear and not yet constructed market environment. The accumulated potential of incentives and desire ffir self-development - so called "entrepreneurial spirit in the bottle" can be the "motor" of the new private sector in the limiting conditions the restrictive policy creates.

2. The fundamental problem is how to choose the object of activity and to diverse that activity. The case of "shortly flying away commercial speculative firms" shows it is necessary to create a good starting position for business. The change from one extreme (commercial speculative) to the other (the difficult development of production-oriented firms) proves the lack of a normal backgrounds for private sector development. The question is till when internal power and enthusiasm to realize one's ego, will overcome difficulties and will survive in this inadequate environment.

3. As we saw before, a large number of firms are between entrepreneurial phase and the phase of growth. The example with Tribo is an exception that confirms the rule that production-oriented firms' growth is the most difficult. The question is not only how to grow and when. Or what the growth should be: internal or external; qualitative or quantitative. The most important problem is about **the price of growth**. That price at the present moment is enormous.

4. The question about state's role and activity and state institutions in terms of their help for the private sector is also important. The lack of a clear state policy on small business and entrepreneurs leads to the present situation: the energy of enthusiastic entrepreneurs does not move the locomotive, it only makes it whistle.

5. The development of a consulting infrastructure is of great importance and it should be oriented mainly to entrepreneurs and entrepreneurial management. Many actions based on trial and error method would have been useless if such consulting help had been on hand. The organizing of a better and practically oriented training for beginners in entrepreneurship and the development of those who are in business is also important. Here the experiment of industrial developed countries is very useful (as theory and practice of entrepreneurial activity) but the specific characteristics of the national economy should be considered carefully.

References

CSI (1991), *An Annual Book*, Central Statistical Institute, Sofia.

Cooper, A.C. (1972), 'Technical Entrepreneurship: What to Know?', *R & D Management*, Vol. 3, No. 2

Johannisson, B. (1989), *To Grow and Not To Grow - On The External Growth of Small Firms*, Paper presented at the Third Workshop on Recent Research in Entrepreneurship, November 30th- December 1 st, 1989, Durham University Business School, Durham, England.

MI (1992) *An Investigation of Small Business Sector in Bulgaria* /by Programme PHARE/, Ministry of Industry, Sofia, 1992.

Monsted, M. (1985), *Flexibility and Growth in Small Manufacturing Enterprise - The Case of Denmark*, Copenhagen.

Todorov, K., Nikolov, N./eds/(1992). *Small Business Management*, Publishing House Vek 22, Sofia.

Todorov, K. (1992), *Strategies for Competitive Behaviour of Bulgarian Industrial Enterprises in The Context of Transition from Planned to Market Economy*, Paper presented at the 22nd IIAS Congress, subtopic: Autonomy and Control. Basic Issues for Public Enterprises in a Competitive Environment, July 13th-17th, 1992, Vienna.

UNWE (1992), *EntrepreneurActivity*. Research project, 1991-1992, Sofia.

25 Development of small business sector in Poland as the Fisher-Pry process

Krystyna Wilczewska and Witold Wilczewski

Introduction

None of the contemporary economic changes in Europe causes as many emotions and passions as the transition from central planned economy to market economy in countries of Central and East Europe.

The high level of the concentration has been typical for the economy of Central and East European countries. The economy was dominated by big business units with considerable property. These companies created work places for millions of people. The existing small business sector had an inconspicuous share in the economy. Its development has been restricted by law and fiscal regulations.

Creation of big business units was dictated not only by technical causes. It resulted from ease of control and management.

The beginning of the process of reform leads to fundamental economy changes in Central and East European countries. The role of the private sector rapidly increases as a consequences of privatization of state owned companies and also of establishment a new private firms. As the result of this changes we observe the increasing share of small and medium size enterprises in the economy structure.

Changing in Economy as the Fisher-Pry Process

Decisively most of technical, economical innovations spread through replacement of existing products, technologies, systems of economy and organization by new solutions. This means that the technical, economical progress is inseparably bound with the displacement of solution existing earlier. This phenomenon is called substitution. The development of economy provides many examples of substitution processes in each field.

The processes of technological substitution became the object of research by economic sciences in the seventies. They were began by Fisher and Pry who presented in [1] the model describing the above phenomena in the aspect of time.

This model verified by various investigations, turned out to be useful in describing the process of technology development. It was applied, among others, in the description of the process of replacement of horses by tractors in the USA in the years of 1920-1960, water-power plants by thermal power station in Canada in the years of 1917-1972 [2], conventional power plants by nuclear power plants in the years of 1970-1986 [3]. The essence of the model and its basic elements are formulated as follows.

Let X(t) indicate an optional level of applying the new solution in the moment (t), and Y(t) the stage of using old solution at the same moment. The participation of the new solution is measured by:

$$f(t) = \frac{X(t)}{X(t) + Y(t)}$$

and the conventional solution

$$f'(t) = \frac{Y(t)}{X(t) + Y(t)}$$

while f(t)+f'(t)=1

The basic assumption of Fisher and Pry is the ascertain, that the speed of the substitution process varies in time. At given moment the rate of substitution is proportional to the achieved level of substitution and the difference between the current and final level of utilizing of the given technology. We may express this as

$$\frac{df(t)}{dt} = 2\alpha f(t)[1-f(t)] \qquad (1)$$

where:

2α rate of substitution process in the initial period,
f(t)   level of application of the new solution at the moment of t.

Let t_{50} define the moment of time, in which the process of substitution was achieved in half, i.e. $f(t)_{50} = 1/2$. Integrating the equation (1) with consideration of the above condition we obtain the following form of logistic function.

$$f(t) = [1+\exp(2\alpha(t-t_{50}))]^{-1} \qquad (2)$$

or

$$\ln\left[\frac{f(t)}{1-f(t)}\right] = a+tb \qquad (3)$$

where: $a = -2\alpha \, t_{50}$, $b = 2\alpha$.

Equation (3) express the basic idea of the Fisher-Pry model. It may be formulated as follows: if the process of substitution began and achieved a specified level, than this process will lead to the supplanting of conventional solution. The above, very simple model, is very convenient in a formal description of various processes of diffusion of the innovation. Its graphic illustration (Equation 2) is the substitution curve presented in Figure 1.

It is characterized by three phases. The first depicts the introduction of new solutions for utilization. In this phase they are not competitive yet, in the economic and technical aspect, in comparison to conventional solutions. This situation causes that the potential buyers and users treat them with a certain reserve and distance. The rate of the substitution process is still not very great. The second phase is called the period of conquest (T). Now a rapid acceleration of the substitution process follows related with attaintment of an economic and technological supremacy of new solutions over

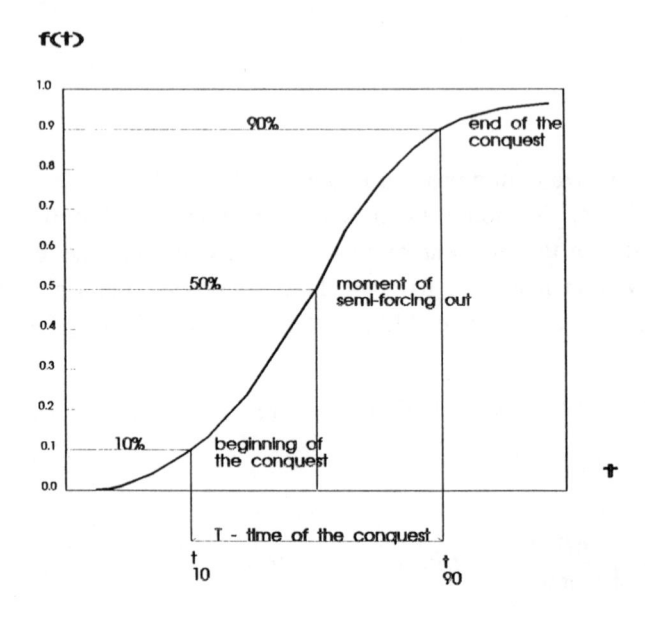

Figure 1. The substitution curve.

conventional ones. In this period the number of producers and users of such products increases fundamentally. In this phase the function f(t) increases from the value f(t)=0.1 to the magnitude f(t)=0.9. This period is inversely proportional to the value of parameter a and amount to $T = t_{90} - t_{10} = 2.2/\alpha$.

In the final phase we observe lowering of the application rate of the given solutions. As a result of the occurring processes they become conventional and one can be expect that in the nearest future they will be replaced by newer solution.

Substitution of Big Company Sector by Small Business

In the seventies participation of small business sector in the overall economic structure was stable and amounted to 4.4-4.6%. Since 1980 the process of growing participation of small business enterprises has began.

These enterprises created spontaneously new places of work. Number of employees in small business sector comprises 30% of overall employees in economy excluding agriculture. Rapid development of small business sector observed since 1990 is caused by privatization and demonopolization of economy and advantageous conditions for establishment of new private enterprises.

The forming of the process of substitution of big company sector by small business sector (outside agriculture) is illustrated by statistic data in Table 1.

On the basis of the above table we calculated the parameters of the mode (3) for the period 1980-1992. Estimating them we assumed that small business sector in not only substitutional in relation to big company sector, but also complementary. Small business sector can force out 70% of big company sector. According to the above statement the obtained substitution curve concerns only this part of the forced out sector which remains after subtracting non replaceable quantities (30%). Only in this sense the course of function $f(t)/[1-f(t)]$ in time should be understood. The results of the estimation are presented in Table 2.

Table 1. Forcing out of big company sector by small business sector

Year	Number of employees in small business sector [thousands] X(t)	Total number of employees. [thousands] X(t)+Y(t)	f(t)
1970	442	9,980	0.044
1971	446	10,211	0.044
1972	470	10,555	0.045
1973	491	10,906	0.045
1974	552	11,613	0.045
1975	531	11,793	0.045
1976	550	11,852	0.046
1977	559	12,050	0.046
1978	555	12,197	0.046
1979	565	12,190	0.046
1980	602	12,296	0.049
1981	667	12,106	0.055
1982	829	11,921	0.061
1983	816	12,060	0.068
1984	897	12,245	0.073
1985	957	12,186	0.079
1986	1,107	12,332	0.090
1987	1,250	12,384	0.101
1988	1,421	12,406	0.115
1989	1,636	12,401	0.132
1990	2,231	12,390	0.188
1991	3,032	11,800	0.257
1992 *)	3,563	11,790	0.302

*) 30 June.

Table 2. Values of parameters of FISHER-PRY Model (3)

Parameters of the model	
Leveling of the forcing out process	0.1783t - 2.9763
Rate of the process _=b/2	0.0892
Correlation coefficient	0.9538
R - squared	90.99 percent

The above parameters characterize the process of forcing out present structure of small business sector in the investigated period. The degree of consistence of the obtained theoretical function with empirical magnitudes is high. The course of the process responds to the assumption of FISHER-PRY model. (Fig.2)

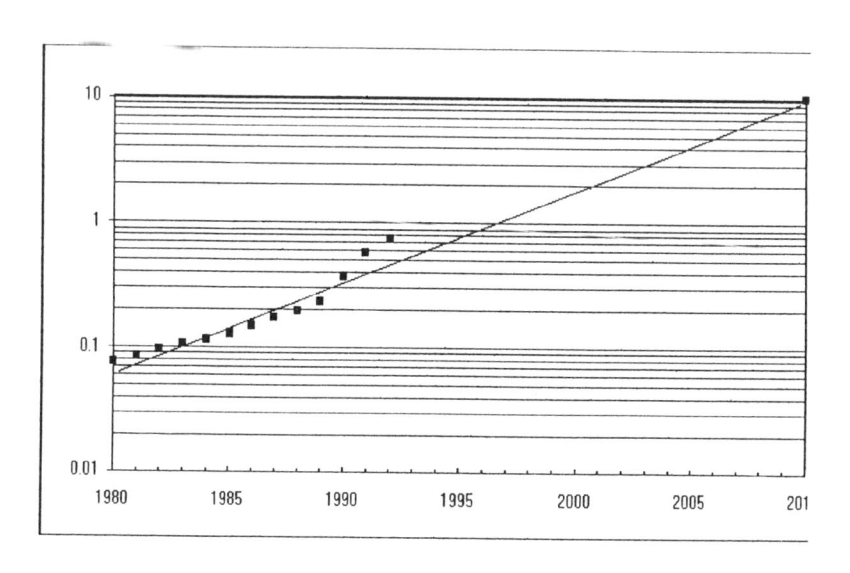

Figure 2. The forcing out process.

The results presented in Table 2 allow for determination of the parameters characterizing forcing out process . For better clarity they have been grouped in the form of Table 3.

Table 3. Parameters of the process of substitution

	Parameters of the process
Beginning of the conquest t_{10}	1984
Moment of semi-forcing out t_{50}	1996
End of the conquest t_{90}	2008
Period of the conquest T	25 years

On the basis of the obtained results is it possible to ascertain, that the beginning of the period of conquest of small business sector in Poland took place in the year 1984, in which $f(t)/[1-f(t)] = 0.11$. The period of conquest is 25 years. This means that the process of forcing out will terminate in the year of 2008, when the function $f(t)/[1-f(t)] = 9.0$.

Conclusion

The model presented in this paper may be treated as a scenario of consequences of the present development of small business sector in Poland. Obviously, it is not without imperfections. It does not embrace factors influencing the course of development processes of the small business sector. And so, we know nothing of the inner mechanism of the examined phenomena. Since inference for the future is made exclusively on the basis of the data from the past, these conclusions should not be treated in an absolute way as unavoidable consequences of the hitherto existing development. The results obtained are, as stressed by Fisher and Pry, suggestions according to which, in unchanged conditions, with no interference from stronger factors, the processes of substitution lead to afore determined situations.

References

Fisher J.C., Pry R.H.A. A simple substitution model of technological change. Technol. *Forecast and Soc. Change* 1971, vol. 3. p. 75-88.

Sahal D., *Patterns of Technological Innovation*, Addison-Weseley Publishing Company Inc. London-Amsterdam-Don Mills, Ontario-Sydney-Tokyo 1981

Wilczewska K., Wilczewski W., Kernenergieentwicklung in den EWG-und RGW-Laendern. Jahrestagung Kerntechnik'89 Kerntechnische Gesellschaft e.V. *Deutsches Atomforum e.V. Tagungsbericht* p.671-674.

Part E
ENTREPRENEURS

26 Entrepreneurial scripting

David Johnson

Abstract

Transactional Analysis (T.A.) is a theoretical model of human psychology and communication which provides a framework for understanding the softer aspects of entrepreneurship. According to the T.A. concept of scripts at an early age individuals make decisions about what their lives are going to be like and what they are going to achieve. The assumption to be explored within this paper is that during the start up and survival stages of business development key figures within the business are making decisions as to how successful it will be and how people will work within the business. These decisions which constitute the organisations script are influenced by significant events within the environment, and have a determining effect upon the ongoing success or failure of the business.

A model is developed which explores the component parts of an organisations script, and evidence derived from interviews with a sample of twenty owner-managers of emerging businesses is presented in support.

The implications of organisational scripting for the success and failure of new business ventures are discussed.

Introduction

The aim of this paper is to introduce the concept of 'Scripts' as used within Transactional Analysis (Berne 1961) with a view to contributing to our understanding of success and failure amongst small and medium sized businesses. This approach focuses upon the 'softer' aspects of small business development although the implications for survival profit margins, market share, etc are significant and will be discussed throughout the paper.

Transactional Analysis was defined by Eric Berne (1961) as: "*a systematic and consistent theory of personality and social dynamics*" which essentially considers how and why people think, feel and behave the way they do. To date Transactional Analysis has been primarily used in the diagnosis and treatment of individuals. However it is equally valid for application to organisations and organisation development. As such it is particularly suited to an investigation of small business development and could provide a powerful explanation for the success, failure or indifferent performance of emerging business ventures.

Although there is a wealth of material underpining the clinical usage of Transactional Analysis the application of T.A. to organisations is in its infancy and in order to avoid the dangers of reification of a Clinical Model to an organisational setting, there is a need for the development of sound and cmpirically verified models of T.A. as applied to organisations. The aim of this paper is to present a model of the T.A. concept of 'script' as applied to small business development, supported by empirical data.

Scripts

According to Berne (1972) a script is: "*a life plan made in childhood, reinforced by parents, justified by subsequent events and culminating in a chosen alternative*"

Berne is using the term script analogous to its usage in a theatrical setting denoting, 'a story to be acted out before an audience' (Hay 1992). In essence what Berne is suggesting is that early on in our lives, as a consequence of the interactions we have with our parents and significant others, we make decisions about the kind of people we are, whether or not we are going to be successful and what the quality of our lives is going to be. There is a wealth of literature in support of this (Steiner 1974, Berne 1972) and the following cases may illustrate the point further.

Claudia was reared in a family in which her parents were continually telling her that she was a quick developer and very clever. This was reinforced by family friends who commented upon Claudia's interest in reading books suggesting that she will be successful at school. In order to ensure the love and attention of her parents Claudia accepts these labels and decides to continue to read and show an interest in school world In terms of her life plan Claudia could become a successful academic and theoretician, thus confirming the decisions she made early on in her life.

Michael grows up in a lower class family in which his parents, in response to their own frustrations, are continually telling him that 'if he fights for what he wants and is determined he will eventually achieve his aims'. Michael chooses to accept these parental messages and as an adult becomes the highly aggressive owner of a financially successful business venture.

Although these two examples are oversimplified and underscore the complexity of scripts and scripting they provide an illustration of the way in which early experiences can influence later developments and achievements. Stapleton and Murkison (1988, 1989, 1990) have explored directly the relationship between the individual scripts of entrepreneurs and the success or failure of business. Key influences were the age at which the entrepreneur decided to go into business and the fantasies they have as children concerning success and failure. The implications of this work for the ownermanagers of small businesses at the start-up, consolidation or growth stages of development are quite significant. However, before considering these implications we need to further explore the theoretical basis of scripts and scripting.

A script contains information about the destination and outcome of an individuals life plan and also about the process involved in achieving that outcome.

SCRIPT = PROCESS + OUTCOME

There are many types of script, and it is beyond the scope of this paper to explore these fully. For a more detailed exploration of the various classifications of script see Berne 1961, Woollams and Brown 1978, Berne 1972, Steiner 1974. However in 1961 Berne outlined three types of script which illustrate the process and outcome facets of scripting and which provide a useful basis for a typology of scripting as applied to organisations. The three types of script are Winners, Losers and Banal scripts.

'Losers' are continually caught up in grief, hardship and tragedy at all levels. We can recognise a losers script in people who are continually in trouble at school they choose the wrong job, may get fired or become redundant or they may be in conflict with the authorities. Berne described the different degrees of severity of the outcome of a losers script. A first degree losing script is one where the failures and losses are mild enough to be discussed in the persons social circle, for example mild depression, failure at college examinations or inability to hold down a job. Second degree losers experience outcomes which tend not to be the topic of social conversation. This could involve being fired from a series of jobs or experiencing a number of very distressing relationship breakdowns. A third degree losing script culminates in death, serious injury or a legal crisis. For example imprisonment for the embezzlement of funds, death from a stress induced heart attack or suicide following the collapse of a small business venture.

Steiner (1974) focuses more upon the process of achieving the script outcome and suggests that people achieve their script outcome as a consequence of either not thinking, not experiencing closeness and intimacy with others or not experiencing joy and fulfilment throughout life. This focus upon process is easily recognisable in the case of the losers script, although it also operates with the winners and banal script.

'Winners' are apparently successful and achieve what they set out to do. For example the student who achieves top grades in their chosen subject could be a winner. The owner-manager who establishes her own small firm which achieves a turnover of 2 million pounds within three years could be a winner. However, if the person is following a winners script this suggests that winning is more of a response to an early script decision than genuinely satisfying the individuals needs in the here and now. A typical example is the successful business person who reaches their mid 40's having built up a successful company only to lose interest, become disillusioned and wonder why they spend so much time at work.

Berne also outlined the 'Banal' or 'Non-Winner' script to describe individuals whose early decisions lead them towards living in the middle of the road. The non-winner plods along from day to day not making any big wins but not making any big losses either. Berne suggests that the majority of us fit the non-winner script to some extent. To summarize so far script theory postulates that the decisions individuals make in their early years in response to the influences of significant others and events in the environment, have a significant and predictive effect upon the process and outcomes of their lives. Moreover, this paper suggests that the decisions made by key figures in the early years of the emergence of a business venture, will have a powerful influence upon the process and outcome of the business itself. Indeed the suggestion is that organisations have scripts in a similar way to the scripts of individuals.

Organisational Scripts

An organisational script can be defined as:
> *'A life plan for the business made at the time of its birth and during its early developmental stages. A life plan which is moulded by key figures in the business, influenced by key factors in the surrounding economic, social and political environment and reinforced by subsequent events. This life plan culminates in a particular outcome for the business'*

The following is an illustration of the effect of an hypothetical organisation's script. Company A, an industrial cleaning contractor was founded in 1976 by a hard working and determined husband and wife partnership. During the first five years the business established a sound customer base, took on 31 full and part-time employees and provided a satisfying level of income for both the owners and the employees. In the second year of operadon the husband and wife attempted to take a major potential customer away from a competitor and suffered financial losses which almost led to receivership. A decision was made to stay relatively small and focus upon survival rather than growth. In 1984 the major competitor folded and there was every opportunity for Company A to take over many of its competitors established customers if only it would take the risk of a substantial capital investment. In view of the events of 1978 the Board of Directors decided against investment and expansion. In 1986 Company A folded having lost over 60% of its customer base to a highly aggressive successor to its previous competitor.

This example shows quite clearly how decisions made by key persons in response to events within the business environment had a powerful and determining effect upon the eventual destiny of the company.

Design of the study

This model of organisational scripts is a novel approach to understanding the process of entrepreneurship. Theoretically it is still in its infancy and requires conceptual development in order to assess both its predictive value as an explanation of entrepreneurial success and failure and as the basis for planned interventions.

A sample of 20 owner-managers of SMEs based in the North East of England were interviewed about their organisation script. The semi-structured interview was based upon the components of an organisational script outlined in Figure 1. The interviews were audio recorded and transcribed for later analysis. Analysis of the interviews involved listening to the interview tapes and picking out the major themes. The themes provided the basis for a classification system to be reapplied to the transcripts with a view to exploring its validity and reliability in a further investigation. Quotations taken from the interviews are included within the results and analysis section to illustrate the different components of organisational scripts. When appropriate this is supported by already existent literature.

The results and analysis section concludes with a case study drawn together from comments of the owner-managers studies. Although based upon actual businesses it is hypothetical to protect the confidentiality of companies involved in the study.

Results and analysis

1. Business life plan: outcomes

As was mentioned in the discussion of individual scripts some people choose to be winners. The same occurs with organisational scripts and this became apparent during the interviews. During the early years of a businesses development some owner-managers decide that their firm is going to be hugely successful no matter what the cost. This was expressed directly by one owner-manager who said 'We are going to be the best'. Alternatively, although this may sound rather irrational some owner-managers suggest that they 'don't really think they will be able to survive in face of the steep competition'. Although this did not manifest within the present study this was probably due to the sample of businesses and the methodology used. The literature already exists which shows how such statements can act as a self-fulfilling prophec:y. Further, certain owner-managers suggest that they do not want to produce the most successful business, as indicated by the following comment, 'I don't want this business to be a huge success. It is a means of providing income and security. I actually resist it growing'. According to script theory these three predicted and/or desired outcomes can set the scene for everything else to follow in the firms on going development.

2. Business life plan: process

Individual script theory suggests that people have one or two preferred styles of living and working and these can be seen quite clearly in the operation of a business. Within Transactional Analysis these styles of living and working are referred to as 'Drivers' to reflect their driven or compulsive quality. In terms of individual development, Driver behaviour is both a response to the messages we received from our parents as to how we should behave and the decisions we made about what we needed to do to satisfy our parents.

There are five primary working styles which are seen in organisations and constitute a significant part of the organisations script.

Organisations with a 'Be Perfect' driver are striving for perfection and expect others to do so. This is based upon the assumption that if everything is not exactly right then as an organisation they are not OK Be Perfect organisations can go into excessive detail in order to ensure the highest quality standards. The positive side of a Be Perfect organisation is the achievement of excellence in output (Clarkson 1992), however the negative side of the Be Perfect dnver is over attention to unnecessary detail in an attempt to avoid making a mistake at all costs.

A number of businesses had Be Perfect drivers as the following comments illustrate, 'We need to be very careful with a lot of procedural checks and a high level of supervision', 'Quality overrides everything'.

The emergence of Total Quality Management (TQM) in recent years provides an illustration of how a Be Perfect driver can have positive and negative effects. On the one hand focussing upon quality in procedures and output can draw attention to flaws and lead to genuine improvements. On the other hand this could interrupt the organisations spontaneity and output by imposing too many 'quality control' restrictions. The introduction of BS5750 in the United Kingdom is an illustration of how procedures can stifle an organisation.

Organisations with a 'Please People' driver feel responsible for making other people feel good. Underlying this is a need to be liked by people. The positive side of a Please People driver is care and attention being paid to the needs of customers, and this driver is at the heart of many 'customer-care' and 'customer-delight' philosophies. In itself this is not a bad thing as many organisaffons have for too long ignored the needs of their customers, a factor which could lead to their own downfall. However the negative side of a Please People driver is where the organisation goes out of its way to satisfy the needs of others to the detriment of its own needs. Please People organisations may avoid criticism of others and are liable to accept interruptions in a pleasant and assuming fashion which again could disrupt the organisations effectiveness.

The following comment illustrates a Please People driver, 'It's all about building up relationships with customers. I've got to find out what they want and provide it. I am always wanting to know if we are giving our customers what they want'.

Organisations with a 'Try Hard' driver focus upon the effon required to do something and are often enthusiastic and motivated when it comes to new ideas and new projects. The positive side of the Try Hard driver is the enthusiasm and energy they generate and a willingness to think about lots of new ideas and potential projects. The negative side of Try Hard is the emphasis upon commitment to Trying rather than completing and succeeding as interest seems to wear off before the project is finished.

The following comment is illustrative of a Try Hard driver, 'Opening up was very exciting and very thrilling. We were very enthusiastic then ... Now I can see other branches and divenifications which are very attractive and exciting'.

In individual terms the Try Hard is the opposite of Belbins team role description of Completer-Finisher (Belbin 1981), and at an organisational level one can picture quite clearly the danger to a small emerging business of becoming overly enthusiastic in many projects because of the excitement of newness and not successfully completing any or enough of them.

Organisations with a 'Be Strong' driver give off the impression that they are always able to cope, even under high degrees of pressure and stress. These organisations are good at staying calm and appear to be able to address the task at hand even though there may be many other things to do. Should a crisis occur these organisations will structure their work in order to be able to address the crisis and continue to produce the goods. During the recession which has hit Britain in the past couple of years Be Strong organisations have been able to cope and thus survive as a result of their Capacity for Endurance (Clarkson 1992).

However, the negative side of a Be Strong organisation is that it is liable to take on too much work and become overloaded and eventually fail to satisfy the needs of its customers. With a Be Strong organisation the overload of work tends to increase gradually and the difficulties of managing the load are ignored and denied. Eventually, a Be Strong organisation may crack as evidenced by the loss of significant orders and customers or indeed the loss of key members of staff who are no longer able to maintain the 'I can cope' image.

The following comment illustrates a Be Strong driver, 'You need to give off the impression that you can cope for the banks and customers to maintain confidence in you. If you look as if you can't people will take their business else where and the bank may takes its support away'.

The 'Hurry Up' organisation operates as if everything has to be done 'right now'. They operate quickly and get a lot done in a short time and can thus achieve a rernarkable output of work. Hurry Up organisations respond well to deadlines and have a functional sense of urgency. These organisations do have a capacity for working out the quickest and most effective way of getting a job done.

A comment from one owner-manager illustrates this, 'We do seem to work best under pressure, you know when the Adrenalin is pumping'.

However, the negative side of the Hurry Up driver is that jobs are left until a sense of urgency arises as deadlines become nearer and this can lead to errors and mistakes and the quality of work can at times be poor. People in Hurry Up organisations tend to think quickly, speak quickly and interrupt others by finishing their sentences. As such they may not hear what their customers are actually saying and thus not provide what they are actually asking for. This can compound the sense of urgency when the customer returns the product which requires modification because the original specifications have not been met.

3. Key Influences: Internal

Individuals within the business clearly have a powerful effect upon, and are a significant aspect of, an organisations script, and there are numerous accounts within the literature of the influence of founding fathers upon the operation of a company. Beynons (1984) 'Working for Ford' is a powerful expose of the influence Henry Ford had upon the style and direction of The Ford Motor Company. More recently studies by Hennessy (1980) and Banks (1982) have shown how the personality and behaviour of entrepreneurs such as Terrance Conran and Freddie Laker have influenced the development of their businesses. In an interesting commentary upon the growth of the Trust House Forte empire Hennessy (1980) noted Sir Charles Forte's belief that the 'cardinal sin in this company is unpunctuality'. Those words having a powerful effect throughout the organisation. When considering script development within an emerging business venture it is necessary to acknowledge all of the key influences in addition to the owner-manager. When asked who they saw as having a significant influence upon the way the business operates owner-managers listed a range of people including themselves, their business partners, their spouses and early employees.

The influence of different individuals upon the development of an organisations script can be explored in terms of the drivers discussed in the previous section. If the owner-manager of a business has a Try Hard driver and a senior partner has a Be Perfect driver this could be a recipe for great success or disaster. On the positive side the Try Hard driver could facilitate the development of a creative and enthusiastic organisation, the quality of which would be maintained by the influence of the Be Perfect driver. However the enthusiasm of the Try Hard driver could lead to the initiation of many new and exciting projects none of which come to fruition as a consequence of the Be Perfect's over attention to detail.

A number of authors have highlighted the influence of newly appointed Chief Executives in some of the major established companies. Deal and Kennedy (1982) refer to Adolph Oches at the New York Times and Harold Geneen at I.T.T. whose 'personality and management style' had a powerful influence upon attitudes and behaviour throughout their respective organisations. Script theory would Inake two observations here. Firstly, many of the difficulties experienced by these two Chief Executives could be explained as a conflict between the dictates of their own individual scripting and the already established script of the organisation. Secondly, one can hypothesize that a clash between the new scripting and the established scripting could affect the physical and emotional health of employees within the organisation.

4. Key Influences: External

It would be overly deterministic to view an organisational script as a consequence of internal events. There are very powerful events within the economic, social and political environment. Those most commonly referred to by the owner-managers being the banks, customers, suppliers, the support network and the economic life cycle.

During the start-up phase and early development of a business the banks and other sources of financial support can influence the development of an organisations script. If the banks behaviour towards the business is controlling and restricting this could have a direct effect upon the company's capacity to grow. In addition key personnel within the business may decide that the bank is not a source of support for 'risky' investments and may hold back from approaching the bank in the future, when in fact they may be sympathetic to and supportive of new developments. One owner-manager commented that he had 'a bad experience in the early days and I keep away from the bank if I can'. Alternatively the bank may take the role of a steady supporting influence offering both financial resources and business advice. This could provide a huge source of stability for the emerging business venture allowing it to develop a sense of self-confidence which forms the basis for its future development. One owner-manager described the bank as a 'huge source of support. They have been very good for us'.

Certain businesses are more prone to the control and dictates of suppliers than others and in the early stages of development the organisation may not have the business experience required to establish a fair business relationship as the following comment illustrates 'We were very naive at the start and too reliant upon our suppliers who really hindered our progress'. This could lead to the development of a very aggressive or passive attitude to suppliers which could have negative effects upon the future success of the business. Customers are another major influence upon the development of an organisations script. In certain businesses there may be an established customer base for the new business to move into and this could lead the organisation to become complacent about the need to ensure an on going market for products. The consequences of this for the business are obvious. For example one owner-manager acknowledged, 'I moved into an already structured customer base and this has made me a little complacent'. The influence of the support network can also have a crucial effect upon an organisations script. The advice and guidance offered by consultants, business schools and other training agencies can offset the establishment of bad practice before it is ingrained into the organisations script. This can lead to the development of an evaluated and rational approach to business as opposed to a driven approach. One owner-manager acknowledged that 'the Business School has had a very good effect upon this business'.

In addition to these sources of external influence there are more general influences. Government initiatives and support can provide a useful support to a business in the early days as the following comment illustrates, 'Government legislation is becoming increasingly stringent and that means more scope for people like me'.

5. Significant Events

The final area to be touched upon in both the development and content of an organisations script is the significant events in the companrs early history. The event may be a key staff member leaving which leads to the loss of a necessary company resource. This was apparent in one business and made the senior partner 'very careful when it comes to employing staff'.

Another example of the influence of significant early events is the case of a business which invested a lot of money into the opening a new factory. The effect of this was to create to the business world the impression that the firm was well grounded and able to cope with a wide range of requests. However, the infrastructure of the business was unable to meet the orders and requests from customers and underwent a very stressful two year period of meeting some orders, but missing other deadlines and occasionally producing low quality output. The event is remembered as presenting too confident an image too quickly and as such this organisation now has a very cautious script which occasionally means it misses out on orders which it could adequately cope with.

A case study

The idea to form company B arose in November 1989 and the business was founded in July 1990. The two senior partners were Sheila, a very industrious and enthusiastic pharmaceutical sales representative with lots of ideas who saw an opportunity for the skills of Kevin, a quieter and very meticulous industrial designer. At the time of start up Colin, another industrial designer with a flair for creativity and enthusiasm, was brought into the business. The aim at the beginning was to fonn a team of three with Sheila representing the business to the outside world.

During the late 1980's there were many industrial design businesses in the North of England, with a glut of qualified designers emerging from local colleges. In addition the 'recession' in Britain had imposed constraints upon the market place. Sheila, Kevin and Colin were entering a difficult sector. Although the business plan was put together in fine detail by Kevin, the banks were uncertain as to the viability of the venture and imposed heavy interest rates on their financial support. As a consequence of this Sheila had to be overly aggressive in seeking out contracts and Kevin and Colin had to work vely long hours to be able to produce the highest quality work which Kevin demands.

As a consequence of Sheila's marketing ability a major contract was secured in January 1991 which all three employees saw as a 'great opportunity' for the business. However, in order to meet the strict time deadline two designers were employed on a temporary basis. Due to their lack of experience at recruitment Geoff fitted in well whereas Simon was a bad selection and caused a lot of difficulty within the business by arriving late for work and not producing quality output. In addition this caused difficulties between Kevin and Sheila, particularly as Sheila's marketing was temporarily not required as the 'books were full'. In May 1991 Simon was finished. Eventually the contract was completed two days beyond schedule to bring to an end a tumultuous and distressing period in the company's history. The contract was viewed as a huge success and in view of all of the difficulties Kevin and Sheila decided that 'if we can go through all of that and still produce the goods we should make it big'.

Towards the end of 1991 Sheila secured another major contract in the face of stiff competition from two competitors. To ensure she gained the contract Sheila promised a completion date before the one agreed with Kevin. Once again there was a need for temporary support and Kevin was quite insistent that following their previous experience he would ensure they employed the correct person. As such he spent a great deal of time recruiting another member of staff, time which should have been allocated to the actual project. Eventually Martin was employed and proved to be very efficient and became so integral to the business that Colin was feeling pushed out and alienated. In April 1992 Colin left to form his own business. Fortunately this was right at the end of the contract and only had the effect of delaying the final designs by eight days and once again high quality work was produced if a little late and with a great deal of personal distress amongst the remaining employees.

Company B is still in existence.

Script Analysis

Key internal influences upon the development of Company B were Sheila, Kevin, Colin, Geoff, Simon and Martin. Sheila and Colin's enthusiasm and creative energy has led to the development of a Try Hard' organisation where by new projects are greeted with huge enthusiasm even though the business does not always have the resources necessary to complete them on time. In addition, Kevin's influence has led to the development of a 'Be Perfect' driver with high attention being paid to quality, even at the cost of missing completion dates.

The stringent constraints imposed by the bank at the start led Kevin and Sheila to decide that they will go it alone in future and not take out any unnecessary loans. 'We've done it so far without the support of the bank so we can continue to do so'.

The earliest employees in Company B have also affected the script. The experience with Simon has enhanced Kevin's desire to get it right even if that requires a level of input which takes him away from the actual design work of the company. Both Kevin and Sheila now find it difficult to delegate and have an expressed plan not to take a holiday for the next three years. This high work load could lead to 'Burnout' for one or both of them. In addition the experiences with the bank, with new staff and with missing deadlines has lead both Kevin and Sheila to recognise that 'although we can do it and do make money, we now know that its always going to be difficult'. As such the organisational script of Company B contains the seeds of potential disaster and although it is too early to make fir˜n

predications script theory suggests that the following issues be addressed:
- There is a need for Kevin and Sheila to recognise their own 'Driver' behaviour and how it is a potential source of conflict between them and could also have a detrimental effect upon the business.
- Although Kevin's Be Perfect behaviour leads to high quality output it needs to be integrated with Sheila's enthusiasm for securing new contracts and to take into account the possibility that some firms will not accept late completion dates.
- The human resource issues of recruitment and delegation of work also need to be addressed and Kevin and Sheila need to become aware of the dangers of not doing so as this could affect both the economic viability of the business and their own personal health.

Conclusions

Script theory provides a theoretical model of small business development which incorporates individual psychology, interpersonal relationships and organisation development and shows how one can be affected by the other. The interviews with owner-managers illustrate its validity as a means of understanding process and outcomes for a small business. However there is also a need for longitudinal studies of businesses to trace the determining effects of organisational scripting and thus the predictive capacity of this model.

Although the model of organisational scripting is deterministic it acknowledges the influence of factors internal and external to the organisation. Moreover, by understanding the determining aspect of an organisations script interventions can be made to overcome the negative effects.

Implicit within the Transactional Analytic approach to small business development is the call for a more holistic model of success and failure. After all is it really correct to refer to a business as a success if the senior partner is divorced from bis wife, estranged from bis cbildren and suffering from hypertension and angina at the age of 48 years?

References

Banks, H (1982) *The Rise and Fall of Freddie Laker*, Faber and Faber Ltd. London

Belbin, M R (1981) *Management Teams: Why They Succeed or Fail*, Butterworth-Heinemann Ltd

Berne, E (1961) *Transactional Analysis in Psychotherapy*, Grove Press. New York Berne, E (1972) *What Do You Say After You Say Hello?*, Corgi Books. London Beynon, H (1984) *Working for Ford*, Penguin 2nd Ed. London

Clarkson, P (1992) In Praise of Speed, Experimentation, Agreeableness, Endurance and Excellence: Counterscript Drivers and Aspiration. *Transactional Analysis Journal*, Volume 22, No. 1, January, pp 16-20

DeaL T and Kennedy, A (1982) *Corporate Cultures: The Rites and Rituals of Corporate Life*, Penguin Books. London

Hay, J (1992) *Transactional Analysis for Trainers*, McGraw Hill. Maidenhead, England

Hennessy, E (1980) *The Entrepreneurs*, Scope Books. Newbury, England

Stapleton, R J and Murkison, G (1990) Scripts and Entrepreneurship. *Transactional Analysis Journal*, Volume 20, No. 3, July, pp 193-197

Stapleton, R J and Murkison, G (1988) Entrepreneurial Learning and Small Business Failure Rates. In H Desai (Ed.) *Proceedings of The Institute for Management Science, 24th Annual Meeting*, pp 180-190

Stapleton, R J and Murkison, G (1989) Entrepreneurial Autonomy and Success. In J R Baker and R T Sumichrast (Eds.) *Proceedings of The Institute of Management Science, 25th Annual Meeting*, pp 98-100

Steiner, C (1974) *The Scripts People Live. Transactional Analysis of Life Scripts*, GrovePress. NewYork

Woollams, S and Brown, M (1978) *Transactional Analysis*, Huron Valley Institute Press. Michigan

Figure 1. Components of an Organisational Script

Business life plan: outcomes

To succeed
To fail or struggle
To be safe

Business life plan: process

To work hard
To produce high quality
To be enthusiastic
To please customers
To be quick

Key influences: internal

Founding partners
Key directors
Earliest employees

Key influences: external

Banks
Customers
Suppliers
Economic Cycle
Network

Significant events

Initial order
Opening factory
Product success

27 Psychological profiling: Implications for the training of entrepreneurs

Rachel Mulholland and Elizabeth McVeigh

Summary

Business schools and enterprise agencies continue to design courses aimed at the development of entrepreneurs. Many are aimed specifically at training entrepreneurs in functional business skills but some would question whether such knowledge is essential, (Vesper et al 1989). How effective then are the courses offered to entrepreneurs and how can they be improved?

In this paper it is suggested that psychological instruments can be used to improve the design of entrepreneurial training courses and be of assistance to the entrepreneurs in their own development.

Psychological devices have been extensively used in the search for the definitive description of the 'entrepreneur'. Whilst this debate still goes on practitioners should use the psychological information already gained to optimise the effectiveness of the programmes offered to entrepreneurs.

Using psychological information can help in the assessment of the strengths and weaknesses of individuals in relation to their businesses. Such insights are relevant not only to entrepreneurs but also very much to trainers. In the former case a greater sense of self-awareness can assist in all areas of business interactions. Trainers can use the information for example, to design training which matches the preferred styles of those in the group, to cater for individual development needs and to co-ordinate team work.

The present study was carried out with thirty-three entrepreneurs embarking on an entrepreneurial training programme. The majority had been in business between one and five years. Before the programme commenced a range of psychological inventories was used to give a broad profile of each participant. The inventories used were: the Entrepreneurial Style and Success Indicator (ESSI), the General Enterprising Tendency Test (GET), the Herrmann Brain Dominance Inventory (HBDI) and the 16PF.

Individual feedback of the results of each inventory was given in a follow-up counselling session. A group session was also carried out to improve the group awareness of their individual differences. The programme co-ordinator also took part in the general profile talk and exercise in order to increase his awareness of the group characteristics.

On the basis of the information obtained a number of recommendations were made about the design and content of the programme.

Introduction

Most development programmes for entrepreneurs in Ireland involve the participants attending local training courses with their peers at which they can acquire the functional knowledge and skills considered necessary to successfully run their business. This would seem to be typical of training programmes in other countries, where the teaching of such subjects as marketing, finance and general management skills are considered important (Moran and Lamshead (1991), Vesper et al (1989), Sexton and Bowman-Upton (1987, 1988)). Vesper et al (1989) would question whether training, which focuses on such subjects as separate and distinct categories of activity alone, is sufficient to effectively develop entrepreneurs. They suggest that "entrepreneurship has a concern with the various functional aspects of a business but in a much more holistic sense. Small new organisations simply cannot afford much functional specialisation." (p.63). The lack of emphasis on an integrative and holistic approach may be related to the characteristics of programme co-ordinators and trainers whose own background is often one of concrete and specific business expertise. Moran and Lamshead (1991) point out an imbalance among small business support services with 'insufficient emphasis on strategic issues and future possibilities for the business as compared with a concern for the concrete, here-and-now realities of the business.' (p.8). Raj Jain and Akbar Ansari (1989) also emphasise the detrimental effects of a short-term focus and suggest that business owners need to be assisted in developing a more long term perspective on their business.

Recent research on the training and development of entrepreneurs have suggested a number of areas which should be addressed to improve the effectiveness of entrepreneurial development programmes. Sexton and Bowman-Upton (1987, 1988) evaluated and validated an innovative approach to the teaching of entrepreneurship. They profiled their participants and on the results of this designed a programme to increase the overall effectiveness of the learning experiences of their participants. They suggested that entrepreneurship training should be unstructured, more focused on independent study and provide opportunities for problem solving in situations involving greater ambiguity and risk. Vesper et al (1989) put forward a similar argument stressing the need for entrepreneurial education to offer individual entrepreneurs greater responsibility in determining their own educational needs and move beyond a microcosm of MBA-type courses and instead a microcosm of real-life business creation and development, offering opportunities to learn and develop ones skills in order to be able to operate in the complex and uncertain environment of entrepreneurial business. Sexton and Bowman-Upton (1987, 1988) also highlighted the importance of developing the individual entrepreneur's interpersonal skills as their participants profiles suggested tendencies to be more independent, unpredictable and aloof.

These findings and commentaries emphasise the challenge to programme designers not to shirk the responsibility to examine the traditional training methods used and design programmes to the specific needs of their participants.

If programmes are to be designed to meet individual needs a psychological input is crucial . Although some researchers in the past have said this element is unimportant it is becoming increasingly recognised, not only by professional psychologists but also by practitioners in the field that a person-focussed approach to the development of entrepreneurs will lead to more effective learning. Moran and Lamshead (1991) word it more strongly in arguing that the 'business counsellor needs to be as much psychologist as business expert.' (p.11)

The Present Study and Background

The programme on which the present study was based was designed as an innovative approach in response to the training needs of Irish entrepreneurs. With the support of government agencies the "Development of Entrepreneurs in soston for Ireland" (DEBI) was launched in 1989 in an attempt to stimulate the growth of small business enterprises. From the outset it was intended that the entrepreneurs, (selected from the whole of Ireland) should, as the contemporary research was indicating, be offered more than specific management skills training. Along with core topics such as strategy formulation, finance and marketing the training is customised to the needs of the individuals' businesses. As far as possible training is practical, challenging and flexible. An interesting feature is that the main training component takes place in the USA presenting a greater challenge to their entrepreneurial skills.

Although the programme tried to incorporate many of the findings of the entrepreneurial research literature it was still felt that an important element was not being fully addressed, namely, catering for the needs of the entrepreneur as an individual. To redress this imbalance a psychological input was considered. As stated previously, Moran and Lamshead (1991) consider the psychological input in training to be as important as business knowledge but the problem in the past has been how to sift from the mass of information available that which is most relevant and practical to both the immediate and longer term needs of the small business owners.

Much of the entrepreneurial research of late has focused on narrow psychological aspects, in an effort to determine the definitive description of the entrepreneur.

However, there is still much debate about who the entrepreneur is and what motivates their decision to set up in business. It is widely suggested that a combination of factors, such as, family background, personal characteristics, educational experience and work histories influence the decision to set up in business (de Vries (1977), Shenson and Anderson

(1989)). Some place more emphasis on the key role that personal characteristics play in determining business founding. Many studies have been conducted to determine the characteristics of entrepreneurs. The importance of high need for achievement (nAch) has been cited by many researchers (e.g. McClelland (1961), Lachman (1980), Johnson (1990)). Other characteristics such as lower need for support, greater independence and leadership are also said to differentiate successful entrepreneurs from other groups. Cromie and Johns (1983) said that entrepreneurs display greater achievement motivation, persistence, self-confidence, autonomy and internal locus of control. In a literature review conducted by Caird (1988) she concluded that the major entrepreneurial tendencies are need for achievement, need for autonomy, an internal locus of control, creativity and calculated risk taking.

Herrmann (1988) suggests that entrepreneurs have a thinking preference which is characterised by curiosity, imagination, future orientation, intuition and enjoyment of risks. However technical entrepreneurs have a dual thinking preference which combines logic, analysis and facts with those listed above. Similar results were obtained by INC (1988). High-growth company founders were found to favour the intuition (future orientation) category of the Myers-Briggs Inventory.

But the emphasis for psychological input in entrepreneurial research should not be on either person or environment. As Shaver and Scott (1991) state 'psychology combines external circumstance with intrapsychic processes' (p.25) and thus its 'focus on the person as the unit of analysis should not be construed as equivalent to a search for personological variables that, regardless of the situation, produce behaviours that lead to the creation of new ventures',(p.28).

The present study aimed to apply psychology in entrepreneurial training and development in the way suggested by such people as Shaver and Scott (1991) i.e. focusing on individual entrepreneurs and their businesses rather than on a composite 'entrepreneur'. Stammers and Patrick (1975) also stressed that by designing training programmes aimed at addressing the needs of an 'average' trainee one was not necessarily optimising the effectiveness and efficiency of the programme. They pointed out the importance of being aware of the profiles of all trainees and not just the average profile of a group. In this way one would be able to develop courses which could accommodate both the similarities and differences between trainees, thereby maximising the benefits of training and development for each participant.

It was felt therefore that the DEBI programme could benefit from the use of psychological profiling of its participants. It was decided that a range of inventories should be used to give a broad profile of each participant. The inventories administered were: the Entrepreneurial Style and Success Indicator (ESSI), the General Enterprising Tendency (GET), the Herrmann Brain Dominance Instrument (HBDI) and the 16PF. Further details of the instruments can be found in the Appendices.

On the basis of the information gained from the inventories the individual entrepreneurs could understand themselves more fully and programme trainers/co-ordinators and counsellors could also make more accurate assessments of the needs of the participants at both a group and individual level.

In this paper the applications and usefulness of the psychological profiling of entrepreneurs will be discussed.

Subjects

The subjects were 33 entrepreneurs wishing to be considered for acceptance onto the DEBI Programme. There were 6 female entrepreneurs and 27 males ranging in age from 22 to 60 years. Figure 1 illustrates the distribution of ages within this range.

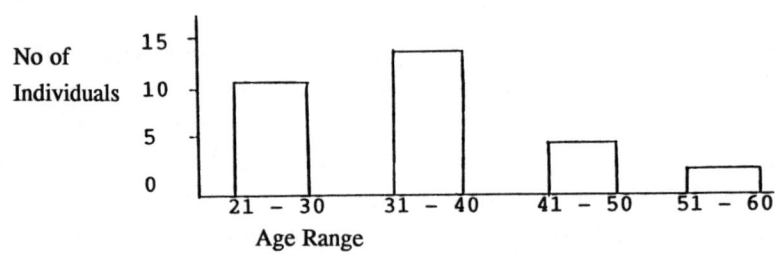

Figure 1. Age range of business owners

The group were also representative of a range of business types at varying stages of development.

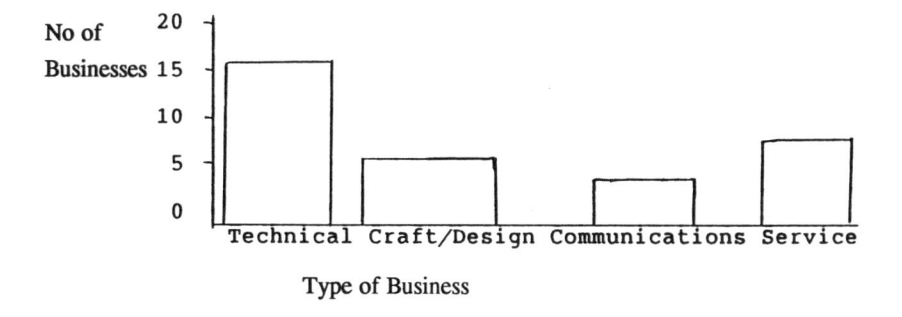

```
No of      20
Businesses 15
           10
            5
            0
              Technical Craft/Design Communications Service
                          Type of Business
```

Figure 2. Type of business

The majority of businesses (63.6%) were new, having been established less than one year. 21.2% of the businesses had been established for between one and five years, while 15.2% were over five years in existence.

Method

The subjects were all tested under standardised conditions using the four psychological measures described, (E.S.S.I., G.E.T., and the 16PF). Three hours were given for completion of the tests, which included a break of fifteen minutes.

Results

E.S.S.I. Part 1

For the entrepreneurial style and success indicator the results are presented as scores on each of the four dimensions, (Behavioural (s),

Cognitive (C), Interpersonal (I) and Affective (A)).

The pattern of scoring for the DEBI group was as shown in Table 1.

Table 1. Average scoring for the DEBI Group on the ESSI Dimensions.

DIMENSION	B	C	I	A
Mean Score	46.1	35.7	36.7	41.1
Maximum score	57	49	57	52
Minimum score	27	27	25	29
Standard Deviation	7.9	5.9	8.9	6.7

(Any score above 40 is considered as a high dimension area, while any score below 35 is considered a low dimension area). As Table 1 illustrates none of the mean scores of dimensions were in the low range of the scale, although the Cognitive and Interpersonal dimensions were in the borderline score levels. The maximum and minimum scores for each dimension highlight the diverse range of scores existing within the group. Some peoples scores were in the 'very high' range of dimensions whereas other members scores fell within the 'low' score range for the dimensions.

The Behavioural dimension was the highest scoring of the four, for the group. The most prevalent pattern of scoring, (made up of those dimensions scoring above 40), was the Behavioural/Cognitive : pattern, termed 'Self reliant' type. Of the group 35.5% showed this pattern. The Behavioural/Affective ('Confident' type) and the Affective/Behavioural ('Freelancing' type) patterns made up 41.9% of the group. The Interpersonal/Affective pattern ('Networking' type) made up 12.9% of the group. The remaining 9.7% of the group comprised the Affective/Interpersonal ('Flexible' type), the Cognitive/Affective ('Astute' type), and the Interpersonal/Cognitive pattern ('Conscientious' type).

E.S.S.I. Part 2

Part 2 of the ESSI related to entrepreneurial attitudes and experiences. 94% of the group scored in the mid range of the scoring band, which is described as indicating that 'the individual has somewhat similar attitudes and previous experiences to successful entrepreneurs and may experience entrepreneurship as desirable, motivating and stimulating' (Shenson and Anderson 1988).

6% scored in the upper range and none scored in the lower range. On average there was agreement within the group with 19 of the 28 entrepreneurial attitudes/life experiences, (i.e. 67.8% agreement).

Table 2 shows the five statements with which there was most agreement and the five with which there was least agreement.

Table 2. Entrepreneurial Attitudes/Experiences Statements with which there was Most and Least Agreement

Statement No.	Statement	Av. Score (Max. =10)
1	I showed an early inclination towards hard work and achievement that has not diminished.	8.8
26	I understand my personal strengths and weaknesses and am willing to modify to improve performance.	8.6
8	I exhibited a strong need early in life to take charge of situations and to be the one in control.	8.4
16	I have the philosophy that I can succeed at just about anything I put my mind to.	8.4
12	I felt strong pressure from my family to appreciate the value of education and learning.	8.3
21	I generally dislike and try to avoid work activities which involve management or supervision.	2.3

6	I have been fired from at least one job or have quit a job in anticipation of being fired.	2.4
4	I tend to establish somewhat difficult barriers such as incurring debt, as a means of motivating myself into action.	2.6
15	I tend to be unsuccessful with and not particularly interested in, outside investments.	3.2
14	I suffer from stress related illnesses and/or problems but find stress exhilarating.	3.5

General enterprising tendency

The average, maximum and minimum scores for the group on the five factors measured by the GET are given in table 3. Included in the table is also the group average for total enterprising tendency score. These can be compared with those expected of enterprising individuals.

Table 3. Group Results for Enterprising Attributes as Measured by GET

FACTOR	Ach	Aut	LC	C	CRT	TOT
Av. Score	10.3	4.3	9.6	9.0	9.7	42.8
Av. Ent. Score	9	4	8	8	8	
Maximum Score	12	6	12	12	12	52
Minimum Score	7*	3	6*	6*	6*	33*

Ach - Achievement
Aut - Autonomy
LC   - Internal Locus of Control
C   - Creativity
CRT - Calculated risk taking
TOT - Total enterprising tendency score

The group showed higher than average scores on each of the measured factors. 'Internal locus of control' and 'calculated risk taking' were the factors with the greatest difference from the entrepreneurial average. Group variability again existed with some enterprising tendencies falling into the 'low' range (see results *) for enterprise attributes of entrepreneurs.

Sixteen personality factors

The group average results for the sixteen primary factors are shown on figure 3. As can be seen they are above average on three of the factors. These are dominance (dominant, aggressive, stubborn, competitive), parmia (bold, venturesome, uninhibited, spontaneous) and radicalism (experimenting, liberal, analytical, free-thinking).

Table 4 shows the ranges of scores within the group for each of the sixteen primary factors.

Table 4. Sixteen primary factors score ranges

Factor	Sten Scores Maximum	Minimum
A	10	2
B	9	3
C	9	4
E	10	5
F	10	2
G	8	2
H	9	5
I	9	2
L	10	2
M	9	2
N	10	2
O	7	2
Q1	10	3
Q2	9	3
Q3	10	2
Q4	8	2

Figure 3. Group Average Results for 16 PF Primary Factors

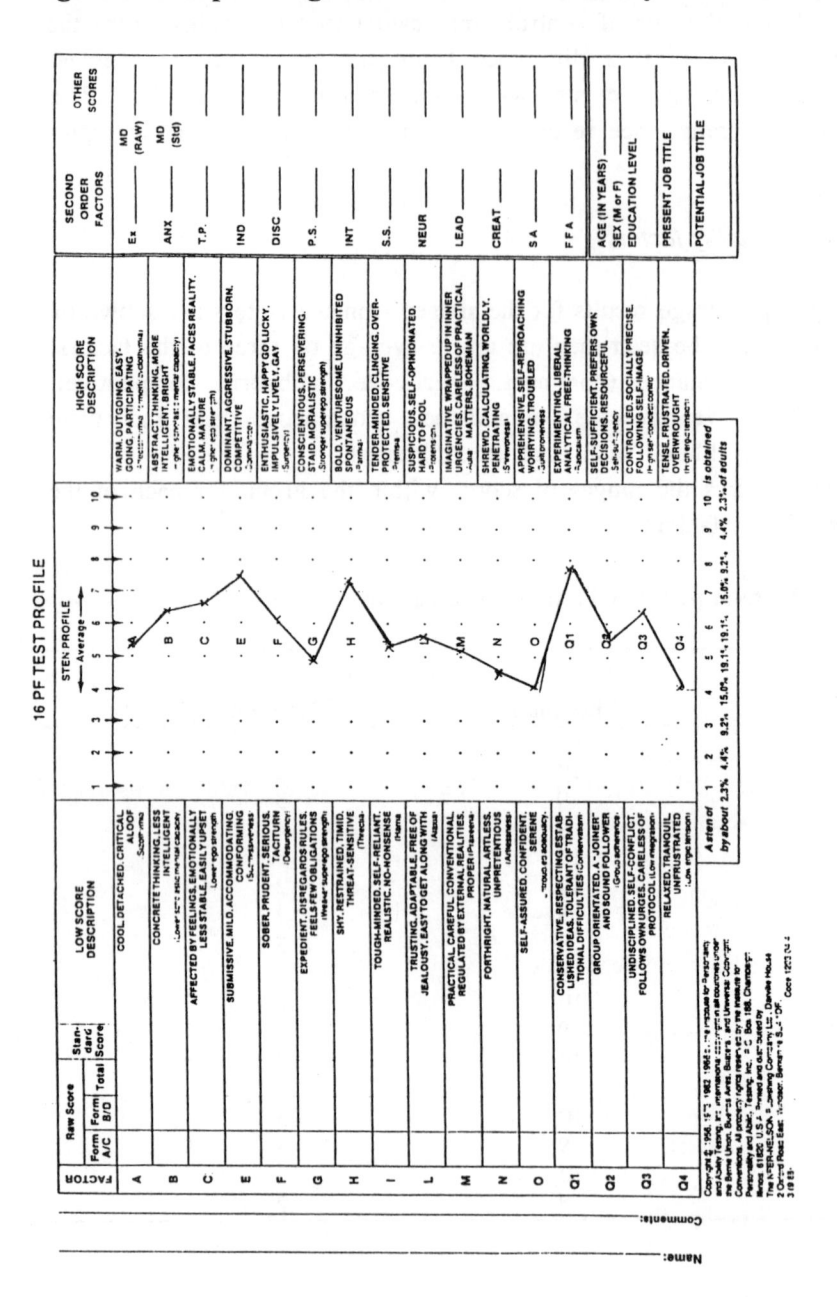

Table 5 shows the conversion of the group primary scores to second order factors.

Table 5 Second Order Factors for 16PF

FACTOR	EX	ANX	TP	I	CTL	AD	L	C
Score	6.4	3.9	5.6	8.1	5.4	7.6	6.8	6.9

EX - Extraversion
ANX- Anxiety
TP - Tough Poise
I - Independence
CTL- Control
AD - Adjustment
L - Leadership
C - Creativity

(High Scores > 7, Low Scores < 4)

The group showed higher than average scores for adjustment and independence and had a lower than average anxiety score.

The 16PF profile pattern derived from the above results is 2123. Individuals with this profile pattern are creative and independent and are 'likely to be unpredictable on occasion', (Krug 1981). Such people value autonomy. Their self confident and radical pattern may cause difficulties in interpersonal relationships. Career theme scores point towards innovation and away from following routine. Again within the group there were individual differences in the extent to which this profile represented individual entrepreneurs and individual Second order Factors and profiles were calculated for each entrepreneur.

Herrmann Brain Dominance Inventory

Thinking preferences are given as four figures representing the four quadrants of A, B, C and D respectively. Primary preferences are represented by 1, secondary preferences by 2 and avoidances by 3.

The HBDI composite scores for the group are presented in Figure 4.

The profile pattern is 1121, indicating primary preferences for A, B and D quadrants with the strongest preference in the D quadrant. There is a secondary preference in the C quadrant. Of the group 15.2% indicated this preference pattern. The 1221 pattern, indicating primary preferences for A, and D quadrants was the most common pattern of the group with 18.2%. The 2111 pattern made up 15.2% and the 2211 pattern 9.1% of the group. The remaining 42.3% of the group encompassed 11 different profile patterns.

THE VISUAL PROFILE DISPLAY

HERRMANN BRAIN DOMINANCE PROFILE

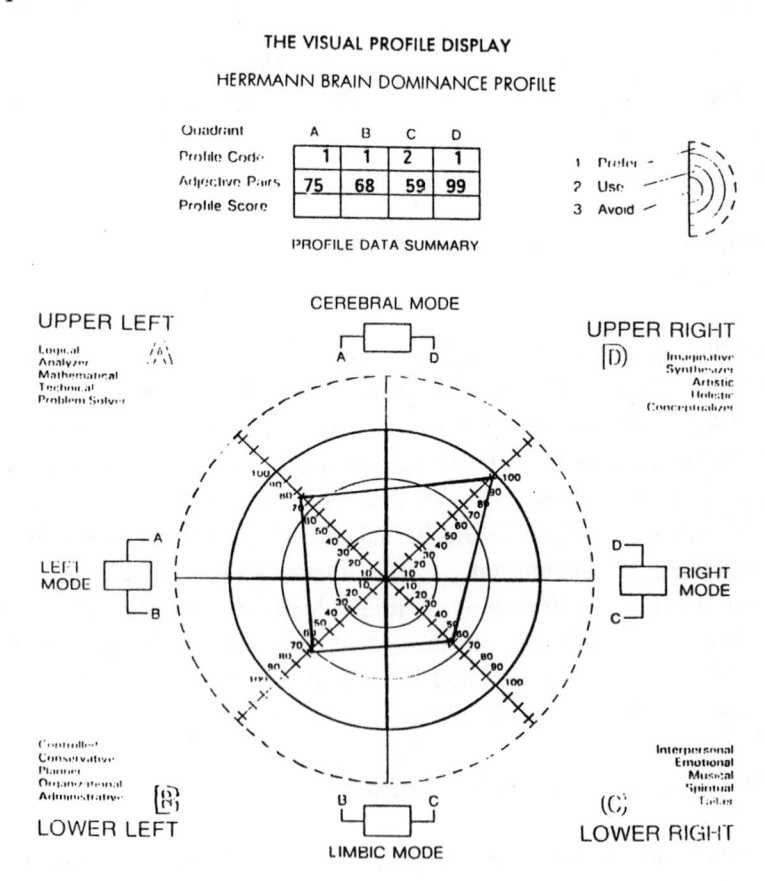

Quadrant	A	B	C	D
Profile Code	1	1	2	1
Adjective Pairs	75	68	59	99
Profile Score				

1 Prefer
2 Use
3 Avoid

PROFILE DATA SUMMARY

UPPER LEFT
Logical
Analyzer
Mathematical
Technical
Problem Solver

CEREBRAL MODE

UPPER RIGHT
Imaginative
Synthesizer
Artistic
Holistic
Conceptualizer

LEFT MODE

RIGHT MODE

Controlled
Conservative
Planner
Organizational
Administrative
LOWER LEFT

Interpersonal
Emotional
Musical
Spiritual
Talker
LOWER RIGHT

LIMBIC MODE

Figure 4. HBDI Composite Scores for the DEBI Group Discussion

Group Characteristics

Despite the diversity of ages, types of business and length of time in their present business the group displayed many common characteristics. Well over half of the group (76.6%) had high scores in the Behavioural dimension of the ESSI. This entrepreneurial style is characterised by 'a strong tendency towards shaping the environment in ways which will achieve goals,' (Shenson and Anderson, 1989). The two main profile patterns of the group were 'confident' and ' self-reliant'.

Those with the former pattern tend to be innovative and driven to action, self-assured and leaders. However problems may arise because they may seem to others to be too self-oriented and 'bull-headed'. People with this pattern are apt to neglect detail, and find it very difficult to relax. In times of stress they become more impatient and aggressive, (especially with other people).

The 'self-reliant' type tends to want total control of the business, and focuses on getting things done whilst attending to detail. They have a strong orientation towards future events and logically plan ahead. Their tendency to critically evaluate often results in others seeing them as insensitive. Under stress they tend to become depressed and moody.

Both of the ESSI profiles are similar to the results of the 16PF, where the profile pattern (2123) for the group suggested that people would encounter difficulties in interpersonal relations. The second order factors indicated that 'independence' and 'adjustment' were higher than average for the entrepreneurs. This suggests that they are more aggressive, daring, incisive, self-confident, assertive, adaptive and flexible than the normal population.

The higher than average internal locus of control, autonomy, and achievement motivation scores (as measured on the GET) are similar to the findings of researchers such as, Caird (1988), Cromie and Johns (1983) and McClelland (1961).

A feature of the group was a free-thinking, liberal attitude and a certain unpredictability (see 16PF sten scores). Similar characteristics are described by the 'D' quadrant preference on the HBDI shown by the group (see Figure 4). However the DEBI group also had strong preferences for 'A' and 'B' quadrant thinking, which reflects the large proportion of technical entrepreneurs tested (see Figure 2). These results confirm Herrmann's (1988) profiles of entrepreneurs.

The group also had a tendency towards calculated risk-taking and experimentation as seen in the GET, HBDI and ESSI results.

The findings support the results of previous research studies (e.g. McClelland (1961), Herrmann (1988), INC (1988) and Bailey) with respect to such things as the influences, characteristics and thinking preferences of entrepreneurs. However what is also highlighted is the fact that several of the entrepreneurs profiles do not conform to standard. For example, several of the profiles indicated that the entrepreneurs did not have strong drives for autonomy, risk-taking or action. Instead they had a concern for working with others in an organised and traditional business framework. For such entrepreneurs it would be predicted that they would experience greater difficulties in succeeding in the rough and tumble business environment, resulting in the need for them to receive more individual support during the programme.

Practical applications of psychological profiling on the Debi Programme.

The programme developers found that the use of psychological inventories enabled more in-depth information to be gathered (about each participant and the group), than observations and interviews had alone allowed.

Much of the previous research applying psychology to the field of entrepreneurship has focused on the search for the "entrepreneur". The present project was instead concerned with applying psychology in a more immediate and practical way, in order to add value to the training and development of entrepreneurs.

The wide range of participant profiles resulting from the testing session indicated that designing the programme to satisfy the needs of the 'average' entrepreneur would satisfy some entrepreneurs needs whilst being of little benefit to others. It was therefore decided that, (with the consent of participants) the information gained should be disseminated not only to the entrepreneurs but also to the programme trainers and developers. In this way the course could be modified to the more specific needs of individual entrepreneurs and the group.

One of the major findings from the profiles was that the majority of the group would encounter problems in the interpersonal aspects of business. Qualities such as, drive, autonomy and independence are factors in entrepreneurial success (Raj Jain and Akbar Ansari (1989)). However when coupled with lower regard for other peoples feelings the individuals may lose the support of needed others, through insensitivity, impatience and aggression.

Based on such knowledge it was decided that each entrepreneur should be given a personal counselling session. During this feedback each person was made aware of their own particular profiles. The counsellors were able to give in-depth analyses of the results and the implications of these for the individual in relation to communication, interpersonal relations, reactions to stress, motivations and preferred thinking styles. One of the interesting results to emerge from the individual session was that of increased openness and trust between the entrepreneurs and counsellors. The participants valued the 1:1 counselling, reporting that it gave them valuable self-insights allowing them to better understand themselves in relation to their business operations.

The results also indicated areas where particular development was needed for the entrepreneurs. For example, sessions on communication skills, presentation skills, negotiation skills, and working alone and in teams were emphasised. williams (1985) highlighted that setting up in business is a rich source of psychological stress especially in the formative years of the business. The profile results and the age of businesses indicated that the entrepreneurs needed particular development in stress awareness and management. Prior to the research and testing some of these areas had not been considered of importance in entrepreneurial training.

Because of the international dimension of the course and the results of profiling a number of interactive group sessions were developed. For example, during an initial training module the group and the co-ordinator were introduced to the field of individual differences. The group members were positioned according to their profile similarities and various exercises were conducted to highlight how diverse people react differently under the same conditions. In this way for example real communication differences were made apparent and the group started to share information and experiences with each other as they gained a deeper appreciation and understanding of their fellow entrepreneurs.

The co-ordinator also gained valuable insight into the group make-up and dynamics and also learnt that more effective training could be achieved by noting trainees preferred thinking and learning modes, and so designing modules which more closely match their preferences.

It was also recognised by both the programme co-ordinator and the entrepreneurs that the personal awareness session was a useful tool for personal and group development because it highlighted many areas of strengths and weaknesses which would not otherwise have been apparent.

Because the programme developers/co-ordinators more fully understood the psychological make-up of individuals they were better able to communicate and deal with participants on an individual basis. This was particularly useful to the co-ordinator in Boston who had to place participants with host organisations in the USA and also provide guidance and support to the entrepreneurs whilst they underwent training in a new country.

Because use was made of psychological profiling the programme developers themselves are now more aware of their own inclinations and preferences. As a result of this they are aware that personal biases may influence the effectiveness of the course and as such have taken up the challenge of continually reviewing, assessing and revising the course to better facilitate the training and development of entrepreneurs selected for courses.

Summary implications of using psychological profiles in the training and development of entrepreneurs.

- Programme designers should focus equally on the development of the individual entrepreneur as well as the business.

- Entrepreneurs should be given a range of psychological inventories in order to compile a detailed profile of each entrepreneur.

- Profile programme designers, to enable them to be aware of their own characteristics and their impact on the training programme.

- Give each person individual feedback of their profile results.

- Based on profile results design programmes to more closely address the individual needs of each entrepreneur.

- Based on profiles develop programmes to optimise the effectiveness and efficiency of the course for the group to be developed. (e.g. alter the use of training media in the light of preferred modes of thinking and learning, include particular units and sessions as required).

- Profiling entrepreneurs means that it is no longer enough to offer traditional courses year after year. Instead based on the increased information made available courses must be reviewed and revised to be flexible enough to achieve their objectives whilst accommodating needs of different entrepreneurs at different times.

References

Bailey, J. E. *Learning Styles Of Successful Entrepreneurs.*
Caird, S. (1990). What Does It Mean To Be Enterprising: *British Journal of Management,* 1.
Caird, S. (1988). *Report On The Development And Validation Of A Measure Of General Enterprising Tendency.* Durham University Business School, Small Business Centre.
Chell, E. (1984). The Entrepreneurial Personality: A Few Ghosts Laid to Rest? *International Small Business Journal,* 3, 3.
Cromie, S. and Johns, S. (1983). Irish entrepreneurs: Some personal characteristics. *Journal of Occupational Behaviour, 4.*
Cunningham, J. B. and Lischeron, J. (1991). Defining Entrepreneurship. *Journal of Small Business Management.*

Herrmann, N. (1988). *The Creative Brain*. Brain Books, North Carolina.

Hornaday, R. W. (1990). Dropping the E-Words From Small Business Research: An Alternative Typology. *Journal of Small Business Management*, 28, 4, Oct.

Hyatt, J. (1991). Mapping the Entrepreneurial Mind. *INC*, Aug.

The Entrepreneurial Personality, (1988). *INC*, Aug pp.18.

Johnson, B. R. (1990). Toward a Multidimensional Model of Entrepreneurship: The case of Achievement Motivation and the Entrepreneur. *Entrepreneurship Theory and Practice*, 14, 3, Spring.

Kets de Vries, M. F. R. (1977). The Entrepreneurial Personality: A Person At the Crossroads. *The Journal of Management Studies*, Feb.

Krug, S. E. (1981). *Interpreting 16pf profile patterns*. Institute for Personality and Abiity Testing, Inc., Illinois.

Lachman, R. (1980). Toward Measurement of Entrepreneurial Tendencies. *Management International Review*, 20, 2.

Liles, P. R. (1974). Who Are the Entrepreneurs? *MSU Business Topics*, Winter.

Moran, P. and Lamshead, C. (1991). Working with the growth-oriented entrepreneur: implications for counselling support services. *Paper presented at the 21st European Small Business Seminar*.

Raj Jain, G. and Akbar Ansari, M. (1989). Self-made Impact Making Entrepreneurs: A Research Study. Paper presented at *EIASM: Third Workshop on Recent Research In Entrepreneurship*.

Sexton, D. L. and Bowman - Upton, N. (1987). Evaluation Of An Innovative Approach To Teaching Entrepreneurship. *Journal of Small Business Management*, 25, 1.

Sexton, D. L. and Bowman - Upton, N. (1988). Validation of Innovative Teaching Approach for Entrepreneurship Courses. *American Journal of Small Business*, 12, 3, Winter.

Shaver R. G. and Scott L. R. (1991). Person, Process, Choice: The Psychology Of New Venture Creation. *EntrePreneurship Theory and Practice*, 16, 2, Winter.

Shenson, H. L. and Anderson, T. D. (1989). The Entrepreneurial Style and Success Indicator: Professional's Guide. *Consulting Resource Group International*, Inc., Canada.

Stammers, R. and Patrick, J. (1975). *The Psychology of Training.* Methuen & Co Ltd., London.

Walden, J. (1979). Entrepreneurship: It Takes More Than a Dream. *Business Education Forum,* April.

Williams, A. (1985). Stress And The Entrepreneurial Role. *International Small Business Journal,* 3, 4, Summer.

Ulrich, T. A. and Cole, G. S. (1987). Toward More Effective Training of Future Entrepreneurs. *Journal of Small Business Management,* 25, 4.

Vesper, K H., McMullan, W. E. and Ray, D. M. (1989). Entrepreneurship Education: More Than Just an Adjustment to Management Education. *International Small Business Journal,* Oct - Dec.

Appendix 1

Inventories Used

ESSI

The instrument was developed by Shenson and Anderson(1989).It assesses entrepreneurial style and the extent to which an individual possesses 'success' factors common to successful entrepreneurs.

The entrepreneurial style results are given as four style dimension scores:

1. Behavioural - action orientation, extroversion, greater task orientation, need for challenge, freedom and responsibility;
2. Cognitive - verbal orientation towards tasks and the need for safety and respect;
3. Interpersonal - action orientation towards people, care and a need for security, appreciation and harmony in relationships;
4. Affective - expression towards people, influencing, selling, need for attention, acceptance and recognition.

The degree of similarity between respondents and successful entrepreneurs histories and attitudes gives an indication as to what degree an individual will find entrepreneurship a desirable and fulfilling approach to life and work.

GET

The GET devised by Caird (1988) gives a measure of an individual's enterprising tendency, defined as 'the extent to which an individual has a tendency to set up and run projects.'

The inventory measures the extent of an individual's; Internal Locus of Control i.e. belief that one can act on the environment and control reinforcement contingencies, Creative Tendency i.e. sensitivity to opportunities and needs, Need for Achievement-i.e. goal setting and planning to realise ideas, Need for Autonomy i.e. predisposition to persevere, be self reliant and maintain motivation and Calculated Risk Taking, (to facilitate the implementation of plans).

Results are given as a score on each of the enterprising attributes described above as well as a general score for enterprising tendency. These can then be compared with a range of scores obtained for enterprising individuals.

16PF

Cattell's well known 16PF gives information about the individual on sixteen primary personality dimensions and eight second order dimensions. The latter include : extraversion, anxiety, tough poise, creativity, independence, control, adjustment and leadership.

These scores can be compared to those obtained from a sample of the general population.

Appendix 2

HBDI

The instrument developed by Herrmann (1988) measures an individuals thinking preferences. Four major measures are given, indicating a four quadrant, 'A','B','C','D',dominance (preference) profile.

'A' denotes a preference for logical, analytical, fact-based and quantitative thinking. 'B' represents preference for organised, sequential, detailed and planned thinking. 'C' highlights a preference for interpersonal, feeling based and emotional thinking and 'D' shows a preference for holistic, intuitive and integrative thinking.

28 Successful women entrepreneurs in Fiji: Their profile, vision and motivation: An exploratory study

Ken Khi Pang and Godwin Nair

Abstract

Women entrepreneurship is a recent phenomena worldwide. This paper seeks to compare successful women entrepreneurs in the formal sector in Fiji to those in developed and developing countries. This paper goes a step further to make recommendations to government, non-government and private bodies to take women entrepreneurs into consideration in their small business development policy.

Introduction

Women as entrepreneurs has been coming out as a distinct class on the industrial scene around the world in the past decade. In some countries, their economic contribution is being considered as significant (Shad,1988). In United States, women-owned businesses are the fastest growing segment of the small business population. Nearly one-third of the small businesses in the US today belong to women. Between 1980 and 1986, sole proprietorships owned by women rose from 2.5 million to 4.1 million - a 62.5 per cent jump during a period when the number of male-owned businesses increased by 33.4 per cent (Nelton,1989). In Canada, the growth in the female portion of self-employment has increased by an annual average rate of 5.8 per cent as compared to 2.8 per cent for males (Stevenson,1986). In other Asian countries such as India, Singapore, Malaysia, Indonesia, Philippines, participation of women as industrial entrepreneurs is also a recent phenomena. India is generally recognised as one of the pioneers on women development in Asia. In India, a survey of women in small-scale industries in 1986-1987 revealed that there are less than 100,000 of them among the 1.6 million small scale industry entrepreneurs (Alchouri,1988). In Singapore, study revealed that the number of women entrepreneurs had grown from 2,760 in 1974 to 55,127 in 1988. This represented 20% of all partnerships and sole proprietorships in Singapore (Boey,1988). In Malaysia, the number of women entrepreneur as compared to men is significantly small. There are no statistics available to show exactly the proportion of women in business (Abdullah,1988; Reduan,1988). In Indonesia, there are successful women entrepreneurs among the 1.5 millions small enterprises but the exact number is not known (Pratiwi,1988). This lack of statistics in some of these developing countries revealed that interest in women entrepreneurs as research subjects is not singled out or has only developed recently.

There are two separate streams in the literature, reflecting the two quite different constituent groups of women. The first stream concentrate on low-income women with few employment prospects. These are the females that abound in the informal sector involving in microbusinesses such as vegetable sellers, peddlers, hawkers and vendors (Lazo,1988). As for those in the rural-based industries, they are the women homemakers who are involved producing products under the subcontracting agreement with the middlemen or the larger companies who supply them with the materials and equipments or women may produce goods in their homes at their own initiative and the goods are collected and sold by a third party which could be a petty trader. Examples, producing artefacts, rootcrops or gathering fisheries products such as beche-de-mer, prawns,etc. They engaged themselves in such activities basically to earn income for the family's subsistence. All these have hardly been taken into account in the economy of most developing countries (Helter,1986; ILO Reports). This group of women is not aware of the potential for starting an enterprise, and needs to be informed, encouraged and nurtured to consider to start business as an option.

The second stream relates to women in the formal sector. Much of this literature focuses on personal and demographic characteristics of female entrepreneur, and differences, if any, from the male entrepreneur, issues and problems women entrepreneurs face, case studies of successful women entrepreneurs, women entrepreneurship programs. The consensus is that there is a need for much more and better information on women entrepreneurs and how best to foster them and uplift their status and role in society (Chico,1988; El-Namaki,1988; Stevenson,1986; Hirsch,1984).

Small Business Development in Fiji

Fiji is a developing country situated in the hub of the South-West Pacific. It comprises about 332 islands of which one-third are inhabited. It has one of the most developed economy in the South Pacific Island countries.

It has an economy which is agro-base with sugar being the major export and income generating commodity. The large decade has seen the drift away from the country's dependence on sugar and diversification into broader agricultural production, secondary industries and tourist industry which is becoming the largest foreign exchange earner (Basha, 1989)

It is a multiracial country of 715,375 peoples of which 329,305 are the indigenous Fijians, 348,704 are Indians and 37,366 are mixture of part-Europeans, Chinese, Europeans and other Pacific Islanders (Census,1986).

The Indians, Europeans and Chinese participate in the commercial and industrial sectors whereas the indigenous Fijians have only marginal participation. To balance the participation between the indigenous and others, the government has recently given major priority to increase Fijian participation in commerce as business owners and operators. Some of the incentives to encourage Fijian participation include a 20 year tax free holiday, easy access to low interest loan, 10 per cent cash grant on investment on fixed asset.

The focus of government policy on small business development in Fiji is still blurred. The government does not have a special policy for the development of small scale enterprise as a separate sector of the economy but development in this important sector is embraced within the overall industrial development objectives (Mataiciwa,1988; Fiji Ninth Point Plan, 1986-1990).

Women in Small Business Development in Fiji

The number of female population in Fiji is close to 49.3 per cent of the total population of 715,375. Of these, only 51,231 (23.35 per cent) of the 219,596 females who are above 15 years of age, are economically active. As compared to male population, 189,929 (85 per cent) of the 222,316 males are economically active. Of those women who are economically active, only 8,294 (16.2 per cent) are self-employed and as compared to male, 72,706 (38.3 per cent) are self-employed. A large per cent of the women are unpaid family worker (60.9 per cent) or unemployed (15.3 per cent), and as compared to men, only 4.2 per cent are unpaid family workers and 5.4 per cent unemployed (Census 1986).

The number of women operating in the formal sector, like any developing countries, is observed to be much smaller in number as compared to those women operating in the informal sector ie. outside the modern industrial sector. The ratio is not known as there is no available data compiled specifically for women entrepreneurs in formal and informal sectors in Fiji. However, a survey done by National Training Council, Fiji, in 1986 revealed that self-employment in informal sector or micro-businesses (i.e. home-industries and small trade like selling agricultural or waterbased produce) was found to be relatively widespread. The majority of them engaged themselves on productive activities such as agriculture, fishing, handicrafts and production of other household items in addition to fulfilling their main role relating to household duties. Those self-employed usually sell their produce for cash income to supplement the family needs (i.e. when the husband's wage is small) (Helter,et al,1986). There are also a large sector of economically nonactive women which accounts for 76 per cent of the women population. These women's silence or invisibility in the economy could be due to their economic activities as being relegated to supplementing their spouses' income. In times of difficulties,these women often turn to income generating activities such as growing subsistence crops, animals rearing, selling or bartering self produced goods, cooking food and selling, and offering sewing activities, to make ends meet.

Methodology

Very little research has been done on women and entrepreneurship in the South Pacific Islands. Therefore this paper seeks to acquire information about successful entrepreneurs who are operating registered businesses in Fiji. This survey was carried out by use of postal questionnaire and supplemented by personal interview. The questionnaire consists of 22 questions, classified under six headings namely, nature of business run , motivational factors, entrepreneurial qualities and behaviour pattern, barriers encountered in running a business, demographic profile and finance. A mixture of scaled, open-ended, multiple choices, fixed response rank-order items questions were used in the questionnaire.

Since there is no documented record available on the number of women entrepreneurs existing in Fiji, the method used in identifying them were done through Chambers of Commerce, banks, personal contact, referral by one woman entrepreneur to another. There was no limit to how many women entrepreneurs were to be studied because the number of women entrepreneurs in Fiji is very limited and not listed in any form of directory. Therefore studies were carried out on as many women entrepreneurs as possible, who have some success in their respective business. The samples taken were women entrepreneurs from the cities and towns of Fiji like Suva, Lautoka, Sigatoka, Nadi, and Rakiraki.

The identified women entrepreneurs were first contacted by telephone informing them of the purpose of the survey. The questionnaire was then mailed to 43 willing participants. Some of them were also approached to be interviewed when information given was found incomplete. Only women entrepreneurs with 1 or more employed staff were included in this study. 36 questionnaires were returned giving a response rate of 84 per cent. Out of 36 questionnaires, only 31 useable ones were used for analysis. This sample number is estimated to represent more than 50 per cent of the successful women entrepreneur who employed more than 1 employees.

Findings

The findings were based on thirty one successful women entrepreneurs in the formal sector, who employed one or more staff. The discussions revolved around on six areas: business description, the motives or reasons of starting business, the entrepreneurial personality traits, problems attributed of being a woman, demographic profile of women entrepreneurs, and finance.

Business Description

45 per cent of them operated in the service business, 36 per cent in retailing and 19 per cent in manufacturing. Those involved in manufacturing are also involved in retailing their own products. This finding agreed with most of the other research findings which said that most women entrepreneurs go into more service-orientated and retailing types of business (Birley,1989; Hajba, 1986; Matthew,1988; Neider,1987). As compared to those in developing countries like India and Thailand the preference for women to go for non-technical or service business over manufacturing is dispelled (Singer,1990; Suthawara,1988).

The type of business venture in this survey varied from male dominated business like steelwork, boat building to traditionally females dominated areas like beauty saloon, florist and clothing boutique.

Majority of the businesses were general partnerships (42 per cent), mostly with husbands. 19 per cent were private limited companies; 36 per cent were sole proprietorships; and 3 per cent were co-operatives. 77 per cent of the businesses have been operating for less than ten years (32 per cent for 0 to 3 years, 13 per cent for 3 to 6 years, 32 per cent for 6 to 10 years) of which 32 per cent are below 3 years. This shows that the phenomenon of women entrepreneurs in Fiji is a recent one. This phenomenon is very similar to the kind of situation in US and Canada in 1986. The major study done in US in 1986 on women entrepreneurs found that 75 per cent of the business have been running for less than ten years, and 46 per cent for less than five years. In Maritime Provinces of Canada, 74 per cent of the women entrepreneurs have been running their businesses for less than ten years, of which 32 per cent are below 3 years (Stevenson, 1986).

The present business worth varies from F$5000 to above 1 million dollars. Almost 90 per cent of the businesses are F$100,000 and below, as shown in Table 1. In Fiji, there is no specific definition for small business, but according to the Fiji Ninth Development Plan(1986-1990), any business under the F$100,000 category is defined as small industry. As such, almost 90 per cent of these businesses surveyed can be classified as small businesses.

It appears that the number of medium and large size companies ie. above $100,000, owned by women in Fiji are few (only 13 per cent). One of the reasons for this, is their short history as business owners and more than three quarters of the companies are less that than ten years old and are considered to be still, in the embryonic stage of development.

It is interesting to note that 71 per cent of the businesses have expanded since inception. Of the remaining 29 per cent, 23 per cent said they have been the same (with 13 per cent of them on the borderline of success and failure) and 6 per cent said they experienced some contraction. According to feminine model (Chaganti,1986), women owned enterprise would normally remain small and marginally profitable. This is because the types of products and services they offer tend to be primarily local in scope, and partly because women entrepreneurs lacked the vision and the strategic and operating abilities needed for expanding them into large-sized businesses. This model may or may not apply to Fiji and it is too early to draw a comparison since women entrepreneurs are a recent phenomenon in Fiji. It is interesting to note that 71 per cent of the female entrepreneurs had actually expanded their businesses since inception see (see Table 1) and almost three quarter of them have been operating over 3 years and above. One company (3 per cent) which has been operating over 10 years has in fact gone into overseas markets.

More than a third of the firms engage both full-time and part-time employees. Majority employed 1 to 4 employees. Two of the businesses (one food catering and one manufacturing) also engaged casual or contract labour on a `as required' basis. Totally, they have generated a total of 224 full-time and 50 part-time jobs, in addition to the 31 jobs the women business owners had created for themselves, and also `casual' labour who were employed on an `as required' basis. This indicates that women too can play an important role in developing the country's economy by creating employment through entrepreneurship.

Table 1. Initial investment versus present business value (number of companies)

PRESENT VALUE (x '000)	BELOW 5	5.001 - 10,	10.00 - 50	50.001 - 100	100.001 - 250	250.001 - 1,000	ABOVE 1,000	TOTAL
INITIAL VALUE (x '000)								
BELOW 5	0	2	3	1	0	0	1	7
5 - 10	0	1	5	3	0	0	0	9
10.001 - 50	0	0	6	5	0	1	0	12
50.001 - 100	0	0	0	1	1	0	0	2
100.001 - 200	0	0	0	0	1	0	0	1
ABOVE 200	0	0	0	0	0	0	0	0
TOTAL	0	3	14	10	2	1	1	31

Reasons/Motives for Starting a Business

A study of the motivational factors that drove these women to become entrepreneurs, revealed that these respondents enter business not primarily out of economic factors, or in other words, to make money to support the family. The survey indicates that the first and foremost factor chosen by them was to pursue own interest, followed by to supplement family income, satisfaction of being your own boss and to secure social prestige (See Table 2). It is consistent with other findings in US and even India that the foremost reason for start-up tended to involve "personal satisfaction" issues except to supplement family income was not an important reasons to start a business (Singh,1990; Neider, 1987). In this findings, husband's interest and support is too an important factor. This may be due to Fiji `clannish' culture which strongly emphasises on the prime role of male in the family (Fairbairn,1988).

Table 2. Motives/reasons for starting a business

REASONS	* WEIGHTED SCORE	RANK
To secure social prestige	181	4
To supplement family income	213	2
To pursue own interest	222	1
Insufficient educational qualification to seek for a job	86	8
Satisfaction of being your own boss	193	3
To provide employment to others	132	7
Does not affect family life	135	6
Husband's (or family) interest and support	165	5
By accident, or by circumstances beyond control such as family death,etc.	77	9

* The weighted score was calculated for the nine factors according to the ranking to them by the respondents. The reasons ranked first were given 9 points, the reason ranked second received 8 points and so on.

Insufficient educational qualification to seek a job was not a motive at all that prompt them into starting a business. In fact, 91 per cent of them have completed secondary school and above and therefore were qualified enough to get jobs else where. Forty-eight (48) per cent of the women entrepreneurs surveyed of which 6 per cent are in inherited business, had actually resigned from their jobs to go into business. Personal crisis related to marriage (eg. divorce, death of a spouse, an unemployed spouse.) was also not an important reason for starting a business in Fiji as unlike in US and also in India (Singh 1990; Neider,1987). These difference in motive in starting a business may be explained by the difference in social and cultural environment that they are in. For instance, extended family where family members taking care of one another is dominant in Fiji.

Factors Responsible for Choosing the Particular Business

The respondents were asked to identify factors responsible for choosing the particular business from a list of 7 factors (see Table 3). A look at the first four factors indicate that they possess some professionalism and also have prepared themselves to face challenges when choosing their products or services. More than half of them based their choice of the particular business on either past experience or special skills they possessed. These percentages are very similar to the survey done on 129 successful women entrepreneurs in Australia in 1988 (see Table 3). Other important factors influencing the choice of their business are ideal product and service and product/service gap in the market. These were considered as unimportant factors in the survey done in Australia. The respondents considered flexible hours as not important factor even though 75% of them were married and have a multiple role to play, that is as a wife, a mother and a full time business woman. The Australian women also considered flexible hours as unimportant reason for choosing their businesses.

Table 3. Reasons for choosing the particular business

REASONS	PERCENTAGE	
	AUSTRALIA (1988)	FIJI
EXPERIENCE	58	50
SPECIAL SKILLS	55	50
FLEXIBLE HOURS	19	9
IDEAL FOR PRODUCT/SERVICE	45	12
GAP IN THE MARKET	42	19
INHERITED FROM FAMILY	23	-
OTHERS	0	-

Note: These response are multiple choice, as such the total of various percentage may not add up to 100.

Entrepreneurial Personality Traits

The lack of self-confidence, assertiveness and drive, is mentioned to be the biggest obstacle in women's success in business (Hisrich and Brush, 1984). However, the present survey clearly indicates a departure from the accepted pattern of thinking. The survey indicates that the first and foremost entrepreneurial personality traits that these successful women possessed were self-confidence, followed by originality, task-result oriented, people-oriented and future oriented. This shows that the general traits of the entrepreneurial qualities of women entrepreneur in Fiji tend to resemble the `generic' trait profile described by McClelland, which consist of independence, leadership, originality, people-oriented, task/result-oriented and future-orientated (El-Namaki, 1985). This findings also show resemblance to the generally accepted trait profile of a male entrepreneur which consists of self confidence, originality, task-result orientation, future orientation, people-orientation (East West Center, 1977). Low masculinity index, connoting femininity, such as interdependence, sympathy for the unemployed, being a female are found to be unimportant entrepreneurial personality traits in this findings (see Table 4). This pattern is similar to those findings in Western Europe and North America, which suggest a resemblance between the trait profile of a male and a female entrepreneur and that the differences, if any, are marginal.

Table 4. Entrepreneurial personality traits

DESCRIPTION	* WEIGHTED SCORE	RANK
Self confidence	268	1
Originality	251	2
People-oriented	205	4
Task-result oriented	223	3
Future-oriented	176	5
Risk taker	167	6
Interdependence	98	9
Intuition	101	8
Sympathy for the unemployed	93	10
Being a female	112	7

* The weighted score was calculated for the ten factors according to the ranking to them by the respondents. The reasons ranked first were given 10 points, the reason ranked second received 9 points and so on.

Extensive research on entrepreneurship has time and again proved that entrepreneurs are risk-takers (Brockhaus 1980). However, this survey indicates there is some departure from the accepted pattern of thinking. Risk taking was ranked sixth in the entrepreneurial qualities. Therefore whether most of the women entrepreneur will take the risk to expand their businesses to large businesses are yet to be seen.

Problems Attributed to Being Women

In this survey, an attempt was made to find out from the respondents the problems they faced in being a woman. 71 per cent or more of them did not feel that they faced any problems listed in Table 5 by virtue of being a woman. This indicates a good turning point, in the sense these women were able to understand and work effectively in a male dominated business environment. An entrepreneur even quoted that being a female is an asset in the business world. They are similar to successful women entrepreneurs in the West and in developing countries like India and Singapore (Singer, 1990; Boey, 1988; El-Namaki, 1985). Therefore, it is quite heartening to find that the majority of the women entrepreneurs are aware of their competence and possessed a sense of confidence in their business. This is very encouraging to many contemplating and forthcoming Fiji women entrepreneurs who are to venture into business.

Table 5. Problems attributed to being a woman in business

DESCRIPTION	PER CENT OF BUSINESSES
Lack of support from family members	19
Lack of support from employees	13
Discriminated against by bankers	19
Discriminated against by suppliers	29
Discriminated against by customers	16
*Others	6

These response are multiple choice, as such the total of various percentage may not add up to 100.

*One of the entrepreneurs said that at times it is difficult to delegate work to employees, and also emotional factors sometimes make it difficult to make sound decisions. Another entrepreneur said being a female is an asset in the business world.

However, a small percentage felt that the general competence of women was still suspect. Those that have these attitudinal problems were also mostly those who have been operating their businesses for not more than three years or were on a borderline of success and failure or younger in age. This reveals that once the business is established and financially sound and the owners become more mature and less vulnerable, discrimination of any form does not appear to exist any more for a woman entrepreneur.

Demographic Profile

Interestingly, 74 per cent of the women went into business before the age of 35 years (see Table 6), the prime child-rearing years. Although running a business is time- and effort demanding, family responsibilities did not seem to deter a married woman from entering her own business.

Table 6. Age (years old) starting business

AGE RANGE	% OF RESPONSES
15 - 24	29
25 - 34	45
35 - 44	19
45 - 54	7
55 - 59	0
60 +	0
	100

Women entrepreneurs surveyed come from different levels of education, from primary school to undergraduate degree level. 68 per cent had secondary school certificate or trade certificate, 13 per cent have diploma, 13 per cent have primary education and only 6 per cent were graduates. On the whole, their education background is average and comparable to the female working population in Fiji and women entrepreneurs in developing countries. None of them had any formal business educational background.

Seventy-seven (77) per cent had gained work experience, varying from 2 years to 32 years, from working as employees for others or from their previous businesses or from parents/relatives, before setting or running their present businesses. Most of these experiences were in the technical and managerial areas, which seemed to have contributed to the starting of and managing successfully of their present business. This resembles with other findings which said women entrepreneurs tend to start businesses in fields in which they have had job experience (Matthew,1988; Scott,1986; Hirsh and Brush,1984). The other 23 per cent had no experience of any kind before venturing into business, and all except one who is a sole trader, are in partnership with husbands or male partners.

According to some surveys in United States, most of the women entrepreneurs are first born in the family (eg. Neider,1987; Hisrich and Brush,1984). In this survey, only 26 per cent were first born and 61 per cent are in the middle position of the family. This demonstrates that position in the family is not an important factor as is initiative and determination to succeed.

There is a school of thought, particularly among the Chinese and Indian merchants, that entrepreneurship training should commence early in life (Singh,1990; Snidvongs,1988). In other words, orientation to business must be acquired in an individual's formative year. However, this survey only showed 23 per cent of their fathers and none of their mothers (84 per cent are homemakers) were entrepreneurs. In other words, 77 per cent of the women entrepreneurs surveyed came from family with no business background. Even so their assumed disadvantage positions have not deterred them from being successful in business. This is an encouraging point for those women from non-business family background who are contemplating of going into business, to note.

Finance

Excluding those who inherited businesses (23 per cent) and those who borrowed loans only from friends and relatives (3 per cent), 74% of the women entrepreneurs involved their own savings together with other means to initially finance their businesses (see Table 7). Most of them said they did not know how to approach a bank for financial help at the inception of their businesses. Of those who finally did, 19 per cent of them said they experienced discrimination from bankers. A closer examination of the discrimination revealed that 6 per cent of the women entrepreneurs surveyed faced discriminations from the bankers at the inception of their businesses and were only granted loans when their businesses were proven successful. The other 13 per cent who face discriminations from bankers now relied on their own savings and loans from friends and relatives. Of these 13 per cent, 6.5% have been in business for 6 to 10 years but are on the borderline of success and failure and the other 6.5% are in business only between 0 to 3 years. Based on these samples, the discrimination faced from bankers by the 19 per cent women entrepreneurs is not exceptional and is very similar to the discriminations faced by any male entrepreneur.

Table 7. Ways of Financing Business

DESCRIPTION	PERCENTAGE
Own Savings	19.5
Own Savings + loans From friends and relatives	13.0
Own savings and loans from financial institutions	32.5
Owning savings and shareholders	6.0
Loans from friends and relatives	3.0
Inherited and loans from financial institutions	13.0
Inherited and own savings	10.0
	100.0

Discussions and Recommendations

This study proves beyond doubt that successful women entrepreneurs in Fiji are just like any other successful women entrepreneurs in other parts of the world with each having their unique sets of problems and abilities. They can be equally successful and will rapidly increase in number in future if government, non-government bodies and private agencies actively participate in the promotion of both indigenous entrepreneurs in general and women entrepreneurs in particular. Even though government in Fiji does not distinguish between genders in terms of education, employment and entrepreneurship, the ratio of economically active women to men is only 1 to 3.7 (Fiji Bureau of statistics, 1986).

Entrepreneurship has long been recognised as an important factor in development process. Many developed and even developing countries such as India, Singapore and Indonesia have made planned efforts to increase national production and provide better employment opportunities by encouraging entrepreneurship among women. However, although women constituted nearly half of the population in Fiji, hardly any effort is made to inculcate entrepreneurship amongst women. In other words, the government has not yet fully recognised that women too have an important role to play in developing the nation's economy. If the climate for female-owned and operated businesses is enhanced, the national economies will benefit from increased revenues, greater employment opportunities and hence a better living standard and a more dynamic private sector (Fairbairn,1988).

In Fiji, employment opportunities in large industries are also few. Therefore, small businesses are critically important to the economy as providers of employment and as major sources of earning income to the country. The pressure for women to be economically active also increased in recent years and will continue to do so as the need for cash increases with the economic development and rapid social and cultural change in South Pacific Island countries. Therefore, the support and encouragement of entrepreneurship among women is timely and relevant part of economic policy in this part of the world.

The following recommendations are made based on the survey's findings and respondents' suggestions:

1. The experience gain from this study has indicated that comprehensive data base on women and enterprise development is needed to be developed. Such data base is required to enable one to accurately measure the equity of women's access to business opportunities, education services designed to support small business ventures and women representation in the economy.

2. Easy access to finance. Most women who took part in this survey faced difficulty in getting finance or they did not know how to get access to finance at the inception of the business. Therefore they relied on their own savings or borrowed from relatives or friends. Sometimes this inaccessibility may become one of the main factors that cause many potential business women from venturing into business or from expanding their business from informal to formal sector and from small to medium size.

3. Encourage and provide funding to women to enrol in appropriate education and training programmes. All the women participated in this study did not have business education background. Running a business is not only involved with buying and selling, it needs skills in all aspects of management functions like marketing, finance, operations, human resource. Therefore in order to survive and to be able to expand a business successfully, these women need to be educated and trained in various aspects of business management.

4. Women Entrepreneur Network - Lack of network of contacts has always prevented many potential women from starting a business. The complex procedure for business registration, the fear of competition, the lack of information on social guidelines are some of the main problems. There may be so much verbal information about setting up businesses but there is often a lack of published information in Fiji. All these often baffled and intrigued the potential business women who do not know where to begin. The network also can help women entrepreneurs to meet one and another to learn and share their experiences. Successful ones can act as role model and mentor to the

younger ones and other potential entrepreneurs.

REFERENCES

Abdullah R., First Person Case Story: A Woman Entrepreneur In Malaysia, *International Workshop On Women Entrepreneurship*, Philippines, 15-18th August, 1988.

Akhouri M.M.P., Entrepreneurship For Women In India, International *Workshop On Women Entrepreneurship*, Philippines, 15-18th August, 1988.

Apted T.J., Fiji-Women In The Work Place -Personal Perspective, *Workshop paper*, 1990.

Bradley D. and Saunders H., Problems Women Face In Entrepreneurial Development, *Proceedings of Small Business Institute Directors Association*, San Antonio, February, 1987.

Birley S., Female entrepreneurs: Are They Really Any Different?, *Journal of Small Business Management,* January, 1989.

Bowen D. and Hisrich R., The Female Entrepreneur: A career Development Perspective, *Academy of Management Review,* Vol.11, No.2, 1986, pp. 393-407.

Boey K.Y., Women Entrepreneurship In Singapore, International *Workshop On Women Entrepreneurship*, Philippines, 15-18th August, 1988.

Bureau of Statistics, Report on Fiji Population census, 1986, *Parliamentary Paper* No. 10 of 1988.

Chaganti R., Management In Women-owned Enterprises, *Journal of Small Business Management*, October, 1986.

Chico L., Quo Vadis, Entrepreneuse, *International Workshop On Women Entrepreneurship,* Philippines, 15-18th August, 1988.

East West Center, Entrepreneurial Discovery and Development, *Progress of Action Research*, Honolulu, East West Centre, 1977, pp. 46-48.

Fairbairn T.J., *Island Entrepreneurs -Problems And Performances In The Pacific*, The East-West Center, Hawaii, 1988.

Hailey J.M., *Entrepreneurs and Indigenous Business in the Pacific, Honolulu: Pacific Islands Development Program*, East-West Center,1988.

El-Namaki M.S.S., *Could women be equally entrepreneurial?* Readings from a Conference: Delft, the Netherlands, 1-3 May, 1985.

Hajba S., Male and female entrepreneurs: similarities and differences, *Women in Small Business: focus on Europe*, Netherlands, 1986.

Hetler C. and Khoo S.E., Women's Participation In The South Pacific Economy, *Paper for Human Resource Development Workshop, Canberra,* 1986.

Hisrich R.D. and Brush C., The Woman Entrepreneur: Management Skills And Business Problems, *Journal of Small Business Management,* January 1984.

Kamal B., Fiji Development of Small Scale Business - Policy Environment and Institutional Infrastructure, *Conference Report of the International Conference and Workshop*, Singapore, 1989.

Lazo L.S., Women Entrepreneurs: Issues and Problems, *Workshop on Entrepreneurship Development for Small Scale Enterprise,* Malaysia, 22-27 February,1988.

Licuanan V., Entrepreneurship And Women: Opportunities For Management Training, *International Workshop On Women Entrepreneurship,* Philippines, 15-18th August, 1988.

Mataiciwa L., Country Paper - Fiji, *Workshop on Entrepreneurship Development For Small Scale Enterprise,* Malaysia, 22-27 February, 1988

Matthew R., *Women and Small Business - A Report For The Premier - Victoria,* Victorian Women's Consultative Council, March,1988.

Neider L., A Preliminary of Female Entrepreneurs In Florida, *Journal of Small Business Manager, July, 1987.*

Nelton S., The Age Of The Woman Entrepreneur, *National Business,* May, 1989.

Pratiwi M., *The Role Of Women In Industrial Development In Indonesia,* International Workshop On Women Entrepreneurship, Philippines, 15-18th August, 1988.

Reduan S.H., Women And Entrepreneurship Development In Malaysia, *International Workshop On Women Entrepreneurship,* Philippines, 15-18th August, 1988.

Scott C.E., Why More Women Are Becoming Entrepreneurs, *Journal of Small Business Management,* October, 1986.

Semesi F., Promotion Of Equality For Women Workers, *ILO Asian/Pacific Regional Symposium,* 1990, Australia.

Shad H., Strategic Approach To Development Of Women Entrepreneurs, *International Workshop on Women Entrepreneurship,* Philippines, 15-18, August, 1988.

Singh N.P. and Gupta R.S., *Potential women entrepreneurs- Their profile, vision and motivation,* Research Report serial 1, National Institute For Entrepreneurship And Small Business Development, New Delhi, 1990

Snidvongs S., Women Entrepreneurs in Small Scale Entrepreneurs - Issues and Problems, *Workshop on Entrepreneurship Development For Small Scale Enterprise,* Malaysia, 22-27 February, 1988.

Stevenson L., Against All Odds: The Entrepreneurship Of Women, *Journal of Small Business Management,* October, 1986.

Suthawaree N., Women Entrepreneurship In Thailand, *International Workshop on Women Entrepreneurship,* Philippines, 15-18, August, 1988.

Va'a L.R. and Teaiwa J.M. (Editors), *Environment And Pacific Women - From Globe to Village,* The Fiji Association of Women Graduates in association with The Institute of Pacific Studies, The University of the South Pacific, 1988.

29 Gender and ownership in UK small firms

Peter Rosa, Daphne Hamilton and Helen Burns

Abstract

The emphasis on the individual "female entrepreneur" in much of the small business literature in the last decade disguises the fact that many women in business ownership are in partnership with others, usually with men. How "gender" impinges on the process of small business ownership has been little studied.

The paper examines gender and ownership using evidence from a three year study on the impact of gender on small business management, involving interviews with 377 male and female UK business owners, drawn from three industrial sectors.

Difficulties were encountered in interpreting sex differences as "gender" trends, owing to significant sectoral variation. Nevertheless some marked gender differences were identified. These referred to differential patterns of kinship with the owner manager; the allocation and perception of specialist roles within the business; and the fact that female owners are less likely to be associated with more than two businesses. Overall sole traders were in the minority in both sexes, implying that most owners shared responsibility and management in some way with other owners. The paper concludes with methodological implications of co-ownership to common approaches to sampling and analysis of small business owner managers from a gender perspective.

Introduction

In July 1986 an article appeared in the business magazine Venture, entitled "Women Entrepreneurs, the new business owners". It reported

"True, women entrepreneurs are rare in a wide field of men. But startups have swelled their number so that now the woman who heads her own company is no longer the exception. Indeed for an ambitious and capable woman, entrepreneurship is a sensible choice, devoid of conflict between her professional and working life." (p.33).

Implicit in this quotation is the view of the female entrepreneur as an individual owner, pioneering new opportunities in a previously male dominated area of economic activity, and in control of her own enterprise. This theme is implicit in much of the academic small business literature too. Solomon and Fernald (1988:24) estimate that there are some three million female owned businesses in the United States. Their article focuses-on describing the characteristics of the "new phenomenon" of the female entrepreneur (p.24). There are many other similar studies reinforcing notions of female individualism through identifying the characteritics of the female entrepreneur (for example Fischer 1992; Carter and Cannon 1991; Brush 1988; Birley, Moss and Saunders 1987; Cromie and Hayes 1988) This preoccupation with the female entrepreneur is rooted in the debate of whether proprietorship represents an opportunity of liberation for women, or whether it is yet another form of subordination of women in an exploitative capitalist system - where proprietorship "promises autonomy, but in fact offers serfdom" (Bechofer quoted by Scase and Goffee 1983: 641).

The positive role of proprietorship for women relies on the idea that in the capitalist system, members of economically and socially deprived groups can "escape" deprivation through business ownership, which provides opportunities for self-determination through owning and controlling resources, and through an increased ability to flexibly interface work and domestic life (Goffee and Scase 1983:626). By exploiting social and economic conditions in the 1970s and 1980s it has been easier for women to aspire to self-determination though proprietorship. Prominent, successful women entrepreneurs have not only bettered their own lives, but have made a dramatic impact on the perception of women in society as a whole. As Goffee and Scase put it, "female entrepreneurs have a symbolic importance which implicitly questions popular conceptions of the position of women in society" (p.627).

On the negative side proprietorship could be seen as supporting capitalist institutions which "sustain the dominance of men over women"; and as reinforcing economic deprivation of women in employment - from whose ranks the entrepreneurs often come (Goffee and Scase 1983 627). Moreover, as these authors show in their analysis of case studies, subordination does not necessarily cease with proprietorship. The influence of husbands and male relatives can undermine the quest for self-determination. Many female proprietors may feel that they "have failed to obtain full legitimacy and credibility as proprietors" as a result of experiences with dealing with bank and business support officials, customers, suppliers, and clients.

A researcher's views on this debate may be crucial on how "ownership" is treated in a study. A belief in the benefits of proprietorship for women tends to stress "individuality". The struggle for self-determination through proprietorship is a personal one, to be undertaken alone. It is an exploration of "self" rather than a competitive "game". Likewise business success is inseparable from the achievement of the female entrepreneur who owns and manages the business. The rewards are the consequences of her struggle and achievement. This line of argument tends to be undermined by co-ownership, especially if the co-owner is male. Consequently there tends to be no mention of this complication in the literature where the female entrepreneur is the focus of interest.

If a researcher takes a less unidimensional view of proprietorship, then the concept of the "lone female entrepreneur" is simplistic. A woman in business is not an island, even if a sole legal owner, and cannot 'escape' from the wider society. The social conditions that reinforce gender inequalities may impinge on her business and personal life at several levels (Hamilton, Rosa and Carter 1992). These may well be manifest in the types of relationships she has with others in both the business and domestic domains. In this scenario, the analysis of co-ownership is vital in our attempts to study gender from a more holistic perspective (Hamilton 1990).

The preoccupation with "individualism" in entrepreneurial and small business studies has disguised the potential complexity of small business ownership, a complexity compounded by the influence of gender. Large numbers of small businesses are partnerships.

Partnerships may comprise:

Married couples
Non married couples
With relatives
With non relatives
With relatives and non relatives
Single sex
Mixed sex

Where partnerships comprise both men and women, gender roles and relationships can be potentially extremely intricate.

Sole traders are not necessarily on their own either. Many have domestic partners that contribute significantly to the business even though they may not be legal co-owners (Goffee and Scase 1983; Meijer 1986; Meittinen 1986). Even single people with no domestic partner contributing to the business may have father, mother, sisters or brothers contributing.

The question of "ownership" is then fundamental in any study of gender and small business management. It is an area we know little about, as previous studies (for example those mentioned in the first paragraph) have tended to side-track the issues raised by co-ownership, by focusing on "female entrepreneurs" alone. By focusing on "females" or "women", moreover, males have been unfortunately relegated to a functional research role as "controls"; or merely as examples of gender antagonists (eg. the interfering or hostile husband). Consequently even less is known about male business ownership, and the way women and men interact as business co-owners. Because so little is known, we regard it as important to find out what small business ownership empirically looks like. Until this is done, it is perhaps premature to address theoretical debates in detail.

Materials And Methods

Ownership is one element in a study of gender in small business management drawing to its close at the University of Stirling. Over six hundred owner managers have been interviewed, using a structured questionnaire comprising over 100 questions (some 650 variables). Each interview took approximately an hour.

The sample is a random statistical "quota" sample, half male and half female. It was also stratified by sector. One third are from the textile and clothing sectors; one third from business services; and one third from hotel and catering. The sectors were limited to enable us to control for sectoral effects in evaluating gender relationships.

Included in the questions on ownership were details on other owners in the business (sex of other owner; when met; whether they are active; their managerial roles). Similar questions were also asked about owners that had left the business.

A significant section of the questionnaire contains questions about home life, and the contribution of domestic partners and children. To obtain further insights, thirty qualitative interviews have also been conducted on the domestic partners of some owner managers from the survey.

At the time of writing, not all the interviews have been processed for analysis. The paper is thus based on data from only the first 377 respondents, and is a preliminary analysis of gender and ownership in a small business context.

Table 1. Legal status of the Firm by sex of respondent.*

	TEXTILE & CLOTHING		BUSINESS SERVICE		HOTEL & CATERING		ALL SECTORS	
	F	M	F	M	F	M	F	M
	%		%		%		%	
Sole Trades	35	24	34	40	30	29	32	32
Partnership	41	47	40	31	53	54	47	43
Limited Company	24	29	26	29	16	15	20	23
	100	100	100	100	100	100	100	100

* Figures do not itemise 3 "others" franchises/co-operatives.

Deciphering gender relationships.

Identifying gender relationships using statistical analysis is a deceptively simple process. A "gender" relationship is usually deemed to exist if a statistically significant difference between male and female respondents is found for a given variable. All this really tells us, however, is whether a statistically significant "sex difference" exists. A sex difference may indeed correspond to a genuine agender" difference, that is one which is attributable to the action of socially determined forces that differentiates the sexes. Alternatively, a significant sex difference may merely reflect the influence of non social forces. The most important of these are sectoral factors (see Hamilton, Rosa and Carter 1992). It is possible that most apparent gender differences at an aggregate level may be explicable in terms of underlying trends of sectoral variation. To give a hypothetical example, women could appear to be significantly more likely to own a business in partnership with a spouse than men are. A gender explanation is implied. However, this difference may simply be a consequence of having a sectoral mix where far more women respondents are hotel owners than men are. Were the sample equally matched by sector, this difference would disappear.

Our decision to obtain an equal quota sample for three industrial sectors has reduced the sectoral problem. Unfortunately, however, there is still considerable variation in markets within each of our sectors chosen (for example a respondent owning a business in the business services sector could be a solicitor, accountant, employment agent, a provider of typing services and so on). The analysis that follows, therefore, will consistently examine sex differences in relation to sectoral trends.

Glossary

Statistical significance is tested through chi square. This is usually based on the overall table. Where a significant **"separate effect"** is recorded in a table, this means that the chi square was performed for that row versus all other categories pooled.

Results

Legal Ownership

The status of the firm is nearly identical between the sexes, as Table 1 shows. A third are sole traders, which means that two thirds of the sample are involved in legal co-ownership of some kind. Analysis by sector reveals a highly significant overall difference between the three sectors. This is attributable to differences-in the occurrence of partnerships, which are much higher in the hotel/catering sector than in the other two sectors. The distribution of types of legal ownership is thus sensitive to sectoral variation.

When sex differences were examined <u>within</u> each sector, no statistically significant relationships were found. We conclude that legal ownership is not affected by gender in our sample, but that it varies significantly by sector.

Table 2. Mechanism of Business Entry by Sex of Respondent

	TEXTILE & CLOTHING		BUSINESS SERVICE		HOTEL & CATERING		ALL SECTORS	
	F	M	F	M	F	M	F	M
	%		%		%		%	
Inherited firm	0	0	0	3	4	6	2	3
Bought firm	3	5	9	5	58	45	32	22*
Bought into firm	5	3	6	11	8	8	7	8
Married into firm	0	2	4	0	1	1	2	1
Started up firm	92	90	68	72	27	36	52	61
Other	0	0	13	9	2	4	5	5
	100	100	100	100	100	100	100	100
Chi-square	NS		NS		NS		NS	

*Separate effect: Chi-square 0 0.025

A sectoral variation is considerably stronger than any detectable "gender" effects.

Mechanism of becoming on owner

Only 57 per cent of the sample overall started from scratch. A sizeable minority (33%) bought or bought into the business. Surprisingly, only 10 respondents (3%) inherited the business.

Table 2 demonstrates a non-significant overall relationship with sex. When each category is compared separately with all others pooled, there is one very significant effect. Females are much more likely to have bought a business than males (chi square p = 0.025).

This result, however, coexists with a highly significant sectoral difference (see Figure 2). More than half of owners from the hotel and catering sector bought their business, compared to six per cent or less in the other two sectors. Conversely, most owners in the textile/clothing and business services sectors started their own business, compared to only 31% in the hotel and catering sector.

When trends by sex are examined within each sector, no relationship is significant. Within hotel and catering, however, there are some marked differences, though not quite significant. Women are more likely to have bought the business and less likely to have started one from scratch.

Other owners

Table 1 showed that two-thirds of the sample were in partnership with at least one other person. In both sexes a majority of those with other partners only have one other (see Table 3). Differences by sex are not significant either overall or within sectors. There is, however, a significant "separate effect" (see methods section) in the overall figures, pointing to women owners being more frequently associated with only one other owner than men.

This trend is replicated in the textile and business services sectors, where the proportion of owners with 2 or more partners is nearly 2:1 in favour of men. This trend, however, is not replicated in the hotel and catering sector, where differences are slight.

Table 3. Number of other owners by Sex of Respondent.

NUMBER OF OTHER OWNERS	TEXTILE & CLOTHING		BUSINESS SERVICE		HOTEL & CATERING		ALL SECTORS	
	F	M	F	M	F	M	F	M
	%		%		%		%	
One	72	60	71	48	80	78	76	63*
Two	20	20	4	13	10	16	13	21
Three Or More	8	20	5	12	10	7	11	16
	100	100	100	100	100	100	100	100
Chi Square	NS		NS		NS		NS	

* Significant separate effect: Chi Square = 4.49 (2df) P = 0.03

Table 4. Sex of other owners by sex of Respondent

SEX OF OTHER OWNERS	TEXTILE & CLOTHING		BUSINESS SERVICE		HOTEL & CATERING		ALL SECTORS	
	F	M	F	M	F	M	F	M
	%		%		%		%	
Female	17	40	25	21	16	51	19	35
Males	83	60	75	79	84	49	81	65
	100	100	100	100	100	100	100	100
Chi Square	P = 0.03		NS		P = 0.000		P = 0.001	

Distribution of sex of other owners

Table 4 shows that the sex of other owners is not distributed randomly when associated with the sex of the respondent. For both sexes other owners are predominantly male, though male respondents are much more likely than females to be ass-ociated with another female owner. This overall trend is replicated in the hotel and catering sector and the textile and clothing sector.

In the case of business services, however, there is no significant difference at all between the distribution of other owners in regard to sex. It is unclear why business services should stand out in this way.

Original founder by sex of owner

Two-thirds of the sample of other owners were original founders, a trend which differs little between the sexes. There are no significant differences within sectors either, although in the textile and clothing sector women are more likely than men to have been original founders. It is possible that this fairly large difference may become significant when the full sample is available for analysis.

The relationship of other owners to the respondent

Women respondents are much more likely to be related to one or more of the other owners in their business than men are (Table 6). This variable, however, shows enormous sectoral variability. Over three-quarters of the respondents in the textile, clothing and hotel and catering sectors are related in some way to other owners, in contrast to business services where the proportion of respondents related to other owners is only a third or less. In contrast, too, to the overall result, only one of the sub-sectors, business services, shows a significant difference in the degree of relatedness between the sexes. In business services, females are more likely than males to be related to another owner.

Table 7 explores the nature of the relationship of related other owners to the sex of the respondent. In all sectors it is the domestic partner which tends to be dominant category of relationship. In all sectors, too, it is the female respondent who is much more likely to be related to a domestic partner than male respondents. This relationship is significant overall and also in the textile and clothing sector. This means, therefore, that women are much less likely to be associated with other categories of relatives than men are. This is particularly evident in certain categories of kinship. In the textile and clothing sector for example, nearly a fifth of male respondents have other owners who are their children, usually or almost invariably sons rather than daughters, whereas women respondents have no example of children being co-owners in their firm. In all three sectors as well as in the overall sample siblings are relatively common as other owners where the respondent is a male, and extremely uncommon where the respondent is female. Breaking down siblings into brothers and sisters shows that nearly all the relationships mentioned happen to be brothers rather than sisters.

Table 5. Original Founder by Sex of Owner

ORIGINAL FOUNDER	TEXTILE & CLOTHING		BUSINESS SERVICE		HOTEL & CATERING		ALL SECTORS	
	F	M	F	M	F	M	F	M
	%		%		%		%	
YES	84	67	55	51	69	79	68	65
NO	16	33	45	49	31	21	32	35
	100	100	100	100	100	100	100	100
Chi Square	NS		NS		NS		NS	

Table 6. Other Owners: Related to respondent? By sex of respondent

RELATED TO OTHER OWNERS?	TEXTILE & CLOTHING		BUSINESS SERVICE		HOTEL & CATERING		ALL SECTORS	
	F	M	F	M	F	M	F	M
	%		%		%		%	
YES	77	77	35	20	85	77	67	51
NO	23	23	65	80	15	23	33	49
	100	100	100	100	100	100	100	100
Chi Square	NS		$P = 0.05$		NS		$P = 0.001$	

Of note, too, referring to the textile and clothing sector is the fact that female respondents are much more likely than male to have other owners who are related outside the nuclear family. This probably reflects the influence of in-laws. This is not surprising given that a male domestic partner is much more likely in this sector to have relatives drawn from his nuclear family. On marrying the person, the woman obviously acquires these relationships with marriage. In the business services sector, the fact that relatives are much less common than other sectors reflects the professional nature of many of these businesses. It is interesting that not a single woman respondent has any relative in the business services sector other than domestic partners, whereas 25 per cent of male partners do. This, in its extreme, obviously reflects the structure of ownership of many of the business services professional practices, where sons and fathers are often co-owners of the business and daughters seldom are. For example, a firm called Hogg, and Hogg, Solicitors, would usually refers to 3 male Hoggs. Given the rarity of involving daughters in such practices, it is almost inevitable that the only way a woman can enter them through a kinship route is through marriage. This is clearly reflected in Table 7.

Active management/business roles

Two-thirds of other owners were perceived to be "active" in the management of the business. As Table 8 shows, differences by sex were slight in the total sample. There was, however, a significant difference in the business services sector, where women were perceived to be appreciably less active than men.

Differences by sex of owner were also small overall when the respondents were asked whether each owner had a specialist role in the business (Table 9). Sex differences within sectors were also non-significant. It is interesting to note that in the textile/clothing sector, women other owners are ten per cent more likely to have a specialist role than men; whereas in the business services the trend is almost the exact reverse. This may be due to the fact that specialisation in business ownership carries more prestige in the business services sector than it does in textiles, where specialisation is associated with the more "tradesmen" skills.

If a specialist role was indicated for an owner, the respondent was asked to itemise what the role actually was in an open-ended question. A variety of answers were obtained. A large number of categories has led to low cell numbers in cross tabulations which has made it difficult to meaningly analyse the results. We expect that clearer trends will emerge when the full sample is available for analysis.

Table 7. Other Owners: How related to Respondent by sex of Respondent

HOW I RELATED?	TEXTILE & CLOTHING		BUSINESS SERVICE		HOTEL & CATERING		ALL SECTORS	
	F	M	F	M	F	M	F	M
	%		%		%		%	
Parents	4	15	0	10	13	15	9	14
Children	0	19*	0	0	10	8	6	10
Siblings	7	19	0	10	2	15*	3	16***
Other relatives	22	8	0	5	7	6	8	6
Domestic partners	67	39*	100	75*	69	56	74	54***
	100	100	100	100	100	100	100	100

Chi Square	P = 0.001	NS	NS	P = 0

SEPARATE EFFECTS: * = Chi Square Significant
                   *** = Chi Square Highly Significant

Table 8. Whether an Active Manager by sex as other owner

ACTIVE MANAGER?	TEXTILE & CLOTHING		BUSINESS SERVICE		HOTEL & CATERING		ALL SECTORS	
	F	M	F	M	F	M	F	M
	%		%		%		%	
YES	79	84	76	91	76	67	65	67
NO	21	16	24	9	24	33	35	33
	100	100	100	100	100	100	100	100

Chi Square	NS	NS	NS	NS

An example of one gender trend, however, is discernible in the figures. A specialist role in the hotel/catering sector is cooking food. There are two labels used to describe this role in English. A person doing the cooking is either the "cook" or the "chef". The word "chef" conveys considerably more status and prestige than "cook".

Table 10 demonstrates a highly significant gender difference. Of 83 respondents with a specialist role in the hotel and catering sector, 48 per cent are "cooks" if women, but only 8 per cent if men. Conversely, 27 per cent of male owners are "chefs" but only 5 per cent are women. This distinction is clearly irrelevant in other sectors where no cooking takes place as a business role. Specific business roles are thus heavily influenced by sectoral factors, but within relevant sectors, can be associated with significant gender components too.

Owners who have left the business

Sixty-five owners altogether (19 per cent) indicated that at least one other owner had left the business during the time they had been involved with the ownership and management of the business. Of the sixty-five, twenty-seven, a substantial minority, had had more than one owner leaving the business. Five businesses had four or more owners leaving. Men are more likely than women to have had one other owner leaving the business as Table 11 shows. This difference, however, if not significant overall, however, in one sector, the textile and clothing, the difference is very significant. The hotel and catering sector actually goes against this general trend, though the difference is too low to achieve significance.

Considerable information was obtained in the questionnaire on the characteristics of other owners who had left the firm. Most of these results will not be reported here in this paper. However, it is interesting to note that whereas in Table 6 two-thirds of the other owners were related in some way to the respondent, when the other owners who had left were examined, only 22 per cent were related to the respondent. This indicates that it is usually non-relatives who leave the firm. The sexes do not differ very much in the proportion of ex-owners who are related to the respondent. There is, however, a notable difference when the distribution of relatives who have left is considered. In the case of female respondents, ex-owners include father, mother, sister and ex domestic partners. There is no instance of a brother or of another relative having left a firm where a female respondent was working. In contrast, only two ex male owners fall into these categories. The majority of male ex owners were either brothers or other relatives, categories which do not appear at all in relation to female respondents.

Table 9. Whether the other owner has a specialist role by sex of other owner

SPECIALIST ROLE?	TEXTILE & CLOTHING		BUSINESS SERVICE		HOTEL & CATERING		ALL SECTORS	
	F	M	F	M	F	M	F	M
	%		%		%		%	
YES	68	59	58	69	67	69	65	67
NO	32	41	42	31	33	31	35	33
	100	100	100	100	100	100	100	100
Chi Square	NS		NS		NS		NS	

Table 10. Cook versus Chef as specialist roles in the Hotel and Catering sector, by sex of other owner.

	F		M		TOTAL	
SPECIALIST ROLE	N	%	N	%	N	%
CHEF	2	8	14	27	16	21
COOK	13	48	5	10	18	23
OTHER	12	44	32	63	44	56
	27	100	51	100	78*	100
Chi Square			P = 0.000			

Table 11. Owners who have left the business by sex of respondent.

AT LEAST ONE OWNER HAS LEFT	TEXTILE & CLOTHING		BUSINESS SERVICE		HOTEL & CATERING		ALL SECTORS	
	F	M	F	M	F	M	F	M
	%		%		%		%	
YES	11	32	19	28	15	9	15	22
NO	89	68	81	72	85	91	85	78
	100	100	100	100	100	100	100	100
Chi Square	P = 0.03		NS		NS		NS	

Table 12. Multiple business ownership by sex of respondent

RESPONDENTS OWNING MORE THAN ONE BUSINESS	TEXTILE & CLOTHING		BUSINESS SERVICE		HOTEL & CATERING		ALL SECTORS	
	F	M	F	M	F	M	F	M
	%		%		%		%	
YES	3	25	11	24	8	18	8	22
NO	97	75	89	76	92	82	92	78
	100	100	100	100	100	100	100	100
Chi Square	P = 0.02		P = 0.08		P = 0.08		P = 0.001	

Table 13. Additional businesses owned by sex of respondent of those that own additional businesses

NUMBER OF ADDITIONAL BUSINESS OWNED	FEMALE RESPONDENT N	%	MALE RESPONDENT N	%
ONE	10	83	19	47
TWO	2	17	9	22
MORE THAN TWO	0	0	13	31
	12	100	41	100

Chi Square $P = 0.04$

Multiple business ownership

Just under a fifth of respondents overall own more than one business. Men are far more likely to own more than one business than women are (Table 12). This trend is highly significant in the total sample, and is either significant or close to being significant within each sector. Unlike most of the trends illustrated in this paper where at least one sector does not follow the general trend of the total sample, all three sectors show the same type of trend in this particular case. Of those who own more than one business, there is a highly significant gender difference in the distribution of numbers of additional businesses owned (Table 13). The table shows quite clearly that men are much more likely to own multiple businesses than women are.

Conclusions

Of the variables examined in this paper, most showed statistically significant differences between sectors. Only a minority varied significantly by sex. This pattern is broadly repeated over all sections of our study.

Sector, therefore, is the primary factor in differentiating small business owners in their ownership and management practices.

This fact makes the identification of "gender" differences extremely difficult. The covariation between sector and sex is considerable, and complex to separate. To help this process, this study repeated cross-tabulations by sex separately in each of the three sectors.

A sex difference is truly a gender one if the difference by sex is significant and in the same direction in all three sectors. None of the variables examined in this paper fell into this category. A gender difference is also strongly implied if at least one of the sub-sectors displays similarly large differences and patterns falling short of statistical significance. Of the variables examined in this paper, only "multiple business ownerships" meets this criterion. Men are much more likely to own more businesses than women in all sectors examined.

All other variables exhibiting some significant variation by sex display "discordant" trends. A "discordant" trend is one where a relationship is one group is not replicated in another. It is common in our results for two sectors to display similar differences and for the third to contradict this trend. Two sectors showing similarity are not invariably the same ones as different variables examined.

Discordant variation by sex should not be necessarily interpreted that no gender trends exist. This is possible, but we showed in Table 10, when referring to the "cook/chef" gender difference, that instances may arise where gender relevantly impacts only on one sector. (Cooks and chefs have no relevance to management practice in the textile or business services sectors.)

We also detect the influence of gender on female business owners in the business service sector are only related to other owners who are domestic partners, while men are more frequently related to other categories of kin, such as fathers, brothers and other relatives.

Overall the study demonstrates that the truly individual owner-manager, particularly the individual woman in business, is less common than the literature implies. Two thirds of businesses involve partnership of some kind. Even sole traders tend to have domestic partners and other relatives who are contributing to the business in some way (we have a great deal of evidence for this which could not be reported in this paper).

Gender, surprisingly, does not impinge on the form of legal ownership undertaken by men and women. Distributions of types of ownership (i.e. sole traders versus partners versus limited companies) are remarkably similar by sex. This runs counter to Brush (1992:13) who states that "comparable to male-owned businesses, women most often choose sole proprietorship as the preferred form of business structure (Hisrich and Brush 1983; Cuba, Decenzo and Anish, 1983; Mescon, Stevens and Vozikis 1983/4)". This difference may be accounted for by sectoral factors, in that our study covers three sectors, not all sectors. Table 1. however, shows that female business owners are not always proportionally the majority of sole traders in all sectors (male sole traders tend to be proportionally more common in business services). This would indicate that it is not so much that women **PREFER** sole trading, but that in sectors where women are commonly self employed, sole trading is the dominant form of business ownership in that sector for those sizes of business commonly owned by women. Sectoral factors again complicate the identification of gender differences on this issue.

The most spectacular and consistent gender difference involves multiple business ownership. Why men tend to own more businesses than women begs many gender-related explanations. (For example, men are reputed to have more resources; are less likely to value financial security; have more opportunities and choice of establishing new ventures, and so on.) A major possibility too is that in practice many women may not have the total control of their own resources necessary for lateral business expansion. Most women either share their business resources with legal partners, and/or share their domestic resources with their domestic partner. This is also true for male business owners to a large extent, but social custom arguably allows men more freedom to separate and "ring fence" resources for their own ends. These conclusions, however, need to be modified to take into account the inherent heterogeneity of female business owners in their relationships with spouses and partners. For example the detrimental impact of the husband to a woman's business, indicated as common by Goffee and Scase (1983), is often contracticed in our study. The qualitative interviews commonly portrayed a positive contribution of husbands to a woman's business. We hope to pursue these issues more systematically when the full sample is available.

The findings also have implications for the methodology of small business gender studies. As most variables vary so widely between sectors, precise "gender" findings of a study may be a consequence of the sectoral mix of the sample as much as genuine social trends impinging on the small business community. We concur with Thomas, Uribe-Echevarria and Romijn when they state:

"The so-called small scale sector is far from homogenous and does not constitute a single sector of the economy in any real sense. Reality shows a sectoral labour market, regional heterogeneity that cannot be ignored. A most disaggregated view of small scale economic activity should therefore reduce the emphasis on broad and highly aggregated analysis and policy." (Page 5)

Secondly, the practice of comparing samples of female and male "entrepreneurs" without taking into account wider ownership issues in the sampling and analysis phases is simplistic. Fischer (1992:6), for example, extracted 2724 firms from the Dun and Bradsheet data base in Canada and identified 60 female owned firms out of 508 usable replies. She does not explain what is meant by "female owned", or whether the male owned sample is totally male owned, or a mixture of male and female co-owners. What does Brush (1988:612) mean by "women owned enterprises now account for more than 25% of all small businesses?" Even Kalleberg and Leicht's otherwise commendable and thorough longitudinal analysis of Indiana firms, does not elaborate on what they mean by "businesses headed by women" (1991:136,139), or what differential success and performance between male and female headed businesses really means in the light of the authors' failure to control for co-ownership.

This paper shows that a majority of owner-managers, whether female or male, share decision making in some way. What are we comparing when we compare "random" sample of female and male entrepreneurs or business owners? Are we comparing management of female and male ways? Or are we comparing perceptions of a common process of decision makings, female and male perspective? Or merely the compromise between the negotiated decisions between male and female owner-managers within the firm? These questions are obviously much more complex to answer than the implication of a simple male versus female sampling strategy, where there is a strong implication that each owner manager in the sample is entirely responsible for the decisions of the firm he or she manages and that he or she does not share the burden with others.

Finally, the evidence from this paper suggests that, for many women, proprietorship tends to provide only a limited opportunity for "liberation through self-determination" (Scase and Goffee 1983:627). Most women have to accommodate their own ambitions in business ownership with those of others. The impact of "gender" on small business ownership is thus not interpretable in simple uni-dimensional terms, but can only be fully understood by taking a more holistic approach to research.

References

Birley, S.; Moss, C. and Sanders, P. (1987) Do women entrepreneurs require different training? *Journal of Small Business*, pp.27-35.

Brush, C. (1988) Women entrepreneurs: strategic origins impact on growth. *Frontiers of Entrepreneurship* Research Babson Conference, Calgary. pp. 612-625.

Brush, C. (1992) Research on women business owners: past trends, a new perpective and future directions. *Entrepreneurship Theory and Practice.* summer, pp. 5-30.

Carter, S. and Cannon, T. (1991) *Women as Entrepreneurs* Academic Press.

Cromie, S. and Hayes, J. (1988) Towards a typology of female entrepreneurs. *The Sociological Review* 36(1) pp. 87-113.

Cuba, R,; Decenzo, D,; and Anish, A. (1983) Management practices of successful female business owners. *American Journal of Small Business* 8(2) pp. 40-45.

Fischer, E. (1992) Sex differences and small business performance among Canadian retailers and service providers. *Journal of Small Business and Entrepreneurship.* 9(4) pp. 2-13.

Goffee, R. and Scase, R. (1983) Business ownership and women's subordination: a preliminary study of female prorietors. *The Sociological Review* 3(4) pp. 625-648.

Hamilton, D. (1990) *An Ecological Basis for the Analysis of Gender Differences in the Predisposition to Self Employement*. University of Stirling: SEF monograph 73/90.

Hamilton, D.; Rosa, P. and Carter, S. (1992) The impact of gender on the management of small busiiness: some fundamental problems. In Welford, R. (ed) *Small Businesses and Small Business Development - A Practical Approach* Bradford: European Research Press pp. 33-40

Hisrich, R. and Brush, C. (1983) The woman entrepreneur: Implications of family, educational and occupational experience. *Frontiers in entrepreneurship research.* pp. 54-77. Wellesley, M.A: Babson College.

Kalleberg, A. and Leicht, K. (1991) Gender and organisational performance: determinants of small business survival and success. *Academv of Management Journal* 34(1) pp. 136-161.

Meijer, J.; Braaksma, R. and Van Uxem, F. (1986) Contributing wife partner in business; in Donckels, R. and Meijer, J. *Women in Small Business.* Maastricht: Van Gorcum. pp. 65-77.

Meittinen, A. (1986) Contributing spouses and the dynamics of entrepreneurial families; in Donckels, R. and Meijer, J. *Women in Small Business.* Maastricht: Van Gorcum. pp. 78-86.

Mescon, T.S.; Stevens, G.E and Vozikis, G.S. (1983/4) Women as entrepreneurs. *Wisconsin Business Forum.* 2(2) pp. 7-17.

Solomon, T. and Fernald, L. (1988) Value profiles of male and female entrepreneurs. *International Small Business Journal* 6(3) pp. 24-33.

Thomas, H.; Uribe-Echevarria; F. and Romijn, H. (1991) *Small-Scale Production.* London:Intermediate Technology Publications.

Part F
VENTURE CAPITAL

Part I
VENTURE CAPITAL

30 Financial structure and profitability of SMEs vs large companies: An international study

Enric Genescà, José Mª Veciana and Teresa Obis

Introduction

The hypotesis that the rate of return increases with the size of the firm has not only been defended in the economic field but is also a generalized belief. Baumol put forward the hypotesis that "... increased money capital will not only increase the total profits of the firm in a higher echelon of imperfectly competing capital groups, it may very well also increase its earning per dollar of investment (2, p. 33).

The question of profitability and size of firms has been a subject of study by many researchers. See, for instance, CRUM (1939), McCONELL (1945), ALEXANDER (1949), OSBORN (1951), STECKLER (1963), HALL & WEISS (1967), SAMUELS - SMYTH (1968), JACQUEMIN & CARDON DE LICHTBUER (1973), MANCKE (1974), JACQUEMIN & SAEX (1976), WHITTINGTON (1971), QUARTZ (1976), etc. Previous studies of the effect of size on profitability have provided contradictory results. Some researchers have found confirming results, some not. Perhaps one of the most outstanding shortcomings of previous research is the size of the sample used. Most of the studies have worked with a small sample and/or restricted to a country. They have also used different methodologies so that the results are generally not comparable.

The results presented in this paper are based on a sample of 285.550 firms and 11 countries.

Our research focusses not only on the relation between profitability and size of firms but also enables one to draw additional, and we think, interesting conclusions from the financial structure in regard to size of firms.

General characteristics of the data base

The BACH project (Bank for Accounts of Companies Harmonised) was promoted in 1985 by the Directorate-General for Economic and Financial Affairs of the Commission of the EEC with the aim of creating a data base of aggregated economic and financial data from industrial and service (non financial) enterprises classified by size from the following countries:

>Germany (G)
>Belgium (B)
>Spain (S)
>U.S.A (USA)
>France (F)
>Holland (H)
>Italy (I)
>Japan (J)
>Portugal (P)
>United Kingdom (U.K.)

The Agency balance sheet centralizing data of the above countries sends to the above mentioned Task Force the aggregated data in a standard form in order to make possible international comparisons. The sample of firms participating in each of the above mentioned Agency is rather large, i.e.

	Sample
Germany	71.000 firms
France	18.000
Italy	29.000
United Kingdom	3.200

Belgium	118.000
Holland	3.000
Portugal	7.000
Japan	20.000
U.S.A.	7.500
Spain	7.500

In order to be able to make a comparative analysis of the Catalan firms with those of other countries, we have calculated for the Spanish firms with base in Catalonia (C) each of the items used in the BACH project from the data collected by the Spanish Agency, Banco de España. The sample of Catalan firms is 1.500. Therefore, in this paper when we say Spain we always mean Spain, excluding Catalonia.

Annex 1 shows the structure of the Balance Sheet and Profit and Loss Acount used in the BACH project. In this paper we shall base our analysis on the study of the following ratios expressed, usually, in percentage form:

1 - FIXED ASSETS / TOTAL ASSETS
2 - FINANCIAL ASSETS / FIXED ASSETS
3 - TOTAL LIABILITIES / TOTAL ASSETS
4 - LONG-TERM LIABILITIES / TOTAL ASSETS
5 - OPERATING PROFIT / NET TURNOVER
6 - LABOUR COST / VALUE ADDED
7 - FINANCIAL PROFIT / NET TURNOVER
8 - INTEREST CHARGES / BORROWED CAPITAL
9 - NET TURNOVER / TOTAL ASSETS
10 - NET PROFIT PLUS INTEREST CHARGES / TOTAL ASSETS

the meaning of which is, in our view, self-explanatory. The fact that other relevant ratios, such as operating profitability and operating turnover or working capital, are not selected for analysis is because they cannot be calculated for all countries on the basis of the data available.

When comparing the value of a certain ratio for a given year it must be taken into account that there are still some differences of criteria in the data base that can distort the analysis. Whenever possible international comparisons should be based on trend analysis because when such analysis is referred to the same country the criteria in question are uniform.

Due to its significance, we should also like to single out the fact that, in view of the definition used of the rate of return (10) and cost of debt (8) ratios, their direct comparison does not give the sign of the leverage due to the lack of uniformity of the denominators.

In the next sections we present the main conclusions that may be drawn from this information, in an initial approach. The analysis will primary refer to the manufacturing industry companies (excluding Energy and Building) as it is the segment best covered in a more homogeneous and uniform way by the Balance Sheet Agency of the countries considered. The samples of the Services sector are, on the other hand, much less representative and also less uniform, so that the conclusions reached about it will have to be viewed with a certain caution.

International comparisons at global level

The comparisons at global level, i.e. without size distinction, of the economic and financial situation of the companies of the different countries included in the study will act as a general framework of reference for the next two sections, which are the one making up the central core of our study.

The first series of graphs (1.1 to 1.5) summarize the economic situation in financial year 1990 (1989 for Germany) of the companies of the different countries considered in the study. In graph 1.1. a line has been drawn through the coordinates origin and the point corresponding to Catalonia so as to have a bench mark thereby for making comparisons since, as it has been said before, direct comparison between profitability and the cost of debt is not strictly valid. Obviously, the bench mark could have been any other country without this altering the sense of the conclusions.

Based excepcionally on comparisons at gloval level, it can be asserted with the usual precaution that as regards Industry, the best relative situation, which is obtained by relating profitability and the cost of debt, appears in Germany (G), Holland (H), United States (US), United Kingdom (UK),

Japan (J), France (F) and Portugal (P)[1]. To the contrary Italy (I), Spain (S), Belgium (B), and Catalonia (C) exhibit a lower profitability-cost of debt ratio. The conclusions are similar for the Service sector.

Through not having information on operating profitability and operating turnover, the reasons for this wide variety of situations cannot be pinpointed easily. What we can see is that precisely in the worse situated countries (with the exception of Belgium) financial results (fiancial assets income minus interest charge) has a strong negative impact.

As regards the financing sources the most significant fact to point out is that the external source of financing, especially the long term debt, is lower in Catalonia, Spain (excluding Catalonia), Portugal and Italy in comparison to other countries.

The reason for the higher leverage in the other countries is the lower cost of the debt, on the one hand, and the existence of more transparent and dynamics financial markets, on the other.

The only information that allows us to relate the quantities of "Assets" to "Claims on Assets" is the liquidity ratio (current assets / current liabilities). In general, the situation of the Italian, Catalan and Portuguese firms are in a slightly worse position in this respect.

As regards the evolution of the main financial variables in the 1986-90 period the most remarkable fact in our opinion is the existence of basic similar trends in spite of the differences at the outset. For example, the percentage of the financial assets on total assets increases between 6 and 9 points in all the countries considered in the period in question (1986/90).

The liquidity ratio decreases in general terms and total assets rotation deteriorates in all countries, except Catalonia, due to the above mentioned increase of the financial assets.

As far as the Profit and Loss Account is concerned, similar trends are observable in most countries, the most significant facts being a) the general decline of the operating margin, b) the financial results and c) the ROI in the last year. These changes are due to the increase of financial expenses

---

[1] The information pertaning to this sample exhibits wide fluctuations from one year to another, so the conclusions stemming from it should be viewed with a certain caution.

(interest charges) and the labour cost on the value added.

In the general framework of similar trends, some differences may, however, be pointed out. First, Germany, Japan and Belgium show a greater stability in all indicators; even the general trend change in 1990 is less noticeable. At the other extreme, we find Catalonia, Spain, United Kingdom and the U.S.A. with great variations and/or declines.

Another remarcable point is that Italy and Catalonia are the only two countries where the ratio Labour cost / Value added increases in all periods considered in this trend analysis. Both operating and net margin also systematically decrease. Contrary to Italy, in Catalonia this margin decline has not a full and direct effect on ROI, this being due to an improvement ot the rotation.

As far as the firms in the service sector are concerned, the most significant trends for the 1986-90 period are the following:

- In all countries, except Catalonia, there is an important increase of the financial assets in the total asset structure.

- There is general trend to increase the long term debt over proportionally except Catalonia, Spain, Portugal, Belgium and Italy.

- A general trend to decrease the rotation of total assets, due, in part, to the increase of the financial assets and, in part, to the management of the working capital.

- In the financial year 1990 (and in some cases already in 1989) a rather general trend in the decrease of margins and ROI and an increase of the financial cost, can be identified, these trends being specially striking regarding Catalonia, Spain, United Kingdom and U.S.A.

From this general framework, we will now go on to analyze the main differences in profitability and economic and financial structure by size of firms. We shall make a distinction between SMEs, on the one hand, and large ones on the other. The frontier between the two differs according to the country. The standard practice, however, is to consider SMEs as companies with fewer than 500 employees and large companies as those exceeding that figure.

Comparisons of the ratios by size of firms within the same country are not affected by the armonization problem referred to above, and therefore they can be considered as valid.

Economic and financial structure by size of firms

Unfortunately, we have no data available for Germany and the United Kingdom under this head because, for the time being, there is no breakdown by size in the data base.

From the data for 1990, we see the existence of clearly differentiated economic and financial structures in almost all the countries depending on the size of firms (see graphs 2.1 to 2.4).

As far as the industrial sector is concerned, large firms have proporcionate larger assets (especially financial assets), lower total asset rotation, higher depreciation and lower labour cost. In general, there are not great differences regarding operating margin by size of firms, because one factor may be compensated by another. We venture the hypotesis that the cash flow of large firms is higher that in SMEs due to higher depreciation volume. On the contrary, the financial results are significantly higher in large firms than in SMEs.

On the other hand, large firms have a higher long term debt, in relative terms, than SMEs. The former also show lower unit cost of the external financing. Despite this, however, profitability of total assets of SMEs is significantly higher than large firms. This is probably due to the greater flexibility of the former.

The structural differences by size of firms, whith undoubtedly fit the conventional theorethical model, are present in practically all countries. Furthermore it is worth ponting out that in Catalonia, Spain and Italy the operating margins of SMEs are also clearly higher that those of large firms. The reason for this difference lies in the fact that the labour cost and the depreciation volume are higher in large firms in these countries. Consequently, the SMEs' ROI in 1990 is 3 points higher than in large firms.

Regarding the companies in the service sector, the differences by size are similar to those in the industrial sector. SMEs generally have a higher rotation and lower margin than large ones. The ROI of the former is slightly higher, but the differences are also smaller than in industry. Unitary cost of debt is here also higher in SMEs.

To confirm the stability of these conclusions, obtained from the analysis of the data referring to financial year 1990, we proceed to compare for each item the economic and finantial structures of the companies by size, based on an average of the ratios of the periods 1986-90 both inclusive. As may be observed in graphs 3.1 to 3.5, the clearest and most significant differences are, in line with that stated above, as follows:

- Both the proportion of fixed assets to total assets and that of fiancial assets to fixed assets are substantially higher in the large companies than in the SMEs.

- Long-term liabilities are also grater, in relative terms, in large firms.

- Barring Catalonia, Spain and Italy, the operating margin in greater in large companies than in the SMEs, primarily because of the different impact that labour costs have on added value.

- On the other hand, total asset turnover is higher in the SMEs. Unfortunately, we are unable to learn how far this is due to working asset management or to the lesser weight of the fiancial assets.

- In all the countries except Portugal, the larger the size of the company, the higher the financial result, mainly because of enjoying a lower unitary cost of debt and of the greater weight of the financial assets.

- Except in the United States, Portugal and Belgium, the ROI is higher in the SMEs.

If we relate profitability and unit cost of debt, the resulting ratio is, in almost all the countries, the same or higher in the SMEs than in the large companies. According to this syntesis ratio, the ranking of countries is as follows:

SMEs	LARGE COMPANIES
USA	HOLLAND
HOLLAND	JAPAN
JAPAN	USA
FRANCE	ITALY
BELGIUM	FRANCE
SPAIN	BELGIUM
CATALONIA	SPAIN
ITALY	PORTUGAL
PORTUGAL	CATALONIA

According to the results of our analysis we can confirm the diffent economic and finantial structure of the industrial SMEs vs large companies, their higher profitability in strongly competitive situations and, lastly, their greater weakness in the management of financial resources.

Countries can also be ranked on the basis of these criteria. If the ROI and cost of debt are taken into account simultaneously, this ranking does not differ much by size of firms. As may be seen, this ranking largely depends on the differences in the cost of debt from one country to another. For this reason, the liberalization of the financial markets may especially benefit the industrial companies of the bottom-ranked countries.

The differences in ROI in favour of the SMEs are more structural, as they arise in the majority of the countries and, albeit to a lesser extent, both whether the cost of debt is taken into account or not.

Analysis of trends in the period 1986-90

To conclude this study, let us lastly take a look in this section at the main trends observed in the period 1986-90. Graphs 4.1 and 4.2 show the development by countries of the ROI ratio of the industrial and services SMEs and large companies. The most significant thing to be observed from the study of these graphs is the widespread change in trend that ocurred in year 1990 (1989 in some countries). Another aspect to be singled out is the higher stability of the indicators relating to the SMEs. The advances in the period 1986-89 are not so spectacular and the decline in 1990 in not so sharp either. In fact it represents a more flexible and adaptable structure. Although in periods of expansion it cannot benefit to the same extent as the large companies from the improved profitability stemming from rising levels of occupancy of the production capacity available, in times of recession, however, it benefits from its ability to adapt more quickly to the changes in demand.

By countries, the most significant factor would be the high stability of results both of the SMEs and of the large companies of Japan an the decline in profitability of the Italian companies of both sizes throughout the period in question.

Graphs 5.1 to 5.8 show the mean annual variation in percentage of the selected ratios for the period 1986-89 on the one hand, and 1989-90 on the other. The most salient common features are:

- An increase in proportion of the financial assets to total assets throughout the period considered, although this growth is greater in 1986-89 than in 1989-90.
- The decline in results and consequent decrease in the possibilities of self-financing bring about a sharp increase in long-term liabilities in the last year nearly all countries.
- The labour costs/added value ratio, which displayed a certain tendency to decrease up to 1989 up to 1989, changed direction generally and in particular marked way in the large companies in 1990. This leads to a fall in operating margins in the all the countries and company sizes.
- In 1990 there was also a break in the trend towards improved fiancial result on account of the rise in the unit cost of debt.

The first conclusion in this section is that the trends that occur in the period 1986-90 in the economic and finantial variables considered are very similar from one country and one size of company to another. The second conclusion is that we may confidently state that the SMEs display less variance in the value of the indicators than the large companies. Lastly, the bottom-ranked countries according to the earlier classification are the ones that most suffered the impact of the drop in profitability in 1990.

These conclusions are the other reached in the previous section on the basis of a static analysis, regarding the different finantial structure and higher profitability of the SMEs, help to reach a better understanding of their different features and competitive possibilities. However, this analysis should be completed whith a study of the creation and failures of SMEs. An interesting hypothesis to be tested would be wether the SMEs adaptation to the changes in the economic cycle takes place through bankruptcies and the creation of new SMEs rather than through the adaptation of the existing ones.

References

Alexander, S.S. (1949): "The Effect of Size of Manufacturing Corporation on the distribution of the rate of return", *The Review of Economics and Statistics, 31*.

Baumol, W.J. (1959): "Business Behavior, Value and Growth", *New York, MacMillan*.

Crum, W.L. (1939): "Corporate Size and Earning Power", *Cambridge, Mass*.

Gale, B.T. (1972): "Market Sahre and Rate of Return", *The Review of Economics and Statistics*.

Genesca, E. & Luria, J. et alt (1992): "Estudi economico-financer de l'empresa catalana", *n° 2 Direcció General de Programació Econòmica*.

Hall, M. & Weiss, L. (1967): "Firm Size and Profitability", *in Review of Economics and Statistics, August*.

Jeacquemin, A. & Cardon, M. (1973): "Size Structure, Stability and

Performance of the Largest British and EEC Firms", *European Economic Review, n° 4*.

Mancke, B.B. (1974): "Causes of Interim Profitability Differences: A new interpretation of the evidence", *Quaterly Journal of Economics, Vol. LXXXVIII, May*.

McConnell, J.L. (1945): "Corporate Earnings by Size of Firms", *Survey of Current Business XXV, n° 5*.

Osborn, R.C. (1951): "Efficiency and Profitability in Relation to Size", *HBR, March*.

Quartz, H.W. (1976): "Rendite, Finanzstruktur und Risiko - Eine empirische Unternsuchung bei deutschen Aktiengesellschaften", *Dissertation Saarbrücken*.

Samuels, J. & Smyth, D. (1968): "Profits, variability of profits and firm size", *Economica, May*.

Singh, A. & Whittington, G. (1975): "The Size and Growth of Firms", *Review of Economic Studies*.

Steckler, H.O. (1963): "Profitability and Size of Firm", *Institute of Business and Economic Research, University of California, Berkley*.

Steckler, H.O. (1964): "The Variability of Profitability with Size of Firms", *in Journal of the American Statistical Association", December*.

Vogt, H. (1982): "Unternehmensgrösse und Produktivität", *in ZfO*.

Whittington, G. (1971): "The Prediction of Probability", *Cambridge, Mass*.

ANNEX 1. Table Of Harmonization Codes

CODE	BALANCE SHEET DESCRIPTION
A.	SUBSCRIBED CAPITAL UNPAID
B.	FORMATION EXPENSES
C.1	Total intangible assets
C.2.1.	Land and buildings
C.2.2.	Plant and machinery
C.2.3.	Other fixtures
C.2.4.	Payments on acc. & constr. in progress
C.2.	Total tangible assets
C.3.	Total financial assets
C.	TOTAL FIXED ASSETS
D.1.1.	Raw materials and consumables
D.1.2.	Other stocks
D.1	Total stocks
D.2.1.	Trade debtors
D.2.4.	Other debtors
D.2.	Total debtors
D.3.	Investments in marketable securities
D.4	Cash at bank and in hand
D.	TOTAL CURRENT ASSETS
E.	PREPAYMENTS AND ACCRUED INCOME
P.	TOTAL CURRENT ASSETS AND PREPAYMENTS
F.0.2.	Bank loans and overdrafts
F.0.4.	Trade creditors
F.0.8.	Other creditors
F.	TOTAL CREDITORS (SHORT TERM : < 1 YEAR)
G.	NET CURRENT ASSETS / LIABILITIES
H.	TOTAL ASSETS LESS CURRENT LIABILITIES
I.0.2.	Bank loans and overdrafts
I.0.8.	Other creditors
I.	TOTAL CREDITORS (LONG TERM : > 1 YEAR)
J.	TOTAL PROVISIONS
k.	ACCRUALS AND DEFERRED INCOME
Q.	TOTAL LIABILITIES (LONG TERM)
R.	NET ASSETS
L.1	Subscribed capital
L.2	Share premium account
L.4	Total reserves
L.M.	Minority interests
L.6	Profit to the financial year
L.	TOTAL CAPITAL AND RESERVES (EQUITY)
X.X.	TOTAL ASSETS (MEMORANDUM ITEM)

CODE	PROFIT AND LOSS ACCOUNT DESCRIPTION
1.	Net turnover
2.	Change in stock levels
3.	Capitalised production
4.	Other operating income
S.	TOTAL OPERATING INCOME
5.	Purchases
T.	GROSS PROFIT (OR LOSS)
6.a.	Wages and salary
6.b.	Social security costs (incl. pensions)
6.	Total staff costs
7.	Depreciation and amortisation
8.	Other operating charges
U.	TOTAL OPERATING EXPENSES
V.	OPERATING PROFIT
11.	Investment income
12.	Investment provisions
13.	Interest and other charges
W.	Income from investments net of charges
X.	PROFIT AND ORDIN. ACTIVITIES BEFORE TAX
14.	Tax on profit on ordinary activities
15.	PROFIT ON ORDIN. ACTIVITIES AFTER TAX
M.	Minority interests
N.	PROFIT AFTER TAX AND MINOR. INTERESTS
16.	Extraordinary income
17.	Extraordinary charges
Z.	PROFIT AFTER TAX AND EXTRAORDIN. ITEMS
21.	PROFIT FOR THE FINANCIAL YEAR

Source: BACH (European Comission: DG2)

RATE OF RETURN AND COST OF DEBT
MANUFACTURING
Year 1990

Net profit+interest charges / Total assets

Interest charges / Borrowed capital

+ Catalonia
* Spain (ext. Catalonia)
■ U.S.A
× Japan
♦ Belgium
▲ U.K.
⊻ France
◉ The Netherlands
▼ Italy
★ Germany
⊠ Portugal

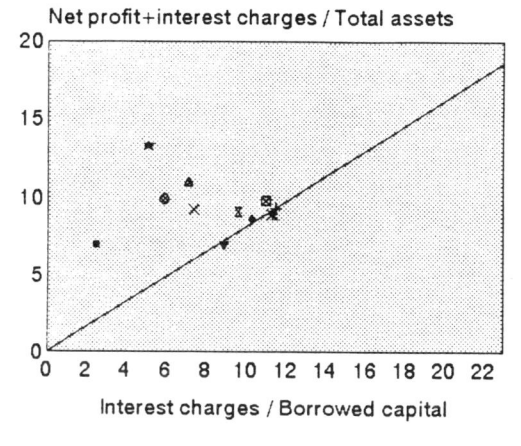

1.1

L.T. LIABILITIES / TOTAL ASSETS
MANUFACTURING
Year 1990

Cat.   S (ext.C)   U.S.A   J   B   U.K   F   N   I   G   P

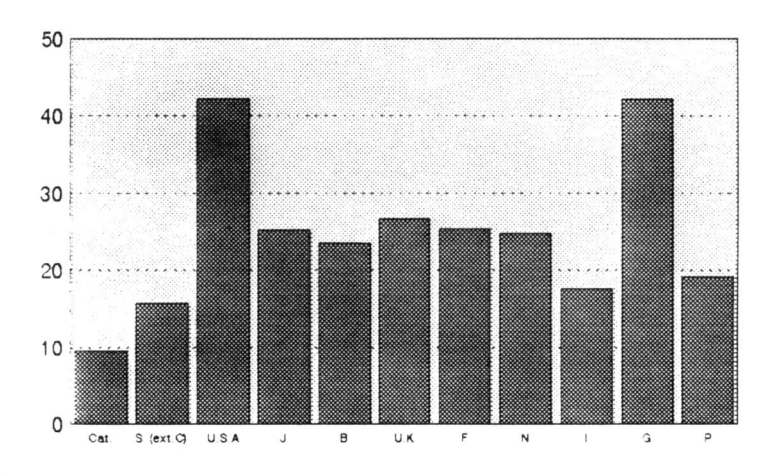

1.2

NET PROFIT+INTEREST CHARGES / TOTAL ASSETS
MANUFACTURING
Variation 1986-90

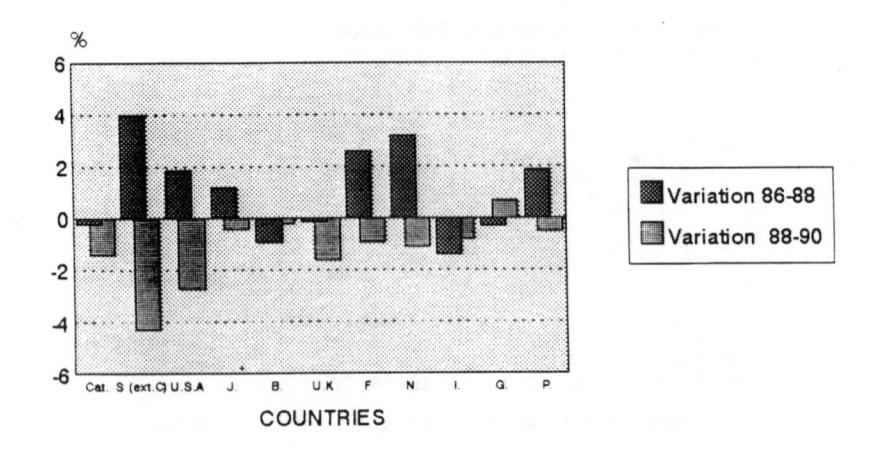

■ Variation 86-88
▨ Variation 88-90

COUNTRIES

OPERATING PROFIT / NET TURNOVER
MANUFACTURING
Variation 1986-90

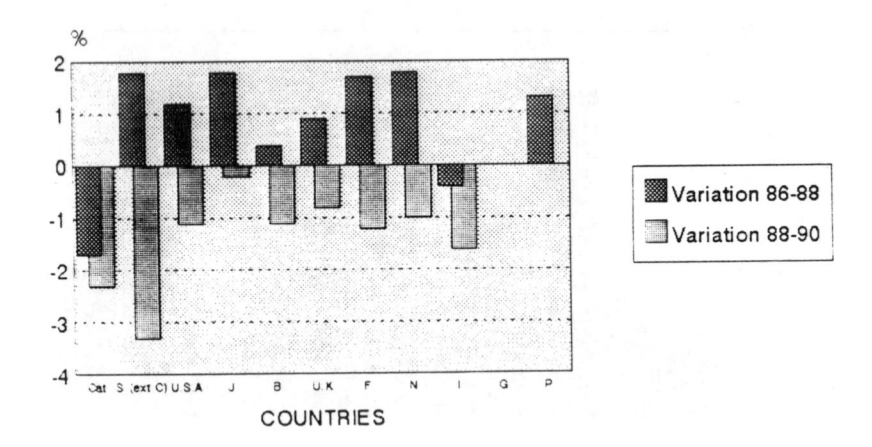

■ Variation 86-88
▨ Variation 88-90

COUNTRIES

NET TURNOVER / TOTAL ASSETS (X 10)
MANUFACTURING
Variation 1986-90

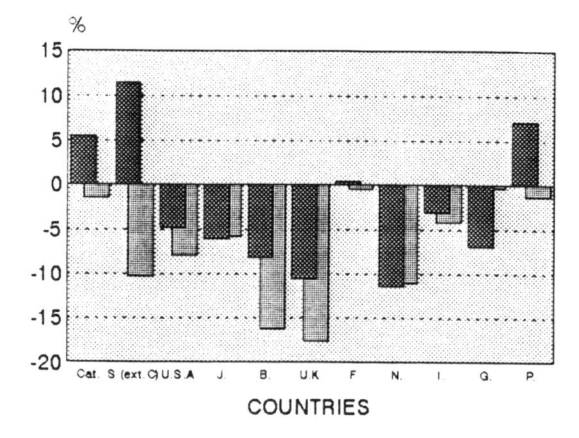

1.5

NET PROFIT+INTEREST CHARGES / TOTAL ASSETS
MANUFACTURING
Year 1990

Large firms

Legend:
- + Catalonia
- ✶ Spain (ext. Catalonia)
- ■ U.S.A
- × Japan
- ♦ Belgium
- ᚼ France
- ● The Netherlands
- ▼ Italy
- ⊠ Portugal

SMES

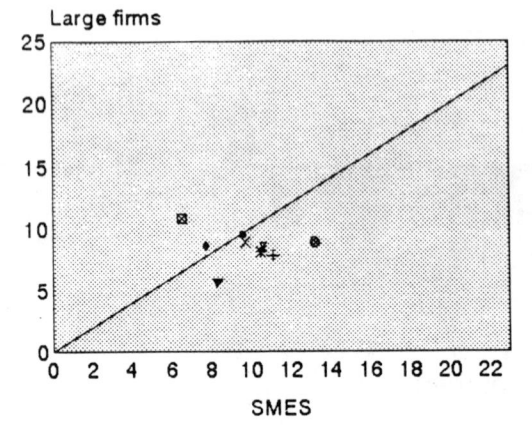

2.1

INTEREST CHARGES / BORROWED CAPITAL
MANUFACTURING
Year 1990

Large firms

Legend:
- + Catalonia
- ✶ Spain (ext. Catalonia)
- ■ U.S.A
- × Japan
- ♦ Belgium
- ᚼ France
- ● The Netherlands
- ▼ Italy
- ⊠ Portugal

SMES

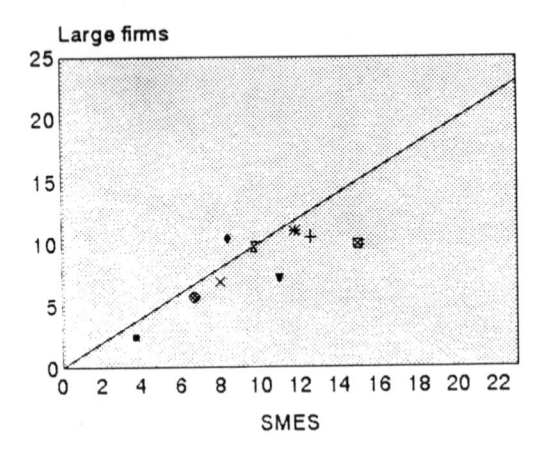

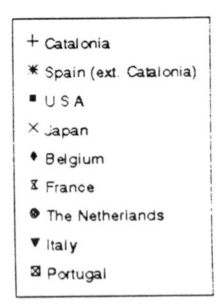

2.2

NET TURNOVER / TOTAL ASSETS (X 10)
MANUFACTURING
Year 1990

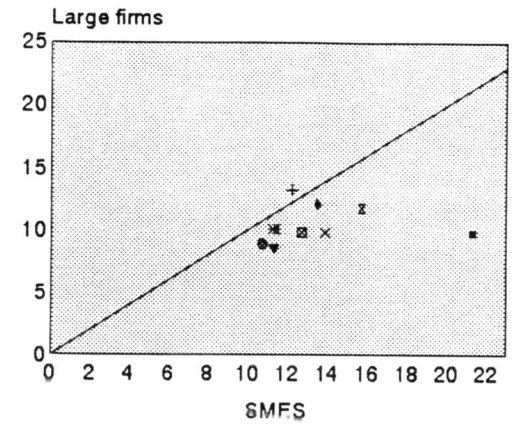

Large firms vs **SMES**

- $+$ Catalonia
- ✱ Spain (ext. Catalonia)
- ■ U.S.A
- × Japan
- ♦ Belgium
- ℐ France
- ⊕ The Netherlands
- ▼ Italy
- ⊠ Portugal

OPERATING PROFIT / NET TURNOVER
MANUFACTURING
Year 1990

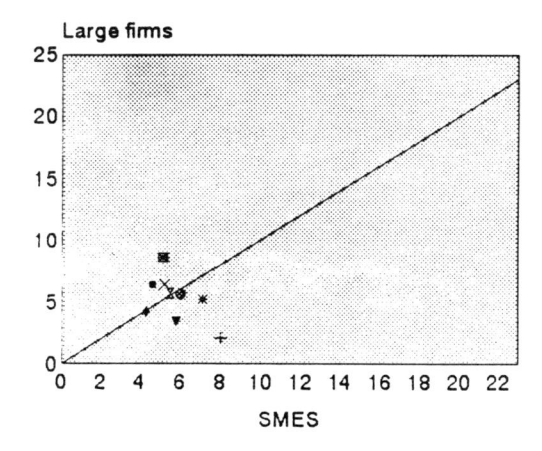

Large firms vs **SMES**

- $+$ Catalonia
- ✱ Spain (ext. Catalonia)
- ■ U.S.A
- × Japan
- ♦ Belgium
- ℐ France
- ⊕ The Netherlands
- ▼ Italy
- ⊠ Portugal

NET PROFIT+INTEREST CHARGES/TOTAL ASSETS
MANUFACTURING
Mean ratios 1986-90

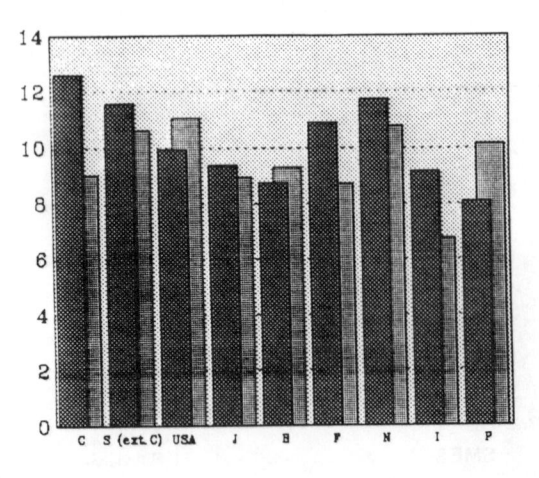

3.1

OPERATING PROFIT/NET TURNOVER
MANUFACTURING
Mean ratios 1986-90

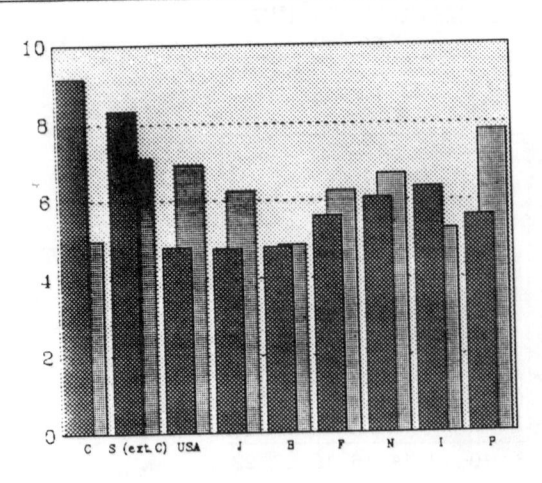

3.2

NET TURNOVER/TOTAL ASSETS (X 10)
MANUFACTURING
Mean ratios 1986-90

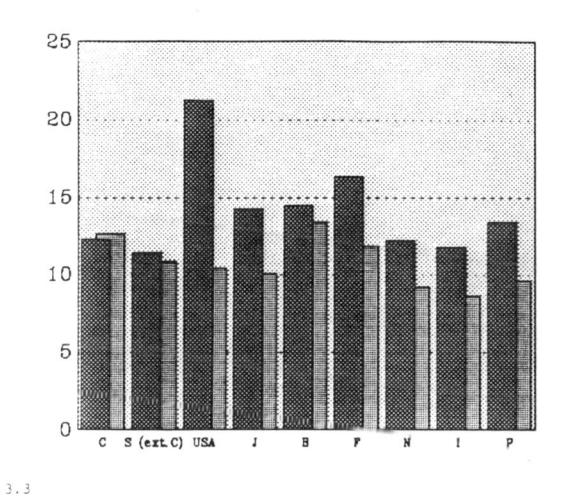

FIXED ASSETS/TOTAL ASSETS
MANUFACTURING
Mean ratios 1986-90

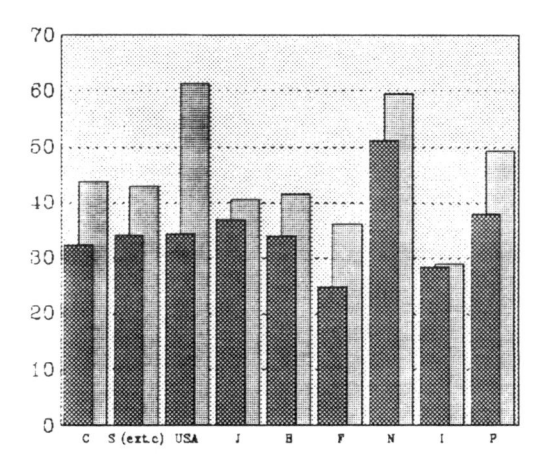

L.T. LIABILITIES/TOTAL ASSETS
MANUFACTURING
Mean ratios 1986-90

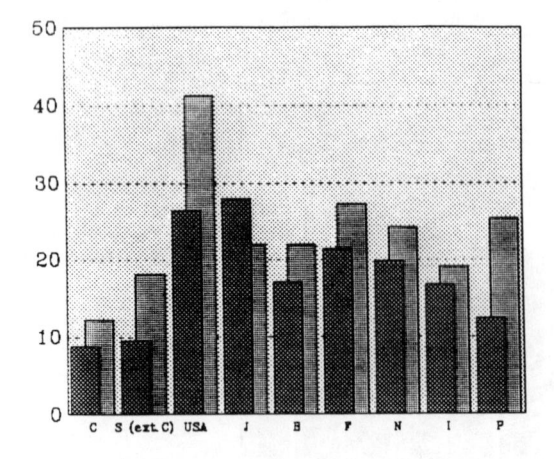

4.1. Net profit + Interest charges/Total Assets. Manufacturing.SMES

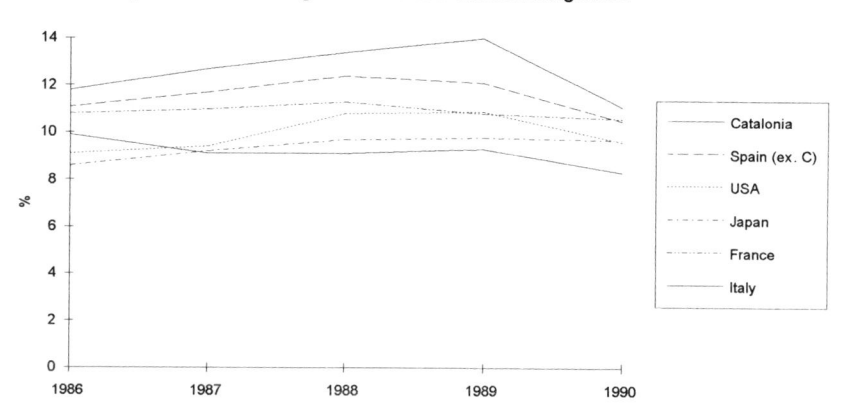

4.2. Net profit + Interest charges/Total Assets. Manufacturing. LARGE FIRMS

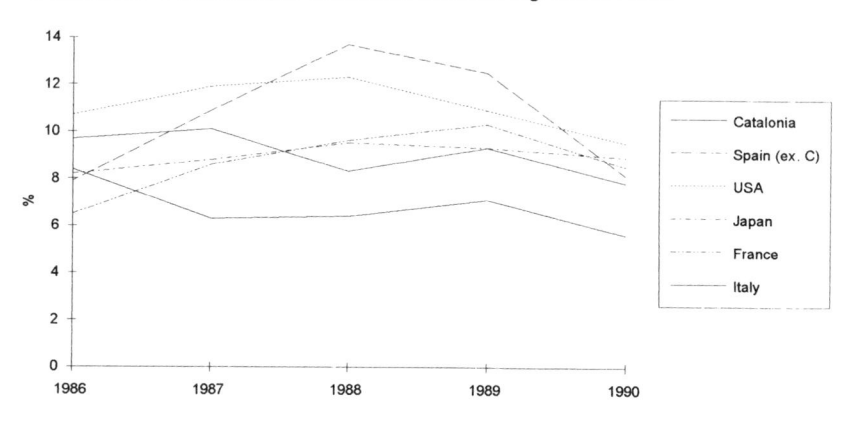

L.T. LIABILITIES / TOTAL ASSETS
MANUFACTURING
Yearly mean variation 1986-89

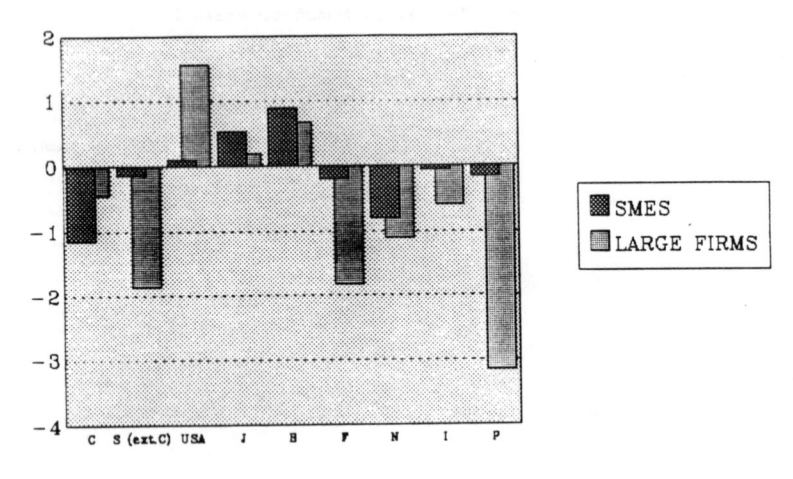

5.1

L.T. LIABILITIES / TOTAL ASSETS
MANUFACTURING
Variation 1989-90

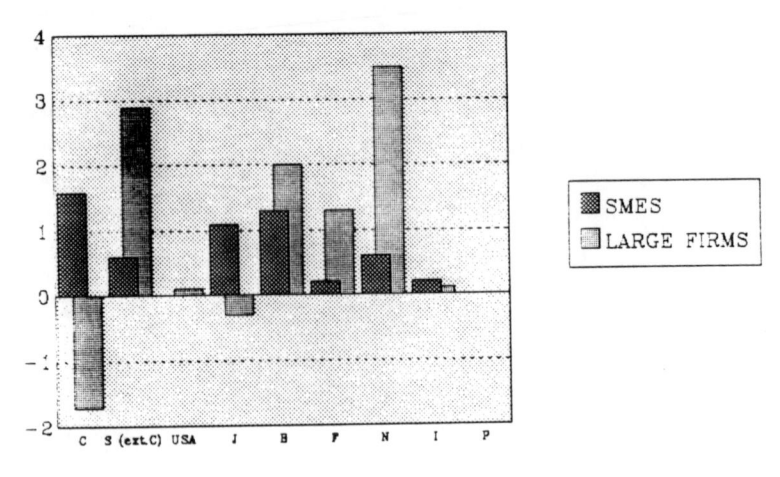

5.2

NET PROFIT+INTEREST CHARGES / TOTAL ASSETS
MANUFACTURING
Yearly mean variation 1986-89

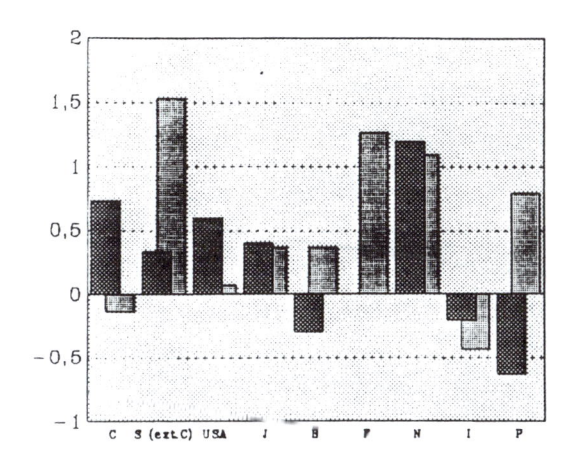

5.3

NET PROFIT+INTEREST CHARGES / TOTAL ASSETS
MANUFACTURING
Variation 1989-90

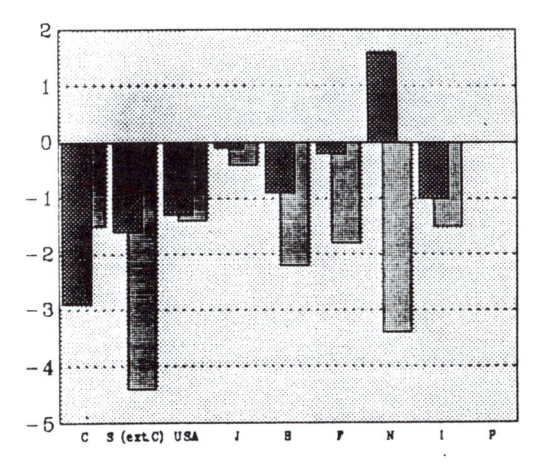

5.4

OPERATING PROFIT / NET TURNOVER
MANUFACTURING
Yearly mean variation 1986-89

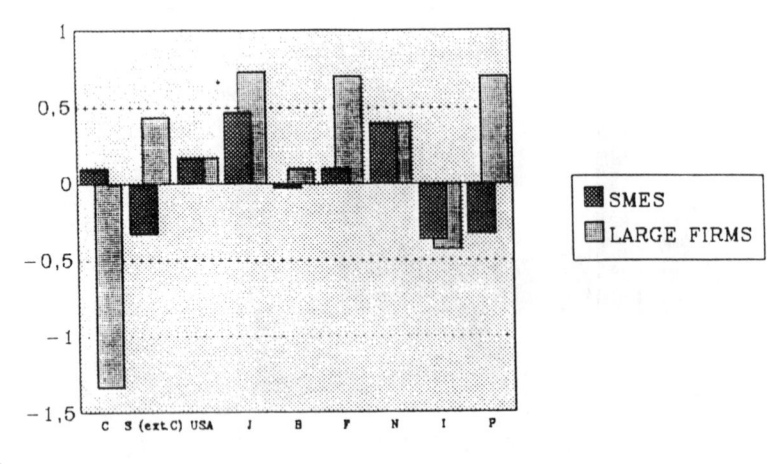

5.5

OPERATING PROFIT / NET TURNOVER
MANUFACTURING
Variation 1989-90

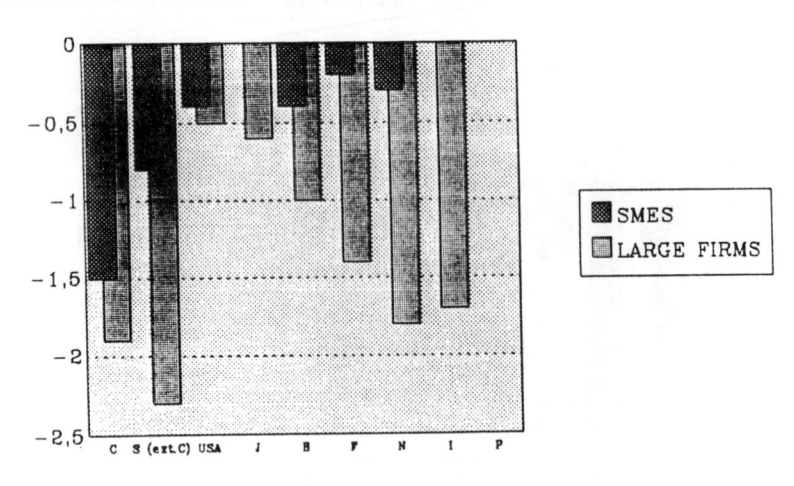

5.6

INTEREST CHARGES / BORROWED CAPITAL
MANUFACTURING
Yearly mean variation 1986-89

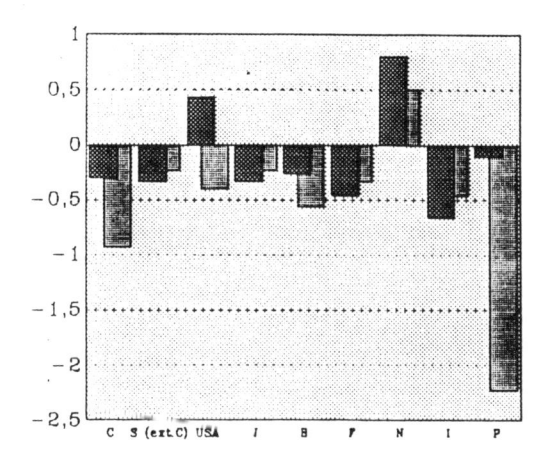

5.7

INTEREST CHARGES / BORROWED CAPITAL
MANUFACTURING
Variation 1989-90

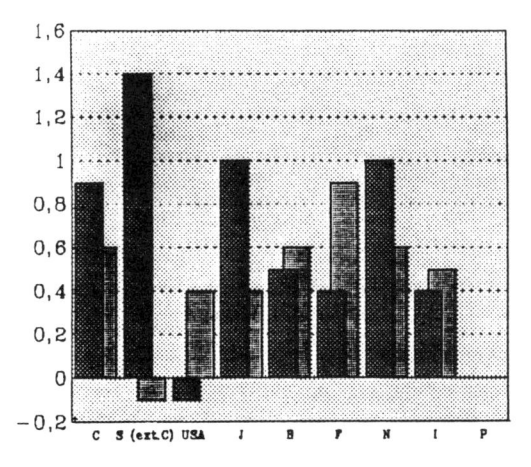

5.8

31 Venture capital investment process in a decision theory framework

Hans Landström

Introduction

The venture capital market has, in many countries, received much attention from policy makers. The small companies' low share of equity capital has been identified as a large problem and policy makers have looked at the venture capital market as a solution to this problem. However, experience has shown that this has not always been the case (EVCA, 1990, and 1991). Even among researchers, the venture capital companies have experienced much attention. The research has been mainly focused on the venture capital companies' decision process in connection with investments in new portfolio companies.

The venture capital companies' investment decisions differ in many important respects from investment decisions in large companies and decisions to acquire established companies, where the decisions can be carried out according to well known financial models. Investments in young and small companies are characterized by such factors as high risk, shortage of prior historical data, quick changes in the company's requisites, etc., which mean that established financial models are not fully applicable. In this paper I will discuss the venture capital companies investment process in a decision theory framework. Hopefully, such discussion will contribute to a better understanding of venture capitalists investment decisions.

The objective of the present paper is; (I) to examine the existing research concerning the venture capital companies' investment decisions, (II) to put the empirical results into a decision theory context, and (III) to present several tentative results from my own empirical research.

The paper will be organized in the following way. In section 2 the decision theory is summarized. In section 3 earlier research relating to the venture capital companies investment decisions is presented. Section 4 gives an account of several tentative results from the empirical research which I have carried out. Finally, the conclusions of the reasoning in the paper are summarized in section 5.

Decision theory

The literature within the area of decision theory is very extensive. Many academic fields have discussed the subject and different aspects of decision-making have been observed. In light of this, it is only possible, in a limited space, to highlight the most central principle of the theory. Therefore, in this paper I will only describe the traditional and basic models within the theory. On the other hand, I will exclude more applied aspects of the decision theory, such as decision-support systems, capital budgeting, etc.

To begin with, a number of process-oriented theories will be presented. Second a number of cognition-oriented theories are described, and finally the individual's relation to risk-taking is discussed.

Decision process theories

There is extensive literature dealing with theories which view decision-making as a process over time. These theories have different starting points and the theories can be divided into decision theories which originate from a rationality norm, a political norm or an action norm.

Theories which originate from a rationality norm Theories which originate from a rationality norm have their starting point in a logical-deductive way of thinking. A categorization can be made in completely rational decisions and limited rational decisions.

The completely rational decision theories are directed towards developing normative models for how decisions shall be made. This has caused the models, above all, to be used within such areas as econometrics, game theory and statistical decision theory. The rational decision process is characterized by distinct and stable goals, the decision-maker is supposed to have complete information about the action alternatives and their consequences, and it is assumed that the decision-maker will maximize his/hers utility. Furthermore, the decision-process can be described in the following phases; (I) define the problem, (II) determine the goals to be fulfilled, (III) look for action alternatives which help to achieve the set goals, (IV) assess the consequences of the different action alternatives, and (V) select the alternative which leads to the highest goal fulfillment.

The completely rational decision theories have been exposed to much criticism (March and Simon, 1958, Cyert and March, 1963, and Simon, 1965). The criticism has, on the one hand, meant that the rational decision models do not give a correct description of reality and, on the other hand, that rational decision-making is not something to strive for.

In relation to completely rational decision-making, limited rational decision-making is characterized by a goal formulation which can include indistinct goals. There is a tendency for a sequential observation to occur at the different goals, i.e., a prioritizing of the goals is made. Furthermore, in the limited rational decision-making, the action alternatives are not completely known. The action alternatives must be searched for, and the search process is often limited to a search for solutions in the area of the problem, in the area of old solutions and to a sequential search process where the decision-makers look at one action alternative at a time (Cyert and March, 1963). The evaluation of the various consequences of the alternatives is made by concentrating on criteria which is documented. The choice of action alternatives usually occurs with the decision-makers comparing one alternative at a time with the goals, and with the question being whether the alternative is good enough in relation to the goals. In many situations simple rules of thumb are used in the decision-making process.

Theories which originate from a political norm The political decision processes are based on the assumptions that; (I) many decision-makers (groups) participate in the decision and that the groups are organized in relatively clearly-defined fractions, (II) the partners have relatively well-formulated goals but the partner's goals are partly conflicting, and (III) the conflicting goals create a base for negotiations between the partners (Schelling, 1960, Lindblom, 1965, and Bauer and Gerger, 1971). The political decision processes can be divided into the following categories:

- Compromise models, which means that the partners are united as to either the goals (goal compromise), i.e., where the partners try to agree on common goals, or the means (mean compromise), i.e., where the compromise occurs on the alternative side and the partners can retain their respective goals.

- Theories about "muddling through", where the basic idea is that the decision-makers develop a number of decision criteria in order to muddle through the decision situations and, in this way, tackle uncertainty and complexity (Lindblom, 1959). The main principle is that a successive adaptation of the original alternative takes place. The decision is developed in a "zig-zag" rather than in a straight-line process and different groups of decision-makers influence the decision at different points in time.

Theories which originate from an action norm   Common to the theories which originate from an action norm is that rational decision-making, on the whole, is lacking or is so limited that it can not be used as a starting point for an analysis. Instead, it is the action itself which should be analyzed. The decisions consist as a consequence of, not a reason for, the action. Within this category the following theories can be referred to:

- "The Garbage Can Model" (Cohen, *et.al.*, 1972, Olsen, 1972, and Cohen and March, 1973) builds on the assumption that the decision process is not some well-arranged process, but is composed of many input-flows; decision situations, problems, solutions and participants. When the input-flows are set into motion, a decision process arises where coincidences and "timing" have great significance for the outcome.

- Action rational theories, which assume that irrationality is a fundamental feature in organizations. People's actions often arise as autonomous processes without previous planning or analyses and where clear and well-defined ideologies in the organization can make the decision-making easier (Brunsson, 1982, and 1985). Furthermore, Brunsson (1985) believes that the conditions for action are that the individual has expectations about success, is motivated and is committed.

- Hidden decision processes, where it is hard to perceive the decision process and to identify the point of time for the decision. Danielsson and Malmberg (1979) have pointed out that many small and separately indiscernible steps, together, give a new direction to the action. The decision comes about gradually and, in a way which is hard to comprehend for an outsider, and can lead to the real decision already being made and carried out before the formal decision is made (Hedberg, 1980).

Cognitive-oriented theories

Extensive research has also been carried out concerning the individual's capacity to manage information. The decision-maker must interpret and create meaning in the information. In this respect, the individual is often dependent on his own cognitive categories in order to channel his experiences and actions. Thus, the decision-maker uses a "map" in order to identify what is relevant to the decision-making (Kelley, 1955). This cognitive map is built up from the decision-maker's function, experiences, expectations, etc.

Some research has been carried out concerning the cognitive style which the individual uses in the decison-making process. Cognitive style refers to the relatively stable and firmly organized method which the private individual uses in order to handle all the types of information he/she receives (Grimsø, 1979).

In the research on cognitive styles, it appears that it crystallizes into two central dimensions; creative and rational thinking, and intuitive and analytical thinking. Creative thinking refers to pattern-breaking thinking, in contrast to rational thinking which follows traditional paths. Analytical thinking is based on quantifiable knowledge which is built up piece by piece. The fundamental features in intuitive thinking are, on the other hand, less systematic. More diffuse and qualitative factors are taken into consideration. However, different authors use different terminology. Guilford (1967), who is one of the forerunners in the field, distinguishes, for example, between convergent and divergent thinking. DeBono (1979) discusses vertical and lateral thinking, while Huysman (1970) makes a division between analytical and heuristic thinking.

A starting point for many discussions around cognitive styles is Jung's

(1933) classification of the concept pairs "perception-intuition" and "feeling-thought". A person with "perception" prefers structured problems and concentrates on routine work. The opposite is true for "intuitive" persons who seek a comprehensive view and do not focus on single units, and prefer unstructured problems. "Feeling" refers to individuals who take into consideration feelings, while "thought" concerns individuals who tend to be impersonal in their evaluation. Jung combines these dimensions into four fundamental styles where each one has advantages and disadvantages, but where one is not superior to other.

Jung's dimensions have established the starting point for many studies. Hellriegel and Slocum (1975) assert, for example, that decision-makers often can not be described in any of these isolated forms, but can be placed on a continuous scale. There is also a tendency for the individual to pull towards a balance and integration of the four styles. Henderson and Nutt (1980) examined the decison maker's experience of risk in connection with the investment projects. The results showed that the cognitive style is a significant explanation for the individual's decision. The "perception-feeling" individuals saw fewer risks and had a stronger tendency to accept, while the "perception-thought" individuals experienced greater risks and had a tendency not to accept the investments. McKeeney and Keen (1974), using Jung's reasoning as a starting point, make a classification of information collection (perceptive versus receptive individuals) and information evaluation (systematic versus intuitive individuals). McKeeney and Keen use this categorizing in order to analyse different management problems. The results showed, *inter alia*, that the systematic individual has a tendency to direct the work towards planning assignments while the intuitive individual prefers to work with less structured work assignments with higher grades of uncertainty.

The treatment of risk

A central concept in decision-making is "risk". In daily speech this is not some distinct concept. Risk is often associated with an outcome which is influenced by factors which the decision-maker has no control over. In terms of a definition, it is important to distinguish between decision-making in a risk situation, i.e., when the decision-maker does not know, with certainty, the true outcome but can state a probability distribution about the outcome, and decision-making in cases of uncertainty, i.e., where the decision-maker neither knows the true outcome nor the probability distribution of the outcome. When the decision-maker can estimate and state a personal probability distribution, an intermediate position exists between risk and uncertainty, which some authors call partial uncertainty while others see it as a transference from an uncertain situation to a risk situation.

The research concerning decision-making in cases of risk and uncertainty has, for a long time, started out from the theory about expected utility (von Neumann and Morgenstern, 1944). An assumption is that the decision-maker chooses from the utility which the total assets give and not only the marginal utility the change of asset will give. Other assumptions are that the individual is assumed to be adverse to risk-taking (Pratt, 1964), and that the attitude towards risk is looked at as stable person dependent. Several studies have also related the individual's risk perception to different personality features (McClelland, 1961, Atkinson, 1964, and Kogan and Wallach, 1964).

Recent research has shown, however, that decision-makers do not always act rationally according to the traditional risk theory. For example, the results indicate that the attitude towards risk is only partly related to the individual's personality but is influenced by other factors such as feelings and the way in which the problem is presented (Johnson and Tversky, 1983). Thus, the studies point out that the individual's attitude towards risk is contextually dependent. This has been observed by Kahneman and Tversky (1979) who found that in situations where the possible outcome is positive, the individual tends to be adverse to risk-taking. But in situations with a possible negative outcome, the individual tends to be more risk-seeking. From these observations, Kahneman and Tversky (ibid.) proposed an alternative theory, "prospect theory", whose fundamental assumptions are (Wahlund, 1989): (I) The individual's value function is defined from the deviation from a reference point and this reference point varies depending on how the problem is formulated. (II) The marginal utility is assumed to be decreasing, but is steeper for loss than for profits. The probability is weighed with a subjective weight which does not need to be equal to 1.

Empirical studies show that company managers often look at risk in a different way than what is assumed within the traditional risk theory. For instance, March and Shapira (1987) showed that company managers do not define risks in accordance with the risk theory. Also, company managers try to control the risks and modify the odds in risk situations and view the risk as manageable. Furthermore, earlier studies (Cyert and March, 1963) indicate that company managers avoid risks by, for example, delaying or delegating the decision.

Decision rationality versus action rationality

In my analysis I will originate from Brunsson's (1976, and 1985) discussions about decision rationality and action rationality. Therefore, I will finish this section with a description of Brunsson's reasoning. Brunsson (1976) distinguishes between a "decision rationality", which means that a function of choice is reached, i.e., it leads to a choice between different courses of action, and "action rationality" which means that action can be initiated. The concept of "uncertainty" is of central importance for the discussion. The concept, in this context, refers to the decision-maker's understanding of which decision is best. Uncertainty influences the decision-maker's motivation, i.e., the individual's wish to participate through action. An individual who feels uncertain about whether the decision is good or bad cannot be expected to be motivated to act. The uncertainty also has consequences for the decision-maker's positive expectations, i.e., the individual's understanding of the action leads to a positive result, and commitment, i.e., people signal to one another their endorsement of any proposed action.

From the above discussion, Brunsson (ibid.) identifies two extremes concerning evaluation modes.

- "Rationalistic evaluation mode" means that abstract elements are used in the assessment, which means a deduction from abstract elements to more operational elements. Also, there is a balance between positive and negative elements.

- "Impressionistic evaluation mode" means that operational elements are used in the assessment, an induction from concrete to increasingly abstract elements, and a concentration on either positive or negative elements.

The conclusion is that a rationalistic evaluation mode generates a high uncertainty potential in decision-making and is therefore not a good basis for action. The high uncertainty means that the decision-maker has low motivation to act, has negative expectations regarding the outcome of the decision, and has weak commitment to the proposal. The result will be that the decision-maker is not interested to act.

On the other hand, an impressionistic evaluation mode means that assumptions are created for an action rationality. The situation is characterized by low uncertainty. The low uncertainty means that the decision-maker has high motivation to act, has positive expectations regarding the outcome of the decision, and strong commitment to the proposal. The result will be that the decision-maker can act.

Earlier research relating to the venture capital companies' investment decisions

Relatively extensive research has been carried out in order to ascertain how the venture capital companies make their investment decisions. In the following subsections, the research relating to the venture capital companies' investment decisions is summarized. First, the decision-making is described as a process. Second, the decision criteria used by the venture capitalists are described, and third, the handling of risk-taking in the investment decision is discussed. Finally, the research is put into a decision theory framework.

Decision -making as a process

The venture capital companies' decision-making, in connection with new investments, contains certain characteristic features which distinguishes it from the more traditional investment decisions. Carleton (1986) points out, for instance, that an information asymmetry exists between the venture capitalist and the entrepreneur, to the entrepreneur's advantage. Naturally, the information asymmetry is particularly pronounced in investments in young, high technology-based companies. As an answer to the information asymmetry, the decision process tends to become sequential, which allows the venture capital company to limit its investments until more information has been received.

Several researchers have described the decision-making process in connection with the venture capital companies' investments. For example, Tyebjee and Bruno (1984a) have, from earlier studies, e.g., Poindexter (1976), and Timmons and Gumpert (1982), described the decision-making process in five steps (for a summary see also Hall and Hofer, 1993):

Step 1: Deal origination - a phase in which a business possibility is identified and considered.
Step 2: Deal-screening - an assessment of key variables (for example, an assessment of the company's technology and market, and financing stages) which limit the investment proposals to a manageable number.
Step 3: Deal evaluation - an evaluation of the potential proposals and decisions about investments.
Step 4: Deal-structuring - negotiations about the conditions in the agreement between the venture capital company and portfolio company.
Step 5: Post-investment activities - a competence and capital supply during the time of investment.

A study by Van Auken and Carter (1990) showed that the venture capitalist judges the evaluation stage as the most important activity in the operation. The result is not unexpected, keeping in mind that the venture capital companies often receive several hundred investment proposals but invest in only a few of them. Other empirical studies show that the venture capitalist spends 30-50% of his time with activities before the investment decision (Tyebjee and Bruno, 1981, and Robinson, 1987). The average time from the contact to the agreement is 4-5 months among the US venture capital companies (Tyebjee and Bruno, 1984b). These results correspond with Swedish conditions (Olofsson and Klofsten, 1985, and Fredriksen, et.al., 1990).

Decision criteria

The part of the investment decision which attracts the largest interest in research are the decision criteria used by the venture capitalists in the evaluation of new investment proposals (Wells, 1974, Bean, *et.al.*, 1975, Poindexter, 1976, Tyebjee and Bruno, 1984a, Robinson, 1987, and Riquelme, 1991). Most of these studies have emphasized the following criteria as important for the investment decision:

- The company's management capability, competence and capacity.
- Factors relating to the company's market.
- Factors relating to the product and the technology.
- The company's financial situation.

Carter and Van Auken (1992) found that the decision criteria which the venture capitalists used in the assessment of new investment proposals differ depending on the potential portfolio company's development phase. Venture capitalists who, on the whole, invest in early development phases were more interested in the possibility of "bailing-out" of the investment if the need arose. They were also open to different types of investment proposals, more interested in listing the portfolio companies on the stock exchange and more inclined to changing the manager in the portfolio company if it was considered necessary, compared to the venture capitalists who prefer investments in later development phases. An interpretation of the results is that venture capitalists who prefer investments in early development phases are more risk-inclined but require, at the same time, a higher potential return.

Van Auken and Carter (1990) showed that venture capitalists with non-business backgrounds seem to be more adverse to risk-taking compared to venture capitalists with prior company experience. There is also a tendency for the venture capitalists to use different decision criteria in their assessment of new investment proposals. For example, venture capitalists without previous company experience place more weight on the uniqueness of the product, the entrepreneur's health and the project's cost structure.

MacMillan, *et.al.*, (1985) qualify the descriptions by dividing the venture capital companies into three categories. The first company category can be characterized as "balanced" venture capital companies. These companies use many different criteria in order to balance the different risks in the investment. The second company category is characterized by companies who consider a minimum of criteria. Finally, the third company category can be looked on as "parachute companies". They are prepared to invest in most of the investment proposals, provided that the investment gives sufficient liquidity and, in this way, makes it possible for the company to pull out if something should go wrong.

However, Hall and Hofer (1993) are rather critical of the existing research results regarding the decision criteria used by venture capitalists, because most of the studies have not specified the stage of the decision process that is studied. Therefore, it is likely that the criteria identified came from different stages of the venture capitalists' assessment process, which means that the existing findings have probably "mixed" different stage criteria, and it is probable that different criteria are used in different stages. Hall and Hofer's study shows that venture capitalists screen and assess investment proposals very rapidly, and they seem to reach a GO/NO-GO decision in an average of less than six minutes on initial screening and less than 21 minutes on proposal assessment.

Similarily, Riquelme and Richards (1992) mean that in the screening stage, the venture capitalists focus on a small subset of criteria in a non-compensatory process, i.e., an unacceptable value on one criterion cannot be offset by a high value on another one. The screening step is more judgemental than analytical. In the evaluation stage, venture capitalists end a detailed examination by choosing the most preferred ventures through processes approximating compensatory rules, i.e., a low but acceptable value on one criterion can be compensated by a high value on another.

Even other researchers have questioned earlier results in the field. Sandberg, et.al., (1987, and 1988) have, for example, pointed out that impressions which were received early in the decision process, influenced the venture capitalist's assessment of the entrepreneur's qualities. Hisrich and Jankowicz (1990) emphasize the importance of intuition for the venture capitalist's assessment. In comparison with bank credit managers (Jankowicz and Hisrich, 1987), the venture capitalists' assessments can be characterized by a lower cognitive complexity, with a strong focus on a few factors. This is explained by the fact that the venture capital company's credit assessment is often made by senior credit managers, while the banks' credit assessment is made by credit managers on a lower level within the organization. One explanation can also be that in complex decision situations, the individual tends to use a cognitive strain-reducing strategy which allows only a few factors to be considered (Khan, 1987a). However, Sjöberg (1990, and 1991) has pointed out the intuitive assessment's low prognosis value for the future result. A large number of empirical studies have clearly shown that intuitive assessments are consistently worse than simple statistical weighing of information (Khan, 1987a, and 1987b).

A large number of studies have thus been carried out in order to ascertain the decision criteria used by venture capitalists in their assessment of new investment proposals. De Castro (1991) makes an interesting reflection, when he points out that a venture capital investment requires a closer cooperation between the venture capitalist and the entrepreneur over a relatively long period of time. Despite this, there are not many studies which have observed the significance of the relationship between the partners as an essential criterion in the venture capitalist's decision-making. However, one study in this direction is by Sargent and Young (1991), who stress the significance of the social context for the venture capitalist's decision-making. They contend that the entrepreneur's social context (social background, education, social network, etc.) is important for the venture capitalist's assessment. When people share a social context, a base is formed for common evaluations and goal-setting which makes it possible for the partners also to interpret information in a similar way. This makes it easier to understand and build confidence in one another.

Beyond the lack of studies concerning the relationship between the venture capitalist and entrepreneur during the selection phase, there are few studies which consider the decision criteria's importance for future success. An exception is Khan (1986) who compared the venture capitalists' expected outcome of an investment with the real outcome. The result showed a very low correlation, i.e., the venture capitalists' original assessment was not related to the final outcome. MacMillan, et.al, (1987) have identified decision criteria which are predictors of the success or failure of the investments. The results show that three types of unsuccessful investments can be identified; (I) companies where the management lacks experience, the product does not have any prototype, and there is no clear market need, (II) companies which are confronted with early competition and the company's management lack perseverance, and (III) companies which have inadequate product protection. In a similar way, two decision criteria are identified as predictors of success, namely, "the absence of competition in the introductory stage" and "the product's market acceptance". These results are supported by Rea (1989) who found that when seed capital and start-up investments are made, the business aspects, e.g., a market which offers expansion possibilities, are more important for a successful investment decision than the nature of the product. On the other hand, the product does not need to be superior to competing products, or the management team complete in this development phase.

The venture capital companies' treatment of risk

The venture capital companies' investment decisions are considered, in many cases, to be characterized by high risk. The risk-taking is due to the fact that many investments are made in small and young companies. Many investments never reach the exit stage which means that there exists a "success risk". This risk is increased by an uncertainty concerning the capital market's susceptibility when the company is ready to be sold. Poindexter (1986) classified 45% of the investments made by the US venture capital companies as high risk investments. Ruhnka and Young (1987) have, however, shown that the venture capitalists' experienced risk diminishes significantly when investments are made in more established companies. The results correspond with Jog, *et.al.*, (1989) who found that there were differences in the venture capitalists' risk assessment and risk-handling among portfolio companies in early as opposed to later development phases. An interesting result in the study was that there were not any differences in the treatment of technology-based and non-technology-based companies.

Tyebjee and Bruno (1981) have studied how the venture capital companies estimate the risks in the portfolio and they identify three categories of venture capital companies:

- Venture capital companies which do not explicitly estimate the risk.
- Venture capital companies which manage the risk by balancing the portfolio.
- Venture capital companies which explicitly consider the risk in the expected return.

Ruhnka and Young (1991) contend, in a similar way, that the venture capital companies develop different strategies in order to identify and limit the risks. One such strategy is to require a detailed business plan from the potential portfolio company which clearly identifies the risks involved in the company. Another strategy is a sequential financing which makes it possible for the venture capital company to break off the financing if certain "benchmarks" are not reached. A third strategy is where the venture capital company spreads its risks by creating a differentiated portfolio. Finally, the venture capital company can develop a unique knowledge among its employees so that the employees can manage different situations in the portfolio company's development.

A further way of managing risks is through making syndicate investments. Bygrave (1987, and 1988) found that the larger the risks associated with the investment, the more common it was to have syndicate investments. Thus, syndicate investments are made with the purpose of sharing risks. But the syndicate also functions as an information carrier both internally and in respect to other investors (Chan, 1983).

The venture capital research in a decision theory framework

The earlier research relating to the venture capital companies' investment decisions has, on the whole, originated from a rationality norm where the decision-maker is expected to act in a planned and methodical way. With this starting point, the decision-maker is assumed to have goals which he wants to achieve and will therefore choose the means which best or sufficiently well meets these goals. Rational action further assumes that the decision-maker considers a large number of alternatives and has the opportunity to calculate both the positive as well as the negative consequences of every alternative.

The research also describes the venture capitalist as analytical in his decision-making where quantifiable information is focused on and where knowledge is built up step by step, and where traditional models are used in the assessment. In Jung's (1933) terms, the venture capitalist would be almost looked on as a "perception-thought" person who prefers structured problems and who is objective in his assessments. According to Hellriegel and Slocum (1975), these persons tend to stress external data and detailed information. They also tend to analyse the data in a logical step by step process. Studies by Henderson and Nutt (1980) point out that these people experience greater risks and have a greater tendency to reject investment proposals. This is in accordance with Brunsson (1976, and 1985). The research relating to the venture capitalists' investment decisions describes, to a large extent, the decision as "decision rational" where the selection function is stressed. The decision rationality leads to an increased feeling of uncertainty in the decision-making which causes the decision-maker to be less willing to make risky decisions.

However, I wish to remain a little critical about the results which are presented in the research within the area. A large part of the existing research treats the investment decisions in too oversimplified and inexact a way (see also Sandberg, *et.al.*, 1987). Often wide concepts, such as the "company's market" and the "management competence" are used as examples of criteria which the venture capitalist uses in his decision-making. Furthermore, there is a tendency to treat all venture capitalists as a homogeneous group when it is really a matter of a relatively heterogeneous group of investors who can be expected to manage the investment decisions in various ways. The oversimplified description of the investment decision is, to a large extent, a consequence of the major part of the studies using a method which does not fully capture the complexity of the decision-making. For instance, the studies often use a retrospective method and survey technique. The methods mean that the answers often reflect "desirable" decision processes and criteria rather than the decision processes and criteria which are really used. There is also a tendency to overestimate the number of criteria instead of pointing out the importance of different criteria, where perhaps a few criteria are of major importance for the decision.

A study of the venture capital investment process

In the present section, several results will be presented from a research project relating to venture capital companies in Sweden (Landström, 1990a). The studies are based on a multi-methodological approach which means that the venture capital companies' investment decisions have been studied with the help of a combination of different methodological approaches and methods of gathering data. In the research project, in-depth case studies have been carried out on three venture capital companies and five portfolio companies. The case studies were in progress for two years and involved different methods of gathering data, primarily interviews and the review of secondary data. Besides case studies, two survey studies have been carried out. The survey studies consisted of a questionnaire sent to 59 venture capital companies, and a questionnaire sent to their portfolio companies. The questionnaire contained questions concerning decision-making in connection with the venture capital company's investments, the co-operation between the venture capital company and the portfolio company, and the result of that co-operation. The methodology of the studies has been presented in other contexts (Landström, 1990a, and 1990b) and therefore will not be further presented in this paper.

Several tentative results from the studies will be presented below. Attention will be focused on a number of conditions which have not been mentioned extensively in the earlier research relating to the venture capital companies' investment decisions. Furthermore, the section will mainly contain a theoretical discussion, and to a lesser extent empirical descriptions. First, the early relationship between the venture capitalist and the entrepreneur is discussed. Second, the venture capital companies' risk management strategies and their consequences for investment decisions are discussed.

The early assessment's character

In this subsection I will present some tentative results from the study and discuss some concepts which characterize the first meeting between the venture capitalist and the entrepreneur.

Some tentative results A reflection which was made at the time of the research project was that many investment decisions appeared to be made at a very early stage of the decision process. For instance, many venture capitalists expressed the following opinion: "After only a half-hour, I know if I will invest in the project/company". A study was also made of one of the venture capital companies which implied that 88 new investment proposals were studied and followed during the investment process. The results showed that 51% of the proposals were rejected during the first contacts, 27% were rejected after a careful assessment of the company, and a further 15% were rejected in connection with the investment negotiations. Of the 88 investment proposals, the venture capital company made investments in six companies, or 7% of the original investment proposals.

The results thus suggest that assessments in the early stages of the process and the first meeting between the venture capitalist and entrepreneur have great significance for the final investment decision (see also Sandberg, *et.al.*, 1987, and 1988). What characterizes this early assessment? It is naturally a very complex situation which can be difficult to describe. However, one observation which was made was that the venture capitalist's early assessment of a new investment proposal and first meeting was, to a large extent, characterized by something that can be called a "momentary relationship". The "momentary relationship" can, *inter alia*, be characterized as;

- intuitive decision-making,
- an assessment of the social attraction (personal chemistry), and
- a possibility for trust in the entrepreneur.

The result is in accordance with Hall and Hofer (1993) and Riquelme and Rickards (1992) who emphazise that the early assessment is characterized by a very rapid decision which seems to be of a GO/NO-GO nature, and where the decision is more judgemental than analytical.

The decision is seldom an acceptance decision. On the contrary, the decision seems mainly to be a rejection decision, i.e., it is a decision that excludes a number of investment proposals.

A result of the momentary relationship is that the venture capitalists experienced a feeling of certainty in the assessment. The decision can be characterized as a one direction decision ("black or white decision"). This assessment directed the work of the continuous assessment by dismissing a large number of investment proposals, and selecting the areas which should be focused on in the continuous analysis of the remaining proposals. Thus, this early assessment seems to reduce the uncertainty in decision-making, and therefore create good conditions for an action rationality in the decision-making.

Momentary relationship As described above, central concepts in the "momentary relationship" are intuition, social attraction, and trust. In this subsection I will try to make some clarifying notes regarding these concepts.

The concept **intuition** is a concept which has been discussed by philosophers and psychologists for a long time. However there seems to be no concensus in the results that have been presented. It is even difficult to find an unambiguous definition (for a summary see Green, 1992). However, the definitions often contain concepts like immediate and unconscious decision-making, characterized by a synthesized and comprehensive view, based on diffuse and qualitative factors.

The significance of **social attraction** for the venture capitalist's decision-making has only been hinted at in the existing venture capital research (see for example Sargent and Young, 1991). This, despite the fact that social attraction in other contexts, for instance, employment interviews, has proven to be of great importance for the assessment of a person. What is meant by social attraction? In my opinion (and according to Sjöberg and Tollgerdt, 1986), social attraction can be seen as an intuitive and unconscious process consisting partly of a perception of the attractiveness of a person, and partly of an assessment of the attractiveness of the person. According to Sjöberg and Tollgerdt (ibid.), the social attraction seems to be a function of factors such as physical attraction, similarities in central attitudes and values, and verbal and non-verbal behavior etc.

It is probable that social attraction is of great significance for creating trust and a generally positive attitude towards a person. It is still not certain that these early assessments lead to a correct understanding of the person. If anything, it can lead to the decision-maker attaching too much importance to very incidental conditions at the first meeting.

A condition for a long-term commitment is that **trust** exists between the partners. The concept of "trust" is often used in everyday contexts and most people have a certain understanding of the concept's meaning. Within sociology, the concept has been defined in different ways (see for example Garfinkel, 1964, and Zucker, 1986). Several common features in these definitions are that trust is based on common expectations, these expectations constitute a part both of our "social knowledge" and our knowledge of those individuals who are part of the interaction, and on the existence of trust in the absence of means of coercion (Neu, 1991). Trust is already created in the early contact between the venture capitalist and the entrepreneur, and Zucker (1986) identifies three trust-creating mechanisms; (I) process-based trust, which is based on earlier and expected future exchanges and where the individual relies on information specific to the transaction, (II) character-based trust, which is generalized from a large number of exchanges where ascribed characteristics are used in order to arrive at trust, and (III) institutional-based trust, which means that generalizations are made outside a specific transaction and specific partners.

Conclusions Earlier research relating to the venture capital companies' investment decisions has thus assumed that the venture capitalists act from a decision rationality (Brunsson, 1976, and 1985) where the objective is to choose the investment proposals which best or sufficiently fulfil the venture capital company's goal.

However, from the discussion above, the momentary relationship between the venture capitalist and entrepreneur seems to give a good basis for an action rationality in the decision-making (Brunsson, ibid.). The momentary relationship is characterized, from the venture capitalist's side by, *inter alia*, intuitive decision-making, an assessment of social attraction and an assessment of the trust in the entrepreneur. The result is that many investment proposals are rejected at an early stage and that the venture capitalist experiences certainty in his assessment, which constitute the condition for acting.

It must be emphazised that this is not sufficient for finding out which decision rationality are used in the venture capital companies. One reflection that was made in the study was that the venture capital companies varied in their way of making their investment decisions. One factor that seems to determine which type of decision rationality is used in the venture capital company is the venture capital company's risk management strategy. In the next section I will develop this reasoning further.

The venture capital company's risk management strategies

In an earlier article (Landström, 1990b), a categorization was made of the Swedish venture capital companies and the companies' method for co-operating with their portfolio companies. I will not develop further the categorization in this context, but will only point to an observation which was made in the study which showed that the different categories of venture capital companies tended to manage the risks associated with investments in young and small companies in different ways. From this, a polarizing can be made between operative risk management and risk management via the portfolio.

Venture capital companies which worked with a form of "operative risk management" assumed that the venture capital company, by supplying resources in sufficient quantity and of the right quality, would be able to reduce the potential risk of "failure" in the individual portfolio company. Operative risk management often means active work in the portfolio companies and strong control of the company. An operative risk management strategy also has consequences for the venture capital company's investment strategy, where an operative risk management strategy often leads to a relatively "narrow" portfolio of similar companies, e.g., companies within approximately the same business areas.

Other venture capital companies tended to "manage risks via the portfolio" where the aim was to differentiate the portfolio in such a way that the risk in the portfolio as a whole could be reduced. This type of risk management leads to an investment strategy in which the venture capital company tries to spread its investments in portfolio companies which are in different development phases, different areas of business, etc. In this way, a "wide" porfolio is created where, for instance, investments in mature companies balance the risk and the return on investment in young companies.

What consequences do the venture capital companies' risk management strategy have for the investment decision? Brunsson's (1976) discussion of how action is created in organizations will be taken as a starting-point. The company's strategy constitutes an important explanation variable for the evaluation mode which is used in the decision-making. An operationally defined strategy, which is accepted and well known by the decision-makers, means that the selection can be shifted from the evaluation phase to earlier phases in the decision process. Through the strategy, it also becomes easy to anticipate which proposals will be rejected or accepted. It provides a little room for different interpretations and the proposals are assessed in the same way by all those involved in the assessment. In addition, an operationally defined strategy makes it easier for the person assessing to become familiar with the specific decision area and narrows the area within which knowledge must be obtained. The early selection and the increased knowledge within the area allow an impressionistic evaluation mode to be used, which means that conditions are created for an action rationality.

In accordance with this reasoning the two categories of venture capital companies can be discussed. Venture capital companies which use an operative risk management strategy generally have an investment strategy which is narrowly defined as regards the market and products. Such an investment strategy means that entrepreneurs who seek external capital do not turn to such a venture capital company unless the entrepreneur does works within the defined business area. At the same time, it is easy for the venture capitalist to judge quickly whether the investment proposal lies within the defined business area or not. The strategy thus functions as a "selector". Furthermore, a narrow investment strategy means that the venture capitalist can build up competence and experience within a relatively specific business area. This also leads to the venture capitalist being able to assess the investment proposals more easily. The consequence of the reasoning is that when an operative risk management strategy and a "narrow" investment strategy are used, the uncertainty is reduced in the decision situation. The possibilities to use action rational decision-making are increased, and all the energy can be directed towards creating motivation and a strong commitment for carrying out the decision.

Venture capital companies which manage risk via the portfolio often have a broader investment strategy, which is characterized by the venture capital company's ability to make investments within several different business areas, in companies in different development phases, etc. This means that the strategy does not function as a selector. The venture capitalist can be expected to receive a large number of different investment proposals, which tends to cause the selection to be shifted to later phases of the decision process and much work to be spent on a careful analysis of the investment proposal. The work is thus focused on the function of choice. The broad investment strategy also means that the venture capitalist cannot be expected to have sufficient knowledge within all the areas. For the venture capitalist, the number of investment proposals and insufficient knowledge mean that the uncertainty in the decision situation increases, and the decision-making can be characterized as decision rational. If the decision-maker is uncertain about whether the investment proposal is good or not, he becomes less willing to commit himself to the investment proposal. Several investment proposals also mean that the decision-maker's motivation becomes divided, and this weakens the motivation which is attached to any one of the proposals.

The conclusion is that differences exist in the conditions for making an action rational decision depending on the venture capital company's risk management strategy. In venture capital companies which work with an operative risk management strategy within a narrowly defined business area, there exist conditions that strengthen the action rationality by the strategy functioning as a "selector" and by the venture capitalist having the chance to build up competence within the specified business area. On the other hand, a risk management strategy which means a differentiated portfolio, tends to weaken the action rationality since the uncertainty in the decision situation increases.

Conclusions

The research regarding the venture capital companies' investment decisions can, to a large extent, be characterized as descriptive. There is little analytical research, where the results are related to a theoretical framework. Therefore, in this paper I have tried to place the empirical results in a decision theory framework. In this section I will try to summarize the conclusions that can be derived from the discussion above.

One conclusion in the study is that earlier research relating to the venture capital companies' investment decisions has to a large extent assumed that the venture capitalists act according to a decision rationality. However, my tentative results in this paper indicate that the venture capitalists in some of the venture capital companies studied act less in accordance with a decision rationality, and more according to an action rationality.

The results suggest that the assessments in the early stages of the investment process, and the "momentary relationship" between the venture capitalist and entrepreneur during the first meeting have great significance for the investment decision. The "momentary relationship" is characterized by an intuitive decision-making, an assessment of the social attraction, and a possibility to get trust in the entrepreneur. One result of this relationship is that the venture capitalists experience a feeling of certainty in the assessment, which gives good conditions for an action rationality. However, this is not sufficient. As I see it, the venture capital company's risk management strategy seems to constitute an important explanation variable to determine which type of decision rationality is used in the organization.

- Venture capital companies which use an operative risk management strategy with a narrowly defined investment strategy seem to increase the conditions for using an action rationality in the decision-making.

- Venture capital companies which manage risks via the portfolio and use a broader investment strategy seem to a larger extent use a decision rationality in their decision-making.

During the 1980s the Swedish venture capital companies have tended to work less active in their portfolio firms. They work more and more "hands-off", and as passive investors. Also, their way of managing risks have changed. They have changed from an operative risk management strategy, to managing risks via the portfolio, and they usually have rather differentiated and wide portfolios with portfolio companies in different industry sectors, different development phases, etc. In accordance with the reasoning above this change in risk management strategy also leads to a change in their way of assessing new investment proposals; from an action rationality to a decision rationality. This change will reinforce the discrimination against risky investments such as investments in young and technology-based firms.

References

Atkinson, J.W. (1964), *An Introduction to Motivation*, Nostrand, New York.
Bauer, R.A. and Gerger, K.J. (1971), *Study of Policy Formation*, Free Press, New York.
Bean, A.S. and Schiffel, D.D. and Mogee, M.M. (1975), The Venture Capital Market and Technology Innovation, *Research Policy*, No 4.
Brunsson, N. (1976), *Propensity to Change: An Empirical Study of Decision on Reorientations*, BAS, Göteborg.
Brunsson, N. (1982), The Irrationality of Action and Action Irrationality: Decisions, Ideologies and Organizational Actions, *Journal of Management Studies*, Vol 19, No 1.
Brunsson, N. (1985), *The Irrational Organization*, Wiley&Sons, N.Y.
Bygrave, W. (1987), Syndicated Investments by Venture Capital Firms: A Networking Perspective, *Journal of Business Venturing*, Vol 2.
Bygrave, W. (1988), The Structure of the Investment Networks of Venture Capital Firms, *Journal of Business Venturing*, Vol 3.
Carleton, W.T. (1986), Issues and Questions Involving Venture Capital,

Advances in the Study of Entrepreneurship, Innovation and Economic Growth, JAI Press, Vol 1.

Carter, R.B. and Van Auken, H.E. (1992), Venture Capital Firm's Preferences for Projects in Particular Stages of Development, unpublished paper, Iowa State University, Ames, Iowa.

Chan, Y. (1983), On the Positive Role of Financial Intermediation in Allocation of Venture Capital in a Market with Imperfect Information, *Journal of Finance*, Vol 38, No 5.

Cohen, M.D. and March, J.G. (1973), *Leadership and Ambiquity: The American College President*, McGraw-Hill, New York.

Cohen, M.D. and March, J.G. and Olsen, J.P. (1972), A Garbage Can Model of Organizational Choice, *Administrative Science Quarterly*, Vol 17, No 1.

Cyert, R.M. and March, J.G. (1963), *A Behavioral Theory of the Firm*, Prentice-Hall, Englewood Cliffs.

Danielsson, A. and Malmberg, A. (1979), *Beslut fattas*, SAF, Stockholm.

DeBono, E. (1970), *Lateral Thinking*, Penguin Books, Harmondsworth, Middlesex.

DeCastro, J.O. (1991), The Relationship Between Venture Capital and Performance: A Review with Propositions, in *Proceedings of the 36th ICSB World Conference*, Vol 1, University of Economics, Vienna, Austria.

European Venture Capital Association (1990), *Venture Capital in Europe*, Peat Marwick McLintock, London.

European Venture Capital Association (1991), New Phase in European Venture Capital, *Venture Info*, No 2.

Fredriksen, Ø. and Klofsten, M. and Landström, H. and Olofsson, C. and Wahlbin, C. (1990), Entrepreneur-Venture Capitalist Relations: The Entrepreneurs' View, in Churchill, N.C. and Bygrave, W.D. and Hornaday, J.A. and Muzyka, D.F. and Vesper, K.H. and Wetzel Jr., W.E., *Frontiers of Entrepreneurship Research 1990*, Babson College, Wellesley, MA.

Garfinkel, H. (1964), Studies in the Routine Grounds of Everyday Activities, *Social Problems*, No 2.

Green, E. (1992), *Kreditbedömning och intuition*, Företagsekonomiska Institutionen, Lunds Universitet.

Grimsø, R.E. (1979), Tenkestil og problemløsning, *Bedriftsøkonomen*, nr 7.

Guilford, J.P. (1967), *The Nature of Human Intelligence*, McGraw Hill, New York.

Hall, J. and Hofer, C.W. (1993), Venture Capitalists' Decision Criteria in New Venture Evaluation, *Journal of Business Venturing*, Vol 8.

Hedberg, B. (1980), *Konsten att inflyta. Handbok för omäktiga*, Liber, Malmö.

Hellriegel, D. and Slocum, J.W. (1975), Managerial Problem-Solving Styles, *Business Horizons*, December.

Henderson, J.C. and Nutt, P.C. (1980), The Influence of Decision Style on Decision Making Behavior, *Management Science*, No 4.

Hisrich, R.D. and Jankowicz, A.D. (1990), Intuition in Venture Capital Decisions: An Exploratory Study Using a New Technique, *Journal of Business Venturing*, Vol 5, No 1.

Huysman, J.H.B.M. (1970), The Effectiveness of the Cognitive-Style Constraint in Implementing Operations Research Proposals, *Management Science*, Vol 17, No 1.

Jankowicz, A.D. and Hisrich, R.D. (1987), Intuition in Small Business Lending Decisions, *Journal of Small Business Management*, Vol 25, No 3.

Jog, V. and Lawson, W. and Riding, A. (1989), Venture Capitalists and Technology Entrepreneurs: Expectations and Contractual Provisions, Working Paper Series 89- 27, Carleton University, Ottawa, Canada.

Johnson, E.J. and Tversky, A. (1983), Affect, Generalization and the Perception of Risk, *Journal of Personality and Social Psychology*, Vol 45, No 1.

Jung, C.G. (1933), *Psychological Types*, Brace & World, Harcourt, New York.

Kahneman, D. and Tversky, A. (1979), Prospect Theory: An Analysis of Decision under Risk, *Econometrica*, March.

Kahneman, D. and Slovic, P. and Tversky, A. (1982), *Judgement under Uncertainty: Heuristics and Biases*, Cambridge University Press, Cambridge.

Kelley, G.A. (1955), *A Theory of Personality: A Psychology of Personal Constructs*, Norton, New York.

Khan, A.M. (1986), Entrepreneur Characteristics and the Prediction of New Venture Success, *Omega*, Vol 14, No 5.

Khan, A.M. (1987a), Assessing Venture Capital Investments with

Noncompensatory Behavioral Decision Models, *Journal of Business Venturing*, Vol 2, No 2.

Khan, A.M. (1987b), Modelling Venture Capital Investments, *Technovation*, Vol 6.

Kogan, N. and Wallach, M.A. (1964), *Risk Taking*, Holt, New York.

Landström, H. (1990a), *Riskkapitalföretagens resurstillförsel till små företag*, IMIT, Lund.

Landström, H. (1990b), Co-operation Between Venture Capital Companies and Small Firms, *Journal of Entrepreneurship and Regional Development*, No 4.

Lindblom, C.E. (1959), The Science of Muddling Through, *Public Administrative Review*, Vol 19, Spring.

Lindblom, C.E. (1965), *The Intelligence of Democracy*, Free Press, New York.

MacMillan, I.C. and Siegel, R. and Subbanarasimha, P.N. (1985), Criteria Used by Venture Capitalists to Evaluate New Venture Proposals, in Hornaday, J.A. and Shils, E.B. and Timmons, J.A. and Vesper, K.H., *Frontiers of Entrepreneurship Research 1985*, Babson College, Wellesley, Massachusetts.

MacMillan, I.C. and Zemann, L. and Subbanarasimha, P.N. (1987), Criteria Distinguishing Successful from Unsuccessful Ventures in the Venture Screening Process, *Journal of Business Venturing*, Vol 2.

March, J.G. and Olsen, J.P. (1976), *Ambiguity and Choice in Organizations*, Universitetsforlaget, Bergen.

March, J.G. and Shapira, Z. (1987), Managerial Perspectives on Risk and Risk Taking, *Management Science*, Vol 33, No 11.

March, J.G. and Simon, H.A. (1958), *Organizations*, Wiley&Sons, New York.

McClelland, D.C. (1961), *The Achieving Society*, Nostrand Co, Princeton, New Jersey.

McKeeney, J.L. and Keen, P.G.W. (1974), How Managers Minds Work, *Harvard Business Review*, May-June.

Neu, D. (1991), Trust, Contracting and the Prospectus Process, *Accounting, Organizations and Society*, Vol 16, No 3.

Olofsson, C. and Klofsten, M. (1985), Bäst med ven-capsatsningar. Riskkapital och samtalspartner, *Affärsvärlden*, nr 39.

Olsen, J.P. (1972), Public Policy-Making and Theories of Organizational

Choice, *Scandinavian Political Studies*, Vol 7.

Poindexter, J.B. (1976), *The Efficiency of Financial Markets. The Venture Capital Case*, New York University, New York.

Pratt, J.W. (1964), Risk Aversion in the Small and in the Large Firms, *Econometrica*, Vol 32.

Rea, R.H. (1989), Factors Affecting Success and Failure of Seed Capital/ Start-up Negotiations, *Journal of Business Venturing*, vol 4, No 2.

Riquelme, H. (1991), Hybrid Conjoint Analysis: An Estimation Probe in New Venture Decisions, paper at RENT V - Research in Entrepreneurship Fifth Workshop, Växjö University, Sweden.

Riquelme, H. and Richards, T. (1992), Hybrid Conjoint Analysis: An Estimation Probe in New Venture Decisions, *Journal of Business Venturing*, Vol 7.

Robinson, R.B. (1987), Emerging Strategies in the Venture Capital Industry, *Journal of Business Venturing*, Vol 2, No 1.

Ruhnka, J.C. and Young, J.E. (1987), A Venture Capital Model of the Development Process for New Ventures, *Journal of Business Venturing*, Vol 2, No 2.

Ruhnka, J.C. and Young, J.E. (1991), Some Hypotheses about Risk in Venture Capital Investing, *Journal of Business Venturing*, Vol 6.

Sandberg, W.R. and Schweiger, D.M. and Hofer, C.W. (1987), Determining Venture Capitalists' Decision Criteria: The Use of Verbal Protocols, in *Frontiers of Entrepreneurship Research 1987*, Babson College, Wellesley, M.A.

Sandberg, W.R. and Schweiger, D.M. and Hofer, C.W. (1988), The Use of Verbal Protocols in Determining Venture Capitalists' Decision Processes, *Entrepreneurship Theory and Practice*, Vol 13, Winter.

Sargent, M. and Young, J.E. (1991), The Entrepreneurial Search for Capital: A Behavioural Science Perspective, *Journal of Entrepreneurship and Regional Development*, Vol 3.

Schelling, T. (1960), *The Strategy of Conflict*, Harvard University Press, Cambridge, Mass.

Simon, H.A. (1965), *Adminstrative Behavior*, Free Press, New York.

Sjöberg, L. (1990), Diagnosen otillförlitlig och utan prognosvärde vid psykodynamisk arbetsmodell, *Läkartidningen*, vol 87, nr 11.

Sjöberg, L. (1991), Personbedömning i ljuset av samtida empirisk psykologi, stencil, Centrum för Riskforskning, Handelshögskolan i

Stockholm.
Sjöberg, L. and Tollgerdt, I. (1986), Vad är personkemi, stencil, Handelshögskolan i Stockholm, Stockholm.
Timmons, J.A. and Gumpert, D.E. (1982), Discard Many Old Rules About Getting Venture Capital, *Harvard Business Review*, January-February.
Tyebjee, T.T. and Bruno, A.V. (1981), Venture Capital Decision Making, in Vesper, K.H., *Frontiers of Entrepreneurship Research, Babson College 1981*, Wellesley, Massachusetts.
Tyebjee, T.T. and Bruno, A.V. (1984a), A Model of Venture Capital Investment Activity, *Management Science*, Vol 30, No 9.
Tyebjee, T.T. and Bruno, A.V. (1984b), The Entrepreneur's Search for Capital, in Hornaday, J.A. and Tanpley Jr., F. and Timmons, J.A. and Vesper, K.H., *Frontiers of Entrepreneurship Research 1984*, Babson College, Wellesley, Massachusetts.
Van Auken, H.E. and Carter, R.B. (1990), Affect of Professional Background on Venture Capital Proposal Evaluation, unpublished paper, Iowa State University, Ames, Iowa.
von Neumann, J. and Morgenstern, O. (1944), *Theory of Games and Economic Behavior*, Princeton University Press, Princeton, N.J.
Wahlund, R. (1989), *Att fatta beslut under osäkerhet och risk*, Norstedts, Stockholm.
Wells, W.A. (1974), *Venture Capital Decision Making*, Carnegie-Mellon University.
Zucker, L.G. (1986), Production of Trust: Institutional Sources of Economic Structure, 1840-1920, *Research in Organizational Behaviour*, Vol 8.

32 The impact of venture capital funding on small high technology manufacturing firms in the United Kingdom

Heather I.M. Wilson

Abstract

This paper considers venture capital funding in relation to small high technology manufacturing firms located in Scotland and the South East of England. Empirical information is cited from two surveys, one postal questionnaire and one personal interview questionnaire, involving a total of 153 firms in the scientific instruments and electronics industries. This is supplemented by qualitative interviews with a small number of venture capital organisations. The resulting data are used to investigate a number of issues including the distribution of venture capital finance within the study firms and regions, the unique role played by venture capital organisations in relation to other financial services and the characteristics of firms which were successful in obtaining venture capital funds. Explanations are also offered for the pattern of venture capital distribution according to the venture capitalist investment criteria of management, market and product. The results provide a better understanding of UK venture capital industry investment preferences and behaviour, and indicate that venture capital organisations in the United Kingdom are not totally risk-averse, that the management investment criterion is secondary to the market investment criterion and that venture capital organisations rarely adopt a 'hands-on' management role.

Introduction

Evidence on the importance of the venture capital industry to technology funding and economic growth first emerged in the US in the late 1970s and early 1980s [1]. Venture capitalists in the US financed a disproportionate share of rapidly growing high technology companies such as Digital Equipment Corporation, Scientific Data Systems, Apple Computer, Compaq, Lotus and Genentech [2-5]. In turn, successful investee companies contributed to the economic prosperity of the US by providing, inter alia, new jobs, tax revenues and export sales [1].

Given the example of the above spectacular investment successes and the fact that there is only a limited general body of knowledge concerning the operations of the venture capital industry in the UK [6], especially with regard to high technology investments, this research aimed to investigate venture capital provision in the UK from the perspective of the high technology entrepreneur, and to attempt to assess its impact on small firms in the high technology manufacturing sector. As a result, this paper offers explanations for both the extent of venture capital provision to firms in the same industries in different regions of the UK, and observed differences in the propensity of entrepreneurs to apply for, and obtain, venture capital funding.

Three major observations provided the impetus for this research. First, venture capital funding in the UK did not appear to be of a similar type or extent to the venture capital services available historically in the US. A generally accepted definition of venture capital is "... a way in which investors support entrepreneurial talent with finance and business skills to exploit market opportunities, and thus obtain long-term capital gains" [7]. The critical components of this definition, which distinguish venture capital from other forms of finance, are the long-term orientation and the active hands-on involvement of the financier to add value to the investment [8]. These components are typical of traditional venture capital investment behaviour in the US [9]. By contrast, venture capital organisations in the UK focus on later-stage investments [10] which come to fruition over a comparatively shorter time period, and they rarely become involved in the management of the investee company [11], although many appoint, or reserve the right to appoint, directors to the board of management [12]. As a result of these observed differences in investment behaviour, this research sought to investigate whether UK venture capital organisations actively sought early-stage investment opportunities and whether they attempted to add value to the investment.

Second, there was some concern that venture capital organisations in the UK were not assisting small high technology manufacturing firms to any significant degree. Evidence from the US indicates that traditional venture capitalists primarily invest in new ventures with a high technology content [9, 13]. Indeed, many venture capitalists located in financial centres like New York and Chicago export investment funds to technology-related centres such as San Francisco and Boston [14]. However, UK venture capital providers have focused their investment interests on well-established companies in the consumer product and/or service industries [10] to the possible detriment of high technology companies [15]. This research, therefore, attempted to determine the investment criteria applied by UK venture capital companies when deciding their investment priorities, and to list the characteristics of high technology firms which were successful in raising investment funds.

Third, venture capital providers and investments appeared to be concentrated in the South East of England to the possible detriment of other regions in the UK. Indeed, the South East and East Anglia regions not only received a disproportionate share of total investments, but also a disproportionate share of total technological investments over the years [16]. This regional investment bias has been attributed to both demand and supply factors: on the demand side, a disproportionate number of new and growing technological businesses are located in the South East planning region and East Anglia; and, on the supply side, hands-on contact necessitates spatial proximity between venture capital investors, which are primarily located in the South East, and their investee companies [16]. This research aimed to determine whether this regional bias was justified on the grounds of need for hands-on contact and/or a dearth of suitable technological investment opportunities outside of the South East and East Anglia regions.

The terms of reference of this paper are wide, serving as a summary of the principal findings of the research project. These principal findings will be investigated in greater detail in subsequent publications. Meanwhile, the more general issues raised above will be addressed in the results and discussion parts of the paper prior to the formulation of conclusions and recommendations to encourage future venture capital investments in the small high technology manufacturing sector. The following section details the methods employed to generate the data for the research.

Methodology

The aim of this section is to demonstrate that the methods employed during the research process were adequate to address the following questions:
- are venture capital organisations in the UK actively involved in seeking early-stage investment opportunities?
- what investment criteria appear most important to the investment decision at the post-investment stage, management, market or product?
- what are the characteristics of those small high technology manufacturing firms receiving venture capital funds?
- do UK venture capital organisations attempt to add value to their investments?
- is the regional investment bias due to the hands-on nature of the venture capital investment and/or a lack of suitable investment opportunities outside the South East and East Anglia regions?

The target population for the research were high technology industries well represented in the two regions of Scotland and the South East and East Anglia, notably Hertfordshire, Bedfordshire and Cambridgeshire. This was to test for the regional investment bias since, if Scotland was under-represented in terms of venture capital investments with its strong indigenous financial community, then this would have significant implications for regional development in all areas outside of the South East regions. The electrical and electronic engineering industry (SIC 34) and the instrument engineering sector (SIC 37) are well represented in the two survey regions and, after eliminating those firms which did not employ 200 people or less, were not independent at the time of formation and were not primarily involved in manufacturing, the remaining population were selected to take part in a postal questionnaire survey. Questionnaires were sent to a total of 535 firms, 355 located in the South East and East Anglia and 180 companies in Scotland, and were designed to elicit precise information about the size of the company, ownership status and nature of the operation of the company, and to generate preliminary data on the distribution of venture capital in the target industries. After eliminating ineligible firms and those which had gone out of business, the effective response rate to the postal questionnaire survey was 42 per cent comprising 154 useable questionnaires from an effective universe of 370 firms.

The second stage of the research involved selecting a sample of companies from the 154 respondents to take part in a semi-structured personal interview survey, the aim being to gain more detailed information about the background of the companies and their financial histories. In order to test for differences between firms receiving venture capital funds and those operating without such finance, 90 firms were randomly selected in equal proportions according location and also venture capital status; that is, firms receiving venture capital funds, firms which had been in contact with venture capital providers and not taken up or received such finance, and firms which had not had any contact with venture capital providers (Figure 1). Withdrawals and the lack of replacements due to the limited overall number of firms receiving venture capital finance (see later) meant that 83 firms in actual fact took part in the semi-structured personal interview survey (Figure 1).

Finally, in order to set the information obtained from the high technology companies in context, unstructured personal interviews were conducted with a small number of venture capital organisations which have a high technology investment focus and which are located in or near the two study regions.

Results

Early-stage investments and UK venture capital companies

Given the evidence that management buy-outs and other later-stage investments are the popular investment target of the UK venture capital industry [10], respondents to the personal interview survey were asked who had established the initial contact between the firm and the venture capital organisation, and whether the investment resulted. This was linked to the age of the survey firm in order to ascertain whether firms at an early stage in their development were, first, contacted by venture capital organisations and, second, received investment funds. Table 1 illustrates that a total of 61 firms had contact with venture capital providers, comprising an almost equal split between recipients and non-recipients due to the use of the proportional stratified random sampling technique described earlier. In terms of who initiated the contact, it emerged that a significantly greater percentage of firms received venture capital funds when they initiated the contact with venture capital organisations than when firms were approached by such financiers. A third category was included in this table for firms which could not determine specifically who had first made contact, and the majority of firms in this instance had received venture capital funds. Investigating these results further revealed that venture capital providers were significantly more interested in initiating contact with firms which had been operating for more than ten years (Table 2). Coincidentally, a large percentage of such firms were exhibiting currently positive growth levels as measured by growth in turnover per employee over a five year period (Table 3). When the firm was less than ten years old, the firm itself tended to apply for venture capital funds (Table 2), and a high percentage of these applicants were experiencing no growth or decline in terms of turnover per employee (Table 3). Despite the attempts of venture capital providers to target funds to currently growing firms, Table 4 illustrates that the actual supply of funds is evenly distributed between growing and no growth/declining firms with just over a 45 per cent incidence for both categories.

The above results must reflect partly the emergence of venture capital in the 1980s as a source of funding, and newer firms learning of the existence and possibility of venture capital funding when seeking start-up and early development finance. By implication, older firms would be more familiar with more traditional sources of finance, and venture capital companies may themselves have had to create awareness amongst such firms. Thus, to a certain extent, venture capital organisations in the UK are marketing their services. However, it would appear that they still have some way to go when over 47 per cent of the respondents to the postal questionnaire survey indicated that they had neither approached or been approached by venture capital organisations. Indeed, Tables 1 and 3 point strongly to the fact that venture capital providers in the UK are largely reactive in terms of their delivery of funds and that they target less marginal firms. Nevertheless, the financiers are not averse to supplying venture capital funds to a number of these more marginal investment opportunities. Indeed, over 50 per cent of the recipients of venture capital finance believed that they owed their current existence to the timely investment of the venture capital organisation.

Investment criteria

At the pre-investment stage, the three criteria considered most important by venture capital organisations when deciding whether to invest in a firm are the management, the market and the product [17], and the management team is often cited as the most critical factor in the appraisal process. This research investigated these criteria at the post-investment stage in order to determine the critical differences between firms receiving venture capital finance, firms which had not taken up such finance after contact with venture capital organisations and firms which had not had any contact with such financiers.

The management criterion was investigated from two angles: the qualifications of the principal founder of the company and prior experience of the management team. However, the qualifications of the founder appeared to have, if anything, only a marginal effect on the distribution of venture capital funds. It might be the case that the qualifications of the founders are considered to be supplanted by the expertise they gain in business after leaving an academic environment. On-thejob management experience was examined by asking the respondents to the personal interview survey whether any members of the management team had management experience with other firms in the same industry prior to working with the current company. A surprising, although not significant, result is that a greater percentage of firms without prior management experience in the industry had received venture capital finance (Table 5) when compared with firms with two or more managers possessing relevant industrial experience. In terms of the market investment criterion, the survey enquired after what percentage of the output of the firm was sold to customers located in the UK and abroad, and this was cross-tabulated with venture capital status. According to Table 6, a strong exporting orientation is associated with receipt of venture capital funds although, it should be noted, this result just fails to be significant at the $p=0.05$ level. It might be the case that the venture capital investment was used to develop these export opportunities, however, further investigation revealed that venture capital monies were used to finance the marketing efforts of only two export-oriented companies. It is also interesting to note that the majority of firms in the no contact category concentrated on sales to the UK market (Table 6). The personal interview survey investigated the product technology in terms of whether the main product of the firm was an imitation of something already available on the market, whether it was an improved product compared to other products on the market or whether it was totally new to the market. This was an attempt to gauge whether UK venture capital organisations prefer to invest in products involving existing or new applications of technology. Table 7 indicates that there is no significant pattern of investment behaviour when it comes to the character of the main product of the firm, however, a higher percentage of firms manufacturing imitation-based products had received venture capital funds when compared to those firms with improvement or totally new products. However, in terms of actual numbers, more firms manufacturing totally new products had received venture capital funds than the combined total of firms receiving venture capital finance when manufacturing imitation-based and improvement products.

The lack of management expertise does not appear to inhibit the ability of the firm to attract venture capital funds. What is not clear is whether experienced founders and managers found themselves involved in the current business as a result of the failure of a previous venture. It might be the case when seeking venture capital finance that no previous business experience in the industry is preferable to having failed in the running of a similar company. Another explanation for this result could be that more weight is put on the ability of the personnel in the organisation to relate to and get along with the people in the investee firm than on the actual experience of the management team. It also seems reasonable to postulate that venture capital organisations are interested in investment opportunities involving companies with a strong emphasis on exporting. Perhaps this is because the investee firms are not dependent upon the fortunes of one market, and demand abroad is a reflection of the strength of the third investment criterion, the product technology, whether or not it is an imitation, improvement or totally new product.

Characteristics of investee companies

It has already been stated that younger firms and firms with a propensity to export tended to receive funds from UK venture capital providers. This research also attempted to determine which other characteristics were typical of firms in receipt of venture capital finance. Generally speaking, firms which utilised venture capital funding had, at some previous stage, received some form of rejection from venture capital providers (Table 8). A significant ninety per cent of firms refused venture capital funding previously had become eventual recipients. This is surely a consequence of the aforementioned observation that survey firms approached the financiers for assistance and, thus, exposed themselves to rejection. In addition, Table 9 illustrates that firms which realised that venture capital finance involved more than just the injection of funds, for example the appointment of a non-executive director, had become recipients. The direction of the cause and effect in this significant relationship is uncertain, since awareness of the role venture capital organisations play over and above the provision of capital may have come about as a result of involvemen˜ with the venture capital organisation. Nevertheless, some of the entrepreneurs interviewed had sought venture capital funding precisely because of the perceived added advantages of managerial input and other benefits. This aspect of venture capital behaviour will be discussed in the next subsection of this paper.

A further characteristic of recipients of venture capital funds is the greater tendency to be 'higher technology' as measured by R&D inputs to the organisation. Working on the principle that the higher the R&D spend and the larger the number of R&D employees the greater the level of technical commitment, the input measure of R&D was considered a reasonable approximation to the technological sophistication of the firm. This variable was then cross-tabulated with venture capital status and revealed that a higher percentage of firms in the high technology category had received venture capital funding when compared to the lower technology category (Table 10). The chi-square test on this data produced a result significant at the $p=0.062$ level indicating a strong relationship between the higher technology firms in this survey and the adoption of venture capital funds.

The above result might indicate that UK venture capital organisations have a strong technology-based investment orientation. However, given the observation that the firms themselves initiate contact with the financiers, it would seem more likely that a high R&D commitment compels small high technology firms to apply for venture capital funding. It is also apparent that applicants for venture capital funding should not be discouraged by initial refusals of finance. A number of applications for funding will lead to familiarity with the application procedures, and generate greater awareness and acceptance of the non-financial components of the venture capital investment.

Added value

What distinguishes venture capital from other institutionalised sources of finance is the added value aspect of the investment. Traditionally, venture capital companies nurture their investments by providing, in addition to finance, hands-on assistance in the form of strategic planning, management restructuring/recruiting and access to networks involving companies, investors and other useful contacts [18]. The recipients of venture capital funding in the personal interview survey were asked about the non-financial contribution of the financier. Table 11 summarises the assistance listed by the 31 firms which had received venture capital finance and, noticeably, there is higher incidence of responses across most of the categories for the younger firms in the survey. However, a total of 12 firms (40 per cent) had received no assistance whatsoever and believed that the main advantage of venture capital was receiving the finance itself. In addition, not all investee companies had venture capital representation on the board of management. Nineteen firms had venture capital directors, and a further two venture capital organisations had reserved the right to appoint directors. Eight such firms indicated that the venture capital firm played an active role on the board of management, and the remaining 13 companies with an appointed or appointee director maintained that the financier either played no role in the running of the company or intervened only in times of trouble.

Venture capital directors effected limited changes to management and/or strategy only in a very small number of cases. Perhaps this was because venture capital organisations obtained mostly minority equity shareholdings which meant that they were not required, or did not seek, to participate actively in the running of the company. These results are promising for those firms which hesitate to adopt venture capital funds due to a fear of losing control to the financier. However, they also call into question the claims that venture capital providers add value to the investment beyond the provision of finance.

Regional investment bias

Given the above evidence, it does not appear that the local nature of investments can be attributed to the need for hands-on management or monitoring by venture capital organisations. Another explanation might be the lack of suitable investment opportunities in areas other than the South East and East Anglia regions. However, any regional difference in venture capital status would not be evident from the 83 personal interview firms due to the otherwise justified use of the stratified random sampling technique described earlier. However, the regional question can be approached from a different angle by considering the data obtained during the postal questionnaire phase of the research.

Surprisingly, a substantial percentage of firms in Scotland not only had contact with venture capital organisations, but also had received venture capital funds (Table 12). In contrast, a significantly higher percentage of firms located in the South East of England compared with Scotland had not been in contact with venture capital providers. However, it should be remembered that the South East comprised a larger population of firms in the study industries, and there were also a number of firms about which there was no information because they did not respond to the initial postal survey. Considering the location of the venture capital organisations in relation to the personal interview survey firms, Table 13 indicates that a small number of Scottish firms had contact with Southern-based venture capital organisations and, in some instances had received the required funds. The same was not true of firms based in the South East and Scottish venture capital companies.

Thus, there is the implication that Scottish firms benefit not only from their association with indigenous financial organisations, but also from contact with a significant minority of venture capital providers based in the South East of England. Given the recent emergence of venture capital firms in the more peripheral regions, it might have been expected that Scotland would benefit from an appreciable provision of venture capital finance. It was not anticipated, however, that the outcome would so strikingly imply that Scottish firms benefited proportionately more from the supply of venture capital funds in comparison to companies located in the South East of England. Notwithstanding the previous comments, the strong significance level associated with Table 13 suggests that there is still a certain amount of investment parochialism associated with the distribution of venture capital funds in the UK.

Discussion

In terms of this research it appears that management with no previous experience in the industry are just as likely, or even more likely, to receive venture capital funds as firms with experienced management teams. This contradicts a stated aim of many venture capital organisations to target firms with relevant management expertise. It also raises the question as to whether the firm is likely to obtain venture capital funds if members of the management team have been involved in prior business ventures which have failed. Venture capital organisations in the US acknowledge that as much valuable business experience will be gained from failed ventures as from successful enterprises. The UK venture capital industry appears to place a greater emphasis on the market investment criterion, particularly the existence of exporting opportunities, and this may be the result of the limited home market for UK businesses when compared to the US for example.

In addition to the exporting orientation, firms which are successful generally in obtaining venture capital funds tend to possess some combination of the following characteristics: relative youth, a high technological commitment in terms of R&D spend, knowledge of the non-financial contribution of venture capital organisations and, perhaps, stubbornness by persevering in the application for venture capital finance. The onus is on the potential recipient to actively and tenaciously seek venture capital funding. This would seem logical given that the firm itself, rather that the venture capital organisation, would know when investment funds were required. However, venture capital is not a short term form of finance and cannot be compared with a typical application for a loan or overdraft from a bank. The venture capital provider should be investing in the future prosperity of the firm, as distinct from banks which are concerned with current performance. Effectively, venture capital organisations fulfil a shareholding role and, like any other investor, they should carefully research and select company shares with a view to seeing the investment grow.

Given the role model of traditional venture capital providers in the US, it seems natural that the financier would get involved in some form of search process in order to target the firms most likely to grow. This type of activity could lead to accusations of the venture capital providers ' skimming the cream ' of current investment opportunities, however, the skill of the venture capitalist lies in finding currently marginal investment opportunities and investing at an early stage to obtain significant returns in the long term. The nature of traditional venture capital is such that the investor not only provides finance, but also takes a hands-on role in the running of the company in order to add value to the investment. However, evidence indicates that UK venture capital organisations generally take a hands-off stance, and even where venture capital providers attempt to offer assistance beyond the provision of finance there are few perceived benefits.

A substantial number of venture capital organisations choose the different and, perhaps, easier option of investing in situations which do not require much involvement beyond the initial provision of funds. Thus, the venture capital industry can be criticised for becoming too 'institutionalised' in relation to the example of the US, and too similar in nature to other available sources of finance. However, a number of venture capital organisations in the UK are prepared to invest in firms which believe they will go out of business without the injection of venture capital funds. These firms are unable to obtain finance from other sources, perhaps because the collateral of the firm is tied up by prior investments. In addition, given the aforementioned characteristics of recipients, many of these firms are young and require investment capital for expensive R&D purposes. Therefore, the distinguishing aspect of venture capital funding in the UK is that it is risk finance without the requirement for collateral. This is a different lending strategy from that pursued by other financial institutions which, in general, seek comprehensive assurance that investment capital will be repaid in full with interest within a defined time period, even if the firm collapses.

Finally, it is extremely interesting to note from this research that the disparity in the distribution of venture capital exists within the target sector, not in terms of a disproportionate number of firms in the South East attracting such finance, but in terms of venture capital providers from both regions investing in Scottish firms. This indicates that Southern-based venture capital organisations are prepared to invest at some distance in a limited number of cases, perhaps because they perceive these projects to be exceptional, especially since a commonly expressed complaint of venture capital providers concerns the dearth of suitable investment opportunities. However, this investment on a remote rather than local basis is facilitated by the fact that UK venture capital organisations tend to pursue a hands-off investment strategy, which means that frequent contact with the investee company is not necessary. Ultimately, this positive result in terms of the regional distribution of venture capital funds means that the nurturing/adding value aspect of the investment relationship becomes difficult to promote.

Conclusions

A major aim of this research is to provide a better understanding of both the investment behaviour and investment preferences of UK venture capital providers, with regard to firms in the high technology manufacturing sector, in order to dispose of some of the confusion surrounding the term venture capital. Much of this confusion arises from the fact that traditional venture capital investment behaviour in the US is very different to what has transpired in the UK, namely hands-on management to add value to the investment, and this is compounded by the many different players on the UK venture capital scene which offer varying combinations of equity and loan finance with associated conditions to firms in different industries and at varying stages in their development. The current generic term venture capital might be better described as investment capital, and venture capital designated as equity investment in early-stage high risk companies where the investors take an active role in adding value to the investment. Thus, there should be some reorganising of the UK venture capital industry to better distinguish between seed capitalists, venture capitalists, providers of later-stage development capital, management buy-out/buy-in specialists and so forth. This would assist considerably the marketing efforts of organisations in the UK venture capital industry and avoid wasteful applications on the part of potential investee firms.

Several misconceptions have been dispelled somewhat by this research. Venture capital organisations in the UK generally do not participate extensively in their investee firms, either in equity or management terms; the management investment criterion appears secondary to the market investment criterion, so that prior management experience is less important than the demonstration of exporting opportunities; venture capital is a form of risk finance, since venture capital providers are prepared to invest in firms which other financiers will not consider; and the regional investment bias is not due to the need for hands-on contact or the lack of suitable investment opportunities in more peripheral regions. Future research should be aimed at determining whether the hands-on style of venture capital investment behaviour is beneficial, either to the investor or the investee, and whether/how it should be promoted. Further work in the area of venture capital investment criteria could also establish whether selection procedures are systematical, and which pre-investment criteria are indicative of post-investment performance. It would also be worthwhile to investigate, both in the UK and internationally, the performance of venture capital organisations specialising in the provision of funds to early-stage high technology firms compared with other investment specialists, for example venture capitalists concentrating their efforts on later-stage consumer product companies. Finally, there should be some assessment of the mechanisms which encourage contact between venture capital providers and potential investee firms in order to promote future venture capital investments in the small high technology manufacturing sector.

Acknowledgements

I would like to thank the Economic and Social Research Council (ESRC) which provided financial support for the research. I would also like to thank Professor Ray Oakey of Manchester Business School, Dr Wendy Faulkner of Edinburgh University and colleagues at Heriot-Watt Business School for their advice and encouragement.

References

S.E. Pratt, Preface. In: S.E. Pratt (Ed.), *How to Raise Venture Capital*. Charles Scribner's Sons, New York, 1982, pp. XV-XVII.

W.R. Hambrecht, Venture Capital and the Growth of Silicon Valley. *California Management Review*, XXVI(2) (1984) 74-82.

J.W. Wilson, *The New Venturers: Inside the High-Stakes World of Venture Capital*. Addison-Wesley, Wokingham, 1986, 237 pp.

Venture Capital Drought. *The Economist*, 311(7607) (1989) 95-96.

H. Lancaster, Sevin Rosen's New Venture Capital Fund Hopes to Find Gemsas Rivals Seek Safety. *Wall Street Journal*, 16 December 1991, pA6.

R.C. Sweeting, UK Venture Capital Funds and the Funding of New

Technology-Based Businesses: Process and Relationships. *Journal of Management Studies,* 28(6) (1991) 601-622.

D. Shilson, Venture Capital in the United Kingdom. *Bank of England Quarterly Bulletin,* 24(2) 207-211.

C.M. Mason and R.T. Harrison, Venture Capital, the Equity Gap and the 'North-South Divide' in the United Kingdom. In: M.B. Green (Ed.), *Venture Capital: International Comparisons.* Routledge, London, 1991, pp. 202-247.

E.B. Roberts, Initial Capital for the New Technological Enterprise. *IEEE Transactions on Engineering Management,* 37(2) (1990) 81-94.

British Venture Capital Association, *Report on Investment Activity.* BVCA, London, 1985-1991.

M. Dodgson and R. Rothwell, Financing Early-Stage Innovation in Small Firms (Flexible and Broad-Ranging Support Packages). *Proceedings of the European conference on Enterprise, Innovation and 1992: Innovation Support Services in Europe,* 1989, 57-69.

T. Lorenz, *Venture Capital Today.* Woodllead-Faulkner, Cambridge, 1985, 214 pp.

L. Orsenigo, *The Emergence of Biotechnology: Institutions and Markets in Industrial Innovation.* Pinter, London, 1989, 230 pp.

R. Florida and M. Kenney, Venture Capital and High Technology Entrepreneurship. *Journal of Business Venturing,* 3(4) (1988) 301-319.

G. Pratt, Venture Capital in the United Kingdom. *Bank of England Quarterly Bulletin,* 30(1) (1990) 78-83.

R. Martin, The Growth and Geographical Anatomy of Venture Capitalism in the United Kingdom. *Regional Studies,* 23(5) (1989) 389-403.

S. Gopalan, To Get Your Cash, First Get Your Plan Right. *The Accountant,* 194(5780) (1986) 17.

J. A. Timmons, Venture Capital: More than Money? In: S.E. Pratt (Ed.), *Guide to Venture Capital Sources.* Capital, Wellesley Hills, Mass., 1983, pp. 71-75.

Appendix

Figure 1   The research design

		Location	
		Scotland	SE England
Venture capital status	Received venture capital	Target 15 Actual 15	Target 15 Actual 16
	Not received venture capital after contact	Target 15 Actual 13	Target 15 Actual 17
	No contact with venture capitalists	Target 15 Actual 10	Target 15 Actual 12

Table 1   Whether received venture capital by nature of contact with venture capital providers

	Who initiated contact							
	Firm		Venture capitalist		Combination		Total	
	n	(%)	n	(%)	n	(%)	n	(%)
Received venture capital	20	(66.7)	2	(11.8)	9	(64.3)	31	(50.8)
Not received venture capital	10	(33.3)	15	(88.2)	5	(35.7)	30	(49.2)
Total	30	(100.0)	17	(100.0)	14	(100.0)	61	(100.0)

Chi-square (2 d.f.) = 14.405 $p = 0.0007$

Table 2 Who initiated contact by year of formation

	Prior to 1980		1980 onwards		Total	
	n	(%)	n	(%)	n	(%)
Firm	14	(40.0)	16	(61.5)	30	(49.2)
Venture capitalist	14	(40.0)	3	(11.5)	17	(27.9)
Combination	7	(20.0)	7	(26.9)	14	(23.0)
Total	35	(100.0)	26	(100.0)	61	(100.0)

Chi-square (2 d.f.) = 6.055 $p = 0.048$

Table 3 Who initiated contact by incidence of growth

	Positive growth		No growth/decline		Total	
	n	(%)	n	(%)	n	(%)
Firm	13	(41.9)	9	(69.2)	22	(50.0)
Venture capitalist	11	(35.5)	1	(7.7)	12	(27.3)
Combination	7	(22.6)	3	(23.1)	10	(22.7)
Total	31	(100.0)	13	(100.0)	44	(100.0)

Table 4 Whether received venture capital funding by incidence of growth

	Positive growth		No growth/decline		Total	
	n	(%)	n	(%)	n	(%)
Received venture capital	15	(48.4)	6	(46.2)	21	(47.7)
Not received venture capital	16	(51.6)	7	(53.8)	23	(52.3)
Total	31	(100.0)	13	(100.0)	44	(100.0)

Table 5 Incidence of venture capital funding by number of managers on management team with prior management experience in the industry

	0		1		2+		Total	
	n	(%)	n	(%)	n	(%)	n	(%)
Received venture capital	13	(46.4)	8	(36.4)	10	(31.3)	31	(37.8)
Not received venture capital	9	(32.1)	7	(31.8)	14	(43.8)	30	(36.6)
No contact with venture capitalists	6	(21.4)	7	(31.8)	8	(25.0)	21	(25.6)
Total	27	(100.0)	22	(100.0)	32	(100.0)	82	(100.0)

Table 6 Venture capital status by predominant customer location

	United Kingdom		Abroad		Total	
	n	(%)	n	(%)	n	(%)
Received venture capital	11	(26.2)	20	(48.8)	31	(37.3)
Not received venture capital	16	(38.1)	14	(34.1)	30	(36.1)
No contact with venture capitalists	15	(35.7)	7	(17.1)	22	(26.5)
Total	42	(100.0)	41	(100.0)	83	(100.0)

Chi-square (2 d.f.) = 5.644 $p = 0.059$

Table 7	Incidence of venture capital funding by nature of main product							
	Imitation		Improvement		Totally new		Total	
	n	(%)	n	(%)	n	(%)	n	(%)
Received venture capital	5	(50.0)	6	(24.0)	20	(41.7)	31	(37.3)
Not received venture capital	3	(30.0)	9	(36.0)	18	(37.5)	30	(36.1)
No contact with venture capitalists	2	(20.0)	10	(40.0)	10	(20.8)	22	(26.5)
Total	10	(100.0)	25	(100.0)	48	(100.0)	83	(100.0)

Table 8	Incidence of venture capital funding by whether refused venture capital finance					
	Refused venture capital		Not refused venture capital		Total	
	n	(%)	n	(%)	n	(%)
Received venture capital	18	(90.0)	11	(35.5)	29	(56.9)
Not received venture capital	2	(10.0)	20	(64.5)	22	(43.1)
Total	20	(100.0)	31	(100.0)	51	(100.0)

Chi-square (1 d.f) = 14.730 p = 0.0001

Table 9	Venture capital status by beliefs of founders on involvement of venture capital providers					
	Solely money		Money plus		Total	
	n	(%)	n	(%)	n	(%)
Received venture capital	11	(39.3)	19	(70.4)	30	(54.5)
Not received venture capital	17	(60.7)	8	(29.6)	25	(45.5)
Total	28	(100.0)	27	(100.0)	55	(100.0)

Chi-square (1 d.f) = 5.357 p = 0.021

Table 10 Venture capital status by technological sophisticiation

	High technology		Low technology		Total	
	n	(%)	n	(%)	n	(%)
Received venture capital	20	(46.5)	11	(27.5)	31	(37.3)
Not received venture capital	16	(37.2)	14	(35.0)	30	(36.1)
No contact with venture capitalists	7	(16.3)	15	(37.5)	22	(26.5)
Total	43	(100.0)	40	(100.0)	83	(100.0)

Chi-square (2 d.f.) = 5.554 p = 0.062

Table 11 Assistance received from venture capital organisations by year of formation

	Prior to 1980		1980 onwards		Total	
	n	(%)	n	(%)	n	(%)
No assistance	8	(61.5)	4	(23.5)	12	(40.0)
Management advice	0	(0.0)	6	(35.3)	6	(20.0)
Accounting/bank assistance	2	(15.4)	3	(17.6)	5	(16.7)
Venture capital firm experience	1	(7.7)	4	(23.5)	5	(16.7)
Recruitment help	1	(7.7)	2	(11.8)	3	(10.0)
Network contacts	0	(0.0)	2	(11.8)	2	(6.7)
Legal assistance	1	(7.7)	0	(0.0)	1	(3.3)
Other	2	(15.4)	2	(11.8)	4	(13.3)
Total responses	15	---------	23	---------	38	---------
Total firms	13	---------	17	---------	30	---------

Table 12   Venture capital status by location of postal survey firm

	South East		Scotland		Total	
	n	(%)	n	(%)	n	(%)
Received venture capital	17	(15.9)	16	(34.0)	33	(21.4)
Not received venture capital	32	(29.9)	16	(34.0)	48	(31.2)
No contact with venture capitalists	58	(54.2)	15	(31.9)	73	(47.4)
Total	107	(100.0)	47	(100.0)	154	(100.0)

Chi-square (2 d.f.) = 8.625 $p = 0.013$

Table 13   Location of venture capital provider by location of interview firms in contact with these financiers

	Survey firm location					
	South East		Scotland		Total	
	n	(%)	n	(%)	n	(%)
South East	30	(100.0)	9	(32.1)	39	(67.2)
Scotland	0	(0.0)	19	(67.9)	19	(32.8)
Total	30	(100.0)	28	(100.0)	58	(100.0)

Chi-square (1 d.f) = 30.275 $p = 0.00001$